A PORTRAIT OF PAY, 1970–1982

A Portrait of Pay, 1970–1982

An Analysis of the New Earnings Survey

edited by
MARY B. GREGORY
and
ANDREW W. J. THOMSON

CLARENDON PRESS • OXFORD
1990

Oxford University Press, Walton Street, Oxford OX2 6DP
Oxford   New York   Toronto
Delhi   Bombay   Calcutta   Madras   Karachi
Petaling Jaya   Singapore   Hong Kong   Tokyo
Nairobi   Dar es Salaam   Cape Town
Melbourne   Auckland
and associated Companies in
Berlin   Ibadan

Oxford is a trade mark of Oxford University Press

Published in the United States
by Oxford University Press, New York

British Library Cataloguing in Publication Data
A Portrait of pay, 1970–1982: an analysis of the New
earnings survey.
1. Great Britain. Personnel. Remuneration
I. Gregory, Mary   II. Thomson, Andrew W. J.   III. New
earnings survey
331.2941
ISBN 0-19-828576-0

Library of Congress Cataloging in Publication Data
A Portrait of pay, 1970–1982: an analysis of the new earnings survey
/edited by Mary B. Gregory and Andrew W. J. Thomson.
1. Wages—Great Britain.   I. Gregory, M. B. (Mary B.)
II. Thomson, Andrew W. J.
HD5015.P67   1990   331.2'941'09047—dc20   90-6705
ISBN 0-19-828576-0

Set by Graphicraft Typesetters Ltd., Hong Kong
Printed in Great Britain by
Bookcraft (Bath) Ltd,
Midsomer Norton, Avon

Preface

This portrait of pay depicts the structure and evolution of earnings in Britain over the years 1970–82 as recorded through the New Earnings Survey. During this period issues of pay were virtually continuously at the centre of political and economic debates. Throughout the 1970s the growth of earnings was seen by many—including successive governments—as a main cause of inflation, then proceeding at unprecedented rates. Even for those who saw wages as a reactive rather than an initiating force in the inflation process, the apparent leap-frogging and uncoordinated growth in earnings produced by decentralized collective bargaining could be seen to threaten the position of those unable or unwilling to exercise industrial muscle. In 1981–2, as the economy plunged into the deepest recession of the post-war years, wages were again the focus of attention; but where previously the excessive upward adjustment of pay had been held to be the cause of inflation, within two years the failure of wages to adjust downwards with sufficient flexibility was being blamed for the high levels of unemployment.

For the purposes of these debates developments in pay can be represented, not too misleadingly, by a single summary statistic, such as the rate of growth of average earnings. In practice, however, pay is an extremely complex matter, with the rate of price inflation only one out of many determining factors. Comparability or relativities between groups, both broadly and narrowly defined, inequality and the dispersion of earnings, the make-up of pay, hours of work, and the role of collective bargaining are all essential features. Our objective in this book is to present an appropriately multi-faceted picture of pay by considering many of these dimensions individually while also setting them within a unified overall framework.

The New Earnings Survey, carried out annually by the Department of Employment since 1970, is by far the largest and most comprehensive source of data on earnings in Britain and compares very favourably with those available for most other countries. Its published tabulations are widely used within government, by employers and trade unions in collective bargaining, and as a primary source for informed comment on many aspects of pay. Its importance was endorsed in the Rayner Review in the early 1980s, which examined the functions and costs of a wide range of statistical services provided by government departments:

The NES is used within the Department as the major source of reference for all questions involving pay statistics. The results by agreement and industry are seen as essential for monitoring and briefing about pay settlements. The distribution and structure of earnings is needed for policy questions concerning tax and benefit. Relativities between men and women are used in briefing on equal pay. Information about basic hours and overtime hours is used in questions arising on the shorter working week. Occupational pay differentials are relevant to any study of skill shortages. Earnings levels can be significant in studying the role of Wages Councils. Regional earnings information can illuminate an aspect of regional policy. Thus the NES results are used as a data base for all labour market questions in which pay is a relevant factor. (Department of Employment 1981: 113)

The review recommended that the NES continue largely unchanged while other of the Department of Employment's surveys of earnings were discontinued or reduced in scope.

In spite of the richness of the material and its potential as a research data base, only limited use has been made of the NES outside government, beyond the information available directly from the published tabulations. Two major obstacles have impeded more extensive utilization. Firstly, the returns from employers are obtained under the Statistics of Trade Act 1947, which places on the Department of Employment the statutory duty of ensuring their confidentiality. This precludes the release of the data in its original form either directly to outside users or more generally into the public domain. The Department of Employment, as custodians of the data, are empowered and willing to provide further tabulations for researchers and others, on request, but limited resources within the Department have inevitably restricted access by this route. For more elaborate data retrieval outside programming has been necessary which, given the size of the Survey and the need to develop the programs on a remote basis, has been a daunting prospect. These difficulties of access have been widely known for some years; in 1979 the Royal Commission on the Distribution of Income and Wealth drew attention to the underutilization of the NES:

The Department rightly gives higher priority to maintaining the regular publication timetable than to producing tabulations to meet special requirements of individual users. However, we consider that such an invaluable source should be exploited as fully as possible ... The Department should give serious consideration to the possibility of making the data available, on a basis which protects confidentiality, to users to carry out their own analyses. If this should not prove possible, then the Department might consider developing the facility to respond readily and flexibly to requests for analyses from *bona fide* users of their data. (Royal Commission on the Distribution of Income and Wealth 1979: para. 4.8)

Solutions have, happily, now been devised, and this book, with the research project from which it is derived, represent the first major study from outside government to be based on access in full to the original NES data.

The project has, inevitably, had a lengthy and complex gestation. Its origins go back to two much earlier projects involving the editors. These studies (Thomson, Mulvey, and Farbman 1977, Gregory and Thomson 1981), which were concerned with the relationship between bargaining structure and earnings, drew on information collected through the NES questionnaire but not processed for the published tabulations. In both cases access and data extraction, under safeguards, were authorized by the Department of Employment, and their co-operation, combined with financial support from the Economic and Social Research Council, allowed the necessary programming to be undertaken. The successful completion of this early work established the practicality of access via outside programming.

Negotiations were then instituted with the Department of Employment to explore the terms on which extensive access to the data could be authorized, to open the way for wide-ranging analysis. Because of the important issues of principle involved these negotiations were protracted. Under the guidance of the Central Statistical Office the interpretation of the confidentiality requirement was clarified as precluding the release of information relating to any individual, irrespective of issues of identifiability or anonymization. Discussions were therefore pursued on methods of pre-processing the data to allow its release in a form which respected these restrictions while retaining as much information as possible for research purposes. The form eventually agreed involved a process of 'minimal aggregation', the mechanics of which are fully described later.

While these negotiations were being carried forward a group of academics was formed to begin the planning of the research strategy. It had very quickly become clear that the potential of the data far exceeded the resources of individual researchers or of any one university department. From its initial Glasgow and then Scottish base the group was soon extended to seven different universities throughout the UK, as individuals with known expertise in the various dimensions of pay recorded through the NES agreed to participate.

A successful application for research support was made by the group to the Economic and Social Research Council, which awarded a substantial grant over three years. This financed the extensive programming required to pre-format the data in accordance with the conditions agreed with the Department of Employment, as well as other research costs.

The project has had two objectives throughout. The first, of bringing the NES into the public domain, has already been achieved. The data extractions obtained through the project have been deposited with the ESRC Survey Archive at the University of Essex, who are now responsible, in conjunction with the Department of Employment, for making them available for further research.

The present book fulfils the second objective, to use the enhanced access to the NES records to produce an extensive account of developments in pay over the period. Most of the major facets of the growth and structure of earnings are examined in the context of prevailing macro-economic developments, changes in the labour market, and contemporary policy issues and debates. While much detailed evidence is assembled and sifted, the main perspective sought is one of overview, assessing the pay climate over the period rather than the year-to-year pay-setting weather.

Pay determination is, as is well known, one of the most complex and controversial areas of economic analysis. This is only partly due to the fact that it is not an exclusively economic issue. A variety of themes run through the literature on pay, and these are, for the most part, taken up in the relevant chapters. However, while many pointers emerge from the analysis, the authors do not seek to adduce support for any one school. Rather, we aim to extend the evidence against which existing theories can be assessed, extended, or revised.

Likewise, it is hoped that the relevance of the work to the formulation of policy, in both public and private spheres, is self-evident, although it is not part of our purpose to offer policy advice directly. Decisions on pay in its many aspects are unavoidable, for government, companies, and unions, and one of the major lessons of the period analysed here, in which a great deal of desynchronization of established pay relationships occurred, is that issues of pay can generate a great deal of uncertainty, resentment, and controversy. A more informed basis for debate on pay in its many dimensions can be only beneficial.

The New Earnings Survey, with the comprehensiveness and richness of the picture of pay which it gives, has a major contribution to make to the improved quality of information, analysis, and debate. We hope these will follow from the public access to the Survey data, now established, and the studies initiated in this book.

M.B.G.
A.W.J.T.

St Hilda's College
Oxford

The Open University
Milton Keynes

Acknowledgements

This book is the outcome of a research project which had two major objectives: to bring into the public domain a very large data set held within a government department and not previously accessible to outside users, and to carry out extensive economic analysis based on it. The ambitious nature of these objectives, and the consequent scope and complexity of the project, have brought the involvement of numerous individuals and institutions in varying capacities and at different stages in its development. We wish to acknowledge the help and co-operation we have received from them; they have all, in their varied ways, made essential contributions to the successful realization of these objectives.

Our biggest debt is to the Department of Employment. Their support has been of crucial importance and unstintingly given throughout. Without their willingness firstly to open negotiations on the issues of principle involved in establishing access to the New Earnings Survey data, and then to persist with the venture through the complexities of devising a method for releasing the data consistent with their statutory obligations, the project could never have been launched. When we made our first approach to them, Stuart Rusby at Statistics Division in London provided a major initial impetus through his enthusiasm for the research potential of the NES. Daniel Capron then steered us through the complexities of defining and making operational the terms for the release of the data. Cathy Gibbins, as the book moved into draft, and Clive Lewis as we finally went to press, helped us ensure that the Department's requirements were suitably met.

At the Department of Employment's Computer Centre at Runcorn, where the NES files are created and kept, successive generations of DE officers advised on file structure and accessing, tested the final versions of our many programs, carried out the data-extraction runs, and organized the dispatch of the output files. We were welcomed first by Alan Jones and Trevor Williams, who organized the initial arrangements and ensured that our work got smoothly under way. Alan Jones put many weeks of work into that crucial but most unwelcome of tasks, extending and updating the documentation we required on the full series of Survey data files. As the project continued John Hague, Gordon Davies, Des Partington, and later Chris Bertera, Dave Coglan, Tony Muckelt, and Karl Wissgott gave friendly help and advice whenever called upon, while Marjorie Jones, Bill Spencer, Hilary Roe, Margaret Freedman, Julian Worker, and Robert Hepworth repeatedly fitted our work into already busy schedules. At Watford, Eddy Burton answered many queries when the complexities of the special section in the 1979 Survey were causing difficulties.

The economists at the Department of Employment, David Stanton, William Smith, and latterly Mark Adams, of the Employment Market Research Unit, did much to maintain commitment within government to the role of the NES as a research data set in the public domain. Their continuing efforts in this area are already carrying forward the use of the NES as a research data set beyond the work of this project.

The support of the Economic and Social Research Council has been of central importance throughout, no less so for taking widely differing forms at various stages of the project. Most prominently, since money is an essential lubricant in research of this scope no less than in other activities, the considerable financial support provided by the Economic and Social Research Council made possible the extensive programming and other costs incurred by the project.

We have drawn heavily on the expertise and services of the ESRC's Survey Archive at the University of Essex. During the initial negotiations on the release of the data, Eric Tannenbaum, its Deputy Director, became a valued participant, contributing the Archive's substantial expertise in issues of data confidentiality and the custody and distribution of major data sets for research purposes. Subsequently, the staff of the Archive, under Eric Roughley, gave valuable advice on organizing the release of the data to the members of the project and on smoothing the path for future users through the Archive. When, at their own suggestion, they took over the final stage of data dispatch to the project participants, their knowledge of the computer installations in the various universities and their expertise in data distribution spared us what was threatening to be a major headache.

When the data became available research assistance was provided firstly by Jim Malley and subsequently by Carmen Sanjines, both based at Glasgow University. Their help in checking the output from the initial extract files, in preparing files and documentation to be lodged with the Survey Archive, and in handling the large volume of data was invaluable throughout.

Glasgow University Computing Service provided the facilities on which all work on program development was carried out, and where the test data and many extract files were stored for considerable periods.

The largest single contribution to the successful extraction of the data was the skilled programming work of Sophie Houston, who prepared the suites of programs required to obtain and organize the several hundred different extract data sets which the project eventually involved. That this was achieved virtually without error or mishap speaks volumes for the quality of her work. She rapidly established herself not only as a key member of the team but also as without question the outstanding expert on the NES computer files outside the DE itself.

We are grateful to them all for their varied contributions, without which the project could not have been carried through. We hope that the present work, and the future work with the NES which is now in prospect, will repay our debt.

Contents

List of Abbreviations

B. & CE	Building and Civil Engineering
BHR	basic hourly rates of pay
CBI	Confederation of British Industry
CODOT	Classification of Occupations and Directory of Occupational Titles
CSEU	Confederation of Shipbuilding and Engineering Unions
CSC	Civil Service Commission
DE	Department of Employment
DEP	Department of Employment and Productivity
DHSS	Department of Health and Social Security
EMRU	Employment Market Research Unit
ESRC	Economic and Social Research Council
JC	Joint Committee/Joint Conference
JCC	Joint Co-ordinating Committee
KOS	Key Occupations for Statistical Purposes
MLH	Minimum List Heading
NACE	General Industrial Classification of Economic Activities within European Community
nae	not allocated elsewhere
NBPI	National Board for Prices and Incomes
nec	not elsewhere classified
nes	not elsewhere specified
NES	New Earnings Survey
NHR	national hourly rates of pay
NHS	National Health Service
NI	National Insurance
NJB	National Joint Board
NJC	National Joint Committee/Council
NJIC	National Joint Industrial Council
NJNC	National Joint Negotiating Committee/Council
OECD	Organization for Economic Co-operation and Development
PAYE	pay-as-you-earn
PBR	payment-by-results
PRU	Pay Research Unit
SEG	socio-economic group
SHE	standard hourly earnings
SIC	Standard Industrial Classification
SIC(R)	Revised Standard Industrial Classification

TUC	Trades Union Congress
VAT	value added tax
WIRS	Workplace Industrial Relations Survey

List of Figures

1

The New Earnings Survey

M. B. Gregory, S. Houston, C. Sanjines, and A. W. J. Thomson

1.1. The Survey

(a) The establishment of the Survey

The origins of the New Earnings Survey lie in the emergence of inflation as a major issue in macroeconomic policy in the latter half of the 1960s. As pay increases, particularly those set under collective bargaining, became a central focus of attention, the inadequacy of the available information on pay levels and trends became increasingly apparent. The National Board for Prices and Incomes, as the body charged with investigating proposed increases in prices and wages as part of the government's policy for restraining inflation, was particularly exposed to these deficiencies; as Fels (1972: 91), in his study of the work of the Board, succinctly comments, 'the NBPI very often encountered industries in which practically the only knowledge available was basic rates of pay'. It was this dissatisfaction with the existing data sources on earnings, when the orientation of macroeconomic policy required the detailed and accurate monitoring of pay developments, which led to the establishment of the New Earnings Survey.

The various series of earnings statistics compiled at that time by the then Ministry of Labour (from mid-1968 the Department of Employment and Productivity, and from 1971 the Department of Employment) consisted of several enquiries covering, separately, the earnings of manual workers, non-manual workers, earnings by occupation, and short-term trends.

For manual worker earnings the main source of information was the biannual enquiry into earnings and hours, held in April and October. These enquiries combined the use of a postal questionnaire to firms with information available from official sources, to give coverage of the whole of manufacturing industry, utilities, construction, and mining and quarrying (excluding coal-mining), and of parts of transport and communications, the NHS, national and local government, and miscellaneous services. Workers in agriculture, coal-mining, the dock labour scheme, and, latterly, British Railways were not formally included in the enquiry, but related information was made available for them from official sources. Thus while the coverage of the index of production industries was comprehensive, the coverage of the service sector left major gaps, notably in distribution, catering, and commerce and banking. The survey was a large one, with some 50,000 establishments supplying returns covering around six million manual workers, two-thirds of the total in the relevant industries. The questionnaire was a simple one, asking only for total earnings for the survey week, the number of employees involved, and the total number of hours worked. Five groups were distinguished—men, full-time women, part-time women, youths and boys, and girls. Average figures for weekly earnings, weekly hours, and hourly earnings were compiled at the level of 129 MLH industries, of which 110 were in manufacturing. These were further aggregated to the 20 relevant SIC Orders, with the individual MLH averages weighted by their total employment to offset disparities in sample coverage. For adult males only, average earnings at the SIC Order level were also compiled for the eleven standard regions. In addition to the limitations of coverage, the usefulness of these enquiries, even for comparisons across industries, was restricted by their lack of information on skill-mix and the make-up of pay. As the Department itself acknowledged with each set of enquiry results as they were published,[1] they were 'general averages covering all classes of manual workers, including unskilled workers and general labourers as well as operatives in skilled occupations', and

In view of the wide variations, between different industries, in the proportions of skilled and unskilled workers, in the opportunities for extra earnings from overtime, nightwork and payment-by-result schemes and in the amount of time lost by short-time working, absenteeism, sickness, etc., the differences in average earnings shown in the tables should not be taken as evidence of, or as a measure of, disparities in the ordinary rates of pay prevailing in different industries for comparable classes of workpeople employed under similar conditions.

For non-manual workers earnings were recorded annually in the October salary survey of 'administrative, technical and clerical employees'. The enquiry itself, conducted under the Statistics of Trade Act, covered manufacturing, mining and quarrying (excluding coal-mining), construction, and the water industry. Postal questionnaires were sent to all large firms, with 100 or more employees, and to a 50 per cent sample of firms known to have between 25 and 99 employees. This gave around 20,000 returns, covering more than two million salaried workers, over 80 per cent of those in the relevant sectors. The enquiry thus covered all staff in the relevant occupational groups, regardless of salary level, but excluding those in small firms. The methodology was essentially similar to that of the surveys of manual earnings. Information was collected on the pay-bill, for weekly and monthly paid workers separately, and on the number of employees, distinguishing men, full-time women, and part-time women. The results were collated for publication into 16 SIC Orders, 13 of them in manufacturing. These gave average weekly earnings for the weekly paid, monthly and equivalent weekly earnings for the monthly paid, and average weekly earnings for all employees combined. Corresponding information was supplied on a voluntary basis for the nationalized transport industries, coal-mining, gas, electricity, national and local government, education (teachers), the NHS hospital sector, and insurance and banking. This gave average earnings on a weekly basis, for males and females separately, but without distinguishing part-time women. Where available, earnings were also quoted for clerical and analogous workers only. The limitations indicated above in the context of the surveys of the earnings of manual workers applied equally to these surveys of non-manual earnings; as the Department warned in publishing the enquiry results:[2]

when considering the information for separate industry groups it should be remembered that because of the variations between industries in the proportion of adults and young persons, and of highly qualified staff and routine office workers, the differences in average earnings in the tables cannot be taken as evidence of, or even as a measure of, disparities in the ordinary rates of pay prevailing in different industries for comparable classes of employee working under similar conditions.

The fact that over the whole field covered the average salary for males was about double that for females does not mean that males and females with similar qualifications and responsibilities received such widely differing remuneration.

For these non-manual workers comparisons across industries and over time were made more imprecise by the shifting boundary in the use of weekly and monthly pay.

For manual workers some coverage by occupation was provided in the January and June occupational earnings enquiries. These were, however, limited to adult male workers in five major industry groups (engineering, iron and steel, shipbuilding and repairing, chemicals, and construction). A graduated sample was again used, involving all firms with 500 or more workers, half of those with between 100 and 499, and 10 per cent of those with between 25 and 99; firms with fewer than 25 employees were not covered. Around 6,500 returns were obtained to each survey. Only a small number of skill and payment-system categories were distinguished: skilled workers, semi-skilled, labourers, time- and PBR-workers. Workers not directly involved in production, such as storemen, cleaners, and canteen workers, were excluded. Some breakdowns by region and by size of firm for the engineering industry were also prepared.

The monthly index of average earnings (1963 series) was designed to provide a rapid and up-to-date indicator of the trend in average earnings, covering salaries as well as wages. Again it was sample based, via a postal questionnaire to firms, supplemented by information from government departments and public bodies. In the interests of speed the returns requested only the minimum information necessary for the calculation of an overall average earnings figure for each industry: the total amounts paid in the relevant week to weekly paid employees and in the month to monthly paid, plus the numbers involved. Monthly earnings were converted to a weekly basis, and average weekly earnings calculated by the straightforward division of the weekly pay-bill by the number of employees. Average earnings were calculated for a large number of MLH industries, and aggregated for publication into 20, mainly index of production, industries. The coverage of the index omitted major areas of the service sector, such as distribution, catering, professional and scientific services, insurance, banking and finance, and national and local government. No distinction was made between men and women, full- and part-time workers, adults and juveniles, or manual and non-manual workers, and no information was recorded on the skill-mix of the employees involved, the incidence of overtime rates, or other factors affecting earnings.

The information on earnings available in the mid-1960s was, therefore, in spite of the range of sources, far from comprehensive in either coverage or content.[3] The existing surveys were confined to simple measures of average earnings, predominantly by industry, with little information by occupation, and essentially none on the distribution of earnings within either industries or occupations. The relationship between earnings and basic pay, and between earnings and hours of work, was scarcely addressed. In these respects, as the Department of Employment and Productivity noted in introducing the first New Earnings Survey in 1968, 'there has been far less information available in recent years than was collected by the Government in surveys held as long ago as 1886 and 1906' (*NES* 1968: 2).

Moreover, the 1960s saw growing concern with the relationship between collective bargaining and pay. Collective bargaining had become the dominant mode of pay determination in Britain, spreading from its traditional base among manual workers to an increasing number of white-collar groups. Moreover, with the rise of shop-floor bargaining under the impetus of continuing full employment, the bargaining agenda expanded from its traditional sphere of basic rates to many other elements, as pay premiums, and indeed the payment systems themselves, became of increasing importance to actual earnings.

It was to give an adequate representation of the complexity of pay in these many dimensions that early in 1967 the National Board for Prices and Incomes called for the establishment of an ongoing, comprehensive survey of earnings. As the DEP recounted in introducing the NES, in order to obtain the extensive range of information envisaged while keeping the survey of manageable scope, the NBPI put forward the further suggestion that the survey be designed as a statistical random sample, through the use of employees' National Insurance numbers. This would allow the survey results to be generalized on a statistical basis while keeping to a minimum the number of employers from whom returns would be required. These proposals introduced the essential principles on which the new survey was based.

From that point the development and launch of the New Earnings Survey followed relatively rapidly. After a small-scale pilot study in 1967 the first Survey proper was carried out by the DEP in September 1968. This 1968 Survey collected information on earnings for about 84,000 employees in a 0.5 per cent sample of employees, and a substantial amount of information was published, particularly on the distribution of earnings. The questionnaire design and format of results of this Survey were then appraised by a group of experts and interested parties appointed by the Department and including representatives of the NBPI, the CBI, and the TUC.[4] Following their recommendations, the Survey date was altered to April, the size of the sample was doubled to 1 per cent of employees in employment, and a number of revisions were made to the questionnaire, principally in order to reduce its length.

The Survey proper was then launched in April 1970 and has been repeated in each year since then. A companion Northern Ireland New Earnings Survey is carried out and published by the Northern Ireland Economic Development Department, complementing the Department of Employment's Survey for Great Britain.

(b) The Survey questionnaire

The new Earnings Survey was thus designed, in the words of the official introduction,

to provide answers to a great many questions which are of concern to the Government and to industry, and for which other earnings enquiries are inadequate. For example, it provides information about the way in which the earnings of individuals are spread about their average, about the variations in earnings between regions, about lower paid workers, about the composition of pay and about the earnings of employees under the main collective wage agreements, in particular occupations, and in sectors of employment not covered by other enquiries.

This was to be on the basis of coverage of 'employees in all categories, in all occupations, in all types and sizes of businesses, in all industries' (Department of Employment, *NES* 1970: 3). The sample was to be random and sufficiently large to ensure representativeness in all dimensions and to provide reliable information on the distributions of earnings and hours as well as on averages. Compulsory response under the Statistics of Trade Act 1947 was to ensure a high response rate, with the discontinuance of the April earnings enquiry for manual workers and the October enquiry for non-manual workers giving a compensating reduction in administrative data collection and in the burden of form-filling on employers. All information provided by the employer was to be treated as strictly confidential, to be used only for the statistical purposes of the survey. The employee's name would appear only on a tear-off identification slip, which the employer would be requested to remove before returning the form. Neither the employee's nor the employer's name or address would be held in the data file. These basic principles, elaborated when the NES was first introduced, applied throughout the period which is the subject of this study and continue to the present.

The structure and content of the main questionnaire have remained largely unchanged throughout the subsequent period, after an initial streamlining between 1970 and 1971, when the report form was slimmed down from five pages to two. Subsequently, the order of questions on the form has been rearranged on occasion, and a number of revisions have been made to the wording of individual questions for greater clarity, but the thrust of the questions themselves has not been altered. The questionnaire form for 1982, with its accompanying notes, is reproduced as Appendix A below. The structure of the questionnaire is straightforward. The industry classification of the establishment is inserted by the Department of Employment. Questions 1, 2, and 3 provide the basic information on the sex, age, occupation, and workplace location of the employee. Question 4 identifies the role of collective agreements. Question 5 records hours of work. Question 6 defines and records gross earnings, and question 7 the make-up of pay. Each of these will be discussed in turn, in the form and sequence used in 1982.

Industry/MLH. This is allocated by the nominated local office of the DE on the basis of the principal product of the establishment, the standard procedure applied in the compilation of the many official data series classified by industry. Until 1981 the Standard Industrial Classification 1968 was used, involving a three-, sometimes four-digit level of disaggregation for initial allocation, aggregated to 181 Minimum List Headings for publication.

When the Revised Standard Industrial Classification 1980, based on activity headings and divisions, was introduced in the early 1980s, 1982 was chosen as the cross-over year for the NES, with the full tables published on the old basis and a small number repeated on the new basis. Since 1983 only the SIC(R) has been used. The matching of SIC(R) with SIC 1968 and its implications for the project data set are described in Appendix C.

1. *Sex and year of birth/age*. Since 1974 the calendar year of birth has been asked, from which age in years as at 1 January is recorded in the data file. Prior to 1974 age was recorded at the date of the Survey. In 1970 only, nine broad ranges were specified. In 1971 and 1972 sex and age were recorded jointly, with the four-way classification male under 21, male 21 and over, female under 18, female 18 and over. In 1973 only this classification was extended to a symmetric six-way basis, with those under 18, those between 18 and 20, and those 21 and over, both males and females, distinguished separately.

2. *Occupation: (a) job title; (b) description of work*. The guide-lines to employers on completing this question are reproduced following the questionnaire form. From the job title and work description provided by the employer the DE assigns the employee to the appropriate occupational category. Since 1973 the occupational classification has been based on the KOS/CODOT system. KOS provides the main divisions of the system, which are built up from the CODOT list of detailed job titles. In 1973, 441 KOS codes were established as standard, increased temporarily to 442 in 1979 and permanently to 445 in 1981. These are arranged into 18 main groups for publication. In addition, through the KOS classification each occupation is designated as either non-manual or manual, one of the primary divisions adopted in the processing of the Survey results. Employees described as apprentices or trainees in their job title or job description are classified to the occupation for which they are being trained.

Prior to 1973 the NES used its own occupational classification, in which only 189 codes, in 16 main groups, were used. The changeover to the KOS/CODOT system brought major conceptual and definitional changes as well as greater disaggregation to the classification. Because of the resulting discontinuity, only very limited linkage of individual occupations is possible between 1970–2 and subsequent years.

The occupational classifications are described in more detail in Appendix B, where the full lists of occupations used in the Survey, both since 1973 and 1970–2, are reprinted.

(c) At least 12 months. Since 1977 this question on continuity of employment has specified 'in this job' or 'doing the kind of work described', with the current employer, for at least 12 months. The surveys of 1970–4 asked only whether the employee had been employed with his current employer for more than 12 months. In 1975 and 1976 two questions were asked: how many years the employee had been with the company, busi-

ness, or organization, to be answered as a number of years, and whether the employee had been in his present job for more than 12 months. The first of these questions was repeated in 1979 as part of that year's special EEC section.

3. *Location of workplace*. This is identified by the DE on the basis of the address and post-code supplied. Since 1974, with the reorganization of local government in England and Wales in that year and in Scotland in the following year, the new administrative units have been used. Addresses are coded into local employment areas, which are then aggregated into sub-regions, comprising the London Boroughs and counties or Metropolitan counties in England and Wales, and the administrative regions in Scotland. The Standard Regions are now based on these new counties and Boroughs. The list of regional units identified in the data files is given in Appendix A, after the Survey questionnaire.

In 1970–3, the address given by the employer allowed the return to be coded to the appropriate local employment office.

4. *Wages Board or Council/collective agreement*: (a) *Wages Board or Council*. This question identifies those to whom Wages Board or Council Orders apply, whether or not these are the primary determinants of actual rates of pay or conditions of employment.

(b) *Collective agreements*. The major collective agreements to be identified are listed with each year's questionnaire. The list for 1982 is reproduced in Appendix A. The list is reviewed each year, and usually subject to minor revision as agreements are consolidated or discontinued, or new ones introduced. Revisions to the list were particularly substantial in 1977. The 'direct or indirect' effect of an agreement is intended to cover those employees whose employer follows the rates of pay or conditions of employment set in one of the collective agreements, regardless of membership of the employers' organization or other formal commitment to the agreement.

5. *Normal basic hours:* (a) *normal week*. These are the number of hours which the employee is normally expected to work per week, excluding main meal breaks and overtime hours. They may include hours not actually worked, if the employee has been available for work and guaranteed payment has been made. Where normal basic hours are specified for a period other than one week these are converted to a weekly basis.

(b) *Full-time worker*. Where normal basic hours cannot be given as a specific figure because of the nature of the job, the employer specifies whether the job is regarded as full-time or part-time.

6. *Total earnings:* (a) *length of period*. The length of the pay-period is recorded to allow all earnings to be converted to the equivalent weekly basis.

(b) *Earnings affected*. This forms the criterion for the separation of the sample into Basis A, all employees, and Basis D, the main sample for the analysis of earnings, those with no loss of pay in the Survey period. This is discussed further on p. 10 below.

(c) Total gross earnings. This is the figure from which both gross weekly and gross hourly earnings are constructed. The question is designed to encompass all earnings attributable to the Survey pay-period, whether paid then or not. Overtime and all premium pay is included, as are bonuses, commission, and similar elements of pay, attributed as far as possible to the appropriate period, and gratuities or tips where these are shown in the employer's pay records. The value of benefits in kind is not included, except for agricultural, catering, and other workers where employers provide accommodation, meals, and other benefits for which reckonable values for pay purposes are laid down in Wages Orders. Arrears and advances are excluded, as are any expenses reimbursed. Earnings are reported gross, before any statutory or other deductions.

7. *Make-up of earnings: (a) overtime earnings and hours.* (i) Overtime earnings relate to the pay for overtime hours, and refer to the total pay for these hours, not just the premium element. Overtime pay may be recorded even in the absence of overtime hours worked, if a guaranteed overtime pay scheme is in operation. Overtime pay may be recorded where normal basic hours are not specified. (ii) overtime hours are recorded as time-measured hours, not multiplied up by the overtime premium. Overtime hours may also be recorded where normal basic hours are not specified.

(b) Incentive pay. This is divided between (i) payments made in each pay period; (ii) payments made less frequently. The different types of incentive pay in the two categories, such as payment-by-results (piece-work), commission, bonuses, profit-sharing, productivity, or performance-related pay, are not distinguished.

(c) Shift premium pay. This is the amount of gross weekly pay paid in respect of shift, night, or weekend work not treated as overtime work. The nature of the shift-working, late evening, overnight, or weekend, is not distinguished.

In 1971 and 1972 the only category of pay distinguished was overtime pay. In 1970 the question was much more detailed, distinguishing ten categories: basic, overtime, shift and other premium, PBR, commission, bonus, holiday, sickness, arrears or advances, and other pay.

Certain further classifications are regularly used in the preparation of the published tables. These are:

Adult/juvenile. Adults are defined as males aged 21 and over and females aged 18 or over; juveniles are those below these ages. Since the work reported here was based on access to the full data files, where age can be identified directly from question 1, the authors of some chapters have felt it more appropriate to adopt an alternative definition.

Full-time/part-time. A full-time employee is defined as one who would normally work more than 30 hours per week, excluding overtime and main meal breaks. Two further groups are also classified as full-time: (1) teachers or academics, provided their normal working week is of 25 hours or more; (2) an employee whose hours of work are not specified but who is described by his employer as in full-time employment. The definition of full-time employment thus relates to the number of hours which a worker is normally expected to work, and not to the actual hours worked. If he normally works more than 30 hours per week but works fewer hours in the Survey week, due to illness, holiday, short-time, or other interruptions, he is classified as full-time.

Employee whose pay for the Survey period was affected by absence. Absence within normal basic hours in the pay-period may include: employment starting or terminating within the period; interruption of work due to plant breakdown, inclement weather, and other causes of short-time working; approved absence, including holidays, leave, time off for study; certified or uncertified sickness; voluntary absenteeism, late arrival, or early finish; stoppage of work due to an industrial dispute in which the employee was involved, directly or indirectly.

The full sample is referred to as on 'Basis A', those whose pay was not affected by absence as on 'Basis D'. The main analyses of pay are carried out on Basis D, while the analysis of sample characteristics, and limited pay analyses, are on Basis A.

Non-manual/manual employees. Each occupation on the KOS/NES list is classified as either exclusively non-manual or exclusively manual. The classification of the employee as manual or non-manual is thus determined by his job title or description and the consequent allocation by KOS occupation. The intermediate classification, by socio-economic group within the non-manual and manual categories, used extensively throughout this book, is described in Appendix B.

Certain further measures of pay are calculated from the information given in the questionnaire replies:

Hourly earnings. These are calculated as total earnings for the group divided by the total hours which they worked. They are calculated only for those employees whose total numbers of hours worked is specified, and whose pay is not affected by absence. The numbers covered are at most equal to the numbers for whom gross weekly pay is given, but usually smaller due to the presence of full-time employees without specified hours of work. By the method of calculation, they are earnings averaged over hours for the group as a whole, *not* the average of the hourly earnings of all individuals in the group.

Hourly earnings excluding overtime. These are calculated as total earnings for the group, excluding overtime pay, divided by total normal basic hours. The group is restricted to those for whom normal weekly hours are specified, as with hourly earnings.

Residual pay. This is calculated as gross earnings less any reported overtime earnings, incentive, or shift premium payments for the Survey period.

Special questions

In addition, in most years since 1973 the questionnaire has also included a 'special question' on a particular topic; these tend to be varied from year to year, although some have been repeated after an interval. Although space exists in the questionnaire and the data file for a special question, it is not always used; in 1982, for example, when the new Standard Industrial Classification was introduced, the special question was omitted to reduce the burden of processing. On two occasions, in 1975 and 1979, when particular information on earnings was required by the EEC, a special section was included in the NES to provide this information, with no special question set by the DE in that year.

The following special questions were asked between 1973 and 1982:

1971–4 (*Current training*): 'Please indicate whether the employee is currently (1) working as an apprentice (whether or not indentured) (2) receiving some other formal vocational training (within your organisation and/or elsewhere).'

1973 (*Collective agreements*): 'Please indicate the type of negotiated collective agreement, if any, which affects the pay and conditions of employment of this employee, either directly or indirectly: (1) a national agreement and a supplementary company/district/local agreement (2) a national agreement only (3) a company/district/local agreement only (4) no agreement.'

1974 (*Annual holiday entitlement*): 'Please indicate (in working weeks and days) this employee's annual entitlement to paid holidays.'

1975: Special EEC section for employees in wholesale and retail distribution, banking, and other credit institutions and insurance.

1976: No special question.

1977 (*Types of incentive payments*): 'Please indicate (1) payments based upon the performance of the *individual* employee (2) payments based upon the performance of a *group* of employees (to which the individual may or may not belong) *within* the establishment, company or business organisation (3) payments based on the performance of the *whole* of either the company or business organisation, or one of its separate establishments, branches or divisions.'

1978 (*Collective agreements*): The 1973 question was repeated identically.

1979 (*National Insurance category*): 'Please indicate the National Insurance Contribution Table Reference Letter relevant to this employee.'

Special EEC section on the size of company and establishment.

1980: 'Please indicate if the employee is registered as being paid on adult rates i.e. where, subject to a minimum age, rates are not determined with reference to age. If there has been a recent pay settlement not yet implemented, is the figure given above an estimate of the gross earnings which would have been payable had the settlement been implemented?'

1981 (*Annual holiday entitlement*): 'Please indicate (in working weeks and days) this employee's entitlement to paid holidays during a calendar year *excluding* public holidays but including additional entitlement for seniority and any local (floating) days above the eight public holidays.'

1982: No special question.

(c) The sample

The sampling frame for the NES consists of all recorded National Insurance numbers of employees in employment. Since the allocation of NI numbers is random this method is designed to yield a statistically random sample of all employees in employment; in the words of the Department of Employment's introduction to the first full Survey:

The survey, therefore, was based on a sample of persons selected in a completely impersonal way according to their national insurance numbers, so that each employee in the country had an equal chance of being included. In view of the way national insurance numbers are allocated, this provides a random sample. (*NES* 1970: 4)

with the survey thus 'covering employees in all categories, in all occupations, in all types and sizes of businesses, in all industries' (*NES* 1970: 3). In particular, the NES sample frame avoids the under-representation of small employers characteristic of many surveys of firms or establishments, although in practice the great majority of small firms need not complete any Survey returns. The use of National Insurance numbers automatically confines the sample to employees in employment, excluding the self-employed and members of the armed forces; employees of the Royal Household and, since 1982, employees in establishments located within Enterprise Zones are also not included.

Since 1975 the basis for inclusion in the sample has been an NI number terminating in the digits '14', giving a sample of 1 per cent as all digits are used equally in the allocation. Until 1974 the employee's NI record was kept on a card which the employer was required to exchange annually. In order to spread card exchanges across the year, each NI number also included a terminating letter, A, B, C, or D, identifying the three-month period in which the card was due for exchange. The NES, as an April survey, used cards exchanged in the period March–May, suffixed A. Since only one quarter of the total NI numbers with any pair of terminating digits would be due for exchange in any three-month period, four pairs of terminating digits were specified (04, 14, 84, 94), each with suffix A, to take the sample base to 1 per cent.

Under both selection systems the same identifiers have been used in each year, reducing the effort required to locate the sample. Since an individual's NI number remains with him once it has been allocated, many of the same individuals appear in successive samples. This cohort of those present in adjacent years constitutes the 'matched sample' element in the Survey, and in practice around two-thirds of any year's respondents are also included in the following year. When NI cards, and with them the annual card exchange, were abolished after 1974 the terminating letter became superfluous and was dropped from the selection criteria; the digits '14' alone then became sufficient to provide the 1 per cent sample. As a result of this changeover a maximum of 25 per cent of the sample from 1974 could also be present in 1975 and subsequent years.

A particular feature of the NES is that, while the employee is the unit of observation, it is the employer's responsibility to complete the Survey return; employer as well as employee must therefore be identified. However, since no source holds a systematic record of NI numbers accompanied by the employer's name and address, indirect precedures have had to be devised to allow the relevant employees and their employers to be located. Since the absorption of the employee's NI deduction records into the PAYE records in 1975, the majority of employees in the sample have been located through the assistance of the Inland Revenue, from the PAYE records which employers lodge with their local tax office. These list their employees who are members of the PAYE scheme, along with their NI numbers. Until 1980 PAYE deduction cards were still in use, and the local tax office screened for employees with NI numbers terminating in the designated pair of digits for the NES when PAYE records were being checked in preparation for the issue of new cards around February–March. With the phasing-out of deduction cards from 1981 the process has been essentially similar, but the screening has taken place slightly later, around early March, when the tax offices go through employers' lists to issue tax returns. The search is predominantly on a manual basis, although with the movement towards computerization of Inland Revenue records in the course of the 1980s the search is beginning to become automated. The Inland Revenue then provide the

Department of Employment with the names and addresses of the relevant employers, under authorization from Section 58 of the Finance Act 1969.

In order to reduce the burden which this screening places on tax offices, the Department of Employment has introduced a second source of identification, inviting larger companies and organizations in both the private and public sectors to scrutinize their own records and supply a list of those employees with the relevant NI numbers. This 'nominal roll' is supplied by the employer under a 'special arrangement' with the DE. With the increasing computerization of employee and payroll records the cost which this places on companies can be small. However, while the use of 'nominal rolls' was increasing, by 1982 it was still only being extended to employers with over 1,000 employees, while around four-fifths of the sample were being located through the process of screening of Inland Revenue records by tax offices. Information on employees in government departments and the NHS has always been obtained under administrative arrangements.

Between 1970 and 1974, when the employee's NI deduction record was maintained through the NI card system, the location of the NES sample was a relatively straightforward matter, the employer being identified when the employee's card was exchanged at the local DHSS office. For civil servants and Post Office employees whose NI contributions were paid without the use of cards, the sample was located through departmental or office records.

Once the sample has been identified, one questionnaire form per selected employee is sent to the employer. Where the tax office has provided the list of employees and employers the questionnaire form is dispatched by the nominated local office of the DE. Where the employer has supplied nominal rolls under the special arrangements Statistics Division of DE dispatches the forms directly. Once the questionnaire has been received the employer is under the legal obligation to return it duly completed. For certain categories of employee the questionnaire need not be completed, but simply returned with the exemption category indicated:

(A) domestic servants in private employment (since 1971);
(B) former employees now retired and receiving an occupational pension;
(C) wives working for/with their husbands or vice versa;
(D) those employed outside Great Britain;
(E) those who left the employer before 1 March;
(F) company directors receiving no salary;
(G) clergymen holding pastoral appointments.

For all other employees the employer must complete and return the questionnaire within one month.

(d) The Quality of the Survey Data

The quality of the data provided by the NES depends, as with all surveys, on the quality of the Survey process at each stage: the representativeness of the sample; the accuracy with which the individual respondents complete the questionnaire; and the accuracy with which the responses are coded and collated. At each stage the Department of Employment applies a series of procedures designed to maintain the response rate within the sample, to minimize the incidence of incomplete or unusable records, and to prevent the intrusion of errors as the information is transcribed into the data files.

The employer's responses to the questionnaire are checked in two separate stages, firstly for completeness, by way of a direct scan, and then for credibility, as part of the checking of the data entry. The majority of the Survey returns, for those employees identified through the tax offices, are returned in the first instance to the DE's nominated local office, which is responsible for the initial check that the form has been completed in full. Once it has been established that this is the case, the local office passes the form to Statistics Division for processing. If the form is incomplete the local office contacts the employer to obtain the missing replies; this is usually done by telephone. A strict timetable is, however, imposed on the local offices, and at the specified date they are required to forward the returns, complete or not, to Statistics Division.

A further process of checking is then carried out by Statistics Division. This is applied to all returns, both those forwarded through the local offices and those received directly from employers who have supplied nominal rolls. Statistics Division implements the same follow-up procedures as are applied by the local offices, involving up to two letters and telephone calls.

Once the form has been passed as duly completed the replies are coded and the information keyed into the Survey data files. The keying of the questionnaire responses, carried out at the DE's NES Computer Centre at Runcorn, is scrupulously checked. The number of records entered are checked against batch numbers, to prevent oversight or double-entry. All entries are keyed twice, and any discrepancies checked against the questionnaire form. In addition, a range of credibility checks are applied, to try to capture errors introduced either in the original return or in the transcription process:

1. where the survey reply indicates that the employee has been with his employer for more than 12 months the previous year's record is located. This is necessary for establishing the matched sample, but in addition it allows consistency checks on the record content; age should progress by one year between Surveys, while sex should remain unchanged.

2. all NI numbers are checked for duplicates; these may be either genuine 'double-jobbers', to be identified in the file, or errors.
3. where code numbers are used, as for industries, occupations, collective agreements, or other information, checks search out any invalid entries; pay and hours figures are checked for arithmetic consistency; relationships such as between the overtime rate of pay and the normal rate are scrutinized for credibility.
4. where possible, the mutual consistency of occupational, industry, and collective agreement entries is checked.
5. extreme values for the level of earnings are scrutinized for possible errors, if necessary with reference back to the employer.

Even after this intensive process of scrutiny and checking errors will remain from each stage of the Survey process. How far inaccuracies are important depends on the extent to which they introduce systematic bias into the Survey results. Errors by the employer in completing the questionnaire can be expected to be largely random, although possibly more prevalent for newer employees where information is less securely established. Likewise, errors of coding and transcription can probably be expected to be largely random, introducing variability and inaccuracy into the figures, but not systematic bias.

The main area in which the accuracy of the Survey process for the NES has come into question has centred on the sample itself, in particular on the incidence of non-response and possible biases which it may introduce. Specific procedures are implemented to minimize non-response. After each tax office has screened its PAYE records for members of the NES sample, the number of employees identified is compared with the number implied by 1 per cent of its total records; if the discrepancy appears significant the sample selection is checked again. Where returns are not received the DE local office and Statistics Division both use reminder letters and telephone calls to try to obtain a response. In the relatively rare event of explicit refusal to complete a return, the employer is contacted by Statistics Division; the Department's power to prosecute for non-return has not so far been used, persuasion being preferred to coercion.

In the early years of the Survey rather little information was provided on the response rate, but since 1976, and particularly since 1982, the DE has sought to identify and report on the various sources of non-response. In analysing the response rate we draw on the notes to each year's Survey and comments supplied by the DE. The information available for the years 1970–82 on response rates and the sources of non-response is presented in Table 1.1. The DE has most frequently reported the Survey response rate as a grossing-up factor, of the form '1 in 123 of all employees were included in the year's sample.' We follow the approach adopted by Micklewright and Trinder (1981) in their study of the NES

Table 1.1. *Sample sizes and returns, 1970–1982*

Year	(1) Potential sample	(2) Forms issued	(3) Returned complete and usable	(4) Undelivered by Post Office	(5) Not returned or returned incomplete			(6) Returned as requested but not usable						(7) Compliance Rate [(3) + (6)] ÷ (2) (%)	(8) Response rate (3) ÷ (1) (%)
					Outstanding queries at time data base was closed	Not returned at all	Total	Employer unable to trace employee	Employee left employer before March	Receiving only occupational pension	Non-salaried director	Not known	Total		
1970	220	195	171												77.4
1971	216	193	170												78.8
1972	216	192	175												81.3
1973	221	186	172												77.8
1974	221	186	162												73.2
1975	221	..	157												71.0
1976	219	195	170				9					16	16	95.4	77.7
1977	220	197	172	1			8	2	10	1	1	2	17	95.9	78.4
1978	221	193	173	0.5			4	2	9	1	1	2.5	16	97.9	78.4
1979	222	202	163	..	10	12	22	3	10			4	17	89.1	74.9
1980	220	202	171	..	1	12	13	2	11			5	18	93.6	77.5
1981	213	198	174	1	1	4	5	1	9	2	1	3	16	96.0	81.5
1982	207	192	169	1	2	4	6	1	9	1	1	3	15	95.8	81.5

Notes: All figures from NES reports for cols. (4), (5), and (6) are rounded to the nearest 1,000 and we have followed this practice for presentation in the other columns. The response rate in col. (8) is calculated from the unrounded figure for the potential sample.

Col. (1) represents 1% of the March estimate of civilian employees in employment in GB (seasonally unadjusted). 1970–1 figures are on the NI card count basis adjusted by the ratio of the NI card count to the Census of Employment count in June 1972. 1972–82 figures are based on the annual Census of Employment held in June. The Census was not held in 1979 or 1980 and the figures for those years are provisional.

.. Not reported.

Source: Col. (1): *DE Gazette* (Oct. 1973), Table 101; (July 1977), Table 101; (Sept. 1980), Table 101; (July 1981), Table 1.1; (July 1983), Table 1.4; (Jan. 1987), 33. Cols. (2)–(6): NES Reports 1970–82.

sample, in measuring the response rate as the ratio of actual to potential returns, and taking as the potential sample 1 per cent of the estimated civilian population in employment in Great Britain (seasonally unadjusted) in March of each year, the nearest quarterly figure to the NES survey week in April. The response rate is then calculated as the actual number of complete and usable returns received, including exempt categories, as a percentage of the potential sample. The response rate in the NES (column (8)), at a maximum of 81.5 per cent and a minimum of 71.0 per cent between 1970 and 1982, is significantly lower than might be expected, given the universality of the NI and PAYE systems, and the statutory obligation on the employer to complete the return. It shows substantial fluctuation over the thirteen years, but no significant trend. The response rates for 1974, 1975, and 1979 are particularly low. From the information available, the loss of sample responses can be grouped into three sources: the failure of sample selection, shown by the discrepancy between the potential sample and the number of forms issued (columns (1) and (2)); non-compliance by the employer, shown in forms issued but not returned (columns (5)); and unusable returns, most commonly having been sent to the wrong employer (columns (6)). These will be considered in turn.

The main obstacle to efficient and reliable sample selection lies with the lack of a single source which identifies the employee by NI number, with his current employer, and the necessity therefore of adopting the indirect procedures of tax office searches and employers' nominal rolls. Reliance on Inland Revenue records means that, although the Survey is formally designed to draw a 1 per cent sample of all employees in employment, the sample base, strictly construed, comprises those employees recorded in tax office records as at March of any year as paying NI contributions through the PAYE scheme, and whose NI numbers are included in the records. Any employee not on his employer's list is liable to be excluded. Two groups are systematically affected by this. Firstly, the NI and PAYE systems incorporate an earnings or hours threshold before the employee is liable for deductions. Where earnings fall below the deduction threshold for NI contributions, employees need not feature in the employer's returns. This will, however, actually occur only if earnings never exceed the limit in the relevant year; moreover, once registered in the tax office's files, an employee may remain there, even if his earnings subsequently fall below the limit. Conversely, where an employee is a member of more than one PAYE scheme two different records of his earnings are made, and he is liable to be located twice for the NES sample. These 'double-jobbers' have been identified in the NES Survey files since 1975. The process of identification based on the exchange of National Insurance cards prior to 1975 likewise implied the exclusion of those whose hours of work were below the number required for a card to be issued. The second restriction to the sample base through the use of PAYE records arises from the time-lapse between the date of identification of the sample (typically early March) and the Survey pay week in April. Those unemployed at the first date but back into employment by the second will not be present on the employer's return at the earlier date. These sources of omission are less likely to occur when the sample is located through special arrangements rather than tax office searches, as the employer's payroll records can be expected to be more complete and up-to-date; on the other hand, it may be that, in establishing their nominal rolls, firms themselves tend to omit certain categories of employee, such as senior management, or those on secondment or at remote sites.

In addition to these two systematic sources of exclusion, any failure by the employer to cite the NI number correctly on the PAYE return likewise precludes identification, as does oversight by the tax office in the screening process. Similarly, some oversights and errors must be expected in the preparation of the nominal rolls. Omissions of this sort are believed to be the source of the low response rates in 1974 and 1975; in 1974 difficulties for the employer were caused by the reorganizations of local government and the administration of the NHS in that year, while 1975 was the first year in which the tax offices were involved in screening for the sample following the withdrawal of NI cards.

The number of forms issued but not returned is available only from 1976 (columns (5)), and apart from 1979 (see below) tends to be the smallest of the three categories of non-response. In column (7) we give an estimate of the compliance rate for these years. Ideally, this would be measured as the percentage of the forms delivered which are returned by the due date and in usable condition. However, the number which the GPO were unable to deliver is available only for four years, and was small, while the fact that certain categories were to be excluded from the Survey would encourage non-response there. Column (7) therefore shows the employer compliance rate measured as the percentage of all forms issued which were returned, usable or not; this is likely to give an under- rather than overestimate of compliance, since it counts against employer compliance forms which did not reach the employer or to which he could not or need not reply, although crediting him with compliance for returning unusable forms. Even with the probable underestimate, compliance is generally high, as would be expected for compulsory response. Moreover, the final compliance figure for 1979 is higher than appears from the Table; the questionnaire in that year was exceptionally lengthy and complex due to the inclusion of a special section for EEC purposes, giving rise to a large number of queries and late returns; once these had eventually been dealt with, the final data file was significantly larger than that on which the published tabulations were prepared.

Forms which are returned but are unusable (columns (6)) occur most commonly when the employer contacted is no longer the current employer. This originates in the time-lapse between the tax office screening for the sample, by early March, and the Survey data in April, a gap of some six weeks. Those changing jobs during this period, and possibly in the early part of the year more generally, may not be identified, if their new employer does not include them in his list of PAYE records.

Table 1.2 disaggregates the response rates by the four major groups, full-time and part-time, male and female, employees. The low response rates in 1974, 1975, and 1979 characterized all groups. For full-time employees the response rate was normally in excess of 80 per cent, and tended to be higher for men than for women, although the gap was narrowing. The response rate was substantially lower for part-time than for full-time employees, typically just over 60 rather than over 80 per cent. This seems to confirm the importance for sample selection of the earnings threshold for the PAYE system, a threshold much more likely to exempt part-time workers. The DE, who consistently draw attention to this in the published reports, have estimated that exclusion from the PAYE scheme accounts for one-third of the part-timers omitted from the NES. Contrary to the situation for full-time employees, among part-timers the response rate is systematically lower for men than for women, rarely exceeding 50 per cent, and under 40 per cent in 1973 and 1974. Part-time employment is, however, rare among men, with only around 5 per cent of male employees working part-time, representing under 20 per cent of part-timers.

While non-response is considerably more prevalent in the NES than might be expected, it affects the quality of the Survey only to the extent that it is non-random, involving the systematic under-representation of particular groups. Of the various sources of non-response discussed, several seem likely to distort the composition of the sample. The non-issuance of a form due to the absence of a PAYE record because of the earnings threshold leads directly to the exclusion of the lowest paid, in terms of weekly if not necessarily hourly earnings. Loss of response among re-entrants from unemployment and recent movers is a more subtle source of bias. Re-engagement and labour turnover both vary directly with the pressure of demand and will, therefore, vary across labour markets and cyclically. Unemployment spells and job changes are more frequent among younger people and the less skilled, and in certain low-paying industries and occupations, all tending on average to under-representation of the lower paid. Moreover, since earnings in general rise with length of service under-representation of recent recruits may contribute an upward bias to reported earnings.

While non-compliance by employers is not high, it is plausible to expect it to be concentrated among smaller employers, for whom the administrative burden of completing the return is relatively greater, and where the cost to the DE of follow-up is likewise proportionally greater. While one of the great merits of the use of NI numbers as the sampling frame for the Survey is that it formally eliminates the under-sampling of small employers, this probably re-emerges in a minor way through non-compliance. Moreover, earnings are on average lower in smaller establishments and companies, suggesting that this source of under-representation also contributes some upward bias to reported earnings. Non-compliance by a large employer, on the other hand, would lead to the loss of a larger number of returns, but probably with less tendency to distort the pattern of earnings.

The important issue, however, is not whether sources of possible or even probable bias exist, but whether they are quantitatively significant. This cannot be answered directly, since no alternative data source has comparable coverage to act as the standard of comparison. Some indication can, however, be gleaned from the work of Atkinson, Micklewright, and Stern (1981, 1982), who set out to assess the biases in the earnings information recorded in the Family Expenditure Survey, taking the New Earnings Survey as the bench-mark, but were forced, by recognition of the non-responses in the NES, to conclude that they confronted what was 'in a general sense a "two-sample" rather than a one-sample problem'. They confirm the probable under-representation of part-timers, particularly women, in the NES: 'At very least the NES information on part-time work by women should be used with caution' (Atkinson, Micklewright, and Stern 1981: 46). More generally, however, their conclusion is optimistic:

The fact that the level and distribution of earnings is close in the two sources, with their independent approach and methods, does indeed provide support for the use of both sets of data. The difference of 2% in the median earnings of full-time adult males is impressively small, as is the similarity in the shape of the distribution. (Atkinson, Micklewright, and Stern 1982: 56)

Thus in spite of the apparent universality of NI numbers as the sampling frame for the NES, reinforced by compulsory response, the response rate to the NES is significantly lower than might be expected, and the realized sample seems to fall some way short of the DE's claim of giving all employees an equal chance of selection. Nonetheless, the biases which this may introduce seem, for the most part, to be minor, while the coverage, particularly in the full-time sample, makes it by far the most comprehensive and detailed source of information on earnings available.

Table 1.2. *Sample response rates, 1970–1982*

	Total			Males			Females		
	Potential sample	Forms returned complete	Response rate (%)	Potential sample	Forms returned complete	Response rate (%)	Potential sample	Forms returned complete	Response rate (%)
All employees									
1970	220	171	77.4	n/a			n/a		
1971	216	170	78.8	135	109	80.6	81	62	75.9
1972	216	175	81.3	132	111	83.4	83	65	77.8
1973	221	172	77.8	134	108	80.2	87	46	53.4
1974	221	162	73.2	133	102	76.2	86	61	70.3
1975	221	157	71.0	132	99	75.1	89	57	63.9
1976	219	170	77.7	131	107	81.7	89	64	71.9
1977	220	172	78.4	130	107	81.9	90	66	73.4
1978	221	173	78.4	130	107	81.7	91	67	73.5
1979	222	163	74.9	130	100	76.4	92	64	69.5
1980	220	171	77.5	129	103	80.4	92	67	73.5
1981	213	174	81.5	122	104	85.4	91	69	76.2
1982	207	169	81.5	118	100	85.1	89	68	76.7
Full-time employees									
1970	n/a	150		n/a			n/a		
1971	183	148	81.2	129	106	82.4	54	42	78.4
1972	181	152	84.0	126	108	85.4	55	44	80.7
1973	183	148	80.9	128	105	82.3	55	43	77.7

Year									
1974	181	139	76.8	126	99	78.4	52	40	73.0
1975	179	135	75.5	125	96	77.2	54	39	71.7
1976	177	145	82.0	124	103	83.2	53	42	79.1
1977	177	146	82.4	123	103	83.5	54	43	80.1
1978	177	146	82.4	123	103	83.5	54	43	80.2
1979	178	138	77.1	123	96	78.1	55	41	74.9
1980	177	144	81.4	122	100	82.3	55	44	79.5
1981	168	146	86.7	115	101	87.8	53	45	84.3
1982	162	141	86.9	111	97	87.4	51	44	85.9

Part-time employees

Year									
1970	n/a	21	n/a	n/a	n/a	n/a	n/a	n/a	n/a
1971	33	22	65.8	5.9	2.5	41.8	27	19	70.9
1972	35	23	67.0	6.0	2.5	41.4	29	21	72.4
1973	38	24	62.9	6.6	2.6	39.7	32	21	67.8
1974	41	23	57.5	6.9	2.5	36.7	34	21	61.7
1975	42	22	51.5	7.0	3.4	48.6	35	18	52.0
1976	43	25	59.9	7.0	3.8	54.6	36	22	61.0
1977	43	26	61.7	6.8	3.6	53.4	36	23	63.2
1978	43	27	61.5	7.0	3.6	51.1	36	23	63.5
1979	44	26	65.8	7.0	3.2	45.7	37	23	61.5
1980	44	27	61.9	6.9	3.3	47.9	37	24	64.5
1981	45	28	61.9	7.2	3.3	45.6	38	25	65.0
1982	45	28	61.8	7.0	3.4	48.1	38	24	64.3

Source: Figures and sources for all employees are as in Table 1.1. Division of the potential sample between full- and part-time employees is achieved by using the percentages of each type in the Census of Employment in June of each year. For 1979 and 1980, when no Census was held, the proportion of part-time workers was estimated by extrapolation of the trend 1971–8. The breakdown of employees by category is not available for 1970.

1.2. The Method of Data Extraction

The New Earnings Survey enquiries are conducted by the Department of Employment under the Statistics of Trade Act 1947, which places on the Department the statutory duty of ensuring the confidentiality of statistical information obtained under it. The interpretation of this statutory duty is that no data so obtained and relating to any individual may be released into the public domain. The duty of confidentiality is thus interpreted as relating to the Survey return and the information which it contains, rather than to the identity, and hence identifiability, of the individual respondent. This interpretation precludes the release of the data in the form in which they are held in the NES data files, where each record contains the questionnaire return for one individual in the Survey. The only way consistent with this statutory obligation that the data could be released into the public domain was not as a micro-data set but in aggregated form.

Discussions with the DE on ways in which the data could be made available for research purposes centred, therefore, on devising acceptable methods of aggregation. For the published NES tabulations the Department imposes a minimum group size, on occasion of 100, on occasion of 25; this, however, is to ensure statistical reliability of the averages published rather than to safeguard confidentiality. For the general release of the data the DE proposed that a 'minimally aggregated' form would be consistent with their duties under the Act, where the minimal aggregation acceptable would be that each record released relate to no less than three individuals.

A data-structuring procedure had therefore to be devised to effect this minimal aggregation while retaining as much as possible of the information contained in the original data files. The basic principle adopted was that each 'group of three' to be formed should comprise individuals who are as alike as possible, so that, in spite of its synthetic nature, each of the new units of observation should directly transmit the information relating to its constituent individuals. The implementation of this concept was, however, far from straightforward. The main problem arose from the richness of the data set itself, where the number of possible combinations of characteristics which it offers for defining alike individuals vastly exceeds the number of individuals in any year's survey. With 440 occupations distinguished, 180 MLH-level industries, and 11 Standard Regions, the number of possible combinations of these three variables alone is over four times greater than the 200,000 individuals in any year's Survey. Seeking to define alike individuals on the basis of all the characteristics recorded in the Surveys was therefore totally impractical, making some form of prior selection inescapable. However, because of the high level of aggregation used in the published tables, and their predominantly one-dimensional focus (earnings by industry or by occupation, rarely by occupation within industry, not at all by industry within occupation), little was known about the distribution of individuals across a more extensive set of dimensions. In order to gain some insight into this, and help establish how much disaggregation was feasible in defining alike individuals, the DE agreed to a preliminary exploration based on the 1974 Survey. From sets of characteristics proposed by the researchers on each topic a head-count of the distribution of individuals was generated. This revealed that while a substantial number of the combinations implied would indeed turn out to be void, the attempt to retain more than a quite restricted number of the potential classificatory variables from the Survey would in many instances jeopardize the required minimum group size of three. It also became clear that, given the restricted number of variables which could be retained, the most appropriate set for the identification of alike individuals would vary from issue to issue. The concept of a single aggregation process had therefore to be superseded by a series of differing grouping criteria for each of the fourteen areas of analysis which had been identified in the research strategy, with a specific data set generated for each of them.

The steps in the 'minimal aggregation' process were then worked out as follows.

1. In the light of the outcome of the head-count on the 1974 Survey, the researchers involved with each dimension of pay made their prior selection of the number and identity of the variables considered to be the most important for that analysis. In seeking the optimal level of disaggregation they had to balance the objective of retaining as much relevant information as possible against the risks of losing from the sample those individuals who were insufficiently alike on more stringent criteria to form the group of three necessary for the release of the data. Moreover, while the head-count for 1974 provided a very useful insight into the patterns prevailing in that year, there could be no presumption, given the ongoing changes in the structure of employment, that these would be closely paralleled in other, particularly more distant, years. A priori guidance from knowledge of the substantive considerations affecting the various dimensions of pay seemed the most prudent course. Four basic divisions are adopted in every case: whether pay was affected by absence in the survey period, full- or part-time employment status, whether the employee is adult or juvenile, and sex. No aggregated record forms a group of three which mixes individuals across these boundaries; thus each new record always relates to a group comprising exclusively men, or

women, and either all working full-time or all part-time. Groups of mixed sex or employment status are precluded. In a number of cases, notably where pay was affected by absence, these individuals were excluded from the analysis altogether. Further variables extensively adopted as important influences on earnings are occupation, particularly at the level of the socio-economic group,[5] main industry division, age group, and region. Where an analysis has a particular focus, such as the position of the public sector or the role of national agreements, this is brought to the fore as one of the major variables defining alike individuals. Likewise, features of pay itself, where they are of central importance, are also used as defining variables, as with the presence or absence of a shift premium or of incentive pay for the studies of shift-working and the role of incentive pay. Where only small numbers of individuals are present in the Survey, for example with part-time men or juveniles, the number of identifying variables is typically reduced in order to minimize the loss of individuals from the sample; thus the occupational grouping may be compressed to a non-manual/manual division in place of the eight socio-economic groups. The full list of variables selected for the analysis of each dimension is given in Appendix 1.1 to this chapter.

2. The records in the original data file for any year, held by the DE in sequence by National Insurance number, were then re-sorted on the basis of the sequence of classificatory variables chosen for each analysis, to give a series of cells, each indexed by a unique combination of these variables. All individuals within any cell were alike in terms of the variables specified. This process of sorting on the basis of selected variables was repeated for each area of analysis.

3. Where fewer than three individuals appeared in a cell these records have been discarded, in accordance with the DE's duty of confidentiality.

4. Within each cell of alike individuals the records were re-sorted in ascending order of a chosen measure of pay, most commonly either gross weekly earnings or residual pay. This placed individuals adjacent to each other within the cell on the basis of similarity in pay levels, so preserving as much as possible of the dispersion in pay among individuals.

5. The required 'groups of three' were then formed as an aggregate of each set of three sequential records. Each group of three retains all the classificatory information defining the cell, which is common to them all, while its pay and hours information is the aggregate for the three specific individuals.

6. Information on non-pay variables not adopted as part of the cell definition may also be retained at this stage, in the form of a group-of-three aggregate similar to the pay information. For variables such as age this is a useful way of retaining further information, although the aggregation (and therefore averaging) implies a loss of precision from the original

data. Likewise, for variables with only a very small number of possible replies, a counter is used; thus two out of three within a group may be in receipt of shift pay. However, for variables processed as code numbers and taking a large number of values, such as industry, this is impracticable.

7. Where the number of individuals in a cell was not divisible exactly by three, a record comprising four or five individuals has been constructed in order to retain all the individuals in the cell.

Table 1.3 shows, for each data file generated on the minimally aggregated basis, the number of individuals lost through the need to discard individuals where a group of three was not generated. This was, for the most part, quite limited, sometimes less than 1 per cent of the sample. However, the trade-off between retention of the sample and the specificity of the grouping criteria is evident, the losses being slight when only broad grouping criteria are used, but quite substantial with a finer classification, such as the presence of a particular national agreement.

These data sets are the material on which the analyses reported in the remainder of this book are based. Thirteen topics have been selected, representing the major dimensions of pay recorded through the NES. Eleven of these are examined across the period, giving a perspective over time as well as extensive evidence within each year. Of those, nine use the period as a whole, while the remaining two confine themselves to the period 1973–82; in one case (the relationship between earnings and wage rates set in national wage agreements) this is because of the incompatibilities in the occupational classification before and after 1973, and in the other (shift-working) because of the absence of the relevant variable (shift premium pay) from the Survey questionnaire before 1973. The other two chapters take advantage of special questions asked in a single year only, but of sufficient significance to warrant inclusion even on that basis.

1.3. Outline of the Book

In designing the research strategy to exploit the wealth of new information made available through the release of the 'minimally aggregated' records of the NES the intention was to present a portrait of pay in the many dimensions recorded in the Survey data, using the Survey itself as a unifying framework. Each of the chapters which follow therefore explores a particular aspect of pay within the period 1970–82 as recorded through the NES.

The 1970s were above all the decade of 'stagflation', the combination of slackening growth, increasing unemployment, and accelerating inflation

Table 1.3. *Losses in aggregation due to small cells (% of individuals)*

Topic	Year												
	1970	1971	1972	1973	1974	1975	1976	1977	1978	1979	1980	1981	1982
Manual skill differentials	2.3	0.9	0.8	5.0	4.4	4.6	4.3	4.2	11.2	4.8	4.8	4.9	4.7
White-collar pay	1.7	0.3	0.3	0.5	0.0	1.7	1.6	1.5	1.7	1.5	1.5	1.4	1.4
Sex differentials	0.6	0.5	0.5	1.2	1.2	1.2	1.2	1.1	1.2	1.2	1.2	1.3	1.2
Public sector	0.3	0.1	0.0	0.1	0.3	0.3	0.3	0.2	0.3	0.3	0.3	0.3	0.3
Distribution of earnings	0.5	0.1	0.1	0.2	0.8	0.8	0.8	0.6	0.6	1.6	0.6	0.6	0.7
Regional differentials	1.1	1.1	1.0	1.2	1.3	1.3	1.3	1.3	1.3	1.2	1.3	1.3	1.2
Age and earnings	0.6	0.1	0.1	0.2	0.7	0.7	0.6	0.7	0.7	0.7	0.4	0.6	0.7
Size of company and plant	—	—	—	—	—	—	—	—	—	1.7	—	—	—
Size of company and region	—	—	—	—	—	—	—	—	—	0.8	—	—	—
Hours of work and pay	1.3	1.2	1.1	2.1	2.3	2.4	2.3	2.2	2.3	2.4	2.5	2.4	2.4
Shiftworking	—	—	—	1.0	1.1	1.1	1.1	1.1	1.1	1.1	1.1	1.1	1.1
Incentive payment schemes	—	—	—	—	—	—	—	1.0	—	—	—	—	—
Incentive pay and age	—	—	—	—	—	—	—	0.3	—	—	—	—	—
National wage agreements	—	—	—	12.3	15.8	16.6	15.0	15.7	22.1	17.2	17.7	18.0	17.6
Collective bargaining and pay	1.1	1.1	1.0	1.2	1.3	1.3	1.3	1.3	1.3	1.2	1.3	1.3	1.2

seen as bringing to an end two decades of full employment, sustained prosperity, and rising living standards. This deterioration in macroeconomic performance was accompanied by a diminishing faith in the efficacy of demand management and increasingly frequent use of incomes policies as a major measure against inflation. It was also a period of substantial change in the labour market, with falling employment in manufacturing accompanied by the growth of the service industries, white-collar jobs, and the employment of women, particularly on a part-time basis. Chapter 2 gives a brief review of these developments and the policy themes of the period as the historical context to the developments in pay over the period.

The next group of four chapters looks at the major dimensions of pay and how relativities in these respects have moved over the period. Bob Elliott and and Phil Murphy re-examine skill differentials among manual workers, one of the oldest-established areas of investigation in pay. The central years of the period gave forceful confirmation of the importance attaching to these when the perceived erosion of established skill differentials became a source of industrial conflict. The different measures of pay available simultaneously from the NES along with the full industrial and occupational coverage allow an exceptionally detailed exploration of this issue. Ken Mayhew and Amit Ray, in Chapter 4, consider white-collar earnings, one of the main areas where the introduction of the NES has provided much fuller information. As well as considering occupational structure and pay differentials, this chapter draws particularly on the length-of-service information to examine the implications of the widespread role of internal labour markets and career jobs for white-collar employees. The narrowing of the male–female earnings differential over the first part of the 1970s, subsequently checked, has been one of the most challenging and widely researched aspects of earnings over this period. In Chapter 5 Peter Sloane extends his analysis of this issue beyond previously published work, making particular use of the occupation-by-industry disaggregation which the NES data set allows to separate the effects of occupational and industrial change on female earnings from changes in pay rates for women. In Chapter 6 Mary Gregory addresses an issue which loomed large in the 1970s and has never been far from the centre of attention in the 1980s: pay relativities between the public and the private sector. This area shows the sharpest changes in earnings differentials to be found among the major divisions of the labour force, a consequence of the degree of intervention in pay-setting for the public sector.

The next group of three chapters continues to focus on the structure of pay but through less direct comparisons. In Chapter 7 David Bell, Laurie Hunter, and Mike Danson address the important topic of inequality and the distribution of earnings, and the way in which these have moved over time, looking at the position of occupations in the pay hierarchy over time and at the dispersion of earnings within a number of selected occupations. Richard Harris re-examines the issue of regional differences in earnings, using the scope of the NES data to standardize for a range of structural and compositional influences to establish whether there is an irreducible 'regional' element to the level of earnings, and of what magnitude. Boyd Black reviews the age structure of earnings for the principal groups distinguished in the NES, looking particularly at relative pay levels for younger workers.

In Chapter 10 Andrew Thomson and Carmen Sanjines use the results of the special section incorporated in the 1979 NES for EEC purposes to break new ground in the examination of the earnings gradients for different categories of worker across different sizes of establishment, company, and establishment within company. This documents, at a level of detail and comprehensiveness not previously attained, a major empirical regularity for which, as yet, there are more hypotheses than explanations.

Two chapters, both by Derek Bosworth and Rob Wilson, examine the structure of the working week and its relationship to pay. In Chapter 11 they document the changes in normal hours of work, the growth of part-time work and the use of overtime, and their implications for the level and structure of earnings. In Chapter 12 they examine the incidence of shift-working, particularly its relationship to the use of overtime, and the evidence on the role of shift-work in shaping earnings.

Two chapters then explore different dimensions of the institutional aspect in pay determination, linking the NES data on earnings with other information. Bob Elliott and Phil Murphy, in their second contribution, return to the ever-topical issue of wage drift, the relationship between the wage rates set in national collective agreements and actual earnings. They do this by linking the NES earnings data to national wage rates data, where appropriate groups can be identified; these include pay set under Wages Council Orders. In examining the premium to unionized wage-setting in Chapter 14 Phil Beaumont and Richard Harris link the NES earnings data to information from the Workplace Industrial Relations Survey.

In Chapter 15 Angela Bowey uses another of the special questions, on the extent and nature of incentive payments, included in the 1977 Survey, to make a contribution to a topical debate.

In the only contribution which has not arisen immediately from the original NES project, Rebecca Endean and William Smith report on some subsequent work of great promise with the NES: the evidence on earnings mobility which can be gained from the matched sample.

In the final chapter Mary Gregory draws together the evidence on all these individual aspects of pay, marshalled in the preceding chapters, to give an overall perspective to the portrait of pay.

Appendix 1.1. The Classification of Alike Individuals

Chapter 3. Manual Skill Differentials
full-time/part-time employment status
sex
industry division
socio-economic group
occupation
age range
type of collective agreement

Chapter 4. White-Collar Pay
full-time/part-time employment status
sex
industry division
socio-economic group
age range
region
public/private sector

Chapter 5. Sex Differentials
loss/no loss of pay
full-time/part-time employment status
sex
industry division
socio-economic group
occupation

Chapter 6. Public Sector Pay
full-time/part-time employment status
sex
socio-economic group
age range
region
public/private sector

Chapter 7. The Distribution of Earnings
full-time/part-time employment status
sex
occupation
age range
region
with/without national agreement or Wages Board/Council

Chapter 8. Regional Earnings Differentials
loss/no loss of pay
full-time/part-time employment status
sex
adult/juvenile
industry division
socio-economic group
region
public/private sector

Chapter 9. Age and Earnings
loss/no loss of pay
full-time/part-time employment status
sex
industry division
socio-economic group
age range

Chapter 10. Earnings by Size of Company and Establishment
loss/no loss of pay
full-time/part-time employment status
sex
industry division
socio-economic group
company size range
plant size range

Chapter 11. Changes in Hours of Work and Pay Developments
full-time/part-time employment status
sex
industry division
socio-economic group
presence of collective agreement or Wages Board/Council
receives incentive pay
range of total hours

Chapter 12. Shift-working and Pay
loss/no loss of pay
full-time/part-time employment status
sex
industry division
socio-economic group
presence of collective agreement, Wages Board or Council
receives premium pay
receives incentive pay

Chapter 13. National Wage Agreements
sex
socio-economic group
occupation

age range
type of collective agreement
national agreement code
Wages Board or Council code

Chapter 14. Collective Bargaining and Relative Wages
loss/no loss of pay
sex
adult/juvenile
full-time/part-time employment status
industry
socio-economic group
region
public/private sector

Chapter 15. The Use of Incentive Payment Schemes, 1977
sex
industry division
socio-economic group
type of main incentive payment
range of incentive pay
range of earnings
range of hours worked

Notes

1. The reports for the April and October enquiries were published in the *Department of Employment and Productivity Gazette* in the following August and February. The summary statistics were repeated in the statistical section of each issue.
2. The enquiry results were published in the March issue of the *Department of Employment and Productivity Gazette*, with the summary statistics reproduced in each month's statistical section.
3. A more comprehensive account of these various earnings series is given in Dean (1980).
4. Extracts from the report of the expert group are printed as Appendix V to the Survey Report on the 1968 NES.
5. The socio-economic groups are described in Appendix B.

2

The Economic Context

Mary B. Gregory

The developments in the various dimensions of pay which are analysed in detail in subsequent chapters share the common economic context of the years 1970–82. In order to set this context this chapter gives a brief review of the economic record of the period, focusing particularly on those features and developments which had a major influence, directly or indirectly, on pay outcomes.

It may be said that the years 1970–82 derive a certain unity from the common feature that, in macroeconomic terms, they were unhappy ones virtually throughout. The quality of the unhappy experience was, however, very different in the 1970s from that in 1980–2. The 1970s were above all the decade of 'stagflation' in which the combination of sluggish growth, high unemployment, and rapid inflation led to increasing disillusion with traditional policies of demand management and almost continual resort to policies of income restraint to control inflation. By the end of the decade, however, it was not just demand management which was being called into question but increasingly the collectivist and interventionist approach to macroeconomic management which had been common to governments of both political persuasions throughout the postwar period. In the rejection of this overall approach to the role and responsibilities of government in the macroeconomic sphere and the concomitant change in the priorities and methods of macroeconomic policy, the change of government in 1979 marked a watershed. Initially, however, the commitment to the control of inflation through monetary stringency and the policy of non-intervention towards the exchange rate brought a further, and much more severe, deterioration in macroeconomic performance as measured by the standard indices of GDP growth, the level of unemployment, and the rate of inflation. Only at the very end of the period, in 1982, were some of the macroeconomic indicators beginning to record improvements, while for others the turn-round still remained in the future.

The period 1970–82 was also one of major change in many dimensions of the labour market, of which the rise in unemployment was only the most conspicuous. In some sectors of industry the contraction of employment had already begun in the latter part of the 1960s, and many more jobs, particularly in the manufacturing sector and the nationalized industries, were to disappear through the 1970s. In terms of job losses in these areas the redundancies and plant closures of 1980–1 were merely a sharp accentuation of a well-established trend. Against this, however, the service sector expanded steadily and the numbers of women in employment set new records at several points in the 1970s before the relatively minor, and temporary, set-back in 1980–2. Partly with the growth of the service sector and partly with the changing nature of many production processes a larger proportion of jobs were becoming administrative rather than production jobs, increasing the proportion of employees in white-collar occupations and the role of part-time work. We will look in greater detail at these various developments.

To complete the context for the subsequent chapters the final section gives an overview of the major developments in pay and pay structures over the period.

2.1. The Macroeconomic Context

The emergence of stagflation, as the British economy entered the 1970s, was seen as marking the end of a quarter of a century of full employment, sustained prosperity, and steadily rising living standards, during which the only shadows on the macroeconomic scene had been cast by recurrent balance of payments difficulties and the awareness that the record of the entire post-war period placed Britain at the bottom of the international league table in terms of the rate of economic growth. Over the thirteen years with which this study deals, by contrast, the macroeconomic situation was dominated, sometimes successively, more often simultaneously, by the twin problems of inflation and unemployment, which economic policy seemed increasingly unable to control and, at worst, economic analysis ineffective in explaining.

Some of the main macroeconomic statistics for 1970–82 are given in Table 2.1. In terms of growth the record of the period was unimpressive, with GDP increasing at an average annual rate of only 1.3 per cent, and labour productivity by only 1.6 per cent, both low by historical standards for Britain and particularly by comparison with most developed countries. Moreover, even this slow growth did not bring stability, with the time-path of output following a markedly cyclical pattern. Sluggish for the first couple of years, output then accelerated strongly in the 'dash for growth' or 'Barber boom' named after the then Chancellor of the Exchequer; this upsurge of growth reached its peak in 1973, which was to be easily the best year of the entire period in terms of both high output growth and low unemployment. The strong growth of output was, however, already faltering in the later months of 1973 when the quadrupling of the price of

Table 2.1. *Macroeconomic indicators, 1970–1982*

Year	Annual change			Unemployment rate (%)	Sterling–dollar exchange rate ($/£)
	Gross domestic product (%)	Retail prices index (%)	Output per employee (%)		
1970	1.9	6.4	2.2	n/a	2.396
1971	1.5	9.4	2.8	2.5	2.444
1972	3.1	7.3	2.7	2.8	2.502
1973	5.8	9.1	3.7	2.0	2.453
1974	−1.5	16.0	−1.9	2.0	2.340
1975	−1.9	24.2	−1.4	3.0	2.220
1976	2.1	16.5	2.7	4.1	1.805
1977	2.9	15.9	2.9	4.4	1.745
1978	3.4	8.3	3.1	4.3	1.920
1979	3.0	13.4	1.6	3.9	2.123
1980	−2.8	18.0	−2.2	5.0	2.328
1981	−1.6	11.9	1.0	8.0	2.025
1982	1.7	8.6	3.7	9.4	1.749
Annual average	1.3	12.3	1.6	4.3	

Notes: All percentage changes are measured as year-on-year.

Gross domestic product is measured on the output basis at 1980 factor cost.

The unemployment rate is the annual average for Great Britain, adjusted to current definitions throughout. Figures for 1970 on this basis are not available.

Source: Economic Trends, Annual Supplement (1988); *Employment Gazette, Unemployment Statistics Historical Supplement* (Apr. 1989).

crude oil by OPEC brought it to a definitive end. The continuity of oil supplies was seen to be under threat; with North Sea oil not yet commercially on stream the balance of trade moved sharply into deficit; Britain, along with most industrialized, oil-importing countries, moved into recession. The decline in output was temporarily exacerbated by the effects of the three-day working week introduced by the government to conserve coal stocks and ration electricity supplies during the miners' strike in the winter of 1973–4, triggered by the rise in the oil price following a period of mounting grievance over pay. An even more important consequence of the rise in the oil price—one of a number of commodity prices which rose steeply at this time—was the major impetus it gave to inflation throughout the industrialized world. By 1974 inflation in Britain had accelerated to well over 20 per cent, and nearer 30 per cent at an annual rate in the worst period. For the next two years inflation continued to be the dominant macroeconomic concern, while output remained sluggish and unemployment persisted at what seemed at the time unprecedentedly high levels. The record of these years 1974–6 did much to undermine belief in the effectiveness of fiscal policy, and in particular deficit spending, as a means for securing full employment and controlling inflation. This disillusion prompted renewed interest in the use of monetary control as the main policy for the control of inflation, a shift in stance which was reinforced when, with the balance of trade continuing heavily in deficit and the exchange rate apparently in free fall, the IMF extracted the 'Letter of Intent' from the British government on its plans to curtail domestic monetary growth as the price for preventing the further collapse of the international value of sterling. Adherence to corporatism, however, not only continued but was enhanced as the government—in the event unsuccessfully—sought restraint in pay settlements through the 'Social Contract', under which the trade union movement was to curb pay demands in return for restraints on prices and various measures of social and industrial legislation from government. Following these traumatic years 1978–9 could be seen as in some respects almost a mini-boom; already in 1977 inflation had begun to slacken following the reduction in the rate of monetary growth and the easing of commodity prices; North Sea oil was coming on stream, moving the balance of trade into surplus; output accelerated, unemployment fell, and the exchange rate moved upwards. But although the underlying economic conditions improved the general economic climate remained bleak, as industrial action, mainly over pay grievances, disrupted a wide range of public services. The experience of this 'winter of discontent' in 1978–9 culminated in the repudiation of corporatism in the election of 1979.

In spite of the new government's commitment to the control of inflation the reduction evident in the early months of 1979 was to be short-lived. The second oil price rise, which brought beneficial effects for output, employment, and government revenue, also gave an upwards boost to inflation which worked through to retail prices later in 1979; this was reinforced for consumer prices, marginally in statistical terms but substantially in public perception, by the increase in VAT to 15 per cent as part of the policy of shifting the balance of taxation from direct to indirect taxes. As a result inflation accelerated again towards the end of 1979 and into 1980. By 1980, however, a radically new approach to macroeconomic policy, the Medium Term Financial Strategy, was being implemented. The control of inflation, the dominant objective of macroeconomic policy, was to be achieved through the progressive reduction of the rate of monetary growth, based on a tightening of fiscal stance to secure the reduction of the Public Sector Borrowing Requirement. The combination

of domestic monetary and fiscal tightness, recession throughout the
OECD following the second oil price rise, and the very high exchange
rate for sterling brought about by the turn-round on the oil account and
the capital inflows stimulated by the high interest rates and the petro-
currency status of sterling forced the British economy in 1980–2 into the
deepest recession of the post-war period. Total output fell by over 7 per
cent from its peak in mid-1979 to its lowest point in mid-1981; the sectors
most severely affected were industrial production, falling by 14 per cent,
and manufacturing, where exposure to international pressures was
greatest, and the fall in output over 20 per cent. The control of inflation
seemed, however, to have been achieved. In 1982 it had fallen to under
10 per cent and was already beginning to stabilize around the level of 5
per cent which was to characterize the middle years of the 1980s. Likewise in 1982 the recovery of output was clearly under way, and was to
continue through the remainder of the 1980s, although only in 1987 did
manufacturing output regain its level of 1979. In these respects 1982
marked both the end of the recession and the beginning of the recovery.

2.2. Incomes Policies

Throughout the 1970s incomes policies frequently played a central role in
the anti-inflation strategies of successive governments. The policies took
a variety of forms, statutory and voluntary, involving freezes, norms,
and targets, with and without exemptions. Since their objective, and
frequently also their effect, was to influence pay outcomes, the evolution
of these policies is of particular interest to us.

Initially, in 1970–2, the government's aim was to set a general climate
of restraint through exhortation rather than direct intervention. The
National Board for Prices and Incomes was abolished and with it formal
scrutiny of pay settlements and enforcement mechanisms for any government norms. For the first six months of 1970 the government relied on the
enunciation of a 'target range' for settlements, of between 2½ and 4½
per cent, but allowing a number of explicit exemptions, for productivity
improvements, the low paid, movements towards equal pay, and adjustments to relativities distorted by previous policy interventions. The same
spirit of voluntarism underlay the next phase, but the content of policy
was more sharply defined. In this so-called 'N – 1' policy the government
urged pay bargainers to keep awards 1 per cent below the level of the
previous settlement. Persuasion was bolstered up by the accompanying
commitment from the CBI to hold price increases below 5 per cent,
although the government also indicated its intention to ensure that the
policy was adhered to in the public sector. As inflation and pay settlements

accelerated, however, the government switched to more stringent policies, with statutory enforcement. A four-month freeze, introduced in
November 1972, was applied even to settlements agreed but not yet
implemented (Stage I). This was succeeded at the beginning of April 1973
by Stage II, where increases were limited to £1 plus 4 per cent, settlements were to take place not less than twelve months after the previous
settlement, and all settlements were to be reported to the newly established Pay Board, which was given the power to impose fines on firms
breaching the norms for pay increases. From November 1973 (Stage III)
the allowable increase was relaxed briefly to 7 per cent or £2.25, whichever was larger. In the only formal commitment to indexation made by
any government during this period, this provision was accompanied by
the guarantee of payments of an additional 40p per week for every 1 per
cent rise in inflation above a 7 per cent threshold. The Conservative
government of 1970–4 thus found itself following the same sequence as
previous governments in this area, initially adopting a voluntary approach
to income restraint but, when this proved ineffective, replacing it by
statutory controls, which were largely effective for as long as they could
be enforced. However, the freeze followed by the provisions on twelve-
month intervals between settlements disrupted the timing of pay settlements, an important consideration given the stylized pattern of the annual
wage-round in British pay-bargaining. The form in which the norms were
expressed, including a significant 'flat rate' aimed at alleviating the impact
on the lower paid, contained a threat to established differentials.
These various factors combined to make incomes policy on this pattern
politically untenable.

The change of government early in 1974 brought a reversal of policy
back to the voluntary mode, in the form of the 'Social Contract'. Under
this 'agreed policy' between the government and the TUC the government committed itself to implementing price controls and various improvements in benefits, while the TUC was to persuade its members to
restrain their pay claims. For its first year the participants did not spell
out explicitly what would constitute restraint; however, as the policy went
through four successive annual phases, August to July of each year from
1975, explicit targets were introduced, again usually in the form of a
percentage increase combined with a flat-rate element: in 1975–6 £6 per
week but zero for high incomes; for 1976–7 5 per cent, subject to a
minimum of £2.50 and a maximum of £4.00; for 1977–8 10 per cent, with
sanctions threatened against firms exceeding this; and finally a reduction
to 5 per cent in 1978, giving way to the loosely structured 'Concordat' just
before the election of May 1979.

The advent of the new government brought to an end the use, and even
the consideration, of incomes policies on the traditional pattern as an

instrument of macroeconomic policy, although the imposition of cash limits in the public sector in the early 1980s could be construed as a form of indirect incomes policy there.

2.3. Unemployment and Employment Change

Through the first two post-war decades the unemployment rate was regarded as the key macroeconomic indicator and the principal signal to the adjustment of fiscal stance, and its responsiveness to fiscal changes provided the basis for the continuing use of demand management. From the end of the 1960s, however, this stable relation with other macro-economic measures disappeared, and unemployment began an apparently inexorable rise, no longer responding in the established way to policy settings. With the repudiation of demand management as a means to full employment from 1979 unemployment lost its pre-eminence as a macro-economic indicator, although the various training and other policies aimed at enhancing the employment prospects of the unemployed were to put it back on the political agenda, albeit in a different form, later in the decade.

Unemployment almost doubled through the 1970s, and more than doubled again by 1982, rising from an annual average of around 600,000 to just over 1 million and then to 2.4 million, from 2.5 per cent of the workforce to 3.9 per cent and then 9.4 (Table 2.2). While male unemployment dominated both the numbers and the increase, rising from around 0.5 million to 1.8 million, substantial unemployment for females, rising from 80,000 to 650,000, was a new phenomenon, contributing significantly to the total, although remaining at just over half of the rate for men. While for men the change in the unemployment rate over the period was dominated by the strongly rising trend, it also followed the cyclical path of GDP, dropping under the impact of the Barber boom in 1973–4 and again in 1978–9. The severity of the trend can, however, be seen from the fact that even at the cyclical peak in 1979 unemployment was above its level in previous cyclical troughs. In the case of women the trend obliterates any cyclical pattern.

The level and structure of employment were also undergoing substantial change (Table 2.3). Total employment, measured either as the employed labour force or the number of employees in employment, fell by one million over the thirteen years. The fall was concentrated among men, where no less than 1.8 million jobs were lost, while the number of women employed rose by 700,000. The fall in employment of men was already evident in 1970, although the numbers remained stable, even increasing slightly, through the years of the Barber boom. From 1974,

Table 2.2. *Levels and rates of unemployment*

Year	Numbers (000s)			Percentage of Workforce		
	All	Males	Females	All	Males	Females
1971	621	538	83	2.5	3.4	0.9
1972	692	594	98	2.8	3.7	1.1
1973	490	415	75	2.0	2.6	0.8
1974	495	422	73	2.0	2.7	0.8
1975	764	636	128	3.0	4.0	1.3
1976	1,048	835	213	4.1	5.3	2.2
1977	1,113	854	259	4.4	5.4	2.7
1978	1,093	815	278	4.3	5.1	2.8
1979	1,023	742	281	3.9	4.7	2.8
1980	1,302	938	365	5.0	5.9	3.6
1981	2,088	1,536	552	8.0	9.6	5.4
1982	2,450	1,797	653	9.4	11.3	6.4

Note: Figures are annual averages for Great Britain, adjusted to current definitions throughout. Figures for 1970 on this basis are not available.

Source: Employment Gazette, Unemployment Statistics Historical Supplement (Apr. 1989).

however, the downward trend was evident, checked but barely reversed, in 1978–9, then falling very sharply in 1981–2. Over these two years one million male jobs disappeared. The growth in the employment of women mostly took place in the early 1970s, with the numbers then remaining largely static until 1981–2, when the fall was less pronounced than for men. As a result, where women had been 38 per cent of employees in 1970 by 1982 they were almost 43 per cent. The manufacturing sector was the main area of job loss, employment there falling by 2.1 million over the period, 1.1 million jobs being lost through the 1970s and a further million in 1981–2. Part of these job losses was recouped through the expansion of the service sector, where employment increased by over 1.6 million, mainly through the 1970s, with employment remaining largely static 1979–82.

To gain further insight into the changing structure of employment we now turn to the NES to examine the balance between full- and part-time employment and blue- and white-collar occupations. Problems of definition in both areas are well known, as are the problems of statistical coverage for part-timers; the qualities of the NES in these respects are discussed in Chapter 1. For present purposes the NES sample has the substantial advantage of providing information which is consistent over the whole period and with the analysis applied in the remainder of the

Table 2.3. *Employment, 1970–1982 (000s)*

Year	Employed labour force	Employees in employment			Employment in Manufacturing	Employment in services
		Total	Males	Females		
1970	24,207	21,983	13,717	8,266	n/a	n/a
1971	23,866	21,554	13,376	8,178	7,910	11,361
1972	24,038	21,725	13,335	8,390	7,640	11,641
1973	24,531	22,211	13,497	8,714	7,693	12,069
1974	24,594	22,311	13,367	8,944	7,737	12,217
1975	24,446	22,183	13,224	8,959	7,365	12,524
1976	24,274	22,055	13,102	8,953	7,131	12,604
1977	24,293	22,121	13,077	9,044	7,183	12,679
1978	24,490	22,328	13,120	9,208	7,147	12,877
1979	24,800	22,622	13,179	9,443	7,113	13,239
1980	24,553	22,262	12,898	9,364	6,804	13,370
1981	23,715	21,321	12,238	9,083	6,100	13,132
1982	23,261	20,821	11,900	8,921	5,788	13,087

Notes: All figures are for Great Britain.

The figures for manufacturing are for divisions 2, 3, and 4 of the SIC(R) 1980. The figures for services are for divisions 6, 7, 8 and 9. Figures for 1970 are not available on a comparable basis.

Source: *Employment Gazette, Employment Statistics Historical Supplement* (Apr. 1985).

book. The structure of employment implicit in the NES sample is shown in Table 2.4. Three main changes are evident; the proportions of women, part-timers, and non-manual employees all increased at the expense of male, full-time, and manual jobs. Men continued to outnumber women overall in employment by a large margin, but falling from 63 to 58 per cent of the total. Part-time employees, as recorded in the NES, increased from 12.9 to 17.4 per cent of all employees, with full-time jobs still overwhelmingly typical but dropping from 87 to under 83 per cent of the total. The most striking change occurred in the relative importance of white- as against blue-collar jobs, with manual workers losing their majority, declining from virtually 60 per cent of employees to 47 per cent; the proportion of employees who were in white-collar jobs increased by almost one-third over thirteen years. In the case of each of these major structural changes the balance shifted steadily and progressively across the thirteen years, largely irrespective of the cyclical position of the economy.

In spite of these changes full-time male manual workers still constituted

Table 2.4. *The composition of employment* (%)

Year	Total						Full-time				Part-time			
							Males		Females		Males		Females	
	Males	Females	Full-time	Part-time	Non-manual	Manual	Non-manual	Manual	Non-manual	Manual	Non-manual	Manual	Non-manual	Manual
1970	63.2	36.8	87.1	12.9	40.3	59.7	20.3	41.6	15.4	9.8	0.4	0.9	4.2	7.4
1971	63.3	36.8	86.8	13.3	41.3	58.8	20.9	41.0	15.5	9.4	0.4	1.0	4.5	7.4
1972	62.6	37.4	86.4	13.6	42.1	57.9	21.0	40.3	15.9	9.2	0.4	0.9	4.8	7.5
1973	62.2	37.9	85.7	14.4	43.0	57.1	21.3	39.4	16.1	8.9	0.5	1.0	5.1	7.8
1974	61.8	38.2	85.0	15.0	43.2	56.8	21.2	39.1	15.8	8.9	0.5	1.0	5.7	7.8
1975	62.8	37.1	85.3	14.6	46.1	53.8	22.6	38.0	16.6	8.1	1.1	1.1	5.8	6.6
1976	61.5	38.6	84.2	15.9	47.2	52.9	22.5	36.7	17.2	7.8	1.2	1.1	6.3	7.3
1977	60.8	39.2	83.9	16.1	47.3	52.7	22.4	36.2	17.5	7.8	1.1	1.1	6.3	7.6
1978	60.4	39.7	83.8	16.3	48.1	52.0	22.8	35.5	17.7	7.8	1.0	1.1	6.6	7.6
1979	59.6	40.4	83.2	16.8	48.2	51.8	22.4	35.2	17.9	7.7	1.0	1.0	6.9	7.9
1980	59.3	40.8	83.3	16.8	49.6	50.6	23.1	34.2	18.3	7.7	1.0	1.0	7.1	7.7
1981	58.7	41.4	83.0	17.1	51.7	48.4	23.8	32.9	19.2	7.1	1.1	0.9	7.6	7.5
1982	58.2	41.9	82.7	17.4	52.7	47.4	24.1	32.0	19.6	7.0	1.2	0.9	7.8	7.5

Note: Figures relate to men 21 years of age and over, and women 18 and over.

Source: New Earnings Survey.

Table 2.5. *The level of earnings, 1970–1982 (£ per week)*

Year	Males			Females		
	All	Non-manual	Manual	All	Non-manual	Manual
1970	29.0	35.4	25.8	15.9	17.8	13.0
1971	31.8	38.8	28.2	17.7	19.6	14.5
1972	35.5	43.3	31.5	19.9	22.0	16.4
1973	40.5	47.8	36.6	22.4	24.4	18.9
1974	46.0	54.1	42.3	26.2	28.3	22.8
1975	58.6	67.9	54.0	36.3	39.3	30.9
1976	69.2	81.0	63.3	44.9	48.5	38.1
1977	75.9	88.4	69.5	49.6	53.4	42.2
1978	85.8	99.9	78.4	54.8	58.5	48.0
1979	97.3	112.1	90.1	61.0	65.3	53.4
1980	120.2	140.4	108.6	76.5	82.0	65.9
1981	135.4	161.2	118.4	88.5	95.6	72.1
1982	150.3	177.9	131.4	96.6	104.3	78.3

Note: All figures are gross weekly earnings for full-time employees, men aged 21 and over, women aged 18 and over.

Source: New Earnings Survey.

the largest of the categories discussed, comprising 32 per cent of all employees in employment; its relative importance had, however, been very substantially eroded from 1970, when it had been more than twice as large as any other category. The rising importance of non-manual employment encompassed both male and female jobs approximately equally, while manual jobs for women remained much the smallest category of full-time jobs. The growing category of part-time employees was dominated by women, with non-manual jobs catching up to equal manual jobs in importance by the early 1980s. The employment of men on a part-time basis, in spite of some expansion, remained minimal.

2.4. Broad Patterns in Pay

As a bench-mark for the discussions in later chapters, the levels of average gross weekly earnings for the principal groups are shown, in current prices, in Table 2.5. Where average earnings for men had been under £30 per week at the start of the period they had risen to £150 per

Table 2.6. *The growth of earnings, 1970–1982 (£ per week; 1975 prices)*

Year	Males			Females		
	All	Non- manual	Manual	All	Non- manual	Manual
1970	53.5	65.3	47.6	29.3	32.8	24.0
1971	53.6	65.4	47.6	29.9	33.1	24.5
1972	55.8	68.1	49.5	31.3	34.6	25.8
1973	58.4	68.9	52.7	32.3	35.2	27.2
1974	57.1	67.2	52.6	32.6	35.2	28.3
1975	58.6	67.9	54.0	36.3	39.3	30.9
1976	59.4	69.5	54.3	38.5	41.6	32.7
1977	56.2	65.5	51.5	36.7	39.6	31.3
1978	58.7	68.3	53.6	37.5	40.0	32.8
1979	58.7	67.6	54.4	36.8	39.4	32.2
1980	61.5	71.8	55.5	39.1	41.9	33.7
1981	61.9	73.7	54.1	40.5	43.7	33.0
1982	63.3	74.9	55.3	40.7	43.9	33.0
Total change (%)	18.3	14.7	16.2	38.9	33.8	37.5
Annual change (%)	1.2	0.9	1.1	2.8	2.5	2.9

Note: All figures are gross weekly earnings for full-time employees, men aged 21 and over, women aged 18 and over.

Source: New Earnings Survey; deflated by the index of retail prices (1975 = 100).

week thirteen years later, while for women they had risen from £16 to £96. In Table 2.6 the earnings levels are shown in constant prices of 1975. This confirms that, while earnings for men increased by 500 per cent and for women by 600 per cent over the thirteen years, less than 20 per cent of this for men and 40 per cent for women represented growth in real terms. In keeping with the sluggish growth of GDP and productivity noted above the trend rate of growth of earnings for men was around just 1 per cent, although women did significantly better. In spite of the huge nominal changes, changes in real pay overall were as limited as real economic performance over this period. Moreover, the year-to-year changes in real earnings are seen to have been quite variable. Since inflation is on-going while pay awards are made intermittently, real earnings change continuously and also erratically. With rapid rates of inflation (and during this period they were on occasion over 2 per cent

Table 2.7. *The level of earnings, 1970–1982 (%)*

Year	Males (Non-manual/manual)	Females (Non-manual/manual)	Females/males		
			All	Non-manual	Manual
1970	137.2	136.9	54.8	50.3	50.4
1971	137.6	135.2	55.7	50.5	51.4
1972	137.5	134.1	56.1	50.8	52.1
1973	130.6	129.1	55.3	51.0	51.6
1974	127.9	124.1	57.0	52.3	53.9
1975	125.7	127.2	61.9	57.9	57.2
1976	128.0	127.3	64.9	59.9	60.2
1977	127.2	126.5	65.3	60.4	60.7
1978	127.4	121.9	63.9	58.5	61.2
1979	124.4	122.3	62.7	58.3	59.3
1980	129.3	124.4	63.6	58.4	60.7
1981	136.1	132.6	65.4	59.3	60.9
1982	135.4	133.2	64.3	58.6	59.6

Note: All figures are gross weekly earnings for full-time employees, men aged 21 and over, women aged 18 and over.

Source: New Earnings Survey.

per month) real earnings undergo substantial erosion in the interval between successive settlements, and the timing of settlements becomes as important an influence as their size. Further year-to-year instability was caused by government intervention by way of incomes policies. While these were at their most dramatic in the periods of freeze, all delays to the implementation of settlements and manipulation of their size would have an immediate distortionary effect on real earnings, even if subsequent adjustments eliminated them.

Table 2.7 reverts to the current price basis used in Table 2.5 to give the patterns of change in the major earnings relativities, with the earnings ratios converted to a percentage basis. For both men and women the earnings differential between non-manual and manual earnings narrowed significantly through the 1970s, to become 10 per cent narrower in the case of men and 12 per cent for women by 1979, before widening again sharply in both cases, almost to their level of the early 1970s. The earnings differentials between men and women, on the other hand, show rather different trends. In each case the differential narrows markedly until 1977–8, with a very slight decline thereafter, to end the period 17 per cent narrower than in 1970.

Table 2.8. *The inequality of earnings*

Year	Males		Females	
	P75–P25/P50	P90/P10	P75–P25/P50	P90/P10
1970	0.496	2.659	0.521	2.736
1971	0.480	2.538	0.482	2.587
1972	0.479	2.556	0.500	2.621
1973	0.469	2.525	0.478	2.541
1974	0.457	2.473	0.467	2.434
1975	0.461	2.464	0.452	2.514
1976	0.460	2.499	0.466	2.088
1977	0.454	2.430	0.438	2.003
1978	0.464	2.499	0.436	1.983
1979	0.475	2.528	0.441	1.959
1980	0.481	2.559	0.465	2.028
1981	0.510	2.642	0.499	2.178
1982	0.518	2.697	0.506	2.153

Notes: P75 is the 75th percentile (upper quartile) earnings level. P50 is the 50th percentile (median) earnings level. P25 is the 25th percentile (lower quartile) earnings level.

Figures relate to full-time employees, non-manual and manual, males aged 21 and over, females 18 and over.

The overall dispersion of earnings, for men and women separately, is summarized in Table 2.8. Two measures are shown; the interquartile range (upper minus lower quartile earnings, relative to the median), concentrating on the central part of the distribution, and the decile ratio (the level of earnings at the 90th percentile relative to the 10th percentile), which gives greater emphasis to earnings at the two extremes. The patterns for men and women show certain broad similarities of trend although the size and timing of relative changes differ. For men the dispersion of earnings on both measures tended to narrow between 1970 and 1974, widened again slightly in 1975–6, before reaching its lowest point in 1977; thereafter it increased sharply, to be significantly greater in 1982 than at the start of the period. For women a similar narrowing over the early years is evident, with the modest reversal in 1975–6; the lowest degree of inequality, however, occurs rather later, in 1978–9, and the subsequent widening of the distribution in the early 1980s still leaves less inequality than in 1970.

The more detailed exploration of these, and other, relativities and the factors shaping them are the subject-matter of the remaining chapters.

3
Manual Skill Differentials[1]

R. F. Elliott and P. D. Murphy

3.1. Introduction

Individuals who invest in the acquisition of skills which enhance their productivity expect to receive a return on their investment, a return which takes the form of a higher wage, *ceteris paribus*, than that of unskilled workers. This premium, the skill differential, provides the incentive for individuals to incur the costs associated with the acquisition of a skill and thus its existence is an essential precondition for the development of the skills demanded in a modern economy. The magnitude of the average return to skills has therefore been the focus of considerable analysis over the years.

Industry studies suggest that over the years since 1945 the differentials enjoyed by both skilled and semi-skilled manual males contracted during the decade to the mid–1950s, stabilized or even widened slightly over the period to the start of the 1970s, and narrowed sharply once again during the period to the mid–1970s.[2] However this picture is based on an analysis of and generalization from a few key industries, largely, it should be noted, in the manufacturing sector, for before the inception of the New Earnings Survey there was no sufficiently comprehensive data source reporting the picture in each of the complete range of industries and services found in Great Britain. Access to the disaggregated New Earnings Survey data files has enabled us to build up a complete picture of the behaviour of skill differentials in the period since 1970. We have been able to distinguish the relative magnitude of the differential in each industry and describe the manner in which it has changed over the period. Moreover we have been able to distinguish the extent to which movements in differentials, expressed in terms of weekly earnings, reflect differences in the hours worked and incentive payments received by workers of differing levels of skill and to distinguish the extent to which changes in the age and occupational structure of the workforce account for the changes in the broad industry averages that we detail. In the following pages we describe the behaviour of the pay differentials enjoyed by full-time manual males and females possessing differing levels of skill for the period 1970–82.

The skill differentials we employ in our subsequent analysis were calculated by assigning individuals to each of four categories—foremen and supervisors, skilled, semi-skilled, and unskilled—according to the occupation in which they work in the manner described in Appendix B. Broadly speaking those manual occupations reported in the NES as involving supervisory work or bearing the title foremen are assigned to the category foremen and supervisors, those occupations populated by time-served craftsmen or individuals with a similar level of *formal* qualification were assigned to the skilled category; those identified as labouring or in un-skilled jobs to the unskilled category, and the balance to the category semi-skilled. For males these represent four homogeneous and distinct skill groups but it is doubtful that the same can be said for females. It seems likely that the criteria used to aggregate occupations into different skill groups is least appropriate in their case, for on the one hand they possess fewer formal skill qualifications and on the other they are less likely to occupy simple labouring jobs. It should be further noted that in 1973 the NES adopted a new system of classifying occupations which resulted in some changes in the coverage of those occupations which comprise in particular the category foremen and supervisors. As a result comparison of the differential for this group in particular between the periods before and after 1973 must be conducted with caution and since this reclassification also affected other groups to a small degree the major part of the subsequent analysis is confined to the period from 1973 onwards.

3.2. Long-Run Skill Differentials

Over the period 1973 to 1982 the average weekly earnings of male supervisors and foremen in all industries and services in Britain exceeded the average weekly earnings of unskilled males by 33.8 per cent. This compares to a differential over the average weekly earnings of unskilled workers of 21.3 per cent for skilled males and 7.9 per cent for semi-skilled males. The corresponding differentials for females are 17.6, 4.7, and 6.1 per cent respectively. Thus while the long-run differentials enjoyed by semi-skilled workers are similar for males and females, those for female supervisors and foremen and skilled workers are appreciably less than those for their male counterparts.

These differentials reflect, for the most part, the long-run returns to the skills acquired by foremen and supervisors, skilled and semi-skilled work-ers and to the responsibilities of foremen and supervisors, but they may also reflect differences in their hours of work and earnings under incentive payment schemes. That is, they may reflect differences in both the quality and intensity of labour input and as such, provide an inaccurate measure of the 'pure' return to skill. On the face of it the most obvious way to estimate the pure skill differential is to control for differences in the quantity and intensity of labour input, that is to calculate the differential in terms of basic pay. However there are objections to this approach. Many workers are paid under incentive schemes and have minimum earnings guarantees which exceed their basic rates, if indeed a basic rate is set. To all intents and purposes they and management come to regard the minimum earnings level as the basic rate of pay and it is this which should be used in the calculation of differentials. It would, therefore, be inappropriate to exclude that element of earnings which contributes to the minimum. In the same way the widespread and sustained resort to overtime in Britain seems less to reflect the immediate labour requirements of firms than to be designed to produce some minimum level of earnings. Again this suggests that earnings, or some part of them, and not basic rates of pay ought to be regarded as the best measure of the effective rates of pay for many jobs and therefore as the basis on which to calculate differentials.

The New Earnings Survey details the composition of earnings on a consistent basis from 1973 onwards and allows us to calculate differentials in terms of weekly, hourly, and basic rates of pay. It therefore enables us to see whether these different measures tell the same story about changes in the differential and whether it matters which is chosen as our unit of analysis. The long-run differentials for males and females calculated for each of these three measures are reported in Table 3.1 which also reveals the substantially different make-up of earnings for the four socio-economic groups for which we calculate skill differentials.

Table 3.1 indicates that it makes little difference to the size of the differentials enjoyed by skilled and semi-skilled males, whether we express this in terms of gross weekly or hourly earnings or indeed in terms of basic pay. It is evident that the share of the earnings of skilled and semi-skilled workers which is accounted for by incentive and overtime pay is very similar to that of unskilled workers. On the other hand it does matter which measure we use for foremen and supervisors and skilled and semi-skilled females. Shift and incentive pay make a much smaller contribution to the earnings of both male and female foremen and supervisors than they do to the earnings of their unskilled counterparts and accordingly the differential is considerably larger when expressed in terms of basic rates of pay than it is when expressed in terms of earnings. It is also clear from Table 3.1 that incentive and shift pay account for a much larger proportion of the earnings of skilled, and in particular semi-skilled, females than they do for unskilled females. In consequence when the skill differential for skilled and semi-skilled females is expressed in terms of basic pay it turns out to be negative. A negative long-run skill

Table 3.1. *Long-run skill differentials and the composition of earnings, 1973–1982*

SEG	Long-run skill differentials						Composition of average earnings (%)					
	Males			Females			Males			Females		
	Weekly earnings	Hourly earnings	Basic pay	Weekly earnings	Hourly earnings	Basic pay	Overtime pay	Incentive and shift pay	Basic pay	Overtime pay	Incentive and shift pay	Basic pay
5. Foremen and supervisors	133.8	135.1	145.6	117.6	117.0	121.8	13.1	6.7	80.2	3.6	3.5	92.9
6. Skilled	121.3	121.9	120.1	104.7	104.5	99.8	14.4	12.5	73.1	2.9	11.6	85.5
7. Semi-skilled	107.9	108.3	107.3	106.1	105.2	97.1	14.6	12.1	73.3	3.1	15.7	81.2
8. Unskilled	100.0	100.0	100.0	100.0	100.0	100.0	14.2	12.1	73.7	3.6	6.7	89.7

Table 3.2. *Long-run differentials by industry, males, 1970–1982*

Division	Foremen and supervisors	Skilled	Semi-skilled
0. Agriculture, forestry, and fishing	135.5	132.9	114.3
1. Energy and water	136.1	116.7	104.6
2. Mineral extraction etc.	127.6	114.3	106.0
3. Metal goods, engineering, vehicles	134.5	118.8	107.9
4. Other manufacturing	124.8	119.1	106.9
5. Construction	133.4	115.5	107.4
6. Distribution and hotels	128.8	119.6	106.5
7. Transport and communications	133.6	115.1	109.2
8. Banking and finance	142.2	136.8	116.3
9. Other services	132.5	120.5	105.5
All industries	135.4	121.9	108.6

Note: Unskilled weekly earnings in each industry = 100.

differential is hardly plausible and suggests that it would be wrong to exclude incentive pay from the calculation of female differentials.

Long-run differentials, expressed in terms of weekly earnings, differ between industries as Tables 3.2 for males and 3.3 for females illustrate. The differentials enjoyed by male supervisors and foremen, skilled workers, and the semi-skilled are greatest in banking and finance but after that no clear pattern emerges. The differential enjoyed by the semi-skilled is smallest in the energy and water industries, while for the skilled it is smallest in mineral extraction and for foremen and supervisors in other manufacturing.

Among females the pattern is even more varied, although there are many fewer observations due to the crowding of female employment into a relatively small number of occupations and industries.[3] The differential for foremen and supervisors is greatest in distribution and hotels and least in engineering and vehicles. For skilled workers the differential is greatest in metal goods and least in other services, where the average weekly earnings of skilled workers are less than those of the unskilled workers in this industry. Again in other manufacturing semi-skilled females have weekly earnings less than those of the unskilled while the differential for the semi-skilled is greatest in transport and communications.

One question naturally arises. Why do skill differentials differ between industries? The theory of net advantages informs us that the pay of a

Table 3.3. *Long-run differentials by industry, females, 1970–1982*

Division	Foremen and supervisors	Skilled	Semi-skilled
0. Agriculture, forestry, and fishing	—	—	—
1. Energy and water	—	—	—
2. Mineral extraction etc.	—	105.5	106.7
3. Metal goods, engineering, vehicles	122.8	109.1	106.7
4. Other manufacturing	118.0	102.8	98.3
5. Construction	—	—	—
6. Distribution and hotels	132.5	107.5	105.1
7. Transport and communications	—	—	131.1
8. Banking and finance	—	—	—
9. Other services	124.4	96.6	111.0
All industries	122.5	105.5	108.0

Note: Unskilled weekly earnings in each industry = 100.

particular occupation or skill group may differ between industries to compensate workers for the different conditions of work they encounter in the various industries. In addition there may be non-compensating differentials due to the influence of unions and/or internal labour markets. Our theory suggests that those skilled or indeed unskilled workers working in the least pleasant conditions or the most highly organized will enjoy the highest rates of pay, and thus earnings for any skill group will differ between industries. Of course it does not follow from this that skill differentials will differ between industries, for the skilled and unskilled may be employed in equally pleasant or unpleasant conditions in each industry. In this case the inter-industry dispersion of earnings for the unskilled will match that for the skilled and there will, as a result, be no difference in skill differentials between industries in the long run. The fact that we observe a substantial variation in the inter-industry structure of skill differentials however suggests that skilled and unskilled workers are often not employed under the same conditions nor subject to the same institutional pressures in each industry and so they require rather different levels of compensation within the same industry. Reflecting this the inter-industry dispersion of earnings, as measured by the coefficient of variation, is, at 9 per cent for skilled and semi-skilled workers, rather smaller than that for unskilled workers, for whom the coefficient of variation is 13 per cent. Thus part of the variation in the level of skill differentials between industries is probably accounted for by the different conditions and institutional context that confront the skilled and semi-skilled on the one hand and unskilled workers on the other in the same industry. In the case of females part of the explanation is also likely to be the rather more heterogeneous skill categories as discussed above.

3.3. Changes in Aggregate Skill Differentials, 1970–1982

Figs. 3.1 to 3.6 map changes in differentials over the period 1970 to 1982 while Table 3.4 records the change over the period since 1973. Both detail three different measures of the differential for males and females. Fig. 3.1 reveals that from a level equivalent to 140.3 per cent of unskilled weekly earnings in 1970 those of male foremen and supervisors declined to 137.3 per cent in 1982. The comparable figures for skilled males were 123.9 per cent in 1970 and 122.0 per cent in 1982, while for semi-skilled males they were 111.0 and 108.1 per cent in 1970 and 1982 respectively. Fig. 3.3 which records hourly earnings reveals a similar picture. Only Fig. 3.5 reporting basic pay reveals a slight widening in the differential of skilled and semi-skilled males. All these charts reveal some year-on-year fluctuation in the differential. During the period to 1975–7 differentials narrowed for all groups but after this time those of the skilled and semi-skilled widened slightly while those of foremen and supervisors widened rather more.

Female differentials reveal rather larger fluctuations over the period since 1970. From levels of 141.3, 109.7, and 115.5 per cent of unskilled weekly earnings for foremen and supervisors, skilled, and semi-skilled workers respectively in 1970 these had declined to 119.2, 103.8, and 105.0 respectively in 1982. Again Fig. 3.4 which reports hourly earnings paints a similar picture to Fig. 3.2 reporting weekly earnings. Both suggest that the differentials of female supervisors and foremen narrowed sharply and those of skilled and semi-skilled less sharply in the period to 1975. All widened slightly thereafter to recover some, though not all, of the ground lost earlier. Here again we see the significance of payments-by-results to skilled and in particular semi-skilled females, for a negative differential emerges for part of the period when it is expressed in terms of basic pay. However the negative differential has disappeared by the end of the period because the contribution of incentive pay to the earnings of skilled and semi-skilled females falls dramatically over the period, as Table 3.5 indicates. In 1973 15.6 per cent of the weekly earnings of skilled females and 19.0 per cent of the earnings of semi-skilled females compared to only 6.6 per cent of the earnings of unskilled females was accounted for by shift and incentive pay, largely incentive pay. By 1982 these proportions had diminished to 8.5 and 11.6 per cent in the case of skilled and semi-skilled females respectively but had increased to 7.2 per cent for the unskilled. Thus by the end of the period the unskilled depended on incentive pay only slightly less than did the semi-skilled and skilled.

3.4. The Cyclical Behaviour of Differentials

Closer inspection of Figs. 3.1 and 3.2 reveals not only that there are periods of contracting and then widening differentials but that there appear to be substantial fluctuations around these broad movements. Earlier writers (Reder 1955) have suggested that skill differentials exhibit a distinct counter-cyclical pattern for the pay of the unskilled falls most in the depression and rises fastest in the boom phases of the cycle. Furthermore it is well known that overtime hours and incentive payments vary positively with the cycle and we should therefore expect the earnings of some of our socio-economic groups to vary in a pro-cyclical fashion. If these pro-cyclical movements in earnings are confined to only some of the skill groups then this also imparts a distinct cyclical pattern to skill differentials. For both these reasons we decided to evaluate the cyclical sensitivity of skill differentials. We therefore regressed the proportional change in the annual skill differential, D_t, on the contemporaneous proportional change in annual output, O_t, and a constant term, C. Thus $D_{it} = C + bO_t + E$ where E represents a stochastic error term. A significant coefficient, b, on O_t, attests to the cyclical sensitivity of the differential for the skill category, i, in question, and the size of this coefficient provides an estimate of the magnitude of this effect.

Part A of Table 3.6 reports the results of this exercise for the period from 1970 to 1982 with the differential measured in terms of average weekly earnings. They provide cold comfort to supporters of the Reder hypothesis for the only significant output effect, among skilled females, is pro-cyclical in nature. Even here, however, the magnitude of the cyclical effect is relatively small suggesting that a 1 per cent increase in output is associated with a 0.45 per cent widening in the proportional differential for skilled female workers; that is, the long-run differential for skilled females as detailed in Table 3.3 widens from 105.5 to 106 as a result of a 1 per cent increase in output.

In one respect the failure to find cyclical sensitivity in male differentials was not surprising particularly when we reconsider the evidence given in Tables 3.1 and 3.5. These reveal that overtime pay was an equally important component of earnings for each of the four male socio-economic groups considered. Our analysis showed that while there are

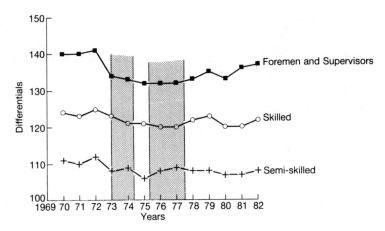

Fig. 3.1. Male differentials, 1970–1982 (weekly earnings)

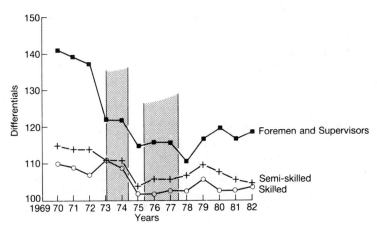

Fig. 3.2. Female differentials, 1970–1982 (weekly earnings)

R. F. Elliott and P. D. Murphy

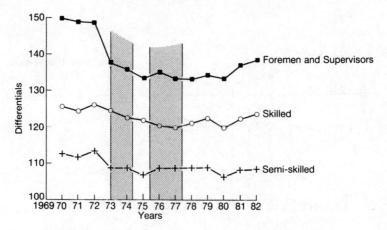

Fig. 3.3. Male differentials, 1970–1982 (hourly earnings)

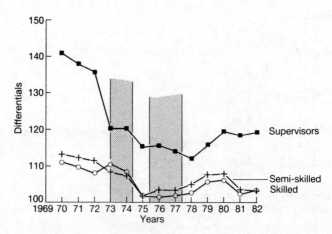

Fig. 3.4. Female differentials, 1970–1982 (hourly earnings)

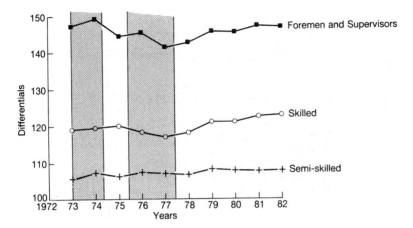

Fig. 3.5. Male differentials, 1973–1982 (excluding overtime, shift, and incentive pay)

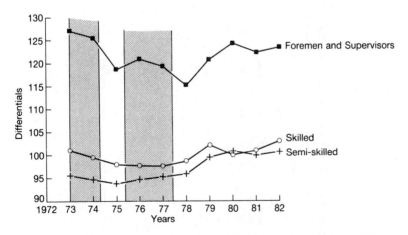

Fig. 3.6. Female differentials, 1973–1982 (excluding overtime, shift, and incentive pay)

Table 3.4. *Differentials in weekly and hourly earnings and basic pay for males and females, 1973–1982*

Year	Foremen and supervisors						Skilled						Semi-skilled					
	Males			Females			Males			Females			Males			Females		
	Weekly earnings (a)	Hourly earnings (b)	Basic pay (c)	Weekly earnings (a)	Hourly earnings (b)	Basic pay (c)	Weekly earnings (a)	Hourly earnings (b)	Basic pay (c)	Weekly earnings (a)	Hourly earnings (b)	Basic pay (c)	Weekly earnings (a)	Hourly earnings (b)	Basic pay (c)	Weekly earnings (a)	Hourly earnings (b)	Basic pay (c)
1973	134.1	137.4	147.3	121.6	120.4	127.1	123.4	124.5	119.1	111.4	110.6	100.1	108.1	108.7	105.6	110.6	108.3	95.6
1974	133.4	135.8	149.3	121.8	120.3	125.6	121.0	122.6	119.6	109.4	108.4	99.5	108.6	108.8	107.4	109.8	107.2	94.7
1975	131.9	133.4	144.4	115.1	115.1	118.8	121.1	121.9	120.2	102.1	101.9	97.9	106.3	107.0	106.2	103.7	102.0	93.8
1976	132.5	135.1	145.4	116.9	115.5	120.9	119.9	120.3	118.4	102.3	101.5	97.7	107.9	108.7	107.5	106.3	103.5	94.8
1977	132.2	133.2	141.5	116.0	114.0	119.3	120.0	119.8	117.1	103.1	102.0	97.6	108.6	108.9	107.2	106.1	103.4	95.3
1978	133.1	133.0	142.7	110.6	112.1	115.2	121.5	122.1	118.2	103.3	102.7	98.6	108.4	108.9	106.8	107.4	105.0	96.0
1979	135.1	134.2	145.8	117.0	115.6	120.9	123.0	122.5	121.2	106.1	105.7	102.2	108.3	109.0	108.4	98.1	107.6	99.6
1980	133.2	133.3	145.5	120.2	119.4	124.4	120.4	119.8	121.2	102.7	106.2	100.0	107.3	106.4	108.0	108.1	107.9	100.8
1981	135.6	136.9	147.3	117.4	118.3	122.4	120.3	122.3	122.7	102.5	102.3	100.9	107.2	108.1	107.8	105.7	103.5	99.9
1982	137.3	138.3	146.9	119.2	119.2	123.5	122.0	123.7	123.1	103.8	103.4	103.0	108.1	108.5	108.0	105.0	103.2	100.7
Mean	133.8	135.1	145.6	117.6	117.0	121.8	121.3	121.9	120.1	104.7	104.5	99.8	107.9	108.3	107.3	106.1	105.2	97.1
Coefficient of variation (%)	1.3	1.4	1.6	2.9	2.5	2.9	1.0	1.3	1.6	3.1	3.0	1.9	0.7	0.8	0.8	3.3	2.2	2.9

Note: Unskilled earnings = 100.

Table 3.5. *Percentage of earnings accounted for by overtime and shift premium and incentive pay, 1973–1982*

Year	Foremen and supervisors				Skilled				Semi-skilled				Unskilled			
	Overtime		Premium and incentive		Overtime		Premium and incentive		Overtime		Premium and incentive		Overtime		Premium and incentive	
	M.	F.	M.	F.	M.	F.	M.	F.	M.	F.	M.	F.	M.	F.	M.	F.
1973	14.2	3.8	6.4	2.7	16.5	3.3	13.6	15.6	16.7	3.7	12.6	19.0	16.8	4.0	10.9	6.6
1974	14.3	4.3	6.1	3.3	15.8	3.1	13.9	15.4	16.8	3.7	12.8	19.1	16.8	4.0	12.1	6.4
1975	12.6	3.0	6.7	3.8	14.6	2.6	12.3	10.9	14.5	2.5	11.9	15.9	14.6	3.3	11.8	6.5
1976	12.1	3.5	5.6	2.4	13.7	2.0	12.3	11.0	13.5	2.5	11.8	16.3	13.3	2.6	11.7	6.4
1977	12.9	3.2	6.0	3.0	14.1	2.8	12.0	11.0	13.8	2.6	11.5	15.5	13.3	3.0	10.9	5.9
1978	13.4	2.8	7.2	3.6	14.8	3.0	13.1	11.2	14.5	3.3	12.4	16.5	13.7	3.4	12.1	6.8
1979	13.9	4.3	7.4	3.9	15.5	3.5	13.4	11.0	15.1	3.4	12.7	16.1	14.5	4.0	13.2	7.2
1980	13.5	3.7	7.4	4.4	14.3	2.8	12.8	11.7	14.7	3.3	12.4	13.9	14.1	3.9	13.4	7.3
1981	11.6	3.0	7.0	4.2	11.9	2.7	10.6	9.8	13.1	3.0	11.5	12.9	12.3	3.9	12.7	7.1
1982	12.8	4.0	6.9	4.1	13.0	3.4	11.3	8.5	13.3	3.2	11.7	11.6	12.4	4.0	12.6	7.2

Table 3.6. *Cyclical sensitivity of skill differentials, 1970–1982*

	Male			Female		
	Foremen and supervisors	Skilled	Semi-skilled	Foremen and supervisors	Skilled	Semi-skilled
Part A (weekly earnings)						
Constant	−0.15	−0.16	−0.24	−1.29	−0.64	−0.60
	(−0.30)	(−0.47)	(−0.58)	(−0.97)	(−1.36)	(−0.45)
Change in	−0.03	0.09	0.05	−0.07	0.45	−0.20
output	(−0.30)	(1.26)	(0.64)	(−0.25)	(4.73)	(−0.76)
R^2	0.01	0.17	0.04	0.01	0.69	0.05
Part B (hourly earnings)						
Constant	−0.56	−0.13	−0.30	−1.22	−0.74	−0.86
	(−0.76)	(−0.31)	(−0.56)	(−1.10)	(−1.52)	(−1.50)
Change in	−0.15	0.04	0.01	−0.18	0.38	0.24
output	(−1.01)	(0.44)	(−0.09)	(−0.79)	(3.82)	(2.06)
R^2	0.09	0.02	0.001	0.06	0.59	0.30

Note: *t*-statistics in parentheses.

cycles in the share of earnings accounted for by overtime pay these cycles were remarkably similar for all four categories of male manual workers. So even though overtime hours and payments move in a pro-cyclical manner they have a similar impact on the earnings of all four groups and in consequence have little impact on differentials. It is therefore hardly surprising that when we standardize for differences in hours worked as is done in the exercise reported in Part B of Table 3.6 this has little impact on the results for males. Among females, however, the standardization produces a rather different picture. Now there is a positive association between the business cycle and the semi-skilled female differential while the magnitude of the positive coefficient for skilled females is reduced.

Over the period analysed here output fell and unemployment rose most sharply during the years from 1974 to 1976 and again from 1979 to 1981. The Reder hypothesis rests on the proposition that in the recession the demand for the skilled declines proportionately less than that for the unskilled and that the relatively greater excess supply of the unskilled acts to depress their relative rates of pay. For this reason skill differentials widen in the recession. However Marsden (1987*b*) has shown that in the years in which unemployment rose most sharply 'unemployment among skilled workers increased faster than for the unskilled in both the 1974–6 and 1979–81 recessions' and that this tendency was most pronounced among males. On this basis we might expect to find a narrowing of the skill differential in both these periods. That we only do so for females is evidently because further forces were at work. One of these is incomes policy which we discuss shortly. One thing is however clear; the simple notion that the end of the period we analysed witnessed increasing skill shortages is far from the truth. Skill shortages existed but for relatively small and highly specialized types of skilled labour while the generality was an excess supply of labour.

Why should unemployment among skilled workers rise relatively faster than among the unskilled? The Reder hypothesis rests on the idea that firms will try to retain their most valuable employees even in the recession and hence will hoard skilled labour while laying off the unskilled. However both of these recessions, and particularly that of 1979–81, were characterized by widespread plant closures. Under these circumstances it is no longer a question of retaining some workers while discharging others; all workers in a plant are dismissed. Again where complete plants were not closed but reductions in the workforce were sought one of the most common methods of achieving this was voluntary redundancies. Those workers with the longest job tenure and highest pay receive the largest payments under redundancy payment schemes in the UK and for this reason are the most likely to elect for voluntary redundancy. The skilled will number prominently among these. Finally these recessions were experienced most severely in the manufacturing sector of the economy, again an area employing a large proportion of skilled workers. Perhaps together these three effects explain Marsden's surprising results.

The regression results are also interesting for they emphasize the quite distinct mechanisms producing changes in the earnings of each of the four female socio-economic groups over the business cycle. Thus we find that the earnings of the skilled rise relative to those of the unskilled during the expansionary phase of the business cycle both because their hours of work rise more and because their output and earnings per hour rise faster than those of the unskilled. The mechanism encouraging this latter is of course payments-by-results and we have already noted in Table 3.1 the much greater role of incentive pay in the earnings of skilled females. Again we find that the hourly earnings of semi-skilled females rise faster than do those of unskilled females during the expansionary phase of the cycle and again this is because of the greater role of incentive pay in the earnings of semi-skilled females. However it is also evident from a comparison of the results for hourly and weekly earnings in Part B of Table 3.6 that during the expansionary phase the hours of work of unskilled females must increase more than those of semi-skilled females. We saw that the gross *weekly* earnings of semi-skilled and unskilled females increased by similar amounts over the cycle, for we could find no cycle in the semi-skilled differential when this was expressed in terms of weekly earnings. Yet if such a cycle emerges when the differential is expressed in terms of hourly earnings, when we standardize for differences in hours worked between the two groups, it is evident that while the semi-skilled increase their earnings because of the link between their pay and their output the unskilled can only increase their output by working longer hours. Semi-skilled females increase the intensity of their work in the upswing while the unskilled work more extensively.

The cyclical nature of female skill differentials stands in sharp contrast to the behaviour of male differentials. The earnings of all male manual workers appear to change in a fairly uniform manner over the business cycle and as a result there is no cycle in male differentials. In contrast the hours and the intensity of work differ substantially between females with different skills and as a consequence there is a marked cycle in pay differentials throughout wide areas of female employment.

3.5. The Impact of Incomes Policy

The incomes policy of the periods from April 1973 to July 1974 (the £1 + 4 per cent, followed by 7 per cent or £2.25 per week) and from July 1975 to July 1977 (first the £6 per week, then the 5 per cent with £2.50 minimum/£4.00 maximum per week) contained substantial flat-rate elements. Yet it is evident from Figs. 3.1 to 3.6 on which these periods are shown that the narrowing that occurred was not confined to these periods. Certainly policies such as the £6 flat-rate increase for all would have caused some narrowing, but as has been indicated elsewhere, Elliott and Fallick (1979) and Ashenfelter and Layard (1983), this narrowing was underway before these policies and the policies were not responsible for the whole of the narrowing that occurred at these times. Part of the narrowing both before and during incomes policies appears to be due to the deliberate intention of bargainers at this time. However Figs. 3.1 to 3.6 also suggest that there was some reversal of this narrowing after 1977 and hence some reversal in the policies of bargainers, despite the relatively greater excess supply of skilled workers during the recession at the end of the period.

Evidently there are a number of important and sometimes conflicting forces at work during this period which require further research to analyse their precise effects. In the remaining part of this chapter we confine ourselves to distinguishing some of those that were at work during the period and which are likely to account for at least part of the changes that we observe. These are changes in the composition of the workforce.

3.6. Change in Differentials due to Change in the Composition of Employment

The basic rates and the earnings series reported to date have been averages across a wide range of different industries, occupations, collective bargaining arrangements, plant sizes, and age groups, and changes in any one of these dimensions could account for part or perhaps all of the changes in skill differentials we have reported. Accordingly the next step is to distinguish the extent to which changes in these dimensions, in the composition of the manual workforce, have been responsible for the changes in the skill differentials we have observed. In the following pages therefore we proceed to distinguish the effects on average earnings of each of the major changes in the composition of the manual workforce that took place over the period since 1970.

Those compositional changes which are likely to have had the biggest impact on average earnings over the period analysed here are changes in the occupational and industrial composition of the manual workforce and changes in age structure. Of course these three are not independent and their effects are not therefore additive. Occupations are often industry specific and therefore a change in industry structure also results in a change in the occupational distribution of the employed population. Again a change in occupational structure is not infrequently associated with a change in the age distribution of the employed population, because many occupations are filled by individuals falling within certain relatively narrow age bands. It may be that they have to reach a certain age before they are eligible for certain jobs or it may be that individuals are not allowed to hold certain jobs once they pass a certain age. Either way changes in age composition and changes in occupational composition are often associated. In fact changes in industry structure may well subsume both these changes. For this reason we proceed to evaluate the effects of occupational structure on skill differentials first, then move on to consider the effects of the changing age structure of the employed population on differentials, and finally analyse the effects of changes in industry structure.

(a) The effects of occupational changes

Over the period 1973 to 1982 there have been substantial changes in the occupational composition of the manual workforce. Table 3.7 details the most important of these for males together with the growth in average weekly earnings that each of these occupations has experienced over the period.

Table 3.7. *Major occupational changes in manual male employment, 1973–1982 (full-time workers)*

KOS	Occupational title	1973		1982		Index of 1982 wages (1973 = 100)
		Share of employment	Average gross weekly earnings	Share of employment	Average gross weekly earnings	
Skilled						
370	Carpenters and joiners	3.5	41.72	3.5	126.49	303
422	Maintenance fitters	5.2	42.49	6.9	153.38	361
424	Motor vehicle mechanics	3.9	37.13	5.1	123.10	332
435	Electricians	3.1	44.65	3.8	160.84	360
462	Other skilled workers in metal and electrical	10.4	39.05	8.1	133.27	341
465	Painters and decorators	3.3	37.00	2.6	119.75	324
472	Inspectors and testers	3.0	40.69	2.4	141.38	347
516	Heavy goods drivers	6.3	40.47	9.3	140.48	347
	Proportion of skilled accounted for	38.7		41.8		
Semi-skilled						
237	Postmen	8.4	34.65	9.5	133.98	387
242	Roundsmen and van salesmen	3.6	33.70	3.2	121.20	360
281	Others in catering, cleaning, hairdressing	2.5	31.46	3.3	112.98	359
290	Gardeners and groundsmen	3.5	27.29	4.5	100.70	369
308	Chemical and gas plant operators	2.4	41.37	3.1	156.72	379
327	Other process workers	7.4	37.79	7.2	134.48	356

No.						
385	Other workers in making and repairing jobs	5.4	37.43	6.1	131.32	351
406	Machine tool operators	4.4	40.06	2.9	126.43	316
470	Repetitive assemblers	3.3	38.41	3.1	119.17	310
477	Other workers in repetitive assembling	3.7	35.57	4.2	123.60	347
517	Goods drivers	5.9	34.71	6.0	112.81	325
528	Storekeepers, warehousemen	13.3	32.08	14.5	111.71	348
	Proportion of semi-skilled accounted for	63.7		67.5		
Unskilled						
268	Hospital porters	1.8	26.99	3.4	102.27	379
271	Caretakers	4.3	28.75	7.2	101.37	353
273	Cleaners	6.4	30.12	8.1	104.49	347
283	General farm workers	3.2	25.35	5.4	95.12	375
476	Bottlers/canners	6.6	35.20	7.4	123.10	350
488	Roadmen	2.8	31.26	3.3	112.53	360
497	Builders' mates	14.9	35.12	12.0	108.86	310
503	Building labourers	4.4	38.11	5.6	147.66	387
531	Warehouse and goods porters	3.7	32.10	3.3	120.13	374
532	Dustmen	2.9	31.48	4.0	112.97	359
533	Drivers' mates	10.0	36.46	10.1	139.03	381
538	General labourers in engineering and shipbuilding	20.9	32.33	14.1	112.97	349
540	Other labourers	5.0	36.31	1.2	150.68	415
	Proportion of unskilled accounted for	80.3		84.9		

Earnings have evidently not grown at uniform rates across all occupations, indeed while they have trebled for builders' mates they have quadrupled for general labourers outside shipbuilding and engineering. These differential rates of growth of earnings between occupations together with the changing shares of employment accounted for by them will have affected the average earnings of each skill group and may therefore be one of the reasons why skill differentials have moved in the manner recorded earlier.

In order to distinguish the impact of changes in occupational composition on skill differentials we adopted the following procedure. We took the first year for which the new occupational classification is available, 1973, and calculated the shares of employment accounted for by each occupation within an SEG. These are the weights which we used in conjunction with earnings by occupation in 1973 to calculate the average earnings of each 'skill' group in that year. These 1973 weights were then applied to corresponding earnings by occupation figures for 1982 to give a hypothetical average earnings figure by SEG for 1982. The resulting earnings were then converted to an index based on 1973 and so constitute base-weighted indices of earnings which abstract from any occupational change that occurred over the period. These indices are detailed in column (2) of Table 3.8 along with indices detailing the actual growth in earnings by SEG for the period.

A far from uniform pattern emerges but in general occupational change has enhanced the growth of female earnings while detracting from that for males. Thus occupational change enhanced the growth in average earnings among female supervisors, unskilled, and semi-skilled workers for here the indices of actual earnings growth exceed the hypothetical indices which indicate what would have happened to average earnings had occupational composition remained unaltered over the period. In contrast occupational change depressed average earnings growth for skilled females and for all males except skilled workers for whom occupational change had no effect on earnings over the period. The magnitude of the contribution of occupational change to earnings growth is calculated as the proportional difference between the actual and hypothetical earnings indices and is reported in column (3) of Table 3.8.

Of course the overall impact on skill differentials depends upon the relative change in earnings in two SEGs. We therefore used the indices calculated in Table 3.8 to construct hypothetical earnings figures for each group in 1982 and then calculated the differential in terms of these. Accordingly, in Table 3.9 we detail the actual skill differentials that existed in 1973 and 1982 and the hypothetical differential that would have existed in 1982 had there been no occupational change over the period, column (*c*).

Table 3.8. *The contribution of occupational change to the earnings growth of full-time manual workers, 1973–1982*

	SEG 5: foremen and supervisors			SEG 6: skilled			SEG 7: semi-skilled			SEG 8: unskilled		
	Actual earnings in 1982 (1)	Hypothetical earnings in 1982 (2)	Contribution to earnings growth[a] (3)	Actual earnings in 1982 (1)	Hypothetical earnings in 1982 (2)	Contribution to earnings growth[a] (3)	Actual earnings in 1982 (1)	Hypothetical earnings in 1982 (2)	Contribution to earnings growth[a] (3)	Actual earnings in 1982 (1)	Hypothetical earnings in 1982 (2)	Contribution to earnings growth[a] (3)
Male	357	359	−0.6	345	345	0.0	349	352	−0.9	349	357	−2.2
Female	412	405	+1.7	391	405	−3.5	399	397	+0.5	420	415	+1.2

Note: Index of average weekly earnings with 1973 = 100.

[a] Contribution to earnings growth = [(Actual, col. (1)/Hypothetical, col. (2)) − 1] × 100.

Table 3.9. *The impact of occupational change on differentials of full-time manual workers, 1973–1982*

	Level of differentials			Proportional change in differentials over the period		
	1973 Actual (a)	1982 Actual (b)	1982 Hypothetical (c)	Actual (d)	Hypothetical (e)	Contribution of occupational change (d) − (e) (f)
Foremen and supervisors						
Male	134.1	137.3	134.7	+2.4	+0.4	+2.0
Female	121.6	119.2	118.5	−2.0	−2.5	+0.5
Skilled						
Male	123.4	122.0	119.4	−1.1	−3.2	+2.1
Female	111.4	103.8	108.5	−6.8	−2.6	−4.2
Semi-skilled						
Male	108.1	108.1	106.4	—	−1.6	+1.6
Female	110.6	105.0	105.8	−5.1	−4.3	−0.8

Note: Differentials expressed in average weekly earnings with those of the unskilled = 100.

Thus we find that had there been no change in occupational composition the differential for male foremen and supervisors would only have risen from 134.1 in 1973 to 134.7 in 1982. Hence most of the widening from 134.1 to 137.3 that actually occurred over this period was accounted for by occupational change and this is detailed in the right-hand part of Table 3.9 where it is revealed that 2.0 of the 2.4 per cent change in the differential of male foremen and supervisors over the period was accounted for by occupational change. Elsewhere occupational changes masked a deterioration in the male semi-skilled differential over the period and led to an understatement of the deterioration of the relative position of skilled males.

The reverse is, however, true for females. In this case occupational change was part of the reason for the narrowing of the differential for skilled and semi-skilled females. Thus had there been no change in occupational composition in either of these groups the differential would have declined from approximately 111 per cent of the unskilled rate in both cases in 1973 to 108.5 and 105.8 per cent respectively for the skilled and semi-skilled in 1982. Thus occupational change accounts for a major part of the narrowing of the skilled differential to 103.8 in 1982 although only a small part of the narrowing of the semi-skilled differential to 105.0.

It is clear from this analysis that although the changes in skill differentials that occurred over the period 1973–82 were not in general very large there were significant changes in the occupational composition of the manual workforce and these had a significant impact on skill differentials. Column (*f*) in Table 3.9 summarizes the changes in differentials that occurred over this period and the part played by occupational change. Evidently occupational change was working to widen male differentials but to narrow those of females.

(b) The effect of the changing age distribution of employees

Figs. 3.7 and 3.8 report the skill differentials in terms of average weekly earnings for male and female workers at different ages. They reveal that male skill differentials increase until around 50 years of age and that thereafter they deteriorate through to until just before retirement when in the case of foremen and skilled workers they increase once again. Fig. 3.7 also reveals that in the years up to age 28 skilled workers earn more than supervisors but that this 'reversal' is more than compensated in later years. In general these profiles reveal that the more skilled the worker, the more pronounced is the positive association between earnings and age. The human capital literature and the literature on internal labour markets provide several explanations for these patterns. They emphasize that the greater productivity of the more highly skilled workers is only fully revealed some years after they enter the labour market, and that firms offer financial inducements in the form of seniority payments in an effort to reduce turnover amongst the more highly skilled. Fig. 3.7 is consistent with these arguments.

The picture for females is rather more complicated for the reversal of the differential between the skilled and semi-skilled occurs at several ages. For females differentials reach a maximum around age 30 again reflecting the rather steep age–earnings profiles of females.

In order to discern the impact of changes in the age structure first on the average earnings of each group and then on skill differentials we adopted the same procedure as we used above to distinguish the effects of occupational change. Thus Table 3.10 details the actual growth in earnings that occurred over the period 1974–82 (detailed information on the age structure of the employed population is only available from this year onwards) and that which would have occurred had there been no change in the age structure of the working population over this period, the hypothetical figures in column (2). The proportional difference between the actual and the hypothetical figures, column (3), reveals the contribution of changing age structure to the earnings growth of each of these four groups in the case of both males and females. In general it appears that at this level of disaggregation the effects of age have been slight.

However it is the impact of these changes on differentials that is of concern to us and accordingly in Table 3.11 we recalculate the differentials for 1982 abstracting from the effects of changing age structure (these calculations are shown in column (c)). Thus it emerges that had there been no change in age structure the differential between male foremen and supervisors and the unskilled would have been 137.7 in 1982 instead of the 137.3 that emerged. Table 3.11 reveals that overall had there been no change in age structure male differentials would have been slightly wider than they were while female differentials would have declined less than they did.

(c) The effects of changing industrial structure

Table 3.2 has already revealed the substantial variation that exists between industries in the differentials for male manual workers in the long run. As might be expected the pattern of change over the period has also differed quite considerably between industries. Fig. 3.9 details the changes that have occurred in the differentials for foremen and supervisors, skilled and semi-skilled males over the period 1970 to 1982 in each of the ten industry groups, and for females in those industries for which it is similarly possible to calculate differentials over this period. From these it is evident that there is considerably more diversity in the movements of female skill differentials in different industries.

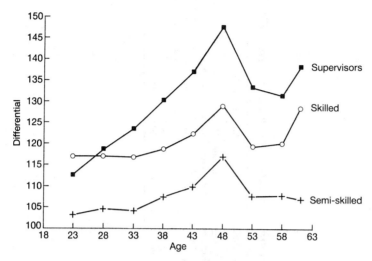

Fig. 3.7. Male differentials by age: all industries and services, 1970–1982

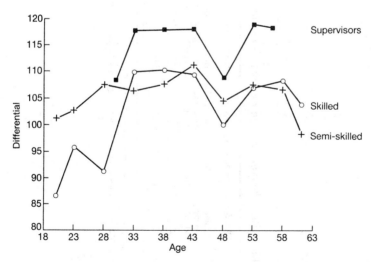

Fig. 3.8. Female differentials by age: all industries and services, 1970–1982

Table 3.10. *The contribution of changes in the age structure to the earnings growth of full-time manual workers, 1974–1982*

	SEG 5: Foremen and supervisors			SEG 6: skilled			SEG 7: semi-skilled			SEG 8: unskilled		
	Actual earnings in 1982 (1)	Hypothetical earnings in 1982 (2)	Contribution to earnings growth[a] (3)	Actual earnings in 1982 (1)	Hypothetical earnings in 1982 (2)	Contribution to earnings growth[a] (3)	Actual earnings in 1982 (1)	Hypothetical earnings in 1982 (2)	Contribution to earnings growth[a] (3)	Actual earnings in 1982 (1)	Hypothetical earnings in 1982 (2)	Contribution to earnings growth[a] (3)
Male	312	311	+0.2	306	306	—	302	302	—	303	302	+0.3
Female	342	342	—	331	338	−2.1	334	336	−0.6	349	347	+0.6

Note: Index of average weekly earnings with 1973 = 100.

[a] Contribution to earnings growth = [(Actual, col. (1)/Hypothetical, col. (2)) − 1] = 100

Table 3.11. *The impact of changes in age structure on differentials of full-time manual workers, 1974–1982*

	Level of differentials			Proportional change in differentials over the period		
	1974 Actual (a)	1982 Actual (b)	1982 Hypothetical (c)	Actual (d)	Hypothetical (e)	Contribution of change in age structure (d) − (e) (f)
Foremen and supervisors						
Male	133.4	137.3	137.7	+2.9	+3.2	−0.3
Female	121.8	119.2	120.2	−2.1	−1.3	−0.8
Skilled						
Male	121.0	122.0	122.7	+0.8	+1.4	−0.6
Female	109.4	103.8	106.7	−5.1	−2.5	−2.6
Semi-skilled						
Male	108.6	108.1	108.6	−0.5	—	−0.5
Female	109.8	105.0	106.4	−4.4	−3.1	−1.3

Note: Differentials expressed in average weekly earnings with those of the unskilled = 100.

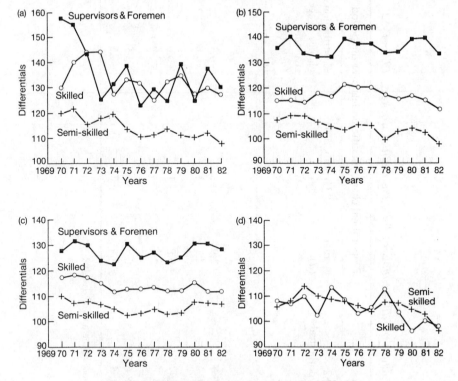

Fig. 3.9. Skill differentials by industry, 1970–82
(*a*) Division 0: agriculture, forestry, and fishing (male)
(*b*) Division 1: energy and water (male)
(*c*) Division 2: mineral extraction etc. (male)
(*d*) Division 2: mineral extraction etc. (female)

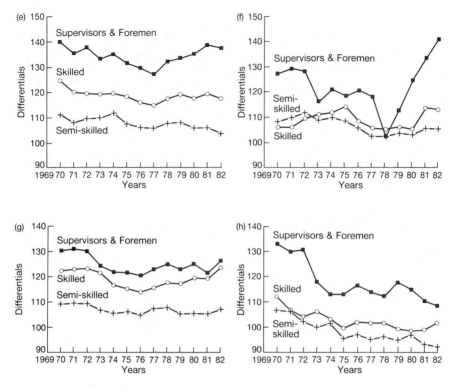

(*e*) Division 3: metal goods, engineering, vehicles (male)
(*f*) Division 3: metal goods, engineering, vehicles (female)
(*g*) Division 4: other manufacturing (male)
(*h*) Division 4: other manufacturing (female)

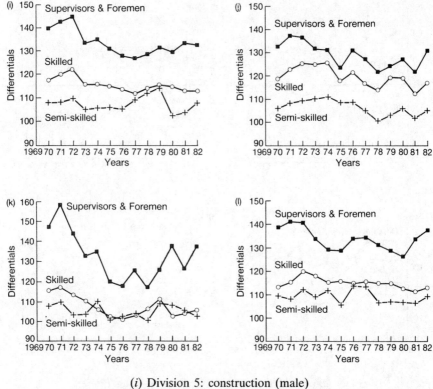

(*i*) Division 5: construction (male)
(*j*) Division 6: distribution and hotels (male)
(*k*) Division 6: distribution and hotels (female)
(*l*) Division 7: transport and communications (male)

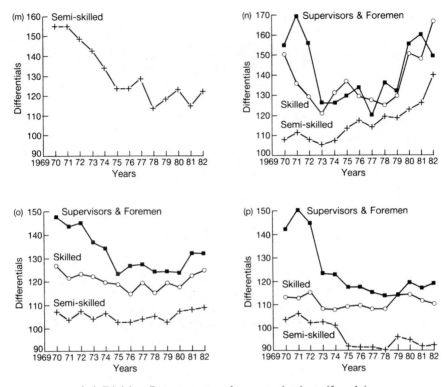

(*m*) Division 7: transport and communications (female)
(*n*) Division 8: banking and finance (male)
(*o*) Division 9: other services (male)
(*p*) Division 9: other services (female)

Table 3.12. *The industrial distribution of employment, 1970 and 1982 (%)*

Division	Males					
	SEG 5: foremen and supervisors		SEG 6: skilled		SEG 7: semi-skilled	
	1970	1982	1970	1982	1970	1982
0. Agriculture, forestry, and fishing	1.0	2.1	0.2	0.1	3.9	5.0
1. Energy and water	4.5	7.0	11.3	8.1	4.2	3.2
2. Mineral extraction etc.	11.6	8.7	7.5	7.3	11.3	8.9
3. Metal goods, engineering, vehicles	27.5	24.4	26.7	30.0	23.6	16.5
4. Other manufacturing	18.2	16.9	14.8	11.7	14.9	19.3
5. Construction	12.7	14.7	14.1	14.1	3.7	2.5
6. Distribution and hotels	7.3	8.1	7.1	9.5	8.2	12.4
7. Transport and communication	8.2	8.4	11.7	13.9	15.7	16.4
8. Banking and finance	1.2	1.0	0.5	0.4	1.5	2.0
9. Other services	7.8	8.7	6.1	4.9	13.0	13.8
Total	100.0	100.0	100.0	100.0	100.0	100.0

Over the period 1970 to 1982 there has been a substantial change in the industrial distribution of manual employment as Table 3.12 reveals, so that when taken together with the quite different patterns of differentials in different industries it seems likely that these changes in industry structure account for a major part of the changes we have observed in aggregate skill differentials.

Table 3.12 reveals that the share of male manual employment and in particular the share of unskilled and semi-skilled male employment which is accounted for by manufacturing industries, divisions 2–4, has declined substantially while that of distribution and hotels, communications, and other services has increased. Amongst females there is also a decline in the share of manufacturing and a sharp rise in the share accounted for by 'other services' in particular.

In order to distinguish the effects of industrial change on movements in skill differentials over the periods since 1970 and 1973, the latter to enable us to compare with occupational change, we adopted the same procedures as used earlier. Accordingly Table 3.13 details the contribution of changes in industrial structure over the complete period 1970–82 to the growth in earnings while Table 3.14 details the effect of these on differentials. The right-hand part of Table 3.14 then details that part of the proportional change in differentials that occurred over the period 1970–82 that can be attributed to changing industrial structure. This reveals that changes in industrial structure reduced the narrowing of male differentials that took place over the period 1970 to 1982, and that in the absence of these effects the narrowing of male differentials that occurred over this period would have been more severe.

For females the results are mixed. Changes in industrial structure again

		Females							
SEG 8: unskilled		SEG 5: foremen and supervisors		SEG 6: skilled		SEG 7: semi-skilled		SEG 8: unskilled	
1970	1982	1970	1982	1970	1982	1970	1982	1970	1982
2.9	5.4	—	0.6	—	—	2.1	0.6	0.6	0.4
3.5	6.7	0.9	0.6	0.3	0.3	0.1	—	0.8	1.0
11.4	6.4	5.7	1.4	2.1	4.0	5.4	4.4	5.7	6.4
15.9	8.6	14.3	7.4	5.5	23.9	33.4	21.2	15.5	6.1
17.0	10.7	38.3	24.5	58.6	21.9	32.7	41.7	25.2	19.6
13.1	20.7	—	—	—	—	—	—	0.3	0.4
7.3	7.1	8.7	12.7	8.6	5.7	8.9	8.8	11.0	14.3
10.6	7.5	6.4	0.6	0.1	1.5	4.3	3.2	2.7	4.3
0.8	1.2	3.0	0.6	0.1	0.7	0.4	0.1	0.9	0.5
17.5	25.7	22.8	51.6	24.7	42.0	12.7	20.0	37.3	47.0
100.0	100.0	100.0	100.0	100.0	100.0	100.0	100.0	100.0	100.0

served to reduce the narrowing of differentials for the skilled while for supervisors and foremen and the semi-skilled they enhanced the narrowing that occurred. In general the effects of changes in industrial structure account for a fairly large part of the change in male differentials that occurred over the period since 1970 but for only a small part of the changes that occurred for females. The change in female differentials over this period was much larger than that for males as column (*d*) of Table 3.14 reveals.

We conducted a similar exercise to that above for the period 1973–82 to enable us to compare the effects of industrial change to that of occupational change distinguished earlier in Tables 3.8 and 3.9. The results are reported in Tables 3.15 and 3.16. Over this shorter period changes in industrial structure work in the same direction as those identified above in the case of males. However in the case of females they appear to be working in opposite directions to those suggested in Table 3.14 suggesting that the changes in the industrial distribution of female employment have been rather different before and after 1973.

The effects of changes in industrial structure over the period since 1973 worked in broadly the same direction as the effects of changes in occupational structure in the case of males. Both widened or reduced the narrowing of differentials over this period although the impact of occupational change was larger than that of industrial change. For female foremen and supervisors and skilled workers again the two effects worked in the same direction tending to widen and narrow differentials respectively, and again the magnitude of the effects of industrial change was smaller than that of occupational change. Only in the case of semi-skilled females did the two effects work in opposite directions.

Table 3.13. *The contribution of changes in industrial structure to the earnings growth of full-time manual workers, 1970–1982*

	SEG 5: foremen and supervisors			SEG 6: skilled			SEG 7: semi-skilled			SEG 8: unskilled		
	Actual earnings in 1982 (1)	Hypothetical earnings in 1982 (2)	Contribution to earnings growth[a] (3)	Actual earnings in 1982 (1)	Hypothetical earnings in 1982 (2)	Contribution to earnings growth[a] (3)	Actual earnings in 1982 (1)	Hypothetical earnings in 1982 (2)	Contribution to earnings growth[a] (3)	Actual earnings in 1982 (1)	Hypothetical earnings in 1982 (2)	Contribution to earnings growth[a] (3)
Male	491	491	—	494	499	−1.0	489	494	−1.0	502	509	−1.4
Female	526	545	−3.5	590	592	−0.3	567	577	−1.7	624	633	−1.4

Note: Index of average weekly earnings with 1970 = 100.

[a] Contribution to earnings growth = [(Actual, col. (1)/Hypothetical, col. (2)) − 1] = 100.

Table 3.14. *The impact of changes in industrial structure on the differentials of full-time manual workers, 1970–1982*

	Level of differentials			Proportional change in differentials over the period		
	1970 Actual (a)	1982 Actual (b)	1982 Hypothetical (c)	Actual (d)	Hypothetical (e)	Contribution of change in industrial structure (d) − (e) (f)
Foremen and supervisors						
Male	140.3	137.3	135.1	−2.1	−3.7	+1.6
Female	141.3	119.2	121.7	−15.6	−13.9	−1.7
Skilled						
Male	123.9	122.0	121.5	−1.5	−1.9	+0.4
Female	109.7	103.8	102.5	−5.4	−6.6	+1.2
Semi-skilled						
Male	111.0	108.1	107.7	−2.6	−3.0	−0.4
Female	115.5	105.0	105.2	−9.1	−8.9	−0.2

Note: Differentials expressed in average weekly earnings with those of the unskilled = 100.

Table 3.15. *The contribution of changes in industrial structure to the earnings growth of full-time manual workers, 1973–1982*

	SEG 5: foremen and supervisors			SEG 6: skilled			SEG 7: semi-skilled			SEG 8: unskilled		
	Actual earnings in 1982 (1)	Hypothetical earnings in 1982 (2)	Contribution to earnings growth[a] (3)	Actual earnings in 1982 (1)	Hypothetical earnings in 1982 (2)	Contribution to earnings growth[a] (3)	Actual earnings in 1982 (1)	Hypothetical earnings in 1982 (2)	Contribution to earnings growth[a] (3)	Actual earnings in 1982 (1)	Hypothetical earnings in 1982 (2)	Contribution to earnings growth[a] (3)
Male	357	362	−1.4	345	347	−0.6	349	352	−0.9	349	355	−1.7
Female	412	413	−0.2	391	407	−3.9	399	395	+1.0	420	422	−0.5

Note: Index of average weekly earnings with 1973 = 100.

[a] Contribution to earnings growth = [(Actual, col. (1)/Hypothetical, col. (2)) − 1] = 100.

Table 3.16. *The impact of changes in industrial structure on the differentials of full-time manual workers, 1973–1982*

	Level of differentials			Proportional change in differentials over the period		
	1973 Actual (a)	1982 Actual (b)	1982 Hypothetical (c)	Actual (d)	Hypothetical (e)	Contribution of change in industrial structure (d) − (e) (f)
Foremen and supervisors						
Male	134.1	137.3	136.7	+2.4	+1.9	+0.5
Female	121.6	119.2	119.0	−2.0	−2.1	+0.1
Skilled						
Male	123.4	122.0	120.7	−1.1	−2.2	+1.1
Female	111.4	103.8	107.3	−6.8	−3.7	−3.1
Semi-skilled						
Male	108.1	108.1	107.3	—	−0.7	+0.7
Female	110.6	105.0	103.5	−5.1	−6.4	+1.3

Note: Differentials expressed in average weekly earnings with those of the unskilled = 100.

3.7. A Summary of Compositional Effects

The results of the previous analysis of the effects of changes in the occupational age and industrial composition of the manual workforce on skill differentials are brought together in Table 3.17. This confirms that occupational changes had the largest impact on differentials over the period since 1973 and that while in general they arrested the narrowing of male differentials they assisted the narrowing for females. Changes in age composition served to minimize any widening and enhance any narrowing of differentials that took place but their effects were generally small. Yet none of the effects we distinguish is trivial. For example over the period 1973–82 the differential of male foremen and supervisors widened by 2.4 per cent. Occupational change alone widened this differential by 2.0 per cent, while changes in industrial structure widened it by 0.5 per cent and changes in age structure tended to narrow it by 0.3 per cent. In the context of this small change in the differential therefore the contribution of each of the compositional changes we identify is important. Of course, as we have emphasized earlier, none of those effects is entirely independent of the others; their contributions cannot therefore be added to give the 'total effect' for this would involve double counting. None the less each measure considered independently tells us something about the forces working to change aggregate skill differentials and gives us some idea of the magnitude of these effects.

3.8. The Effect of Collective Bargaining

Finally there remains one important dimension of skill differentials that we have not discussed, namely the effects of unions. If trade unions successfully pursue equalizing wage policies we should expect to observe lower skill differentials in the union as opposed to the non-union sector. Although we are unable to address this question directly, for we are not able to distinguish those workers who are members of trade unions, we can distinguish those workers who are affected by some form of collective bargaining and this enables us to compare the differentials in the covered and uncovered sectors. This we do in Table 3.18 for the years 1973 and 1978, using the special questions asked in these years.[4]

Table 3.18 reveals that in all but the case of the semi-skilled in 1973, the differentials of male workers not covered by any form of collective agreement are greater than those who are covered. The same is again true for females, although this time with the exception of skilled workers

Table 3.17. *Accounting for changes in 'skill' differentials*

	Proportional change in the differential over the period			Proportional change in differentials due to				
				Occupational change 1973–82	Changes in the industrial distribution of employment			Changes in age composition 1974–82
	1970–82 (a)	1973–82 (b)	1974–82 (c)	(d)	1970–82 (e)	1973–82 (f)		(g)
Male								
Foremen and supervisors	−2.1	+2.4	+2.9	+2.0	+1.6	+0.5		−0.3
Skilled	−1.5	−1.1	+0.8	+2.1	+0.4	+1.1		−0.6
Semi-skilled	−2.6	—	−0.5	+1.6	+0.4	+0.7		−0.5
Female								
Foremen and supervisors	−15.6	−2.0	−2.1	+0.5	−1.7	+0.1		−0.8
Skilled	−5.4	−6.8	−5.1	−4.2	+1.2	−3.1		−2.6
Semi-skilled	−9.1	−5.1	−4.4	−0.8	−0.2	+1.3		−1.3

Table 3.18. *Skill differentials by type of collective agreement*

	Foremen and supervisors		Skilled		Semi-skilled	
	1973	1978	1973	1978	1973	1978
Males						
National and supplementary	132.5	127.8	122.3	118.2	111.5	110.4
National only	136.5	131.8	122.6	120.4	107.1	103.5
Company or district	124.3	133.8	116.8	112.9	105.7	107.5
Some form of collective agreement	133.8	132.2	122.4	119.2	109.4	107.7
No collective agreement	142.1	142.7	126.6	123.4	107.1	108.7
Females						
National and supplementary	111.9	109.2	111.7	110.0	110.6	109.8
National only	121.0	113.9	107.5	100.9	110.2	108.0
Company or district	121.0	114.8	106.6	104.9	105.2	101.7
Some form of collective agreement	119.7	112.0	110.0	104.9	110.5	108.3
No collective agreement	136.0	118.5	112.9	101.6	112.7	110.9

in 1978. Thus differentials in the covered sector are in general lower in both 1973 and 1978 than in the uncovered sector.

Table 3.18 also allows us to distinguish the level of the differential in each of the two years by the type of collective agreement. No simple pattern emerges nor indeed should we expect there to be one. Those covered by national agreements enjoy neither consistently higher nor consistently lower differentials than those covered by company agreements. Instead each year and the period as a whole reveal considerable variation in the level of differentials between the different types of collective bargaining arrangement.

In fact there is no reason to expect any systematic relationship by type of collective agreement, for the types identified here do not coincide with any particular type of union structure. We might expect differentials to be lower in general unions, in which the wage objectives of the skilled minority take second place to those of the majority of unskilled workers. Conversely they might be widest where skilled workers have their own union and can pursue their own objectives unconstrained by the preferences of the unskilled. However we have no way of identifying these different union types and there is no reason to suppose that they coincide in any systematic fashion with the different types of bargaining arrangement identified here.

Table 3.19. *Skill differentials for male manual workers by plant size, 1979*

Size of plant (employees)	Foremen and supervisors	Skilled	Semi-skilled
Under 50	133.3	123.1	106.2
50–99	136.5	125.6	115.5
100–199	132.6	120.0	108.9
200–499	129.7	121.9	110.1
500–999	125.4	117.8	107.9
1,000+	129.0	113.2	103.5

One final piece of evidence corroborates the view that differentials are lower in the covered, predominantly union, sector than they are in the uncovered sector and that is the evidence on differentials by plant size available for 1979. The details for males only are reported in Table 3.19 for it is males which are most heavily unionized and most affected by collective bargaining arrangements. We know from other studies that unionization, and accordingly collective bargaining coverage, is positively associated with plant size. Table 3.19 reveals that large plants have lower skill differentials.[5]

3.9. Conclusions

The period 1970–82 has witnessed a general reduction in skill differentials. Amongst males this reduction has been relatively small but amongst females it has been substantial. The narrowing took place in the years to 1977 and thereafter there was some small reversal of this trend. However this general pattern in the movement of differentials has resulted from a number of conflicting developments. The largest single cause of this narrowing was certainly the narrowing of differentials within each industry. But other changes, most notably in the occupational and industrial structure of employment, tended to widen male and occasionally female differentials and thus to arrest the narrowing that occurred. In contrast changes in age structure, although not as significant, worked in the opposite direction. On balance however the narrowing of skill differentials as a result of changes in the negotiated rates of pay of male workers was more severe than the unadjusted average earnings or basic rates series indicate. Instead of narrowing by some 2 per cent for all male groups over the period since 1970 the actual narrowing may have been as much as 5 per cent. In contrast for females the narrowing has in general been less than the unadjusted series indicates. Again the narrowing that has occurred is predominantly due to the narrowing of differentials within industries although once again there are sizeable occupational and industrial effects.

Changes in male differentials do not appear to be associated with the business cycle. Evidently the basic rates of pay of male manual workers are not cyclically sensitive in the manner suggested by Reder. Hours of work certainly fluctuate over the cycle but such fluctuations are uniform across all groups of male manual workers and thus have no impact on their relative pay. In contrast changes in female differentials seem to be associated with the business cycle both because of the cyclical behaviour of hours worked across skill groups and because of the role of incentive payments in the earnings of the semi-skilled.

From the above it emerges that once we strip away changes in the age, occupational, and industrial composition of the workforce the narrowing of differentials that has occurred over the period since 1970 was predominantly due to the narrowing of differentials within each industry. It is tempting to argue that such narrowing is due to the effects of the several flat-rate incomes policies in force at various times within the period but such an explanation does not square with the facts. Incomes policies were only one of a number of forces narrowing differentials in the first part of the period and this narrowing was partly reversed during the later years. The narrowing in the early part took place both when incomes policies were in force and when they were not while the subsequent reversal as incomes policy restraints were lifted during the latter half of the period took place during years when unemployment among the unskilled and particularly skilled workers was increasing sharply. Complex forces were evidently at work which subsequent research will identify.

Notes

1. In common with other contributors to this volume we are grateful to the ESRC for providing funds to support this research. We are similarly indebted to Sophie Houston whose considerable computing expertise made this whole exercise provide and to Andrew Thomson and Mary Gregory for their initiative in bringing this group of researchers together and for their continuing efforts to administer and co-ordinate the whole enterprise. Back in Aberdeen we also benefited from a small grant from the University of Aberdeen Advisory Committee on Research to whom we extend our thanks. Thanks are also due to Hector Williams for his first-class computational and computing assistance; to Philip Hemmings, Donald Scobie, Angela Houston, and Marie Westoby for their help at various stages of the project; to David Marsden and David Blackaby for their constructive comments; and to Winnie Sinclair for typing the several drafts through which this paper has proceeded.
2. See Phelps Brown (1977), Saunders et al. (1977), and Elliott and Fallick (1979).
3. Throughout this analysis we report only those results which are based on cells which

contain 30 individuals or more. Further discussion of the crowding of women by occupation is given in ch. 5.

4. See ch. 1.1(*b*) for a discussion of the special questions.

5. It is interesting to note that in contrast to this general result Marsden (1987*a*) has revealed that in the engineering industry skill differentials were wider in large plants in 1970 although by 1980 differentials were narrower in the larger plants.

4
White-Collar Pay and Employment
Ken Mayhew and Amit Ray

4.1. Introduction

Many of the chapters in this book cover quite specific topics—sex differentials, for example, or the effect of size of establishment on earnings. White-collar pay and employment, by contrast, involve a complex of issues. So do some other chapters—those on manual workers and on public–private sector relativities, for instance. Yet even for most of these, the recent literature produces a well-defined and restricted set of questions for discussion. This is not true for this chapter, which is hardly surprising since the description 'white-collar' has relatively little economic meaning beyond the dubious one, in this day and age, of distinguishing a group of workers from their manual counterparts. It is a vastly heterogeneous category along almost any dimension—pay, status, extent of union coverage, and so on. For this reason an early strand of literature on white-collar–blue-collar differentials has fallen largely into disuse.[1] At the other extreme of aggregation, some more modern work considers certain specific professions, such as chemists and engineers.[2] Otherwise discussion of white-collar workers has emerged from interest in more general themes—for example, age differentials, the determinants of pay dispersion, and internal labour markets. This chapter attempts to pick out some of these themes. Using, as it does, an unexploited data set and at the same time attempting to cover a broad area, it is predominantly descriptive. Therefore, it raises as many questions as it answers. Later papers will explore particular issues in more detail.

There is another reason for our lack of conclusiveness; and that is the form in which the data were provided. As is explained in Chapter 1, our unit of observation is a 'cell' containing 3, 4, or 5 individuals. The individuals were sorted into cells by pre-defined characteristics. Only one sort was allowed. Clearly a cell is useful for analytical purposes only if its inhabitants possess the relevant common characteristics—e.g. all full-timers or all men. Equally clearly there is a limit to the number of characteristics which can be employed on any one sort. Thus, though we were allowed to use a restricted number of occupational categories (KOSs), it was not/possible to include them as characteristics in the sort.

As a result, if there were potentially, say, 1,000 individuals in a particular KOS, perhaps coincidentally only 300 of them were placed homogeneously in cells; and it is only this 300 which can be included in any analysis. Inevitably usable sample size is always reduced as cross-tabulation is layered on cross-tabulation. The particular presentation of the data set severely compounded this familiar problem. Consequently we have some analysis of KOS level data, but much more is conducted for white-collar workers as a whole and for socio-economic groups.

Even had we not faced the particular problems outlined in the previous paragraph, it will be evident that the form of the NES data restricts our approach. Essentially we have a sequence of cross-sections, whereas many recent advances in the study of earnings dispersion have been made possible by the use of panel data. Further, most of the information on personal characteristics used in such studies is absent from the New Earnings Survey. For all of these reasons it may be that the best we can aim for is codified description rather than analysis.

The period we are considering was one of massive flux in the economy in general and in the labour market in particular. The composition of the labour force was changing rapidly. White-collar work was expanding and blue-collar work was contracting. There was a move out of manufacturing and from large to small firms. Women were becoming an ever-increasing proportion of the labour force, and alongside that went a concomitant growth of part-time jobs. In the macroeconomy, the 1970s witnessed unprecedently high inflation and high unemployment by post-Second World War standards. At the same time the common perception was of an increased threat from the union movement, though the matter is arguable when confronted by the usual indicators such as strike statistics. The end of the decade witnessed a severe downward shock to the world and British economies and a 'shake-out' of labour of a magnitude which few would have predicted. The main background aim of this chapter is to use the NES data to investigate how this period of change impinged on white-collar pay and employment. We concentrate especially on the extent to which white-collar work was in career jobs in internal labour markets and the extent to which it was in 'peripheral' jobs, and ask whether the picture changed during the decade.

In section 4.2 we consider white-collar employment patterns and how they altered over the period. Section 4.3 is concerned with overall earnings dispersion, and section 4.4 with pay hierarchies and differentials. In section 4.5 we present some detailed analysis of particular occupations, while in section 4.6 we turn to the interlinked themes of internalization and the relationships between pay, length of service, and age. Our main findings are drawn together in section 4.7.

4.2. White-Collar Employment Patterns

The size of the sample increased over the years, from just over 59,000 in 1970 to nearly 79,000 in 1982. Its composition yields few surprises. There was a slight fall in the proportion of full-timers and of men (Table 4.1), while there was a rise in the public-sector share of employment until 1980, and a small decline thereafter (Table 4.2). There are very few part-time men in the sample. Consequently we omit them from much of the subsequent discussion; where they are included any inferences should be qualified by awareness of their small numbers. In terms of regional patterns, there was a shift from Greater London to the rest of the South East, and a shift from the North, North West, Wales, and Scotland to East Anglia, the South West, the Midlands, and Yorkshire (Table 4.2). The age distribution of the sample was pretty stable. Among part-time women the young (less than 30 years of age) became slightly less well represented as the period went on, while the old (over 50) became slightly better represented. Amongst full-time women, the only significant change was a fall in the proportion of 18–19-year-olds in the sample. Workers are allocated to one of ten industries. These are:

0. Agriculture, forestry, and fishing;
1. Energy and water supply;
2. Extraction of minerals other than fuel; manufacture of metals, mineral products, and chemicals;
3. Metal goods, engineering, and vehicle industries;
4. Other manufacturing industries;
5. Construction;
6. Distribution; hotels and catering; repairs;
7. Transport and communication;
8. Banking, finance, insurance, business services, and leasing;
9. Other services.

The main features to emerge are the heavy industrial concentrations of women and part-timers. Two industries (distribution and other services) account for a large majority of part-timers—in 1970 for 76 per cent of women and for 72 per cent of men. By 1982 these figures had risen to 80 per cent and 78 per cent, with distribution having become less and other services more important. Of the remaining industries, banking etc. contained the largest number of part-timers, accounting as it did for just under 10 per cent of them in 1982. Full-timers were rather more evenly spread, though distribution and particularly other services still accounted for the majority of women. Banking and finance also took a significant and increasing number—just under 16 per cent by 1982. Metal goods,

Table 4.1. *White-collar workers: composition by sex and full-time/part-time status (%)*

	1970	1971	1972	1973	1974	1975	1976	1977	1978	1979	1980	1981	1982
Men													
Full-time	50.8	50.6	49.9	50.6	50.1	50.0	48.9	48.9	48.6	48.1	47.9	47.2	47.0
Part-time	0.9	1.0	0.9	1.0	1.0	2.0	2.0	2.0	1.9	1.8	1.8	2.0	2.0
Women													
Full-time	38.2	37.8	38.0	37.0	36.4	36.3	36.4	36.6	36.6	36.8	36.8	36.9	37.2
Part-time	10.1	10.6	11.2	11.3	12.5	11.8	12.5	12.5	12.9	13.3	13.5	13.9	13.8
TOTAL NUMBER	59,108	62,620	66,157	66,335	62,667	63,610	69,780	71,856	72,335	72,297	74,686	77,430	78,844

Table 4.2. *White-collar workers: composition by public/private sector and by region (%)*

	1970	1971	1972	1973	1974	1975	1976	1977	1978	1979	1980	1981	1982
Men													
Public sector	35.7	37.2	37.9	37.7	35.7	38.5	38.2	39.7	39.5	40.0	41.2	40.4	40.6
Private sector	64.3	62.8	62.1	62.3	64.3	61.5	61.8	60.3	60.5	60.0	58.8	59.6	59.4
Women													
Public sector	41.1	42.2	42.4	43.0	41.0	45.9	46.7	47.3	46.8	46.7	48.0	47.4	48.0
Private sector	58.9	57.8	57.6	57.0	59.0	54.1	53.3	52.7	53.2	53.3	52.0	52.6	52.0
Men (full-time only)													
Greater London	24.0	24.3	23.8	23.3	22.9	22.0	21.6	21.6	22.0	21.1	21.2	21.5	21.7
Rest of South East	16.8	16.7	17.5	17.5	16.8	16.5	17.4	17.7	17.7	17.8	18.0	18.1	18.3
East Anglia, South West, Midlands, and Yorkshire	30.4	30.5	30.3	30.4	32.0	32.4	32.3	32.3	32.8	33.0	32.7	32.5	32.2
North, North West, Wales, and Scotland	28.8	28.5	28.4	28.9	28.3	29.0	28.7	28.4	27.5	28.1	27.8	27.8	27.8
Women													
Greater London	21.7	22.1	21.2	21.3	20.7	19.7	19.1	19.5	18.9	18.1	17.7	18.8	18.5
Rest of South East	17.0	16.9	17.4	17.7	17.3	16.9	17.6	17.7	18.1	18.2	18.4	18.5	18.4
East Anglia, South West, Midlands, and Yorkshire	29.9	30.1	30.4	29.9	31.5	32.1	32.1	32.0	32.9	33.4	33.5	33.2	33.2
North, North West, Wales, and Scotland	31.4	30.8	31.0	31.2	30.4	31.3	31.2	30.8	30.2	30.2	29.2	29.5	29.8

engineering, and vehicles, and other manufacturing, which between them had contained 17 per cent of full-time women in 1970, contained less than 12 per cent by 1982. Full-time men were most evenly distributed. Other services, however, still had by far the largest number (around 30 per cent throughout the period). Metal goods, engineering, and vehicles, distribution, and banking and finance held the next largest concentrations, as they did in 1982, though by this time metal goods, engineering, and vehicles had diminished in importance.

Non-manual workers are divided into four socio-economic groups (SEGs) as follows:

1. Managers;
2. Professional and technical workers;
3. Intermediate non-manual workers;
4. Junior non-manual workers.

This is not a pure ordering by prestige or pay; the overlap between 1 and 2 is too great for that. Categories 3 and 4, however, are clearly 'inferior' to 1 and 2, while 4 is 'inferior' to 3. Notwithstanding the above qualifications, the subordinate position of women is evident from Table 4.3. For the sake of brevity, the figures are given for just three 'snapshot' years. Comparing full-timers in 1973, a much smaller percentage of women than of men were in the first two SEGs. Indeed a relatively small proportion were in the third. Though by 1982 women had experienced a slight 'upgrading', men had too—so that the striking contrast remained. The occupational crowding of female workers is well known, but Table 4.3 serves as a salutary reminder that the term 'white-collar' means very different things for the two sexes. Among women, part-timers were less well represented than full-timers in SEG 1 and SEG 3. The same general contrast holds for men, but also noteworthy is the high proportion of male part-timers in professional and technical jobs. At the more general level, the often-mentioned upgrading of work is evident but not dramatic on this SEG classification.

As Table 4.4 shows,[3] over the period as a whole there was little change in hours worked. Part-time women worked 20.4 hours per week in 1970 as compared with 20.1 in 1982. Similarly for full-time women and men, falls from 37.1 to 36.5 and from 38.9 to 38.2 respectively were insignificant. Only part-time men experienced a significant fall—from 19.2 to 15.2. At the beginning of the 1970s, employees in the private sector worked longer hours than those in the public sector. By and large that picture remained true in the early 1980s. The tendency amongst full-timers for men to work longer than women also continued throughout the period. By 1982, however, part-time men were on significantly shorter hours than their female counterparts.

Table 4.3. *White-collar workers: distribution by socio-economic group (%)*

		1973	1979	1982
Full-time men				
SEG 1	Managers	22.5	24.7	23.5
SEG 2	Professional and technical	24.8	25.6	28.1
SEG 3	Intermediate	25.6	27.9	27.9
SEG 4	Junior	27.8	21.7	20.6
Part-time men				
SEG 1	Managers	7.4	16.3	12.7
SEG 2	Professional and technical	29.3	36.3	40.3
SEG 3	Intermediate	17.5	12.1	16.0
SEG 4	Junior	45.9	35.2	31.0
Full-time women				
SEG 1	Managers	2.1	3.0	3.1
SEG 2	Professional and technical	4.6	5.8	7.3
SEG 3	Intermediate	24.7	27.3	27.8
SEG 4	Junior	68.5	63.9	61.9
Part-time women				
SEG 1	Managers	0.2	0.9	0.6
SEG 2	Professional and technical	4.6	6.1	7.5
SEG 3	Intermediate	16.0	15.2	17.4
SEG 4	Junior	79.2	77.7	74.5

Turning to the two components of total hours, normal and overtime, we see from Tables 4.5 and 4.6 that there was a slight reduction in normal hours (substantial for part-time men), but no trend fall in overtime. Table 4.6 gives figures averaged across all workers regardless of whether or not they were on overtime, while Table 4.7 presents analogous figures relating just to those who actually worked overtime. The Tables show more over-time working among full-time men than among the other groups. A greater proportion of them were on overtime—about 20 per cent of them as compared to approximately 10 per cent of full-time women and 2½ per cent of part-time men. A relatively high proportion of part-time women worked overtime—7 to 8 per cent. In addition there were workers who received premium payments for shift-work, night work, and weekend work which were not treated as overtime. For part-time men they repre-sented a small proportion of the total—2 to 3 per cent. Larger percen-tages of full-time men fell into this category—7.3, 12.9, and 16.6 in 1975, 1978, and 1982 respectively. Significant proportions of women were also

Table 4.4. *White-collar workers: total weekly hours worked*

	1970	1973	1976	1979	1982
Full-time men					
All	38.9	38.8	38.4	38.8	38.2
Private sector	39.5	39.3	39.1	39.2	38.7
Public sector	38.0	38.0	37.3	38.1	37.6
Part-time men					
All	19.2	18.4	16.0	15.8	15.2
Private sector	20.2	19.9	18.5	18.2	17.8
Public sector	17.8	15.9	12.4	12.2	12.6
Full-time women					
All	37.1	36.8	36.5	36.7	36.5
Private sector	37.7	37.5	37.2	37.2	37.1
Public sector	36.4	36.0	35.7	36.2	35.8
Part-time women					
All	20.4	20.9	20.9	20.8	20.1
Private sector	21.0	21.2	21.6	21.3	20.2
Public sector	19.2	20.4	19.9	20.1	20.0

Table 4.5. *White-collar workers: normal weekly hours worked*

	1970	1973	1976	1979	1982
Full-time men					
All	37.7	37.4	37.2	37.2	37.0
Private sector	38.2	38.0	38.0	37.9	37.7
Public sector	36.7	36.6	35.9	36.1	36.0
Part-time men					
All	19.0	18.1	15.8	15.6	14.9
Private sector	19.9	19.5	18.3	18.0	17.4
Public sector	17.7	15.5	12.3	12.1	12.3
Full-time women					
All	36.8	36.4	36.2	36.3	36.1
Private sector	37.3	37.1	36.8	36.8	36.6
Public sector	36.1	35.7	35.4	35.8	35.5
Part-time women					
All	20.1	20.5	20.6	20.4	19.6
Private sector	20.6	20.7	21.3	20.7	19.6
Public sector	19.0	20.1	19.7	19.8	19.7

Table 4.6. *White-collar workers: weekly overtime hours worked*

	1970	1973	1976	1979	1982
Full-time men					
All	1.3	1.4	1.3	1.6	1.3
Private sector	1.3	1.3	1.2	1.4	1.1
Public sector	1.3	1.5	1.5	2.0	1.7
Part-time men					
All	0.2	0.4	0.2	0.3	0.4
Private sector	0.3	0.4	0.2	0.3	0.5
Public sector	0.1	0.3	0.2	0.2	0.3
Full-time women					
All	0.3	0.4	0.3	0.4	0.4
Private sector	0.4	0.5	0.3	0.4	0.4
Public sector	0.2	0.3	0.3	0.5	0.4
Part-time women					
All	0.3	0.4	0.3	0.5	0.5
Private sector	0.3	0.5	0.4	0.6	0.6
Public sector	0.3	0.3	0.3	0.3	0.3

Table 4.7. *White-collar workers: average number of overtime hours worked per week*

	1970	1973	1976	1979	1982
Full-time men					
All	6.4	6.5	6.6	7.2	6.3
Private sector	6.4	6.5	6.3	6.6	5.8
Public sector	6.4	6.6	6.9	7.8	6.7
Part-time men					
All	5.0	6.5	4.1	5.7	6.3
Private sector	5.2	6.6	5.2	7.2	6.9
Public sector	4.4	6.4	3.0	4.3	5.6
Full-time women					
All	3.3	3.6	3.4	3.9	3.3
Private sector	3.3	3.5	3.0	3.0	2.7
Public sector	3.4	4.0	4.1	5.9	4.7
Part-time women					
All	4.9	5.1	4.7	5.4	4.5
Private sector	5.0	5.4	4.7	5.4	4.4
Public sector	4.6	4.5	4.8	5.2	4.6

covered—amongst part-timers 2.9 per cent, 4.4 per cent, and 6.9 per cent
in the three relevant years, and amongst full-timers 3.3 per cent, 7.8 per
cent, and 12.7 per cent. The upward trend for all three groups is noteworthy. This may well represent the increasing concern of British industry
and commerce with flexible working patterns.

Incentive payments systems used to be generally associated with blue-
collar workers. Yet over the last few years there has been increasing talk
of their application to white-collar employees, through schemes such as
merit-related pay rather than via 'old-fashioned' payments-by-results.
Our NES data record information on the numbers who received payments under the broad category 'piecework and other payments-by-
results systems, bonuses including profit-sharing, commission and other
incentive payments, with the possible exception of any relating to overtime hours and treated as overtime earnings'. Very few part-time men
received such payments. More of the other three categories did. They
seemed more popular amongst both part-time and full-time women,
affecting over 7 per cent of them in 1975 and over 10 per cent in 1982,
than amongst full-time men of whom 5 per cent to 6 per cent were
affected. Interestingly, over the period they became increasingly common
for women, but not for men. Given the recent stress on profit-sharing
arrangements and individual merit-related pay, this is probably an area
where the years since 1982 have shown considerable change.[4]

The most important point to emerge from this section is that white-
collar employment patterns were very different for men and women, the
latter being crowded at the low end of the group. As we shall see later,
even within the higher SEGs, the position of women seems to have been
disadvantaged. This will become evident when we consider the management class (SEG 1). What this serves to underline is the 'fuzziness' of
occupational definitions in this area of the labour market. A critical
aspect of this, one suspects, is the range of human capital endowment
embodied in individuals with the same or similar-sounding jobs. Unfortunately it is in this very dimension that the NES lacks data.

4.3. The Dispersion of Earnings and Differentials by Region, Industry, and Occupation

For the men in our sample real gross weekly earnings increased by 13.1
per cent between 1970 and 1982, and real gross hourly earnings by 15.7
per cent. The corresponding figures for women are 33.4 per cent and 34.9
per cent. By way of comparison, for male and female manual workers
real weekly earnings increased by 13 per cent and 32 per cent respectively.
Thus aggregate white-collar/blue-collar pay differentials appear to have

Table 4.8. *White-collar workers: dispersion of earnings*

	Weekly earnings				Hourly earnings			
	BD	LQ	UQ	TD	BD	LQ	UQ	TD
	M	M	M	M	M	M	M	M
1970								
Full-time men	62.2	77.2	131.0	173.0	61.9	76.1	136.7	187.1
Part-time men	46.8	63.2	219.8	356.6	47.6	57.6	193.3	291.2
Full-time women	64.3	78.5	129.6	173.2	62.8	77.7	133.1	184.4
Part-time women	52.9	72.6	137.8	181.1	68.6	78.6	130.6	187.4
1976								
Full-time men	62.7	78.1	131.0	165.7	62.6	77.7	135.9	180.7
Part-time men	34.5	59.3	186.3	344.7	45.5	58.6	185.1	238.4
Full-time women	65.6	80.0	128.9	171.9	65.2	80.4	131.5	195.6
Part-time women	53.9	75.0	134.7	175.2	70.9	80.0	128.5	178.8
1979								
Full-time men	65.0	79.9	125.4	156.9	64.7	79.1	128.5	163.9
Part-time men	31.2	54.8	180.6	313.2	46.1	59.7	181.7	245.2
Full-time women	70.2	82.3	124.9	158.4	69.5	82.1	128.4	177.5
Part-time women	56.4	76.0	128.2	163.5	76.9	84.1	121.0	157.4
1982								
Full-time men	61.0	77.5	129.2	167.5	60.1	77.0	131.6	172.0
Part-time men	32.6	52.4	171.6	306.4	42.4	55.9	175.7	247.0
Full-time women	66.6	79.6	130.1	166.1	65.9	79.8	134.0	183.8
Part-time women	49.6	70.3	135.4	184.0	74.3	82.3	129.5	179.3

Note: BD = Bottom decile; LQ = lower quartile; UQ = upper quartile; TD = top decile; M = median.

changed little over the period. What, however, happened to the dispersion of pay within the white-collar group?

As a first pass at this analysis, we calculated four ratios, those of the bottom decile, lower quartile, upper quartile, and top decile respectively to the median. We then examined how these ratios altered over the years and how they varied between groups. Table 4.8 gives the relevant ratios for men and women, split between full-timers and part-timers.[5]

On the measures we have used, there is little difference between the relative ranges of full-time male and full-time female earnings though there is a tighter bunching of low female earners towards the median. Part-time women, however, exhibit a substantially wider dispersion.

In the case of full-time men, the bottom end of the distribution showed considerable stability between 1970 and 1979. If anything, there was a very slight narrowing, with both the bottom decile and lower quartile creeping closer to the median. Most of the movement took place in the late 1970s, as it did at the top end of the distribution, where the narrowing is more evident. Between 1970 and 1979, for example, the ratio of the top decile to the median fell from 173.0 to 156.9, on the weekly earnings measure. These movements were slightly greater for hourly earnings than for weekly earnings. Between 1979 and 1982 there was pronounced widening of the dispersion, with both ends floating away from the median. The movement was particularly marked for the top decile. However, it should be noted that these developments generally did little more than restore matters to their 1976 position. On the hourly earnings measure, there was some net narrowing over the whole period.

For full-time women there was a much more noticeable narrowing at the bottom end between 1970 and 1979. It was particularly pronounced in the last few years of this period. Such squeezing was replicated at the top end of the distribution, but on a scale no greater than for men. Turning to the 1979–82 period, the picture is similar to that for male full-timers— that is a substantial widening, with both ends of the distribution moving further away from the median. The story is broadly repeated for part-time women, though interestingly the widening for the top decile of this group was greater than for full-time women. As far as the latter are concerned, developments in 1979–82 broadly restored the position at the mid-1970s. For part-timers, however, there was some net widening.

The historical pattern of narrowing and widening is repeated if we disaggregate by socio-economic group (SEG). For full-time men the relative dispersion of the four SEGs remained similar across the years. SEG 1, managers, exhibits most dispersion, followed by professional and technical employees (SEG 2). There is little to choose between SEGs 3 and 4, the intermediate and junior groups. The latter exhibit only minor positive skewness. SEGs 1 and 2 exhibit substantially more. This picture of narrowing and then subsequent widening is repeated for full-time women. There is less obvious difference between the dispersions of SEG 1 and SEG 2. Both, however, exhibit more dispersion than the other two SEGs. In contrast to the men, SEG 4 is noticeably less dispersed than is SEG 3. The part-timers of both sexes show the same general narrowing and widening over time, but individual examination of each of the SEGs yields sufficient exceptions to suggest that a more detailed analysis at this disaggregated level would be useful. Comparison of dispersion between the SEGs yields a radically different pattern from that exhibited by full-timers. SEG 2 is dramatically more dispersed than the other SEGs. SEG 1 and SEG 3 have little to choose between them. SEG 4 has least dispersion.

In sum, then, dispersion over time altered in similar ways for men and women. The evidence does not just reflect the difference in occupational composition between the sexes mentioned in the previous section, but also suggests that part-time workers differ yet again. Inferences about changes over time in equality or inequality have to be guarded in the absence of proper panel data.

4.4. Pay Hierarchies and Differentials

Our sample was split into four regional groupings:

1. Greater London;
2. Rest of the South East;
3. East Anglia, South West, Midlands, and Yorkshire;
4. North, North West, Wales, and Scotland.

On both the weekly and hourly measures, earnings differentials were as expected, with Greater London doing better than the rest of the South East, where in turn pay was higher than in the other two regions. Earnings were generally greater in the North etc. than in East Anglia etc. Amongst men there was no tendency for regional differentials to alter over time. For women they widened slightly. This general stability is in spite of a widening of absolute unemployment rates across regions, confirming a lasting feature of the British labour market—the failure of regional pay differentials more than partially to reflect different demand conditions.

Industrial differentials varied somewhat over the period, but the ranking of industries was by and large pretty stable. There was little difference in their pecking order between men and women or between part-time or full-time women. High in the league were energy and water supply; banking etc.; transport and communication. Other services came out better for women than for men. Bottom of the league were agriculture, forestry, and fishing; construction; distribution; hotels and catering; and repairs. Whether the hourly or weekly measure was used usually made little difference, though there were some exceptions—for example, for men other services persistently ranked higher on the hourly than on the weekly measure.

Given our inability to disaggregate satisfactorily by KOS, we also explored disaggregation by 'socio-economic group'. As explained earlier, four SEGs are relevant for white-collar workers. Tables 4.9 and 4.10 present gross earnings for each year, based on SEG 1 = 100. The years prior to 1973 were omitted, because the earnings levels of SEGs 2 and 3 were out of line with later years—an oddity which we have not yet been able to explain.

For full-time men there was no obviously strong trend in differentials

Table 4.9. *White-collar workers: earnings by socio-economic group—full-time men*

		1973	1974	1975	1976	1977	1978	1979	1980	1981	1982
Hourly earnings											
SEG 1	Managers	100.0	100.0	100.0	100.0	100.0	100.0	100.0	100.0	100.0	100.0
SEG 2	Professionals	94.8	92.1	99.1	102.4	100.0	97.8	95.7	97.5	98.0	99.5
SEG 3	Intermediate	77.3	75.6	81.6	85.1	81.6	79.6	80.1	78.4	82.2	79.4
SEG 4	Junior	56.5	56.8	60.4	61.0	61.4	59.7	60.4	61.5	61.3	68.1
Weekly earnings											
SEG 1	Managers	100.0	100.0	100.0	100.0	100.0	100.0	100.0	100.0	100.0	100.0
SEG 2	Professionals	91.9	90.6	94.9	98.8	97.5	93.6	93.1	94.6	96.5	95.5
SEG 3	Intermediate	71.3	70.9	75.2	78.2	77.0	74.9	75.4	73.9	77.2	75.1
SEG 4	Junior	58.3	58.9	62.7	63.9	63.7	61.8	63.6	63.4	62.9	62.4

Table 4.10. *White-collar workers: earnings by socio-economic group—full-time women*

		1973	1974	1975	1976	1977	1978	1979	1980	1981	1982
Hourly earnings											
SEG 1	Managers	100.0	100.0	100.0	100.0	100.0	100.0	100.0	100.0	100.0	100.0
SEG 2	Professionals	106.3	98.7	107.9	110.1	109.1	104.3	103.4	99.7	108.6	106.3
SEG 3	Intermediate	96.9	92.4	110.1	112.4	104.3	99.5	99.2	91.0	104.8	96.6
SEG 4	Junior	59.4	58.6	64.8	65.7	65.2	65.1	66.2	61.6	65.0	63.9
Weekly earnings											
SEG 1	Managers	100.0	100.0	100.0	100.0	100.0	100.0	100.0	100.0	100.0	100.0
SEG 2	Professionals	103.7	97.1	108.0	110.8	109.5	104.0	105.8	103.3	107.9	104.8
SEG 3	Intermediate	84.7	83.2	98.8	100.3	96.9	92.5	91.9	87.4	94.8	88.5
SEG 4	Junior	58.6	59.0	65.0	65.6	66.5	65.6	67.3	63.3	64.4	63.1

between the SEGs. Most noteworthy is the sharp narrowing of differentials between SEG 1 and the rest in the mid-1970s, probably the consequence of incomes policies. This was generally unwound in subsequent years, but, interestingly, there is no systematic evidence of widening during the early 1980s.

While for men there is a clear pecking order in relative pay, the ranking being (1) managers, (2) professional and technical workers, (3) intermediate non-manual workers, (4) junior non-manual workers, the picture for full-time women is very different. SEG 4 is distinctly lower paid than the other SEGs, as is the case of men, but there is a much tighter range of earnings between the other three SEGs. Indeed generally those in SEG 2 earn more than those in SEG 1. This presumably reflects the relatively lower status of women within the management ranks. As with men, there are no obvious systematic trends in differentials between SEGs.

On these various measures of differentials, therefore, the picture in 1982 was not dramatically different from that in 1970; though, as with dispersion, this sometimes masks several offsetting changes within the period.

It is possible that relatively high levels of aggregation hid more substantive changes taking place at, for example, a more finely defined occupational level. As far as the data permit, therefore, we turn to this in the next section, where we discover that to a limited extent our suspicions are confirmed.

4.5. Earnings in Selected Occupations

We selected certain occupations for special consideration. These are listed in Appendix 4.1. For the reasons given in the Introduction, the information we were able to extract was limited. Where possible, however, we examined how earnings in each occupation moved relative to average earnings for men or women as a whole. The results for weekly earnings are presented in Table 4.11.

Making due allowance for large standard errors associated with sometimes small groups, a number of occupations experienced large fluctuations in their relative fortunes, without necessarily experiencing secular declines or improvements. This seems to be particularly true of public sector groups in an era of pay restraint which often not only had differential impacts but altered the relative timing of pay settlements. Cases in point are primary teachers and nurses for women, and secondary teachers for men. As far as secular movements are concerned, nurses were no

Table 4.11. *White-collar workers: earnings in selected occupations*

	1973	1974	1975	1976	1977	1978	1979	1980	1981	1982
Full-time men										
1. Secondary teachers	125.1	117.0	123.7	132.8	125.2	118.8	106.8	97.9	124.5	114.6
2. Production managers	121.7	122.5	—	120.2	—	117.2	121.3	137.2	120.7	124.1
3. Supervisors of clerks	93.9	109.6	96.6	—	99.4	97.4	95.5	101.1	98.6	94.9
4. Production clerks	80.3	84.4	71.1	74.5	74.6	76.2	82.1	69.4	69.1	73.7
5. General clerks	61.2	71.0	65.6	73.3	72.1	67.8	67.6	74.1	68.6	74.9
6. Salesmen	78.9	64.9	63.9	55.6	61.3	74.1	70.5	62.7	59.2	52.6
7. Sales representatives	105.6	107.0	95.1	93.1	102.5	105.6	115.1	115.4	107.6	110.2
8. Accountants	99.3	91.6	80.9	90.2	99.3	96.4	106.3	112.9	85.9	91.9
9. Office managers	139.0	143.7	132.3	139.9	138.2	151.7	145.2	139.1	152.9	152.0
Full-time women										
1. Primary teachers	157.9	151.9	149.7	161.5	155.1	151.8	140.9	134.4	158.1	151.8
2. Nurses	80.4	79.9	94.6	93.1	90.0	83.0	84.6	86.5	88.8	88.7
3. Accounts clerks	—	—	—	89.7	95.6	96.1	96.9	93.9	103.0	97.6
4. General clerks	100.4	112.0	95.8	98.2	97.2	96.2	90.9	96.5	93.6	90.0
5. Secretaries	114.7	122.3	108.4	112.4	111.0	115.4	115.4	114.5	108.9	116.0
6. Sales assistants	62.7	61.5	60.9	58.5	61.5	61.8	67.4	64.5	62.6	61.2
7. Secondary teachers	190.9	186.9	174.9	187.5	176.8	176.7	152.0	139.7	166.2	154.4
8. Nursing auxiliaries	73.9	67.6	—	—	—	—	—	79.3	—	77.7

Note: Full occupational definitions are listed in Appendix 4.1. Average white-collar earnings = 100 (men and women separately).

worse off in the early 1980s than at the beginning of our period, but had lost out since their halcyon days of 1975–7. These latter years also appear to have been particularly good ones for women primary teachers and male secondary teachers. Oddly and in contrast to their male counterparts, women secondary teachers did experience a fall in their relative earnings while female primary teachers did not. More expectedly female general clerks also lost ground, as would be expected at a time when lower-paid groups were losing out. So did junior male clerks. But this was not so obviously the experience of more senior male clerks or higher-grade female secretaries. Surprisingly female shop assistants held their position, while their male counterparts suffered heavily. At the other end of the spectrum, sales reps improved their relative standing.

4.6. Age, Length of Service, and Internalization

Age differentials in the aggregate

Table 4.12 shows age differentials for gross weekly earnings. The years before 1974 are omitted for lack of comparable data, as are part-time men. It should be stressed that these data relate to differentials, and do not necessarily imply anything for the age–earnings profiles of particular individuals. The latter could properly be analysed only by use of panel data. We shall return to this point later. For full-time men peak earnings were reached in the 40–9 age group. Thereafter earnings fell off slightly for the 50–9-year-olds, and rather more for those over 60. As compared to men, women's earnings peaked earlier (at 30–9) and declined less after these peak years. The 20–9 group also did better relative to the peak than did men of similar age. Part-time women reached peak earnings later than their full-time counterparts and there was a larger subsequent fall-off. The earnings of young part-time women were, however, far closer to their peak than were the earnings of full-time women of similar age. For this group, there is no evidence of any systematic movement of age differentials over our period of study. However, for full-timers of both sexes, there was some slight deterioration in the relative earnings of the young. Moving to the hourly earnings measure (Table 4.13), the peak years for part-time women reduce to 30–9. With that exception the same general pattern of age differentials across time and between groups remains. By and large, however, differentials are more marked for hourly than for weekly earnings, reflecting the fact that, to a minor extent, the lower-paid work more hours.

Table 4.12. *White-collar workers: weekly earnings differentials—by age*

	1974	1975	1976	1977	1978	1979	1980	1981	1982
Full-time men									
18–19	—	—	—	—	—	—	—	—	—
20–9	69.9	70.9	71.2	71.9	70.9	71.1	70.1	68.6	67.3
30–9	93.6	93.1	94.2	93.8	93.8	93.3	93.1	92.7	91.8
40–9	100.0	100.0	100.0	100.0	100.0	100.0	100.0	100.0	100.0
50–9	95.6	95.1	95.3	95.5	95.7	95.6	96.0	96.3	95.7
60+	81.8	80.7	81.7	81.1	81.2	81.7	83.9	85.0	81.5
Full-time women									
18–19	62.7	64.0	62.0	63.8	63.7	64.1	63.4	61.2	60.0
20–9	88.3	87.9	87.4	87.2	87.2	86.7	85.9	84.1	83.4
30–9	101.6	99.8	99.8	100.0	100.4	100.9	100.7	100.0	99.0
40–9	100.0	100.0	100.0	100.0	100.0	100.0	100.0	100.0	100.0
50–9	104.5	100.0	100.1	98.4	98.7	98.2	99.2	98.2	97.6
60+	103.0	92.6	95.0	95.6	90.1	88.1	93.1	97.7	96.2
Part-time women									
18–19	51.2	63.3	45.9	57.5	65.9	53.9	61.9	55.4	57.1
20–9	96.0	99.2	97.2	97.1	94.3	94.2	95.2	96.4	94.9
30–9	96.1	99.8	98.2	98.5	99.5	95.9	95.4	96.5	96.1
40–9	100.0	100.0	100.0	100.0	100.0	100.0	100.0	100.0	100.0
50–9	93.1	97.3	97.1	97.1	95.4	95.9	96.9	96.0	95.6
60+	80.9	81.4	82.0	81.3	79.6	81.1	80.7	79.2	78.2

Age differentials within socio-economic groups

Confining ourselves to weekly earnings, first we consider how the age profiles of men divided into SEGs compare with their overall profiles. The results (Table 4.14) are much as expected. In SEGs 1 and 2, the young were further below their peak earnings than were young non-manuals as a whole while the earnings of the older workers fell back by less. By contrast the earnings profile for SEG 4 shows the young doing relatively better, and the old doing relatively worse. By and large, the same is true for SEG 3. Clearly these contrasts reflect steeper early career paths in the higher SEGs, together with a greater ability to maintain earning power later in life.

The earnings profile for full-time women in SEG 4 was noticeably flatter than for non-manual women as a whole—unsurprisingly for this lowly occupational group. By contrast, for SEGs 2 and 3, the earnings profiles were steeper at the young end. Most surprising is the fact that the profile was generally flatter for SEG 1 (managers) than it was for all women. This confirms the general impression that occupational progression is low for women in management jobs.

There is little evidence of a systematic change in age profiles over time. There is some suggestion of a slight gain in the position of youth until the end of the 1970s, followed by a deterioration thereafter.

Dispersion of earnings within age groups

For full-time men the dispersion generally widened the older the age group. Compared with the total distribution, that for men aged 21–39 was usually narrower at both ends, while it tended to be wider (particularly at the top end) for those over 50. There are a few partial exceptions to this picture. In some years, as we move to the 60-plus group, there was some narrowing—usually (and perhaps unexpectedly) at the bottom end. The pattern is slightly different for full-time women. Generally there was initially a widening as we move to the older age groups, but this halted and reversed at 40–9. The widening usually resumed in the 50–9 age group, but on some measures and in some years the reversal continued. In such cases there was further widening in the 60 and above group.

The picture is more substantially different for part-time women. Taking weekly earnings, generally the ratio of bottom decile to median earnings was lower for the 21–9 group than for the 18–20 group. It then rose only to fall again for the over-60s. There are some oddities in the ratio of lower quartile earnings to the median but generally it increased with age until the 60+ group. At the upper end of the distribution, young high earners had bigger differentials than the other groups. Turning to hourly

Table 4.13. *White-collar workers: hourly earnings differentials—by age*

	1974	1975	1976	1977	1978	1979	1980	1981	1982
Full-time men									
18–19	—	—	—	—	—	—	—	—	—
20–9	69.4	71.1	70.3	71.3	70.2	69.7	68.9	67.5	66.1
30–9	93.1	94.8	94.1	94.2	94.1	92.9	92.3	92.4	92.1
40–9	100.0	100.0	100.0	100.0	100.0	100.0	100.0	100.0	100.0
50–9	94.4	95.0	94.5	95.0	94.8	94.6	94.9	95.1	95.7
60+	79.4	79.1	80.3	79.9	78.9	79.4	81.5	82.0	79.2
Full-time women									
18–19	59.1	61.1	59.2	61.3	60.5	60.3	60.9	58.1	57.8
20–9	86.0	87.5	87.2	86.4	85.6	84.0	84.3	81.3	81.4
30–9	100.0	100.0	100.0	100.0	100.0	100.0	100.0	100.0	100.0
40–9	98.1	100.0	100.3	100.0	99.5	99.3	99.4	99.0	99.2
50–9	101.4	100.0	99.3	97.9	97.2	95.9	98.3	96.3	96.2
60+	102.2	90.9	94.6	95.9	88.8	86.4	90.7	93.7	92.0
Part-time women									
18–19	69.9	73.2	70.2	66.7	73.7	73.7	85.0	78.8	70.8
20–9	98.4	98.3	99.4	96.1	94.3	100.1	99.5	102.0	99.6
30–9	100.0	100.0	100.0	100.0	100.0	100.0	100.0	100.0	100.0
40–9	98.8	95.8	97.5	97.2	96.6	97.8	99.2	96.0	97.1
50–9	93.8	92.2	92.8	92.4	91.0	94.0	94.3	93.3	92.0
60+	90.9	86.7	87.5	86.1	84.8	88.8	86.9	89.4	84.5

earnings, the bottom decile median earnings ratio behaved in roughly similar manner as on the weekly earnings measure. The young 1 did particularly well on the lower quartile ratio. There was no obvious age pattern at the upper end of the distribution.

Dispersion within each age group shows broadly similar time series movement as the aggregate. There are some exceptions. For men over 60 the low paid became lower paid, and the high paid less highly paid. The latter tendency was repeated for the top decile of women over 30.

The major phenomena which require further investigation are as follows:

1. A flatter age profile for full-time women than for men;
2. An earlier peak for women than for men;
3. A more pronounced tendency for earnings dispersion to rise with age for men than for women;
4. Among women, better relative earnings for 20–9-year-old part-timers than for similarly aged full-timers, but worse earnings for the over-50s;
5. Some decline over time in the relative pay of younger workers.

Preliminary hypotheses are that the first three of these features reflect the relatively lowly occupational status of women and their lack of career progression, and that the fifth reflects a decline in the relative demand for younger workers. The fourth feature probably reflects the fact that among women, career dislocation caused by bearing children and raising families is evidenced more in part-time than full-time profiles.

There are many possible reasons why earnings show the age patterns that they do. For manual workers, in particular, physical capabilities are stressed, while for non-manuals mention is often made of the benefits of 'experience' which, it is argued, are less prone to be damaged by the ageing process than are physical attributes. A further factor which has to be brought into play is the likely decay of skills with time. Whatever the mix of these and other influences, clearly there is a strong potential relationship between age differentials and length of service with the firm. In other words, it may be that an advantage which is attributed to age may in fact be the consequence of length of service. Why employers should pay more for the latter has itself become the topic of much academic debate in the last few years. It has been argued by, for example, Abraham and Farber (1987) that any length-of-service effect may be illusory. One reason for this may be that the data are 'censored'. In any length-of-service cohort, there is a dispersion of efficiency across workers who are paid accordingly. As the years go by, the least efficient of the cohort 'drop out', either voluntarily or involuntarily. Then the cohort's average efficiency and average pay increases with time. Amongst those

Table 4.14. *White-collar workers: weekly earnings differentials—by age and socio-economic group*

	1974	1976	1979	1982
SEG 1: Managers				
Full-time men				
18–19	—	—	—	—
20–9	68.6	69.2	72.1	67.2
30–9	92.3	89.9	91.9	91.5
40–9	100.0	100.0	100.0	100.0
50–9	100.9	98.1	100.4	100.0
60+	90.9	81.6	86.0	84.3
Full-time women				
18–19	—	47.7	52.4	—
20–9	90.3	91.9	90.8	88.5
30–9	103.7	104.5	101.3	104.6
40–9	100.0	100.0	100.0	100.0
50–9	113.3	114.4	92.5	98.0
60+	80.2	105.4	80.9	109.0
SEG 2: Professionals				
Full-time men				
18–19	—	—	—	—
20–9	68.6	67.6	69.0	66.2
30–9	93.1	92.2	92.3	90.6
40–9	100.0	100.0	100.0	100.0
50–9	100.2	100.0	98.6	97.7
60+	94.6	92.8	90.4	91.3
Full-time women				
18–19	42.0	44.9	54.4	45.4
20–9	81.2	77.2	85.6	78.0
30–9	109.0	96.7	104.3	97.0
40–9	100.0	100.0	100.0	100.0
50–9	109.8	97.3	104.2	100.6
60+	121.8	94.1	80.2	92.8
SEG 3: Intermediate non-manual				
Full-time men				
18–19	—	—	—	—
20–9	78.0	79.1	79.3	75.9
30–9	95.6	98.4	97.5	95.5
40–9	100.0	100.0	100.0	100.0
50–9	95.0	96.0	95.6	94.4
60+	86.9	88.8	88.3	81.5

	1974	1976	1979	1982
Full-time women				
18–19	45.5	53.4	53.8	51.0
20–9	78.5	79.3	77.1	76.1
30–9	95.2	94.7	100.7	95.4
40–9	100.0	100.0	100.0	100.0
50–9	105.2	101.4	100.2	100.8
60+	105.3	96.3	90.4	98.8
Part-time women				
18–19	—	—	—	—
20–9	84.8	88.2	91.9	92.2
30–9	89.2	90.9	95.4	93.5
40–9	100.0	100.0	100.0	100.0
50–9	90.1	101.6	98.4	96.4
60+	90.2	84.3	81.3	70.4
SEG 4: Junior non-manual				
Full-time men				
18–19	—	—	—	—
20–9	85.1	86.8	80.3	82.5
30–9	101.8	100.3	99.1	101.5
40–9	100.0	100.0	100.0	100.0
50–9	92.7	92.3	88.3	89.9
60+	80.8	81.9	78.2	77.6
Full-time women				
18–19	74.4	75.8	76.8	76.3
20–9	96.8	97.1	97.1	97.6
30–9	101.3	100.6	101.6	104.0
40–9	100.0	100.0	100.0	100.0
50–9	103.0	102.7	99.6	101.3
60+	98.3	95.7	92.8	101.4
Part-time women				
18–19	54.7	46.7	57.5	61.5
20–9	97.1	95.5	92.3	88.4
30–9	96.7	97.2	95.0	94.2
40–9	100.0	100.0	100.0	100.0
50–9	94.8	98.6	97.2	99.1
60+	79.6	83.8	84.4	81.6

who believe that the length-of-service effect is more than such 'illusion', there are in turn a variety of hypotheses, mainly concerned with the construction of pay structures in a world where labour is not a fully variable factor of production, where there are turnover costs for employer and employee, and where incentives are used to extract from workers optimum effort in situations where it is not fully observable.[6]

For three years (1975, 1976, and 1979) we have data on the length of time employees had been with their present firm. We give details below, but in brief the evidence suggests that much of the apparent age differential is in fact a length-of-service differential, and that the latter is pronounced.

Age differentials and length of service

These data can be analysed separately for the various age groups. Table 4.15 shows joint distributions by age and length of stay. For example for full-time men, the 20–9 column indicates that in 1975 12.2 per cent of 20–9-year-olds had been with their firm for a year or less. The rows are not cumulative. Generally the impression is one of long tenure, confirming the findings, for example, of Main (1982) on male manual and non-manual workers. In all three years, about 50 per cent of full-time men aged between 40 and 49 had been with their present firm between 10 and 20 years. Clearly many such workers tend to remain with the same firm as they get older, since over 70 per cent of the 50–9 group had stayed between 10 and 30 years. Smaller proportions of full-time women were long stayers, but even then around a quarter of the 40–9 group had been with their present firms for 10 to 20 years, while 45–50 per cent of the 50–9 group had stayed between 10 and 30 years. The figures reflect married women returning to the labour force after having had their families, and remaining with their new firm for the rest of their working lives. Though job tenure is shorter for women who work part-time, this same phenomenon is suggested by the fact that 60 per cent of the 40–9 group had been in post for 1–5 years, 36 per cent of the 50–9 group for 5–10 years, and nearly 70 per cent of the 60 and over group for 5–20 years. Also evident is the small number of men over 40 who enter new jobs. This is less marked for women, and particularly for part-time women. Thus there is strong evidence of a form of internalization for white-collar workers, particularly for men and for full-timers.

Table 4.16 sets out age differentials for all male full-timers, and then considers separately different length-of-service groups. Taking the 40–9 age group as our base, the 20–9 age group has earnings much closer to the base once length of service is taken into account. The same is generally true of the 30–9 age group, but those whose length of service is between 10 and 20 years are a consistent exception to this rule. The same picture of 'squeezing' is given if we examine older workers. Generally age differentials are less when calculated within length-of-service groups. Again a partial exception are the longer-service groups.

A similar effect of allowing for length of service is found in full-time female age differentials. Indeed it becomes evident that women over 40 seem to lose pay on account of their age once service with the firm is allowed for.

Turning the issue on its head, we can examine the effect of length of service within age groups. Generally full-time men continue to gain earnings advantage from length of service, though that advantage diminishes in later years. Such effects seem at least as strong for full-time women, and again tail off as time with the firm increases. Some illustrative figures are given in Table 4.17.

4.7. Conclusions

The NES has not proved to be a particularly rich data set for the analysis of white-collar pay and employment. This was to some extent inevitable, in that the paucity of information on 'personal characteristics' makes conventional earnings regressions impossible. Research problems were compounded, however, by the release of the data in the form of 'cells' rather than of 'individuals'. Assuming that this is an insuperable obstacle, progress will be made only if the initial sort is by KOS occupation, particularly if this is incorporated in a study of the 'panel' subset of the NES sample.

Given the above what limited conclusions can be drawn from our analysis? In many respects, despite the massive changes taking place in the economy at large, things looked very similar in 1982 as compared with 1970. Total hours worked changed little, there being only a slight fall in 'normal' weekly hours. The age distribution of the sample was pretty constant. There were few trend changes in regional or industrial earnings differentials, while, in the aggregate, white-collar/blue-collar differentials altered little. In some dimensions, we discovered considerable variability from year to year without any clear trend. Very often such variability was linked to the operation of incomes policy in a system of largely annual pay bargaining. This was particularly evident, for example, with the relative earnings positions of certain occupational groups at the KOS level—particularly those working in the public sector. Similar effects from incomes policy are found in the sharp narrowing of SEG 1 earnings relative to earnings of other SEGs in the mid to late 1970s, and at the same time in a narrowing of the overall dispersion of pay.

Ken Mayhew and Amit Ray

Table 4.15. *White-collar workers: age and length of service (%)*

Length of service (years)	Age					
	18–19	20–9	30–9	40–9	50–9	60+
Full-time men						
1975						
1 or less		12.2	2.0	0.9	0.7	1.1
5 or less		64.9	28.4	10.4	7.0	5.7
10 or less		22.4	47.0	24.8	12.6	12.5
20 or less		0.5	22.4	51.6	39.9	35.2
30 or less		—	0.2	12.0	31.7	31.1
30+		—	—	0.3	8.2	14.5
1976						
1 or less		10.6	2.0	0.8	0.3	0.4
5 or less		67.2	29.2	10.1	6.8	4.4
10 or less		21.7	45.9	27.4	13.9	33.2
20 or less		0.5	22.8	49.6	40.1	24.4
30 or less		—	0.1	12.1	30.7	25.8
30+		—	—	0.1	8.2	11.8
1979						
1 or less		9.2	1.5	0.4	0.1	0.3
5 or less		66.8	26.8	10.4	4.9	4.3
10 or less		22.9	46.6	26.8	13.1	14.0
20 or less		1.1	23.9	50.8	42.7	36.1
30 or less		[0.1]	0.2	11.3	30.5	35.5
30+		—	—	0.3	8.8	9.8
Full-time women						
1975						
1 or less	52.0	20.1	9.6	5.5	2.1	—
5 or less	47.5	67.0	49.0	38.6	20.4	13.1
10 or less	[0.3]	12.7	33.2	31.4	30.6	24.9
20 or less	[0.1]	0.2	8.2	22.7	38.5	46.0
30 or less	—	[0.04]	—	1.8	8.1	16.1
30+	—	—	—	—	0.5	1.3
1976						
1 or less	45.5	47.8	9.0	3.8	1.3	—
5 or less	54.5	18.3	49.2	37.6	19.7	9.5
10 or less	—	33.6	32.9	33.1	32.7	26.6
20 or less	—	0.3	9.0	24.1	36.6	45.7
30 or less	—	—	—	1.5	9.2	16.2
30+	—	—	—	—	0.5	2.0

Length of service (years)	Age					
	18–19	20–9	30–9	40–9	50–9	60+
1979						
1 or less	52.3	12.7	5.5	1.8	0.5	—
5 or less	47.8	72.0	47.1	31.0	11.7	10.5
10 or less	—	15.2	38.1	41.3	37.3	27.7
20 or less	—	0.2	9.3	24.4	42.5	45.8
30 or less	—	[0.03]	—	1.6	7.6	11.1
30+	—	—	—	—	0.4	4.9
Part-time women						
1975						
1 or less	54.1	43.5	22.2	8.4	2.8	2.0
5 or less	45.9	52.5	65.9	60.4	42.3	20.3
10 or less	—	3.6	11.7	26.0	36.4	40.8
20 or less	—	0.3	0.3	5.0	18.3	28.1
30 or less	—	—	—	0.1	0.2	7.8
30+	—	—	—	—	—	1.0
1976						
1 or less	44.0	35.0	16.4	5.4	3.6	0.9
5 or less	56.0	62.4	73.5	58.8	37.7	25.3
10 or less	—	2.5	10.0	25.5	43.0	34.5
20 or less	—	—	0.4	10.2	15.7	34.5
30 or less	—	—	—	0.1	—	4.4
30+	—	—	—	—	—	0.4
1979						
1 or less	60.3	35.0	14.7	3.8	1.2	1.4
5 or less	39.1	61.1	69.9	53.3	29.4	15.3
10 or less	—	3.9	15.1	36.9	49.8	39.7
20 or less	—	—	0.2	6.0	19.0	38.0
30 or less	—	—	0.1	—	0.5	5.6
30+	—	—	—	—	—	—

Note: Square brackets indicate clearly inconsistent observations.

Ken Mayhew and Amit Ray

Table 4.16. *White-collar workers: age, length of service, and pay—hourly earnings*

Length of service (years)	Age					
	18–19	20–9	30–9	40–9	50–9	60+
Full-time men						
1975 All		71	95	100	95	79
1		85	92	100	71	—
1–5		86	113	100	76	63
5–10		79	100	100	84	65
10–20		—	92	100	90	76
20–30		—	—	100	98	81
30+		—	—	—	108	84
1976 All		70	94	100	95	80
1		100	111	100	—	—
1–5		89	112	100	78	62
5–10		80	102	100	84	68
10–20		69	93	100	88	75
20–30		—	—	100	98	81
30+		—	—	—	110	87
1979 All		70	93	100	95	79
1		93	125	100	—	—
1–5		82	104	100	82	67
5–10		76	98	100	83	68
10–20		78	91	100	91	71
20–30		—	—	100	98	73
30+		—	—	—	74	59
Full-time women						
1975 All	61	88	100	100	91	—
1	77	107	100	90	85	—
1–5	63	93	100	93	78	70
5–10	—	80	100	97	83	75
10–20	—	—	100	104	99	85
20–30	—	—	—	—	—	—
30+	—	—	—	—	—	—
1976 All	59	87	100	100	99	95
1	76	110	100	85	94	—
1–5	60	90	100	93	77	66
5–10	—	82	100	95	83	72
10–20	—	—	100	113	103	97
20–30	—	—	—	—	—	—
30+	—	—	—	—	—	—

Length of service (years)	Age					
	18–19	20–9	30–9	40–9	50–9	60+
1979 All	60	84	100	99	96	86
1	77	101	100	95	—	—
1–5	65	91	100	95	83	71
5–10	—	80	100	93	69	—
10–20	—	—	100	103	96	80
20–30	—	—	—	—	—	—
30+	—	—	—	—	—	—
Part-time women						
1975 All	73	98	100	96	92	87
1	—	107	100	101	100	—
1–5	—	101	100	94	82	88
5–10	—	—	100	82	75	67
10–20	—	—	—	—	—	—
20–30	—	—	—	—	—	—
30+	—	—	—	—	—	—
1976 All	70	99	100	98	93	88
1	—	170	100	107	90	—
1–5	—	98	100	91	84	74
5–10	—	—	100	99	92	82
10–20	—	—	—	—	—	—
20–30	—	—	—	—	—	—
30+	—	—	—	—	—	—
1979 All	74	100	100	98	94	90
1	86	100	100	93	—	—
1–5	—	106	100	94	91	85
5–10	—	77	100	93	87	86
10–20	—	—	—	—	—	—
20–30	—	—	—	—	—	—
30+	—	—	—	—	—	—

Table 4.17. *White-collar workers: length of service and earnings*

Length of service (years)	Age				
	20–9	30–9	40–9	50–9	60+
Full-time men					
1	100	100	100	—	—
1–5	110	103	124	100	100
5–10	119	112	144	122	118
10–20	128	111	153	141	142
20–30	—	—	155	156	155
30+	—	—	—	166	156
Full-time women					
1	100	100	100	—	—
1–5	108	120	120	116	—
5–10	116	146	143	118	—
10–20	—	144	153	161	—
20–30	—	—	162	166	—
30+	—	—	—	—	—

In many areas where permanent change was observed this simply reflected well-recognized developments in the economy at large. The increasing importance of part-time women, movements in the public-sector share of employment, and in the regional and industrial distribution of workers all fall into this category. More interesting are the signs of the 'upgrading' of work (i.e. a greater proportion of workers in the higher SEGs), the relative decline in the earnings of the young, the increased use of incentive and bonus systems (broadly defined) for women, and evidence of greater flexibility of working time and patterns.

Many white-collar workers are in internal labour markets, as evinced not only by length of service but by the correlation between length of service and pay and by other signs of earnings and occupational progression within the firm. Many, by contrast, seem more like what the modern literature describes as peripheral. Such workers are either more loosely attached to the firm, or appear to gain relatively little benefit from length of service. Information on the comparative size of these two groups is scanty. To the extent that there is a correlation—albeit a weak one—between being in a higher SEG and being a core worker, the slight occupational upgrading observed over the 1970s would signal an increase in the relative size of core group. But this is likely to have been more than offset by the growing importance of female part-time workers. Clearly some part-timers are 'high-grade' employees, but about three-quarters are in SEG 4 and highly concentrated in distribution and other services. Their earnings show little tendency to increase with age, and they gain relatively little benefit from long service with the firm. While the widening of the dispersion of earnings for full-time workers had tended by 1982 to do little more than restore the position after the narrowing of the mid-1970s, for part-timers there was a net widening for the period as a whole. In sum, part-time female workers are a larger group than in the early 1970s. This group as a whole is relatively disadvantaged, and even within the group the extremes of disadvantage are greater.

These are compositional effects. The evidence makes it harder for us to assess how many individuals were pushed towards the periphery in the respects highlighted above, but a suspicion is that some were. The net widening of the dispersion of earnings among part-timers, together with signs that some low-grade occupations were 'losing out', are possible indications of this.

Full-time women did substantially better than their part-time colleagues, and like all women experienced an improvement in earnings relative to men. In many other ways, however, they did worse than men. They were concentrated by industry and into the lower SEGs. Even in the higher ones, there is evidence of relatively unfavourable occupational and career structures. In these respects there is little evidence of significant advance.

Perhaps the most interesting preliminary results relate to the effect on pay of age and length of service. Age differentials tend to reduce substantially once length of service is taken into account. Interestingly, full-time women benefited as much from length of service as did men; indeed to such an extent that, once this correction is made, their pay actually fell as they entered their forties. A striking aspect of age profiles is that dispersion of earnings tended to be higher the older the age group, particularly so for men. This dimension of the NES data would repay further study, particularly on the panel subset with KOS being used as one of the initial sorting characteristics.

Appendix 4.1. Occupations Selected for Special Consideration, 1973–1982

Men
  1. Secondary teachers;
  2. Production managers, works managers, and foremen;
  3. Supervisors of clerks;
  4. Production and materials controlling clerks;

5. General clerks and clerks not elsewhere classified;
6. Salesmen, sales assistants, shop assistants, and shelf fillers;
7. Other sales representatives and agents;
8. Accountants;
9. Office managers, national government, local government, others.

Women

1. Primary teachers;
2. State registered and enrolled nurses and certified midwives;
3. Costing and accounting clerks;
4. General clerks and clerks not elsewhere classified;
5. Personal secretaries, shorthand writers/typists;
6. Saleswomen, sales assistants, shop assistants, and shelf fillers;
7. Secondary teachers;
8. Nursing auxiliaries and assistants.

Notes

1. Though for an interesting recent approach to white-collar pay in the aggregate, see Blanchflower and Oswald (1988).
2. See for example Creedy and Whitfield (1982).
3. Again for the sake of brevity, only 'snapshot' years are presented. Full tables are available on request.
4. See Millward and Stevens (1986).
5. See n. 3.
6. For examples of recent work in this tradition, see Lazear (1981), Marshall and Zarkin (1987), Hutchens (1987), Mortensen (1988), and Kostiuk and Follman (1989).

5

Sex Differentials: Structure, Stability, and Change[1]

P. J. Sloane

5.1. Introduction

The objective of this chapter is to review changes in the male–female earnings differential and its components, together with associated changes in the employment of women. The time period 1970–82 is a particularly opportune one for an examination of relative female pay, since the Equal Pay Act was passed in 1970 and became fully operational at the end of 1975, and the Sex Discrimination Act also became law in that year.[2] The upward movement in female relative pay which occurred over this period followed long-run stability in the differential which had lasted from at least the late nineteenth century, so that it is clearly tempting to attribute the improvement in female pay to the legislation. However, it is necessary to consider other factors which were at work at this time. Apart from the fact that the demand for female labour appears to have grown relative to that for men, as reflected in the contraction of employment in manufacturing and its expansion in services and particularly part-time employment, the 1970s were a period during which flat-rate incomes policies were applied, and skill differentials narrowed.[3]

The major advantage of the NES data tapes is the ability to compare earnings classified separately by industry and by occupation, something which is not possible with any published data set. This should enable one to detect much more clearly the extent to which there is job segregation by sex and to measure the degree to which this depresses female pay relative to male. Another variable which obviously has a bearing on the sex–earnings differential is length of service. The NES contains data on those who have been employed by the same firm in the same job for more than 12 months, and for 1975, 1976, and 1979 on the number of years spent with the firm. There are also detailed data on the make-up of pay, including overtime premium payments from 1970 and shift-work premiums and incentive payments from 1973. Most studies of discrimination have compared male and female earnings net of overtime on the grounds that overtime earnings are more likely to represent different preferences between men and women with regard to undertaking such work than differential access. However, such reasoning leads one to conclude that on this basis one should also exclude shift-work and incentive payments and limit the comparison to residual pay. Data are also available on four types of collective agreement for 1973 and 1978 and for whether a collective agreement or Wages Council was present, in other years. In 1979 there is a detailed analysis of earnings by sex by establishment and company size, data which are not available from any other source. Other relevant variables include age from 1974, whether a double-jobber from 1975, and whether currently undertaking training, for 1973 and 1974.

Despite the above advantages the New Earnings Survey is in certain respects not an ideal data source for analysing movements in female pay relative to male. First, as noted in Chapter 1, the use of Inland Revenue records in the NES identification procedure may exclude from the sample workers whose weekly or monthly earnings are below the deduction card limit for tax purposes including in particular part-time women, those who changed jobs two–three months before the time of sample selection, and small firms (amongst whom women may be disproportionately represented). Care should be taken, therefore, in interpreting the absolute size of the gross earnings differential between men and women, though this problem should be less serious for changes in the relativity over time. Second, there are no data within the NES on educational qualifications, which would seemingly render the conventional human capital approach inoperative. However, this problem could be minimized by disaggregating to the KOS occupational level on the assumption that educational qualifications will be fairly uniform within KOS occupational groups. This will obviously be more reasonable for some occupations than others (e.g. for skilled manual occupations it may be reasonable to suppose that all adult workers are time-served). In the case of professional groups, however, there will be differences both in highest educational qualifications obtained and in class of qualification, both of which may have appreciable effects on earnings. Further, we must bear in mind that females do not appear to be placed into such clearly identified occupational groups as is the case for men. A third major omission is the absence of any data on marital status. A large number of studies have shown that marital status (or more precisely presence of children) has a negative effect on the earnings of married women, but a positive effect on male earnings, other things being equal. A fourth omission from the NES is data on earnings classified by individual employment units. The Equal Pay Act 1970 refers to equal pay for the same or broadly similar work or where work has been rated as equivalent under a job evaluation scheme *in the same or associated employer*, where common terms and conditions of employment apply. Thus, there is no legal requirement for earnings to be equalized across employment units.

Record identities in the sex differential data tapes are whether loss of pay, which provides information on the relative absenteeism rates of men and women; full-time/part-time—which enables us to compare earnings of part-time women with those of part-time men, which is not possible from published data; sex; industry division; socio-economic group; and KOS occupational code. In disaggregating the data it is necessary to compromise between industry and occupation. It was decided to retain all information on occupational classification, but because of the problem of empty cells this only permits analysis at the division level under the 1980 SIC. In practice over 400 occupations under the KOS classification are not manageable for many purposes and in the main we report here results for SEG by industry division which proves to be a most informative breakdown. The data files are limited to workers of 21 years and over to overcome the problem of different ages for the receipt of the adult rate. As illustrated in Chapter 1 and Table 5.1 the achieved sample is rather less than 1 per cent of employees in employment and the under-representation is rather greater for women than for men in every year in which the Survey has been conducted. This may in part reflect the fact that many women are secondary workers and when traced may no longer be in employment at the time of the Survey. The under-representation of women in the NES needs, however, to be borne in mind in the analysis which follows since female earnings are likely to be biased upwards in the NES sample. Table 5.2 reveals that sample numbers have been adjusted to reflect declining full-time male employment, increasing female employment, and rising part-time employment for both sexes. Loss of pay affects about 10 per cent of the sample according to the 1982 survey results (Table 5.3). Contrary to expectations a slightly higher proportion of full-time males (though a slightly smaller proportion of part-time males) are affected relative to comparable women.

5.2. The Degree of Sex Segregation

The simplest comparison to make is of the number of KOS occupations by industry in which women are found with those in which men are found. As indicated in Table 5.4 men are found in roughly 2.5 times the number of occupations in which there are women when one includes occupations where even a single man or woman is found. Restricting the sample to cases where there are at least 10 men or women in the sample does not alter this conclusion. Indeed the ratio of 'men's' to 'women's' occupations rises to 3.2. Comparisons over time are complicated by the fact that the occupational classification was altered in 1973, so that there is a much finer occupational breakdown after this date. Thus the number

Table 5.1. *Employees in employment: unadjusted for seasonal variation, Great Britain, and the NES sample*

	Male (000s)	Female (000s)	All
1970	13,880 (0.79)	8,545 (0.72)	22,425
1971	13,424 (0.81)	8,224 (0.75)	21,648
1972	13,241 (0.83)	8,318 (0.78)	21,559
1973	13,430 (0.80)	8,676 (0.74)	22,106
1974	13,325 (0.76)	8,802 (0.69)	22,127
1975	13,240 (0.76)	8,894 (0.64)	22,135
1976	13,050 (0.82)	8,870 (0.72)	21,920
1977	13,018 (0.82)	8,951 (0.73)	21,968
1978	12,984 (0.82)	9,017 (0.74)	22,001
1979	12,980 (0.77)	9,151 (0.70)	22,131
1980	12,817 (0.81)	9,127 (0.74)	21,944
1981	12,299 (0.85)	9,020 (0.77)	21,318
1982	11,775 (0.85)	8,850 (0.77)	20,626

Notes: The figures are quarterly figures for March each year.
Bracketed figures: NES sample as percentage of employees in employment.

of occupations by industry in which men were found rose from 1,056 in 1972 to 1,759 in 1973, the corresponding figures for women being 480 and 660 respectively. That the ability of women to enter a broader range of occupations has been relatively limited is indicated by the fact that in 1982 the corresponding figures were 1,676 for men and 681 for women, so that improvement has occurred more as a result of a decline in the number of occupations in which men are found rather than an expansion in the number in which women are employed. Further, when we confine the comparison to those occupations in which there are at least 10 individuals, the figure for women in 1982 (320) is actually lower than the comparable figure in 1973 (339). In each of the ten industrial divisions there are more occupations in which men are found than is the case for women, the most 'male intensive' industries being construction, energy, agriculture, and transport.

An alternative approach is to categorize KOS occupations by industry into exclusively male or female (where there are more than 100 in the sample), male or female where there are more than 100 in the sample regardless of the number of the other sex found there, and mixed occupations with more than 100 of both men and women in the sample. Using data for 1982 it is clear that there are rather more exclusively male

Table 5.2. *NES numbers in the sample, 1970–1982*

Year	Men 21+		Women 18+		Males		Females		Total		All
	Full-time	Part-time	Full-time	Part-time	Full-time	Part-time	Full-time	Part-time	Males	Females	
1970	97,184	2,106	39,460	18,189	106,723	2,380	42,738	18,760	109,103	61,498	170,601
1971	97,709	2,163	39,216	18,762	106,019	2,449	42,409	19,336	108,468	61,745	170,213
1972	99,924	2,196	40,869	20,161	107,996	2,472	43,948	20,784	110,468	64,732	175,200
1973	96,981	2,287	39,972	20,694	105,059	2,633	42,945	21,377	107,692	64,322	172,014
1974	90,373	2,233	36,986	20,245	99,039	2,522	39,622	20,804	101,561	60,466	162,027
1975	88,891	3,294	36,234	18,192	96,880	3,390	38,508	18,296	100,270	56,804	157,074
1976	94,353	3,649	39,881	21,549	102,797	3,806	42,085	21,658	106,603	63,743	170,343
1977	94,455	3,471	40,784	22,467	102,999	3,622	43,055	22,613	106,621	65,668	172,289
1978	94,043	3,402	41,169	22,871	102,887	3,576	43,425	23,072	106,463	66,497	172,960
1979	87,743	3,032	38,958	22,482	96,347	3,204	41,180	22,687	99,551	63,867	163,418
1980	91,117	3,073	41,296	23,533	100,121	3,313	43,570	23,786	103,434	67,356	170,790
1981	92,294	3,277	42,699	24,564	101,075	3,532	44,698	24,782	104,607	69,480	174,087
1982	89,198	3,345	42,309	24,268	96,976	3,614	43,725	24,529	100,590	68,254	168,844

Note: Figures for males and females include juveniles (under 21 for males, under 18 for females).

Table 5.3. *New Earnings Survey, 1982: comparison of numbers with and without loss of pay*

Age band	No loss of pay				Loss of pay			
	Full-time		Part-time		Full-time		Part-time	
	Male	Female	Male	Female	Male	Female	Male	Female
21–4	3,675	4,486	39	147	243	216	—	15
25–9	8,227	4,560	120	821	692	334	21	69
30–9	28,264	9,696	465	5,834	3,017	1,261	43	615
40–9	24,116	9,166	594	7,931	3,124	1,003	72	812
50–9	15,345	5,101	705	5,979	1,219	231	52	365
60–4	940	54	383	363	21	3	21	6
65–9	30	9	434	40	3	—	9	3
70+			147					
TOTAL	80,597	33,072	2,887	21,115	8,319 (10.32%)	3,048 (9.22%)	218 (7.55%)	1,885 (8.93%)
TOTAL (males and females)	113,669		24,002		11,367 (10.00%)		2,103 (8.76%)	
TOTAL (full- and part-time)	137,671				13,470 (9.78%)			

Note: Total number of employees aged 21 and over in the sample = 151,141.

Table 5.4. *Number of KOS occupations by industry: ratio of male to female occupations*

Industry (SIC(R))	1970[a]	1971[a]	1972[a]	1973	1974	1975	1976	1977	1978	1979	1980	1981	1982
0. Agriculture etc.	2.7	3.3	2.9	3.9	3.7	3.7	2.7	3.3	4.5	3.1	4.1	3.1	3.3
1. Energy etc.	4.1	3.9	4.0	5.3	5.4	5.8	5.4	4.8	5.7	5.1	5.5	5.6	5.0
2. Mineral extraction etc.	2.5	2.3	2.5	3.5	3.3	3.0	3.2	3.5	3.2	3.6	3.2	3.0	3.0
3. Metal goods, engineering, etc.	2.1	1.9	1.9	2.5	2.6	2.3	2.8	2.6	2.3	3.0	2.5	2.4	2.5
4. Other manufacturing	1.7	1.7	1.7	1.9	2.1	2.1	1.8	1.9	1.9	2.0	2.1	2.0	2.0
5. Construction	6.2	5.1	5.7	8.9	8.3	8.8	8.7	8.5	6.4	6.9	6.4	6.8	7.4
6. Distribution, hotels, etc.	1.9	1.7	1.7	1.9	2.0	2.1	1.9	2.0	2.1	2.0	2.0	2.1	1.9
7. Transport and communications	3.5	3.1	2.7	4.1	3.7	3.5	3.3	3.4	3.1	3.2	3.0	3.1	3.0
8. Banking and finance	2.2	2.2	2.1	2.2	2.1	2.1	2.1	1.9	1.9	2.1	2.3	2.3	2.2
9. Other services	1.8	1.8	1.7	1.9	1.9	1.8	1.8	1.7	1.7	1.7	1.7	1.7	1.7
TOTAL	2.3	2.2	2.2	2.6	2.6	2.6	2.5	2.5	2.4	2.6	2.5	2.5	2.5
	(2.8)	(2.7)	(2.7)	(3.2)	(3.3)	(3.2)	(3.2)	(3.1)	(3.2)	(3.2)	(3.0)	(3.2)	(3.2)

Note: These figures are based on hourly earnings net of overtime; full-time workers 21 and over whose pay was not affected by absence. Bracketed figures refer to occupations listed with more than 10 observations in the sample.

[a] In these years there were appreciably fewer KOS occupations listed and this will influence the results compared to later years.

occupations (52) than there are female (41). Exclusively female occupations are found most frequently in other services, with other manufacturing, distribution and hotels, and banking and finance also well represented. There are no exclusively female occupations in agriculture or construction. For men construction, transport and communications, metal goods and engineering, and energy have the greatest number of exclusively male occupations, and only banking and finance has none. Exclusively male occupations tend to be skilled manual jobs, and exclusively female occupations lower skilled non-manual jobs such as clerical occupations. This division is reflected to some extent in occupations in which 100 or more males are found in the sample (170 KOS occupations in 1982) and those in which 100 or more females are so found (58 KOS occupations in 1982). In 1982 there were 32 mixed occupations classified by industry compared to 31 in 1974. There were no mixed occupations (in 1982) in agriculture, energy, mineral extraction, or construction. The main overlap area is in other services, including the public sector with teaching, welfare, and health occupations well represented, together with some less-skilled clerical and cleaning occupations. In manufacturing clerical and semi-skilled manual occupations provide the main overlap area, and sales and clerical jobs in the remainder of the service sector.

Thus, the overall impression gained from this disaggregated analysis of the NES data is that there is a high degree of sex segregation which has modified little if at all over the period 1970 to 1982. This does not in itself, however, necessarily explain the major part of the earnings difference between men and women, as we shall see below. Indeed, as Table 5.5 reveals, earnings in exclusively male occupations are lower than male earnings in mixed occupations for all years other than 1971. This somewhat surprising finding is explained by the fact that the former are predominantly manual, while some of the highest paid jobs are non-manual and, although male dominated, also contain some women employees. Table 5.5 also reveals that the upward movement in relative female earnings was at least as large in exclusively one-sex occupations as in the integrated occupations, perhaps implying that forces additional to equal pay legislation were operating to raise female relative earnings (such as the narrowing of the skill differential referred to in Chapter 3).[4]

5.3. Earnings differences

The KOS occupational breakdown is too detailed for purposes of tracing the movement of the sex differential over time. In order to make the analysis manageable tables were constructed for each year of the Survey classifying hourly earnings net of overtime and employment by sex for

Table 5.5. *Relative hourly earnings and segregation*

Year	Earnings in exclusively female occupations with 100 or more females (pence per hour) (1)	Earnings in exclusively male occupations with 100 or more males (pence per hour) (2)	Ratio (col. (1)/ col. (2))	Female earnings in occupations with 100 or more males *and* females (pence per hour) (3)	Male earnings in occupations with 100 or more males *and* females (pence per hour) (4)	Ratio (col. (3)/ col. (4))
1970	48.67	63.77	76.32	48.75	65.05	74.94
1971	49.28	72.54	67.93	51.01	71.07	71.77
1972	54.57	79.46	68.68	59.56	83.67	71.18
1973	63.68	89.87	70.88	69.10	95.55	72.32
1974	70.34	101.65	69.20	81.46	108.98	74.75
1975	95.53	132.92	71.87	114.35	144.10	79.36
1976	119.73	156.50	76.50	144.22	177.52	81.24
1977	135.40	171.82	78.80	153.39	186.87	82.08
1978	157.50	192.39	81.86	170.63	211.18	80.80
1979	176.97	226.81	78.03	188.85	236.07	80.00
1980	217.18	269.62	80.55	232.66	285.39	81.52
1981	221.54	297.29	74.52	280.77	343.90	81.64
1982	259.68	332.47	78.11	300.13	367.92	81.57

full-time workers whose pay was not affected by absence for the eight
socio-economic groups and ten industry divisions, which provides 80 cells
for each year. For comparative purposes the data for 1970 and 1982 are
provided here as Tables 5.6 and 5.7 (the pattern in the intervening years
does not differ markedly from these years). For men the SEGs are
aligned extremely well with earnings levels. Invariably earnings decline in
each industry division as one moves from SEG 1 to 4 (non-manual) and
from SEG 5 to 8 (manual). However those in SEG 5 (foremen and
supervisors) in most divisions earn more than those in SEG 4 (junior
non-manual)—exceptions in 1982 being other manufacturing and other
services. For women, however, the relationship between SEG and pay is
not so close. Thus women managers often receive substantially less than
female professional workers within industry divisions. This suggests that
female managers may often be employed in small units where responsibilities are relatively limited and pay is comparatively low. There are also
some cases where semi-skilled manual women earn more than skilled
manual women within divisions. Thus, in general, it appears that female
occupations are less well defined in terms of pay than male. Further,
though this is not true of all divisions, the sex–earnings differential widens
as one moves up the occupational structure, both for manual and non-
manual workers. This is not in accordance with theory as far as the supply
side is concerned, since one would expect that women who had invested
in skill acquisition would be more committed to work because of opportunity cost considerations. Clearly, this is worthy of closer investigation.

In 1970 there were ten cells in which there were no women in the
sample even at this level of aggregation and a further eleven in which
there were fewer than ten females. In 1982 the corresponding figures
were seven and twelve respectively. Over the whole period 1970 to 1982
relative female earnings rose from 67.0 per cent of male to 75.3 per cent,
whilst relative female employment increased from 35.2 per cent of male
to 41.4 per cent, suggesting that the sharp upward adjustment in relative
female earnings was not in itself sufficient to reduce female employment
relative to male. However, there were some interesting variations across
socio-economic groups. For SEG 1 (managers) female relative pay
actually fell over the whole period from 69.9 per cent to 67.9 per cent,
while relative female employment increased from 4.2 per cent to 10.7 per
cent. Likewise in SEG 2 (professional workers) relative female earnings
fell from 80.2 per cent to 76.0 per cent, while relative female employment
increased from 8.8 per cent to 19.9 per cent. There was also an inverse
relationship between relative pay changes and relative employment
changes in SEGs 4, 6, and 8.

It is important to determine, however, to what extent women's pay is
depressed relative to that of men as a consequence of sex segregation and

to what extent it is depressed by lower pay given occupation. There is a simple standardizing procedure to test for this.[5] First one may assign females in their existing KOS occupations in each industry division the level of male mean earnings within each occupation by industry cell (of which there are potentially over 4,000). Second, one may redistribute females to accord with the expected occupation-by-industry distribution on the basis of the proportion of the sexes in the total labour force. There are three bases upon which such an analysis may be conducted. Type A includes all KOS occupations where female earnings data are available and assumes that where there are no male earnings women are effectively paid as men, thus biasing the procedure against finding a large earnings differential effect. Type B includes all KOS occupations where male earnings data are available. Where females do not exist in a cell it is assumed that they would have received male earnings had they been so employed and the occupational redistribution is carried out after the above assumption is applied consistent with the procedure in the Type A exercise. Type C conducts the analysis for those cells containing both males and females. Since there are more 'male' than 'female' occupations the Type B procedure includes most cells and Type C the least, but as shown in Table 5.8 the general finding of a greater earnings effect is not altered by whichever procedure is adopted. Remarkably, given the upward movement of female relative pay, the proportions explained by pay differences given occupation and by occupational differences given pay remain virtually constant and are no smaller than revealed in the earlier analysis using published data.[6] That is, the residual diminishes over time as female relative pay increases, but the proportions attributable to differences in pay and differences in occupational distribution within this smaller residual remain virtually constant. In 1982 sex segregation can only 'explain' between 20 per cent and 27 per cent of the difference in earnings with the remainder being explained by different levels of pay in current occupations. The Type B procedure suggests a lower degree of occupational segregation than either Type A or Type C procedures and might be preferred on the grounds that it contains the largest percentage of the sample (100 per cent of men and generally over 90 per cent of women). Further, it contains many more KOS occupations within divisions, reflecting the fact that men are employed in many more occupations than women (two-thirds of these cells contain no women). Over the period 1973–82 the percentage of women employed in occupations where males are found and the percentage of males employed in occupations where females are found have both increased (by three or four percentage points), suggesting that the labour force is becoming marginally more integrated. Within each industry division it is also generally true that pay inequality exceeds the effect of occupational segregation. Thus in 1982

Table 5.6. *Pay and employment by sex for industrial divisions and socio-economic groups, 1970*

SEG	(0) Agriculture etc.						(1) Energy etc.						(2) Mineral extraction etc.					
	Pay			Employment			Pay			Employment			Pay			Employment		
	F. (p)	M. (p)	F./M.%	F.	M.	F./M.%	F. (p)	M. (p)	F./M.%	F.	M.	F./M.%	F. (p)	M. (p)	F./M.%	F.	M.	F./M.%
Non-manual																		
1. Managers	—	77.49	—	—	49	—	—	150.13	—	—	126	—	73.14	140.32	52.1	7	444	1.6
2. Professional and technical workers	—	106.60	—	—	15	—	—	113.89	—	—	462	—	78.37	104.94	74.7	9	432	2.1
3. Intermediate non-manual workers	48.38	65.29	74.1	10	22	45.5	52.76	73.39	71.9	111	433	25.6	46.23	74.29	62.2	255	805	31.7
4. Junior non-manual workers	36.39	—	—	21	—	—	47.25	60.02	78.7	281	159	176.7	43.99	65.74	66.9	394	165	238.8
Manual																		
5. Foremen and supervisors	—	63.00	—	—	47	—	49.47	73.48	67.3	4	210	1.9	41.83	75.43	55.5	28	532	5.3
6. Skilled manual	—	45.43	—	—	50	—	35.01	59.96	58.4	7	2,658	.3	36.08	62.21	58.0	44	1,788	2.5
7. Semi-skilled manual	27.13	39.02	69.5	70	672	10.4	38.24	54.34	70.4	5	723	.7	35.27	60.53	58.3	200	1,924	10.4
8. Unskilled manual	24.75	34.69	71.3	29	296	9.8	32.57	48.52	67.1	38	359	10.6	32.92	52.66	62.5	251	1,147	21.9
TOTAL	29.84	41.59	71.7	130	1,151	11.3	47.10	66.76	70.6	446	5,130	8.7	40.76	69.81	58.4	1,188	7,237	16.4

Table 5.6. (*cont.*)

| SEG | (3) Metal goods, engineering, etc. | | | | | | (4) Other manufacturing | | | | | | (5) Construction | | | | | |
| | Pay | | | Employment | | | Pay | | | Employment | | | Pay | | | Employment | | |
	F. (p)	M. (p)	F./M.%	F.	M.	F./M.%	F. (p)	M. (p)	F./M.%	F.	M.	F./M.%	F. (p)	M. (p)	F./M.%	F.	M.	F./M.%
Non-manual																		
1. Managers	101.40	133.07	76.2	11	933	1.2	90.58	121.51	74.5	38	855	4.4	—	110.59	—	—	264	—
2. Professional and technical workers	58.65	94.56	62.0	18	1,553	1.2	74.27	97.12	76.5	30	412	7.3	—	93.11	—	—	403	—
3. Intermediate non-manual workers	42.70	73.11	58.4	586	2,063	28.4	42.97	72.64	59.2	603	1,363	44.2	41.82	69.34	60.3	82	283	29.0
4. Junior non-manual workers	41.67	72.08	57.8	1,146	985	116.3	40.65	61.87	65.7	804	248	324.2	41.70	62.43	66.8	160	62	258.1
Manual																		
5. Foremen and supervisors	42.39	76.09	55.7	66	1,264	5.2	40.83	68.03	60.0	178	834	21.3	—	67.30	—	—	582	—
6. Skilled manual	35.86	64.28	55.8	130	6,271	2.1	35.89	60.01	59.8	1,160	3,490	33.2	26.57	54.55	48.7	3	3,310	0.1
7. Semi-skilled manual	36.96	58.58	63.1	1,184	3,983	29.7	33.76	53.47	63.1	1,100	2,547	43.2	—	49.02	—	—	634	—
8. Unskilled manual	34.18	50.57	67.6	678	1,595	42.5	31.00	48.10	64.4	1,059	1,711	61.9	30.87	45.81	67.4	16	1,319	1.2
TOTAL	39.10	69.83	56.0	3,819	18,647	20.5	36.81	64.25	57.3	4,972	11,460	43.4	40.89	58.27	70.2	261	6,857	3.8

Table 5.6. (*cont.*)

SEG	(6) Distribution, hotels, etc.						(7) Transport and communications					
	Pay			Employment			Pay			Employment		
	F. (p)	M. (p)	F./M.%	F.	M.	F./M.%	F. (p)	M. (p)	F./M.%	F.	M.	F./M.%
Non-manual												
1. Managers	69.50	103.93	66.9	72	857	8.4	80.75	119.28	67.7	6	472	1.3
2. Professional and technical workers	62.19	86.46	71.9	8	175	4.6	65.30	96.87	67.4	3	282	1.1
3. Intermediate non-manual workers	39.62	63.41	62.5	996	1,784	55.8	54.74	68.09	80.4	324	961	33.7
4. Junior non-manual workers	31.05	47.17	65.8	2,401	752	319.3	46.60	59.59	78.2	616	374	164.7
Manual												
5. Foremen and supervisors	39.79	58.62	67.9	43	337	12.8	61.12	75.18	81.3	31	380	8.2
6. Skilled manual	31.78	49.83	63.8	174	1,709	10.2	38.76	56.14	69.0	5	2,764	0.2
7. Semi-skilled manual	28.35	44.24	64.1	334	1,406	23.8	47.50	54.93	86.5	163	2,642	6.2
8. Unskilled manual	26.24	41.55	63.2	501	739	67.8	35.41	48.95	72.4	133	1,070	12.4
TOTAL	32.97	57.46	57.4	4,529	7,759	58.4	48.14	61.12	78.8	1,281	8,945	14.32

Table 5.6. (*cont.*)

SEG	(8) Banking, finance, etc.						(9) Other services					
	Pay			Employment			Pay			Employment		
	F. (p)	M. (p)	F./M.%	F.	M.	F./M.%	F. (p)	M. (p)	F./M.%	F.	M.	F./M.%
Non-manual												
1. Managers	109.18	172.08	63.4	20	635	3.1	108.10	133.13	81.2	72	777	9.3
2. Professional and technical workers	75.21	106.40	70.7	46	817	5.6	90.09	124.46	72.4	500	2,411	20.7
3. Intermediate non-manual workers	53.11	79.31	67.0	745	1,734	43.0	74.33	92.62	80.3	4,769	3,788	125.9
4. Junior non-manual workers	48.40	63.69	76.0	1,262	367	343.9	44.26	62.51	70.8	2,747	1,493	184.0
Manual												
5. Foremen and supervisors	55.70	73.71	75.6	14	57	24.6	41.23	62.00	66.5	108	366	29.5
6. Skilled manual	50.30	58.68	85.7	9	159	5.7	31.44	51.72	60.8	451	1,469	30.7
7. Semi-skilled manual	31.86	48.03	66.3	22	277	7.9	32.56	43.88	74.2	477	2,208	21.6
8. Unskilled manual	29.67	43.45	68.3	43	96	44.8	29.26	41.66	70.2	1,698	1,766	96.1
TOTAL	50.71	94.27	53.8	2,161	4,142	52.2	56.37	76.94	73.3	10,822	14,278	75.8

Notes: Sample comprises 29,186 women reporting basic hours for whom mean hourly earnings = 45.41 pence; 82,946 men reporting basic hours for whom mean = 67.81 pence; yielding wage ratio = 67.0 (mean employment ratio F/M = 35.2%). Ratios are only estimated where there are more than 9 men and 9 women in the sample cell. Earnings are based on those workers reporting basic hours.

Hourly earnings net of overtime; full-time workers aged 21 and over whose pay was not affected by absence.

The employment figures reported in the table refer to all employees in the sample.

Source: New Earnings Survey Data Tapes 1982.

Table 5.7. *Pay and employment by sex for industrial divisions and socio-economic groups, 1982*

SEG	(0) Agriculture etc.						(1) Energy etc.						(2) Mineral extraction etc.					
	Pay			Employment			Pay			Employment			Pay			Employment		
	F. (p)	M. (p)	F./M.%	F.	M.	F./M.%	F. (p)	M. (p)	F./M.%	F.	M.	F./M.%	F. (p)	M. (p)	F./M.%	F.	M.	F./M.%
Non-manual																		
1. Managers	0.00	547.48	0.00	0	28	0.00	502.67	637.27	78.88	3	267	1.12	385.74	593.92	64.95	31	530	5.85
2. Professional and technical workers	0.00	456.62	0.00	0	4	0.00	488.63	630.27	77.53	14	546	2.56	370.47	518.22	71.49	39	460	8.48
3. Intermediate non-manual workers	478.80	273.35	175.52	3	88	3.41	357.36	450.25	79.37	58	214	27.10	317.24	408.85	77.59	83	358	23.18
4. Junior non-manual workers	238.44	270.73	88.07	24	3	800.00	306.74	365.63	83.89	395	323	122.29	254.77	326.07	78.13	428	218	196.33
Manual																		
5. Foremen and supervisors	262.55	280.07	93.74	3	90	3.33	344.40	459.46	74.96	5	285	1.75	252.73	381.76	66.20	13	374	3.48
6. Skilled manual	0.00	229.12	0.00	0	41	0.00	225.62	398.45	56.63	4	1,715	0.23	221.61	321.57	68.92	62	1,599	3.88
7. Semi-skilled manual	196.88	214.31	91.87	27	616	4.38	0.00	342.27	0.00	0	420	0.00	216.85	307.94	70.42	175	1,121	15.61
8. Unskilled manual	164.99	204.21	80.79	12	314	3.82	190.33	348.11	54.68	28	389	7.20	213.10	282.14	75.53	141	378	37.30
TOTAL	214.36	224.68	95.40	69	1,184	5.80	312.01	432.40	68.30	507	6,159	8.20	253.29	370.80	68.3	972	5,038	19.3

Table 5.7. (cont.)

SEG	(3) Metal goods, engineering, etc.						(4) Other manufacturing						(5) Construction					
	Pay			Employment			Pay			Employment			Pay			Employment		
	F. (p)	M. (p)	F./M.%	F.	M.	F./M.%	F. (p)	M. (p)	F./M.%	F.	M.	F./M.%	F. (p)	M. (p)	F./M.%	F.	M.	F./M.%
Non-manual																		
1. Managers	338.59	522.40	64.81	66	1,492	4.42	359.65	533.45	67.42	93	1,227	7.58	268.44	489.13	54.88	9	323	2.79
2. Professional and technical workers	357.09	468.58	76.21	62	1,896	3.27	409.88	509.14	80.50	96	585	16.41	361.27	444.48	81.28	4	602	0.66
3. Intermediate non-manual workers	289.00	415.08	69.62	123	893	13.77	299.85	390.91	76.71	214	647	33.08	289.32	416.42	69.48	15	544	2.76
4. Junior non-manual workers	240.71	324.13	74.26	1,277	1,060	120.47	247.26	336.92	73.79	1,036	432	239.81	231.08	302.16	76.48	276	160	172.50
Manual																		
5. Foremen and supervisors	276.41	361.16	76.53	50	1,003	4.99	221.50	335.96	65.93	131	716	18.30	0.00	334.60	0.00	0	596	0.00
6. Skilled manual	231.65	312.52	74.12	311	6,265	4.96	213.28	324.92	65.64	276	2,473	11.16	0.00	292.97	0.00	0	2,943	0.00
7. Semi-skilled manual	215.90	279.86	77.15	811	2,036	39.83	196.82	276.89	71.08	1,455	2,389	60.90	0.00	282.96	0.00	0	320	0.00
8. Unskilled manual	206.64	260.63	79.29	154	505	30.50	206.61	259.68	79.50	451	625	72.16	148.47	259.83	57.14	9	1,196	0.75
TOTAL	238.00	354.42	67.20	2,854	15,150	18.80	228.47	348.10	65.60	3,752	9,094	41.30	234.43	319.83	73.30	313	6,684	4.70

Table 5.7. (*cont.*)

SEG	(6) Distribution, hotels, etc.						(7) Transport and communications					
	Pay			Employment			Pay			Employment		
	F. (p)	M. (p)	F./M.%	F.	M.	F./M.%	F. (p)	M. (p)	F./M.%	F.	M.	F./M.%
Non-manual												
1. Managers	315.88	445.08	70.97	250	1,715	14.58	440.16	533.90	82.44	53	885	5.99
2. Professional and technical workers	383.39	528.53	72.54	31	266	11.65	498.92	576.91	86.48	36	391	9.21
3. Intermediate non-manual workers	240.00	330.77	72.56	752	1,749	43.00	360.05	454.15	79.28	96	732	13.11
4. Junior non-manual workers	199.58	256.55	77.79	2,763	1,033	267.47	276.93	337.02	82.17	997	703	141.82
Manual												
5. Foremen and supervisors	230.26	293.84	78.36	69	355	19.44	341.22	371.41	91.87	4	353	1.13
6. Skilled manual	194.64	259.90	74.89	64	2,017	3.17	274.42	304.56	90.10	20	2,900	0.69
7. Semi-skilled manual	174.88	234.14	74.69	307	1,534	20.01	279.01	289.51	96.37	141	2,007	7.03
8. Unskilled manual	172.73	223.61	77.25	317	413	76.76	220.82	264.78	83.40	115	446	25.78
TOTAL	209.85	306.35	68.50	4,553	9,495	48.00	289.63	348.92	83.00	1,462	8,417	17.40

Table 5.7. (*cont.*)

SEG	(8) Banking, finance, etc.						(9) Other services					
	Pay			Employment			Pay			Employment		
	F. (p)	M. (p)	F./M.%	F.	M.	F./M.%	F. (p)	M. (p)	F./M.%	F.	M.	F./M.%
Non-manual												
1. Managers	437.73	728.54	60.08	138	1,116	12.37	392.33	571.43	68.66	289	1,142	25.31
2. Professional and technical workers	400.71	583.63	68.66	270	1,720	15.70	411.03	561.11	73.25	1,519	3,918	38.77
3. Intermediate non-manual workers	373.56	462.16	80.83	284	953	29.80	406.05	495.49	81.95	5,949	4,140	143.70
4. Junior non-manual workers	286.43	350.90	81.63	2,891	1,213	238.33	253.63	356.65	71.12	4,686	2,508	186.84
Manual												
5. Foremen and supervisors	236.30	365.32	64.68	3	45	6.67	231.60	309.94	74.72	249	361	68.98
6. Skilled manual	290.46	348.06	83.45	9	104	8.65	197.06	285.61	69.00	384	1,023	37.54
7. Semi-skilled manual	214.88	301.08	71.37	8	256	3.13	212.12	251.34	84.40	735	1,721	42.71
8. Unskilled manual	214.93	232.77	92.34	20	85	23.53	193.19	228.49	84.55	1,156	1,484	77.90
TOTAL	306.27	514.62	59.5	3,623	5,492	66.0	318.77	418.34	76.20	14,967	16,297	91.80

Notes: Sample comprises 30,586 women reporting basic hours for whom mean wage = 279.75 pence; 73,859 men reporting basic hours for whom mean wage = 371.30 pence; yielding wage ratio = 75.3 (mean employment F/M ratio = 41.4%). Ratios are only estimated where there are more than 9 men and 9 women in the sample cell. Earnings are based on those workers reporting basic hours.
Hourly earnings net of overtime; full-time workers 21 and over whose pay was not affected by absence.
The employment figures reported in the table refer to all employees in the sample.

Source: New Earnings Survey Data Tapes 1982.

Table 5.8. *Pay inequality vs. occupational segregation: KOS occupations categorized separately by industry division (pence per hour (net of overtime))*

Year	W_1	W_2	W_3	W_4	$\frac{W_2 - W_1}{W_3 - W_1}$ %	$\frac{W_3 - W_2}{W_3 - W_1}$ %	$\frac{W_4 - W_2}{W_4 - W_1}$ %	Total number of cells with observations	% of missing male cells	% of missing female cells	Percentage of sample Male	Percentage of sample Female
Type A												
1970[a]	45.41	60.77	65.26	67.85	77.4	22.6	31.6	450	18.9		60.8	100.0
1971[a]	48.90	65.75	71.98	76.05	73.0	27.0	37.9	478	15.3		62.1	100.0
1972[a]	55.35	73.92	80.72	82.25	73.2	26.8	37.9	480	15.8		61.9	100.0
1973	64.39	86.84	92.19	95.79	80.8	19.2	28.5	666	17.7		54.8	100.0
1974	75.01	99.37	106.42	110.98	77.6	22.4	32.3	679	16.8		55.6	100.0
1975	104.44	131.87	139.27	144.02	78.8	21.2	30.7	640	16.9		56.4	100.0
1976	130.82	157.84	168.39	175.59	71.9	28.1	39.6	652	17.6		54.7	100.0
1977	142.00	170.17	180.95	188.38	72.3	27.7	39.3	645	18.6		54.8	100.0
1978	157.30	187.57	203.68	214.16	65.3	34.7	46.8	677	18.2		58.6	100.0
1979	176.28	209.39	227.15	240.02	65.1	34.9	48.1	560	18.6		53.4	100.0
1980	217.89	263.73	283.32	296.74	70.1	29.9	41.9	658	16.3		57.6	100.0
1981	258.70	317.43	335.11	347.28	76.9	23.1	33.7	665	15.6		58.3	100.0
1982	279.75	342.92	366.00	382.26	73.2	26.8	38.4	681	14.1		58.8	100.0
Type B												
1970[a]	45.57	62.74	66.60	67.81	81.6	18.4	22.8	1,045		65.1	100.0	89.5
1971[a]	49.09	67.47	73.67	75.99	74.8	25.2	31.7	1,068		62.1	100.0	91.7
1972[a]	55.66	75.73	82.29	84.80	75.4	24.6	31.1	1,056		61.7	100.0	92.6
1973	65.02	89.53	93.80	95.24	85.2	14.8	18.9	1,756		68.8	100.0	91.6
1974	75.76	102.45	107.45	109.09	84.2	15.8	19.9	1,762		67.9	100.0	91.3
1975	105.65	135.84	140.18	141.61	87.4	12.6	16.0	1,645		67.7	100.0	90.9
1976	132.31	161.99	167.75	169.70	83.4	16.3	20.6	1,647		67.4	100.0	87.6
1977	143.59	175.21	182.12	184.45	82.1	17.9	22.6	1,644		68.1	100.0	89.1
1978	158.34	193.02	204.62	208.48	74.9	25.1	30.8	1,651		66.4	100.0	87.3
1979	177.68	214.09	230.95	236.90	68.3	31.7	38.5	1,440		68.3	100.0	90.9
1980	219.38	268.72	284.97	290.90	75.2	24.8	31.0	1,666		67.0	100.0	92.9
1981	261.63	324.24	333.57	337.08	87.0	13.0	17.0	1,664		66.3	100.0	93.8
1982	281.84	348.57	364.90	371.30	80.3	19.7	25.4	1,676		65.1	100.0	94.7

Type C

1970[a]	45.57	62.74	66.11	67.85	83.6	16.4	22.9	365	60.8	89.5
1971[a]	49.09	67.47	72.83	76.05	77.4	22.6	31.8	405	62.1	91.7
1972[a]	55.66	75.73	81.62	82.25	77.3	22.7	22.2	404	61.9	92.6
1973	65.02	89.53	93.40	95.79	86.4	13.6	19.6	548	54.8	91.6
1974	75.76	102.45	107.81	110.98	83.3	16.7	24.2	565	55.6	91.3
1975	105.65	135.84	141.00	144.02	85.4	14.6	21.3	532	56.4	90.9
1976	132.31	161.99	170.38	175.59	78.0	22.0	31.4	537	54.7	87.6
1977	143.59	175.21	183.37	188.38	79.5	20.5	29.3	525	54.8	89.1
1978	158.54	193.02	206.51	214.16	72.0	28.0	37.9	554	58.6	87.3
1979	177.68	214.09	229.72	240.02	70.0	30.0	41.6	456	53.4	90.9
1980	219.38	268.72	285.83	296.74	74.3	25.7	36.2	551	57.6	92.9
1981	261.63	324.24	338.24	347.28	81.7	18.3	26.9	561	58.3	93.8
1982	281.84	348.57	368.78	382.26	76.8	23.2	33.5	585	58.8	94.7

Notes: W_1 = female earnings using female employment as weights (i.e. actual mean female earnings); W_2 = male earnings using female employment as weights (i.e. what women would receive if they earned the same as men in their existing occupations). W_3 = male earnings using expected female employment as weights (i.e. what women would receive if they earned the same as men and possessed the KOS occupation by industry distribution suggested by their percentage employment in the total labour force); W_4 = male earnings using the male expectation for female employment in the industry as weights (i.e. what women would receive if they earned the same as men and possessed the KOS occupation by industry distribution implied by the male employment distribution in each industry).

Type A analysis is based on all cells containing females. A cell is a KOS occupation within an industry division. Where males do not exist in a cell it is assumed that females earn 100% of the male level of earnings.

Type B analysis is based on cells containing males. Where females do not exist in a cell it is assumed that females would have been paid 100% of the male level of earnings if they had been employed in that cell.

Type C analysis is based on cells containing both males and females.

[a] In 1970, 1971, and 1972 there were many fewer KOS occupations in the Survey than in later years (189 compared to 445) and consequently the data for these years are not comparable with those for later years.

using the preferred Type B analysis and the W_3 occupational adjustment measure only in one industry, energy, which employs relatively few women, did the occupational adjustment account for a larger proportion of the difference in earnings than the earnings adjustment. However, only in one industry—transport and communications—did the size of the earnings adjustment exceed the average for all divisions. This suggests that occupations are more segregated within industry than across industries. It seems clear, however, that despite the conventional wisdom differences in occupational distribution are not the major explanation for differences in relative pay between men and women. It is not the particular occupations that women enter at the start of their working lives that depress their pay, so much as their failure to advance up the occupational ladder to promoted or better-paid posts once entry into particular occupational groups has been made,[7] though ideally we require longitudinal data to confirm this proposition. This has implications for the recent equal value amendment to the equal pay legislation.

In the literature much has been made of the fact that the timing of the upward movement in relative female earnings corresponds to the full implementation of equal pay in 1975.[8] As Table 5.9 indicates overall female earnings relative to male increased from 68.7 in 1974 to a peak of 77.1 in 1976. However, the peak in earnings by industry division varies between 1976 (other services), 1977 (energy; metal goods, engineering; other manufacturing; transport and communications; banking and finance), 1981 (agriculture; distribution, hotels), and 1982 (mineral extraction; construction). This suggests lagged effects of varying dimensions or the presence of influences other than that of equal pay. Even in 1982 there remain remarkable differences in female earnings relative to male among industry divisions with a range from 59.5 per cent in banking and finance to 95.4 per cent in agriculture. Similarly, in the case of SEGs, while the lower-skilled non-manual and non-manual female–male earnings ratios peak between 1976 and 1978, for managers and professional and technical workers across all divisions the ratio has declined from its peak attained in 1970 and for supervisors the peak was not reached until 1980. From 1978 and including the period from 1982 when our data set ceases women's earnings as a percentage of men's have been very stable overall at between 73 and 75 per cent. Convergence has therefore ceased.

Data on part-time earnings are available for men only on an industry division basis, but these seem to suggest that the improvement in female relative earnings has not been confined to full-time women.[9] Part-time female earnings as a proportion of male rose from 59.6 per cent in 1970 to 77.6 per cent in 1982, and in agriculture female part-time earnings exceeded those of male part-timers by 12.4 per cent. Female part-time earnings averaged 75 per cent of those of full-time women in 1982

Table 5.9. *Sex–earnings ratios by industry: full-time workers aged 21 and over whose pay was not affected by absence*

	(0) Agriculture	(1) Energy	(2) Mineral extraction	(3) Metal goods, engineering	(4) Other manufacturing	(5) Construction	(6) Distribution, hotels	(7) Transport and communication	(8) Banking and finance	(9) Other services	Total
1970	71.7	70.6	58.4	56.0	57.3	70.2	57.4	78.8	53.8	75.8	67.0
1971	74.0	67.7	57.9	55.9	55.9	66.9	56.2	74.8	50.4	68.2	64.4
1972	70.8	67.4	57.8	56.9	56.3	67.5	56.1	75.9	51.1	69.6	65.3
1973	77.1	68.6	58.9	58.4	58.7	64.9	59.2	77.9	55.6	72.2	67.6
1974	74.0	65.1	61.9	61.1	60.3	64.5	60.8	80.9	57.9	71.5	68.7
1975	79.9	67.0	64.4	66.2	64.3	67.4	63.4	82.5	60.1	76.7	73.8
1976	82.3	70.4	66.3	69.7	66.7	66.5	65.4	83.8	61.0	78.7	77.1
1977	92.9	74.4	67.6	70.6	68.4	69.4	66.4	85.4	61.4	78.4	77.0
1978	90.9	70.0	67.7	69.8	67.8	71.1	66.7	83.3	60.9	77.3	75.5
1979	93.9	70.2	66.7	68.5	66.0	71.1	65.6	82.3	58.8	76.8	74.4
1980	92.1	67.0	67.9	69.0	66.9	72.1	68.3	82.6	60.2	75.5	75.1
1981	99.4	71.0	67.7	68.6	66.1	73.0	68.6	83.2	59.6	77.5	76.7
1982	95.4	68.3	68.3	67.2	65.6	73.3	68.5	83.0	59.5	76.2	75.3

Note: The maximum ratio is in italics.

compared to 88 per cent in the case of part-time men relative to full-time men. This improvement in the relative position of part-time workers is surprising in the light of difficulties in obtaining a male comparator under the terms of the equal pay legislation and again suggests that other forces were at work.

The extract data files prepared for the analysis reported in Chapter 10 contain data for 1979 on average weekly pay by plant and company size, though on a slightly different basis from in our file since only juveniles under 18 years are excluded. As regards the former there is a clear positive relationship between pay and size of unit as one progresses from plant size 50–99 to 1,000+ with men earning 13.2 per cent more in the largest-sized establishment compared to the former and women 27.0 per cent more. As a consequence the sex differential narrows with female relative earnings increasing from 54.6 per cent to 61.2 per cent. However, women in the sample make up only 18.8 per cent of employees in the large plant size (compared to 35.4 per cent in the 50–99 category). An exception to the relationship between plant size and earnings is the fact that earnings for both men and women are relatively high in the very smallest plants (0–50)—with only men in plants of 500+ and only women in plants of 1,000+ earning more. Further, small plants are relatively female intensive with 51 per cent of employees in these being female. Turning to company size there is a very clear relationship between size and pay with the smallest units exhibiting lower earnings. Thus, for men those in the largest companies (5,000+) earn 16.9 per cent more than those in the smallest, while for women the gain to size is 26.7 per cent. Correspondingly the female–male earnings ratio rises from 60.0 to 64.9 per cent, though the ratio in the smallest companies is higher than in the medium-sized ones. In the case of company size female employment intensity is positively related to size being 36.7 per cent in the smallest companies and 53.2 per cent in the largest. These findings are confirmed when the analysis is conducted separately by SEG and industry division and suggest that differences in employment by size of unit are an important explanation of differences in earnings by sex. This is consistent with the job search of women, particularly married women, being constrained in a way in which it is not for men. This is made more explicit in Table 5.10 which suggests that 11.5 per cent of the difference in male and female pay is accounted for by a difference in employment distribution by plant size while the corresponding figure for company size is 10.8 per cent.

Another reason for differences in pay between the sexes is differences in age distribution. In both 1974, the first year in which earnings data by age became available, and 1982 the mean age for men was 41.4 and for women 39.2, so that on average women in employment are slightly younger than men. The age distributions of men and women were,

Table 5.10. *Pay inequality vs. segregation by plant and company size, 1979*

	W_1	W_2	W_3	W_4	$\dfrac{W_2-W_1}{W_3-W_1}$	$\dfrac{W_3-W_2}{W_3-W_1}$
Plant size						
Under 50 employees	1.73	2.31	2.36	2.38	92.4	7.6
50–99	1.37	1.93	2.07	2.13	79.3	20.7
100–199	1.42	1.92	2.08	2.15	75.5	24.5
200–499	1.47	1.95	2.13	2.20	72.4	27.6
500–999	1.56	2.06	2.23	2.30	73.7	26.3
1,000+	1.71	2.26	2.45	2.48	74.9	25.1
Overall	1.70	2.26	2.33	2.37	88.5	11.5
Company size						
Under 50 employees	1.47	2.04	2.05	2.06	97.0	3.0
50–99	1.47	2.03	2.12	2.15	86.8	13.2
100–499	1.50	2.04	2.20	2.27	76.1	23.9
500–999	1.56	2.13	2.30	2.36	76.7	23.3
1,000–4,999	1.64	2.20	2.38	2.45	75.7	24.3
5,000+	1.87	2.45	2.49	2.51	94.2	5.8
Overall	1.70	2.27	2.34	2.37	89.2	10.8

Note: This table is derived from a slightly different data base from the remaining tables in this chapter.

however, quite different, with 23 per cent of women being found in the age group 21–9 compared with just under 15 per cent of men in 1974. This difference was even more marked by 1982 with the corresponding figure being almost 28 per cent for women and 15 per cent for men. Further, average female hourly earnings are highest in the 25–9 age group in which relatively few women are found, while the proportion of women in the age group 40–9 in which male earnings are highest declined from 35.5 per cent in 1974 to 27.4 per cent in 1982. More precisely constructing age–earnings profiles for each individual age the age at which maximum earnings are obtained is, depending on the year, generally in the late twenties or early thirties for women, and the late thirties or early forties for men. The female–male earnings ratio declines with age reaching its lowest point in the 40–9 age group, thereafter recovering somewhat. In general, therefore, as Table 5.11 shows female employment is adversely distributed relative to men in relation to the age–earnings profile and this situation has, if anything, worsened since 1974. It is possible to carry out a redistribution exercise similar to that above and work out how much more women would earn if they had the same age distribution as men given their KOS occupational code. In 1974 differences in age distribution as opposed to differences in earnings given age accounted for 12.6 per cent of the difference in earnings and in 1982 the figure was 11.3 per cent. This is rather larger than the earlier finding of Chiplin and Sloane (1976) using published NES data for 1974. In order to test whether the effect of experience was independent of that of age the redistribution exercise was repeated for each experience level by age group. This confirmed that the two effects were largely independent as the combined effect of age and experience was virtually identical to the two effects added together but derived separately.

Experience is an important determinant of pay according to human capital theory. The 1975, 1976, and 1979 New Earnings Surveys include data on earnings by number of years with present employer, and though this does not provide us with a measure of experience in general it will cast some light on specific experience. The data for these three years are summarized in Table 5.12 and some clear trends can be observed. For both men and women there is a positive relationship between earnings and length of experience with current employer. Thus, for the whole sample in 1979 males with up to one year's experience earn £2.01 per hour, which rises to a peak of £3.24 for those with 36–40 years experience, while for women, those with up to one year's experience earn £1.61 and a maximum of £2.55 is reached for those with 36–40 years experience. The female–male earnings ratio declines gradually with experience, from 80.1 per cent for those with one year's experience to 72.4 per cent for those with 21 to 25 years experience, though it is not possible from the data available to determine how much this is influenced by breaks in service. Interestingly in 1975 and 1976 there appears to be no relationship between length of service and level of earnings for women for the first seven years' service, but in 1979 female earnings rise *ab initio*. More significantly the number of female employees falls much more rapidly with experience than is the case for men. Thus, 48.5 per cent of women in 1979 have 5 years or less service with their current firm, compared to 29.7 per cent of men, and only 5.2 per cent of women have more than 15 years service, compared with 19.8 per cent of men. Consequently, length of experience is an important determinant of relative female earnings in the sample as a whole. This is particularly true for non-manual workers for whom the relationship between length of service and level of earnings is particularly marked, but even for manual workers there is some relationship between these two variables. Intermediate non-manual women fare much better relative to men at each experience level than is the case for other SEGs, reflecting the importance of incremental scales for this group. Again conducting a redistribution exercise similar to that outlined above we can ask the question, how much of the earnings difference

Table 5.11. *Age, earnings, and employment*

Age	1974					1975					1976				
	Earnings[a]		Earnings ratio	Employment distribution		Earnings		Earnings ratio	Employment distribution		Earnings		Earnings ratio	Employment distribution	
	F.	M.		F.	M.	F.	M.		F.	M.	F.	M.		F.	M.
21–4	0.74	0.91	81.0	12.0	4.9	1.01	1.17	86.5	12.8	5.4	1.24	1.40	88.7	13.0	5.5
25–9	0.79	1.06	75.2	11.0	9.9	1.14	1.38	82.6	11.7	10.7	1.43	1.64	87.1	11.5	10.6
30–9	0.75	1.12	67.3	24.3	29.7	1.06	1.45	72.9	22.3	28.0	1.33	1.75	76.0	23.4	29.0
40–9	0.74	1.13	65.4	35.5	30.0	1.03	1.47	70.3	34.8	28.9	1.29	1.75	73.9	33.9	28.2
50–9	0.75	1.07	69.7	17.0	23.8	1.01	1.40	72.4	17.9	25.2	1.28	1.69	76.0	17.8	25.0
60–4	0.65	0.85	76.3	0.3	1.6	0.83	1.15	72.5	0.4	1.8	1.17	1.36	86.4	0.4	1.8
65–9	—	0.73	—	—	0.1	0.74	1.29	57.2	0.0	0.1	1.25	1.60	78.2	0.0	0.1
70+	—	—	—	—	—	—	—	—	—	—	—	0.59	—	—	0.0
All age groups	0.75	1.09	68.6	100.0	100.0	1.05	1.41	74.3	100.0	100.0	1.31	1.70	77.2	100.0	100.0

Table 5.11. (*cont.*)

Age	1977						1978						1979					
	Earnings		Earnings ratio	Employment distribution			Earnings		Earnings ratio	Employment distribution			Earnings		Earnings ratio	Employment distribution		
	F.	M.		F.	M.		F.	M.		F.	M.		F.	M.		F.	M.	
21–4	1.33	1.52	87.8	12.5	4.8		1.46	1.68	86.9	12.1	4.3		1.62	1.92	84.0	10.4	3.2	
25–9	1.52	1.77	85.9	12.8	11.9		1.66	1.98	83.7	14.1	12.2		1.87	2.23	83.7	13.4	10.2	
30–9	1.45	1.90	76.5	24.4	30.2		1.62	2.15	75.6	24.2	29.7		1.79	2.40	74.4	28.5	33.3	
40–9	1.41	1.90	74.2	30.9	26.3		1.57	2.16	72.7	29.8	27.6		1.76	2.44	72.1	30.0	31.2	
50–9	1.39	1.84	75.5	19.3	25.1		1.53	2.07	73.8	19.7	24.5		1.73	2.36	73.5	17.5	20.9	
60–4	1.17	1.52	77.3	0.2	1.6		1.28	1.72	74.2	0.2	1.6		1.77	1.99	89.0	0.1	1.1	
65–9	0.87	1.76	49.3	0.0	0.1		1.49	1.68	88.4	0.0	—		0.0	2.97	0.0	—	—	
70+	—	—	—	—	—		—	—	—	—	—		—	—	—	—	—	
All age groups	1.42	1.85	77.0	100.0	100.0		1.57	2.08	75.3	100.0	100.0		1.76	2.36	74.4	100.0	100.0	

Table 5.11. (*cont.*)

Age	1980					1981					1982				
	Earnings		Earnings ratio	Employment distribution		Earnings		Earnings ratio	Employment distribution		Earnings		Earnings ratio	Employment distribution	
	F.	M.		F.	M.	F.	M.		F.	M.	F.	M.		F.	M.
21–4	1.97	2.31	85.3	12.6	4.2	2.27	2.62	86.6	12.9	4.1	2.45	2.81	87.2	14.1	4.7
25–9	2.26	2.71	83.5	13.3	10.6	2.69	3.11	86.7	14.0	10.2	2.94	3.39	86.9	13.8	10.3
30–9	2.27	2.97	76.5	27.0	32.3	2.67	3.44	77.6	28.3	33.7	2.89	3.80	76.0	29.2	34.9
40–9	2.17	3.03	71.6	29.0	29.4	2.61	3.53	74.1	28.1	30.0	2.83	3.88	73.0	27.4	30.0
50–9	2.14	2.90	73.8	17.9	22.0	2.55	3.33	76.6	16.5	21.0	2.75	3.73	73.9	15.2	19.0
60–4	1.97	2.45	80.4	0.2	1.2	2.19	2.79	78.5	0.2	1.1	2.34	3.29	70.9	0.2	1.1
65–9	1.64	1.86	88.6	0.0	0.0	2.33	2.97	78.5	0.0	0.0	2.42	2.14	113.3	0.0	0.0
70+	—	—	—	—	—	—	—	—	—	—	—	—	—	—	—
All age groups	2.18	2.91	74.9	100.0	100.0	2.58	3.37	76.6	100.0	100.0	2.80	3.71	75.4	100.0	100.0

[a] Earnings are average hourly earnings net of overtime (£ per hour) for those who reported hours worked and the employment figures refer to these individuals.

Table 5.12. *Average hourly earnings, employment, and number of years employed in the same firm*

Years employed	1975							1976							1979						
	Female earnings	Male earnings	Earnings ratio	Female employment	Cumulative distribution of female employment	Male employment	Cumulative distribution of male employment	Female earnings	Male earnings	Earnings ratio	Female employment	Cumulative distribution of female employment	Male employment	Cumulative distribution of male employment	Female earnings	Male earnings	Earnings ratio	Female employment	Cumulative distribution of female employment	Male employment	Cumulative distribution of male employment
1	1.01	1.23	81.3	2,124	8.1	3,333	4.5	1.26	1.49	84.6	2,170	7.5	3,177	4.1	1.61	2.01	80.1	1,394	5.0	2,327	3.2
2	1.02	1.26	81.0	3,149	20.0	4,559	10.8	1.27	1.50	84.7	3,193	18.6	4,758	10.2	1.64	2.05	80.0	2,438	13.8	3,701	8.4
3	0.99	1.29	76.7	3,297	32.6	4,846	17.4	1.25	1.53	81.7	3,625	31.2	5,685	17.5	1.69	2.11	80.1	3,233	25.5	4,769	15.1
4	1.01	1.31	77.1	2,914	43.6	5,247	24.5	1.26	1.56	80.8	3,483	43.2	5,808	24.9	1.70	2.20	77.3	3,314	37.5	5,319	22.5
5	1.03	1.35	76.3	2,621	53.6	4,926	31.3	1.28	1.60	80.0	3,065	53.9	5,423	31.9	1.74	2.24	77.7	3,119	48.8	5,166	29.7
6	1.02	1.34	76.1	2,200	61.9	4,900	38.0	1.28	1.61	79.5	2,432	62.3	5,395	38.8	1.79	2.28	78.5	2,656	58.4	4,953	36.6
7	1.02	1.38	73.9	1,797	68.8	4,485	44.1	1.29	1.64	78.7	2,091	69.5	4,803	44.9	1.80	2.35	76.6	2,212	66.4	4,654	43.1
8	1.05	1.40	75.0	1,494	74.5	4,111	49.7	1.34	1.70	78.8	1,510	74.8	4,501	50.7	1.82	2.34	77.8	1,842	73.0	4,293	49.1
9	1.12	1.41	79.4	1,194	79.0	3,791	54.9	1.32	1.73	76.3	1,271	79.2	4,119	56.0	1.79	2.38	75.2	1,475	78.4	4,116	54.8
10	1.09	1.42	76.8	1,050	83.0	3,630	59.8	1.39	1.70	81.8	1,093	83.0	3,757	60.8	1.88	2.40	78.3	1,155	82.5	3,725	60.0
11–15	1.12	1.48	75.7	3,077	94.7	13,600	78.4	1.40	1.77	79.1	3,263	94.3	14,354	79.2	1.93	2.45	76.7	3,384	94.8	14,473	80.2
16–20	1.17	1.51	77.5	932	98.2	8,271	89.7	1.51	1.85	81.6	1,131	98.2	8,416	90.0	1.93	2.56	75.4	1,061	98.6	7,505	90.7
21–25	1.30	1.64	79.3	334	99.5	4,451	95.8	1.55	1.92	80.7	403	99.6	4,518	95.8	1.99	2.75	72.4	292	99.7	3,858	96.1
26–30	1.21	1.70	71.2	120	99.9	2,046	98.5	1.88	2.02	93.1	79	99.9	2,076	98.4	2.25	2.83	79.5	70	100.0	1,764	98.5
31–35	1.35	1.77	76.3	18	100.0	800	99.6	1.81	2.17	81.9	31	100.0	943	99.6	2.20	2.84	77.5	16	100.0	749	99.6
36–40	—	1.87	—	—	—	222	99.9	1.92	2.21	86.9	6	100.0	254	99.9	2.55	3.24	78.7	9	100.0	268	100.0
41–45	—	1.72	—	—	—	42	100.0	—	2.02	—	—	—	30	100.0	—	2.94	—	—	—	29	100.0
46–50	—	5.90	—	—	—	2	—	—	—	—	—	—	—	100.0	—	—	—	—	—	—	—
TOTAL				26,321		73,262					28,846		78,017					27,670		71,669	

between men and women is explained by the fact that women have fewer years of experience with their current employer? In 1975 the experience differential accounted for 5.9 per cent of the earnings difference, in 1976 5.2 per cent, and in 1979 6.2 per cent. Apart from breaks in length of service this takes no account of differential labour market experience other than with the current employer.

The make-up of pay on a weekly basis is summarized for 1974 and 1982 in Tables 5.13 and 5.14. Examining the industry division breakdown it is clear that overtime has the biggest impact on the sex differential. Removing the overtime effect increases relative female earnings by 10 per cent or more in seven industry divisions, being particularly significant in transport and communications and construction, but with its effect being relatively small in the service sector. The impact is much less in 1982, a year of recession, when the percentage effect is lower in every industry. This emphasizes the importance of correcting for overtime in time series analysis.

In general the exclusion of shift-work payments has a minor impact on the overall sex differential, being more important in mineral extraction, energy, metal goods and engineering, and in other manufacturing. The exclusion of incentive payments has variable effects according to division, having a major effect in raising female earnings in construction, but a negative effect in other manufacturing.

Table 5.14 performs the same exercise in relation to SEGs. There is a very strong inverse relationship between the effect of the exclusion of overtime on the sex differential and occupational level with a negligible effect for higher non-manual workers and a very marked effect for manual employees. The exclusion of shift-work has a modest effect on raising relative female earnings for skilled and semi-skilled manual workers and a very small impact for other groups. The exclusion of incentive payments raises female earnings substantially for intermediate non-manual and unskilled manual workers, but lowers it substantially for semi-skilled manuals, repeating the variable effect found in the analysis by industry division.

The 1973 and 1978 Surveys allow a detailed analysis to be made of the effect of collective bargaining arrangements on the male–female earnings differential. In both years the average earnings for men are highest for those with no collective agreement and lowest marginally for women who fall into this category. Women do appreciably better where they are subject to national agreements only, reflecting the fact that this is the predominant negotiating form in the public sector, where a substantial number of women and the highest female earnings are found. As a consequence women fare *relatively* worse if they are employed in areas where there are no collective agreements and better where national

Table 5.13. *Make-up of pay by industry, 1974 and 1982: weekly earnings of full-time employees whose pay was not affected by absence*

Industry	(1) Gross weekly earnings			(2) Earnings net of overtime				(3) Earnings net of overtime and shift-work premiums				(4) Earnings net of overtime, shift-work premiums and incentive payments			
	F.	M.	Ratio	F.	M.	Ratio	% inc. over (1)	F.	M.	Ratio	% inc. over (2)	F.	M.	Ratio	% inc. over (3)
1974															
0. Agriculture	20.69	39.40	52.5	19.79	33.51	59.1	12.6	19.79	33.47	59.1	0.0	18.31	29.67	61.7	4.4
1. Energy	29.57	50.44	58.6	28.99	45.46	63.8	10.9	28.97	44.05	65.7	3.0	28.40	41.61	68.3	4.0
2. Mineral extraction	25.60	48.18	53.1	25.15	42.60	59.1	11.3	25.02	40.67	41.5	4.1	23.47	36.29	64.7	5.2
3. Metal goods, engineering	25.92	47.98	54.0	25.25	42.50	59.4	10.0	25.12	41.39	60.7	2.2	23.05	37.32	61.8	1.8
4. Other manufacturing	24.35	46.79	52.0	23.75	41.22	57.6	10.8	23.60	40.17	58.8	2.1	20.06	36.53	54.9	-6.6
5. Construction	23.92	46.71	51.2	23.61	40.44	58.4	14.1	23.61	40.31	58.6	0.3	23.57	34.80	67.7	15.5
6. Distribution, hotels	21.85	40.68	53.7	21.44	37.80	56.7	5.6	21.41	37.59	56.9	0.4	20.99	34.91	60.1	5.6
7. Transport and communication	31.53	48.09	65.6	29.88	39.56	75.6	15.2	29.52	38.41	76.8	1.5	29.22	36.61	79.8	3.9
8. Banking and finance	29.80	54.51	54.7	29.35	52.86	55.5	1.5	29.21	52.76	55.4	-0.2	28.98	49.00	59.1	6.7
9. Other services	32.32	49.86	64.8	31.92	47.39	67.4	4.0	31.57	47.06	67.1	-0.4	31.41	46.20	68.0	1.3

1982															
0. Agriculture	84.25	107.63	78.3	78.60	95.10	82.6	5.5	78.54	94.99	82.7	0.1	77.44	92.67	83.6	1.1
1. Energy	117.06	182.08	64.3	115.52	165.29	69.9	8.7	115.28	160.83	71.7	2.6	112.70	145.06	77.7	8.4
2. Mineral extraction	96.69	157.66	61.3	95.04	144.58	65.7	7.2	94.45	138.11	68.4	4.1	90.68	125.96	72.0	5.3
3. Metal goods, engineering	92.78	151.17	61.4	90.11	138.12	65.2	6.2	89.59	134.96	66.4	1.8	85.20	127.07	67.0	0.9
4. Other manufacturing	88.06	150.50	58.5	85.79	136.73	62.7	7.2	84.94	132.65	64.0	2.1	78.85	125.12	63.0	-1.6
5. Construction	84.72	139.54	60.7	84.11	127.06	66.2	9.1	84.11	126.70	66.4	0.3	83.51	114.63	72.8	9.6
6. Distribution, hotels	80.03	129.44	61.8	78.83	122.65	64.3	4.0	78.55	121.65	64.6	0.5	76.84	114.65	67.0	3.7
7. Transport and communication	111.54	158.68	70.3	107.36	137.25	78.2	11.2	104.79	130.86	80.1	2.4	103.23	126.06	81.9	2.2
8. Banking and finance	109.72	191.01	57.4	107.80	186.05	57.9	0.9	107.65	185.24	58.1	0.3	105.23	177.56	59.3	2.1
9. Other services	118.58	161.55	70.3	112.32	153.80	73.0	3.8	109.79	151.84	72.3	1.0	109.21	148.69	73.5	1.7

Table 5.14. *Make-up of pay by socioeconomic group, 1974 and 1982: weekly earnings of full-time employees over 21 whose pay was not affected by absence*

SEG	(1) Gross weekly earnings			(2) Earnings net of overtime				(3) Earnings net of overtime and shift-work premiums				(4) Earnings net of overtime, shift-work premiums, and incentive payments			
	F.	M.	Ratio	F.	M.	Ratio	% inc. over (1)	F.	M.	Ratio	% inc. over (2)	F.	M.	Ratio	% inc. over (3)
1974															
Non-manual															
1. Managers	42.28	68.61	61.6	42.02	67.48	62.3	1.1	41.97	67.24	62.4	0.2	44.67	65.82	63.3	1.4
2. Prof. and tech. workers	42.17	62.14	67.9	41.85	60.93	68.7	1.2	41.74	60.74	68.7	0.0	41.47	59.98	69.1	0.6
3. Intermediate non-manual workers	36.64	48.60	75.4	36.39	47.17	77.1	2.3	36.09	46.92	76.9	−0.3	35.92	44.13	81.4	5.9
4. Junior non-manual workers	26.29	40.37	65.1	25.91	37.48	69.1	6.1	25.81	37.20	69.4	0.4	25.67	36.27	70.8	2.0
Manual															
5. Foremen and supervisors	26.95	50.38	53.5	25.68	43.16	59.5	11.2	25.37	42.38	59.9	0.7	24.86	40.15	61.9	3.3
6. Skilled manual	24.50	45.79	53.5	23.71	38.57	61.5	15.0	23.41	37.33	62.7	1.6	19.91	32.24	61.8	−1.4
7. Semi-skilled manual	24.08	44.11	58.6	23.18	34.21	67.8	15.7	22.93	32.86	69.8	2.9	18.75	28.95	64.8	−7.2
8. Unskilled manual	21.89	37.85	57.8	20.99	31.53	66.6	15.2	20.52	30.59	67.1	0.8	19.60	26.97	72.7	8.3

1982

Non-manual															
1. Managers	138.64	212.94	65.1	137.42	209.94	65.5	0.6	137.15	209.23	65.6	0.2	135.03	204.80	65.9	0.5
2. Prof. and tech. workers	149.76	203.21	73.7	147.31	198.21	74.3	0.8	146.32	197.26	74.2	-0.1	145.83	195.05	74.8	0.8
3. Intermediate non-manual workers	128.27	160.19	80.1	127.25	155.19	82.0	2.4	124.55	153.86	81.0	-1.2	123.67	147.90	83.6	3.2
4. Junior non-manual workers	92.53	133.01	69.6	91.21	124.19	73.4	5.5	90.55	122.13	74.1	1.0	89.49	119.07	75.2	1.5
Manual															
5. Foremen and supervisors	92.88	157.30	59.0	88.93	137.26	64.8	9.8	87.39	133.36	65.5	1.1	85.22	126.53	67.4	2.9
6. Skilled manual	83.95	140.08	59.9	81.06	121.89	66.5	11.0	79.35	117.72	67.4	1.4	73.65	106.12	69.4	3.0
7. Semi-skilled manual	81.81	124.23	65.9	79.01	107.73	73.3	11.2	77.11	102.32	75.4	2.9	69.40	93.22	74.4	-1.3
8. Unskilled manual	76.73	114.93	66.8	73.60	100.72	73.1	10.9	70.82	97.18	72.9	-0.3	67.95	86.33	78.7	8.0

collective agreements only prevail. Thus, in 1973 the ratio of female to male earnings was 54.5 per cent in the former, compared to 78.3 in the latter case, the corresponding figures in 1978 being 63.4 per cent and 84.3 per cent. Employment trends relative to collective bargaining arrangements appear to have been moving in favour of closing the earnings differential. Between 1973 and 1978 the ratio of females to males employed where there was no collective agreement fell from 44.4 per cent to 39.0 per cent and where there were company, district, or local agreements from 29.7 per cent to 28 per cent, and these are both areas where women fare relatively badly. In contrast, the ratio of female employment rose in the two areas where women fared relatively well; from 21.5 per cent to 26.9 per cent in the case of national plus supplementary agreements, and from 40.6 per cent to 46.1 per cent in the case of national-only agreements. It is germane that these two dates straddle the period when the substantial upward movement in female relative pay occurred. That the improvement is due to changed employment distribution of women relative to collective bargaining arrangements rather than to the activities of the collective bargainers themselves is confirmed by the fact that the relative improvement in the female differential was as substantial in the absence of collective bargaining as with it.

The disaggregated data in Table 5.15 suggest that these effects are far from uniform across SEGs and divisions. Thus, in the case of national plus supplementary agreements female managers and intermediate non-manual workers seem to have benefited the most with an earnings ratio 11.2 per cent and 10.8 per cent, respectively, higher in 1978 when covered by such agreements, using those SEG/Industry divisions where females are found. The ratio is 6.1 per cent less for professional workers so covered and manual women are little affected. As for divisions the earnings ratio was raised by this form of collective bargaining in 1978 by 15.7 per cent in other services and 11.7 per cent in energy but lowered by 2.8 per cent in transport and communications. In the case of national agreements only the earnings ratio of female managers is raised by 14.2 per cent and that of supervisors by 10.9 per cent, with little change occurring for the other SEGs, while in terms of divisions the ratio rises in all cases, but by as much as 10.8 per cent in the case of banking and finance. Where company/district agreements predominate the ratio is lower in six of the SEGs and by 9.9 per cent in the case of intermediate non-manuals, but it is increased by 12.7 per cent in the case of professional and technical workers. The ratio is 8–10 per cent lower in construction, transport and communications, and other services, but 29.2 per cent higher in banking and finance. Where there are no collective agreements intermediate non-manual women fare particularly badly, with an 18.1 per cent reduction in the ratio, but manual women show a slight gain. The

Table 5.15. Collective bargaining arrangements and relative hourly earnings (excluding overtime) by socio-economic group and division, 1973 and 1978

	National + supplementary agreements						National-only agreements						Company/district/local-only agreements						No collective agreement					
	1973			1978			1973			1978			1973			1978			1973			1978		
	F. (£)	M. (£)	Ratio (%)	F. (£)	M. (£)	Ratio (%)	F. (£)	M. (£)	Ratio (%)	F. (£)	M. (£)	Ratio (%)	F. (£)	M. (£)	Ratio (%)	F. (£)	M. (£)	Ratio (%)	F. (£)	M. (£)	Ratio (%)	F. (£)	M. (£)	Ratio (%)
SEG																								
1. Managers	0.9399	1.3446	69.9	2.2054	2.9299	75.3	1.0876	1.4644	74.3	2.3339	3.0186	77.3	0.8036	1.4600	55.0	1.9320	2.9370	65.8	0.8551	1.5874	53.9	1.9777	3.1558	62.7
2. Professional and technical workers	1.0386	1.3630	76.2	1.9979	2.9101	68.7	1.1176	1.4998	74.5	2.3059	3.1762	72.6	1.0240	1.3516	75.8	2.4063	2.9152	82.5	0.9113	1.4100	64.6	2.2260	2.9644	75.1
3. Intermediate non-manual	1.0187	1.1149	91.4	2.6133	2.6627	98.1	1.0584	1.2908	82.0	2.3678	2.6854	88.2	0.7107	0.8683	81.8	1.5290	1.9175	79.7	0.6914	1.0401	66.5	1.5764	2.1744	72.5
4. Junior non-manual	0.5943	0.8801	67.5	1.5136	1.8960	79.8	0.6171	0.8550	72.2	1.4678	1.8867	77.8	0.5961	0.8606	69.3	1.4204	1.8685	76.0	0.5761	0.8505	67.7	1.3699	1.7895	76.6
5. Foremen/supervisors	0.5508	0.9388	58.7	1.3890	2.0011	69.4	0.5701	0.8751	65.1	1.3653	1.7887	76.3	0.5736	0.9689	59.2	1.3793	2.1160	65.2	0.5386	0.9113	59.1	1.3071	1.9352	67.5
6. Skilled manual	0.5420	0.8729	62.1	1.3436	1.8429	72.9	0.5207	0.8462	61.5	1.2645	1.8306	69.1	0.5155	0.8478	60.8	1.2938	1.8318	70.6	0.4888	0.7803	62.6	1.1882	1.6790	70.8
7. Semi-skilled manual	0.5263	0.7981	65.9	1.3294	1.7267	77.0	0.5032	0.7122	70.7	1.2700	1.5735	80.7	0.4910	0.7792	63.0	1.2623	1.7366	72.2	0.4631	0.6645	69.7	1.1659	1.4848	78.5
8. Unskilled manual	0.4861	0.7078	68.7	1.2416	1.5428	80.5	0.4714	0.6763	69.7	1.2192	1.5023	81.2	0.4708	0.7246	65.0	1.2376	1.5922	77.7	0.4185	0.6186	67.7	1.1081	1.3572	81.6
All SEGs	0.5972	0.8877	67.3	1.6234	1.9641	82.7	0.7455	0.9516	78.3	1.7839	2.1164	84.3	0.5707	0.9271	61.6	1.4012	2.0129	69.6	0.5647	1.0353	54.5	1.3927	2.1952	63.4
Division																								
0. Agriculture. etc.	0.4097	0.5725	71.6	1.1417	1.2637	90.3	0.4120	0.5557	74.1	1.2587	1.3021	96.7	0.4333	0.4836	89.6	1.3912	0.9935	140.0	0.4352	0.5382	80.9	1.1708	1.2725	92.0
1. Energy. etc.	0.6666	0.9186	72.6	1.6427	2.1014	78.2	0.6757	0.9478	71.3	1.5996	2.1901	73.0	0.6069	1.0064	60.3	1.6212	2.2941	70.7	0.6419	1.2085	53.1	1.7191	3.0518	56.3
2. Mineral extraction. etc.	0.5438	0.8872	61.3	1.4038	1.9554	71.8	0.5336	0.8857	60.2	1.4155	2.0512	69.0	0.5593	0.9137	61.2	1.4390	2.1157	68.0	0.5925	1.1761	50.4	1.4675	2.4599	59.7
3. Metal goods. engineering. etc.	0.5559	0.8996	61.8	1.4269	1.9063	74.9	0.5453	0.8888	61.4	1.4107	1.9329	73.0	0.5623	1.0071	55.8	1.4443	2.1246	68.0	0.5599	1.1068	50.6	1.4311	2.2894	62.5
4. Other manufacturing	0.5322	0.8757	60.8	1.3306	1.8446	72.1	0.5203	0.8262	63.0	1.2621	1.7737	71.2	0.5469	0.8976	60.9	1.3456	1.9163	70.2	0.5412	1.0363	52.2	1.3369	2.1918	61.0
5. Construction	0.5721	0.8396	68.1	1.3928	1.8555	75.1	0.5523	0.8358	66.1	1.3108	1.7862	73.4	0.5630	0.9930	56.7	1.3658	2.1203	64.4	0.5679	1.0248	55.4	1.3253	2.0991	63.1
6. Distribution. hotels. etc.	0.4553	0.7280	62.5	1.1292	1.6190	69.7	0.4551	0.7354	61.9	1.1169	1.6415	68.0	0.4981	0.8066	61.8	1.1865	1.6988	69.8	0.4843	0.8647	56.0	1.2119	1.8910	64.1
7. Transport and communication	0.6311	0.8251	76.5	1.5176	1.8726	81.0	0.6790	0.8664	78.4	1.5875	1.8741	84.7	0.6337	0.8944	70.9	1.4306	1.8865	75.8	0.6555	0.9540	68.7	1.4669	2.0486	71.6
8. Banking and finance	0.6939	1.2210	56.8	1.7474	2.7813	62.8	0.6939	1.1360	61.1	1.6255	2.4090	67.5	0.7205	0.9454	76.2	1.6224	2.0607	78.7	0.6975	1.2655	55.1	1.6061	2.7328	58.8
9. Other services	0.7609	0.9502	80.1	2.0513	2.2958	89.4	0.8472	1.1482	73.8	1.9610	2.5153	78.0	0.6181	0.9615	64.3	1.5546	2.1874	71.1	0.5789	0.9872	58.6	1.4885	2.2572	65.9
All industries	0.5972	0.8877	67.3	1.6234	1.9641	82.7	0.7455	0.9516	78.3	1.7839	2.1164	84.3	0.5707	0.9271	61.6	1.4012	2.0129	69.6	0.5647	1.0353	54.5	1.3927	2.1952	63.4

ratio declines substantially in several divisions, including a 19.6 per cent reduction in energy, but in agriculture the ratio is slightly higher. A redistribution exercise similar to that above reveals that, if females had the same collective bargaining arrangements proportionately as men, their earnings ratio would improve by less than one-fifth of a penny per hour in 1973 and decline by just over half a penny per hour in 1978. This emphasizes the point that it is the form of collective bargaining arrangement that appears crucial to women's position *relative to men* rather than collective bargaining *per se*.

In years other than the above data are only available on earnings by collective agreement coverage in general or Wage Council provision. Examining the data for 1982 it is confirmed that women as a whole benefit from the presence of a collective agreement, with an earnings ratio of 85.0 per cent compared to 75.3 per cent for the female sample as a whole. This improvement is obtained by all eight SEGs, apart from professional and technical workers, and in all industries other than agriculture. Earnings in the Wage Council sector are substantially lower than those prevailing elsewhere in the economy, but the figures for the ratio of female to male earnings suggest a slightly beneficial effect for women of Wage Council representation with an overall ratio of 76.2 per cent compared to 75.3 per cent for the whole sample in 1982. The gain is spread across all the SEGs other than professional/technical and intermediate non-manuals and across all relevant industries other than energy. A redistribution exercise suggests that if women were distributed in the same proportions as men with respect to overall collective agreement coverage the ratio of female to male earnings would decline by between 4.5 and 9.3 per cent, depending on whether cells containing males or those containing females are used as the basis for comparison, but if women were distributed proportionately to men with respect to Wage Council coverage, the earnings ratio would increase by between 7.2 and 5.2 per cent on the same basis as above. The former finding suggests that collective bargaining coverage has become more favourable to women since 1978.

Therefore collective bargaining as a whole appears to assist in closing the male–female earnings gap, but the level of collective bargaining is also an important factor in this respect, with national bargaining but not local bargaining serving to raise relative female earnings.

5.4. The Decomposition of the Proportional Change in the Relative Wage (1970–1982)

Using published NES data Zabalza and Tzannatos[10] (ZT) concluded that for the period 1970–80 compositional effects (i.e. the redistribution of women towards high-paying industries or occupations) or an overall improvement in the position of those sectors where women were well represented were not important, but rather there had been a genuine improvement of wages within industries or occupations. However, they were forced to use a restricted sample in order to avoid empty cells at the initial and final years of comparison as the published data exclude sample sizes of less than 100 employees and average wages where the standard error of estimate is greater than 2 per cent of the average. Further, the occupational analysis is restricted to the period 1973–80 because of the change in the KOS classification in 1973. The NES data tapes enable us to obtain a much more complete picture of these elements of change, and the SEG mappings are consistent across 1973.

Following ZT we may express overall female relative pay (r) as

$$r = \sum_{i=1}^{n} f_{it} r_{it} s_{it} \tag{5.1}$$

where f_{it} = female employment in sector i at time t as a proportion of overall female employment at time t.

r_{it} = female earnings in sector i at time t as a proportion of male earnings in sector i at time t.

s_{it} = male earnings in sector i at time t as a proportion of overall male earnings at time t.

We are primarily interested in changes in the overall differential over time in each of these three components, which we may indicate by a dot over the corresponding variable. Hence, we obtain

$$r = \sum_{i=1}^{n} k_i \dot{f}_i + \sum_{i=1}^{n} k_i \dot{r}_i + \sum_{i=1}^{n} k_i \dot{s}_i + \text{remainder}$$

where
$$k = \frac{f_i r_i s_i}{r} \tag{5.2}$$

More specifically in our case since we consider the period 1970–82 we have

$$k = \frac{f_{i1970} r_{i1970} s_{i1970}}{r_{1970}}$$

The overall effect can, therefore, be decomposed into a structure effect, which measures the extent to which relative pay has increased holding constant relative wages within sectors and the relative position of sectors within the earnings league table, a differential effect, which measures the extent to which female relative wages have increased within sectors, holding constant other factors, and a sector ranking effect, which measures how much relative wages have changed as a consequence of changes in the relative position of sectors in the earnings league table. That is

$$\text{the structure effect} = \sum_{i=1}^{n} \frac{(f_{i1982} - f_{i1970})}{f_{i1970}} \cdot 100k_i$$

$$\text{the differential effect} = \sum_{i=1}^{n} \frac{(r_{i1982} - r_{i1970})}{r_{i1970}} \cdot 100k_i$$

$$\text{the sector ranking effect} = \sum_{i=1}^{n} \frac{(s_{i1982} - s_{i1970})}{s_{i1970}} \cdot 100k_i$$

$$\text{and the overall change in relative wages (1970–1982)} = \frac{r_{1982} - r_{1970}}{r_{1970}} \cdot 100$$

In Table 5.16 this exercise is conducted for the entire sample divided into ten industrial divisions. It can be seen that the overall change in relative wages (r) over the period 1970–82 was 12.5 per cent and the pure differential effect was 10.0 per cent. While the division ranking effect depressed relative female earnings by some 1.2 per cent, this was outweighed by a positive structure effect of 4.8 per cent. This suggests a much more important role for changes in the distribution of women towards higher-paying industries than was indicated in the ZT study of 8 industries over the period 1970–80. They found an overall increase of 11.9 per cent, of which the differential effect was 13.3 per cent, the industry ranking effect −2.2 per cent, and the structure effect 1.7 per cent.

Occupational structure can be examined for the whole period 1970–82, using the SEG breakdown. In this case (Table 5.17) the growth change divides into a differential effect of 11.6 per cent, an SEG ranking effect of −0.9, and a structure effect of 6.2. Thus there has been a substantial improvement in the female occupational distribution broken down according to levels of pay. This compares with an overall r of 15.3 in the ZT study of 8 selected occupations over the shorter period 1973–80 with a differential effect in this case of 14.6 per cent, an occupation ranking effect of −0.2 per cent, and a structure effect of 1.3 per cent.

We can go a stage further than ZT in breaking down these effects separately for each industrial sector and SEG group (or 80 cells). For reasons of space the detailed results are not presented here, but the differential effect at this level of disaggregation is 10.5 per cent, the division SEG ranking effect −2.3 per cent, and the structure effect 10.0 per cent. These figures imply that the remainder (or combined effects) are substantial, and therefore we should treat these figures with a degree of caution. None the less, our results suggest a much more substantial role for the structure effect in raising female relative pay than suggested by ZT's earlier analysis, and this implies that their regression model designed to isolate the effect of the equal pay legislation may have

Table 5.16. *Industrial decomposition of relative wages (hourly excluding overtime), 1970–1982*

Division	Female employment 1970	Female employment 1982	f_{i70}	f_{i82}	$k_i\dot{f}_i$	Female earnings 1970	Male earnings 1970	Female earnings 1982	Male earnings 1982	r_{i70}	r_{i82}	$k_i\dot{r}_i$	s_{i70}	s_{i82}	$k_i\dot{s}_i$	k_i
0. Agriculture	130.0	69.0	0.00	0.00	-0.151	0.298	0.416	2.144	2.247	0.718	0.954	0.095	0.613	0.605	-0.004	0.003
1. Energy	446.0	507.0	0.02	0.02	0.028	0.471	0.668	3.120	4.323	0.705	0.722	0.036	0.985	1.164	0.285	0.016
2. Minerals	1,188.0	972.0	0.04	0.03	-0.963	0.408	0.698	2.533	3.709	0.584	0.683	0.612	1.030	0.999	-0.107	0.036
3. Metals and engineering	3,819.0	2,854.0	0.13	0.09	-3.675	0.391	0.698	2.380	3.544	0.560	0.671	2.212	1.030	0.955	-0.810	0.111
4. Other manufacturing	4,972.0	3,752.0	0.17	0.11	-4.416	0.368	0.643	2.285	3.481	0.573	0.656	1.981	0.948	0.938	-0.142	0.136
5. Construction	261.0	313.0	0.01	0.01	0.058	0.409	0.583	2.344	3.198	0.702	0.733	0.035	0.859	0.861	0.002	0.008
6. Distribution	4,529.0	4,553.0	0.15	0.14	-1.110	0.330	0.575	2.098	3.063	0.574	0.685	2.154	0.847	0.825	-0.293	0.111
7. Transport	1,281.0	1,462.0	0.04	0.04	0.100	0.481	0.611	2.896	3.489	0.788	0.830	0.247	0.901	0.940	0.195	0.046
8. Banking	2,161.0	3,623.0	0.07	0.11	4.083	0.507	0.943	3.063	5.146	0.538	0.595	0.867	1.390	1.386	-0.024	0.081
9. Other services	10,822.0	14,967.0	0.37	0.45	10.808	0.564	0.769	3.188	4.183	0.733	0.762	1.808	1.134	1.127	-0.310	0.454
	29,609.0	33,072.0			4.761	0.454	0.678	2.798	3.713			10.048			-1.209	

Notes: Overall change in relative wage (1970–82) = 12.514.
Structure effect = 4.761.
Differential effect = 10.048.
Division ranking effect = -1.209.

Table 5.17. *Occupational decomposition of relative wages (hourly excluding overtime), 1970–1982*

SEG	Female employment 1970	Female employment 1982	f_{70}	f_{82}	$k_i\dot{f}_i$	Female earnings 1970	Male earnings 1970	Female earnings 1982	Male earnings 1982	r_{70}	r_{82}	$k_i\dot{r}_i$	s_{70}	s_{82}	$k_i\dot{s}_i$	k_i
1. Managers	226.0	932.0	0.01	0.03	4.101	0.906	1.297	3.751	5.523	0.699	0.679	−0.042	1.913	1.487	−0.339	0.015
2. Professionals	614.0	2,071.0	0.02	0.06	7.960	0.863	1.076	4.086	5.380	0.802	0.760	−0.208	1.587	1.449	−0.342	0.039
3. Intermediate	8,481.0	7,577.0	0.29	0.23	−7.780	0.616	0.778	3.796	4.383	0.792	0.866	3.619	1.147	1.180	1.138	0.389
4. Junior	9,832.0	14,773.0	0.33	0.45	10.381	0.411	0.619	2.511	3.338	0.664	0.752	3.978	0.913	0.899	−0.452	0.301
5. Foremen	472.0	527.0	0.02	0.02	−0.001	0.429	0.707	2.360	3.475	0.607	0.679	0.179	1.043	0.936	−0.154	0.015
6. Skilled	1,983.0	1,130.0	0.07	0.03	−2.497	0.346	0.588	2.144	3.119	0.588	0.687	0.864	0.867	0.840	−0.160	0.051
7. Semi-skilled	3,555.0	3,659.0	0.12	0.11	−0.721	0.347	0.530	2.058	2.738	0.655	0.752	1.353	0.782	0.738	−0.521	0.092
8. Unskilled	4,446.0	2,403.0	0.15	0.07	−5.204	0.305	0.468	1.965	2.539	0.652	0.774	1.890	0.690	0.684	−0.090	0.101
	29,609.0	33,072.0			6.239	0.454	0.678	2.798	3.713			11.632			−0.920	

Notes: Overall change in relative wage (1970–82) = 12.514.
Structure effect = 6.239.
Differential effect = 11.632.
SEG ranking effect = −0.920.

seriously overestimated the extent to which relative female earnings were raised for this reason.

Finally following ZT we may also take into account the effect of changes in age distribution over the period in this case of 1974–82 using 8 age groups as in Table 5.18. Over this period the overall change in relative earnings was 9.6 per cent, the differential effect 11.0 per cent, the age group ranking effect −1.2 per cent and the age structure effect 0.2 per cent. This compares with corresponding figures of 10.8 per cent, 10.3 per cent, −0.1 per cent, and 0.6 per cent in the ZT analysis. Thus our figures suggest a rather more important adverse effect on female earnings from the changing relative pay in different age groups.

5.5. Conclusions

This disaggregated analysis has provided some useful insights into explanations for differences between the pay of men and women. In particular it seems that differences in pay within existing occupations are much more significant than differences in occupational distribution. Therefore, occupational segregation in so far as it is related to pay is vertical rather than horizontal in nature. That is, women earn less than men not so much because they enter occupations which are particularly low paid but because they fail to advance as fast as men within particular occupations. In addition the findings in relation to age, plant and company size, and the analysis of the data for 1975, 1976, and 1979 on number of years' experience with the firm suggest that at least a quarter of the earnings difference is explained by differences between the sexes in relation to these factors. Finally improvements in female relative pay appear to owe significantly more to structural effects than had previously been realized.

What of the four general themes addressed in this book? First, unemployment has increased substantially for both men and women over the period analysed, but while the absolute level of registered unemployment has been lower for women it has increased at a faster rate than that of men. Thus the level of seasonally adjusted unemployment rose from 3.4 per cent in April 1970 to 14.1 per cent in April 1982 for men and from 0.9 per cent to 7.1 per cent over the same period for women. Consequently the ratio of male to female unemployment fell from 3.8 in 1970 to 2.0 in 1982 or, put in a different way, the level of male unemployment was 4.1 times as high in 1982 as 1970, while female unemployment was 7.9 times as high. Such changes would be an expected consequence of a relative increase in the price of female labour resulting from equal pay and equal opportunities policies or from other causes referred to below. As shown

Table 5.18. *Age decomposition of relative wages (hourly excluding overtime), 1974–1982*

Division age group	Female employment 1974	Female employment 1982	f_{i74}	f_{i82}	$k_i f_i$	Female earnings 1974	Male earnings 1974	Female earnings 1982	Male earnings 1982	r_{i74}	r_{i82}	$k_i r_i$	s_{i74}	s_{i82}	$k_i s_i$	k_i
Below 25	3,539.0	4,486.0	0.12	0.14	1.401	0.735	0.907	2.452	2.812	0.810	0.872	0.902	0.832	0.757	−1.067	0.119
25–9	3,243.0	4,560.0	0.11	0.14	2.822	0.794	1.055	2.944	3.387	0.752	0.869	1.836	0.967	0.912	−0.672	0.118
30–9	7,050.0	9,696.0	0.24	0.29	5.169	0.754	1.120	2.887	3.797	0.673	0.760	3.137	1.026	1.023	−0.087	0.243
40–9	10,329.0	9,166.0	0.35	0.28	−7.618	0.742	1.134	2.833	3.879	0.654	0.730	4.093	1.040	1.045	0.175	0.350
50–9	4,911.0	5,101.0	0.17	0.15	−1.409	0.746	1.070	2.754	3.727	0.697	0.739	1.001	0.981	1.004	0.389	0.168
60–5	90.0	54.0	0.00	0.00	−0.126	0.650	0.852	2.336	3.295	0.763	0.709	−0.019	0.781	0.887	0.037	0.003
65–9	0.0	9.0	0.00	0.00	0.000	0.000	0.726	2.420	2.136	0.000	1.133	0.000	0.666	0.575	0.000	0.000
70+	0.0	0.0	0.00	0.00	0.000	0.000	0.000	0.000	0.000	0.000	0.000	0.000	0.000	0.000	0.000	0.000
	29,162.0	33,072.0			0.240	0.750	1.091	2.798	3.713			10.951			−1.224	

Notes: Overall change in relative wage (1974–82) = 9.581.
Age structure effect = 0.240.
Differential effect = 10.951.
Age group ranking effect = −1.224.

in Table 5.9, part of the increase in relative female earnings on the whole sample was concentrated into the period 1974 to 1976. Over this period, using quarterly figures of actual unemployment at March, male unemployment increased from 473,400 to 930,500 or by 96.6 per cent. Female unemployment, on the other hand, increased from 87,400 to 258,900 or by 296.2 per cent, and female unemployment continued to increase faster than male for the subsequent two years. This is consistent with a classical price effect. However, there are two caveats. First, we require a properly specified econometric model to test this adequately. Second, the registered unemployment figures do not accurately reflect relative unemployment rates by sex. Department of Employment estimates of unregistered unemployment for 1971, 1975, and 1977 suggest that male non-registration was in order of 80,000 at each date. Female non-registration, however, increased from 230,000 in 1971 to 320,000 in 1975 and 340,000 in 1977.[11] This would, therefore, tend to reinforce the above conclusion.

It is noticeable that the period of rapid upward adjustment of relative female earnings coincided with unprecedented price inflation. In 1975 the general index of retail prices rose by 24.2 per cent over the level of the previous year and the producer output price index by 23.0 per cent, while in the following year the price index for materials and fuels purchased by manufacturing industry rose by 24.6 per cent. It has been suggested that trade unions prefer flat-rate as opposed to percentage wage increases in periods of rapid inflation, which they are able to implement because skilled employees exhibit a form of money illusion during such periods.[12] This could have the effect of reducing the size of the male–female earnings differential as women tend on average to be less skilled and lower paid than men. In the context of equal pay, employers, too, may suffer from money illusion and be more prepared to grant sizeable increases to female employees as the cost of so doing may seem slight in relation to the rapid general upward movement of earnings and prices in such periods. Again, this hypothesis needs to be adequately tested in the context of a properly specified econometric model.

The question of structural change in the labour force has been more directly addressed in this chapter. There appear to have been substantial increases in relative female employment in SEGs 1, 2, and 3 (the higher non-manual occupations), while their proportion declined in SEG 4. As for non-manual workers there were increases in SEGs 5 and 7 and decreases in SEGs 6 and 8. Overall, then, the movement of females appears to have been favourable in terms of skill levels. There is a similar, though smaller, favourable effect with respect to industry distribution. Likewise, the shift in relative female employment appears to have been favourable in terms of collective bargaining arrangements relative to their impact on pay. Despite these changes, there is still a high degree of sex segregation by occupation, as revealed in the number of KOS occupations which are single sex and the overall number of occupations in which women are represented.

Finally, there is the issue of government policy in relation to pay, and in this context both equal pay and opportunities legislation and incomes policies are relevant. Using published NES data and applying a regression model ZT suggested that equal pay legislation had been responsible for a 19 per cent increase in the ratio of female to male earnings, compared to a very small (less than 2 per cent) effect attributed to flat-rate incomes policies. Our disaggregated analysis, using the unpublished data tapes, suggests that the above authors seriously underestimated the structural effects in the labour market referred to earlier. This, in turn, implies that the effect of equal pay on its own must have been substantially less and the effect of incomes policy or a more general narrowing of the skill differential substantially larger than they found.[13] That is not to say, however, that the impact of equal pay was not considerable.

Notes

1. I am grateful to Hector Williams whose computing skills made this analysis manageable and for the comments in particular of the editors and the Department of Employment.
2. The Equal Pay Act was phased in to ease the process of adjustment, so that full compliance was not required until the end of 1975. The Act established the right of women to equal treatment when they are employed on work of the same as or broadly similar nature to that of men, or where they are employed on work which has been rated as equivalent to that of men under a job evaluation scheme. The Act also required the removal of discrimination in collective agreements, Wage Council orders, and employers' pay structures.
3. See Chiplin and Sloane (1986).
4. The ratio of earnings in female-only occupations to those in mixed female occupations declines over the period. Thus the Equal Pay Act appears to have had little effect on female-only occupations, again consistent with other factors having an effect on male-only occupations.
5. For an earlier analysis adopting this procedure, but utilizing published NES data, see Chiplin and Sloane (1974 and 1976).
6. Ibid. The insensitivity of the results to the level of disaggregation is confirmed by the fact that the results for 1970, 1971, and 1972 when there were fewer (189) KOS occupations included in the NES are virtually identical to those for later years with a much greater number of KOS occupations listed.
7. As has been noted by Pike (1982), the above procedure is a rather crude one in so far as it does not adjust for the effect of redistribution of the labour force on relative wage rates. That is, it is a partial equilibrium rather than a general equilibrium approach which we have adopted. However, the procedure used is most favourable to providing a large occupational effect since it assumes that the entry of women into male occupations will have no downward impact on earnings. Her own analysis suggests that the predominance of the earnings adjustment over the occupational adjustment does not hold when her data are standardized (imperfectly) for differences in education and experience

within occupational groups, but that is essentially a separate question. We do not have any educational data but the effects of experience are considered below.

8. See for instance Zabalza and Tzannatos (1985*a* and 1985*b*).
9. The NES is particularly deficient in the coverage of male part-timers. In addition a change in the way in which the sample was selected in 1975 resulted in a large proportion of those earning below the National Insurance contribution level being excluded, most of which will be part-timers. Thus, these results must be treated with caution.
10. See Zabalza and Tzannatos (1985*b*).
11. See Department of Employment (1983*a*: 266–7). These figures conflict with earlier estimates of the Department of Employment used by Garside to suggest that the percentage of females registering rose substantially in 1975 and 1976. See Garside (1980: 92).
12. See for example Brown (1976 and 1979).
13. For a fuller discussion of this and related issues see Chiplin and Sloane (1986).

6

Public-Sector Pay

Mary B. Gregory

Public-sector pay came to the fore to an unprecedented extent in the 1970s as an issue in public policy and in economic analysis. Where over previous decades concern about levels of pay for public-sector workers had been intermittent and focused on particular groups, in the 1970s it became persistent and broadened to encompass the public sector as a whole. Does public-sector status, with the processes and pressures in pay determination which it involves, lead to levels of pay which diverge from private-sector outcomes? Is the public sector advantaged or disadvantaged in regard to pay, and if so, with what implications? These are the issues with which this chapter will be concerned. The focus will be the public sector as a whole, defined to cover central government, local government, and the public corporations. This is, of course, an analytical division, where in practice pay, in the public as in the private sector, is determined for a multiplicity of disparate groups. Although typically it is a settlement or dispute involving a specific group (coal-miners, civil servants, firemen, teachers, nurses) which draws attention to the wider issues, this chapter will concentrate on features of pay outcomes and the process of pay determination associated with public-sector status, rather than the pay history of an agglomerate of separate industrial and occupational groups.

6.1. The Public-Sector Pay Issue

The major contentions in the debate on the impact of public-sector status on pay determination can be grouped under four heads: the good employer obligation of government, the bargaining power of public-sector unions, the nature of public service employment, and the role of government in national economic management.

The good employer obligation. It is now virtually 100 years since the British government first formally accepted the obligation as employer to pay 'fair wages'. The early commitment given in the 'Fair Wages' Resolutions of 1891 and 1910 centred on manual workers, skilled and unskilled, for whom 'fair wages' could be defined in a relatively straightforward way as the 'rate for the job' set in the relevant collective agreement. This commitment has been periodically reaffirmed and extended, notably in the Acts establishing the major nationalized industries in the period 1945–51 which brought very large numbers of manual workers into the public sector. Although the commitment is a formal one, its implementation is largely indirect, through explicit or tacit acceptance in the process of collective bargaining in Whitley or National Joint Councils through which pay for most manual workers in the public sector is determined. For white-collar workers, lacking the trade and craft basis of job definition and the associated collective agreements, the parallel commitment came later and has always been much harder to define except in rather general terms. A major landmark was the Report of the Royal Commission on the Civil Service in 1955 (the Priestley Commission) which not only endorsed the concept of comparability, as it has come to be known, for civil service pay, but led to the establishment of the Pay Research Unit to provide information on outside pay levels as a standard input into pay determination for the civil service. Following the Priestley Report, the establishment of Standing Pay Review Bodies, successively for Top Salaries, Doctors and Dentists, and the Armed Forces, extended the sphere of formal use of comparability, while the shadowing of PRU processes and findings extended it informally, but pervasively, in pay determination for other non-manual groups within the public sector, notably local government and the NHS.

As a formal commitment of public policy, however, adherence to the principle of comparability has waxed and waned. In the latter half of the 1960s it was initially strongly rebuffed and then partially reinstated by the National Board for Prices and Incomes. It was overridden with the launching of each phase of incomes policy through the 1970s, but in due course re-established. The anomalies and relativities provisions of the Pay Board in 1973–4, for example, were introduced explicitly as a corrective to the impact of the previous years' policies on parts of the public sector. Then, as on other occasions, it was the basis of the recommendations of *ad hoc* committees of review for a number of areas of the public service, of which the Houghton Committee (Committee of Enquiry into the Pay of Non-university Teachers) in 1974 was one of the most prominent examples. After the operation of the PRU had been informally suspended under the Social Contract between 1975 and 1977, the formal implementation of comparability as the criterion for pay determination in the public sector reached its apex in 1978–81 in the work of the Clegg Commission, which had the establishment of bases for comparison as the keynote of its terms of reference as well as of its title (the Standing Commission on Pay Comparability). This however was followed by the sharpest repudiation, when, in 1981, following review by the Megaw Inquiry, not only was the principle rejected as the basis for pay determination but much of the machinery for its implementation, notably the Pay Research Unit, was swept away.[1]

An immediate justification for the principle of comparability can be given in terms of efficiency and equity. The efficiency case is straight-forward. By implementing the principle of like reward for like work, it shadows the equilibrium outcomes which the operation of market forces would generate, were it practicable for the appropriate market to exist. As often in matters of pay, however, the issue of fairness tends to attract greater attention and to arouse strong feelings. This was acknowledged by the Priestley Commission, which emphasized justice to the taxpayer as well as to the employee, in its extended endorsement of the principle of comparability:

First, it looks after the ordinary citizen's interest as a taxpayer. If the Government which represents him pays what other responsible employers pay for comparable work, the citizen cannot reasonably complain that he is being exploited ...

Fair comparison as the primary principle is ... fair to the individual civil servant ... [If] his remuneration and conditions of service taken together approximate to those prevailing in the outside world he cannot legitimately complain of injustice. (Priestley Commission 1955: paras. 97–101)

Almost two decades later similar sentiments were expressed by the Pay Board, again in the case of civil servants:

There are special considerations in view of the Government's dual involvement as employer and as author of the counter-inflation policy. It is important that not only should justice be done in their case but that the rest of the country see it as justice and not privileged treatment. They should not receive less than justice because they are government employees. (Pay Board 1973: para. 5)

The comparability approach is, however, criticized at two levels: that the ways in which it tends to be implemented introduce systematic biases into pay levels, and, more fundamentally, that the principle itself is undesirable. On the first point, in its most extensive implementation through the PRU for the civil service, the comparator groups used were drawn heavily from larger companies (originally *The Times* 500), when it is known that pay levels rise systematically with company size.[2] The public sector was therefore being matched to the pace-setters in the private sector rather than to the representative or average rate of pay. For manual workers, too, the principle could be seen to be operated opportunistically: 'The fact that public sector rates have followed both private sector earnings and rates, whichever was fastest, means that to some extent the public sector have had the best of both worlds' (Elliott 1977: 149). While comparisons should be based on the whole remunera-tion package, including not only indirect financial benefits such as holiday entitlement and pension benefits, but also job security and conditions of service, the practical implementation tends to concentrate heavily on levels of pay. By excluding the value of indexed pensions and job security this can be seen as implicitly to the advantage of the public sector.

These arguments for an upward bias in pay levels under comparability can be contested. Because of the time required for the collation of information and the implementation of awards, the operation of comparability under a system such as the PRU must imply that public-sector pay always lags behind the comparator groups; and the faster the growth of earnings in the comparator groups the greater the erosion. Moreover, the use of large companies to give the comparator groups is an appropriate procedure, as the civil service and other public-sector organizations must properly be regarded as large employers. While index-linked pensions are a valuable perk of public-sector employment, the company car and its favourable tax status gives many private-sector employees an offsetting advantage.[3]

The strongest objections to comparability as a principle came from the NBPI, who, in their thrust for productivity-linked pay, criticized it as a mechanism for spreading increases, regardless of the reasons for which the original increase was given. More recently, the report of the Megaw Inquiry (1982) criticized pay setting on the basis of comparability for concentrating on an external rather than an internal focus; it urged that, although comparability should retain a role in the determination of civil service pay, it should not be the dominant, or even a central, consideration; rather, there should be much greater emphasis on internal relativities, with the pay system used to encourage better management while also paying explicit regard to the government's budgetary position.

The bargaining power of public-sector unions. Many public services are both essential and non-storable, and any withdrawal of the service has a strong and immediate impact on welfare. Moreover, the fact of public provision implies that the commercial criterion of ability to pay applies at most in attenuated form. Both of these considerations potentially greatly enhance the bargaining power of public-sector employees. This argument has been extensively developed in the context of American city and local administrations, while in the UK the emphasis has tended to centre on the growth of union militancy in important areas of the public sector and the deteriorating climate of public-sector industrial relations in the 1970s.[4] Against this, however, inhibitions in the use of the strike weapon in essential services were already observable in the 1970s, while the 1980s have seen a tightening of the public purse-strings and a hardening of political stances against growing levels of public expenditure.

The nature of public service employment. Where the two previous arguments are in general directed towards implying an upward bias in public-sector pay, a more traditional view of the public sector is as low paying. Many areas of public service have a strong vocational element, and it is sometimes suggested that the public-sector employee is equalizing net advantages by accepting a lower level of pay against the greater job satisfaction which the service element implies, possibly reinforced by greater job security, a lower pressure of work, longer holidays, and favourable pension entitlements.

The government and national economic policy. An argument frequently advanced at the time was that the various incomes policies of the 1970s were differentially effective in holding down pay in the public sector. It was politically imperative for the government to be seen to make its policies of income restraint work among its own employees, particularly given the large numbers involved and the high visibility of public-sector settlements; moreover, the use of national pay scales and the importance of basic pay throughout the public sector provided favourable opportunities for monitoring. The private sector, on the other hand, had much greater scope for circumventing the provisions of pay policies through bonuses, job regrading, and productivity deals, genuine or otherwise. Indeed, in one or two variants pay policy was simply a policy of pay restraint for the public sector. Writing in 1975, for example, Winchester concluded:

experience over the last 15 years has proved conclusively that any policies to restrain wages can be applied more effectively in the public sector than elsewhere. Clearly if a government decides that wage restraint is desirable in the interest of national economic policy, it is not surprising that it should apply such restraint to the pay of its own direct or indirect employees. (Quoted in Dean 1981: 58)

Such a view did not, however, pass uncontested. An alternative claim, not infrequently heard, was that the public sector acted as the pace-setter in the wage inflation of the 1970s, public-sector settlements in the periods following the relaxation of incomes policy representing not a catching-up from the previously depressed pay levels, but a leap-frogging ahead made possible by a favourable political position.[5]

It is clear that the a priori argument can be carried back and forth under each of these four heads, and the issue must be largely an empirical one. Early studies of the relationship of public- to private-sector pay had to devote considerable effort to establishing data series for pay in the two sectors, and consequently the coverage tended to be limited and/or the level of aggregation high. None the less some patterns could be discerned, and evidence was progressively adduced to support some of the contentions above, at least in certain periods (Dean 1975, Fallick and Elliott 1981a, Kessler 1983). However, as further work has introduced greater disaggregation, the complexity of the picture has tended to increase (Trinder 1981, Dean 1981) and summary assertions about pay relativities and trends between the public and private sectors have become rarer. It is this complex and possibly shifting picture of the relative pay status of the public sector which we will use the extensive data from the NES to explore.

6.2. Employment in the Public Sector

Within the public sector three broad institutional groups will be distinguished:

1. *Central government*. Formally all bodies for whom a Minister is answerable to Parliament. In addition to central government departments these include the Regional and District Health Authorities of the NHS; various directly funded bodies, including the Research Councils and National Museums; and trading enterprises financed directly from central government, such as the Forestry Commission and, for the period being studied, the Royal Ordnance factories.

2. *Local government*. Local government authorities at all levels which have power to levy rates. Their constituent bodies include education authorities, police and fire services, and the bodies which carry out local authorities' trading activities, predominantly in housing and transport.

3. *Public corporations*. These are public trading bodies with a substantial degree of autonomy in the management of their activities and in finance, including powers to borrow. Over the period 1970–82 the major public corporations included the National Coal Board, British Steel Corporation, British Rail, electricity, gas, and water undertakings, British Road Services, London Transport, British Airways, British Airports Authority, the British Broadcasting Corporation, the Post Office and British Telecom, and ports and inland waterways.

By contrast with the years immediately following, the period 1970–82 was one in which the scope of the public sector remained largely unchanged. The only sizeable discontinuity caused by the transfer of ownership came with the nationalization of aerospace and shipbuilding in 1978, and the subsequent privatization of British Aerospace in 1981. Since these industries were already experiencing heavy public involvement before nationalization, they have been classified to the public sector throughout, so allowing us to deal with an essentially constant set of organizations and enterprises over the thirteen years. The definition of the public sector and further minor changes in status within it are discussed in Appendix 6.1.

The public sector was a major source of employment during the period, with between six and seven million employees (Table 6.1). At around 30 per cent of total employment, it provided more employment than the

Table 6.1. *Employment in the public and private sectors, 1970–1982*

	Numbers (000s)			Percentage of total employment			Growth rate (%)
	1970	1979	1982	1970	1979	1982	
Employees in employment	22,479	23,158	21,400	100.0	100.0	100.0	−0.08
Private sector	16,336	16,023	14,703	72.7	69.2	68.7	−0.54
Public sector	6,143	7,135	6,697	27.3	30.8	31.3	+1.03
Central government	1,559	2,073	2,076	6.9	8.9	9.7	+2.72
NHS	741	1,152	1,227	3.3	5.0	5.7	+4.39
Local government	2,559	2,997	2,865	11.4	12.9	13.4	+0.88
Education	1,241	1,539	1,434	5.5	6.6	6.7	+1.16
Public corporations	2,025	2,065	1,756	9.0	8.9	8.2	−0.35

Note: The figures present a 'head-count' of employees in civilian employment, with full-time and part-time employees combined. They follow the CSO definitions in representing employment in the public sector as at each date. The 1970 figures therefore exclude aerospace and shipbuilding, then in the private sector, but the 1979 figures, after nationalization, include both. In 1982 British Shipbuilders remained in the public sector but aerospace had been returned to the private sector.

Source: CSO, *Economic Trends Annual Supplement* (1986), 201.

whole of manufacturing industry. Of the three institutional groups, local government was substantially the largest employer, with central government and the public corporations very roughly equal in size, each with around two-thirds of the number of employees of local government. Over half of the employees of central government worked in the NHS, with the civil service as the other major group. In local government likewise a single function, education, accounted for over half of total employment. For much of the period the public sector's rising level of employment contrasted sharply with the general trend towards declining employee numbers. Over a period which saw the total number of employees in employment fall by over one million, employment in the public sector increased by more than half a million while private-sector employment fell by 1.6 million. Public sector employment increased at a trend rate of 1 per cent per year, rising steadily through the 1970s to a peak of 7.1 million in 1979, before falling back. In the private sector, on the other hand, employment declined at a trend rate of 0.5 per cent per annum over the 13 years, and even at its cyclical peaks in 1973–4 and 1979 never regained its levels of 1970. Even when employment in the public sector began to decline between 1980 and 1982, it fell less steeply than in the private sector, with the result that the public-sector share in total employment reached its highest level in 1981–2. This record of employment growth was not, however, uniform across the public sector. The expansion was most marked in central government, notably the NHS, although local government also showed significant growth; the public corporations as a group, on the other hand, more closely matched the private-sector pattern of declining employment. This division within the public sector, with central and local government showing generally similar patterns while the public corporations are much more closely matched to the private sector, is one which recurs throughout this study.

To obtain further insight into the structure of employment in the public sector we must use the NES sample, which comprises around 125,000 adults in full-time employment for each year of the period. The Survey itself does not record directly whether an individual or establishment is in the public or the private sector; the allocation is made by applying a set of comprehensive and detailed criteria, as described in Appendix 6.1.

The overall structure of employment is shown in Table 6.2. Both public and private sectors show the familiar pattern of an increasing role for white-collar occupations and a rising proportion of women in the workforce. In the public sector, however, this pattern is much more pronounced and of longer standing; in 1970 the proportions of non-manual and of female employees in the public sector were already at or above the levels reached by the private sector in 1982. Moreover, the trend towards white-collar jobs and jobs for women developed more strongly in the public sector, such that by 1982 the differences in employment structure were even more marked than in 1970. Again, however, the public sector did not perform as a single entity, the features just cited essentially characterizing central and local government only, while in the public corporations the proportions of white-collar workers and women were not only substantially lower than in central and local government, but lower even than in the private sector.

This pattern of relative similarity between central and local government on the one side, and the public corporations with the private sector on the other, is largely repeated at the level of the socio-economic group. Table 6.3 shows the structure of employment for 1979, and other years are broadly similar. For men, the preponderance of white-collar employment in central and local government applies at each level except managerial. This reflects the role of the traditional public-sector professions and the support staff which they require: education, medicine, public administration, the police, fire, and prison services. Conversely, the skilled and semi-skilled manual workers who constitute much the largest groups in the public corporations and the private sector appear in only relatively small numbers in central and local government. Among women rather similar patterns apply, but in more concentrated form. In central and

Table 6.2. *The structure of employment in the public and private sectors (%)*

	1970		1979		1982		1970		1979		1982	
	Non-manual	Manual	Non-manual	Manual	Non-manual	Manual	Male	Female	Male	Female	Male	Female
Private sector	41	59	45	55	50	50	74	26	73	27	72	28
Public sector	50	50	60	40	63	37	69	31	65	35	64	36
Central government	69	31	76	24	78	22	49	51	44	56	43	57
Local government	63	37	72	28	73	27	65	35	60	40	61	39
Public corporations	21	79	36	64	38	62	91	9	87	13	86	14

Source: New Earnings Survey, 1970, 1979, and 1982.

Table 6.3. *Public- and private-sector employment by socio-economic group, 1979 (%)*

SEG	Males				Females			
	Central government	Local government	Public corporations	Private sector	Central government	Local government	Public corporations	Private sector
Non-manual	63.0	66.1	29.0	38.1	85.6	81.0	81.6	65.8
Manual	37.1	33.9	71.0	61.9	14.3	19.0	18.4	34.2
1. Managers	7.3	5.4	5.3	12.0	1.2	1.3	0.7	3.3
2. Professionals	20.8	19.7	8.0	8.3	3.1	12.7	2.4	2.4
3. Intermediate	17.9	26.3	7.1	9.1	39.7	43.5	6.6	7.1
4. Junior	17.0	14.7	8.6	8.7	41.7	23.4	72.0	52.9
5. Foremen	3.2	2.6	5.5	6.0	0.9	2.1	0.2	2.0
6. Skilled manual	13.5	10.1	39.0	30.8	1.0	3.7	2.8	6.1
7. Semi-skilled manual	12.6	8.2	19.1	17.4	5.2	3.4	8.7	19.0
8. Unskilled manual	7.7	13.0	7.4	7.8	7.2	9.9	6.8	7.2

Source: New Earnings Survey, 1979.

local government the intermediate non-manual group, which contains teachers, nurses, and various para-medical occupations, is particularly prominent. The socio-economic level of women employed in the public sector is thus on average higher than in the public corporations and, to a lesser extent, the private sector, where the 'crowding' of women at the junior level is conspicuous.[6] The only significant source of manual employment for women is in semi-skilled occupations in the private sector.

Thus while there are apparently important differences in both employment structure and employment trends between the public and private sectors over this period, the divergent patterns within the public sector, where the public corporations stand apart from central and local government, must be kept in view, along with the relative similarity between the public corporations and the private sector.

6.3. Relative Pay in the Public Sector before 1970

When public-sector pay came to the fore as an issue in public policy in the mid-1970s the first task confronting economists seeking to make a contribution to the debate was to establish, as best they could, the outline facts of the historical record, given that none of the official sources of data on earnings allowed the direct identification of public-sector employees and their pay levels. The pioneering work came from the National Institute of Economic and Social Research, notably the influential study by Dean (1975), subsequently extended in Dean (1981) and Trinder (1981). Dean's first study researched the period 1951–75, extended subsequently to the end of the 1970s; but since we can have a better perspective on the 1970s given the longer time period and our much more extensive data set, we will confine our description of Dean's findings to the period of the 1950s and 1960s. His main source of data for these years was the Department of Employment's April and October enquiries, confining him to male manual workers.[7] Dean's analysis showed that over the 1950s and 1960s average earnings for male manual workers in the public sector moved very closely in line with those for the private sector, as measured by the relatively stringent test of annual percentage rates of change. As he notes, this was in spite of the compositional changes in each workforce which might have been expected to change the ratio over such an extended period of time. Since the data were on a six-monthly basis he was also able to examine the timing of cyclical fluctuations in the two sectors, but found the differences to be slight. The cyclical pattern of earnings growth in the two sectors did, however, differ somewhat, with public-sector earnings generally increasing rather faster than private-sector earnings during a cyclical downswing and the private sector gaining in relative terms in the upswing. Dean interpreted this result as consistent with the lesser exposure of pay-setting in the public sector to market pressures. He also concluded that incomes policy did not appear to have affected relative earnings in any systematic way.

The principal conclusion which Dean emphasized on the relationship between public- and private-sector pay for male manual workers over the 1950s and 1960s was its stability:

In the 1950s, average earnings in nominal terms grew by about 80 per cent in each sector, the relative pay ratio changed on average by only 1.1 points each year (relative to the 1970 index level of 100) and the maximum spread of the ratio was only 4.2 points. In the 1960s . . . average earnings in each sector grew by about 70 per cent, over 10 per cent *less* than in the 1950s, whilst the pay ratio changed by an average of 1.2 points with a maximum spread of only three points . . . these two decades therefore seem to be an era of great stability in relative pay. (Dean 1981: 50).

6.4. Public-Sector Pay Relativities 1970–1982

By contrast with the paucity of data for the 1950s and 1960s, for the period since its introduction in 1970 the NES provides almost an embarrassment of riches, the available data giving not only a direct measure but a choice of measures of pay. The analysis here will be based primarily on total earnings per week. For most employees this is probably the measure of pay which is their primary focus of interest. It is also the measure of earnings reported in the key question in the NES Survey questionnaire (question 6 in 1982) with the various other measures, such as hourly earnings and basic pay, derived from it. By using total weekly earnings we side-step any grey areas in the definition of the various pay supplements which are deducted to give basic pay.[8] While hourly earnings are often used in the analysis of pay to standardize for differing lengths of the working week, this figure is available only for those employees for whom hours of work are recorded. In 1982 13 per cent of non-manual males and 8 per cent of non-manual women were reported as in full-time employment but without specified normal hours of work. Since white-collar employees predominate in central and local government it is important to retain comprehensive coverage of these categories in both the public and private sectors.

The charts in Fig. 6.1 show the level and trend in the public-sector pay relativity, in terms of total weekly earnings, for men and women separately, for the eight socio-economic groups used in this study and the three divisions of the public sector. The actual level of average earnings in each public-sector group is shown relative to its private-sector counterpart

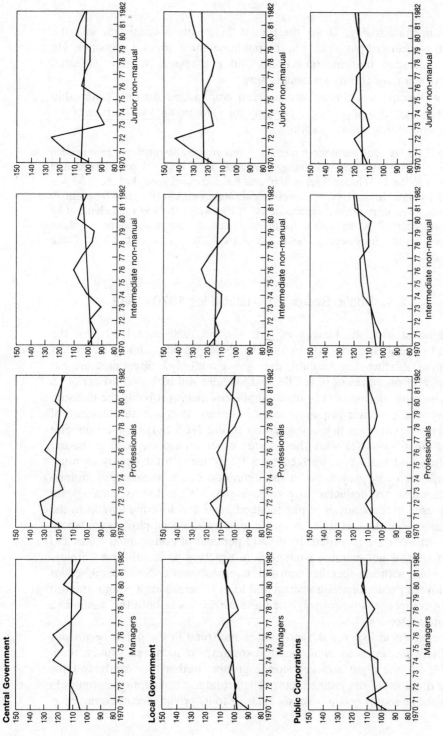

Fig. 6.1. Public–private sector pay relativities, 1970–1982
(*a*) Males: non-manual socio-economic groups

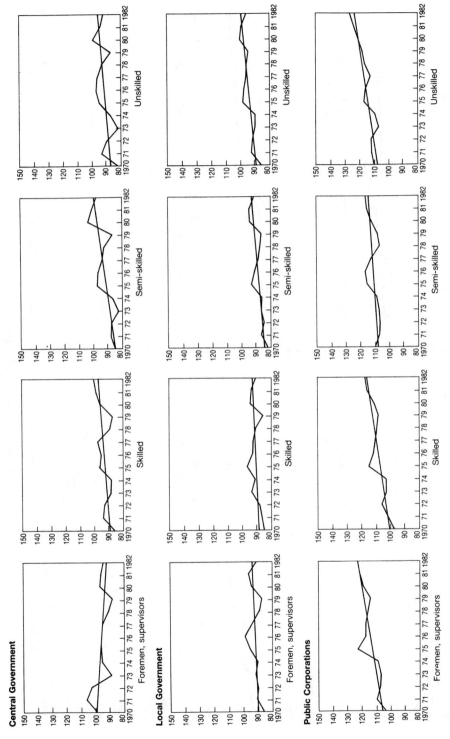

(b) Males: manual socio-economic groups

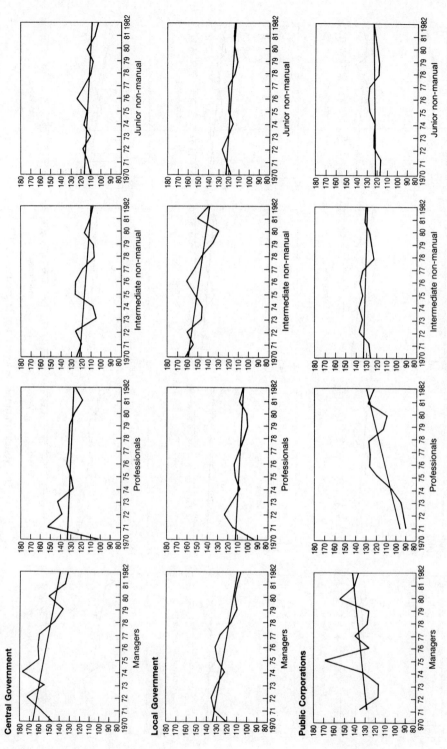

(c) Females: non-manual socio-economic groups

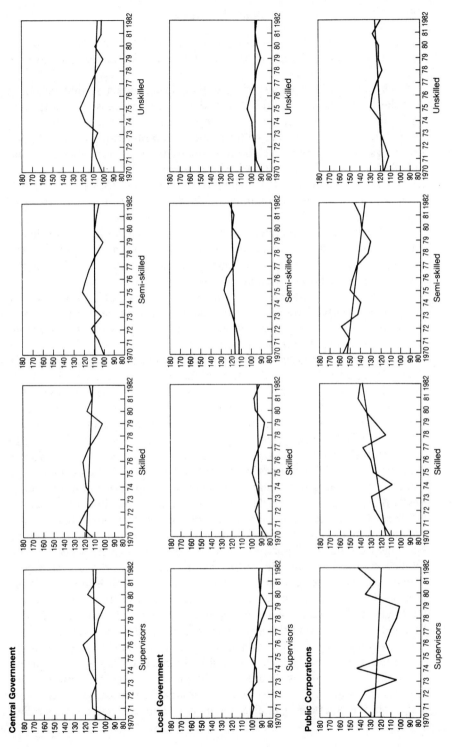

(*d*) Females: manual socio-economic groups

in each year, with private-sector pay taken as 100. The fitted trend line shows the average change in the relative pay level across the thirteen years.

Before the position of specific groups is discussed, it should be noted that the relativities indicated between the two sectors must be interpreted with care. Our perspective is designed to be a broad one, encompassing the public sector as a whole, with the socio-economic categories providing groupings of occupations which are comparable in respect of educational and skill levels and social status. The relativities in the average earnings of the broad socio-economic categories do not constitute like-for-like comparisons between groups matched in all respects except for the employer being a public- rather than a private-sector body. Such like-for-like comparisons are not possible; not only is the public sector the exclusive employer of doctors and nurses, police, fire, and prison officers, tax inspectors, train drivers, and coal-miners, but even where job titles in the two sectors seem closely comparable, as for executives, lawyers, and even secretaries, the content and conditions of the job may differ. Moreover, it is perfectly possible, where a like-for-like comparison can be made, for a pay relativity for specific occupation to be in the opposite direction from that for the relevant socio-economic group.

The evidence on actual levels of relative pay overall in the public sector does not support the claim that the public sector is systematically advantaged in terms of pay, nor that it is systematically disadvantaged; the picture is not a uniform one. Among white-collar groups, both men and women, pay levels in the public sector emerge as virtually universally higher than for the corresponding private-sector groups, by margins ranging from negligible to over 20 per cent for men, and from 8 to over 50 per cent for women. This applies in the public corporations as strongly as in central and local government. For manual occupations, on the other hand, the picture is a very different, and varied, one. For male manual workers at each occupational level in central and local government, and for most female manual workers employed in local government, average earnings were up to 10 per cent below those in the private sector. In the public corporations, on the other hand, earnings for both men and women can again be seen to have been regularly and substantially higher than in the private sector, a position which was also true, although less strikingly so, for manual women employed by central government. It may be noted in passing that the pay advantage or disadvantage for the public sector was not, in general, a simple offset for differences in hours of work which the use of hourly earnings would eliminate. It thus appears, prima facie, that, over quite wide areas of the public sector, including the full spectrum of white-collar jobs and the nationalized industries, pay levels were, on the average, significantly higher than for the corresponding private-sector groups. In other areas, however, the reverse was true, with male manual workers in central and local government and some groups of female manuals having lower levels of average earnings.

Arguably, however, the disputes about public-sector pay through the 1970s were essentially about the perceived erosion or enhancement of relative pay, making the trend of the changes in the relativities over the period the central issue. Moreover, assessment of the trends in the pay relativities over the thirteen years is less affected by influences precluding like-for-like comparisons. For broad socio-economic groups the occupational, age, and regional composition and job characteristics change only slowly. Similarly, thirteen years is, on a trend basis, a sufficiently long period for temporary disequilibria not to be dominant, and for pay levels which are persistently inappropriate to find expression in difficulties of recruitment or retention of employees. Except in areas where chronic difficulties of this sort are established, it can be inferred that pay levels were, on the average, not too inappropriate relative to market conditions, and that the relativities observed were at least broadly acceptable in terms of perceived justness. Given the different rates of employment growth or contraction and other ongoing changes, the presupposition is therefore that trends in pay relativities for the various groups should be relatively modest, but that a zero trend is by no means a necessary index of equal outcomes for the public sector.

The picture on trends, illustrated in the charts and given numerically in Table 6.4, is again a diverse one, with public-sector groups both gaining and losing relative to their private-sector counterparts. Overall, the incidence of gainers and losers is roughly equal. The non-manual groups in central and local government, whose advantage in terms of pay levels was noted above, tended to have this eroded over the period; among men the erosion was slight, except in the professional and technical groups, where it was 7 and 10 per cent respectively in total over the thirteen years. Among women in central and local government the position was more striking, each non-manual group without exception losing relative to its private-sector counterpart. In part, this particular experience can be attributed to the introduction of equal pay, a measure which, in terms of ending differential rates of pay for individual jobs, mainly affected the private sector, as equal pay had already been widely established in the public sector. However, the loss of ground was particularly pronounced among women managers (a small group) and the intermediate non-manual groups in which nurses (in central government) and school teachers (in local government) are much more strongly represented among women than in the corresponding male group. Among manual groups, on the other hand, the reverse pattern emerges, with manual men throughout central and local government tending to improve their relative

Table 6.4. *Levels and trends in pay relativities (%)*

SEG	Average weekly earnings			Trend in earnings		
	Central government	Local government	Public corporations	Central government	Local government	Public corporations
Males						
1. Managers	112	103	108	−0.2	+0.7	+0.9
2. Professionals	122	106	108	−0.7	−0.9	+0.4
3. Intermediate	100	114	111	+0.5	−0.2	+1.2
4. Junior non-manual	103	123	116	−0.2	+0.2	+0.3
5. Foremen	96	92	114	−0.6	+0.4	+1.4
6. Skilled manual	93	91	108	+0.7	+0.4	+1.2
7. Semi-skilled	93	89	112	+1.2	+0.7	+0.5
8. Unskilled manual	91	95	115	+0.7	+0.8	+1.2
Females						
1. Managers	153	122	136	−2.2	−2.0	+1.3
2. Professionals	130	108	113	−0.5	−0.6	+3.0
3. Intermediate	116	149	131	−1.0	−1.8	−0.3
4. Junior non-manual	113	118	123	−0.7	−0.8	+0.1
5. Supervisors	110	96	123	+0.3	−1.0	−0.6
6. Skilled manual	116	94	127	−0.6	+0.2	+1.9
7. Semi-skilled	109	118	145	0.0	+0.2	−1.5
8. Unskilled manual	109	97	121	−0.5	0.0	+0.6

Note: The average weekly earnings of each public-sector group have been expressed as a percentage of average weekly earnings of the corresponding private-sector group in each year, and these relativities averaged across the period 1970–82. The trend measures the average annual change in this relativity. This is also the slope of the trend line in the charts in Fig. 6.1.

position, while women experienced little general change. In the public corporations both manual and non-manual men showed systematic and significant gains in relative earnings, while the outcome for women, a much smaller group, was rather variable. Steep job losses in the nationalized industries over the period thus had as their counterpart substantial improvements in the relative pay position.

It is thus not possible to support the claim that the public sector systematically either gained or lost ground, in terms of relative pay, over the period. Nor is it the case that ground gained or lost either followed or tended to reverse an existing pay advantage. The clear gainers were manual men in central and local government, where average earnings tended to be lower than in the private sector, and also employees in the public corporations, again predominantly men, but a relatively high-pay group. The clearest losers were professional men and all categories of non-manual women employed by central and local government, most notably the intermediate category. While our purpose is not to detail the winners and losers in the pay league on a group-by-group basis, the importance of the health and education services as employers in these categories, their widely acknowledged difficulties of recruitment and retention of certain categories of employee in these two public services, and the erosion of the relative pay position seem ominously correlated.

6.5. The Instability of the Public-Sector Pay Relativity

The most striking feature brought into relief by the charts is not, however, these rather modest trends in relative pay, but the fluctuations around them. The pay relativity for every group was affected by a series of cyclical fluctuations, which in many cases were very substantial. This is in sharp contrast to the conclusion emphasized in Dean's work for the 1950s and 1960s, quoted above, that over these two decades public-sector pay had followed pay in the private sector extremely closely, and to the patterns of change in the other major pay relativities discussed elsewhere in the book.

The maximum deviations above and below trend are shown, as percentages of the trend level of the pay relativity, in Table 6.5. These quantify the impression conveyed from the charts, confirming that not only was every group affected, but in many cases the fluctuations were large relative to the trends in the relativities described above. For a group in a mid-range position in terms of the degree of instability, a typical experience would be alternation between a position 7 per cent above the trend, or normal, level, and one the same degree below it. This spread of around 15 per cent between the maximum deviations above and below

Table 6.5. *Pay relativities: maximum deviations from trend* (%)

SEG	Maximum deviations from trend relativity					
	Above trend			Below trend		
	Central government	Local government	Public corporations	Central government	Local government	Public corporations
Males						
1. Managers	+11.4	+8.6	+8.5	−7.0	−8.6	−6.9
2. Professionals	+7.0	+7.1	+7.1	−6.3	−7.1	−4.8
3. Intermediate	+9.2	+8.6	+4.6	−8.5	−7.6	−6.4
4. Junior non-manual	+21.3	+16.2	+5.5	−14.3	−7.1	−4.9
5. Foremen	+7.4	+7.7	+8.7	−9.0	−5.8	−3.7
6. Skilled manual	+4.6	+6.8	+7.2	−8.0	−7.1	−3.7
7. Semi-skilled	+6.8	+5.9	+5.0	−9.5	−4.9	−5.0
8. Unskilled manual	+6.3	+5.1	+2.6	−8.1	−4.4	−4.2
Females						
1. Managers	+12.8	+8.1	+27.3	−12.8	−10.2	−10.9
2. Professionals	+15.0	+11.2	+13.8	−6.9	−16.9	−11.0
3. Intermediate	+8.7	+8.4	+4.5	−11.9	−9.0	−5.9
4. Junior non-manual	+8.3	+4.4	+5.4	−8.7	−3.6	−3.8
5. Supervisors	+10.7	+5.4	+18.0	−15.5	−8.0	−17.1
6. Skilled manual	+6.4	+6.3	+7.2	−10.1	−7.7	−11.9
7. Semi-skilled	+11.1	+8.0	+7.5	−7.6	−6.7	−7.1
8. Unskilled manual	+11.9	+7.9	+7.4	−9.0	−7.6	−5.4

trend compares with Dean's estimate of a maximum spread of 4.2 points for male manual workers in the 1950s and of only 3 per cent in the 1960s. Between 1970 and 1982 the range was less than 10 per cent for only 4 groups out of our 48; for the great majority (33 groups out of the 48) it was between 10 and 20 percentage points, while for 11 groups it exceeded 20 per cent. In general, the fluctuations had the most pronounced effect on the relative position of central government employees, with those in local government somewhat less acutely affected, and the public corporations less so again. This generalization is more robust in the case of males, with the position for females being more varied. The major development in public-sector pay over the period was thus not that it diverged cumulatively from private-sector levels, but that it veered, first in one direction and then in the other, overshooting its longer-run trend and falling below it, then overshooting again.

In order to bring out the timing of these divergences, Table 6.6 illustrates the years in which the pay level for each individual group was either substantially above or substantially below trend, where a substantial divergence is taken to be in excess of 5 per cent of the trend level, and a very substantial one as in excess of 10 per cent. While there are some differences of timing, a general pattern is clear, confirming that the public sector as a whole shared certain common experiences in pay outcomes, in spite of the wide diversity of groups involved, and the many different pay-setting arrangements in operation. The collective public-sector experience brought out in Table 6.6 can be summarized. In 1970 pay levels for a wide range of public-sector groups were substantially below trend. In 1971 and 1972 a significant number not only recovered ground, but did so to a degree that projected them above trend, a gain which, by 1973 was proving to be short-lived. Beginning in 1974, and most strikingly in 1975 and 1976 the public sector showed a great leap forward, with a very wide range of groups receiving pay settlements which put them well ahead of their normal position *vis-à-vis* the private sector. Virtually every public-sector group moved ahead at this time, with the relative improvement for women being particularly striking. However, for most groups this ground was again progressively lost over the following two years, until by 1979 the majority of groups had seen their pay eroded significantly below its normal level. In the early 1980s the position became quite varied, with some groups moving above trend again, but others not.

While there may be an element of statistical artefact in these fluctuations it will be small. Since the NES is an annual survey based on pay levels for a specified week in April of each year, pay relativities calculated from it are vulnerable to accidents in the timing of pay awards. April is a very common month for public-sector pay settlements, and any

Table 6.6. The time-path of pay fluctuations

SEG	1970	1971	1972	1973	1974	1975	1976	1977	1978	1979	1980	1981	1982
Males													
Central government													
1. Managers	−	−			++	+	++			−	+		−
2. Professionals	−	+	+	−			++			−		+	
3. Intermediate		++	++	− −	−	+ − −	++		−	−	+	+	
4. Junior non-manual	−		+					−		−		+	+
Local government													
1. Managers	−	+	+			+	+++			−			
2. Professionals	−	+	++		−	++				− −			
3. Intermediate			+				++	−	−	−			
4. Junior non-manual	−		+			+				− −			
Public corporations													
1. Managers	−	+				+	++						
2. Professionals	−		+			++				−			
3. Intermediate			+							−			
4. Junior non-manual										−			
Central government													
5. Foremen		+				+	+		−	−			
6. Skilled manual				−						− −	++		
7. Semi-skilled	−	+		− −			+			−			
8. Unskilled manual													
Local government													
5. Foremen						++				−			
6. Skilled manual										− −			
7. Semi-skilled										− −			
8. Unskilled manual									−				
Public corporations													
5. Foremen						++							
6. Skilled manual							+			−			
7. Semi-skilled													
8. Unskilled manual													

Females

Central government											
1. Managers	−−	−	++	++	+	+	+	+	−	+	−
2. Professionals	−−	++	++	− −	+	++	+	−	−	−	−
3. Intermediate			+	−	+	++	+	−	+	+	
4. Junior non-manual	−		−		++	+		−		−	
Local government											
1. Managers	−−	+	−	+	+	+	+	−	+	−	
2. Professionals	−−	++	++	+	++	++	+	−	++	+	
3. Intermediate			+		++	++		−	+		+
4. Junior non-manual			+	−	+	+	++	−	+	−	−
Public corporations											
1. Managers	+	− −	−	++	++	−	−	−	+	++	+
2. Professionals	−	−	−	++	++	++	+	−	++	− −	+
3. Intermediate	−	+		+	+	+	+	−			
4. Junior non-manual					++	++	−	−			
Central government											
5. Supervisors	−−		+	+	++	+	+	− −	−		+
6. Skilled manual		+	−	+	+	++	+	−	−		
7. Semi-skilled			−	++	++	+	+	−			
8. Unskilled manual	−−			+	++	+		−			
Local government											
5. Supervisors			+	+							
6. Skilled manual	−		+	+							
7. Semi-skilled			+	+							
8. Unskilled manual	−		+	+							
Public corporations											
5. Supervisors	++	++	++	−	−	+	−	++	+	++	
6. Skilled manual		+	− −	− −		+	−	+	+	+	++
7. Semi-skilled		+	−	−			−				
8. Unskilled manual	−			+	+		−				

Notes: + denotes a level of relative earnings more than 5% above trend.
++ denotes a level of relative earnings more than 10% above trend.
− denotes a level of relative earnings more than 5% below trend.
−− denotes a level of relative earnings more than 10% below trend.

delay in reaching a settlement, met by subsequent backdating, will distort the picture for a given year. A conspicuous example of this occurred in 1975; non-industrial civil servants, the second largest group of central government employees, received an extremely large pay award, of the order of 30 per cent, partially backdated to January of 1975 and partially to April. Because of the late date of the award, however, neither part was recorded in the 1975 Survey. Had this award been included in the 1975 NES figures, the relativity for the groups involved for that year would have been even more favourable. In spite of their significance for the groups involved, however, the impact of such accidents of timing overall should not be exaggerated. Even large groups, such as civil servants and teachers, are only part of a broader socio-economic group, and the range of further groups involved with their differing procedures and timetables in pay-setting will tend to smooth accidents of timing. Even if particular incidents have a major impact on the short-term interpretation of the evidence, the longer-term perspective sets it in context. Moreover, April is also an extremely common date for the implementation of pay awards throughout the private sector,[9] where late settlements and backdating are also not unknown.

These fluctuations in public-sector pay are so much more pronounced than those in the other major pay relativities that an origin in institutional intervention rather than labour market developments is strongly suggested. We will therefore examine the evolution of the pay relativities to assess whether the stance of government policy towards public-sector pay over this period was the main feature differentiating its experience from that of the rest of the economy.

The 1960s had already sown the seeds of the view that incomes policies were, if not directed predominantly at the public sector, at least likely to be implemented with differential effect there. The 'pay pause' of 1961–2 under Selwyn Lloyd's Chancellorship took the form of an exhortation to the private sector, but backed up by threats of direct intervention against public-sector settlements. Likewise, the implementation of prices and incomes policies through referrals to the NBPI in the latter part of the 1960s involved public-sector groups disproportionately. Our trend figures suggest that there was a significant degree of truth in the view that by 1970 relative pay levels had deteriorated for a number of public-sector groups, notably in white-collar occupations. In the initial variant of incomes policy introduced by the Heath government, the so-called 'N − 1' policy, it was envisaged that the public sector would show the way in the progressive deceleration of settlements: again a policy of exhortation towards the private sector and of at least the threat of coercion of the public sector. Our figures, however, reveal—as was perceived by some commentators at the time—that the outcome was the reverse of the government's intention; for a number of groups the position, as measured by the incidence of earnings levels substantially above or below trend, was significantly better in 1971–2 than it had been in 1970. However, the subsequent Stages I and II, of freeze and £1 + 4 per cent, through 1973, allowed productivity exceptions at a time when output growth was buoyant and labour demand strong. As the private sector outstripped the public sector in earnings growth public-sector resentment found increasing expression in industrial action. It should be noted, however, that public-sector experience at this time was not uniform; the Pay Board's 'Anomalies' report in 1973 led to the granting of pay increases to the civil service and the government scientific service on grounds of comparability, a stance which was to be further elaborated in the Board's report on 'Relativities' in the following year. However, the government's simultaneous refusal to concede the claims of the coal-miners led to the election of February 1974 being won and lost against the background of the miners' strike and the three-day week, with the election outcome seen as a vote against the types of incomes policy being imposed. Under the new 'social contract' approach to pay the government abandoned formal policies in favour of restraint in collective bargaining, co-ordinated by the unions. The first act of the new government in the pay sphere was to concede the pay demand of the miners; this was rapidly followed by related groups, such as the electricity supply workers, and in short order by much of the public sector, with the consequence that later in 1974 and in 1975 pay in the public sector surged ahead of the private sector. Dean has estimated that public-sector male manuals were in 1975 in a position approximately 15 per cent more favourable *vis-à-vis* private-sector manuals than in the 1950s and 1960s. Nor was the upsurge confined to manual workers. During the period of the 'Social Contract' the PRU processes, suspended under the preceding policies, were reinstated leading to a very large award to the civil service after a series of *ad hoc* enquiries, notably the Halsbury Committee for nurses and Houghton Committee for schoolteachers, had also recommended large pay increases for other parts of the public service. The £6 limit for pay increases, introduced in the summer of 1975, served to freeze in place the relativities established by the public sector over the previous year. The subsequent stages of the Social Contract in 1977–9, with 10 and 5 per cent limits but exceptions for productivity improvements, were again seen as operating differentially against the public sector; productivity deals, genuine or otherwise, were felt to be more easily instituted in the private sector, while the government's perceived unwillingness and then inability to take action against Ford Motors for breach of the regulations in 1978 destroyed the credibility of sanctions against private-sector companies breaching the target levels. Our figures for the years 1977–9 support this interpretation of the effects of these policies, and establish a clear factual context for the 'winter of discontent'. In the midst of these general developments the years 1977–8 are also of note for the introduction of settlements, firstly for firemen and subsequently for the police, indexing their pay in the former case to the upper quartile point in manual earnings as recorded in the NES, in the latter to the average earnings index. These arrangements represent an extreme, if simplistic, form of comparability. Comparability was to return to the fore in more sophisticated form in 1979, via the establishment of the Standing Commission on Pay Comparability (the Clegg Commission). The Commission, which could only report on cases referred to it, recommended a number of significant awards to individual public-sector groups, including local authority and health service manual workers, nurses, and teachers, before its disbandment in 1981, but because of its brief its impact could be only partial.

6.6. Conclusions

Our purpose in this chapter has been to gain a broad perspective on public-sector pay over the period 1970–82, and to examine how far and through what channels public-sector status has brought common experiences, in terms of pay outcomes, for the varied industries and occupations which it comprises. These are questions which were scarcely posed before the 1970s, and certainly not with this breadth of focus. The emergence of public-sector pay as a specific issue on the political and economic agenda originated in changes not within the public sector itself but in the scope of macroeconomic policy. With the acceleration of inflation from the late 1960s the government's macroeconomic strategy became more and more dominantly an anti-inflation strategy, increasingly frequently encompassing incomes policies alongside, and sometimes more importantly than, the traditional tools of fiscal and monetary management. Explicit intervention by government in the pay-setting process became virtually continuous, at a time when high rates of price inflation made the timely and adequate adjustment of pay of even greater concern for all groups than in less hectic times. In the case of the public sector, pay and the impact of pay policies had, even by 1970, become an area of contention, and have continued to be so even beyond the abandonment of incomes policies on the traditional pattern in 1979. It was inevitable that the government should feel impelled to make its policies of income restraint effective, and be seen to make them effective, for its own employees, and equally that such attempts, whether effective or not, should be both resented and resisted. The issue thus became contentious, with strongly held beliefs both that public-sector employees were systematically discriminated against in the implementation of public policies, leading to the erosion of their relative pay, and that the political muscle derived from the inconvenience and damage inflicted by strikes in the public service led to unduly favourable treatment for the public sector.

It can be seen from our analysis that both views contain an element of truth. Serious erosion of the relative pay of the public sector as a consequence of the operation of government policies can be substantiated, most conspicuously around 1970 and 1977–9. Likewise, notably in 1975–6, the public sector successfully exploited its political position to establish a substantial pay advantage. In each case, however, the time-perspective adopted is too short. Once the movements in pay relativities are assessed on a longer-term or trend basis, such as thirteen years, each of these claims, in its stronger form, can be rejected. Relative pay movements have, in overall terms, been quite modest. This is not to deny that particular groups have seen a very significant erosion of their position over this period. Rather, our conclusion is that, at the level of the public sector as a whole, and the broad socio-economic groups which we have used, major changes in relativities have not taken place.

The principal characteristic of public-sector pay over this period has been the destabilization of its relationship to private-sector pay, which must be attributed to the impact of government policies. In terms of adjustment processes within broad groups as we have defined them, relativities change only slowly, as evolving patterns of supply and demand in product and labour markets lead to differing rates of recruitment, changing occupational and age mix, and other features. This is confirmed in the analyses of other broad relativities elsewhere in the book. Where pay relativities for major groups deviate from this trend relationship by the types of movements seen in the case of the public sector during the 1970s, these cannot be an accurate reflection of the evolution of the fundamental determinants. The history of the 1970s also confirms that, while public-sector pay levels can be depressed for periods of several years at a time, they have always had ultimately to be restored. Attempts to intervene in the pay-setting process, through the use of public-sector pay as an instrument to achieve alternative policy goals, can force distortions in pay but are ultimately self-defeating. In economic terms such distortions are damaging. Under the impact of poor pay experienced employees leave, vacancies remain unfilled, and the quality of service deteriorates. When relativities are restored, the number of returners attracted by the restored salaries will always be only a small fraction of those lost. Moreover, when restored relativities are seen to be eroded yet again, a credibility problem emerges, compounding the difficulties of recruitment, retention, and re-attraction. Distortionary intervention by government, setting pay levels in pursuit of other policy objectives, undermines the important signalling and allocative function of relative pay. Moreover, the evidence of the 1970s shows that these policy-induced distortions led to feelings of grievance and resentment, as the public and private sectors successively felt the other to be more favourably treated. For much of the public sector, this perceived injustice contributed importantly to a loss of morale and the deteriorating climate of industrial relations.

As has often been remarked, it is impossible for the government not to have an incomes policy, even if its policy is not to have one; the government always has to make decisions about levels of remuneration for its own employees. Our view of the appropriate principles for the determination of public-sector pay follows from our analysis of what went wrong in the years 1970–82. The government as employer cannot 'buck the trend' of market forces other than temporarily and at substantial cost. Public-sector pay must therefore be set at levels consistent with market forces, in terms of the requirement to recruit, retain, and motivate employees. Employees evaluate the multiple attributes of a job and its total remuneration in the public sector just as elsewhere. In this sense the relevance of comparability applies universally, throughout the private and public sectors. The particular message in the case of the public sector is that commitment to it cannot be merely intermittent, conditional on no conflicting policy objective being given priority. One would wish that the 1980s and the ending of the role of incomes policy as an anti-inflation strategy had brought the reintroduction of greater stability into pay-setting for the public sector. The responsibility of the paymaster for public expenditure and the alternative objectives which that has introduced has, unfortunately, meant otherwise.

Appendix 6.1. The Public Sector in the NES

In establishing the appropriate definition of the public sector, an initial choice had to be made between seeking to deal with as constant a body of employees as possible, on the one hand, and respecting the changing status of organizations and enterprises as they moved between the public and private sectors, on the other. Since the concern of this study was to analyse the relative position of the public sector over a sequence of years which saw rather few changes in the scope of public ownership, the former course, of standardizing the composition of the public sector over the period at the cost of minor inaccuracies of classification, was preferred. The only sizeable discontinuities caused by the transfer of ownership came with the nationalization of aerospace and shipbuilding in 1978, which brought approximately 150,000 employees from the private into the public sector, and the subsequent privatization of British Aerospace in 1981, which returned

73,000 to the private sector. In view of the heavy public involvement in both aerospace and shipbuilding before nationalization, both of these industries have been included in the public sector throughout. Moreover, within them, the Royal Naval Dockyards and the RAF aircraft repair and maintenance establishments remained in the public sector throughout. In the same spirit, since government involvement in them became negligible, the specialist steel producers have been classified to the private sector throughout. No adjustment has been made for the privatization of Cable and Wireless in October 1981 and of National Freight Corporation in February 1982, occurring at the very end of the period. The privatizations of Britoil in October 1982, Associated British Ports (previously British Transport Docks) in 1983, and British Telecom in 1984 lie outside the period. A full discussion of the definition of the public sector and the constituent public corporations is given in CSO (1985*a* and 1985*b*).

Since 1978 the published tables of the NES have distinguished the three major divisions of the public sector, central government, local government, and the public corporations, which are used in this study. These classifications are coded by the Department of Employment into the Survey files. As the Survey does not record directly whether an individual or establishment is in the public or the private sector, the DE makes the allocation of individuals on the basis of two criteria:

1. where the individual's pay and conditions of employment are reported as covered by one of the listed collective agreements from either the public- or the private-sector list, this is used as an allocator;
2. where none of the listed agreements applies, the allocation is made on the basis of the industry of employment at the MLH level.

We used the opportunity of access to the original files when constructing our own data set to adopt this allocation procedure uniformly back to 1970.

The allocation of the public-sector collective agreements included in the 1982 list (reproduced with the Survey questionnaire in Appendix A) was as follows:

Central government

National Health Service
431 Administrative and clerical staffs Whitley Council
432 Nurses and midwives Whitley Council
433 Ancillary staffs Whitley Council
434 Maintenance staff
463 Ambulancemen Whitley Council

National government
448 Prison officers
449 Government industrial establishments JCC

Civil service National Whitley Council
450 Administration group: middle and higher grades
451 Administration group: clerical grades
452 Professional and technology group

453 Science group
454 Secretarial, typing, and data processing grades
455 Paper-keeping and messengerial grades

Local government

Teaching
England and Wales: Burnham Committee
435 Primary, secondary, and special schools
436 Establishments for further education
Scottish Teachers Salaries Committee
437 Primary and secondary schools
438 Establishments for further education

Universities
466 Academic staff (non-clinical)
467 Clerical and certain related administrative staff JC
468 Technical staff JC
469 Manual and ancillary staff JC

Local authorities' services
England and Wales
439 Administrative, professional, technical, and clerical NJC
440 Building and civil engineering workers JNC
441 Engineering craftsmen and electricians JNC
442 Manual workers NJC
Scotland
443 Administrative, professional technical and clerical NJC
444 Building and civil engineering workers
445 Engineering craftsmen
446 Electricians and plumbers JNC
447 Manual workers NJC

Other services
456 Police service (ranks below superintendent)
458 Fire services—operational ranks from station officer to senior divisional officer
457 Fire services—operational ranks below station officer
459 Fire services—control room and non-operational staff

Public corporations

Coal-mining
401 Management and clerical staff
402 Mining officials and weekly paid industrial staff
403 Underground mineworkers
404 Surface mineworkers

Iron and steel
405 Iron and steel and pig iron manufacture

Gas
406 Gas staffs, and senior officers NJC (not to include Higher Management NJC)
407 Gas plant maintenance craftsmen (CSEU)
408 Gas workers NJIC

Electricity supply
409 Administrative and clerical grades NJC
410 Technical engineering staff NJB
411 Building operatives NJ (B. & CE) C
412 Workers other than building operatives NJIC

Water
460 Water service staffs NJC
461 Water service—craftsmen
462 Water service NJIC—non-craftsmen

Shipbuilding
464 Shipbuilding and ship repairing

British Airways
414 Engineering and maintenance grades NJC
415 Ground services NJC

British Rail
416 Salaried staff
417 Railway workshops
418 Footplate staff
419 Conciliation staff (other than footplate staff) and miscellaneous grades

London Transport
420 Railways, general and operating grades
421 Road passenger transport, drivers and conductors
422 Garages: maintenance staff

British Road Services
423 Engineering maintenance and repair grades NJNC
424 Operating and other wages grades NJNC

Other transport
425 Road passenger transport: municipal undertakings NJIC
426 Omnibus industry: National Council undertakings

British Broadcasting Corporation
465 Non-manual workers

Other services
669 Port transport (dockworkers) NJC

The list of collective agreements is reviewed each year and minor adjustments are made; these include the addition of new groups, such as the ambulancemen in 1978 and the universities in 1981, and amendments to the agreements included on the list when the structure of agreements is altered, as in the gas and electricity industries in 1973 and the civil service in 1976. The criteria for allocating individuals are not affected by this.

The allocation of MLH industries to the public sector has been made as follows:

Central government

MLH 002 Forestry
    342 Ordnance and small arms
    874 Medical and dental services
    901 National government

Local government

MLH 872 Education services
    906 Local government

Public corporations

MLH 098 Coal-mining—underground workers (from 1974)
    099 Coal-mining—surface workers (from 1974)
    100 Coal-mining—nes (from 1974)
    101 Coal-mining (1970–3)
    311 Iron and steel (general)
    312 Steel tubes
    371 Shipbuilding
    372 Marine engineering
    383 Aerospace
    384 Locomotives
    385 Railway carriages and wagons
    601 Gas
    602 Electricity
    603 Water
    701 Railways
    702 Road passenger transport
    706 Ports and inland waterways
    707 Air transport
    708 Posts and telecommunications

While both selection criteria give a high level of accuracy in allocating individuals between the sectors, two types of misclassification are possible under both: failure to identify an individual who is employed in the public sector, and the erroneous assignment to the public sector of an individual actually employed in the private sector. The use of collective agreements to set pay and conditions of employment is virtually universal throughout the public sector.[10] The formal adoption of the terms of a public-sector agreement by a private-sector employer, as distinct from a decision to follow the terms set in one of them, must be virtually unknown. The list of agreements, on the other hand, comprises only major agreements; where other agreements apply, which are not included in the list, identification fails unless, as is most commonly the case, the industry of employment also signals the individual as employed in the public sector. The degree of approximation implied in the allocation by industry of employment is rather greater. While a number of industries are full public monopolies—national and local government administration, railways, electricity, gas, and posts and telecommunications—those teachers, nurses, miners, and others in the small private-sector element of their industries cannot be distinguished and will have been erroneously allocated to the public sector. Forestry, ordnance and small arms, and ports and inland waterways are the industries where the greatest relative misallocation would occur, the substantial presence of both public and private enterprises making the allocation either way subject to significant error. An implication of this is that adjustment of the boundary of the public sector to accommodate the privatization of Cable and Wireless and of National Freight Corporation, constituting only parts of their respective industries at the MLH level, would not have been feasible, had we sought to follow the shifting boundary between the public and private sectors. Conversely, where the public sector forms only a minor part of the industry the employees involved would not be identified unless one of the listed public-sector agreements applied; the Royal Mint in MLH 396 (jewellery and precious metals), HM Stationery Office and the Bank of England Printing Works in MLH 489 (other printing and publishing), and construction workers employed by the Property Services Agency or the New Town Development Corporations in MLH 500 (construction) would be leading instances. Again as a consequence of this, no adjustment could be made for the changing status of any of these bodies, as when the establishment of HMSO as a trading body on 1 April 1980 made it reclassifiable from 'central government' to 'public corporations'.

Before 1978 much more limited use was made in the NES of the division between the public and the private sectors, and this was mainly for internal purposes rather than for the published tables. Between 1975 and 1977 the public sector was classified into nationalized industries and other public services, while between 1970 and 1974 only the broad division between public and private sector was used. As a consequence, various differences occur both in total and in individual sectors between our classifications and those used by the DE for these earlier years. The major differences are that in the NES for 1970–7 the public sector does not include forestry (MLH 002), the Royal Ordnance factories (342), and ports and inland waterways (706), and does include additional parts of the steel industry (MLH 313).

Notes

1. The main official statements on the principle of comparability are contained in Priestley Commission (1955), Pay Board (1973 and 1974), Clegg Commission Reports, especially no. 9 (1980), and Megaw Inquiry (1982). The work of the National Board for Prices and Incomes is described in Fels (1972).
2. An extensive account of this is given in the chapter by Thomson and Sanjines in this volume.
3. The work of the PRU is described in the submission by the Civil Service Department to the Megaw Inquiry (Civil Service Department 1981), and also in Clegg Commission (1980: Appendix 4). Various criticisms of the work of the PRU are discussed in Beaumont (1978).

4. The *locus classicus* in American literature is Wellington and Winter (1971). For more detailed economic analyses see Smith (1976), Fogel and Lewin (1974), and Shapiro (1978). Similar arguments for Canada are given in Gunderson (1979) and Cousineau and Lacroix (1977). Collective bargaining in the public sector in Britain is discussed in Elliott and Fallick (1981: ch. 3) and Kessler (1983).

5. Incomes policy and public-sector pay is discussed in Fallick and Elliott (1981*a*), Elliott and Fallick (1981: ch. 7), and Kessler (1983).

6. For further discussion of the crowding of women into the lower levels of occupational structure, see Chapter 5 by Sloane on sex differentials and Chapter 4 on the white-collar sector by Mayhew and Ray.

7. The data series available on non-manual earnings before the introduction of the New Earnings Survey and their limitations are described in Chapter 1.

8. These difficulties are discussed by Elliott and Murphy in Chapter 3.

9. The monthly pattern of pay settlements in manufacturing industry, overwhelmingly in the private sector, as recorded through the CBI Pay Databank from 1979 is analysed in Gregory, Lobban, and Thomson (1985).

10. As recorded in the NES special question for 1978, substantially more than 90% of employees in the public sector had their pay and conditions set under a collective agreement. See Gregory and Thomson (1981).

7

The Distribution of Earnings

David Bell, Laurie Hunter, and Michael Danson

7.1. Introduction

Economists have a long-standing interest in the inequalities of pay and the extent to which observed inequalities reflect normal market operations or market imperfections. In a clearly defined occupation, with homogeneous labour and a perfect market, the dispersion of earnings would tend to zero. Any disturbance to this equilibrium would be met by adjustments of demand (e.g. hiring rates or standards) or supply (e.g. mobility) resulting in a return to equilibrium and zero dispersion. When dispersion of pay is observed in an occupational market, then, we may be picking up non-homogeneity of labour, market imperfections, or the effects of some recent external disturbance. In practice, we typically observe non-zero dispersion and our expectation is that this will vary systematically according to the structure and characteristics of the human capital and the institutions of the market. The dispersion will also be subject to influence from government policy, perhaps most obviously in the form of incomes policy but certainly not excluding the distributional effects of policy affecting employment and inflation.

Such influences can be expected to affect both the inter-occupational and intra-occupational distribution of pay and hence the degree of equality of pay within society. In recent years there has developed a general acceptance that the degree of inequality in the UK labour market has been increasing, exemplified by a belief in a growing 'North–South' polarization. In particular the view has been expressed that the dispersion of earnings has increased substantially with the rich getting richer and the poor poorer, though the evidence for this is seldom systematically presented. This chapter allows new light to be shed on this particular dimension of inequality and its behaviour over the decade 1973–82 when dramatic shifts took place in the employment levels and market structures and when bouts of rapid inflation apparently disrupted earnings relationships. We cannot claim that this is a comprehensive account because it rests on data for a limited selection of occupations. It does, however, provide an analysis of inter-occupational and intra-occupational earnings distributions at a level of detail and using a better quality of data than have hitherto been available.

Of course, concern over inequality is not the only reason which might motivate a study of the earnings distribution. The earnings distribution is endogenous, the outcome of the interaction of demand and supply in the labour market, and must reflect, in part, the tastes and preference of employers and employees as well as any imperfections in its structure. For example, studies of the role of trade unions in the labour market often seek to isolate a union 'mark-up' above competitive wage levels. Further analysis might seek to examine what effect, if any, collective bargaining has on the width of the earnings spread. It would also be of interest to allocate any changes in overall inequality through time to shifts in *between* and *within* group inequality. For example, one might wish to examine how far changes in the earnings structure are attributable to changes in the earnings distribution *within* occupations and how far to shifts in inter-occupational differentials.

Or again, treating the earnings distribution as exogenous, one might consider how it influences the process of job search. A widely dispersed wage distribution is likely to lead to longer mean search times than one where the distribution is compact, and changes in dispersion might in turn induce changes in search duration and hence in unemployment.

Again, the response of the earnings distribution to changes in *incomes policy* is obviously important. Historically most UK policies such as those based on equal absolute pay settlements should, a priori, have tended to compress the wage distribution.

In this chapter, our concern is mostly with the descriptive analysis of the data set, which is based on the individual returns to the New Earnings Survey. In section 7.2 we discuss a variety of available dispersion measures and in section 7.3 a more detailed account is given of the data used in this chapter. Section 7.4 presents a brief outline of the general earnings relationships conveyed by the data. Section 7.5 examines the stability and compatibility of alternative measures of dispersion, while section 7.6 provides a preliminary analysis of the time pattern of occupational earnings dispersion and the reasons which underlie this pattern. Section 7.7 reports the results of regression analysis based on the argument of section 7.6.

7.2. Measures of Inequality

Some understanding of the problems of the measurement of inequality and the parameterization of the earnings distribution is essential to an understanding of the subsequent results. We first consider the parametric representation of the earnings distribution function before turning to examine some point inequality measures.

(a) Modelling the distribution of earnings

There have been many attempts to fit probability distributions to earnings data. The Pareto, gamma, and lognormal functions have been popular though recently the Singh–Maddala and generalized beta functions have been shown to yield superior fits with particular data sets (see McDonald 1984).

Difficulties arise, however, in the interpretation of the mechanical application of particular statistical distributions to the spread of earnings. Consider the Pareto distribution which is given by:

$$F(y) = 1 - (y/\bar{y})y > \bar{y} \tag{7.1}$$

and was originally recognized as simply an empirical regularity with no basis in economic theory. Champernowne (1953) showed that if earnings are subdivided into a number of groups whose limits form a geometric progression and if the probability of moving from one group to another follows a Markov process and declines as the distance between groups increases, then the earnings distribution will eventually follow the Pareto distribution. Yet it is somewhat unsatisfactory for economists to believe that earnings are determined by essentially random processes. A similar theme is evident in the work of Gibrat (1931), who introduced the 'Law of Proportionate Effect', which simply stated that if, from some initial base, income levels were subject to random independent *proportionate* changes, then due to the Central Limit Theorem the resulting distribution of incomes would tend towards the lognormal. (The 'Law of Proportionate Effect' implies that the log of earnings follows a random walk.) Like the Pareto, the lognormal distribution has no choice-theoretic basis.

If the direct parameterizations of the functional form of the income distribution have no grounding in economic theory then equally theoretical models of earnings determination have had little success in directly characterizing the earnings distribution. In describing the human capital approach to earnings determination, Blinder (1974: 15) concludes that 'While the model cannot predict a precise functional form for the income distribution—*a task far too tall for any realistic theory*— ... unlike almost all of the models considered so far, it lends itself readily to empirical implementation'.

Even more simplistic than the human capital approach are the ability–earnings models which relate earnings to some measure of ability. If the functional form of ability is known then it should be possible to deduce the functional form of the earnings distribution. Here the classic problem is that of deriving a skewed earnings distribution when it is generally presumed that ability is normally or at least symmetrically distributed.

What is required is a set of assumptions which firstly govern other aspects of the labour input such as 'application', 'experience', or 'responsibility' and secondly determine how these jointly affect earnings. It is generally possible to demonstrate a skewed earnings distribution even if these factors are independent of ability and each other and if individually their distribution is symmetric, provided that they are combined *multiplicatively*. Nevertheless such approaches seem somewhat contrived and still omit any choice-theoretic aspect. In this latter respect theories based on human capital clearly supersede their predecessors.

In the simple human capital model the individual seeks to maximize the discounted value of potential lifetime *earnings*. By using potential earnings rather than expected utility as the maximand, the human capital approach neglects the labour supply decision. Nevertheless, by focusing on investment in human capital through schooling, on-the-job training, etc., the theory does provide a framework for explaining observed differences in earnings. Exogenous factors such as race or sex can also be incorporated. Differences in individuals' tastes as well as their inherent limitations in the production of human capital should also play a role. Blinder (1974) develops a model of earnings dispersion based on the human capital approach which incorporates individual tastes in respect of leisure, bequests, and time discounting. However, it does not lead to a parametric representation of the earnings distribution.

Finally we consider the Lorenz curve, which can be defined formally in terms of the distribution functions of earnings and cumulative earnings. That is, the Lorenz curve is the relationship between the inverse functions of $F(y)$ and $F1(y)$, (assuming these exist) where $F(y)$ is the distribution function of y and $F1(y)$ is the 'first moment' distribution function of y defined as:

$$F1(y) = \frac{1}{\mu} \int_0^y yF(y)dy \quad \text{where} \quad \mu = E(y) \tag{7.2}$$

and is therefore defined on the interval $[0, 1]$. $F(y)$ can be interpreted as the number of units having earnings of y or less while $F1(y)$ is the proportional share of total earnings accounted for by units having income of y or less.

One can easily demonstrate the properties of the Lorenz curve such as its positive increasing slope using this formulation. Since it is defined in terms of the earnings distribution function, one can also derive the Lorenz curve which corresponds to a particular earnings distribution. Presuming the necessary inverse transformations exist, one can thus establish a one-to-one relationship between particular earnings distributions such as the Pareto and particular functional forms for the Lorenz curve.

(*b*) Point measures of inequality

An alternative to direct parametric representation of the earnings distribution is a point measure of inequality which attempts to express the dispersion of the earnings distribution in terms of a single statistic. Before discussing particular examples it is worth considering what properties it might be desirable for such statistics to embody so that individual measures which will be utilized in the subsequent empirical work can be critically assessed.

1. An obvious condition is that inequality should be measured on some finite scale whose limits at one extreme represent complete inequality and at the other complete equality. Most often the interval [0,1] is selected with the value 0 representing complete equality (each individual having the same earnings) and 1 complete inequality (all individuals bar one receiving no earnings).

2. A second property which an inequality measure should possess is that any transfer from a poorer person to a richer person should *increase* its value (the *Pigou–Dalton* condition). While it may seem self-evident that this property should be embodied by them, many commonly used measures do not satisfy Pigou–Dalton. All measures based on ordering, such as the range, quartiles, and deciles, can remain unaffected by transfer within the earnings distribution.

3. Thirdly, inequality measures should not be subject to 'money illusion'. That is, they should be homogeneous of degree zero in earnings. More formally:

if $x = ay$ (where y is a vector representing the earnings distribution, a is a scalar, and $\phi(y)$ the inequality measure) then $\phi(x) = \phi(y)$. Thus proportionate shifts in all incomes should not affect measured inequality.

4. The measure should be *symmetric*, where symmetry is taken to mean that if two individuals exchange positions in the distribution, the inequality measure is unaffected: thus it should be impartial between individuals. Formally $\phi(y) = \phi(\Omega(y))$ where $\Omega(y)$ is any permutation of y.

5. The inequality measure should be unaffected by a proportional expansion of the population. Doubling the number of individuals in each earnings band would thus leave the measure unchanged just as would a doubling of earnings themselves.

6. Finally, it might be desirable that the measure be *decomposable* in the sense that overall inequality can be allocated in some (as yet unspecified) way between constituent parts of the total population. Thus, it should be possible to allocate, say, the total inequality within an occupation between the measured inequality of those who are covered by a collective agreement and the inequality of those who are not so covered.

This is a particularly stringent requirement which very few measures satisfy (see e.g. Cowell 1984).

   So far the implication of the discussion has been that inequality measures are 'objective'. Yet there are normative overtones in the presumption that 'less' inequality is to be preferred to 'more' inequality. For given total earnings, successively higher social welfare is taken to be attained as the level of inequality falls. This presumes a specific form of the social welfare function: yet this form has so far remained implicit. One can, however, deduce the characteristics of the function by considering how the measures respond to transfers between groups within the population. For example, the Gini index is particularly sensitive to transfers about the mode of the distribution rather than at the tails. The coefficient of variation is equally sensitive to transfers at all levels of income.[1] It will thus weight a transfer from someone earning £20,000 to someone earning £18,000 the same as a transfer from someone earning £50,000 to someone earning £4,000 even though one might expect transfers at the bottom of the income scale to be given greater weight. Thus we can see that social welfare functions implicit in some of the commonly used inequality measures may have rather unusual properties (see e.g. Deaton and Muell-bauer 1980).
   To circumvent such difficulties Atkinson's alternative approach to inequality measurement is to specify the social welfare function at the outset and from it derive the inequality measure (Atkinson 1970). Normally such a welfare function would be increasing in income and decreasing in inequality and would include a parameter measuring the extent of aversion to inequality. The Atkinson measure requires an assumption that the social welfare function is additively separable in individual utilities: this may not be wholly appealing. It rules out all situations where the utility of one individual is in some way dependent on that of others.
   Another implication is that it is *always* possible to rank different states of the world in terms of inequality. Sen (1973) argues that individuals may not carry an exhaustive list which ranks all possible distributions. It is consequently dangerous for economists and statisticians to impute to these measures a degree of accuracy greater than that embodied in the concept of inequality itself. The possibility of incompleteness is well illustrated by trying to rank different states in terms of their respective Lorenz curves. As shown in Fig. 7.1, this can lead to ambiguous situations where it is not possible to construct a ranking because the Lorenz curves intersect.
   Curve μ is clearly Lorenz inferior to both σ and π, but these latter cannot be ranked since their respective Lorenz curves intersect. Several of the regularly used inequality measures have direct interpretations

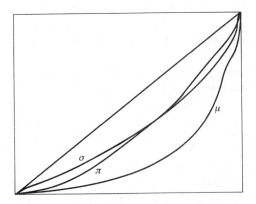

Fig. 7.1. Lorenz curve relationships

within the Lorenz curve framework. The relative mean deviation is equal to the maximum distance between the Lorenz curve and the egalitarian line. The Gini coefficient is equal to twice the area lying between the Lorenz curve and the egalitarian line. Note that if $\sigma < \mu$ then it will be the case that $G(\sigma) < G(\mu)$ where G is the Gini function though the reverse is not necessarily true.

A more general result applicable to Lorenz curves has been shown by Atkinson (1970) who demonstrated that if one distribution is Lorenz superior to another and if the welfare function is separable and additive in identical individual utilities then the social welfare and Lorenz ranking of different distributions will be identical. This result has been generalized to a wider class of social welfare functions.

7.3. The Data

A general description of the data set has been provided in Chapter 1, and we focus here simply on the data organization and arrangement required for this study of dispersion.

For each year in the period 1973–82[2] there are at least 14,000 records, each describing a 'cell' containing three, four, or five persons. In this data set individuals have been allocated to cells firstly on the basis of shared individual characteristics and secondly by the value of their hourly earnings excluding overtime. That is, groups of individuals in the same occupation, of the same sex, working in the same region, having their wages set in the same way (by collective agreement or not), in the same age and socio-economic group were initially constructed. Each of these groups was then ordered by reference to their hourly earnings. Cells were then constructed by taking the first three individuals from this ordered group, the second three, and so on. If the overall number of individuals was not exactly divisible by three, the remainder was added to the last cell.

The very richness of this data set in itself presents problems. To economize on computing costs and to make the analysis more manageable, it was decided at the outset to work with a limited selection of occupations in which there was an expectation of meaningful cell sizes after disaggregation. So far as possible, we also sought a representation of occupational groups throughout the earnings structure, including in particular groups with varying male–female employee ratios and with different degrees of collective bargaining coverage. As noted earlier, the selective approach means that we can offer little authoritative comment on the behaviour of the *whole* earnings distribution.

An initial selection of 78 KOS groups was reduced by excluding those with small populations of cases to a basic data set comprising 60 KOS occupations in each of which there appeared to be sufficient cases to allow some disaggregation.

With sixty representative occupational codes being selected for analysis, split into three large regions, two sex groups, three age groups, eight socio-economic groups, and the presence or absence of collective bargaining coverage, there are potentially 17,280 distinct groups in the data set. Clearly this would mean that some of these groups would be so small as to be statistically unacceptable. While it is possible to conduct analyses along a number of different routes it was decided that, in the first instance, the analysis would concentrate on the distribution of hourly earnings, excluding overtime, by occupation alone.[3]

The data was consequently reordered on the occupational indicator alone. This creates a problem, however, since it was not possible to reorder the original individual information as held by the Department of Employment and construct a new set of cells. Rather it was only possible to reorder the existing cells and hence the possibility of overlap in the earnings of different individuals in different cells of 3, 4, or 5 individuals cannot be ruled out.

To clarify this point consider the following example: in groups identical in all respects except sex, there are two cells. In the female groups there is a cell which has recorded hourly earnings of £4.00. This is the average of three individuals whose hourly earnings are £3.90, £4.00, and £4.10 respectively. In the male cell average earnings are £4.10 and this results from an ordered group of three individuals who have earnings respectively of £3.85, £4.10, and £4.30. When the cells themselves are collected and reordered in a new arrangement of the data based only on occupational characteristics and not sex, the 'male' cell will be placed higher in the new ranking than the 'female' cell even though there is an individual in the male group whose hourly earnings are less than any in the female group.

Thus, while the ordering within cells is unambiguous on the disaggregated data, one cannot be certain that the individual data on which these are based are correctly ordered when the cell data are used in a different aggregation. This problem might be serious were it not for the size of this particular data set. If the cells are all composed of three individuals, then the existing information does permit us to set upper and lower limits on the variation within any cell. Because the original data is completely ordered, the individual with lowest hourly earnings cannot have earned less than the average earnings for the previous cell. (This lower level is only feasible in the event that all individuals in the previous cell had identical earnings and therefore variation in this cell was zero.) Similarly, the individual with highest earnings cannot have earned more than average earnings for the next cell.

Given the large number of cells contained in the overall data set and the small range of variation within cells, we find that the likelihood of individual earnings differing greatly from the recorded mean is low. Certainly the problem of overlap as described here is not nearly so acute as that which arises from the use of data on frequencies within wide income bands to calculate distribution of income measures with no knowledge of the within-band distributions as has typically been the case with previous income distribution studies.

7.4. The Sample Occupations in General

As explained in the previous section, 60 KOS occupations were selected for more detailed analysis, and it is important to establish in what sense this sample is representative of the wider earnings structure.

The sample of 60 KOS occupations is somewhat unevenly spread throughout the eight socio-economic groups, as can be seen from Table 7.1. The absence of representatives from the managerial and foremen/supervisors categories is particularly notable. Apart from this, the list includes both growing and declining numbers in employment, while examples of predominantly male-employing and female-employing occupations are included. The mean wage range among the 60 occupations is wider than that represented by the highest and lowest decile of the full NES data set, and may thus be taken as being inclusive of occupations at the upper and lower reaches of the earnings distribution.

As well as the dispersion measures to which we will be turning our attention, it is useful to set the discussion in the context of the behaviour of the inter-occupational wage structure as represented by our sample.

Table 7.1. *Distribution of selected occupations by socio-economic group*

Socio-economic group	No.
1. Managers	0
2. Professional and technical	3
3. Intermediate non-manual	7
4. Junior non-manual	10
5. Foremen and supervisors	0
6. Skilled manual	26
7. Semi-skilled manual	9
8. Unskilled manual	5
TOTAL	60

From a purely descriptive point of view, there may be some interest in knowing which occupations stand at the extremes of the earnings distribution. But more importantly, there is a question about the stability of the distribution. The wage structure is typically regarded as being somewhat rigid, at least in the short run. What does our evidence on the sixty occupations tell us about these questions?

Table 7.2 shows the comparative 1973 and 1982 situations for the top ten and bottom ten occupations in the sixty cases selected. There is a remarkable degree of similarity, with 7 out of 10 occupations at the bottom end appearing in both years, and 9 out of 10 at the top end: rankings within the groups of 10 change very little. The high-paid occupations are mainly white-collar, the low paid mainly health-related and retail service occupations.

This Table probably overstates the stability when the full range of occupations and the change between years is taken into account. Spearman rank correlation coefficient statistics were calculated for the mean earnings of each pair of different years in the sample: the results are shown in Table 7.3, together with the large sample t-statistics. Although these results show some slight tendency for the strength of the association to fall away as the time span increases, the earnings ranking of 1982 is still significantly associated with that of 1973 and all intervening years.[4]

7.5. Consistency of Measures

In section 7.2 we examined a number of measures of inequality. We now consider the results emerging from the application of some of these measures. Two main questions can be identified. First, do different mea-

Table 7.2. *Rank order of mean wage for top 10 and bottom 10 occupations in sample, 1973 and 1982*

	1973	1982
Top 10 occupations	University academic staff	University academic staff
	Secondary teachers	Secondary teachers
	Primary teachers	Primary teachers
	Accountants	Systems analysts
	Systems analysts	Accountants
	Technical sales reps	Technical sales reps
	Engineering technicians	Engineering technicians
	Draughtsmen	Draughtsmen
	Sales reps (wholesale)	Printing machine minders
	Toolmakers, toolfitters	Sales reps (wholesale)
Bottom 10 occupations	State registered and enrolled nurses	Packers, bottlers, canners, fillers
	Chefs, cooks	Chefs, cooks
	Hospital ward orderlies	Nursing auxiliaries and assistants
	Salesmen, sales assistants	Butchers, meatcutters
	Nursing auxiliaries and assistants	Salesmen, sales assistants
	Sewing machinists (textiles)	Counterhands, assistants
	Petrol pump/forecourt attendants	Sewing machinists (textiles)
	Counterhands, assistants	Petrol pump/forecourt attendants
	Ladies' hairdressers	Ladies' hairdressers

sures of inequality show a consistent picture of the distribution? And if not, what are the implications? Secondly, is the earnings distribution ranking stable over time?

We approach the first question by considering to what extent alternative measures differ in their *ranking of occupational inequality*. Atkinson (1970) indicates that the degree of consistency between different measures is likely to be poor. Using income data from twelve countries he first notes that the Lorenz curves intersect in more than three-quarters of all possible two-country comparisons. Hence, he argues that for these cases ranking will be dependent on whatever social welfare function is chosen. Note, however, that comparisons of inequality measures have normally been carried out in a cross-section context. With the present data set it is possible not only to compare the ranking of different

D. Bell, L. Hunter, M. Danson

Table 7.3. *Spearman rank correlation coefficients:
mean earnings for pairs of years*

Year	1973	1974	1975	1976	1977	1978	1979	1980	1981	1982
1973										
1974	0.506									
1975	0.608	0.438								
1976	0.376	0.407	0.525							
1977	0.528	0.309	0.490	0.494						
1978	0.492	0.370	0.425	0.281	0.306					
1979	0.467	0.368	0.367	0.348	0.226	0.544				
1980	0.454	0.605	0.464	0.415	0.384	0.377	0.284			
1981	0.290	0.321	0.402	0.455	0.471	0.262	0.332	0.357		
1982	0.358	0.267	0.491	0.461	0.524	0.467	0.483	0.296	0.601	
Large sample t-statistics mean										
1973										
1974	4.465									
1975	5.831	3.715								
1976	3.089	3.393	4.700							
1977	4.738	2.474	4.278	4.329						
1978	4.303	3.036	3.580	2.232	2.448					
1979	4.022	3.018	3.004	2.830	1.771	4.934				
1980	3.884	5.793	3.984	3.473	3.168	3.097	2.252			
1981	2.311	2.584	3.322	3.892	4.070	2.069	2.681	2.912		
1982	2.916	2.114	4.288	3.953	4.682	4.020	4.205	2.360	5.720	

measures at a particular point in time, but also to determine whether they behave similarly over a period of ten years. For example, a group of measures might rank a set of occupations differently in a given year, yet if one took a single occupation and examined the time series behaviour of the dispersion statistics calculated for this occupation alone, these time series could be compared to determine if the different measures at least agreed on the evolution of dispersion through time.

For these comparisons a wide range for measures was utilized, but for simplicity of presentation we concentrate on just three, namely the Gini coefficient, the relative mean deviation and the coefficient of variation. These statistics were calculated for our sixty occupations for each of the ten years 1973–82, and their rankings were tabulated along with the ranking of the mean. It was immediately apparent that the different measures generated quite different rankings year by year. (For the sake of brevity we illustrate this by reporting the first six cases by KOS classification number in Table 7.4.)

Thus the correspondence among the rankings under different measures is far from perfect, due partly to the variation in the sensitivities of the measures to differential changes across the earnings range and partly to the statistical error associated with the estimates of the various statistics particularly where the sample size is relatively small.

The fact that the rankings are not identical does not however imply that they are not correlated. Thus where correlation exists, one may make inferences about the behaviour of one conditional on the known behaviour of another. While this is certainly a weaker condition than insistence that the measures be used to form unique rankings, it would imply that, given a particular distribution of earnings ranked according to the Gini coefficient, then the relative mean deviation ranking would be statistically indistinguishable. This is somewhat different from Sen's argument (1973) that the general conception of inequality would not provide a complete ordering of all earnings dispersions. A statistical approach to the rank distribution would imply that while we are interested in a complete ordering we do not insist that it is always precise.

To test whether the rankings are significantly different in the statistical sense, a matrix of Spearman rank correlation coefficients was calculated whose values are shown in Table 7.5. While the coefficients are not, in general, very large, the large sample Student '*t*' tests indicate that the degree of association between the rankings is generally significant. In particular the association between the Gini coefficient and the relative mean deviation is significant in all but one of the ten years of the study. Perhaps this is not surprising in that both measures are related to the Lorenz curve. The association between these and the coefficient of variation is generally not significant though positive. The conclusion is thus somewhat mixed: rankings from measures which are in some way related seem to be at least statistically indistinguishable though clearly they do not produce identical rankings. Our second line of enquiry is an examination of the stability of the earnings ranking over time. Taking a single measure, such as the Gini coefficient, do the data imply that the earnings distribution ranking has remained unchanged in a statistical sense? Clearly, one would not expect this to be the case but it would be of interest to discover whether different measures exhibit statistically significant differences in the time pattern of the changes in ranking. The same non-parametric approach was followed: Spearman rank correlation statistics were calculated for each pair of different years included in the sample (making a total of $(9 \times 8) \div 2 = 36$ comparisons). If the ranking of earnings is serially correlated then we would expect the correlation between rankings to be greatest the shorter the interval between observations. Such serial correlation might be expected for two reasons. First, the employment structure in any particular occupation is unlikely to change

Table 7.4. Rank order of three measures of dispersion of earnings for six selected occupations, 1973–1982

KOS occupation	Rank order of dispersion measure by year									
	1973	1974	1975	1976	1977	1978	1979	1980	1981	1982
126 Primary teachers										
Coefficient of variation	12	13	8	6	9	9	7	8	7	7
Relative mean deviation	19	18	14	16	16	26	27	35	36	43
Gini coefficient	24	19	17	21	18	26	23	38	36	44
Mean	3	3	3	3	3	3	3	4	3	3
138 State registered and enrolled nurses and midwives										
Coefficient of variation	14	15	10	9	10	11	11	13	12	11
Relative mean deviation	15	20	11	20	25	21	25	22	15	20
Gini coefficient	18	21	14	28	31	29	33	26	24	33
Mean	51	53	40	41	43	50	51	41	35	40
139 Nursing auxiliaries and assistants										
Coefficient of variation	6	14	11	7	6	6	6	6	4	4
Relative mean deviation	51	43	51	58	58	60	58	53	54	55
Gini coefficient	50	40	52	58	58	60	56	54	53	55
Mean	56	57	53	50	51	54	55	55	53	53

177 Laboratory technicians

Coefficient of variation	34	29	40	40	42	41	40	34	29	27
Relative mean deviation	5	9	8	8	7	9	7	7	4	7
Gini coefficient	6	10	8	7	8	8	9	7	3	8
Mean	15	21	13	10	10	11	14	13	13	14

178 Engineering technicians and technician engineers

Coefficient of variation	30	30	28	26	26	26	26	25	24	24
Relative mean deviation	23	30	26	19	48	54	54	52	43	50
Gini coefficient	19	28	26	17	43	54	51	50	39	45
Mean	7	8	7	7	7	7	7	8	6	7

213 Costing and accounting clerks

Coefficient of variation	50	51	42	41	17	17	17	18	15	16
Relative mean deviation	9	10	12	13	15	15	18	18	13	16
Gini coefficient	16	17	20	20	21	24	21	24	19	21
Mean	42	42	44	43	42	41	40	42	43	43

Table 7.5. *Spearman rank correlation coefficients among coefficient of variation (CV), relative mean deviation (RMD), and Gini coefficient, 1973–1982*

	1973	1974	1975	1976	1977	1978	1979	1980	1981	1982
CV with RMD	0.23	0.13	0.10	0.07	0.01	0.18	0.07	0.20	0.23	0.01
CV with Gini coefficient	0.10	0.07	0.01	0.13	0.17	0.13	0.25	0.13	0.25	0.11
RMD with Gini coefficient	0.29	0.29	0.60	0.60	0.42	0.39	0.12	0.32	0.36	0.29

dramatically from one year to the next: the hierarchical structure within an occupation is generally subject to a considerable degree of inertia. Employers are likely to maintain short-run stability in the ratio of supervisory grades to other employees. Second, similar inertia probably applies to within-occupation wage differentials. Thus, if the proportions of workers of different grades within an occupation stay reasonably constant and the wage structure also remains relatively stable, there will be no dramatic change in inequality measures for that occupation.

The results in Table 7.6 bear out this crude hypothesis: the ranking of occupations by measures of dispersion is stable over the short term. Large sample *t*-statistics for the ranking of relative mean deviation, coefficient of variation, and Gini coefficient by occupation indicate a stronger association the shorter the time period of comparison. However, there is disagreement between measures on the significance of the association between different pairs of years. Again the coefficient of variation contrasts with the Gini and relative mean deviation agreeing on the significance of the rank correlations in only 50 per cent of the cases.

Another interesting aspect of the comparison of the ranking through time is whether the year-on-year stability of the dispersion ranking has been decreasing. During times of severe 'shake-out', one would expect more rapid change both in the distribution of employees by grade within an occupation and in earnings differentials as employers are forced into radical reappraisal of labour requirements. The results from the measures quoted earlier are indicative of such an effect without being capable of conclusive demonstration. The large sample *t*-statistics for the year-on-year change are generally very significant for the period 1975–8 but tend to fall during 1979–82. But there are considerable variations between measures and this conclusion must remain tentative.

So far the conclusions may appear rather negative. First, rankings across different measures of dispersion are certainly not identical. But we should not necessarily expect them to be so, since their technical derivation and sensitivity to distributional characteristics is different, and what is more important is whether they tell essentially the same story. Second, at a statistical level, correlation coefficients between rankings are not high, but against that the 'solidity' of the association is strong, as measured by the *t*-statistics.[5] Third, the strongest conclusion is that there is a high degree of inertia in the ranking of mean earnings and of occupational dispersions, with change occurring, but only gradually. In economic terms, the implication is that the inter-occupational wage structure is relatively rigid, and that within an occupation the dispersion does not change rapidly from year to year. These factors would seem to confirm the opinion that the British wage structure tends to inflexibility in terms of *relative* change even in the face of substantial external shocks such as

Table 7.6. *Spearman rank correlation coefficients of three measures of dispersion for 60 occupations, 1973–1982*

Inequality measure—coefficient of variation

	1973	1974	1975	1976	1977	1978	1979	1980	1981
1973									
1974	0.35								
1975	0.20	0.31							
1976	0.55	0.33	0.32						
1977	0.28	0.21	0.22	0.35					
1978	0.23	0.13	0.36	0.37	0.22				
1979	0.39	0.40	0.24	0.40	0.00	0.16			
1980	0.03	0.02	0.17	0.23	0.02	0.25	0.17		
1981	0.14	0.54	0.22	0.30	0.32	0.21	0.14	0.15	
1982	0.11	0.00	0.17	0.35	0.15	0.31	0.12	0.21	0.09

Large sample t-statistics

	1973	1974	1975	1976	1977	1978	1979	1980	1981
1973									
1974	2.81								
1975	1.53	2.44							
1976	5.07	2.64	2.55						
1977	2.25	1.62	1.72	2.88					
1978	1.81	1.00	2.94	3.03	1.68				
1979	3.23	3.28	1.87	3.30	0.01	1.21			
1980	0.24	0.13	1.31	1.78	0.12	2.00	1.29		
1981	1.05	4.83	1.75	2.36	2.54	1.60	1.11	1.14	
1982	0.83	0.03	1.35	2.88	1.12	2.48	0.90	1.61	0.69

Inequality measure—relative mean deviation

	1973	1974	1975	1976	1977	1978	1979	1980	1981
1973									
1974	0.31								
1975	0.55	0.33							
1976	0.35	0.50	0.56						
1977	0.29	0.35	0.34	0.49					
1978	0.44	0.29	0.44	0.34	0.30				
1979	0.17	0.27	0.39	0.37	0.38	0.22			
1980	0.39	0.46	0.39	0.34	0.30	0.39	0.26		
1981	0.12	0.43	0.16	0.22	0.34	0.00	0.14	0.41	
1982							0.10	0.17	0.43

Large sample t-statistics

	1973	1974	1975	1976	1977	1978	1979	1980	1981
1973									
1974	2.47								
1975	5.00	2.70							
1976	2.88	4.39	5.09						
1977	2.28	2.85	2.74	4.23					
1978	3.69	2.27	3.71	2.73	2.40				
1979	1.35	2.11	3.25	2.97	3.57	1.81			
1980	2.28	3.20	2.48	3.06	3.15	1.69	2.09		
1981	3.21	3.91	3.27	2.74	2.40	3.25	1.09	3.43	
1982	0.89	3.58	1.23	1.73	2.77	0.02	0.79	1.30	3.61

Inequality measure—Gini coefficient

	1973	1974	1975	1976	1977	1978	1979	1980	1981
1973									
1974	0.29								
1975	0.36	0.46							
1976	0.29	0.59	0.53						
1977	0.22	0.36	0.24	0.46					
1978	0.32	0.41	0.34	0.29	0.32				
1979	0.34	0.36	0.21	0.45	0.21	0.21			
1980	0.27	0.28	0.28	0.42	0.34	0.48	0.34		
1981	0.26	0.47	0.33	0.36	0.39	0.28	0.24	0.25	
1982	0.14	0.26	-0.01	0.25	0.38	0.21	0.33	0.13	0.30

Large sample t-statistics

	1973	1974	1975	1976	1977	1978	1979	1980	1981
1973									
1974	2.31								
1975	2.94	3.89							
1976	2.29	5.54	4.70						
1977	1.72	2.93	1.88	3.93					
1978	2.54	3.43	2.78	2.33	2.53				
1979	2.72	2.94	1.62	3.86	1.63	1.61			
1980	2.14	2.18	2.21	3.49	2.71	4.14	2.75		
1981	2.08	4.04	2.62	2.89	3.27	2.23	1.90	1.97	
1982	1.09	2.05	-0.07	1.96	3.10	1.67	2.66	0.98	2.36

were witnessed over the decade in question. Satisfactory explanations of that relative inflexibility still remain to be given.

7.6. Dispersion: Behaviour and Explanations

So far we have focused mainly on the behaviour of different measures of inequality over the ten-year period and the extent to which relationships between rankings by alternative methods exhibit stability. What then of the behaviour of earnings dispersion itself during a period which witnessed rapid inflation and growing unemployment? Even if the evidence so far indicates considerable stability in the ranking of occupational dispersion of pay, the dispersions themselves may well have altered in response to changes in the economic system. We noted earlier that it is often argued that dispersion has increased in recent years. How far is this true, given the evidence of our sixty occupations? If dispersion has in fact increased, is this true of all cases, and has the dispersion changed steadily or (as we might expect) does it show some cyclical variation?

For reasons which will now be obvious, the answers to these questions are far from clear cut. That different measures tend to behave differently means that it is less justifiable to focus on a particular 'representative' measure of inequality as a general indicator. Even a simple question with regard to the number of sample occupations showing an increased dispersion over the decade gives different answers according to the inequality measure used. Thus a comparison of change in dispersion measured by the coefficient of variation and the Gini coefficient produced results as in Table 7.7.

Clearly the overall trend for this sample of occupations has been towards a reduced dispersion between the end points of the decade in question, but in 17 out of 60 cases (28 per cent) the measures produced conflicting results. Any simple statement about trends in dispersion would seem to run a risk of misrepresenting a complex phenomenon.

We can nevertheless make some progress on the basis of the observation that for most of our occupations the typical time pattern of each measure of dispersion is a truncated U-shape, with dispersion falling from 1973 to 1978 and increasing from 1979 onwards, but not reaching the early 1970s level. A typical case is shown in Figs. 7.2 and 7.3, which illustrate the behaviour of the Gini coefficient and the coefficient of variation for KOS 178 (engineering technicians). Is this, firstly, a reasonable reflection of the behaviour of dispersion across the occupational spectrum? And secondly, if it is, in what ways might we expect to explain the observed pattern of dispersion behaviour?

Strictly, we cannot answer the first question comprehensively, since we are working with a limited sample of occupations. Nevertheless, as we

Table 7.7. *Consistency of coefficient of variation and Gini coefficient in showing direction of change in dispersion, 1973–1982*

	No. of cases
Both increasing	10
Both decreasing	33
Opposite signs	17[a]

[a] Including one case of no change in one coefficient.

shall demonstrate, we can obtain what may be regarded as a reasonable, if provisional, approximation to the overall behaviour of dispersion by estimating the annual dispersion of the means of our sixty occupations; and these results confirm the same broad truncated U-pattern.

Anticipating this result for the moment, we then have to consider its explanations. A number of contenders can be identified, and we discuss each in turn.

(a) Unemployment

The response of pay dispersion to changes in unemployment may be expected to depend upon the relative incidence of the incremental unemployment on different parts of the labour force (Archibald 1969; also Thomas and Stoney 1971). In the process of refining the theoretical underpinnings of the Phillips curve, unemployment dispersion was found to increase in the upswing of the cycle and decline in the downswing, and since unemployment dispersion was believed to be positively associated with the rate of change of money wages, an explanation was offered for the counter-clockwise loops round the long-term Phillips curve.[6] Unemployment dispersion for this purpose was defined in terms of regional unemployment, but occupational markets may behave similarly to regional markets in this respect. That is, as unemployment falls, its dispersion will increase. An increased number of occupational sub-markets will be subject to excess demand, leading their wage levels to escalate relative to the rest and increasing pay dispersion. In the downswing, the reverse will apply, with unemployment dispersion narrowing and wage dispersion following suit as pockets of excess demand are eliminated. Thus we may hypothesize a negative relation between unemployment and wage dispersion.

In the context of the Phillips curve and the implied non-linearity of unemployment dispersion as unemployment changes, consideration has to be given to the possibility of non-linearity in the unemployment–pay

Fig. 7.2. Gini coefficient: KOS 178, 1973–1982

dispersion relation. Beyond some threshold level of unemployment, there are at least two possibilities which might lead to non-linearity. First, even though downwards wage inflexibility is generally regarded as a significant characteristic of the British wage system, a progressive and sustained rise in unemployment may induce some downward flexibility in markets most subject to unemployment, increasing pay dispersion. Secondly, there is a possible composition effect: since pay dispersion data relate only to the employed, high levels of unemployment will remove many from the earnings distribution, and if (as we would expect) the incidence of unemployment is heaviest on the lower-skilled, lower-paid workers, this will tend to reduce their weight in the distribution, and so increase dispersion.

For these reasons, then, we will test for a quadratic relation between unemployment and pay dispersion, hypothesizing an initial negative relation but at high levels of unemployment a positive relation.

(b) Inflation

There does not seem to be any a priori reason for expecting inflation *per se* to influence dispersion. However, one of the reasons for the pre-

Fig. 7.3. Coefficient of variation: KOS 178, 1973–1982

occupation of economic policy with inflation is the recognition that it produces unpopular distributional consequences, since not all sectors of the population are able to keep pace with price increases. In the wage-earning sector itself, different groups are likely to experience varying success in keeping up with price changes, perhaps as a consequence of their bargaining power or the machinery of pay determination. Thus Milton Friedman contends that individual bargaining is much more able to adjust to accelerating inflation than collective bargaining with its more bureaucratic processes. We might then expect that the more rapid the rate of inflation, the greater will be the disparity among occupational groups, depending on the characteristics of their respective pay-determination mechanisms.

(c) Collective bargaining

The influence of collective bargaining on pay dispersion is essentially ambiguous. If trade unions are successful in achieving a mark-up on wages, they will tend to reduce employment in the collective bargaining sector of the economy, increasing competition elsewhere and driving down the non-union wage. This will increase dispersion, especially where collective bargaining is strong among highly paid workers. This argument runs in the face of sentiments which regard unions as working for egalitarianism, which should lead us to expect collective bargaining reducing dispersion.

As Freeman and Medoff (1984) have shown, the increasing dispersion argument is not in itself wrong but incomplete, for it overlooks three other trade union wage effects which reduce inequality: union wage policies lower inequality *within* establishments, they favour equal pay for equal work *across* establishments, and union gains for manual or blue-collar workers reduce inequality between blue-collar and white-collar workers. The question then is an empirical one: do the equalizing forces dominate those producing inequalities, or vice versa? Using US data Freeman and Medoff conclude:

We find that on balance unionism reduces the dispersion of wages, lowering inequality by about 3 per cent—a substantial impact for an organisation encompassing a minority of the overall workforce—and a substantial impact compared with estimates of the effect on inequality of changes in education or the age composition of the labour force. (1984: 3)

This finding is reported to be fairly accurately reflected by other studies.

For the present purpose, concerned as we are with the British case in which union membership and collective bargaining coverage are both significantly higher than in the US, and where union policies seem broadly in line with those outlined by Freeman and Medoff, we may conveniently adopt the hypothesis that collective bargaining will reduce dispersion across occupations.

(d) Incomes policy

Incomes policy is typically concerned both to restrain the growth of pay and to improve distribution in favour of the lower paid, although the latter aspect may be relatively muted in policy pronouncements. The distributional factor may be reflected in some form of exemption for lower-paid workers or in the form of a flat-rate limit which will provide a higher percentage rise for the lower paid. In principle, then, the effects of an incomes policy should be to reduce pay dispersion.

(e) Other variables

Although in this chapter we do not empirically test other variables which may be influential, there are undoubtedly other contenders, such as the effect of changing sex and age compositions of occupational labour forces. To incorporate these into the present chapter would, however, demand a more elaborate model which available space and time do not allow.

7.7. Regression Results

Regression analysis is used here to explain the extent of inequality within a particular occupation at a particular time as a function of variables such as the overall rate of inflation, the coverage of collective bargaining, and unemployment. The findings should be regarded as tentative and further research will be required in order to strengthen our conclusions. Further, we have not, as yet, constructed or tested empirical models where inequality is a causal factor which partly determines other variables. For example, from simple job search theory, one might expect that relatively greater degrees of inequality within an occupation would, *ceteris paribus*, lead to longer durations of search unemployment. For the moment we restrict our attention to the development of models which explain inequality.

Methodology

From our previous discussion, it is evident that one should not seek to make general statements about the determinants of inequality using results based on only one measure thereof. Hence throughout the regression analysis, we tested our model with each of the Gini coefficient, the relative mean deviation, and the coefficient of variation as dependent variable. While aware that these measures respond differently to changes in different parts of a given earnings distribution, we did not expect to find radical differences in the statistical association between each of these dispersion measures and a common group of explanatory variables: this expectation was broadly fulfilled, though there were a few occasions where results under different measures led to different conclusions under the strict application of standard statistical significance tests.

For all of the inequality measures there were ten years of data for each of sixty occupations making 600 observations in all. The regression problem can thus be cast in the standard cross-section–time series framework. Several econometric approaches are available to deal with this problem. One would normally select among these on the basis of their explanatory power as measured by various F statistics. For the moment, however, our results are based on a simple 'fixed effects' model. Each of the explanatory variables is assumed to have the same effect on each of the occupations and these effects are assumed constant through time. However, each occupation is assumed to start from a different but constant level of inequality on which the explanatory variable effects are superimposed.

Thus we presume that some differences in inter-occupational inequality cannot be fully explained by our data and further that these differences remain constant through time. The data certainly reject the more restrictive alternative which precludes any such distinction between occupations.

The data were transformed in such a way as to allow the interpretation of the parameters as elasticities and the data in each regression were weighted by the occupational sample size so that the more robust dispersion measures from the occupations with large samples carried greater weight. Appropriate reduction of the degrees of freedom in each regression was made to allow for the fixed effects.

Dispersion and unemployment

In section 7.4 it was argued that the effects of unemployment on dispersion may be non-linear. This was tested using a fixed effects model as described above with linear and quadratic terms in unemployment as explanatory variables. Unemployment data for each occupation were not available and an aggregate unemployment measure substituted. Nevertheless, as shown in Table 7.8, both linear and quadratic terms emerged as strongly significant under all three measures of inequality. The signs of the coefficient implied a U-shaped response to higher unemployment levels: dispersion initially falls as unemployment rises but starts to rise again as unemployment continues upward.

This finding is not at variance with the view that the initial adjustment of UK occupational labour markets during a reduction in demand is a quantity adjustment with workers in the lower tail of the earnings distribution being made redundant and thus reducing dispersion. This would be the case where the Last-In-First-Out rule is applied and there are seniority premiums. As demand continues to fall, redundancies become more widespread throughout the distribution. If the distribution of redundancies is now random, then we would expect equal proportionate reductions in the size of each earnings cohort. From our initial discussion of the properties of inequality measures such a process would have a neutral effect on measured dispersion. However, if the extent of the depression is now so great that employers renege on their implicit contracts with the workforce, forcing them to accept a greater burden of risk, then there will be increased wage flexibility within occupations and measured dispersion should increase.

This description of the behaviour of the earnings distribution during cycles has implications for its means, i.e. the nominal wage. For it implies, *ceteris paribus*, that the nominal wage will be higher at the start of a downturn than one might otherwise expect due to the composition

Table 7.8. *Regression results: dispersion, unemployment, and collective bargaining coverage*

Dependent variable	Independent variable	Coefficient	Standard error	T-statistic
ZRMD	ZUNEMP	−1.229649	0.1008668	−12.19082
	ZUNEMPSQ	0.2864551	0.2502098E-01	11.44860
	ZPCOL	−0.9490674E-03	0.3550591E-03	−2.67298
	RBARSQ	0.26346523	SEE	0.71095416E-02
ZGINI	ZUNEMP	−1.310117	0.1208628	−10.83971
	ZUNEMPSQ	0.3026075	0.2998117E-01	10.09325
	ZPCOL	−0.1247182E-02	0.4254464E-03	−2.93146
	RBARSQ	0.22787974	SEE	0.85189442E-02
ZCVAR	ZUNEMP	−0.9905882	0.8814132E-01	−11.23864
	ZUNEMPSQ	0.2324487	0.2186430E-01	10.63143
	ZPCOL	−0.5660690E-03	0.3102644E-03	−1.824473
	RBARSQ	0.22681902	SEE	0.62125920E-02

Note: Key to variables:

Dependent variables	ZRMD	Relative mean deviation
	ZGINI	Gini coefficient
	ZCVAR	Coefficient of variation
Independent variables	ZUNEMP	Unemployment
	ZUNEMPSQ	Unemployment squared
	ZPCOL	Collective bargaining coverage
	ZINFLAT	Inflation rate
	ZINCPOL	Incomes policy

effect of less well-paid workers being first to be laid off, thus offsetting
any downward pressure on wages and suggesting a degree of nominal
wage stickiness.

Dispersion and collective bargaining

In section 7.6 we argued that the theoretical effect of collective bargaining on pay dispersion was essentially ambiguous. The empirical evidence
(e.g. Freeman and Medoff, 1984, Metcalf, 1977) tends to favour the notion
that collective bargaining agreements reduce inequality. To test this view a
further variable was added to the model as described above, namely the
percentage of workers in each occupation and time period who were
covered by collective agreement. The results in Table 7.8 are consistent
with the previous studies. Conditional on the effects of unemployment on
wage dispersion, collective bargaining is still capable of exerting a downward effect on inequality. This negative effect was statistically significant
except in the case of the coefficient of variation.

Note that the percentage of workers covered by collective agreement is
not necessarily an ideal measure for the effects of unions on the wage
distribution. There may be a threshold level of the share of an occupational workforce covered by collective agreement beyond which further
coverage has no discernible effect on the wage structure. This is because
the unionized sector so dominates the settlement that the remaining
non-unionized workers are effectively free riders. This would suggest a
non-linear specification for the collective agreement variable. At present,
however, the linear specification seems to perform tolerably well.

Dispersion and inflation

Inflation need not necessarily influence pay dispersion. However, since it
is commonly believed that those groups who are already in strong positions in the labour market are most able to look after themselves during
periods of inflation, our expectation was that higher levels of inflation
would tend to be associated with increasing wage dispersion. This was
confirmed by the addition of an inflation variable to the fixed effects
model which already included the unemployment and collective bargaining terms, as shown in Table 7.9.

Dispersion and incomes policy

During incomes policies and particularly those policies based on flat-rate
wage increases, one would expect some compression of differentials. To
test this hypothesis an incomes policy variable was added to our existing

Table 7.9. *Regression results: dispersion, unemployment, and inflation*

Dependent variable	Independent variable	Coefficient	Standard error	T-statistic
ZRMD	ZUNEMP	−1.407927	0.1067596	−13.18782
	ZUNEMPSQ	0.3381707	0.2700031E-01	12.52470
	ZINFLAT	0.9376745E-01	0.1842139E-01	5.090140
	RBARSQ	0.29094699	SEE	0.69756443E-02
ZGINI	ZUNEMP	−1.422110	0.1302337	−10.91968
	ZUNEMPSQ	0.3372170	0.3293706E-01	10.23822
	ZINFLAT	0.6991600E-01	0.2247183E-01	3.111273
	RBARSQ	0.22960351	SEE	0.85094296E-02
ZCVAR	ZUNEMP	−1.082479	0.9449929E-01	−11.45489
	ZUNEMPSQ	0.2593554	0.2389957E-01	10.85189
	ZINFLAT	0.4963168E-01	0.1630586E-01	3.043793
	RBARSQ	0.23625747	SEE	0.61745561E-02

Note: Key to variables:

Dependent variables

ZRMD	Relative mean deviation
ZGINI	Gini coefficient
ZCVAR	Coefficient of variation

Independent variables

ZUNEMP	Unemployment
ZUNEMPSQ	Unemployment squared
ZPCOL	Collective bargaining coverage
ZINFLAT	Inflation rate
ZINCPOL	Incomes policy

Table 7.10. *Regression results: Unemployment, inflation, collective bargaining, and incomes policy*

Dependent variable	Independent variable	Coefficient	Standard error	T-statistic
ZRMD	ZUNEMP	−1.437576	0.1237854	−11.61345
	ZUNEMPSQ	0.3433743	0.3119801E-01	11.00629
	ZINFLAT	0.9249310E-01	0.1947056E-01	4.750407
	ZPCOL	−0.8903796E-03	0.3887275E-03	−2.290498
	ZINCPOL	0.2046828E-04	0.7288074E-03	0.2808462E-01
	RBARSQ	0.29781258	SEE	0.69417904E-02
ZGINI	ZUNEMP	−1.396780	0.1506411	−9.272233
	ZUNEMPSQ	0.3277849	0.3796654E-01	8.633522
	ZINFLAT	0.7504477E-01	0.2369477E-01	3.167144
	ZPCOL	−0.1017080E-02	0.4730633E-03	−2.149987
	ZINCPOL	0.7911375E-03	0.8869248E-03	0.8920006
	RBARSQ	0.24071568	SEE	0.84478368E-02
ZCVAR	ZUNEMP	−1.106243	0.1099830	−10.05831
	ZUNEMPSQ	0.2639811	0.2771934E-01	9.523356
	ZINFLAT	0.4824171E-01	0.1729954E-01	2.788613
	ZPCOL	−0.5514887E-03	0.3453832E-03	−1.596745
	ZINCPOL	−0.5735944E-04	0.6475431E-03	−0.8858011E-01
	RBARSQ	0.23793803	SEE	0.61677591E-02

Note: Key to variables:

Dependent variables	ZRMD	Relative mean deviation
	ZGINI	Gini coefficient
	ZCVAR	Coefficient of variation
Independent variables	ZUNEMP	Unemployment
	ZUNEMPSQ	Unemployment squared
	ZPCOL	Collective bargaining coverage
	ZINFLAT	Inflation rate
	ZINCPOL	Incomes policy

model. Rather than follow the usual practice of using a dummy variable to represent incomes policy a continuous variable developed by Whitley (1986) was utilized. It seeks to incorporate a number of effects such as the current wage norm, government pressure, and trade union response to calibrate the strength of incomes policy rather than relying on the simple policy on–policy off dichotomy. However, as one might expect, there are some problems of multicollinearity when such a variable is included on the right-hand side of an equation which already includes unemployment and inflation. While the incomes policy variable is not significant when included alongside unemployment and inflation (Table 7.10) it enters an equation where unemployment is the only other explanatory variable as strongly significant and with the correct sign. At an intuitive level, this suggests that incomes policy may have the same sort of effect as high and sustained levels of unemployment. Clearly additional work on the appropriate identification of the model is required before more definite conclusions on the effects of incomes policy can be reached.

Notes

1. For details, see Kakwani (1980: ch. 5).
2. Data available for 1970–2 inclusive were generally not consistent with that for the later period and were excluded from this analysis.
3. The choice of earnings measures is wide and different measures may well produce different distributional characteristics. At least for the initial analysis, however, it seemed appropriate to focus on the most basic measure of hourly earnings without overtime. The inclusion of overtime would be likely to affect the relation between white-collar and blue-collar occupations, and might well influence the within-occupation distributions also. While the effects of overtime on the distributive pattern are a legitimate area of enquiry, they are perhaps a refinement of the basic structure on which we concentrate here.
4. Note that the within-occupation earnings measures are probably more susceptible to sampling error than the individual occupational mean earnings.
5. Part of the reason for this is that when dealing with rank orders, a change of one place will inevitably reorder other observations, which will tend to reduce the correlation coefficient, especially when as many as 60 cases are involved, as here. Thus the relatively low correlation coefficients may be somewhat misleading.
6. In one sense, the observed elasticity of wage dispersion with respect to unemployment will be a measure of the distributional character of changing unemployment. This draws attention to a further problem: unemployment dispersion may itself be seen as an endogenous variable influenced by pay dispersion. This follows from a search-theoretic explanation of unemployment in which increased search and hence extended unemployment duration are induced by higher mean wages and/or by increased wage dispersion, both of which increase the returns to search. While this aspect cannot be pursued here, the existence of the ambiguity should be noted as an issue for further investigation.

8
Regional Earnings Differentials
R. I. D. Harris

8.1. Introduction

This chapter is concerned with relative differences in average hourly earnings between GB regions over the period 1970–82.[1] As will be seen, there were considerable differences between male and female relative earnings, and therefore these two groups are analysed separately. Because of lack of data there has been little UK academic work in this area to date. The availability of the previously unpublished NES data that are used in this chapter should hopefully increase the number (and scope) of studies. For the present purposes, however, five major areas are examined in this chapter:

1. How important is the earnings differential across regions for males and females (i.e., is it a significant factor when compared to occupational and industrial differentials)?
2. Has there been a consistent regional ordering of relative earnings (i.e., did the level of relative earnings in occupational and/or industry groups match the relative earnings position for the region as a whole)?
3. How much of the relative differential in earnings is due to occupational and/or industrial differences in employment structure?
4. How much of the observed differential in regional earnings can be 'explained' by a simple model which includes relative productivity levels and relative output levels as determinants?
5. Is there any discernible difference in collective bargaining structures and/or size of establishments across regions, and do these influence relative earnings?

8.2. The Importance of Regional Differentials

Table 8.1 presents figures for 1970 and 1982 on relative average hourly earnings for each region. These show that the full-time earnings differential varied approximately 30 per cent between the highest- and lowest-paid regions. Excluding the GLC and East Anglia, the other regions are

Table 8.1. *Relative average hourly earnings[a] in 1970 and 1982 (GB = 100)*

	GLC	South East	East Anglia	South West	West Midlands	East Midlands	Yorks– Humberside	North West	North	Wales	Scotland
Males											
1970	117.8	100.3	86.6	94.1	103.5	94.0	91.0	97.5	93.4	96.9	93.2
1982	121.5	100.6	90.9	94.0	93.6	91.4	93.3	96.4	94.2	93.5	97.4
Females											
1970	117.7	101.2	83.3	93.7	97.5	95.0	91.6	95.1	92.1	101.0	92.4
1982	119.5	97.7	91.9	97.3	97.5	88.7	92.9	97.1	93.4	93.2	95.8

[a] Adult full-time workers whose pay was not affected by absence.

Table 8.2. *Analysis of variance of average hourly earnings by region,
occupation, and industry groupings, 1970–1982 (%)*

	Males	Females
Explained variation due to:		
Region	2.1	5.3
Socio-economic group	68.1	47.9
Industry division	8.3	8.4
Year	2.1	10.9
Unexplained variation	19.4	27.6
TOTAL VARIATION	100.0	100.0

Note: All values significant at the 1% level on an *F* test.

mostly well within 10 per cent of the national average, and differences
between these other regions are fairly small. Nevertheless, 10 per cent of
average GB earnings for full-time males in 1982 amounted to £0.38 per
hour, while for females the figure was £0.27 per hour.

The total variation in real earnings,[2] as explained by differences across
industry, occupation, region, and movements over time, is reported in
Table 8.2, which shows the results from analyses of variance for male and
female earnings. Occupational differences are the most important source
of variation, followed by industrial differences (for males) and changes
over time (for females). Regional variations are much smaller, although
highly significant. That is, the regional dimension remains even after
allowing for industrial and occupational mix.

8.3. The Pattern of Relative Earnings Across Regions

The pattern of relative earnings across occupation and industry groupings
was examined to see if relative earnings in each region were ranked
consistently with the overall ranking of that region. (For a previous study
that takes this approach see Mayhew 1976*a*.) It is useful to consider what
has happened at the aggregate level for each region for the period
1970–82. Fig. 8.1 (*a–d*) presents some evidence. This diagram, which
gives relative average hourly earnings for males and females for each
region, shows that there was a marked contrast between the sexes. Male
earnings have been relatively stable. Overall, Scotland, East Anglia, and
Yorkshire–Humberside experienced an increase in relative earnings, while
there was a fairly rapid decline in the West Midlands, and a slower
decline in Wales. Female relative earnings have been unstable with fre-

quent changes in relative rankings over the period, and for the most part no discernible patterns. It is against the backdrop of Fig. 8.1 that the question of consistency needs to be discussed. It may not be very useful to expect consistent rankings across occupations and industries if (1) there is little to distinguish between relative earnings at the aggregate level or if (2) relative rankings at the aggregate level changed rapidly over time (namely the case of females).

Table 8.3 presents (partial) correlation coefficients[3] for socio-economic groups for the periods 1970–5 and 1976–82, for both males and females. These correlations are between relative earnings in each region for a particular SEG and overall relative earnings in each region (in both cases having controlled for time). Hence, the value of the correlation co-efficient in Table 8.3 signifies whether regional rankings for a particular SEG are consistent. A value of 1 would indicate perfect consistency across regions. Male relative earnings by SEG display a certain degree of consistency, especially in non-manual occupations. The figures in Table 8.3 also show that male manual rankings are less consistent after 1975. Female rankings are less consistent overall, again showing a decline in consistency for manual occupations after 1975. In conclusion, Table 8.3 shows that most SEG rankings across regions are approximately consistent with overall rankings for each region.

Turning to rankings by industry across regions, Table 8.4 presents comparable figures to Table 8.3 but for industry divisions (1980 SIC) instead of SEGs. The pattern is similar to that in Table 8.3, and again shows that relative earnings ranked by industry groups are approximately consistent with overall regional rankings (agriculture, fishing, and forestry (division 0) is the exception). Furthermore, there was some decline in consistency after 1975 in most industry groups.

Another way to approach the question of consistent rankings is to compare the *mean* rankings of each SEG by region for a particular year(s). That is, if the relative earnings for each SEG in each region are ranked from highest to lowest, it is possible to calculate the mean rank for each region and compare this to an 'expected' mean rank that would result from a perfectly consistent ranking across regions. Given that there are 11 regions and 8 SEGs, if a perfectly consistent ranking existed, we would expect the highest-paying region to occupy the first 8 places, in order of relative earnings, and hence have a mean rank of 84.5.[4] The lowest-paying region would occupy the last 8 places and its mean rank would be 4.5.[5] Table 8.5 presents the observed and expected mean ranks for 1970, for both males and females. It shows that, for males, there is a fairly close correlation between the two series (expected and observed) apart from Yorks–Humberside and East Anglia. A chi-squared test of the hypothesis that there is no significant difference between the two

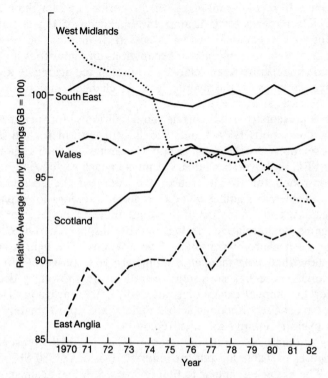

Fig. 8.1. Relative average hourly earnings in selected GB regions, 1970–1982
(*a*) Males

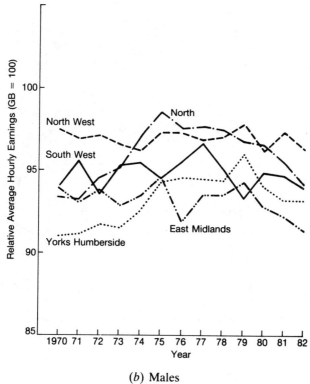

(*b*) Males

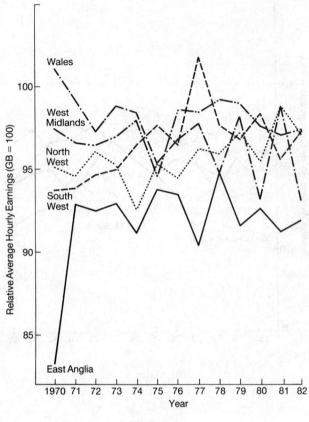

(*c*) Females

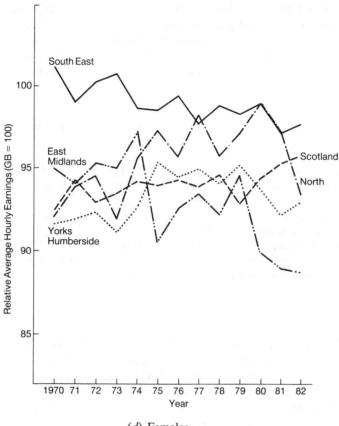

(*d*) Females

Table 8.3. *Partial correlation coefficients of relative earnings for each SEG with relative total regional earnings, 1970–1975 and 1976–1982 (males and females)*

SEG	Males		Females	
	1970–5	1976–82	1970–5	1976–82
1. Managers	0.893	0.879	0.703	0.708
2. Professionals	0.815	0.846	0.463	0.663
3. Intermediate non-manual	0.758	0.731	0.477	0.451
4. Junior non-manual	0.871	0.877	0.897	0.859
5. Foremen	0.730	0.631	0.677	0.576
6. Skilled manual	0.718	0.588	0.612	0.521
7. Semi-skilled manual	0.639	0.608	0.726	0.640
8. Unskilled manual	0.739	0.581	0.792	0.738

Note: All coefficients are significant at the 1% level.

Table 8.4. *Partial correlation coefficients of relative earnings for each industry division with relative total regional earnings, 1970–1975 and 1976–1982 (males and females)*

Industry division	Males		Females	
	1970–5	1976–82	1970–5	1976–82
0. Agriculture	0.492	0.154	0.047[a]	0.382
1. Energy	0.664	0.789	0.668	0.775
2. Metals and chemicals	0.883	0.754	0.570	0.498
3. Engineering and vehicles	0.817	0.823	0.743	0.598
4. Other manufacturing	0.921	0.854	0.801	0.759
5. Construction	0.871	0.830	0.741	0.643
6. Distribution	0.940	0.869	0.886	0.827
7. Transport and communication	0.894	0.887	0.858	0.806
8. Business services	0.842	0.773	0.853	0.828
9. Other services	0.861	0.702	0.739	0.713

Note: All coefficients are significant at the 1% level, except [a] which is insignificant at the 10% level.

Table 8.5. *Mean ranks of relative earnings by region based on socio-economic groups, 1970 (males and females)*

Region	Number of observations	Mean rank	
		Expected	Observed
Males			
GLC	8	84.5	81.9
West Midlands	8	76.5	65.5
Wales	8	68.5	63.5
South East	8	60.5	51.9
North West	8	52.5	51.1
North	8	44.5	41.4
Scotland	8	36.5	35.0
South West	8	28.5	29.3
East Midlands	8	20.5	28.9
Yorks–Humberside	8	12.5	27.6
East Anglia	8	4.5	13.5
TOTAL	88		
Females			
GLC	8	78.5	76.1
West Midlands	7	71.0	53.9
Wales	7	64.0	45.6
South East	8	56.5	45.4
East Midlands	7	49.0	44.3
South West	7	42.0	40.7
Scotland	8	34.5	37.0
North West	8	26.5	36.3
Yorks–Humberside	7	19.0	33.0
North	8	11.5	30.1
East Anglia	7	4.0	11.7
TOTAL	82		

distributions is only rejected because the observed mean ranks for the two lowest-paying regions are much higher than the values expected from a fully consistent ordering. Hence, these figures indicate that the lowest-paying regions do have some SEGs with relative earnings above what would be expected given the overall ranking of relative earnings in those regions.

For female relative earnings, regions are clearly bunched around the middle order ranking, indicating that they each have a number of SEGs with similar relative earnings. This is to be expected, given the smallness of the differential between these regions and given the pattern of change in relative earnings as seen in Fig. 8.1.

It is useful to compare the observed and expected mean ranks for different years, and to extend the analysis to include industry divisions as well. In Fig. 8.2 (a–d) the expected and observed mean ranks for male and female SEGs are plotted for certain years (Figs. 8.2a and 8.2b), while Figs. 8.2c and 8.2d give information for industry divisions. Fig. 8.2a shows that the distribution of mean ranks across regions for male SEGs is quite close to the expected mean rank distribution, although the gap between the two increased over time until 1979 after which there was a return to greater consistency during the recessionary period post-1979. The situation is similar for male industry divisions (Fig. 8.2c), although regions experiencing relatively low earnings levels have a greater mix of both high and low ranking industries. Female mean ranks by SEG (Fig. 8.2b) indicate less consistency in female relative earnings, and no discernible pattern over time. Finally, Fig. 8.2d suggests that the gap between the observed and expected mean ranks increased for females when industry divisions were looked at, and that there was a movement back to the expected distribution post-1979.

In conclusion, the pattern of relative earnings in different industry and occupation sub-groups across regions does show that there is an approximately consistent ranking with overall regional rankings, that this consistency has deteriorated to some extent over time, and that female relative earnings exhibit generally a less consistent pattern throughout. In fact, given the evidence at the aggregate level for each region (Fig. 8.1), and that changes in earnings in industries and occupations tend to be highly correlated with what happens at the national level, it is interesting that the degree of consistency is as high as it is. This suggests that there is an important and discernible local labour market effect on earnings. To consider the latter in any detail is, however, the topic of another study. Nevertheless, as a momentary aside, we present some results in Tables 8.6 and 8.7 to illustrate that it is a topic worthy of future research. Changes in real regional average hourly earnings for each industry division were matched with changes in real earnings at the regional level, while at the same time controlling for the effect of changes in real earnings in the industry at the national level. Similar partial correlation coefficients were calculated for the relationship between changes in earnings in each regional industry sub-group and changes at the national level for that industry while controlling this time for the effect of changes in real earnings in the region. The two sets of (partial) correlation coefficients are compared in Tables 8.6 and 8.7, to indicate which effect dominated—regional effects, or changes at the national level. In the case of male workers, the regional effect is obviously important and dominates

45 per cent of the time. It is especially important in East Anglia and the West Midlands regions (which has interesting connotations for the results presented in Fig. 8.1 for these regions), and for industry divisions 2, 3, 4, and 6 (manufacturing and distribution). For female workers, Table 8.7 shows that changes in real earnings at the regional level were better correlated with regional earnings change by industry 65 per cent of the time. Only in the GLC and South West regions, and industry divisions 0, 1, and 5 (agriculture, energy, and construction, all of which are traditionally not associated with female full-time employment), was there a higher correlation coefficient for national real earnings changes with regional changes by industry.

If the same exercise is performed for SEGs, very different results are obtained. Changes in real earnings across regions at the occupation level are very closely correlated with what happens at the national level for each occupation group. However, the regional effect is much smaller, although significant in a majority of cases.

8.4. Employment Structure as a Determinant of Earnings Differentials

Part of the regional earnings differential may be explained by differences in the number of employees in high- and low-paying sub-groups, rather than by separate regional or local labour market effects. The usual test for this is the standardization procedure known as 'shift-share' analysis. Basically, each region's employment structure is adjusted to be consistent with the national average, so that any divergence between actual regional average earnings and 'expected' average earnings (using national employment weights) provides evidence of a structural effect. It is usual to perform a shift-share analysis at the industry level[6] (using the 27 groupings of the 1968 SIC, since disaggregation is argued to affect the results obtained) or by using a breakdown by SEG. A more exacting test of the data involves the use of each SEG/industry SIC sub-group.[7] The results for two years, 1970 and 1982, and for males and females, are presented in Table 8.8. These show that for males there was a strong 'structural' effect in the South East region, in both 1970 and 1982. The earlier year also points to a strong structural effect in the West Midlands, while in both years other regions generally experienced a strong residual or unexplained effect. For females, there is a strong structural component in the South East and Wales in 1970, but by 1982 no region was disadvantaged by having too many workers in low-paying industries. In general, the pattern for females is one of strong residual effects; differences

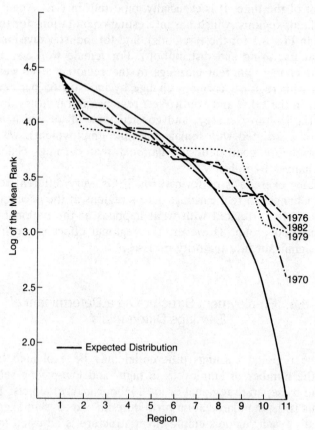

Fig. 8.2. Actual and expected distributions of the mean rankings for each region
(selected years)
(*a*) By male socio-economic groups

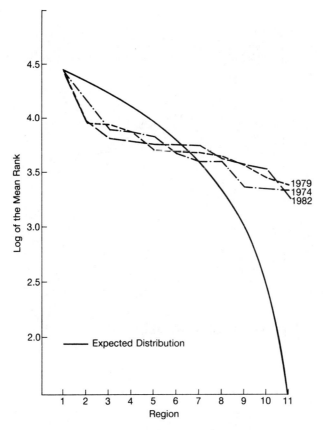

(*b*) By female socio-economic groups

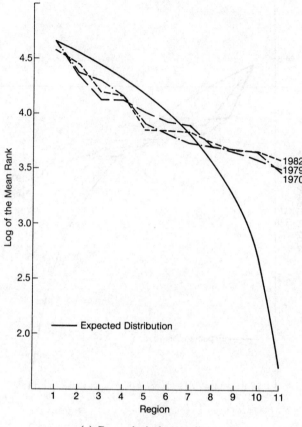

(c) By male industry divisions

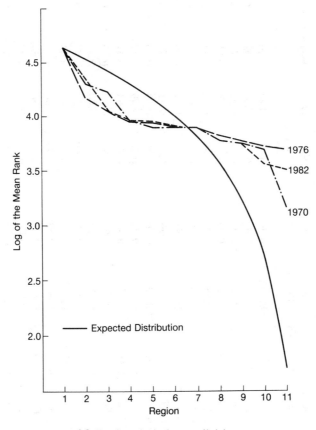

(*d*) By female industry divisions

Table 8.6. *Partial correlations between the change in real earnings by industry by region with changes at the aggregate regional level or national industry level, 1970–1982 (males)*

Industry division	GLC	South East	East Anglia	South West	West Midlands	East Midlands	Yorks–Humberside	North West	North	Wales	Scotland
0. Agriculture	0.46	0.58	0.61	0.19	0.31	0.50	0.30	0.55	0.44	0.13	−0.22
	0.69	*0.90*	*0.92*	*0.87*	*0.57*	*0.66*	*0.84*	*0.87*	*0.67*	*0.52*	*0.83*
1. Energy	0.23	0.59	0.61	0.38	0.77	0.62	0.61	0.54	0.52	0.44	0.50
	0.83	*0.68*	*0.29*	*0.94*	*0.91*	*0.72*	*0.90*	*0.82*	*0.76*	*0.95*	*0.80*
2. Metals and chemicals	0.49	0.72	0.56	0.18	0.82	0.85	0.74	0.48	0.76	0.81	0.82
	0.19	*0.72*	*0.51*	*0.37*	*0.50*	*0.16*	*0.68*	*0.65*	*0.69*	*0.55*	*−0.12*
3. Engineering and vehicles	0.70	0.85	0.63	0.67	0.89	0.76	0.88	0.70	0.64	0.79	0.83
	0.81	*0.88*	*0.29*	*0.69*	*0.29*	*0.46*	*0.50*	*0.70*	*0.71*	*0.77*	*0.72*
4. Other manufacture	0.88	0.83	0.68	0.87	0.85	0.89	0.86	0.78	0.53	0.79	0.68
	0.61	*0.75*	*−0.41*	*0.26*	*0.37*	*0.04*	*0.79*	*0.62*	*0.49*	*0.11*	*0.63*
5. Construction	0.80	0.25	0.30	0.52	0.66	0.47	0.45	0.41	0.54	0.44	0.47
	0.75	*0.94*	*0.73*	*0.81*	*0.66*	*0.77*	*0.93*	*0.92*	*0.79*	*0.56*	*0.75*
6. Distribution	0.39	0.75	0.50	0.58	0.38	0.65	0.65	0.60	0.60	0.79	0.57
	0.73	*0.14*	*0.37*	*0.57*	*0.35*	*0.26*	*0.49*	*0.69*	*0.24*	*0.41*	*0.17*
7. Transport and communication	0.76	0.68	0.82	0.72	0.80	0.78	0.87	0.87	0.66	0.63	0.80
	0.95	*0.42*	*0.77*	*0.83*	*0.86*	*0.81*	*0.49*	*0.46*	*0.60*	*0.81*	*0.91*
8. Business services	0.58	0.28	0.54	0.63	0.44	0.15	0.10	0.42	0.36	0.34	0.27
	0.91	*0.68*	*0.68*	*0.21*	*0.36*	*0.64*	*0.71*	*0.82*	*0.49*	*0.20*	*0.33*
9. Other services	0.75	0.94	0.85	0.83	0.69	0.09	0.76	0.70	0.45	0.62	0.81
	0.92	*0.94*	*0.87*	*0.20*	*0.79*	*0.68*	*0.80*	*0.65*	*0.86*	*0.72*	*0.90*

Note: Figures in italics are partial correlation coefficients between each industry by each region with national changes for that industry, controlling for changes in regional earnings.

Table 8.7. *Partial correlations between the change in real earnings by industry by region with changes at the aggregate regional level or national level, 1970–1982 (females)*

Industry division	GLC	South East	East Anglia	South West	West Midlands	East Midlands	Yorks–Humberside	North West	North	Wales	Scotland
0. Agriculture	—	0.07	0.47	-0.45	0.92	-0.09	0.39	—	—	—	0.33
	—	*0.43*	*0.55*	*0.69*	*0.80*	*0.26*	*0.65*				*0.49*
1. Energy	-0.08	0.40	0.17	-0.20	0.63	0.54	0.71	0.06	0.20	0.50	-0.32
	0.81	*0.09*	*0.47*	*0.21*	*-0.58*	*-0.33*	*-0.30*	*0.52*	*0.27*	*0.18*	*0.80*
2. Metals and chemicals	0.36	0.72	0.56	-0.42	0.18	0.63	0.67	0.69	0.24	0.35	0.73
	0.42	*-0.31*	*-0.16*	*0.45*	*0.61*	*0.42*	*0.19*	*-0.39*	*0.33*	*0.29*	*0.38*
3. Engineering and vehicles	0.73	0.80	0.11	-0.05	0.70	0.51	0.52	0.49	0.30	0.41	0.52
	0.42	*-0.06*	*-0.06*	*0.58*	*0.04*	*0.55*	*0.15*	*0.67*	*0.17*	*0.31*	*0.28*
4. Other manufacture	0.45	0.75	0.51	0.21	0.67	0.48	0.69	0.23	0.51	0.46	0.63
	-0.40	*-0.17*	*0.20*	*0.25*	*0.52*	*-0.08*	*-0.07*	*0.32*	*-0.01*	*0.25*	*0.21*
5. Construction	0.21	0.32	-0.54	0.52	-0.02	0.64	0.39	-0.05	0.40	-0.21	0.03
	0.04	*0.53*	*0.29*	*-0.46*	*-0.30*	*0.59*	*0.02*	*0.15*	*0.41*	*0.16*	*0.09*
6. Distribution	0.49	0.53	0.57	-0.02	0.41	0.49	0.62	0.79	0.72	0.17	0.52
	0.09	*0.50*	*-0.08*	*0.35*	*0.41*	*0.37*	*0.17*	*0.30*	*0.15*	*0.51*	*0.55*
7. Transport and communication	0.77	0.71	0.53	0.21	0.72	0.54	0.33	0.47	0.17	0.22	0.50
	0.31	*0.22*	*0.40*	*0.39*	*0.51*	*0.71*	*0.41*	*0.43*	*0.11*	*0.12*	*-0.06*
8. Business services	0.87	0.40	0.24	-0.23	-0.04	0.32	0.22	0.56	0.60	0.59	0.52
	-0.54	*0.21*	*-0.17*	*0.39*	*0.35*	*0.27*	*0.56*	*-0.12*	*0.25*	*0.26*	*-0.08*
9. Other services	0.90	0.97	0.87	0.83	0.81	0.57	0.71	0.38	0.53	0.67	0.80
	0.56	*0.75*	*0.46*	*0.16*	*0.56*	*0.57*	*0.52*	*0.42*	*0.41*	*0.10*	*0.92*

Note: Figures in italics are partial correlation coefficients between each industry by region with national changes for that industry, controlling for changes in regional earnings.

Table 8.8. *Shift-share of average hourly earnings by region, 1970 and 1982 (pence per hour, 1975 prices)*

Region	1970				1982			
	Actual	Expected	Structural[a]	Residual[b]	Actual	Expected	Structural[a]	Residual[b]
Males								
GLC	150.3	137.8	12.6	10.1	193.6	175.8	17.7	16.5
South East	127.1	124.5	2.6	−2.2	159.6	156.9	2.7	−1.7
East Anglia	108.6	116.9	−8.3	−8.5	143.6	149.3	−5.6	−8.8
South West	118.5	118.3	0.2	−7.7	148.5	149.7	−1.2	−8.3
West Midlands	131.0	126.8	4.2	0.2	148.2	150.0	−1.9	−8.3
East Midlands	117.3	117.1	0.2	−7.8	144.9	149.3	−4.4	−9.2
Yorks–Humberside	115.1	117.8	−2.8	−8.6	147.7	150.2	−2.5	−8.2
North West	123.3	123.2	0.0	−3.3	152.8	154.0	−1.3	−4.4
North	117.2	118.9	−1.7	−6.6	149.1	153.2	−4.0	−5.1
Wales	121.7	122.1	−0.3	−3.6	148.7	149.6	−0.9	−9.5
Scotland	117.7	121.5	−3.7	−4.8	154.3	156.6	−2.3	−1.8
Females								
GLC	95.3	91.1	4.2	10.2	135.9	128.0	7.9	14.2
South East	81.5	79.7	1.8	−0.9	111.3	111.1	0.1	−2.8
East Anglia	68.9	72.4	−3.5	−10.3	104.4	105.5	−1.1	−8.0
South West	75.8	76.4	−0.6	−4.5	110.1	108.2	1.9	−4.9
West Midlands	78.5	78.6	−0.0	−2.0	110.3	110.1	0.3	−3.1
East Midlands	76.5	77.5	−1.0	−3.0	100.3	105.9	−5.5	−7.2
Yorks–Humberside	73.6	74.4	−0.7	−6.0	105.2	106.9	−1.7	−6.3
North West	76.6	77.5	−0.9	−3.0	110.0	109.7	0.3	−3.6
North	74.6	75.2	−0.6	−5.8	106.1	107.8	−1.7	−5.7
Wales	82.1	78.4	3.8	−2.9	106.0	106.1	−0.0	−7.7
Scotland	74.7	75.1	−0.4	−5.7	108.5	108.1	0.5	−5.2

[a] Defined as average hourly earnings in the region minus 'expected' average hourly earnings.
[b] Defined as 'expected' average hourly earnings in the region minus national average hourly earnings.

between regional and national earnings were the result of factors other than employment structure.

The shift-share approach can also be used to consider the effect of employment structure on the *growth* of regional earnings. In this instance there are two underlying changes that need to be taken into account: changes in employment levels, and changes in average hourly earnings. During the period 1970–82, not only did real average earnings grow, but the distribution of employment also changed across industries and occupations.

Hence, the 'expected' growth rate of regional earnings is obtained from weighting total regional earnings (average hourly earnings multiplied by the number of employees) for each SEG/industry SIC in the base year (1970) by the change in total earnings for the comparable sub-group at the national level (see Appendix 8.1 for the actual formulae used). The 'expected' regional growth rate thus obtained is not a pure measure of whether the region specialized in industries/occupations that experienced on average higher or lower real earnings growth, since it also captures changes in the distribution of employment. To obtain a 'pure wage' measure, it could be assumed that the region experienced changes in employment levels equivalent to those that occurred at the national level. In Appendix 8.1, it is shown that such an assumption allows us to isolate the effect of earnings growth alone, although only after making the above (tenuous) assumption about employment changes.

Table 8.9 contains the results of applying the 'shift-share' technique to real earnings growth over the whole period 1970–82. Two sets of figures are given: the first allows both wage levels and employment levels to change, while the second assumes that the national employment structure changed in the same proportion as the region's employment structure. To interpret the results, it is necessary to recall that the structural effect is the 'expected' regional growth rate minus the national growth in earnings, i.e., it is the difference between the rate at which regional earnings are expected to change (given the region's own distribution of employment and initial earnings levels, and applying national rates of change of earnings and employment in each SEG/industry SIC) and the national growth rate. Hence, if the region has a favourable mix of occupations and industries, the structural effect should be positive. Turning to Table 8.9, it can be seen that the structural effect is often large and even dominates (positive residual effects), but in all cases, except the GLC, it is negative. In the case of males, the first set of results (which incorporate changes in wage and employment levels) show that the structural effect dominates the GLC, West and East Midlands, North West, and Wales. The GLC and the West Midlands also have negative residual effects, although in the latter case this enhances the negative structural effect giving the worst

Table 8.9. *Shift-share of the growth in real average hourly earnings by region, 1970–1982 (%)*

Region	Total measure[a]				'Pure wage' measure[b]			
	Actual	Expected	Structural	Residual	Actual	Expected	Structural	Residual
Males								
GLC	28.44	55.69	31.8	−27.25	28.44	25.99	2.10	2.45
South East	25.40	19.79	−4.99	5.61	25.40	23.14	−1.65	2.26
East Anglia	33.06	−3.99	−29.73	37.05	33.06	21.56	−4.17	11.50
South West	25.29	5.57	−19.39	19.72	25.29	20.67	−4.28	4.62
West Midlands	13.31	16.77	−8.45	−3.46	13.31	18.58	−6.64	−5.27
East Midlands	23.20	10.54	−16.1	12.66	23.20	15.23	−11.4	7.97
Yorks–Humberside	28.24	18.91	−6.33	9.33	28.24	23.36	−1.88	4.88
North West	23.74	20.95	−4.06	2.79	23.74	22.39	−2.62	1.35
North	27.05	21.62	−4.12	5.43	27.05	22.99	−2.75	4.06
Wales	22.07	11.35	−15.03	10.72	22.07	17.98	−8.41	4.09
Scotland	31.10	24.33	−1.28	6.77	31.10	23.67	−1.94	7.43
Females								
GLC	42.25	77.55	38.23	−35.30	42.25	39.38	0.07	2.87
South East	35.65	−28.51	−11.50	7.14	35.65	29.97	−10.04	5.68
East Anglia	50.34	8.24	−26.90	42.10	50.34	29.20	−5.95	21.14
South West	43.02	2.05	−35.80	40.97	43.02	32.37	−5.47	10.65
West Midlands	39.39	24.99	−13.85	14.40	39.39	33.75	−5.09	5.64
East Midlands	30.36	16.18	−23.45	14.18	30.36	24.11	−15.51	6.25
Yorks–Humberside	41.27	30.09	−9.38	11.18	41.27	28.45	−11.02	12.82
North West	42.98	39.14	−1.08	3.84	42.98	35.18	−5.03	7.80
North	40.93	32.84	−5.90	8.09	40.93	29.77	−8.97	11.16
Wales	26.27	14.60	−22.80	11.67	26.27	21.15	−16.25	5.12
Scotland	43.86	32.06	−6.22	11.80	43.86	35.49	−2.78	8.37

Note: National growth rates are 25.38 (males) and 38.63 (females) on average.

[a] Allows for wage levels and employment levels to change over time.
[b] Assumes the national employment structure and the region's employment structure change in the same fixed proportions.

overall performance for any region. The 'pure wage' results for males have a similar pattern, but the *dominant* structural effect for the GLC and West Midlands disappears. This last result suggests that for the GLC much of the change over the period was made up of an above average employment loss in high-paying industries, the effects of which disappear when the 'pure wage' measure is considered on its own. As to the West Midlands, the structural effect no longer dominates because the negative residual effect is stronger in the 'pure wage' measure.

Turning to female workers in Table 8.9, the results are similar to those for males, except that real earnings growth was much higher; the West Midlands performed relatively well; and the South East relatively poorly. Overall, the results from Table 8.9 are in line with prior expectations: the structural effect is large in those regions where it might be expected to be large (e.g., East Anglia, South West, East Midlands, Wales, and the GLC), but it is often diminished by a strong positive residual effect which *overall* is the more important factor for both male and female earnings growth.

Finally, it is useful, when comparing the results from Tables 8.8 and 8.9, to remember that the 'shift-share' technique applied to the distribution of earnings in any given year and to the growth of earnings over a period of years produces different effects. For example, East Anglia had the lowest real earnings levels throughout, but experienced the highest growth rates. The residual effect for 1970 and 1982 earnings levels was strongly negative, indicating that earnings were well below the national average (even after correcting for structure), but the residual effect in the growth rate results is strongly positive, since relative earnings in East Anglia in all SEGs/industry SICs 'caught up' to a large degree over the period (see Fig. 8.1).

8.5. Productivity and Output Effects on Relative Earnings

Employment structure is not the major determinant of differences in earnings across regions. Other factors need to be considered, such as differences in productivity and/or output levels across regions. Moore and Rhodes (1981) looked for a relationship between the pressure of demand (proxied by the rate of change in *relative* vacancies across regions), relative productivity levels, and regional earnings levels. However, they included a term in their model which reflected the earnings level to be expected if each region experienced national wage rates within its own employment structure. Since national changes in earnings and regional changes in earnings are highly correlated over time, this additional term tended to 'explain' most of the variation in their data.

In this section, a simple model of *relative* earnings is proposed, with explanatory variables consisting of relative productivity levels and relative output levels. The former is measured as real regional gross domestic product per employee-hour in each industry, divided by the comparable national figure. Employment figures were taken from the June Annual Census of Employment (including full-time and part-time employees) and multiplied by average hours for all employees taken from the NES data base. Hence, the average hours figures reflect high levels of part-time working in some non-manufacturing industries. Regional GDP figures were available from various *Economic Trends* (November issues), and these were deflated by the implied GDP deflators used by the CSO in the *National Income Blue Book* (1982 edition). Since regional GDP data only cover certain industries, it has been necessary to combine manufacturing into a single industry. Other data constraints required SIC Orders 25 and 26 (1968 SIC) to be combined into a single Order, hence leaving 10 industry groups for each region for the period 1971–81 (regional GDP data start in 1971 and change to the 1980 industry classification in 1982).

Regional unemployment data at this level of disaggregation are not readily available, and even if they were constructed there are good reasons for preferring GDP data as a measure of the pressure of demand. If real regional GDP grows at a faster rate than national GDP in an industry then this suggests that demand for the goods produced by the region's industry is higher. Moreover, higher growth may also be linked to an employer's ability to pass on some of his relatively higher profits in the form of wage increases. Unemployment data, which are an end result of changes in labour demand *and* supply, are a less straightforward measure of demand pressures on firms.

The actual model need was initially specified as follows

$$\ell n \left[\frac{AHE_{ir}}{AHE_{in}} \right]_t = \alpha_1 + \sum_{i=2}^{10} (\alpha_i - \alpha_1) \, D_i + \beta_{11} \, \ell n \left[\frac{Y_{ir}}{Y_{in}} \right]_t +$$

$$\sum_{i=2}^{10} (\beta_{1i} - \beta_{11}) \, D_i \, \ell n \left[\frac{Y_{ir}}{Y_{in}} \right]_t + \beta_{21} \, \ell n \left[\frac{Y_{ir}/EH_{ir}}{Y_{in}/EH_{in}} \right]_t +$$

$$\sum_{i=2}^{10} (\beta_{2i} - \beta_{22}) \, D_i \, \ell n \left[\frac{Y_{ir}/EH_{ir}}{Y_{in}/EH_{in}} \right] + \beta_{31} \, t + u$$

where $D_i = \begin{cases} 1 \text{ for an observation in industry } i \quad i = 2, \ldots, 10 \\ 0 \text{ otherwise} \end{cases}$

and   *AHE* is real average hourly earnings in region r or the nation n;
      Y is real GDP;
      EH is employee-hours;
      ℓn refers to natural logarithm;

t refers to time $t = 1971, \ldots, 1981$;
α, β are the parameters of the regression equation to be estimated;
u is the error term $N(0, \sigma^2 I)$.

This equation may look complicated, but it simply shows that the model was estimated by pooling the ten separate industry equations for each region (r) and estimating as a single equation. The model allows intercepts and regression slopes to vary across all industries, with one industry (industry 1) not represented by a dummy variable so that the coefficients of all other variables are differences from the coefficients of that industry. The model was estimated in this form in order to test for similar intercepts and regression slopes across industries, which if found allow for a pooled cross-section time series approach. To go ahead with the latter approach, without testing for the homogeneity of intercepts and slopes, imposes serious potential misspecification on the model; indeed, initial results were very unsatisfactory when an untested 'pooled' approach was used.

The final results obtained for male workers for certain regions are given in Table 8.10. Omitted regions gave unsatisfactory results, as did equations estimated for female earnings (and so results are not reported here). The parameter estimates for East Anglia show that for agriculture, banking, manufacturing, and other services there was an important relative output effect (the estimated coefficient for these pooled industries equals 0.77). However, mining, gas, electricity and water, distribution, transport and communication, and public administration all show strong *negative* relative output effects.[8] This means that as output in East Anglia changed over time relative to national changes, average earnings moved in the opposite direction for these industries. There was also an important, though weaker, positive effect on earnings through productivity changes (the β_2 parameter estimates) in East Anglia. The results for the West Midlands region suggest a much smaller output effect on male earnings for the period. In fact, banking and manufacturing have large negative coefficients. There was also a strong negative estimate for the time trend, which is to be expected given Fig. 8.1a.

Overall, the results presented in Table 8.10 suggest that relative output effects were generally positive in important industries like manufacturing although rarely above one in value. Since the coefficients in the model are elasticities (the model is estimated in log-form), this suggests that local industry effects on earnings were generally smaller than comparable national effects. Moreover, negative output effects are important in a significant number of cases, and *these* often have values greater than one. It is not clear from Table 8.10 whether there is a straightforward link

Table 8.10. *Estimated coefficients for relative earnings model (selected regions), 1971–1981 (males full-time)*

Region/parameters	Industry (SIC)									
	2	3	4	5	6	7	8	9	10	Remainder
East Anglia α	0.046 (0.2)	−0.768 (1.0)	−12.874 (2.2)	0.140 (1.9)	−0.093 (1.3)		0.144 (2.0)			0.150 (3.5)
β_1		−0.402 (2.9)	−0.353 (4.6)	−0.139 (1.9)	0.095 (1.3)		−0.142 (1.92)			0.770 (5.5)
β_2			0.233 (3.0)	−0.100 (1.3)		0.226 (2.9)	0.133 (1.8)			0.147 (1.0)
β_3										0.078 (1.0)
	$\bar{R}^2 = 0.43$	$DW = 1.8$	$n = 108$							
West Midlands α		0.163 (3.6)	0.158 (3.5)			−0.403 (8.9)			−0.03 (0.6)	0.272 (4.0)
β_1			3.849 (2.4)	0.122 (2.7)		−1.228 (1.0)		−0.697 (15.3)		0.130 (1.8)
β_2		0.086 (1.5)	0.077 (1.7)		0.054 (1.2)		0.083 (1.8)			0.081 (1.5)
β_3										−0.196 (4.5)
	$\bar{R}^2 = 0.79$	$DW = 2.3$	$n = 110$							
East Midlands α		0.242 (1.3)		−0.243 (4.8)	−0.173 (3.1)	−0.526 (9.1)	−0.067 (1.3)	−3.576 (1.6)	−0.244 (5.0)	0.092 (3.5)
β_1		−0.208 (1.2)				−1.923 (1.7)	0.069 (1.3)	0.238 (3.3)		0.316 (5.3)
β_2		0.091 (1.1)			−0.115 (2.2)	−0.094 (1.8)	0.071 (1.4)	0.155 (2.2)		−0.235 (5.0)
β_3										−0.049 (1.1)
	$\bar{R}^2 = 0.80$	$DW = 1.9$	$n = 110$							
Yorks–Humberside α						−0.426 (6.5)		−0.045 (1.0)		−0.054 (0.9)
β_1						−3.748 (2.2)				0.500 (8.8)
β_2					0.115 (2.5)	−0.257 (4.4)		0.055 (1.2)	0.055 (1.1)	−0.299 (5.8)
β_3										0.148 (3.0)
	$\bar{R}^2 = 0.77$	$DW = 1.6$	$n = 110$							
α	0.081 (0.8)		−0.114 (1.8)	−0.111 (1.7)				16.292 (2.5)		0.042 (0.5)

Region	Param	(1)	(2)	(3)	(4)	(5)	(6)	(7)	(8)
North West	β_1	0.083 (1.1)	−0.093 (0.8)	0.116 (1.9)	0.112 (1.7)	0.381 (6.1)	0.168 (2.5)		−0.537 (4.9)
	β_2		−0.882 (4.3)				−0.085 (1.3)		1.126 (6.4)
	β_3								−0.140 (2.3)
		$\bar{R}^2 = 0.61$	$DW = 1.8$	$n = 110$					
North	α		−0.492 (5.8)		−0.253 (5.0)		−0.138 (2.6)		0.222 (2.5)
	β_1	−0.404 (7.7)	−0.724 (1.6)	−0.327 (4.9)	−4.909 (1.2)	−0.088 (1.0)			0.934 (13.2)
	β_2		−0.212 (1.3)						−0.638 (8.2)
	β_3								0.147 (2.8)
		$\bar{R}^2 = 0.73$	$DW = 1.9$	$n = 110$					
Wales	α	0.362 (5.1)		−0.074 (1.1)	−0.208 (2.5)	0.122 (1.9)	−0.123 (1.9)		0.097 (1.8)
	β_1	4.686 (2.0)	−0.076 (1.1)	0.075 (1.1)	−3.816 (1.6)	−0.122 (1.9)	0.121 (1.9)		0.295 (3.2)
	β_2					−0.067 (1.1)			−0.094 (1.4)
	β_3								0.056 (0.9)
		$\bar{R}^2 = 0.55$	$DW = 2.4$	$n = 110$					
Scotland	α	−0.336 (4.5)	−0.165 (3.6)		−0.198 (3.5)	−0.113 (2.4)	0.413 (8.7)	0.208 (4.5)	0.641 (11.1)
	β_1	−3.373 (9.0)	−4.313 (1.2)						1.246 (11.9)
	β_2	−4.214 (10.5)							0.067 (0.7)
	β_3								0.060 (1.3)
		$\bar{R}^2 = 0.80$	$DW = 1.8$	$n = 110$					

Notes:

$\bar{R}^2$ coefficient of determination; DW Durbin Watson statistic; n number of observations (figures in parenthesis are t-values).

Industrial classification is as follows: 2. Agriculture, fishing, forestry; 3. mining and quarrying; 4. gas, electricity, and water; 5. distribution; 6. transport and communications; 7. banking, insurance, and finance; 8. public administration and defence; 9. manufacturing; 10. other services.

'Remainder' represents any industry not reported separately, including construction.

All coefficients, other than those labelled 'remainder', are differences from the 'industry' labelled 'remainder'. Hence, the actual value for α_2 in East Anglia is (0.046−0.15), i.e., −0.104.

between regional earnings differences and relative output changes over time. This is also true of productivity differences. Although these are positive for manufacturing in most regions (the North West and the North being the exceptions), again the values associated with these coefficients are low. In general, the major conclusion to be drawn is that, for this group of industries, the results provide little evidence of a strong local labour market effect. It may be that the model needs to be tested on (disaggregated) manufacturing industries alone, where economic reasoning suggests a larger effect is more likely. Data is not readily available with which to undertake such a study, although research is in progress.

8.6. Collective Bargaining and Establishment Size Differences across GB Regions

This final section examines briefly two areas in which we might expect to find some explanation of relative earnings differentials across regions. It is widely argued that there is a positive pay differential between those workers covered by a collective agreement and those not covered (see Chapter 14 for some new results using the NES data base). Therefore, we should expect to see regions with above average coverage experiencing higher relative earnings. Similarly, Chapter 10 shows a positive relationship between firm size and earnings, so that if there are differences in average plant size across regions we should expect this to contribute to any explanation of relative earnings differentials.

Table 8.11 presents some evidence on the differences across regions in collective bargaining structures. The percentage of the workforce actually covered by agreements is tabulated in the first column for each year, 1973 and 1978. The 'expected' figures are produced by adjusting for employment structure (both occupational and industrial). The GLC, South East, and East Anglia are all below national average levels of coverage by agreements; the North and Wales are particularly 'high coverage' areas, largely because of their employment structure. Overall, Table 8.11 suggests that there is a discernible 'North–South' difference in the level of coverage by collective agreements that is not entirely explained by 'industrial mix' (see Beaumont and Harris 1988 for a more extensive treatment).

Table 8.12 shows the effect of collective bargaining on an *intra*-regional basis, i.e. it shows the outcome of correlating earnings by industry *within* each region with the percentage of the workforce covered by collective agreements. The earnings and 'percentage covered' figures have been adjusted for occupational structure, because of important differences in

Table 8.11. *Shift-share of coverage by collective agreement by region, 1973 and 1978 (% covered by agreement)*

Region	1973				1978			
	Actual	Expected	Structural[a]	Residual[b]	Actual	Expected	Structural[a]	Residual[b]
Males								
GLC	63.3^{11}	67.1	−3.76	−7.79	60.8^{11}	62.7	−1.86	−6.89
South East	69.2^{10}	69.9	−0.67	−4.86	63.9^{10}	64.6	−0.72	−5.00
East Anglia	72.2^{9}	74.3	−2.04	−1.31	67.4^{9}	69.5	−2.11	−0.92
South West	77.8^{8}	77.2	0.50	1.79	73.0^{5}	72.0	1.00	2.16
West Midlands	78.3^{6}	76.6	1.68	1.38	70.1^{8}	70.6	−0.48	0.26
East Midlands	78.0^{7}	75.8	2.17	0.14	72.7	71.5	1.28	0.81
Yorks–Humberside	79.6^{3}	76.9	2.69	1.55	74.3^{4}	73.0	1.25	2.72
North West	78.6^{5}	78.1	0.54	2.98	75.2^{3}	74.4	0.73	4.11
North	84.8^{2}	79.9	4.86	3.79	81.0^{1}	75.9	5.10	4.86
Wales	85.1^{1}	79.3	5.79	2.89	80.0^{2}	75.4	4.58	4.46
Scotland	79.3^{4}	78.0	1.30	2.60	72.8^{6}	72.0	0.74	1.30
Females								
GLC	57.2^{11}	61.8	−1.78	−8.15	59.4^{11}	59.4	0.04	−8.92
South East	63.4^{10}	61.8	1.63	−5.36	62.8^{10}	64.2	−1.46	−3.84
East Anglia	64.7^{9}	65.2	−0.54	−1.52	67.5^{9}	69.3	−1.77	0.67
South West	68.5^{8}	68.2	0.36	0.40	68.7^{8}	68.9	−0.16	0.41
West Midlands	72.3^{2}	69.8	2.59	1.91	72.6^{4}	71.8	0.85	2.80
East Midlands	70.9^{6}	69.4	1.50	1.99	71.8^{5}	73.7	−1.89	5.06
Yorks–Humberside	71.6^{4}	71.1	0.51	3.40	68.9^{7}	70.0	−1.06	1.22
North West	71.8^{3}	72.7	−0.89	5.04	74.0^{3}	73.1	0.89	4.51
North	71.4^{5}	70.3	1.05	2.62	77.5^{2}	74.7	2.84	5.58
Wales	76.8^{1}	73.2	3.61	4.58	79.2^{1}	75.6	3.65	6.03
Scotland	70.4^{7}	69.2	1.14	1.75	69.8^{6}	69.2	0.64	0.75

Note: The sum of the structural and residual components equals the difference between the region and the national percentage covered. Superscripts denote the rank of the region in terms of percentage covered.

[a] Defined as % covered in the region minus the 'expected' % covered.
[b] Defined as the 'expected' % covered in the region minus the % covered in the nation.

Table 8.12. *Simple correlations between regional earnings and coverage by collective agreement, by industry,[a] 1973 and 1978*

Region	Average hourly earnings with % coverage by agreement					
	Males				Females	
	1973		1978		1973	1978
GLC	0.066	(0.338^d)	−0.080	(0.568^b)	0.389^c	0.427^c
South East	0.196	(0.433^c)	0.111	(0.280^d)	0.414^c	0.622^b
East Anglia	0.254	(0.412^c)	-0.324^d	(0.389^c)	0.431^c	0.444^c
South West	0.300^d	(0.635^b)	0.139	(0.431^c)	0.264	0.604^b
West Midlands	0.266^d	(0.514^b)	0.294^d	(0.732^b)	0.456^c	0.613^b
East Midlands	0.162	(0.631^b)	0.294^d	(0.543^b)	0.569^b	0.580^b
Yorks–Humberside	0.285^d	(0.691^b)	0.062	(0.663^b)	0.596^b	0.677^b
North West	0.406^c	(0.721^b)	0.299^d	(0.487^b)	0.663^b	0.437^c
North	0.202	(0.577^b)	0.292^d	(0.607^b)	0.684^b	0.416^c
Wales	0.358^c	(0.570^b)	0.352^c	(0.588^b)	0.535^b	0.249
Scotland	0.303^d	(0.697^b)	0.388^b	(0.564^b)	0.764^b	0.615^b

Note: Figures in parenthesis are coefficients obtained when the effects of the 'worst' outliers are removed (see text). No new result is given when there was no improvement.

[a] Both earnings and coverage figures are adjusted for occupational (SEG) structure.
[b] Significant at the 1% level.
[c] Significant at the 5% level.
[d] Significant at the 10% level.

bargaining structure across occupations. The data show that industry earnings were higher when there were large numbers of workers covered by collective agreements, although this is clearly more important when the effects of the 'worst' outliers are removed for male workers (see the figures in parenthesis). In 1973 the 'worst' outliers comprised the leather goods, fur, banking, and professional services industries; in 1978 the outliers were the coal and petroleum, instrumental engineering, and banking industries. Table 8.13 has the results of an *inter*-regional comparison for different industries, and it shows that the effect of collective bargaining across regions is mostly neutral, i.e. having little or no significant independent effect. There are a large number of significantly *negative* correlation coefficients, showing that those regions with high coverage rates also experienced proportionately lower earnings. (Note, no causal linkages are implied—the simple correlations reported do not 'control for' the other factors affecting earnings.) Mining, metal

Table 8.13. *Simple correlations between industry earnings and coverage by collective agreement,[a] by region, 1973 and 1978 (1968 SIC)*

Industry (SIC Order)	Average hourly earnings with % coverage by agreement			
	Males		Females	
	1973	1978	1973	1978
1. Agriculture	0.449^d	-0.011	0.647^d	0.018
2. Mining	0.557^d	0.725^b	0.066	0.780^b
3. Food, drink, tobacco	-0.711^b	-0.399	-0.489^d	-0.396
4. Coal and petroleum	0.425	-0.892^b		0.396
5. Chemicals	0.083	0.356	0.027	0.419^d
6. Metals	0.642^c	-0.153	-0.102	-0.684^c
7. Mechanical engineering	-0.085	-0.343	-0.280	-0.073
8. Instrumental engineering	-0.402	-0.671^c	0.295	0.289
9. Electrical engineering	0.034	-0.198	0.254	0.089
10. Shipbuilding	-0.167	0.437^d	0.311	0.529
11. Vehicles	0.579^c	-0.264		
12. Other Metals	0.086	0.259	-0.566^c	0.007
13. Textiles	0.378	-0.109	0.224	-0.607^c
14. Leather and fur	-0.721^c	0.292	-0.113	-0.698^d
15. Clothing, footwear	0.086	0.025	-0.576^c	0.338
16. Bricks, pottery	-0.110	-0.216	-0.389	0.611^d
17. Timber, furniture	-0.162	-0.279	-0.185	0.255
18. Printing	-0.147	0.086	-0.157	0.460^d
19. Other manufacture	0.307	0.373	0.375	-0.215
20. Construction	-0.281	-0.219	0.360	0.076
21. Utilities	-0.200	-0.322	-0.070	-0.604^c
22. Distribution	0.033	-0.069	-0.208	0.180
23. Transport	-0.745^b	-0.789^b	-0.779^b	-0.535^c
24. Banking	-0.446^d	-0.272	-0.456^d	-0.718^b
25. Professional services	-0.513^c	0.193	-0.246	-0.440^d
26. Miscellaneous services	-0.536^c	-0.385	-0.386	-0.345
27. Public administration	-0.420^d	-0.853^b	-0.625^c	0.036

[a] Both earnings and coverage figures are adjusted for occupational (i.e., SEG) structure.
[b] Significant at the 1% level.
[c] Significant at the 5% level.
[d] Significant at the 10% level.

manufacture, and vehicles are, to some extent, the exceptions, while services are particularly important examples of the negative relationships that do exist.

Overall, collective bargaining structure has a fairly strong intra-regional effect on earnings (i.e. industries with large numbers of workers covered by collective agreements tend to have higher earnings) but no inter-regional effect.

As to the effect of plant size on average hourly earnings, Table 8.14 presents evidence on an *intra*-regional basis. It shows the results from correlating earnings with the 'average' plant size by industry in the region, where average plant size is measured as total employment divided by the 'equivalent' number of equal-sized plants. The latter is the Herfindahl measure of concentration,[9] which is a better measure to use than the total number of firms when calculating 'average' plant size. The relationship between earnings and plant size was found to be non-linear in a majority of cases (i.e. convex upwards) indicating that as size increased earnings increased at a decreasing rate. The figures in parenthesis in Table 8.14 are correlation coefficients when the effects of the 'worst' outlier are removed. The 'badly behaved' industries were either the coal and petroleum industry, shipbuilding, or instrumental engineering for males, and the timber and furniture industry and other metals (SIC Order 12), as well as coal and petroleum, for females. Overall, the results in Table 8.14 suggest that differences in plant size within a region had an important effect on earnings, especially for female workers.

The final column in the Table shows the 'average' plant size for each region for all manufacturing industries, indicating that there is a considerable inter-regional difference, even at this highly aggregated level.

Table 8.15 shows the effect of size on an *inter*-regional basis for different manfacturing industries. For males, size is important, except for the instrumental engineering, timber, and furniture industries. The relationship between average hourly earnings and size in the textiles and clothing industries is important but negative. For females, inter-regional differences in 'average' plant sizes are just as important, if not more so.

Hence, in contrast to the effect of collective bargaining structure on earnings, 'average' plant size differences help to explain a large proportion of both intra- and inter-regional differences in earnings.

8.7. Summary and Conclusions

Differences in earnings across the regions of Great Britain were significant during the period 1970–82, although relatively small by comparison with occupational and industrial differentials. Indeed, these differences

Table 8.14. *Simple correlations between regional earnings and 'average' plant size by industry,[a] 1978*

Region	Average hourly earnings with 'average' plant size				'Average' plant size (no. of employees)
	Males		Females		
South East[b]	0.554[e]	(0.691[d])	0.344[f]	(0.411[f])	335
East Anglia	0.516[e]	(0.598[d])	0.822[dc]	(0.930[d])	106
South West	0.483[e]	(0.710[d])	0.734[dc]		249
West Midlands	0.099	(0.396[f])	0.720[d]		377
East Midlands	0.435[e]	(0.702[d])	0.444[fc]	(0.595[e])	247
Yorks–Humberside	0.011	(0.244)	0.676[dc]		269
North West	0.331[f]	(0.511[e])	0.351[f]	(0.577[e])	408
North	0.473[e]	(0.640[d])	0.737[d]		464
Wales	0.384[fc]	(0.610[e])	0.648[ec]		269
Scotland	0.133	(0.592[d])	0.637[dc]	(0.756[d])	350

Note: Figures in parenthesis are coefficients obtained when the effects of the 'worst' outliers are removed. No new result is given when there was no improvement.

[a] Only manufacturing industries are covered.
[b] GLC and South East are amalgamated.
[c] Linear relationship; all other figures for average plant size are represented by − (1/size).
[d] Significant at the 1% level.
[e] Significant at the 5% level.
[f] Significant at the 10% level.

Table 8.15. Simple correlations between industry[a] earnings and 'average' plant size by region,[b] 1978

Industry (SIC Order)	Average hourly earnings with 'average' plant size				'Average' plant size (no. of employees)
	Males		Females		
3. Food, drink, tobacco	0.339	(0.578^e)	0.246		342
4. Coal and petroleum	0.672^e	(0.737^d)	0.921		124
5. Chemicals	0.465^f	(0.510^f)	0.642^e	(0.797^d)	465
6. Metals	0.741^d	(0.820^d)	−0.035	(0.784^e)	743
7. Mechanical engineering	0.545^e	(0.712^e)	0.502^{fc}	(0.618^e)	256
8. Instrumental engineering	−0.166	(0.256)	0.627^e	(0.862^d)	201
9. Electrical engineering	0.283	(0.482^f)	0.525^e	(0.633^e)	906
10. Shipbuilding	0.496^f	(0.669^e)	0.779		1,617
11. Vehicles	0.687^{ec}		−0.150		3,779
12. Other metals	0.669^e	(0.747^d)	−0.050	(0.356)	93
13. Textiles	−0.767^d		0.142		137
14. Leather and fur	0.119		−0.443		41
15. Clothing, footwear	−0.507^{fc}	(0.220)	−0.246		86
16. Bricks, pottery	0.454^f	(0.621^e)	0.648^f		193
17. Timber, furniture	−0.163	(0.016)	0.150		43
18. Printing	0.585^e	(0.880^d)	0.866^d		179
19. Other manufacture	0.735^d	(0.806^d)	0.320	(0.523^f)	177

Note: Figures in parenthesis are coefficients obtained when the effects of the 'worst' outliers are removed. No new result is given when there was no improvement.

[a] Only manufacturing industries are covered.
[b] GLC and South East are amalgamated.
[c] Linear relationship; all other figures for average plant size are represented by −(1/size).
[d] Significant at the 1% level.
[e] Significant at the 5% level.
[f] Significant at the 10% level.

exhibit a weakly consistent ranking across different industry and occupational groups within regions, which suggests that there is an important and discernible local labour market effect on earnings. This 'regional effect' cannot be fully explained by poor industrial or occupational employment structures although these do influence earnings growth. The effects on regional earnings of output and productivity levels were examined, to try to explain differentials, but the results obtained were not particularly conclusive. Similarly, differences in collective bargaining structures across regions were examined, but these do not explain why inter-regional earnings differences exist, although they do help to explain intra-regional differences. Finally, differences in the size of establishments across regions were found to have an important effect on both intra- and inter-regional differences in average hourly earnings. Clearly, the NES data merit much more disaggregated research. In particular, a more formal econometric approach might prove fruitful as well as careful study of the detailed information contained in the NES beyond what is used for this chapter.

Appendix 8.1. 'Shift-Share' Formulae Used

The 'shift-share' analysis of growth in real average hourly earnings used the following formulae (note that for clarity the equations only use a single summation sign for each sub-group, while summation is actually performed across each industry SIC and then across each SEG).

$$g_r = \frac{\dfrac{\sum_i w_{ir}^t e_{ir}^t}{\sum_i e_{ir}^t} - \dfrac{\sum_i w_{ir}^o e_{ir}^o}{\sum_i e_{ir}^o}}{\dfrac{\sum_i w_{ir}^o e_{ir}^o}{\sum_i e_{ir}^o}} \tag{8.1}$$

where g_r = growth of average hourly earnings in region r;
w_{ir} = real average hourly earnings in sub-group i in region r;
e_{ir} = employment in sub-group i in region r;
o, t = time period o or time period t.

The comparable national growth rate replaces r with n (representing Great Britain) in (8.1).

$$g_{rn} = \frac{\dfrac{\sum_i \left[\dfrac{w_{in}^t e_{in}^t}{w_{in}^o e_{in}^o} \cdot w_{ir}^o e_{ir}^o\right]}{\sum_i e_{ir}^t} - \dfrac{\sum_i w_{ir}^o e_{ir}^o}{\sum_i e_{ir}^o}}{\dfrac{\sum_i w_{ir}^o e_{ir}^o}{\sum_i e_{ir}^o}} \tag{8.2}$$

where g_{rn} is the growth of average hourly earnings in region r if we adjust for national changes in earnings *and* employment levels.

For the 'pure wage' formula, we assume

$$\frac{e_{in}^t}{e_{in}^o} = \frac{e_{ir}^t}{e_{ir}^o} \tag{8.3}$$

so that (8.2) becomes

$$g_{rn}^p = \frac{\dfrac{\sum_i \left[\dfrac{w_{in}^t}{w_{in}^o} \cdot w_{ir}^o\right] e_{ir}^t}{\sum_i e_{ir}^t} - \sum_i \dfrac{w_{ir}^o e_{ir}^o}{\sum_i e_{ir}^o}}{\dfrac{\sum_i w_{ir}^o e_{ir}^o}{\sum_i e_{ir}^o}} \tag{8.4}$$

Notes

1. Only full-time adults whose pay was unaffected by absence from work have been included. Note, however, that the data base does include (for the first time) these omitted categories of workers. As should become apparent, the NES permits a breakdown of employees by both industry and occupation and, therefore, much of the material in this chapter is based upon data not previously available.
2. Deflated by the Retail Price Index (1975 = 100).
3. For the reader not familiar with this statistical technique, partial correlation between two variables x and y calculates how much of the variation in x is associated with the variation in y ($-1 \leq r \leq +1$, where r is the correlation coefficient), having controlled for a third variable z which is potentially correlated with x and y). Ice-cream sales may seem to be strongly correlated with the wearing of summer clothes, but both are correlated with temperature and failure to take account of this third variable would lead to a biased value of r, when only ice-cream sales and clothing are included in the calculation of r.
4. Since it would have the rank positions of 81 to 88, and so an average of 84.5.
5. i.e., 1 to 8, with an average of 4.5.

6. See for example Bell (1967), Black (1985).
7. This is a unique feature possible because of the data base generated from the NES project. Note, however, that the results are very similar whichever breakdown is used. The comparable national average earnings figures were computed for each sub-group using only those industries/SEGs that existed within the data set at the regional level.
8. Although the regression coefficient is positive, the estimate of β_{16} is in fact (0.095 − 0.770), i.e., −0.675. See footnotes to Table 8.10 for an explanation.
9. That is, exp-Σs_i (log s_i), where s_i is the employment share of the ith firms within the industry and region. Note the employment data used to calculate 'average' size is taken from the Census of Employment for 1978 (unpublished data).

9
Age and Earnings[1]
Boyd Black

9.1. Introduction

The period 1970–82 saw considerable changes in the structure of employment. There was a shift of employment out of manufacturing and production industries and into the service sector (divisions 6–9). Employment in services rose from 51.4 per cent of employees in employment in 1970 to 62.5 per cent in 1982, while that in manufacturing fell from 37.1 per cent of employees in employment in 1970 to 27.7 per cent in 1982. Over the same period non-manual employment rose from 40 per cent of employees in employment in 1970 to 51.8 per cent in 1982. The female share of employees in employment rose from 36.0 per cent to 40.1 per cent between 1970 and 1982. Part-time working became more prevalent, up from 12.2 to 16.0 per cent of the total. The number of non-manual females in part-time work increased particularly rapidly, up from 4.1 per cent of employees in employment in 1970 to 7.2 per cent in 1982.

In addition there were changes in the age structure of employment, in part reflecting the impact of the changes outlined above. The percentage of full-time employees under 40 increased between 1970 and 1982. This shift to a more youthful employment structure was true for males and females and for manual and non-manual workers (Table 9.1) despite the raising of the school-leaving age to 16 in 1972. There was a marked increase in the percentage of full-time non-manual females in the 25–9 and 30–9 age groups and of full-time non-manual males in the 30–9 age group. Also the proportion of part-time females (manual and non-manual) in the 30–9 and 50–9 age groups increased. At the same time the percentage of full-time males 60 years and over fell.

This chapter examines the age dimension of the pay structure. Age is intrinsically a less important determinant of pay than other factors such as occupation, industry, and sex. Its direct impact is primarily to be found in the lower age groups. For many occupations, collective agreements specify minimum rates of pay to be paid to young workers, which may be considerably less than the adult rate. In addition, minimum rates in Wages Orders are often age related. For males, these youth rates may be payable up to the age of 21 before the adult rate becomes applicable. For females, the full adult rate is usually payable at the age of 18.[2] These

Table 9.1. *Age structure of employees in employment, 1970 and 1982 (%)*

Age group	Full-time males		Full-time females		Part-time males		Part-time females		Full-time manual males		Full-time non-manual males		Full-time manual females		Full-time non-manual females		Part-time manual males		Part-time non-manual males		Part-time manual females		Part-time non-manual females	
	1970	1982	1970	1982	1970	1982	1970	1982	1970	1982	1970	1982	1970	1982	1970	1982	1970	1982	1970	1982	1970	1982	1970	1982
18	3.2	1.8	7.7	3.2	8.4	4.1	3.0	1.0	3.8	2.5	2.0	0.8	7.4	3.6	7.9	3.0	4.0	3.6	17.6	4.5	0.5	0.5	7.0	1.5
18–20	5.7	6.1	12.8	13.0	2.8	3.3	1.0	1.5	5.9	7.6	5.4	4.1	9.3	12.4	15.0	13.2	1.7	4.3	4.5	2.4	0.7	1.3	1.8	1.7
21–4	9.6	9.4	15.6	16.4	1.9	4.1	2.9	2.3	8.8	9.9	11.2	8.7	9.1	11.9	19.5	18.0	0.7	4.8	4.4	3.6	2.4	2.3	3.9	2.4
25–9	10.8	12.0	8.9	12.7	1.4	5.8	6.2	6.0	9.9	11.3	12.5	13.1	6.4	7.6	10.4	14.4	0.6	4.3	3.2	7.1	5.6	5.4	7.2	6.6
30–9	20.3	24.7	14.0	17.8	3.8	17.3	23.9	27.3	19.6	21.9	21.8	28.6	14.4	16.3	13.7	18.4	1.4	9.8	8.7	23.5	22.8	24.8	25.7	29.8
40–9	22.1	20.3	20.6	18.5	4.3	13.3	29.6	29.5	22.1	19.9	22.1	20.9	25.1	22.7	17.7	17.0	2.4	10.2	8.0	15.9	29.4	29.1	30.0	29.9
50–9	19.6	19.5	17.2	16.4	5.3	13.6	21.8	24.7	20.3	20.2	18.2	18.5	23.4	22.7	13.4	14.2	3.4	10.9	9.1	15.9	24.7	27.6	17.0	21.9
60–4	7.4	5.7	2.6	1.7	4.7	7.8	7.6	5.4	8.2	6.4	5.8	4.7	3.6	2.3	1.9	1.5	3.0	7.8	8.4	7.8	9.0	6.7	5.3	4.2
65+	1.3	0.4	0.7	0.3	67.3	30.7	3.8	2.4	1.4	0.3	1.1	0.5	1.2	0.4	0.4	0.2	82.7	44.3	36.2	19.4	4.9	2.3	2.0	2.1

Source: NES.

youth–adult differentials may be linked to a training or apprenticeship scheme.

More broadly, we are interested in the pattern of earnings over the entire life-cycle. While age may have an important independent influence on earnings, particularly for younger workers and those near retirement age, the shape of the age–earnings profile is likely to be more a reflection of the growth of skills with age and work experience.

Typically, we expect these age–earnings profiles to be concave to the age axis. The usual age profile of earnings shows low earnings on entering employment which then rise to some sort of peak between the years 30 and 50, and then start falling in the years preceding retirement. This is explained by the fact that earnings are depressed at younger ages, in part because of investment in human capital.

Using United States data, Lazear (1976) has estimated that young workers receive approximately one-third of their total employment compensation in the form of human capital. The effect of current work experience on wage growth is therefore substantial. Lazear found that, for individuals in the 14–24 age group, ageing *per se* was an important determinant of wage growth, but its importance declined with age. While, for a 19-year-old, one year of ageing implied about twice as much wage growth as did a year of experience, by the time the individual had reached 25.2 years, the effect of work experience exceeded that of ageing *per se*. Earnings continue to increase as a result of on-the-job training and possibly seniority. On-the-job training usually diminishes with age and experience. Eventually, obsolescence and depreciation of human capital, together with ageing and the associated decline in productivity, cause a flattening and usually a decline in earnings.

The chapter will examine changes in the distribution of earnings by age group over the period 1970–82. Following Wells (1983) particular attention will be paid to movements in the pay of young workers.

9.2. The Data

Ideally age–earnings profiles will be based on longitudinal data describing homogeneous groups of employees. Such longitudinal profiles will be influenced by broad macroeconomic trends in the economy. If these trends are isolated, however, the longitudinal profiles should be similar to those derived from cross-sectional data.[3]

The NES data are cross-sectional, providing average earnings of people in the same age group. This means certain qualifications have to be made before we can draw conclusions about the lifetime earnings profiles of individuals (Jolly *et al.* 1980: 53). The industrial composition of the workforce varies between age groups and over time. Also, individuals move from one socio-economic group to another. In the case of females, participation in the labour force is so intermittent that it is impossible to make generalizations about the lifetime earnings patterns of individuals.

Data are now available from the NES by age group for 1970 and 1974–82.[4] For 1971 and 1972, data for males are available only on the basis of under 21 years and 21 years and over. Data for females for these years are available on the basis of under 18 years and 18 years and over. For 1973, data for males and females are available only for under 18 years, 18–20 years, and 21 years and above.

The other serious limitation of the NES data is that they include virtually no information on human capital characteristics. In 1975, 1976, and 1979 data were collected on the number of years individuals had been employed by their organization, but we do not have data on their over-all work experience. In the early 1970s, information was collected on apprentice training. However, the Department of Employment's project restriction of a minimum cell size of 3 means we are unable to make use of even this limited information. We are, however, able to analyse the data at the level of socio-economic groups, a level of disaggregation not previously publicly available.

9.3. Male Earnings

The variation of average gross weekly earnings with age group for full-time males whose pay for the survey period was not affected by absence is given in Table 9.2. The age group–earnings profile shows an increase in earnings through the younger age groups, reaching a peak in the 40–9 age group. Earnings as a percentage of the mean then fall in the older age groups. A similar pattern is found for average hourly earnings excluding overtime pay and overtime hours.

The shape of the full-time male age group–earnings profile has remained fairly constant during the years under review (Fig. 9.1). The main exception is that it has become less steep over the early age groups. Relative earnings (both including and excluding overtime) of males under 21 rose quite sharply as a percentage of the mean in the early 1970s, reaching a maximum in 1975, before levelling off and falling back slightly between 1980 and 1982. This reduction in the 'youth' differential was accompanied by a slow decline in relative earnings in the 20–4 and 25–9 age groups. Overall, there was a compression of the differentials between age groups (as measured by the sum of the percentage differentials from the mean) which continued up to 1977. After that year, age group differentials began to widen slightly again.

Table 9.2. *Average gross weekly earnings of all full-time males whose pay for the Survey period was not affected by absence, 1970–1982 (age group as % of the mean)*

Year	<18	18–20	<21	21–4	25–9	30–9	40–9	50–9	60–4	65+
1970	33.1	58.4	49.3	83.9	99.0	111.6	113.0	106.4	93.3	80.2
1971	n/a	n/a	47.7	n/a	n/a	n/a	n/a	n/a	n/a	n/a
1972	n/a	n/a	45.9	n/a	n/a	n/a	n/a	n/a	n/a	n/a
1973	34.7	56.6	48.3	n/a	n/a	n/a	n/a	n/a	n/a	n/a
1974	39.5	62.6	54.8	84.3	100.5	111.0	111.8	104.9	92.3	76.8
1975	42.1	64.3	57.0	84.0	99.1	110.0	111.8	104.8	92.7	82.1
1976	40.6	62.9	55.9	83.5	98.5	110.4	111.9	104.7	93.1	82.9
1977	41.8	63.1	56.7	83.6	98.6	110.2	112.0	104.7	91.9	82.7
1978	41.4	63.7	56.7	83.0	97.9	110.4	112.0	104.8	91.7	83.1
1979	41.3	63.7	56.8	83.1	97.5	110.5	112.5	104.8	91.8	80.1
1980	40.5	63.5	56.4	82.0	96.3	110.3	112.6	105.2	93.7	85.6
1981	40.2	61.0	55.1	80.2	95.5	110.7	113.1	105.7	94.0	89.1
1982	40.3	59.8	55.4	78.6	94.1	110.6	113.6	105.9	92.6	86.7

Manual and non-manual

The age group–earnings profiles for manual and non-manual males differ considerably (Fig. 9.2). For manual males, gross weekly earnings rise with acquired experience and seniority to exceed average manual earnings in the 25–9 age group. Earnings are highest in the 30–9 age group, when average gross weekly earnings reach about 110 per cent of the mean. They then decline increasingly rapidly to less than 80 per cent of the mean in the 65+ age group. This may in part reflect declining physical productivity.

There was a particularly rapid relative increase in the case of manual workers less than 18 years old—up from 37.0 per cent of the mean in 1970 to 46.9 per cent in 1975 (Table 9.3). This was part of a general reduction in the dispersion of manual earnings by age group which occurred up to 1975/6, after which differentials started to widen again.

There is a greater dispersion of earnings of non-manual workers by age group. Weekly earnings of non-manual male workers are lower than manual workers until the 25–9 age group. Also, earnings in the lower age groups are lower, relative to the mean for non-manual workers, than is the case for manual workers. This may reflect the greater investment in training and the acquisition of relevant qualifications by non-manual workers.

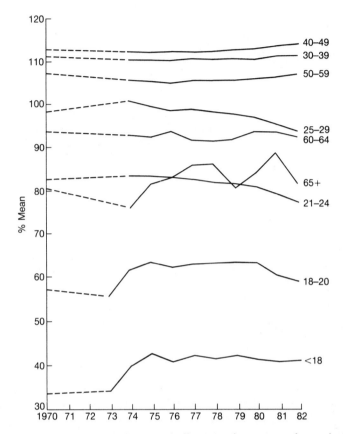

Fig. 9.1. Average hourly earnings, excluding overtime pay and overtime hours, all full-time males whose pay for the Survey period was not affected by absence, 1970–1982 (age group as % of the mean)

Typically, non-manual workers are placed on a salary scale which offers increases in pay with accumulated experience and seniority. They are also more likely to have the opportunity to move on to higher incremental scales as a result of promotion than are manual workers. Not surprisingly, we find that earnings of non-manual male workers peak in a higher age group than manual male workers. Earnings both including and excluding overtime reach between 115 and 120 per cent of the mean in the 40–9 age group. Total earnings then decline to about 90 per cent of the mean in the 65+ age group (earnings excluding overtime to about 80 per cent). Earnings in the 50–9 age group are also higher than those in the 30–9 age group. Relative earnings in the two highest age groups may have been

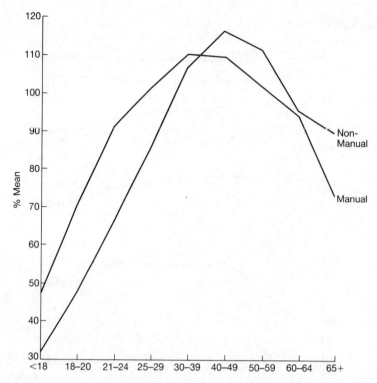

Fig. 9.2. Average gross weekly earnings, full-time manual and non-manual males whose pay for the Survey period was not affected by absence, 1982 (age group as % of the mean)

reduced by the retirement of higher earners with sufficient pension rights and savings to live on.

The same general reduction in the dispersion of age group differentials noted for male manual workers is evident in the earnings of non-manual males. The narrowing of the differentials for non-manual males continued until 1977/8, before widening again.

Socio-economic groups

Disaggregating further to the level of SEGs, it can be seen that while the age group–earnings profiles of different broad occupational groups are similar in shape, earnings of younger males in SEGs 1 and 2, managers and professionals, are relatively low as a percentage of the mean for the SEG compared to SEGs 3 and 4, reflecting the higher levels of investment in training in these groups (Table 9.4). Similarly, earnings of young

Table 9.3. *Average gross weekly earnings, full-time manual and non-manual males whose pay for the Survey period was not affected by absence, 1982 (age group as % of the mean)*

Year	<18	18–20	<21	21–4	25–9	30–9	40–9	50–9	60–4	65+
Manual										
1970	37.0	69.0	56.3	96.5	105.8	111.2	109.3	101.3	92.6	79.7
1971	n/a	n/a	53.4	n/a	n/a	n/a	n/a	n/a	n/a	n/a
1972	n/a	n/a	52.3	n/a	n/a	n/a	n/a	n/a	n/a	n/a
1973	39.0	66.9	55.0	n/a	n/a	n/a	n/a	n/a	n/a	n/a
1974	44.3	73.2	62.4	97.2	106.8	110.7	107.5	101.1	91.8	76.0
1975	46.9	74.3	64.5	95.5	104.8	109.8	107.5	101.5	93.7	90.0
1976	45.9	72.5	63.5	94.9	104.5	109.7	107.9	101.9	94.0	83.9
1977	46.8	72.7	64.1	95.0	104.4	110.1	108.2	101.7	93.1	77.3
1978	46.5	73.2	64.2	94.7	104.3	110.2	108.5	101.8	93.0	76.4
1979	45.9	73.2	64.0	93.6	104.1	110.8	109.3	101.7	92.7	73.3
1980	45.4	73.4	64.1	93.8	102.8	110.2	109.5	101.9	94.1	78.4
1981	46.9	72.4	64.5	93.3	103.3	110.3	109.4	102.0	94.1	79.4
1982	47.2	70.6	64.7	91.5	101.6	110.4	109.7	101.8	94.3	73.7
Non-manual										
1970	26.9	42.8	38.6	67.2	87.9	110.2	118.6	117.4	101.8	86.1
1971	n/a	n/a	37.7	n/a	n/a	n/a	n/a	n/a	n/a	n/a
1972	n/a	n/a	36.5	n/a	n/a	n/a	n/a	n/a	n/a	n/a
1973	26.9	41.3	37.5	n/a	n/a	n/a	n/a	n/a	n/a	n/a
1974	30.9	46.6	42.7	68.0	90.9	109.7	117.2	112.0	98.0	81.1
1975	34.3	49.4	45.5	69.7	90.7	108.4	116.5	110.9	96.0	82.9
1976	32.4	49.6	45.4	69.9	89.9	106.6	116.0	110.5	97.1	81.5
1977	34.4	50.0	46.8	70.3	90.5	108.1	115.3	110.2	94.7	87.2
1978	34.2	50.5	46.6	69.5	89.2	108.1	115.1	110.3	94.2	92.2
1979	34.6	50.4	46.7	70.7	89.0	107.8	115.5	110.4	95.2	88.7
1980	34.9	51.0	47.1	69.1	88.1	107.5	115.5	110.8	96.8	95.9
1981	33.3	48.9	45.6	67.9	86.9	107.3	115.7	111.4	99.1	94.6
1982	32.5	48.7	46.0	66.6	86.1	106.9	116.5	111.5	95.8	89.8

skilled workers (SEG 6) are relatively low compared to the semi-skilled (SEG 7), which are in turn relatively low compared to the unskilled (SEG 8). There is also relatively little decline in earnings in SEGs 1 and 2 until the 60–4 age group. Earnings in SEGs 4, 6, 7, and 8 all start to decline relative to the mean for the SEG above the 30–9 age group.

The reduction in the dispersion of earnings by age group in the mid-1970s was evident in all SEGs except foremen and supervisors, SEG 5.[5]

Table 9.4. Average gross weekly earnings, full-time males whose pay for the Survey period was not affected by absence, 1982 (age group as % of the mean by SEG)

Age group	SEG 1: managers	SEG 2: professionals	SEG 3: intermediate	SEG 4: junior	SEG 5: foremen	SEG 6: skilled	SEG 7: semi-skilled	SEG 8: unskilled
<18	*	26.6	41.9	45.0	*	43.9	51.0	59.4
18–20	41.0	42.3	53.7	67.5	64.5	68.0	75.2	82.1
21–4	59.4	62.0	74.3	87.4	79.1	93.9	91.5	93.5
25–9	78.2	82.5	89.8	106.5	93.7	102.8	101.3	104.5
30–9	98.5	103.3	105.7	118.9	104.4	110.5	109.1	111.5
40–9	108.6	114.3	110.9	118.3	105.4	110.1	107.7	109.2
50–9	108.1	112.2	105.0	105.8	97.9	102.3	102.2	101.6
60–4	94.8	103.5	93.2	93.2	93.5	90.5	96.3	93.2
65+	84.2	106.8	81.8	80.3	*	87.3	70.7	63.6
Average gross weekly earnings (£)	212.13	201.07	158.34	125.38	157.28	133.62	120.83	111.61

* Insufficient data available.

Overtime working

Paid overtime working is more prevalent among manual males than non-manual males with 47.7 per cent of manual males working overtime in 1982 compared to 18.3 per cent of non-manuals. Average overtime hours worked in 1982 are greater among manual workers (4.6 hours) than among non-manuals (1.1 hours). Overtime earnings of non-manual males in SEGs 1–3 peak as a percentage of gross weekly earnings in the 21–4 and 25–9 age groups, while for non-manuals in SEG 4 and for manual males overtime earnings peak later in the 30–9 and 40–9 age groups (Tables 9.5 and 9.6).

When we examine average hourly earnings excluding overtime and overtime hours, the dispersion of the age group differential is somewhat reduced for manual workers (Table 9.7). Overtime working is most prevalent in those age groups where earnings excluding overtime are highest, so that the age group–earnings profile of total earnings rises more rapidly than that for earnings excluding overtime, and maximum total earnings are a higher percentage of the mean. There is a corresponding more rapid relative fall in total earnings in higher age groups.

Overtime earnings declined in importance as a percentage of average earnings of manual workers between 1970 and 1982. This decline occurred across all age groups (Table 9.8).

PBR and shift etc. premiums

Payment-by-results (PBR) and shift etc. premiums are also more important components of the total weekly earnings of manual workers than of non-manual. As with overtime earnings the proportion of earnings of manual workers accounted for by PBR and shift etc. premiums rises to a peak in the 30–9 and 40–9 age groups (see Tables 9.9 and 9.10).

The age group distribution of total earnings of those manual males in receipt of PBR differs from those without incentive pay (Table 9.11). The overall dispersion of age group earnings of those on incentive schemes is less.

9.4. Female Earnings

Relative weekly earnings for full-time females by age group are given in Table 9.12. Female age group–earnings profiles are flatter than those for males in every SEG. Female workers in the younger age groups earn a higher proportion of average female earnings than do male workers in the

Table 9.5. *Overtime working by SEG: full-time males whose pay for the Survey period was not affected by absence, 1982*

Age group	SEG 1: managers		SEG 2: professionals		SEG 3: intermediate		SEG 4: junior non-manual		SEG 5: foremen		SEG 6: skilled		SEG 7: semi-skilled		SEG 8: unskilled	
	% sample working overtime	Av. hrs overtime per person	% sample working overtime	Av. hrs overtime per person	% sample working overtime	Av. hrs overtime per person	% sample working overtime	Av. hrs overtime per person	% sample working overtime	Av. hrs overtime per person	% sample working overtime	Av. hrs overtime per person	% sample working overtime	Av. hrs overtime per person	% sample working overtime	Av. hrs overtime per person
<18	*	*	*	*	*	*	17.6	0.7	*	*	22.0	1.1	30.8	2.5	26.4	1.7
18–20	*	*	*	*	14.7	1.0	30.1	1.1	*	*	32.6	2.2	40.3	3.2	40.3	3.3
21–4	17.9	1.5	23.3	1.25	18.0	1.0	32.6	1.5	43.8	3.6	44.3	3.6	46.0	4.4	38.4	3.6
25–9	14.3	0.7	18.1	1.20	17.7	1.1	36.5	1.8	53.2	5.0	48.7	4.8	50.4	5.0	47.8	4.4
30–9	9.9	0.6	16.3	1.01	15.7	1.1	38.9	2.6	49.2	4.9	53.6	5.5	50.7	5.4	49.3	5.0
40–9	10.1	0.6	15.1	0.9	15.1	1.1	35.0	2.6	53.4	5.0	53.2	5.5	50.1	5.2	51.1	5.5
50–9	8.5	0.5	11.3	0.7	15.1	0.9	29.7	2.4	46.9	3.8	47.5	4.4	48.2	4.8	51.5	4.9
60–4	8.1	0.5	9.1	0.5	13.7	0.8	21.6	1.6	46.3	3.6	41.9	3.6	46.4	4.4	45.6	4.3
65+	*	*	*	*	*	*	*	*	*	*	*	*	*	*	*	*
Average all ages	10.1	0.6	15.4	0.9	15.8	1.1	32.9	2.0	49.5	5.7	47.5	4.5	47.9	4.8	46.7	4.5

* Insufficient individuals in sample.

Table 9.6. *Overtime earnings as % of total weekly pay, full-time males whose pay was not affected by absence, 1982*

Age group	SEG 1: managers	SEG 2: professionals	SEG 3: intermediate	SEG 4: junior	SEG 5: foremen	SEG 6: skilled	SEG 7: semi-skilled	SEG 8: unskilled
<18	*	*	*	3.1	*	3.5	7.9	5.5
18–20	*	*	3.3	4.0	*	7.2	10.0	9.7
21–4	3.1	4.3	3.7	5.3	10.0	10.7	12.4	10.2
25–9	1.8	3.7	3.9	6.2	14.5	12.6	13.9	11.6
30–9	1.5	2.7	3.3	7.5	13.5	14.4	14.0	12.9
40–9	1.5	2.2	3.0	7.9	13.6	14.4	13.7	13.0
50–9	1.2	1.5	2.6	6.8	11.4	11.9	12.9	13.3
60–4	1.3	1.4	2.3	4.6	11.3	10.1	12.0	12.0
65+	*	*	*	*	*	*	*	*
Average all age groups	1.5	2.5	3.2	6.4	12.8	12.6	13.1	12.1

* Insufficient data available.

Table 9.7. *Average hourly earnings, excluding overtime pay and overtime hours, full-time males whose pay for the Survey period was not affected by absence, 1982 (age group as % of the mean)*

Age group	SEG 1: managers	SEG 2: professionals	SEG 3: intermediate	SEG 4: junior	SEG 5: foremen	SEG 6: skilled	SEG 7: semi-skilled	SEG 8: unskilled
<18	*	25.7	*	46.8	*	48.6	53.7	65.5
18–20	39.8	41.5	49.9	69.8	64.9	72.0	77.7	85.1
21–4	57.7	60.5	70.6	89.0	79.5	96.1	92.3	94.4
25–9	76.8	81.3	87.0	107.2	91.3	102.7	100.0	103.9
30–9	98.0	102.8	107.1	117.1	102.2	107.9	107.8	109.6
40–9	108.0	115.7	112.4	115.7	104.5	107.8	106.9	108.5
50–9	110.4	113.5	105.3	105.3	100.8	103.4	102.7	100.9
60–4	94.4	103.2	91.3	94.8	92.7	99.1	98.2	93.8
65+	68.5	96.1	77.0	79.7	*	101.6	76.6	73.0

* Insufficient data available.

Table 9.8. *Overtime earnings as % of total weekly earnings, full-time manual males whose pay for the Survey period was not affected by absence, 1970 and 1974–1982*

Age group	1970	1974	1975	1976	1977	1978	1979	1980	1981	1982
<18	7.9	8.4	6.7	5.9	6.3	5.9	6.8	5.9	4.7	5.0
18–20	13.1	12.3	10.3	9.1	9.0	8.2	10.1	9.1	8.0	8.4
21–4	16.0	14.9	12.8	11.4	12.2	9.4	13.1	12.6	9.8	11.1
25–9	17.4	16.5	14.5	13.8	13.8	9.0	15.2	13.8	12.3	13.0
30–9	17.7	17.3	15.6	14.8	15.2	9.4	16.3	15.4	13.4	14.0
40–9	16.7	16.8	15.1	14.5	14.7	9.1	16.3	15.4	13.0	14.0
50–9	15.3	15.2	13.7	12.6	13.1	8.6	14.3	13.3	11.4	12.3
60–4	13.8	13.7	12.3	11.2	11.4	8.4	12.4	12.1	10.5	11.1
65+	13.4	13.1	12.9	11.6	8.9	6.1	8.6	12.1	10.8	8.1
Average all ages	16.1	15.8	14.1	13.2	13.4	8.9	14.7	13.8	11.9	12.6

same age groups, suggesting that the latter are in receipt of more intensive on-the-job training. The relatively flat shape of the non-manual female age group–earnings profile suggests that women's earnings may also suffer from discontinuous work experience and lack of opportunities for advancement. An exception to this is SEG 3 (intermediate non-manual), where relative earnings continue to rise until the 60–4 group, perhaps reflecting the importance of incremental pay scales and promotion opportunities for some older women.

Relative earnings by age group for manual females have remained fairly stable over the period. There was a slight compression of differentials in the mid to late 1970s which was followed by a slight widening. A similar slight compression and later widening occurred in the relative earnings by age group of non-manual females (Table 9.13).

9.5. Part-Time Females

Part-time female employment is predominantly in the 30–9, 40–9, and 50–9 age groups (Table 9.1). Average hourly earnings excluding overtime of both part-time manual and non-manual women reach a maximum in the 25–9 age groups (Table 9.14). Weekly earnings are maximized in the 40–9 age group for both non-manual and manual female part-timers, while hours worked reach a peak in the 50–9 age group.

Table 9.9. *PBR as % of total weekly earnings, full-time males whose pay for the Survey period was not affected by absence, 1982*

Age group	SEG 1: managers	SEG 2: professionals	SEG 3: intermediate	SEG 4: junior	SEG 5: foremen	SEG 6: skilled	SEG 7: semi-skilled	SEG 8: unskilled
<18	*	*	*	1.1	*	3.4	4.7	7.6
18–20	*	2.6	4.3	1.5	*	5.4	5.9	7.2
21–4	2.5	1.1	4.1	2.1	*	7.6	6.9	9.6
25–9	2.7	1.0	3.8	2.1	4.6	8.3	7.1	10.6
30–9	2.3	1.2	3.9	2.5	4.3	8.3	7.8	10.6
40–9	2.2	1.1	3.9	2.9	5.2	8.8	7.9	10.5
50–9	1.5	0.9	3.4	2.1	3.9	8.1	7.0	8.4
60–4	1.7	1.2	2.4	1.6	3.4	7.2	6.5	6.3
65+	*	*	*	*	*	*	*	*
Average all ages	2.1	1.1	3.7	2.2	4.4	8.0	7.3	9.3

* Insufficient individuals in sample.

Table 9.10. *Shift etc. premiums as % of total weekly earnings, full-time males whose pay for the Survey period was not affected by absence, 1982*

Age group	SEG 1: managers	SEG 2: professionals	SEG 3: intermediate	SEG 4: junior	SEG 5: foremen	SEG 6: skilled	SEG 7: semi-skilled	SEG 8: unskilled
<18	*	*	*	*	*	*	*	0.9
18–20	*	*	*	1.0	*	0.9	1.7	1.4
21–4	0.7	*	1.1	1.0	*	2.0	3.3	2.0
25–9	0.3	0.5	1.0	1.0	1.7	2.8	4.3	2.7
30–9	0.4	0.5	0.8	1.7	2.8	3.1	4.8	3.3
40–9	0.4	0.5	0.7	2.2	2.7	3.4	4.6	3.4
50–9	0.3	0.4	0.8	1.8	2.5	3.1	4.5	3.4
60–4	*	*	*	2.0	1.7	0.7	3.3	2.9
65+	*	*	*	*	*	*	*	*
Average all ages	0.3	0.5	0.8	1.5	2.5	2.8	4.2	2.9

* Insufficient individuals in sample.

Table 9.11. *Average gross weekly earnings of those with and without incentive pay, full-time manual males whose pay was not affected by absence, 1981 (age group as % of the mean)*

Age group	Receiving incentive pay	Not receiving incentive pay
<18	52.7	46.0
18–20	78.8	69.6
21–4	94.5	91.6
25–9	102.2	103.9
30–9	107.8	112.7
40–9	106.6	111.8
50–9	99.4	104.3
60–4	93.1	94.7
65+	84.9	71.4

In SEG 3 (intermediate non-manual) total earnings fall off relative to the mean in the 25–9 and 30–9 age groups, before peaking in the 40–9 age groups (Table 9.15). Average weekly earnings (excluding overtime) in SEG 3 are above the mean in the 60–4 age group. Average hours worked fall below the mean in the 30–9 age group and then rise again to a maximum in the 50–9 age group.

In SEG 4 (junior non-manual) total earnings rise to just below the mean in the 21–4, 25–9, and 30–9 age groups, and then reach maximum relative earnings in the 40–9 age group, which are almost sustained through the 50–9 age group before declining. Average hourly earnings excluding overtime vary little about the mean in SEG 4, except in the two youngest age groups and in the 65+ age group. Average hours worked rise to reach a maximum in the 50–9 age group.

Part-time female manual workers are mostly concentrated in the lower skill groups, SEGs 7 and 8. In SEG 7 (semi-skilled manual) total pay, pay excluding overtime, and average hours worked reach a maximum relative to the mean in the 40–9 and 50–9 age groups. In SEG 8 (unskilled manual) pay with and without overtime rises to a maximum relative to the mean in the 21–4 age group. Average earnings and hours worked then decline in the late twenties and thirties, before rising again.

9.6. Changes in Age Group Differentials

Attention has already been focused on the movements in relative pay of young workers in Britain (Wells 1983). There was a sharp upward rise,

Table 9.12. *Average gross weekly earnings, full-time females whose pay was not affected by absence, 1982*
(age group as % of mean)

Age group	SEG 1: managers	SEG 2: professionals	SEG 3: intermediate	SEG 4: junior	SEG 5: foremen	SEG 6: skilled	SEG 7: semi-skilled	SEG 8: unskilled
<18	*	*	45.0	62.1	*	53.5	70.8	74.9
18–20	*	55.0	60.5	83.4	*	78.4	88.7	94.0
21–4	77.9	78.7	80.3	100.3	88.4	99.8	100.0	104.0
25–9	98.6	97.0	95.5	111.6	105.7	107.7	105.8	105.9
30–9	106.4	107.9	107.9	109.1	105.6	112.1	104.2	104.9
40–9	104.9	109.0	112.9	105.5	100.0	112.3	105.5	100.5
50–9	100.4	108.8	113.6	106.4	99.5	107.0	102.5	99.5
60–4	*	104.6	117.4	108.4	*	*	100.3	87.8
65+	*	*	*	96.7	*	*	*	*

* Insufficient data available.

Table 9.13. *Average gross weekly earnings, full-time females, manual and non-manual, whose pay for the Survey period was not affected by absence, 1970–1982 (age group as % of mean)*

Year	<18	18–20	21–4	25–9	30–9	40–9	50–9	60–4	65+
Manual									
1970	70.2	94.0	107.4	109.1	105.3	103.2	100.6	93.7	89.7
1971	66.3	n/a	n/a	n/a	n/a	n/a	n/a	n/a	n/a
1972	65.3	n/a	n/a	n/a	n/a	n/a	n/a	n/a	n/a
1973	66.3	91.3	n/a	n/a	n/a	n/a	n/a	n/a	n/a
1974	73.2	95.9	103.4	105.9	101.3	102.8	102.7	94.1	82.6
1975	75.4	91.5	103.5	105.5	103.3	102.9	101.3	99.5	85.9
1976	69.7	91.5	99.2	104.4	104.3	103.2	102.9	97.4	82.3
1977	69.3	90.8	102.0	106.8	105.2	103.9	102.4	96.3	85.1
1978	69.3	90.3	101.3	106.8	106.3	103.5	102.5	97.8	84.0
1979	72.0	91.2	101.3	107.9	105.6	103.5	101.9	92.6	83.9
1980	69.9	90.3	103.2	109.9	105.7	103.7	101.7	94.4	82.1
1981	67.9	89.8	101.0	108.0	105.4	104.2	102.0	97.4	81.8
1982	66.6	86.9	100.2	105.9	105.9	104.7	102.1	94.8	88.4
Non-manual									
1970	47.2	70.5	94.4	110.0	115.5	115.8	123.7	122.9	107.1
1971	48.5	n/a	n/a	n/a	n/a	n/a	n/a	n/a	n/a
1972	46.4	n/a	n/a	n/a	n/a	n/a	n/a	n/a	n/a
1973	48.6	68.7	n/a	n/a	n/a	n/a	n/a	n/a	n/a
1974	54.6	73.3	94.8	109.1	113.1	111.2	116.4	120.1	97.1
1975	56.3	74.4	94.4	108.9	111.6	111.7	111.8	107.5	87.5
1976	53.9	72.5	93.6	108.8	111.7	111.9	112.1	110.8	90.8
1977	54.7	74.2	92.9	109.0	111.8	111.8	110.1	111.4	86.6
1978	53.8	74.2	92.3	109.4	112.2	111.7	110.3	105.3	86.0
1979	55.8	74.9	92.7	108.3	113.1	112.0	110.1	101.1	84.6
1980	55.4	74.4	92.1	107.1	113.0	112.3	111.2	107.5	86.3
1981	54.1	71.8	90.3	107.8	114.2	113.4	111.2	111.4	92.5
1982	52.5	71.0	89.4	106.9	113.4	112.1	110.4	111.1	104.5

relative to the mean, in the total earnings and earnings excluding over-time of full-time manual and non-manual males in the <18 and 18–20 age groups in the years 1973–5 (Table 9.16). This increase was sustained for manual males under 18 up to 1982, but there was a fall in relative earnings in the manual 18–20 group after 1979. Relative earnings of non-manual males followed a similar pattern except that relative earnings in the 18–20 age group fell after 1980.

Table 9.14. *Average gross weekly earnings, average hourly earnings excluding overtime pay and overtime hours, average hours worked, part-time females whose pay was not affected by absence, 1982 (age group as % of mean)*

	<18	18–20	21–4	25–9	30–9	40–9	50–9	60–4	65+
Manual									
AGWE	62.2	97.6	93.0	98.1	98.0	103.6	102.9	93.8	78.4
AHEexO	83.4	95.8	100.5	101.7	101.1	100.5	100.8	95.6	87.9
Av. hrs.	66.9	88.9	82.9	96.0	96.5	102.4	105.7	98.2	82.7
Non-manual									
AGWE	34.4	66.7	99.4	101.8	101.6	105.9	101.0	89.0	71.7
AHEexO	55.5	74.3	99.6	106.8	105.9	101.6	96.0	93.8	82.3
Av. hrs.	68.8	88.0	95.2	90.8	95.1	105.9	108.2	91.4	79.2

Note: AGWE: average gross weekly earnings; AHEexO: average hourly earnings excluding overtime.

Table 9.15. *Average gross weekly earnings, average hourly earnings including overtime pay and overtime hours, and average hours worked, part-time females whose pay for the Survey period was not affected by absence, 1982 (age group as % of the mean)*

Age group	<18	18–20	21–4	25–9	30–9	40–9	50–9	60–4	65+
SEG 3: intermediate non-manual									
AGWE	*	*	103.2	96.3	98.3	104.7	101.8	92.1	*
AHEexO	*	*	90.3	*	102.4	101.4	98.1	105.9	*
Av. hrs.	*	*	107.7	101.7	93.6	103.0	112.8	75.8	*
SEG 4: junior non-manual									
AGWE	38.6	73.8	90.7	95.1	100.0	105.8	105.2	92.1	80.0
AHEexO	66.1	87.1	*	99.1	101.2	102.6	101.1	97.7	87.2
Av. hrs.	63.5	84.0	93.7	92.8	98.1	104.9	105.2	92.1	85.6
SEG 7: semi-skilled									
AGWE	*	84.9	74.0	89.3	100.2	107.7	108.5	92.0	77.9
AHEexO	*	*	91.4	98.6	101.7	101.9	103.5	94.2	82.9
Av. hrs.	*	74.4	62.5	86.5	98.6	108.5	105.7	102.8	74.3
SEG 8: unskilled									
AGWE	62.3	104.3	107.6	102.5	95.8	103.1	102.9	93.7	78.3
AHEexO	85.3	101.8	108.0	103.5	100.1	100.5	100.6	96.0	89.7
Av. hrs.	67.7	104.9	100.2	101.5	95.8	100.7	104.9	96.1	85.2

Note: AGWE: average gross weekly earnings; AHEexO: average hourly earnings excluding overtime.

* Insufficient or inconsistent data available.

Table 9.16. *Average gross weekly earnings and average hourly earnings excluding overtime pay and overtime hours, full-time males whose pay was not affected by absence, 18 and 18–20 age groups, 1970 and 1973–1982 (age group as % of the mean)*

Year	SEG 1: managers		SEG 2: professionals		SEG 3: intermediate		SEG 4: junior		SEG 5: foremen		SEG 6: skilled		SEG 7: semi-skilled		SEG 8: unskilled	
	<18	18–20	<18	18–20	<18	18–20	<18	18–20	<18	18–20	<18	18–20	<18	18–20	<18	18–20
Total weekly earnings																
1970	*	28.7	24.1	33.7	36.1	53.5	37.9	60.8	*	82.9	33.4	63.6	41.5	73.8	45.6	84.3
1973	*	34.2	23.1	32.2	31.6	47.0	37.6	57.9	*	70.5	35.8	61.7	43.5	72.5	47.0	81.9
1974	*	38.9	27.2	33.7	31.8	53.7	43.5	64.1	*	74.8	40.7	69.3	48.7	78.4	57.9	86.3
1975	*	43.0	30.1	40.6	38.9	57.9	46.5	66.1	*	65.7	43.5	71.8	52.1	78.4	59.3	85.5
1976	*	42.8	28.4	40.7	35.1	53.6	44.4	68.1	*	66.5	43.4	70.0	52.9	77.2	56.4	83.5
1977	*	43.7	*	41.0	41.8	55.5	46.9	68.2	*	63.9	43.8	70.4	51.0	77.0	58.3	83.2
1978	*	43.9	28.3	43.5	38.3	57.0	47.2	68.9	*	65.0	43.0	70.0	51.3	78.6	57.9	82.9
1979	*	44.5	29.3	41.4	36.9	56.2	47.5	68.4	*	65.3	42.4	70.9	52.1	77.4	56.2	83.5
1980	*	46.2	29.2	43.6	41.2	58.5	47.2	68.5	*	66.4	42.2	71.3	50.2	78.1	57.3	82.9
1981	*	44.7	28.0	43.2	41.4	52.1	46.0	68.0	*	68.9	44.7	70.5	50.4	75.8	56.2	83.7
1982	*	41.0	26.6	42.3	*	53.7	45.0	67.6	*	64.5	43.9	68.0	51.0	75.2	59.4	82.1
Weekly earnings excluding overtime																
1970	*	25.8	22.0	32.3	35.1	50.7	39.7	63.0	*	71.8	37.8	67.0	44.4	75.8	49.4	86.8
1973	*	33.5	21.8	31.8	28.2	41.6	38.3	59.6	*	76.7	39.4	66.0	47.8	74.9	51.3	82.9
1974	*	37.0	25.7	37.1	29.1	47.7	44.7	66.5	*	71.5	44.3	73.0	53.0	80.0	61.3	88.1
1975	*	42.8	28.5	38.7	33.8	50.7	49.3	69.1	*	66.1	47.8	75.4	55.5	80.9	63.3	88.7
1976	*	40.5	28.0	40.0	32.1	49.0	46.3	70.9	*	67.8	47.6	74.1	52.5	80.4	60.9	85.8
1977	*	40.9	30.1	39.8	38.8	51.6	47.6	71.5	*	65.5	48.3	75.1	54.2	79.9	62.7	85.6
1978	*	41.3	26.3	41.4	35.5	51.5	48.9	71.5	*	70.0	47.4	75.4	55.0	80.6	62.1	87.0
1979	*	43.2	27.5	40.9	34.9	51.4	49.8	71.4	*	70.0	46.9	75.6	56.2	80.4	60.5	88.5
1980	*	43.0	27.6	41.3	39.6	54.0	49.5	71.1	*	70.0	46.7	76.2	54.7	81.5	60.4	87.0
1981	*	42.2	26.9	41.4	37.7	48.0	48.4	70.7	*	65.9	48.7	74.6	54.4	78.6	60.8	86.1
1982	*	39.8	25.7	41.5	*	49.9	46.8	69.8	*	65.9	48.6	72.0	53.7	77.7	65.5	85.1

* Insufficient data available.

Female relative earnings in the under 18 and 18–20 age groups have been comparatively stable. There was a sharp increase in earnings both with and without overtime relative to the mean for both manual and non-manual females under 18 years in 1973–5. This increase was reversed somewhat for young manual females in the mid-1970s and was followed by a period of relatively stable differentials until 1979/80. Since then there has been a slight decline in the relative earnings of manual females in the under 18 and 18–20 age groups, a decline which is common across all SEGs for which data are available (Table 9.17). Following the increase in relative earnings up to 1975, the earnings of non-manual females in the under 18 and 18–20 age groups remained stable up to 1980, since when there has been a slight decline relative to the mean for non-manual females.

Wells (1983) concluded that little of the movement of relative earnings of young people up to 1979 could be attributed to compositional changes, whether changes in employment or in hours worked within broad industrial groups. He attributed much of the increase in relative average earnings in the early 1970s to increases in the age composition of youth employment resulting from the raising of the school-leaving age to 16 in 1972. He attributed the increase in relative pay for the same employment mostly to factors other than the demand for, or the supply of, labour. The lowering of the age of majority from 21 to 18 in 1969 was followed by a lowering of the age at which adult rates of pay were paid and a consequent increase in the rates of pay of young men relative to adults (Wells 1983: 12).

It is also likely that the April–November 1973 incomes policy (£1 plus 4 per cent), the threshold payments of £4.40 paid in 1974, and the £6 lump sum entitlement in 1975/6 will also have contributed to the general narrowing of age group differentials in this period of the early 1970s.[6] The matter is further complicated by the passage of the Equal Pay Act 1970 which came into effect in 1975, and which may have had a differential effect on the pay of women of different age groups, so disguising other influences on age group differentials. It is impossible to disentangle these various influences.

While there is some evidence of a slight widening of the youth–adult differential since 1979/80, this may be due as much to the raising of relative pay of the more highly paid workers, who tend to be older, rather than to a widening of age group differentials *per se*. The stickiness downwards of relative earnings of workers in the under 18 and 18–20 years age groups in the face of a more than doubling of the youth unemployment rate since 1975 is one of the most notable features of the pay structure. In SEG 8, unskilled manuals, relative earnings of males under 18 years have actually risen since 1979, but this is largely the result

Table 9.17. *Average gross weekly earnings and average hourly earnings excluding overtime pay and overtime hours, full-time women whose pay was not affected by absence, 18 and 18–20 age groups; 1970 and 1973–1982 (age group as % of the mean)*

Year	SEG 1: managers		SEG 2: professionals		SEG 3: intermediate		SEG 4: junior		SEG 5: foremen		SEG 6: skilled		SEG 7: semi-skilled		SEG 8: unskilled	
	<18	18–20	<18	18–20	<18	18–20	<18	18–20	<18	18–20	<18	18–20	<18	18–20	<18	18–20
Total weekly earnings																
1970	*	*	*	47.5	42.3	61.7	57.3	84.5	*	*	65.9	91.0	69.0	94.1	77.4	98.3
1973	*	*	*	50.7	38.2	52.5	56.8	80.1	*	*	52.7	86.8	70.6	91.9	68.5	95.4
1974	*	*	*	51.4	39.8	56.1	62.7	83.9	*	*	56.9	89.8	77.3	97.2	73.8	99.5
1975	*	*	*	56.1	47.1	62.0	66.2	86.4	*	*	71.0	81.1	76.0	93.6	79.1	96.3
1976	*	*	*	55.1	45.6	62.6	64.2	84.6	*	*	55.8	83.6	71.6	93.8	75.9	96.7
1977	*	*	*	61.4	45.7	64.3	64.3	85.7	*	*	57.0	84.6	72.5	92.1	75.2	96.4
1978	*	*	*	57.1	42.3	61.0	62.7	86.1	*	*	57.6	81.5	71.4	93.0	76.2	94.8
1979	*	*	*	60.3	*	63.7	64.5	85.8	*	*	56.2	85.7	74.4	92.1	80.0	96.2
1980	*	*	*	57.4	50.3	66.4	64.6	85.5	*	*	57.7	84.0	73.7	91.2	77.0	97.8
1981	*	*	*	53.5	44.5	60.3	64.8	85.2	*	*	50.8	81.8	72.6	91.5	77.4	97.4
1982	*	*	*	55.0	45.0	60.5	62.1	83.4	*	*	53.5	78.4	70.8	88.2	74.9	94.0
Weekly earnings excluding overtime																
1970	*	*	*	45.5	38.3	55.4	56.8	84.2	*	*	64.6	89.2	69.6	93.7	74.7	96.3
1973	*	*	*	46.5	32.2	43.6	55.5	79.9	*	*	52.8	84.7	71.0	91.3	67.2	92.0
1974	*	*	*	47.6	33.2	47.2	62.5	83.5	*	*	59.3	87.2	77.0	96.1	72.8	96.0
1975	*	*	*	54.1	39.1	51.7	66.0	86.2	*	*	70.9	80.9	75.6	92.8	77.2	94.1
1976	*	*	*	51.6	38.8	51.5	63.3	84.3	*	*	55.8	83.1	71.1	93.2	74.4	94.7
1977	*	*	*	58.5	40.1	54.3	63.6	85.2	*	*	56.9	83.9	71.6	92.0	73.6	94.3
1978	*	*	*	55.2	36.6	51.2	62.3	85.3	*	*	57.6	81.3	71.6	92.1	73.3	92.2
1979	*	*	*	56.8	38.0	53.0	63.9	85.1	*	*	57.3	85.8	74.4	91.7	76.6	93.5
1980	*	*	*	54.9	40.0	57.1	64.0	84.6	*	*	57.7	85.1	74.4	90.9	73.8	96.5
1981	*	*	*	51.8	39.6	52.5	64.5	84.6	*	*	51.6	81.1	72.7	90.6	74.6	95.2
1982	*	*	*	54.9	39.4	53.3	61.6	83.0	*	*	52.8	77.5	70.9	88.7	72.2	92.2

* Insufficient data available.

of a shift in the structure of employment into higher-paying industry divisions such as energy.

9.7. Summary and Conclusions

1. The age group–earnings profiles for manual and non-manual males differ considerably. Total earnings of non-manual males in the lower age groups are lower relative to the mean for non-manual males than is the case for manual males. Earnings of non-manual males peak in a higher age group than manual males.

2. Overtime earnings of non-manual males in the three higher non-manual groups peak as a percentage of total earnings in the 21–4 and 25–9 age groups. For non-manuals in the junior category and for manual males, overtime earnings peak later in the 30–9 and 40–9 age groups.

3. Female age group–earnings profiles are flatter over the younger age groups than the corresponding profiles for males in every SEG. However, in the intermediate group (SEG 3), relative earnings of females continue to rise to the 60–4 age group, where total earnings are 117.4 per cent of the mean.

4. Part-time female employment is predominantly in the 30–9, 40–9, and 50–9 age groups. In 1982, total earnings are maximized in the 40–9 age group for both non-manual and manual female part-timers. Hours worked reach a peak in the 50–9 age group (except in SEG 7).

5. Over the period 1970–82, the shape of the full-time male age group–earnings profile becomes less steep as a result of the rise in relative earnings of males under 21. Female relative earnings in the under 18 and 18–20 age groups remain relatively stable.

6. More generally there is a compression of age group differentials. For manual males this continues up to 1975 before widening again; for non-manual males it continues up to 1977 before widening (except in SEG 5). This compression of differentials also occurs in the earnings of manual and non-manual females, though it is less pronounced.

7. Several explanations of this compression can be advanced, but it is not possible to disentangle their relative importance. They include the raising of the school-leaving age to 16 in 1972; the lowering of the age at which adult rates of pay are paid; and the impact of various equalizing clauses in incomes policies between 1973 and 1976.

8. There is evidence of a slight widening of the male youth–adult differentials after 1979. However, relative earnings of manual males under 18 in SEG 8 continue to rise up to 1982, despite the rapid increase in youth unemployment. This is largely due to changes in the structure of

employment with an increase in young people employed in high-paying sectors such as energy.

Notes

1. The author acknowledges the assistance of Mary Trainor, Karen Black, and Ann Toman in processing the NES data.
2. For details of time rates of wages negotiated between organizations of employers and workpeople or laid down as minimum rates in Wages Orders, and payable to young workers, see Department of Employment, *Time Rates* (annual: Appendix I).
3. There may also be cohort effects when the relative size of each birth cohort can affect their relative earnings. This could mean that even when broad economic trends have been accounted for the cross-section data may not adequately reflect longitudinal profiles. I am grateful to Cathy Gibbins for this point.
4. The method of calculating gross weekly wages was different in 1970 and therefore the comparison between 1970 and other years may not be strictly valid.
5. Calculated by adding the sum of the percentage differentials from the mean.
6. Ashenfelter and Layard (1983) discuss the equalizing effect of these various measures.

10
Earnings by Size of Company and Establishment

Andrew Thomson and Carmen Sanjines

Many economists have noted a relationship between size of establishment or company and earnings, but as yet the subject has not been satisfactorily explained. Thus Lester (1967) noted of the American data, 'clearly size of establishment differences in employee compensation need much more thorough study and analysis than they have received to date. In the absence of technically competent underpinnings the conventional explanations are not convincing.' More recently in the United States, Weiss and Landau (1984) remarked ruefully: 'one of the unsolved riddles of modern labor economics is why for many occupations wages vary with firm size. Attempts to explain this phenomenon within a model of perfect information with an infinitely elastic supply of labor have encountered dead ends.' Similarly in the British context, Sawyer (1973) commented after trying out various equations: 'size of plant still remains significant and in economic terms this remains something of an enigma.' The most recent major British study of the subject, by George, McNabb, and Shorey (1977), stated the problem as follows:

It would be misleading to pretend, however, that the work which has so far been undertaken has led to decisive results.... It would seem therefore that while the size concept is an operational concept the precise causal mechanism underlying it remains somewhat obscure.... The majority of the cross-sectional statistical studies conducted by economists so far have used industry data because information upon individual units is not available.... Even if a satisfactory specification of the independent variables is achieved a rigorous test of the size effect is difficult to set up because of the complexities of the relationship involved.

In the various studies to date, a considerable number of explanatory variables have been suggested and these will be examined later, after the basic data have been presented. It should be noted however that writers to date have not been able to define whether, rather like bargaining structure, size is an intermediary variable acting as a proxy for other variables, or whether it is an influence in its own right.

The 1979 New Earnings Survey gives a particular opportunity to examine the relationship between size and earnings. Size of plant or company has not been a regular feature of the New Earnings Survey, but was included in 1979 because of the obligations to the EEC regulation 495; further details are given in Appendix 10.1. As a result what is possible through the cross-sectional analysis is limited compared to what is possible over time in most of the other chapters, but nevertheless the data available do permit some of the objectives of George, McNabb, and Shorey to be met, namely to obtain a data base which while permitting disaggregation also allows standardization on such important dimensions as industrial sector and occupational grouping.

The difference between the two has been recognized but largely ignored by writers, except by Marginson (1984), and comments on the relationship between the two will be made during the chapter. The structure of the chapter is to introduce the data according to their internal characteristics in section 10.1, then to discuss possible explanations for the size effect in section 10.2. As with the other data sets in this book, the available data are aggregated according to the methods described in Chapter 1 and the socio-economic categories and industrial classification in Appendices B and C. The total number of observations available is over 38,000 on some 117,000 individuals, and covers the whole of the economy. In this sense it is a major advance over any data set previously available, since previous sets have had to use the industry as the base rather than the individual person or establishment or company. This chapter deals with both establishment size and company size.

10.1. The New Earnings Survey Data

Pay and company size

What is immediately noticeable in Table 10.1 is the almost complete regularity of the pay gradient, with a substantial premium as company size increases. There is only one very minor reversal in the largest category for males, which may be due to public-sector influence in that particular cell, but overall the gradients are extraordinarily monotonic in a way which is rarely found in pay categorizations. The premium for working in the largest size category rather than the smallest is 16.9 per cent for men, and 26.9 per cent for women. The pattern and size of the pay differentials exclude any possibility of random distribution, while the regularity of the dispersions suggests that there are no strong skewing factors at work. Nevertheless, a key part of any explanation of the earnings differentials could lie in the composition of the various size categories. These have been broken down according to a number of

Table 10.1. *Average weekly pay by company size, 1979*

Company size	Males			Females		
	Average (£)	Standard deviation (£)	No.	Average (£)	Standard deviation (£)	No.
0–49	89.56	40.5	4,689	53.95	22.2	1,761
50–99	95.06	38.6	1,227	54.87	18.6	486
100–499	99.61	40.2	3,632	57.05	18.9	1,428
500–999	101.98	36.6	1,871	59.42	17.5	698
1,000–4,999	104.84	41.8	4,303	62.61	20.6	1,729
5,000+	104.73	37.9	10,976	68.01	22.7	5,786
ALL	100.75	39.9	26,698	62.79	22.2	11,888

independent variables, but for present purposes of introducing the data we shall only look at the two most obvious, namely socio-economic group and industrial sector.

The breakdown by socio-economic group presented in Table 10.2 clearly shows that the wage–size hierarchy pattern holds within each group. In fact, the gradients are very similar between the SEGs, with managers at the top end of the occupational classification having an almost identical profile to unskilled manuals at the bottom of regular step increases, with only occasional cells out of line in between. Females have the same pattern as men and again a somewhat larger percentage mark-up by increasing size, especially in the skilled and semi-skilled manual occupations.

Turning now to the breakdown by industrial sector in Table 10.3 the pattern is somewhat less clear than for socio-economic group. The regular hierarchical relationship holds with only two cells out of line for minerals and both metal and other manufacturing for both sexes. However there are some irregularities elsewhere. Finance and transport (for men) peak in the middle size categories, while in several sectors there is a tendency to plateau or a slight downturn in the highest category. Transport, for males, is most unusual in that the 5,000-plus category provides the lowest pay, but this may be connected with the fact that this category was overwhelmingly composed of the nationalized sector. But in spite of these deviations, the overall trends are upward gradients in the size hierarchy, as reflected by the aggregate pattern in Table 10.1.

Table 10.2. *Average weekly pay by socio-economic group by company size (£)*

Company size	SEG 1: managers		SEG 2: professional and technical		SEG 3: intermediate non-manual		SEG 4: junior non-manual		SEG 5: supervisors		SEG 6: skilled manual		SEG 7: semi-skilled manual		SEG 8: unskilled manual	
	Male	Female	Male	Female	Male	Female	Male	Female	Male	Female	Male	Female	Male	Female	Male	Female
0–49	117.86	80.66	114.68	78.96	93.42	68.13	76.71	51.23	90.48	*50.36*	86.15	44.01	72.68	46.14	67.35	42.04
50–99	127.43	75.88	109.37	72.65	97.71	69.61	82.21	53.66	96.81	—	92.74	52.34	80.77	50.20	71.77	45.22
100–499	134.70	82.87	122.68	85.71	99.40	68.98	82.31	55.44	101.33	*61.16*	96.86	55.43	85.08	52.98	77.87	49.23
500–999	137.87	79.23	124.33	82.98	101.66	69.64	81.87	56.81	104.98	64.89	99.60	60.88	88.20	56.98	80.39	52.73
1,000–4,999	142.02	87.68	129.44	98.84	100.61	72.14	83.82	57.80	108.43	65.23	101.31	62.58	91.83	61.30	83.58	55.16
5,000+	144.35	92.47	129.28	91.12	105.07	81.10	89.91	60.22	113.39	60.53	102.31	57.70	89.01	61.10	84.25	52.28
ALL	134.26	85.47	125.88	89.22	101.72	78.11	85.74	57.23	104.63	59.90	97.39	54.81	85.85	55.94	79.13	51.08

Note: An italic number means there were between 10 and 49 observations in the cell; blanks are recorded where there were fewer than 10 observations.

Table 10.3. *Average weekly pay by industrial division by company size (£)*

Company size	(0) Agriculture		(1) Energy		(2) Minerals		(3) Metal manufacturing		(4) Other manufacturing		(5) Construction		(6) Distribution		(7) Transport		(8) Finance		(9) Other services	
	Male	Female	Male	Female	Male	Female	Male	Female	Male	Female	Male	Female	Male	Female	Male	Female	Male	Female	Male	Female
0–49	*67.20*	*44.17*	*118.18*	—	93.92	52.35	101.06	56.76	88.90	51.52	85.96	52.66	80.89	47.28	100.86	*54.74*	103.52	56.83	92.99	58.99
50–99	82.17	—		—	96.26	52.00	98.76	53.95	88.98	51.62	93.38	*50.10*	89.15	50.04	113.94	61.57	109.55	61.91	85.47	61.45
100–499	89.39	—	*115.19*	—	100.27	56.08	99.19	57.42	94.57	54.23	97.83	55.98	91.30	50.82	116.05	61.56	122.75	67.37	98.16	62.27
500–999	—	—	*116.15*	—	104.49	56.98	102.27	61.40	101.41	56.29	97.72	53.30	89.90	52.62	109.95	60.78	125.57	65.13	98.54	66.18
1,000–4,999	—	—	114.47	*69.70*	106.58	66.16	106.78	64.14	104.96	61.24	107.63	55.92	90.23	52.10	100.76	64.49	118.01	64.12	104.64	67.92
5,000+	70.42	—	113.88	69.01	109.97	63.06	106.70	66.70	107.54	63.49	96.66	57.54	97.10	53.77	99.57	69.99	118.50	63.28	101.72	71.26
ALL	69.61	46.97	114.14	68.79	105.61	60.36	103.92	61.95	99.22	56.77	94.76	54.53	88.08	51.07	101.64	66.71	115.35	62.36	100.55	68.97

Note: An italic number means there were between 10 and 49 observations in the cell; blanks are recorded where there were fewer than 10 observations.

Table 10.4. *Average weekly pay by establishment size*

Establishment size	Males			Females		
	Average (£)	Standard deviation (£)	No.	Average (£)	Standard deviation (£)	No.
0–49	99.78	42.1	18,910	63.47	23.6	9,680
50–99	95.58	32.4	609	52.43	12.4	216
100–199	96.89	34.8	878	54.53	13.3	352
200–499	98.23	30.6	1,610	57.18	13.2	595
500–999	101.63	31.1	1,204	61.20	12.5	391
1,000+	108.75	35.0	3,487	66.56	14.2	654
ALL	100.75	39.9	26,698	62.79	22.2	11,888

Pay and establishment size

It is evident from Table 10.4 that there is a relationship between pay and establishment size. We use the term establishment rather than plant, which is more generally used in the literature on size, because this data set, unlike many others, covers the whole economy. Differences between categories are both considerable and highly significant, and it can be seen that pay increases with establishment size for both sexes, with the important exception that the numerically predominant grouping in the smallest size category has a pay level in excess of all but the two largest male categories and the largest female category. The overwhelming number of observations in the under-50 category and the relatively small number of observations in the other size categories clearly create some difficulties for comparisons between the categories, unlike the company breakdown where the distribution of observations was much more even.

Other structural variables that can influence the pay hierarchy are the industrial and occupational composition within the various size categories, and these are taken up in Tables 10.5 and 10.6. The compositional factor also influences the standard deviation, which is, as would be expected, much larger in the heterogeneous under-50 category, but otherwise similar across the size categories. It is, however, again much larger for men than for women, although both are smaller than in the company structure. The premium for working in the highest-paid size category over the lowest is a very substantial 13.8 per cent for males and almost double that for females at 26.9 per cent. These are higher premiums than

Table 10.5. Average weekly pay by industrial division by establishment size (£)

Size of establish-ment	(0) Agriculture		(1) Energy		(2) Minerals		(3) Metal manufacturing		(4) Other manufacturing		(5) Construction		(6) Distribution		(7) Transport		(8) Finance		(9) Other services	
	Male	Female	Male	Female	Male	Female	Male	Female	Male	Female	Male	Female	Male	Female	Male	Female	Male	Female	Male	Female
0–49	69.61	46.97	114.14	68.79	102.92	59.46	106.51	59.05	96.20	56.12	94.69	54.53	87.78	50.97	101.65	66.71	115.27	62.37	100.52	68.97
50–99	—	—	—	—	98.28	*51.78*	97.71	54.25	91.46	52.08	*97.98*	—	*100.09*	—	—	—	—	—	—	—
100–199	—	—	*116.29*	—	100.61	53.77	97.69	57.02	94.42	53.34	—	—	*94.59*	—	—	—	—	—	—	—
200–499	—	—	*112.73*	—	101.62	57.13	98.62	59.83	95.95	55.55	—	—	*95.19*	—	—	—	—	—	—	—
500–999	—	—	*114.43*	—	104.48	61.68	100.26	62.69	101.28	59.81	—	—	—	—	—	—	—	—	—	—
1,000+	—	—	—	—	110.69	65.88	106.90	66.99	112.42	66.00	—	—	100.60	—	—	—	—	—	—	—
ALL	69.61	46.97	114.14	68.79	105.61	60.36	103.92	61.95	99.22	56.77	94.76	54.53	88.08	51.07	101.65	66.71	115.35	62.37	100.55	68.97

Note: An italic number means that there were between 10 and 49 observations; blanks are recorded where there were fewer than 10 observations.

Table 10.6. *Average weekly pay by socio-economic group by establishment size* (£)

Size of establishment	SEG 1: managers		SEG 2: professional and technical		SEG 3: intermediate non-manual		SEG 4: junior non-manual		SEG 5: supervisors		SEG 6: skilled manual		SEG 7: semi-skilled manual		SEG 8: unskilled manual	
	Male	Female	Male	Female	Male	Female	Male	Female	Male	Female	Male	Female	Male	Female	Male	Female
0–49	133.20	85.55	126.56	89.19	101.45	78.33	84.90	56.97	100.37	56.44	94.60	49.88	81.41	52.95	76.61	48.38
50–99	123.98	—	114.43	—	101.08	—	87.80	53.13	100.83	—	93.41	52.56	85.78	51.23	73.42	48.43
100–199	133.48	—	110.61	—	95.60	—	82.69	53.98	104.26	60.41	95.09	55.06	86.42	53.69	78.88	51.85
200–499	133.34	—	114.83	—	99.83	68.49	80.80	56.70	104.43	70.57	98.28	59.82	88.43	56.00	80.06	54.20
500–999	137.74	—	117.59	—	102.13	69.12	83.40	59.21	107.17	69.01	101.59	62.58	93.02	60.87	86.07	59.93
1,000+	147.31	—	128.72	—	107.68	78.34	94.97	63.63	120.96	77.23	106.61	68.44	97.61	66.61	94.24	63.59
ALL	134.26	85.47	125.88	89.22	101.72	78.11	85.74	57.23	104.63	59.90	97.39	54.81	85.85	55.94	79.13	51.08

Note: An italic number means that there were between 10 and 49 observations in the cell; blanks are recorded where there were fewer than 10 observations.

identified for the mark-up due to collective bargaining coverage in Gregory and Thomson (1981) using 1978 NES data.

Unfortunately when we turn to Table 10.5 to examine establishment size by industrial sector, we find that in the primary and service industry sectors establishment size is overwhelmingly below 50, and only minerals and the two manufacturing sectors provide us with a sufficiently large number of observations to identify size gradients. Nevertheless, within these three sectors there is a similar pattern to Table 10.4, namely a very clear-cut ascending gradient of pay with establishment size except for the smallest size band, where pay for both males and females in all three industrial sectors is higher than in the medium size categories, and in one case, males in metal manufacturing, comes close to the pay of the very largest establishments.

We now move to Table 10.6 which examines pay by socio-economic or broad occupational groupings. Here again we get a generally similar picture, although the gradients are much more even all through the size bands in the manual categories; it is noticeable that although the smallest size band is as usual out of line, this is less pronounced in the manual groupings. The non-manual groupings are slightly less regular, with a greater tendency for the smallest size category to reappear providing higher pay than in some of the larger groupings. In fact the substantial premium for the under-50 category comes in the managerial and professional categories, suggesting that they relate to small organizations, probably mainly professional practices. Nevertheless, the same overall trend of increased pay for increasing size of establishment is still present.

The overall conclusion is that there is a very strongly pronounced effect of establishment size, especially when viewed on a socio-economic breakdown, but also on an industrial and overall basis. The higher pay for the larger size bands can be partly explained by compositional factors, especially a higher non-manual–manual ratio in the larger size categories. The irregularly high pay in the smallest size band can be partly explained by the concentration of the non-productive sectors in this band. We now turn to examine some of these compositional issues and the relationship between the company and establishment categorizations.

Company and establishment—composition and earnings

A reordering of the data in Tables 10.7 to 10.9 brings establishment and company size together to evaluate the relative impact of each. Before commenting on the earnings data, however, it is desirable to examine in more detail the distribution of observations within size categories in the company and establishment breakdowns. Table 10.7 indicates that a very high proportion of establishment size observations are in the smallest

Table 10.7. *Average weekly pay by company size, establishment size and sex*

Company size	Establishment size																				
	Under 50			50–99			100–199			200–499			500–999			1,000+			Total		
	Total	Male	Female	Total	Male	Female	Total	Male	Female	Total	Male	Female	Total	Male	Female	Total	Male	Female	Total	Male	Female
0–49																					
£	79.84	89.56	53.95																79.84	89.56	53.95
na.	6,450	4,689	1,761																6,450	4,686	1,761
50–99																					
£	83.88	95.40	56.11	83.22	94.42	52.23													83.66	95.06	54.87
na.	1,129	798	331	584	429	155													1,713	1,227	486
100–499																					
£	89.64	101.89	58.61	83.37	95.31	50.07	84.55	96.58	54.32	85.87	97.35	56.34							87.60	99.61	57.05
na.	2,737	1,962	775	125	92	33	948	678	270	1,250	900	350							5,060	3,632	1,428
500–999																					
£	90.42	102.64	60.07	83.47	96.29	52.13	83.02	98.63	51.80	87.96	100.47	56.57	91.55	101.78	60.49				90.42	101.98	59.42
na.	1,440	1,039	401	31	22	9	78	52	26	249	178	71	771	580	191				2,569	1,871	698
1,000–4,999																					
£	91.39	104.88	62.47	94.50	105.88	58.62	88.42	101.17	57.37	87.34	98.59	59.38	90.43	101.27	61.29	98.78	107.37	65.66	92.73	104.84	62.61
na.	3,754	2,560	1,194	54	41	13	103	73	30	352	251	101	409	298	111	1,360	1,080	280	6,032	4,303	1,729
5,000+																					
£	89.63	103.75	68.36	90.97	98.90	57.63	84.49	94.33	56.10	90.94	99.29	58.79	93.30	101.67	62.63	103.70	109.37	67.23	92.05	104.73	68.01
na.	13,080	7,862	5,218	31	25	6	101	75	26	354	281	73	415	326	89	2,781	2,407	374	16,762	10,976	5,786
TOTAL																					
£		99.78	63.47		95.58	52.43		96.89	54.43		98.23	57.18		101.63	61.20		108.75	66.56		100.75	62.79
na.	28,590	18,910	9,680	825	609	216	1,230	878	352	2,205	1,610	595	1,595	1,204	391	4,141	3,487	654	38,586	26,698	11,888

Note: An italic number means that there were between 10 and 49 observations; a blank is recorded where there were less than 10 observations.

Table 10.8. *Average weekly pay of workers in establishments of less than 50 employees by socio-economic group, company, size, and sex (£)*

Company size	SEG 1: managers		SEG 2: professional and technical		SEG 3: intermediate non-manual		SEG 4: junior non-manual		SEG 5: foremen and supervisors		SEG 6: skilled manual		SEG 7: semi-skilled manual		SEG 8: unskilled manual		Total		Proportion of non-manual workers in total workforce (%)
	Male	Female	Male	Female	Male	Female	Male	Female	Male	Female	Male	Female	Male	Female	Male	Female	Male	Female	
0–49	117.86	80.66	114.68	78.96	93.42	68.14	76.71	51.23	90.48	50.36	86.15	44.00	72.68	46.14	67.35	42.02	89.56	53.95	48.4
50–99	129.18	75.08	109.30	72.65	97.15	70.75	80.52	53.87	93.94	—	93.82	54.00	78.69	47.49	72.21	43.99	95.40	56.11	54.3
100–499	135.27	83.94	126.86	86.34	100.23	69.61	83.02	55.60	100.53	—	97.63	52.49	82.05	49.17	78.57	45.37	101.89	58.61	56.5
500–999	138.42	80.11	128.15	83.63	102.77	70.02	81.47	56.64	101.92	—	97.61	—	83.09	55.91	78.41	47.93	102.64	60.07	59.9
1,000–4,999	144.26	86.87	131.17	98.11	99.89	72.03	81.95	57.11	104.09	60.05	97.88	53.56	86.82	59.73	81.12	50.05	104.88	62.47	62.9
5,000+	143.72	92.58	129.31	91.18	104.64	81.14	89.01	59.93	108.98	58.28	100.21	54.05	85.27	58.72	80.99	50.18	103.75	68.36	66.6
TOTAL	133.20	85.54	126.56	89.19	101.44	78.33	84.90	56.97	100.36	56.44	94.60	49.88	81.41	52.95	76.61	48.37			60.2

Note: An italic number means that there were between 10 and 49 observations; blanks are recorded where there were less than 10 observations.

Table 10.9. *Average weekly pay of workers in small establishments between small organizations and large organizations by socio-economic group and sex (£)*

SEG	Total		Male		Female	
	A	B	A	B	A	B
1. Managers	114.15	137.39	117.86	143.72	80.66	92.58
2. Professional and technical	109.00	121.23	114.68	129.31	78.96	91.18
3. Intermediate non-manual	85.58	92.04	93.42	104.64	68.14	81.14
4. Junior non-manual	57.45	69.14	76.71	89.01	51.23	59.93
5. Foremen and supervisors	86.96	98.19	90.48	108.98	50.36	58.28
6. Skilled manual	83.09	97.01	86.15	100.21	44.01	54.05
7. Semi-skilled manual	66.34	80.73	72.68	85.27	46.14	58.72
8. Unskilled manual	62.74	69.30	67.35	80.99	42.04	50.18
% of non-manual employees in total workforce	48.4	66.6	38.8	54.7	74.1	84.4

Note: A: Establishments of less than 50 employees in organizations of less than 50 employees (6,450 cases).
B: Establishments of less than 50 employees in organizations of more than 5,000 employees (13,080 cases).

category, of under 50 employees, 74 per cent of the total, with only very limited numbers in the other categories, even the 1,000+ category, which only has 11 per cent of the total. By contrast the largest company size category with more than 5,000 employees contains more than twice as many observations as any other category with 43 per cent of the total. Even so, the distribution by company is much more even than that by establishment, and this is one of the reasons why the company will be given rather more attention throughout the chapter. But it should be borne in mind hereafter that we are discussing workers who are mainly in small establishments but large companies.

There are also other notable features of the distribution of observations. One is that large establishments are overwhelmingly in only three industrial divisions (minerals and the two in manufacturing). These have less than one-third of their workers in the under-50 establishment category, whereas every other industrial division has at least 96 per cent of its workers in establishments with less than 50. Thus the under-50 establishment size category is compositionally quite different from the other establishment size categories. The sex breakdown is also important.

The proportion of women in the smallest establishment size category is much larger (33.9 per cent) than in the largest (15.7 per cent). This reflects in part the establishment size breakdown between manufacturing and non-manufacturing, and also help to explain why overall earnings are lower in the smallest establishment category than in the largest. The right-hand column in Table 10.8 gives a further important breakdown by the proportion of non-manual workers in the workforce by size of organization. It will be seen that there is a strong gradient whereby in the smallest company category less than half the workforce is comprised of non-manual workers, but that this rises to two-thirds in the largest company size category. This clearly helps to explain why earnings in the larger organization categories are higher than those in smaller when the earnings by size are not controlled by occupation or socio-economic breakdowns. Table 10.9 illustrates this compositional issue in an even more detailed way; while holding establishment size constant at under 50 employees, it compares this size of establishment in very small and very large companies. In the very small companies there is a very much lower proportion of non-manual workers, especially with respect to males. Again, this helps to explain differentials in company size before standardization for other factors. All the above indicate that there is no simple association between company and establishment size in respect of composition, and one should not necessarily be assumed in terms of earnings.

We now turn to earnings in the rows and columns of Table 10.7, enabling us to hold one size breakdown constant while looking at earnings variations in the other. For establishments of under 50 there is a strong upwards gradient through the organization size categories, with a differential of some £15 for both males (17.1 per cent) and females (26.8 per cent). In other words, holding establishment size constant, the gradient according to company size is still strong. However, in both of the top two company categories, the difference between the lowest and highest establishment size categories is more modest. The implication is that differences in company size are the more important influence on earnings. Moreover, when in Table 10.8 we again hold establishment size constant at under 50 and relate the socio-economic groupings to company size, we find that there is still the same strong gradient within the SEGs as when all establishment sizes are taken into account. Table 10.9 provides an even more vivid illustration of the relative impact of company and establishment size by comparing the smallest and largest category of company size within SEGs. As can be seen, the differentials between these even within the same broad occupational grouping are everywhere very considerable. The implication from these Tables is therefore that company size has a more important effect on earnings than establishment size, somewhat contrary to the emphasis on the establishment in much of the wage and industrial relations literature. There undoubtedly is an establishment size effect, as demonstrated in these and the earlier Tables, but it appears to be less than the company size effect.

Further dimensions of pay

We have seen that the size effect remains after standardizing for broad industrial and socio-economic variables. Some further aspects of the relationship between size and pay arise when we move away from the weekly pay which we have been discussing so far and examine other dimensions of pay, such as incentive pay, overtime pay, hourly earnings, annual earnings, and periodical bonuses. Tables 10.10 and 10.11 show these respectively for company and establishment size categories including in each column only those who receive that type of pay.

Overtime. There is little difference between either company or establishment size categories as far as the absolute level of overtime pay is concerned, although it represents a higher proportion of weekly pay in the smaller company size categories (22.4 per cent for men and 16.1 per cent for women in the smallest) than the larger (19.9 per cent for men and 12.2 per cent for women in the largest). The pattern is similar for establishments. Expectations on the relationship between overtime pay and size could go in either direction; on the one hand smaller units might be expected to have more irregular need for overtime while on the other larger units, being more highly unionized, might be expected to work more regular overtime to enhance earnings. However, the balance is inconclusive.

Incentive pay. Turning to the data on incentive pay, as far as males are concerned, it can be seen from Tables 10.10 and 10.11 that there is a tendency to a diminishing absolute amount for both company and establishment size breakdown with the single and financially small exception of the lowest establishment size category. This is somewhat inconsistent with the view reported in the Workplace Industrial Relations Survey, that larger companies and establishments have more people under incentive pay, although it is of course possible that the fewer workers receiving incentive pay nevertheless get more pay each. Once again the smallest establishment size category is likely to be different because it has a wide industrial spread, while most of the larger establishments are in the manufacturing sectors. Nevertheless the incentive pay for males in this particular cell, unlike females, is not much out of line with those in the other cells, which include a slight downwards gradient with increasing size. The situation for females is different. The smallest establishment

Table 10.10. *Make-up of pay by company size (£)*

Company size	Weekly pay	Weekly overtime pay for those earning any	Weekly incentive pay for those earning any	Hourly basic pay exclusive of overtime/ incentive/ premium pay	Annual periodical bonuses for those earning any	Annual earnings
Under 50						
M.	89.56	20.11	24.68	1.98	807.74	4,293.03
F.	53.95	8.67	15.43	1.42	331.51	2,546.89
50–99						
M.	95.06	20.09	23.90	2.00	589.36	4,456.01
F.	54.87	7.45	18.32	1.39	255.38	2,503.75
100–499						
M.	99.61	21.09	22.65	2.07	501.34	4,647.47
F.	57.05	8.58	16.38	1.40	208.06	2,626.50
500–999						
M.	101.98	20.80	21.07	2.12	391.94	4,771.56
F.	59.42	9.03	14.73	1.44	188.49	2,805.34
1,000–						
4,999	104.84	21.01	20.64	2.21	306.90	4,986.33
M.	62.61	9.48	13.79	1.54	167.55	2,908.13
F.						
5,000+						
M.	104.73	20.87	16.21	2.32	259.57	5,045.16
F.	68.01	8.28	8.10	1.86	165.89	3,251.65
TOTAL						
M.	100.75	20.77	19.87	2.18	428.06	4,803.26
(no.)	(26,698)	(17,607)	(14,510)		(12,878)	(26,692)
F.	62.79	8.59	12.29	1.65	206.98	2,965.42
(no.)	(11,888)	(3,339)	(3,528)		(4,576)	(11,888)

Note: For overtime pay, incentive pay, and periodical bonuses, the number of respondents identified is the number of cells in which at least one person has that breakdown of pay. The pay data refer to the average of all individuals in the cell which may not be the full total of those in the cell. As a result the various components of pay are not additive to weekly or annual pay.

size has a very low amount of incentive pay, due doubtless to the wide distribution of females in this size category between manufacturing and non-manufacturing, but it is also the case that female incentive earnings are considerably out of line in the smallest company size category with what is otherwise a regular downwards gradient with size. It would

Table 10.11. *Make-up of pay by establishment size (£)*

Establishment size	Weekly pay	Weekly overtime pay for those earning any	Weekly incentive pay for those earning any	Annual periodical bonuses for those earning any	Annual earnings
Under 50					
M.	99.78	20.54	20.58	502.20	4,793.76
F.	63.47	8.50	9.45	224.94	3,007.15
50–99					
M.	95.58	20.42	21.00	429.89	4,491.33
F.	52.43	7.04	20.49	247.81	2,342.73
100–199					
M.	96.89	20.38	21.09	470.79	4,456.06
F.	54.53	8.50	22.21	146.89	2,454.75
200–499					
M.	98.23	20.67	19.48	283.74	4,613.15
F.	57.18	8.50	17.67	161.22	2,746.60
500–999					
M.	101.63	21.57	18.84	260.29	4,764.52
F.	61.20	9.27	15.63	132.31	2,778.67
1,000+					
M.	108.75	21.65	17.51	220.02	5,097.83
F.	66.56	9.69	10.87	144.66	3,138.88
TOTAL					
M.	100.75	20.77	19.87	428.06	4,803.26
(no.)	(26,698)	(17,607)	(14,510)	(12,878)	(26,692)
F.	62.79	8.59	12.29	206.98	2,965.42
(no.)	(11,888)	(3,339)	(3,528)	(4,576)	(11,888)

Note: For overtime pay, incentive pay, and periodical bonuses, the number of respondents identified is the number of cells in which at least one person has that breakdown of pay. The pay data refer to the average of all individuals in the cell which may not be the full total of those in the cell. As a result the various components of pay are not additive to weekly or annual pay.

appear that males earn substantial amounts of incentive pay in the services sector but that females do not. The other point is that particularly in the middle size groupings female incentive pay is a considerably higher proportion of total pay than for males; indeed in one category female incentive pay is absolutely higher than that for males. There is also a considerably sharper decline to the largest size category for both establishments and companies.

If we take overtime and incentive pay together (accepting that this is not strictly legitimate because the samples are not the same) the differences between their percentage contribution to the largest and smallest group become considerable, at least at the company level. In the lowest grouping this is 50.0 per cent for men and 44.7 per cent for women, as against 35.4 per cent for men and 24.1 per cent for women in the largest size category. In part this is explained by the fact that the larger size categories have a higher proportion of white-collar staff who would not receive overtime or incentive pay. It should follow that basic pay would be very considerably lower in the smaller size categories to permit this offset.

Hourly pay. The most notable feature of hourly pay exclusive of overtime and incentive pay in Table 10.10 is that there is a sharp increase for both males and females in the two largest size categories, much more than the increase in weekly pay. This conforms with the suggestion in the previous paragraph that in the lower size categories a higher proportion of pay is obtained through overtime and incentive pay, and that this is in part due to compositional factors. Indeed when hourly pay is examined by socio-economic group (not shown in a table due to lack of space) the sharp upwards jump is only found in the intermediate non-manual category and then only for the highest size category. Otherwise the gradients are similar to those for weekly pay. Alternatively, it may well also be that in the smaller size categories, workers make up for the lower hourly rate by working longer hours, not necessarily overtime but longer basic hours. But even though the overall gradient steepens in the higher size categories it is still clearly established throughout the whole range of size groupings.

Annual pay. A further dimension of pay relates to annual pay; this is another statistic which is only available for the 1979 NES. Tables 10.10 and 10.11 indicate that annual pay shows the same gradient in relation to size as weekly pay, as would be expected. The mark-ups between the lowest-paid category and the highest are once again very substantial, being slightly higher in the company size context than for weekly pay at 17.52 per cent for men and 27.67 per cent for women, while for establishment size differentials (not the lowest size category for reasons of distribution) the mark-ups are 13.50 for men and a very large 33.98 for women.

Periodical bonuses. Although annual pay conforms to expectations, a component of annual pay comprising periodical bonuses does not, or at least it relates more closely to the pattern seen in overtime and incentive pay. These bonuses are defined in the NES questionnaire as 'bonuses, commission and similar payments of a kind not included in [weekly] earnings reported above, being paid annually (e.g. Christmas holidays), six monthly or quarterly, for instance'. Tables 10.10 and 10.11 show that periodical bonuses have a very strong inverse relationship with size at both establishment and especially at company level. Not by any means all individuals receive bonuses but a substantial proportion do (21.8 per cent). Managers get considerably higher amounts of bonus than other groups, and have a much sharper gradient. There are large differences between those receiving bonuses in individual sectors, varying from over 80 per cent in finance to around 10 per cent in other services, which of course include public administration where bonuses are virtually unknown. Distribution and transport are also well above average in those receiving bonuses. On the other hand the sharpest gradients in relation to the size categories come in the two manufacturing sectors, at least for men. Overall, nevertheless, the inverse gradient with size is generally well maintained, except for finance, where the biggest bonuses are in the medium size companies.

Other components of labour cost. At this point we introduce a non-NES table, Table 10.12, which is based on a 1981 survey but nevertheless likely to be reasonably accurate with respect to ratios existing in 1979. It indicates that there are ancillary labour costs beyond wages and salaries which are also significantly greater in large establishments than in small, at least within manufacturing, which is the only sector covered by the Table. Amongst the most important of these additional costs are provision for redundancy, voluntary social welfare, subsidized services, and, to a lesser extent, training. Indeed their cost impact for large establishments is much greater than the differential in pay; a mark-up of 38.2 per cent for wages and salaries relates to one of 100.6 per cent for fringe costs between the smallest and largest categories. This situation is also found in the United States, where Lester reported that fringe benefits in large establishments were twice as much as in smaller plants in cents per hour. It is also worth noting that government subsidies provide a disproportionate benefit to the larger plants. However the net overall impact is very much that the larger plants have much higher labour costs per hour than smaller plants, with the difference between the smallest and largest size categories being a massive 47.3 per cent. Again, as with the various elements of pay, a considerable part of the difference is likely to be compositional, relating to differences in industrial and occupational breakdown between the size categories.

Summary of NES size–earnings data

The data for both establishment and company size show differences between size categories which are highly significant, and they bear out all the previous observations in the files, although no previous British study

Table 10.12. *Labour costs per hour in 1981: average expenditure per employee by size of establishment in manufacturing*

Category of labour cost	10–49 employees		50–99 employees		100–199 employees		200–499 employees		500–999 employees		1,000 or more employees	
	Pence per hour	%	Pence per hour	%	Pence per hour	%	Pence per hour	%	Pence per hour	%	Pence per hour	%
Total wages and salaries	274.72	85.5	280.33	84.8	295.69	83.5	309.68	82.1	336.68	81.5	379.73	80.2
Statutory national insurance contributions	32.99	10.3	32.88	9.9	33.98	9.6	34.68	9.2	36.27	8.8	38.02	8.0
Provision for redundancy (net)	1.62	0.5	2.37	0.7	3.51	1.0	7.15	1.9	8.11	2.0	17.02	3.6
Employers' liability insurance	1.47	0.5	1.27	0.4	1.24	0.4	1.35	0.4	1.35	0.3	1.55	0.3
Voluntary social welfare	8.58	2.7	11.52	3.5	15.82	4.5	18.97	5.0	24.19	5.9	30.57	6.5
Benefits in kind	0.46	0.1	0.37	0.1	0.38	0.1	0.43	0.1	0.39	0.1	0.56	0.1
Subsidized services	2.10	0.7	2.46	0.7	4.07	1.2	5.37	1.4	6.76	1.6	6.79	1.4
Training (excluding wage and salary elements)	0.46	0.1	0.81	0.2	1.14	0.3	1.30	0.3	1.42	0.3	1.68	0.4
Government subsidies	−0.96	−0.3	−1.27	−0.4	−1.53	−0.4	−1.84	−0.5	−2.04	−0.5	−2.40	−0.5
Total labour costs	321.45	100.0	330.75	100.0	354.30	100.0	377.09	100.0	413.14	100.0	473.51	100.0

Source: Employment Gazette (May 1983).

has had the wealth of disaggregated data that the NES provides, or has been able to produce such regular gradients. However, the size effect cannot be accounted for by industry or occupational composition nor by unionization unless the whole wage structure of a company is lifted. In any case, given the strength of the trend, it is totally unlikely that wage–size differences could be explained by say a skew in the occupational structure *within* the present socio-economic groupings or in industrial structure.

It is also important that similar size and related pay differences seem to exist elsewhere. Talking to the IRRA in 1984, John Dunlop noted the phenomenon and quoted hourly pay by establishment size category in the grocery industry, namely in ascending order of size category $6.21, $6.78, $6.73, $7.20, $7.60, $8.50, $9.02; and in the sawmill industry $5.43, $5.70, $6.33, $7.43, $7.96, $8.10, $9.00. On the face of it these differences are considerably greater than that which we have reported for Britain, but the pattern of an upwards gradient is very similar. Moreover, Weiss and Landau (1984) report an unpublished study by Antos, who found that even when the data was standardized for race, sex, education, tenure, experience, union membership, time worked, occupation, industry, region, and SMSA there was still a positive size effect.

The size effect seems indisputable and very considerable, with regularities and a distributional pattern which are difficult to explain other than by factors which are a direct function of size. It has been argued by some, e.g. MacKay (1973), that pay has an element of randomness, partly associated with imperfect knowledge, and that as a result theory cannot cope. The regularities in the present data certainly do not suggest that random forces are at work. The problem is, which forces and why?

10.2. Hypotheses Relating to Size

We now have a reasonably disaggregated and standardized data base on which to measure the size effect. But if the dependent variable is for the first time clearly specified, there are still problems in defining and acquiring the statistical base for various independent variables to permit a full cross-sectional analysis to be carried out. It is not, in any case, the intention of this chapter to carry through an econometric analysis. Nevertheless, the results we have just observed are too important and interesting not to attempt some explanation, or rather explanations, since there is a substantial literature in this field and a wide range of different considerations have been examined. We therefore now turn to the most significant of these. Some of them, mainly those relating to external markets, operate primarily through the company size dimension and others, mainly concerned with behaviour and the production process, operate mainly through the establishment dimension. We will therefore also need to evaluate the company/establishment influence on pay in the light of the factors.

(a) Industrial structure

The argument in this context is that a high degree of concentration, which is strongly positively related to size of company and to a slightly lesser extent to size of establishment, will lead either to higher profitability and hence an ability to pay higher wages or to administered prices which through collective bargaining lead to higher wages, or both. Underlying concentration are factors such as higher amounts of capital in individual firms putting the firm into a higher echelon of imperfect competition, and also that investment in economies of scale is possible from which small firms are excluded. Viewed from the side of the demand for labour, the potential for any group of workers to obtain a premium wage is likely to be inversely related to the elasticity of demand for services of that group and the demand for labour is likely to be more inelastic in more concentrated industries. Also dealing with the demand for labour, Weiss (1966) amongst others has noted a potential link between concentration and the quality of labour demanded. Thus size, especially size of company but also size of establishment, may be a proxy for market structure and indeed it is difficult to differentiate the effects of the two because they are different expressions of the same phenomenon, with a high degree of collinearity between them. The NES data breakdown used for this chapter cannot in any case measure true market power, because it is only disaggregated to broad industrial sector, not to MLH level which would be necessary for an adequate measure of concentration. However, to put concentration into context, in one empirical study of this relationship, Masters noted (1969: 344), 'although the concentration ratio has received much more attention, the plant size variable is more important in explaining inter-industry differences in average wages,' while the same has been found in such British studies as Hood and Rees (1974) and Sawyer (1973).

(b) Profitability

Size of company and establishment have generally been accepted as being positively correlated with profitability for reasons connected with economies of scale and market power, although this may not hold above a certain size level. The argument here is that the more profitable the plant or company the higher wages it can afford to pay; it has been argued by

Hall and Weiss and others that firms in such positions may be willing to use some of their economic profits to pay workers so that the accounting profits are less than the true economic profits. In any case the key dimension of profitability is the element of management discretion that it permits in relations to labour market policy. One argument that has been advanced against the profitability argument is that companies with lower profitability may in fact have a more difficult situation under collective bargaining because they will be less able to ride out a strike.

(c) Labour market

Several different issues come under this general heading:

1. *Labour quality*. Larger companies may pay more for higher-quality labour in order to obtain the necessary commitment and performance necessary for their more heavily capitalized operations, and American evidence does suggest a higher human capital input into larger companies. The output can be measured in terms of productivity, which we examine later, but this incorporates other factors as well as labour force quality. Similarly the composition of a labour force can be measured in terms of occupational structure and specialization without access to some indicator of human capital, which the NES data does not give, but it is difficult to measure quality *per se*. Nevertheless the argument from quality of labour would almost certainly be the main one used by firms if they were asked why they paid higher wages. Mayhew has noted (1976b: 154) that size has a significant effect on the earnings of the skilled and semi-skilled more often than on the earnings of the unskilled and females, presumably because the latter are more homogeneous and thus less differentiated in quality.

2. *Labour market information*. Workers are argued to have a very poor knowledge of the labour market (Parnes 1963). While this would not necessarily all point in one direction there would be a tendency for the bigger plants and companies to be better known and hence to be seen as the standard in matters of pay and conditions, and thus attract the better workers.

3. *The size of the labour market*. Sawyer (1973) argues that the smaller the market the lower the wage rates, quoting Lester and others in the American context, although it must be added that the market size effect has been better measured in America than Britain.

4. *Internal and dual labour markets*. A very important fourth dimension of labour markets relates to internal and dual market structures. This issue is well argued by George *et al.* (1977), who comment of internal labour markets:

Well developed internal labour markets tend to have essentially two related characteristics. First they display a fairly rigid system of wage differentials between different groups of workers determined primarily by administrative rules and procedures. The result is a wage structure which in many respects is at odds with the one market forces would produce. Secondly, they encompass a range of jobs which are shielded from the direct influence of external competitive forces. Vacancies are primarily filled from inside with few points of entry to and exit from the internal market. The existence of such internal labour markets can have important consequences for allocative efficiency. However, the question here is whether large units are more likely to encompass strongly structured internal labour markets than small units. There are several reasons for thinking they might do.

The related dimension of dual labour markets is also well defined by George *et al.*:

It has been argued that the total labour market can be divided into two separate segments. The primary market encompasses jobs involving high wages, good work conditions, job security, abundant opportunities for training and promotion, clear well defined and organised job specifications. The secondary market encompasses jobs involving low wages and fringe benefits, poor conditions, high turnover, absenteeism in time keeping, few prospects, little scope for training, badly defined and organised jobs and arbitrary supervision. The relevant question for us is which market will large units in general operate in? Our earlier analysis offer several reasons for thinking that the answer is the primary market.

The implication of internal and dual labour markets, whose existence has been persuasively argued, but not yet proved on a national statistical data base, is that for both internal and external reasons large companies and establishments are likely to pay more than small.

(d) Occupational structures

It is argued that the division of labour will differ between large and small units so as to justify higher pay in the former. The worker in the larger plant will be more specialized and hence more skilled in a narrow job, whereas the worker in the smaller plant will have to do a broader range of activities and hence his marginal productivity will not be as high. Moreover the larger plant will be able to carry a wider range of managerial and back-up services, including a more sophisticated personnel structure, with superior selection procedures which will result in a higher quality labour force and, at least according to George, McNabb, and Shorey (1977), better workplace relationships. Another dimension of this same issue is that it is argued that a higher proportion of women tend to work in smaller plants than in larger and that women are notoriously

associated with lower earnings, in part because of their lower attachment
to the labour force.

(e) Labour Force attitudes and behaviour

There is a good deal of literature which argues (Goldthorpe 1968, Ingham
1970, George, McNabb, and Shorey 1977) that working in large organizations is essentially alienating and that workers need compensation for
doing so. A subsidiary argument is the capacity for stronger and more
cohesive work groups to emerge in large plants, which relates to the
collective bargaining and industrial relations dimension. There are several
reasons for the alienation theory even at the level of the individual, such
as the dehumanizing effect of mass technology, communications and
control problems in large plants, and bureaucratization. A corollary is the
relative performance of large and small plants in relation to turnover and
absenteeism, the assumption being that they represent a personal reaction
against the work situation, with the costs being such that higher wages are
justified to obtain a dependable labour force. The assumption is that both
tend to be higher in large establishments (but not necessarily companies).
On the other hand Ingham's analysis found that absenteeism was higher
in large plants, but that there was no correlation between turnover and
size of unit. However the converse of this, which might be called the
small is harmonious hypothesis, is challenged by others such as Curran
and Stanworth (1981). Attitudes to pay may also differ. Ingham found
that workers in large and small plants had the same relative satisfaction
with pay, although their absolute levels of pay were considerably different. Ingham and Goldthorpe have noted the instrumentalism of workers
in large plants and Ingham has argued that wage incentives and technological advances are more effective in increasing productivity than in creat-
ing identification with the work group. Sawyer also quotes the Prices and
Incomes Board as arguing that payments-by-results systems involve a
disutility to workers which would need to be offset by higher earnings,
and the assumption is that incentive systems are more generally found in
larger organizations. On the other hand there is as counter-argument that
larger organizations have better supervision and more sophisticated pay
systems such as job evaluation which do not require PBR as a means of
motivating workers. Taken overall, however, the general thrust of the
literature is that individual attitude and behaviour patterns in large units
do necessitate higher pay as compensation for the work environment.

(f) Industrial relations and bargaining power

Many studies, including one by the editors of this book (Gregory and
Thomson 1981), have tried to evaluate the impact of collective bargaining

and bargaining power on earnings, and size has been one of the factors involved. The results have not always been convincing. To quote George, McNabb, and Shorey's scepticism:

The variable used has either measured trade union membership coverage or, more directly, capital intensities and labour costs as a proportion of total costs. The conceptual basis, and in some cases the data, for these proxies is extremely doubtful. For example it is not at all obvious that any observed relationship between union membership and wages says anything about bargaining power. As far as they go the results in general indicate that the size effect remains statistically significant even with the inclusion of these variables. The bargaining proxy is sometimes significant as well, sometimes not. There is little empirical evidence on the relationship between bargaining power and size.

Nevertheless, it is frequently argued, not only that there is a mark-up for unionization or collective bargaining coverage, but that power and therefore the size of the mark-up is positively related to size. Since George *et al.* wrote, the Workplace Industrial Relations Survey of 1980, which was carried out at much the same time as the NES data for this chapter was obtained, has become available as the most comprehensive statistical study to date of establishment level industrial relations. It identified a wide range of structural dimensions of industrial relations which are related to size of establishment, which was indeed one of the main variables used in the survey. The following are the main size-related differentiating factors, most of which might be hypothesized as increasing union bargaining power in line with increasing size of establishment:

1. Size of establishment was associated with recognition, with a much higher degree of recognition in larger establishments. Moreover, more separate unions were recognized in larger establishments, and there were also more separate bargaining groups. Finally, recognition in smaller units tended to be more recent.
2. The presence of stewards and full-time convenors was much higher in larger establishments than in smaller.
3. Union representatives were given more training and better facilities and had more dealings with full-time officers in larger establishments.
4. More workers were in closed shops in larger establishments, at any rate in the private sector.
5. Management also was different in industrial relations terms. There was more managerial specialization in industrial relations, management was more qualified for industrial relations, more outside bodies were consulted on industrial relations in larger establishments, and there was more board representation for industrial relations in larger companies.

6. The sophistication of bargaining, consultative, and other machinery of involvement was greater in large establishments than in small.
7. The larger the establishment the greater the role of plant bargaining, although the larger the organization the greater the role of organization bargaining. Indeed, small plants tend to operate according to industry-wide agreement wage rates, in part because of the economies of bargaining jointly rather than separately.
8. Fewer manuals were paid by results in smaller establishments and there was also less job evaluation in smaller establishments.
9. In conflict terms, there were fewer strikes per year in smaller establishments; indeed previous work by the DE had determined that strike frequency is almost directly proportional to size of plant. On the other hand small plants had proportionately more dismissals, but this was explicable in terms of the better grievance machinery in the larger establishments.

The WIRS study also examined possible reasons for the size-related distribution of pay reported in the survey, which, although not as detailed as the NES, nevertheless clearly indicated a mark-up for the larger establishments. Indeed, the broad-ranging nature of the questionnaire enabled it to consider a fairly wide range of factors. In its evaluation of pay, the WIRS found that pay was apparently *not* related to market-orientated measures such as: movements in demand for the product; changes in workplace numbers; the pattern of capital investment; or the financial performance of establishment. It did however find that there were key correlates of pay in terms of unionization, size of unit, and workforce composition, through ratios of both women and part-time workers. Thus the WIRS conclusion would be that there is a union membership benefit which is independent of size of unit, although both lead to higher wages.

Against these arguments that industrial relations-orientated factors help to contribute to the size influence on earnings, there are two counter-factors. One is the threat effect argument, namely that an employer may be willing to pay higher wages in order not to have a union in his organization; this is however not likely to outweigh the positive benefits of union membership, given the level of union membership in Britain. Secondly, from the NES Tables 10.2 and 10.6 earlier in the chapter, there is the strong feature that the mark-up in size terms is the same for managers as it is for unskilled manuals, and indeed seems very similar between those groups who are predominantly unionized and those groups which are not. Thus, unless there is a ratchet effect, whereby a company pays more all through its workforce when it is unionized at the lower levels, there is a difficulty in explaining how unionization can benefit the bottom socio-economic groups when the top groups also appear to benefit equally in relation to size of unit.

(g) Economies of scale and productivity

One of the basic arguments from classical economics is that of economies of scale saying that larger units at least in certain circumstances reap the rewards of more intensive use of certain fixed factors of production, such as capital intensive plant, thus obtaining greater labour productivity per unit of output. Indeed in economic terms this factor ought to be able to pick up the aggregated impact of all the other factors. We have obtained information from the Census of Production relating to a breakdown of sales price by size of unit, and it is apparent from Table 10.13 that there are indeed returns in terms of gross value added to large establishments in relation to small. It should be noted that this definition includes the cost of all inputs to the production process plus gross profit and therefore incorporates some demand and market side dimensions as well as purely supply side factors. Gains in economies of scale can be made for both the supply and demand sides. The difference between the smallest and largest establishment size category is in fact 18.5 per cent, not dissimilar to the earnings mark-up we discussed earlier in the chapter. However it must also be noted that wages actually rise as a proportion of gross value added and thus take a larger share of the total value, especially due to the non-manual element. Nevertheless this is justified by the rise in value added, with the share of the other factors being reduced by the availability of economies of scale. A partial explanation for this is in Table 10.14, which breaks down the overall costs. As will be seen, the costs of raw materials, industrial service, and wages and salaries rise, although not evenly, by size of establishment, while the costs of non-industrial services and the residual fall. Non-industrial services consist of rent, insurance, bank charges, transport, rates, telephone, etc., while the residual consists of such factors as taxes and profits.

Pratten did try to differentiate economic and technical causes from behavioural causes of differences in productivity between the UK and Germany, France, and the United States. The behavioural causes were substantial, amounting to some 40 per cent of the total differential between the UK and Germany, although reducing to less than a quarter in the case of the comparison between the UK and North America. Nevertheless, Pratten (1976) argued that economic factors such as differences in rates of output and differences in plant and machinery were the key factors between Britain and the other countries.

If productivity is indeed higher in larger establishments, this provides an argument that wages would be higher as well. Ball and Skeoch (1981),

Table 10.13. *Workers, wage costs and gross value added by size of establishment*

Production industries (excluding energy): size of establishment	Workers as % of total employment		Wages as % of total costs		Gross value added per head (£)	Wages as a proportion of gross value added		
	Manual	Non-manual	Manual	Non-manual		Manual	Non-manual	Total
1–19	65.8	21.6	69.2	30.7	7,028	34.8	15.4	50.2
20–99	75.0	24.3	69.4	30.6	7,054	39.0	17.2	56.2
100–499	72.5	27.4	67.0	33.0	7,594	36.4	17.9	54.3
500–999	70.3	29.7	65.1	34.9	8,026	35.1	18.8	53.9
1,000+	68.7	31.3	63.0	37.0	8,332	36.5	21.4	57.9
TOTAL	70.5	28.5	65.4	34.6	7,838	36.5	19.3	55.8

Source: Business Monitor (1979).

Table 10.14. *Breakdown of sales value by size of establishment (%)*

Total sales	1–19	20–99	100–499	500–999	1,000+	Total
Cost of raw materials plus cost of industrial services	56.4	59.2	60.3	59.3	60.8	60.0
Cost of non-industrial services	7.9	7.2	6.5	6.5	6.2	6.5
Wages and salaries	18.9	19.9	19.0	19.5	20.6	19.9
Residual	16.8	13.7	14.1	14.7	12.4	13.6

Source: Business Monitor (1979).

in their inter-plant comparison study, found that earnings did increase with establishment size and were also positively correlated with productivity, but concluded that the underlying economic processes were 'extremely unclear'. In this connection, Pratten argues that: 'In practice a substantial benefit, perhaps the main benefit of investment is taken by workers in the form of higher real wages during the life of assets, and yet investment decisions are taken primarily on the basis of return on capital.' Some would argue that British workers tend to take a higher proportion of the return on investment than in other countries. On the other hand the capture of productivity benefits by workers is not necessarily true, as Wragg and Robertson (1978) argue in commenting on Salter's seminal work on productivity: 'Salter's findings that industries with above average rates of productivity growth do not pay above average growth of wages has been confirmed by all subsequent studies. This shows that the growth of productivity is not pre-empted by the workforce through higher wages.' A final thought in this area is that most of the discussions on productivity and economies of scale have been concerned with manufacturing. Yet the size–pay relationships are just as true for services where the technical conditions of production do not hold. What are the implications of this?

(h) Establishment and company pay

The various factors so far considered have not clearly differentiated between the establishment and the company in relation to hypothetical and empirical findings relating to pay. The main relationship measured in the literature has been concerned with establishment size rather than company size. Indeed there has been a tendency to see industry size as the second important size factor. Thus Smith, Hitchens, and Davies note (1982: 82):

It has proved useful to distinguish between industry size—as measured by levels of net output and employment—and plant size. Industry size is perhaps the most appropriate concept for testing whether greater scale yields more scope for specialization and higher productivity. . . . Plant size is a rather more appropriate concept for examining those hypotheses concerned with economies of scale, management control and industrial relations.

Yet there is no denying that the company is the basic unit of modern economic activity. In terms of the above criteria of what is most appropriate for testing at which level, the company level may be most appropriate in relation to profitability and scope of managerial discretion, which are likely to be important influences in wage determination. In one sense the differentiation does not matter too much, since most of the trends in terms of size relationships between establishment pay and company pay are very similar and moreover there is a considerable correlation between size of establishment and size of company in that larger establishments are closely associated with larger companies, especially in manufacturing. Nevertheless there are differences, as we have seen in the basic tables, and the data indicate that of the two levels, size of company is a more significant influence in determining earnings. Unfortunately relatively little work has been done in differentiating the relative significance of the two levels in relation to most of the independent variables discussed in this chapter. Marginson has investigated some differences between plant and company in relation to industrial relations variables. He finds that the major differentiating factor is in relation to aspects of management rather than aspects of union organization or even unionization. Thus the existence of a director with personnel/industrial relations responsibilities will be relatively more influenced by company size than the presence of a specialized personnel or industrial relations manager, which will be relatively more influenced by establishment size. This type of analysis could with advantage be extended to other contextual differences between company and establishment.

10.3. Conclusion

We have examined a number of possible explanations for the clear size effect at both company and establishment level. All of them have some plausibility and it seems very likely that each contributes, perhaps more in one context than another. There are no adequate statistics, however, to measure all in equal degree, and no easy proxies for some. George,

McNabb, and Shorey's comment that 'a rigorous test of the size effect is difficult to set up because of the complexities of the relationship involved' still remains true. Nevertheless the cumulative impact of the various considerations we have examined does appear to justify a wage premium for the size effect. Two issues remain in the memory. One is what sort of variable size is, intermediate or primary. It is difficult to see conceptually how it can be independent of the other factors and one is thus driven to an assumption of combined impact. Yet the other issue is that of the surprisingly high regularity of the size gradient. One would not expect the aggregation of product market, labour market, industrial relations, behavioural, and productivity factors to be so similar in different industries and socio-economic groupings. We know that earnings structures have some degree of independence but the data would indicate that there are similar relativities in all size bands. What may be surmised is that the average level of earnings is determined at some point on the spectrum, due to a range of the factors considered, and that internal relativities follow. This would at least account for behavioural or industrial relations influences, for instance, being apparently carried forward to occupations ostensibly not affected by such factors. What this suggests is that size, more than other dimensions of organizational structure, may be the conduit which carries influences from one group to another. In this limited sense it is an influence in its own right. There are thus still many unresolved issues in a fascinating area.

Appendix 10.1

In order to meet the requirements of EEC Regulation 495 two additional sections were included in the 1979 NES. The questions from these sections which have been used in this study relate to company and establishment size.

In both cases nine size ranges were distinguished: under 10 employees, 10–19, 20–49, 50–99, 100–199, 200–499, 500–999, 1,000–1,999, 2,000–4,999, and 5,000 or more. In constructing the data-files both company and establishment size have been used as cell boundaries. The individual cells are therefore defined in terms of size of establishment within each size of company. These can then be aggregated to give a classification by company size alone, and a classification by establishment size across all sizes of company. A separate aggregation by region for each size of company has also been prepared.

11

Changes in Hours of Work and Pay Developments

D. Bosworth and R. Wilson

11.1. Introduction

This paper presents detailed evidence from the NES data tapes about what has happened to basic, overtime, and total hours of work since 1970. It analyses how the changing level and structure of hours of work have affected pay over this period. Like the other studies reported in this volume, the unit of observation is a 'three (or more) headed person' for reasons of confidentiality. The analysis is essentially descriptive, concentrating upon frequency distributions, cross-tabulations, and shift-share techniques. Multiple regression analysis using the data base is reserved for future research. Nevertheless the approach provides a useful preliminary exploration of the properties of the data and the interrelationships between pay and hours.

   Hours of work influence pay in two main ways: first, through the direct effect of hours worked on total weekly earnings at a given premium rate; and second, through the impact of different premium rates for various lengths of overtime working. There are at least two important aspects associated with the direct effect: the long-run downward trend in average weekly hours and the increasing importance of part-time working (the latter defined by reference to the number of hours worked). The effects of these two influences on hours and pay form a central theme of the discussion below. A further major theme concerns the importance of overtime working in terms of both hours worked and pay.

11.2. A Brief Review of the Hours Literature

A great deal of interest has surrounded hours of work. Much of the early literature was concerned with the unsocial aspects of long hours of work and the welfare gains associated with the movement to a shorter working week.[1] This debate has received renewed impetus in recent years with a further examination of the role of shorter working hours in providing greater numbers of job opportunities, in the light of the sustained high

rates of unemployment.[2] More recently, these concerns have been en-
capsulated in a variety of theoretical and empirical work which focuses
on factor demands. This represents the tip of an iceberg of research
connected with the demand for labour services by firms and the choice
between hours and persons.[3] Interest has particularly centred on the
reasons for the use of overtime working. A further section of the literature has been concerned with the supply side and the decisions by individuals about the allocation of time between work in the formal economy
and leisure.[4]

More recently, attention has focused on the development of certain
'new' forms of employment and working patterns. These are often not
strictly novel, but they have started to emerge as significant dimensions of
employment. They include temporary and casual work, homeworking,
and, perhaps of greatest importance, part-time working.[5] The latter is
clearly intimately connected to hours of work and pay. The role of hours
in determining pay has perhaps been less of an issue in the literature, but
at least two important themes have been discussed. The first of these
involves relative earnings. Much of this work has been carried out across
industries, although it might equally (given sufficient data) have been
undertaken across occupations. In particular, a number of attempts have
been made to explain average hourly earnings of manual male workers in
UK manufacturing industries.[6] However, increasing concern has been
voiced about the treatment of hours in such models. Perhaps the most
sophisticated response was the attempt to endogenize hours and earnings,
estimating separate supply and demand functions for labour services.[7] A
later but less sophisticated treatment was to attempt to account for
overtime by excluding it from the measure of earnings, focusing on basic
average hourly earnings.[8]

The second main area of work on hours of work and developments in
pay has been associated with models of the inflationary process, which
can be traced from the Phillips curve, through the concept of the augmented Phillips curve, to the ideas of adaptive and rational expectations.[9]
Much of this work, as it stands, is not relevant to this study, because it
does not explicitly focus on the role of hours. However, more recently,
concern has been voiced about whether total unemployment is an adequate measure of the tightness of labour markets. This line of argument
appears to take two directions. First, linked with the idea that the non-
accelerating inflation rate of unemployment changes over time, the unemployment measure should be adjusted to allow for the potential economic
contribution of the various types of unemployed (i.e. the longer-term
unemployed should, other things being equal, be weighted less).[10]
Second, and more importantly, in terms of the subject-matter of this
study, the idea has been put forward that intra-firm tightness (i.e. in the

internal labour market, and represented by some measure of overtime working or deviation from trend hours) might be more important than tightness in the external labour market.[11] No results are available to date which test the joint role of the internal and external tightness variables, but work is currently going on in this area.

11.3. Some Details of the Data Base

The NES has provided information about hours of work on an annual basis since 1970. The analyses of hours of work are published in Part F of the Reports.[12] Detailed information is available about the various dimensions of hours (normal, overtime, and total), broken down by industry, occupation (e.g. manual and non-manual workers), age, and region. In general, only one pairing is dealt with at a time. So, for example, total hours are available by industry, but not by industry, occupation, and region. The one exception to this is the availability of data about hours by each of these dimensions, broken down by manual males, manual females, non-manual males, and non-manual females. A number of joint distributions are published, but these mainly deal with the distribution of one of the dimensions of hours and the distribution of a particular dimension of pay.

The hours of work data developed for the present study are formed by stratifying the observations in a number of ways, before amalgamating to 'three-headed people' on the basis of closest-ranked pay. Stratification was undertaken in the following order: (1) full-time and part-time workers; (2) by gender; (3) according to the hours interval in which they reside; (4) whether or not they receive incentive pay; (5) whether they are covered by collective agreement or Wages Councils; (6) according to a seventeen industry breakdown; (7) by eight socio-economic groups. The stratification was designed partly with the future analysis of the data base in mind. A key dimension of interest (which effectively distinguishes this from the other data bases) is the stratification of the observations according to broad bands of total hours of work. Clearly, it would have been interesting to have very detailed breakdowns by hours worked, but there was a trade-off here with detail in other dimensions (i.e. industry and socio-economic group) if the exercise was not to result in a large number of empty cells (i.e. containing less than three people). It was not possible to repeat the exercise for, say, basic hours, overtime hours, and total hours.

It is perhaps worth stressing the importance of the prestratification by hours. The intervals chosen organize the persons into similar hours bands before aggregation takes place. With prior stratification, a full-time (three-headed) individual with average hours of less than 35 per week is likely to be formed from three persons all on relatively low hours; likewise an individual averaging over 60 is also likely to be formed from persons with relatively high hours. Thus, stratification of hours ensures a more meaningful aggregation process and a less compressed frequency distribution of hours compared with purely random aggregation across persons. Part-time workers are divided into those above and below the 30-hours mark (which has, at least until recently, been accepted as the dividing line between part-time and full-time working); full-time workers are divided into bands of 2, 5, and 10 hours, with smaller intervals employed closer to the 40-hours per week mark.[13] These bands are somewhat less detailed than those reported in the published NES tables, for the reasons outlined above. The intervals chosen still enable a separate examination of workers at the extremes of the hours range. It should be emphasized that because of the way the sample is selected for the NES a significant proportion of part-time workers are excluded (notably all those who fall below the National Insurance contribution threshold). The DE estimates that as many as a third of all part-time workers may be excluded from the NES. The information drawn from the NES effectively excludes individuals whose pay is affected by absence and those for whom there are no reported basic hours. There is a further group which is, in principle, covered by the Survey, those on short-time working, for whom total hours should be less than their normal hours. In practice, this group could not be distinguished from those absent from work for a variety of other reasons, including sickness, and they were therefore excluded from the sample.

The preceding discussion outlines a number of cross-tabulations and, by implication, joint frequency distributions that can be constructed using the hours tapes, which are not available in the published NES tables. In the next section we draw on evidence from a variety of published sources and focus on a number of hypotheses that can be tested more thoroughly using the new data base. In particular, we concentrate upon weekly hours. Although changing holiday entitlements and changing economic activity rates for both young and old have significantly affected yearly and lifetime hours of work, these issues lie outside the scope of the current paper. Hours of work are a composite, including overtime and normal basic hours, full-time and part-time working. Given that hours worked over and above normal hours are, in general, paid overtime premiums, which may be as high as 33 per cent for the first 10 hours per week and 50 per cent thereafter, it seems likely that the extent of overtime may be a major determinant of differences in pay between groups of workers and from year to year.[14]

11.4. Hours and Pay

(a) Normal hours

The published evidence indicates that normal basic hours did not alter dramatically over the period 1970 to 1982, although they fell steadily. In the case of full-time males, for example, they fell from an average of 39.4 hours per worker in 1970 to 38.3 in 1982. The equivalent figures for full-time females were 37.5 and 36.5. The movement in normal hours amongst part-time workers was somewhat more complicated (note we are dealing with *average* observed normal hours and not those reported in collective agreements) with a rise for female workers during the mid-1970s, followed by a decline. For males there was also a peak in the mid-1970s. This may reflect compositional and structural changes, as well as cyclical phenomena.

While the average values have been changing, with one exception, which we outline below, the modal values remained unaltered for all of the groups for the whole period (see Bosworth and Westaway 1985). The modal value for full-time males was 40 throughout. The equivalent figure for full-time females was 40 until 1982, when it fell for the first time to 37½ (which was the only change throughout). The picture emerges of a changing distribution of normal hours, with the average moving away from the mode as lower levels of negotiated normal hours diffuse through the economy, eventually resulting in a rather sudden and dramatic change in the modal value. While these changes are not as marked as in earlier years, there is clear evidence of a downward movement in normal hours.

The implications for total hours of work and pay are not entirely clear as overtime hours may be substituted for normal hours.[15] Earnings may be affected in several ways. First, the reduction in normal hours tends to reduce total hours of work, but overtime working may also increase (particularly in the short run, but perhaps also in the long run). The loss of income from lower normal and/or total hours may therefore be partly, wholly, or more than offset by a growth in earnings from overtime premiums. Thus, reductions in normal hours of work can have short- and long-run implications for earnings, because of lagged adjustment of hours to their desired level.

(b) Overtime working

Overtime working has a number of relevant dimensions: incidence, length, and premium level. Incidence and length should be viewed against the background of the level of normal basic hours of work. All of these dimensions affect the overall level and growth of earnings within the economy: (1) a higher incidence with given average length at given premium rates will raise average pay; (2) longer hours of overtime with given incidence and given premium will raise average pay; (3) a higher average premium with constant incidence and length of overtime will also increase pay.

Even fairly casual observation of other data reveals that, in the period since 1963, high levels of overtime have been worked by operatives. In the manufacturing sector, approximately 30 per cent of operatives have typically received overtime pay, working an average of approximately 8 hours of overtime per operative on overtime.[16] Even at the first rung of the overtime ladder (i.e. around the 25–33 per cent premium mark), this implies that approximately 6 per cent of all operatives' pay comes from overtime. If we focus wholly on those operatives working overtime, around 20 per cent of their earnings may be the result of overtime payments.

One important question therefore concerns the extent to which overtime hours were affected by various factors during the period, and, in particular, the degree to which they were squeezed by the recession. The evidence from other sources indicates that, while overtime working was maintained at unexpectedly high levels during the recession, significant variations occurred in both the incidence and (to a lesser extent) the length of overtime worked.[17] Given the high weight of overtime hours within pay, such variations can cause important cyclical variations in earnings. Given that overtime is not distributed evenly across different groups in the economy, there will also be changes in pay with shifts in the industry, occupation, and gender mix of the employment.

The incidence of overtime working varies significantly between males and females, part-time and full-time, and between manual and non-manual workers, as shown in Table 11.1. In 1970, the incidence of overtime working was 54 per cent amongst full-time males, but only 20 per cent amongst full-time females. The relative amounts of overtime working were similar in 1982, although both incidence levels were considerably down on their 1970 values, particularly in the case of full-time males. The incidence of overtime differs substantially between occupations. Even at the aggregate level there is a clear distinction between manual and non-manual workers. For full-time manual males, for example, the incidence of overtime in 1970 ranges from a minimum of 44 per cent in mineral oil refining etc. to a maximum of 100 per cent in bricks, pottery, and glass, and construction. By 1982 incidence levels had fallen somewhat but still remained well over 50 per cent in most industries. In contrast, for non-manual males the incidence levels are normally only half this size. This distinction is nowhere near as pronounced for females or for part-time workers, where the incidence is much lower.

Table 11.1. *Incidence of overtime working for various categories (%)*

	1970	1976	1979	1982
All industries				
All workers	42.1	39.4	40.6	32.0
All full-time	45.5	42.5	44.5	34.2
All part-time	18.1	13.1	17.0	19.6
Full-time				
Males	54.4	51.8	55.0	41.6
Females	19.7	17.9	17.5	17.9
Manual	57.2	54.1	61.2	43.8
Non-manual	21.5	20.5	19.0	21.5
Manufacturing				
All workers	49.1	46.2	46.3	37.8
All full-time	51.1	47.8	47.9	38.7
All part-time	25.2	25.9	24.8	21.5
Full-time				
Males	58.8	55.8	55.6	44.2
Females	23.9	22.1	19.9	19.3
Manual	58.8	55.5	54.7	45.0
Non-manual	25.2	22.5	26.5	23.8

Source: NES data base.

The published data from the NES show important differences in hours of work across industries and across occupations particularly in overtime hours (Bosworth and Dawkins 1981: 69–83). Thus, industry and occupational variables have figured strongly in the literature on hours of work. In the past, however, information has generally not been available by both industry *and* occupation which enables their joint impact on hours of work (and pay) to be investigated. One aspect we explore below, therefore, concerns the way in which the changing industry/occupational matrix has influenced hours of work.

The information contained in Table 11.1 shows that, overall, the incidence of overtime exhibits a significant downward trend. The incidence amongst all workers was 42 per cent in 1970 and by 1982 this had fallen to 32 per cent although this decline is probably at least partly cyclical. However, the fall was not evenly distributed across the different types of workers. For example, for part-time workers the incidence of overtime grew slightly, while in the case of full-time workers the incidence fell appreciably. Interpretation of this result requires further detailed analysis; nevertheless it has clearly been influenced by the recessions that characterized the UK economy over this period. In addition, it may reflect the fact that entry and re-entry into the workforce has increasingly been through part-time employment, although the workers concerned would often prefer full-time jobs.

The longer-term trends take place within the context of quite important cyclical movements in the incidence of overtime. Bearing in mind their overall downward trend, the published NES data indicate that full-time males started from an incidence level of around 55 per cent in 1970, fell to 49 per cent in 1972, before jumping again to over 52 per cent in 1973 and 1974. The next trough was in 1976, peaking again three years later. The equivalent, full-time female incidence levels show an analogous pattern over time. This cyclical pattern can to some extent also be discerned in Table 11.1.

The duration of overtime hours per worker on overtime series exhibit somewhat similar trends to the incidence of overtime working. However, although average hours of overtime fell from 7.7 in 1970 to 6.1 in 1982, the major part of this difference occurs between 1980 and 1981. The average duration of overtime in 1980 was 7.8 hours, which was the highest value of any of the years. The sharp decline between then and 1982 may be a unique response to the strength of the 1981 recession. Data from other sources, such as the DE's monthly survey of operatives in manufacturing industries, suggest that there is normally comparatively little cyclical pattern in the average length of overtime; the main variation occurs through its incidence.

In parallel with the uneven distribution of the incidence of overtime there are major differences in the number of overtime hours per worker on overtime between males and females, and between part-time and full-time workers. In 1980, for example, full-time males worked 7.2 hours of overtime (about 20 per cent of total hours) while full-time females only worked 2.4 hours (around 8 per cent) (see also Table 11.2). In absolute terms, part-time employees worked significantly less overtime than their full-time counterparts. However, Table 11.2 shows that this result no longer holds for females when the overtime hours are taken as a proportion of basic or total hours. On average overtime hours account for some 8 per cent of total hours for females as a whole but for over 10 per cent for part-time workers. None of the groups appears to show significant trends over time, but the degree of variation in hours of overtime appears much greater for some groups than others. Part-time female workers particularly stand out in this respect. This may be consistent with the view that employers are using part-time workers as a source of increasing flexibility in the UK labour market. However the lion's share of overtime hours is again worked by full-time males (in particular manual workers).

Weekly overtime pay per person on overtime varies considerably

Table 11.2. *Ratio of overtime hours to total hours*

	1970	1973	1976	1979	1982
All workers	0.19	0.19	0.18	0.19	0.16
All full-time	0.19	0.19	0.18	0.19	0.16
All part-time	0.10	0.10	0.09	0.11	0.10
Males	0.20	0.20	0.18	0.20	0.18
Females	0.08	0.08	0.07	0.08	0.07
Male full-time	0.20	0.20	0.18	0.20	0.17
Male part-time	0.10	0.11	0.11	0.15	0.11
Female full-time	0.07	0.07	0.06	0.08	0.06
Female part-time	0.10	0.10	0.09	0.10	0.10

Note: Based on the average overtime hours for those working overtime.
Source: NES data base.

between groups, as we would expect given the different hours of overtime worked. It ranges from around £20 per week amongst full-time males, to as little as £3 per week for part-time females (constant, 1979 prices). It also varies over time for each of the groups, peaking at over £20 (1973) in real terms for full-time males, with a minimum of £17 (1977). Again there are very substantial variations in the ratios of overtime pay to total pay for the different categories within the workforce as shown in Table 11.3. Overtime pay accounts for approximately 20 per cent of total earnings amongst full-time males and around 8 per cent in the case of full-time females (with part-time females again showing a somewhat higher proportion). The data in these tables are based on the average overtime hours and pay of those working overtime. They do not therefore reflect differences in incidence which, as Table 11.1 indicates, are also significant.

No simple relationship emerges between hours of work and plant or company size. Further analysis of this data set using multiple regression analysis will be needed to establish the separate effects of these two influences. Nevertheless, it is clear from the existing results that overtime pay per person on overtime is significantly higher in the largest plants and companies *vis-à-vis* the smallest.

(c) Part-time working

Table 11.4 illustrates the incidence of part-time work for different categories in somewhat greater detail. Another factor related to hours of work, with important implications for pay, is the increasing tendency for people to be employed on a part-time basis. As with changes in the

Table 11.3. *Ratio of overtime pay to total pay*

	1970	1973	1976	1979	1982
All workers	0.21	0.23	0.20	0.21	0.19
All full-time	0.20	0.22	0.19	0.20	0.18
All part-time	0.10	0.11	0.09	0.11	0.10
Males	0.20	0.21	0.19	0.20	0.18
Females	0.08	0.09	0.08	0.09	0.08
Male full-time	0.20	0.21	0.19	0.20	0.18
Male part-time	0.11	0.12	0.12	0.16	0.12
Female full-time	0.08	0.09	0.07	0.09	0.08
Female part-time	0.10	0.11	0.09	0.11	0.10

Note: Based on the average overtime hours for those working overtime.
Source: NES data base.

Table 11.4. *Incidence of part-time working (%)*

	1970	1976	1979	1982
All industries				
All workers	12.4	13.1	14.4	15.1
Males	2.0	1.8	1.9	1.9
Females	19.7	17.9	17.5	17.9
Manual	13.5	14.4	15.4	16.3
Non-manual	10.9	11.4	13.4	14.0
Manual males	2.1	2.1	2.0	2.0
Manual females	46.1	48.2	51.8	53.2
Non-manual males	1.7	1.3	1.8	1.7
Non-manual females	20.8	21.8	24.7	25.3
Manufacturing				
All workers	7.7	7.5	6.9	5.3
Males	1.2	1.0	1.0	0.7
Females	24.5	24.4	23.8	18.7
Manual	8.7	8.3	7.5	5.5
Non-manual	5.2	5.5	5.6	4.9
Manual males	1.6	1.2	1.2	0.8
Manual females	30.3	29.2	28.7	22.3
Non-manual males	0.3	0.2	0.5	0.4
Non-manual females	14.3	15.4	15.9	14.1

Source: NES data base.

incidence and average length of overtime, changes in the pattern of part-time working have a direct impact on weekly pay. This highlights the very different incidence rates compared with overtime. While for the latter the highest rates were for male manual workers in manufacturing, the incidence rates of part-time working are greater for female, non-manual workers in the service sector. The table also highlights the growth in incidence over the period, which has primarily affected females (although in recent years there has been an increase for males as well). This increase has mainly been in the service sector. The data indicate a decline in incidence for manufacturing, especially for manual females.

11.5. Compositional and Structural Changes and Pay

Changes in the incidence of overtime working are only one example of the way in which changes in the composition of the workforce (in this case between those working and those not working overtime) can, in principle, affect average pay and hours. Other possible determinants are the trends in the other dimensions related to the composition and structure of employment. In particular these include such features as: the increasing importance of part-time working; the shift from manual to non-manual work; and changes in the industrial structure of employment. The differences in hours worked between different groups have been highlighted above. In Table 11.6 the differences in pay between different groups are illustrated. This demonstrates the well-known differentials in hourly earnings between males and females, manual and non-manual workers, and part-time and full-time workers. In this section, using a simple shift-share technique we attempt to establish the influence (if any) of changes in composition over the period 1970–82 on average hours and pay across all groups.

Table 11.5 provides a broad summary of the structure of employment. This illustrates how the NES sample has altered over time, in line with changes of the overall structure of employment indicated in other sources.[18] The main features are:

1. the shift in employment between industries in favour of services as opposed to the primary and manufacturing sectors;
2. the growth in the employment share of part-timers;
3. the increasing proportion of females in employment;
4. the shift in employment towards white-collar and professional occupations and against lower-skilled, blue-collar workers.

We begin by considering structural and compositional effects on hours of work. Adopting the methodology described in Appendix 11.1 the total

Table 11.5. *Changes in the structure of employment*

	1970	1973	1979	1982
All industries				
% of females	35.5	36.6	38.5	40.7
% of part-timers	12.5	13.1	14.4	15.1
% of non-manual	42.3	43.9	48.8	53.0
% of workers employed in				
Primary	5.39	4.67	4.59	4.50
Engineering	17.71	17.02	15.75	14.15
Remainder of manufacturing	20.98	20.25	17.23	14.96
Construction	5.67	6.50	5.74	5.40
Private services	25.94	27.38	28.51	29.95
Public services	24.31	24.18	28.17	31.04
Manufacturing				
% of females	27.8	27.8	26.1	25.7
% of part-timers	7.7	7.5	6.8	5.3
% of non-manual	28.9	28.1	30.0	34.2

Source: NES data base.

Table 11.6. *Ratios of hourly earnings*

	1970	1973	1976	1979	1982
Manual–non-manual	0.74	0.78	0.78	0.79	0.74
Females–males	0.60	0.61	0.70	0.68	0.68
Part-time–full-time	0.59	0.59	0.66	0.65	0.64

Note: Gross pay including overtime etc.
Source: NES data base.

change in hours worked between any two years can be attributed to the following factors:

1. *Hours effect*: changes in the average level of hours worked by each category of the workforce distinguished *ceteris paribus*.
2. *Industry effect*: changes due to shifts in the industrial structure of employment between the two years, for example, between industries which typically work longer hours (e.g. agriculture and mining) and those which work shorter hours (e.g. parts of the service sector).
3. *Composition effect*: changes due to shifts in composition *within*

industries between categories working longer and shorter hours. These can be further decomposed into:

(a) changes due to composition by gender (the *gender effect*), because, for example, women may work shorter hours, *ceteris paribus*;
(b) changes due to composition by employment status between those working full-time and part-time (the *part-time effect*);
(c) changes due to occupational composition (the *occupational effect*), for example, changes in composition in favour of white-collar workers, working shorter hours.

The results of conducting such an analysis on the NES data base are summarized in the following Tables. The industry effect is based on changes in composition across 17 industries (8 of which are in manufacturing). The occupational effect covers 8 occupational categories, while the gender and part-time effects are based on a two-way split.

Table 11.7 illustrates the results for total average weekly hours, for all industries and services. Separate estimates are also presented for the manufacturing sector. Between 1970 and 1982 the length of the average working week declined by almost 3 hours. Just over half of this was attributable to the hours effect (1.6 hours). The remainder was due to structural or compositional effects. Changes in industry structure, particularly after 1973, in favour of services resulted in a decline of about 0.9 of an hour. Compositional effects within industries were less important, totalling about 0.5 of an hour. About a half of this was due to shifts in occupational composition away from blue-collar and towards white-collar work.

Within manufacturing the overall decline in hours was substantially less (1.8 hours). This reflected a modest decline in normal hours compared with other sectors (see Table 11.8). The hours effect however was greater than in all industries and services (2.1 hours), being offset to some extent by compositional factors. The negative hours effect in manufacturing reflected a substantial reduction in overtime hours (see Table 11.9). The industrial effect within manufacturing was insignificant. However, the compositional effect was more important, amounting to +0.3 of an hour between 1970 and 1982. This compares with the figure of −0.5 for all industries and services. The part-time effect was considerably more important than the gender effect. In the case of manufacturing the share of females and part-timers actually fell over most of this period and consequently this had a positive effect on hours worked.

Tables 11.8 and 11.9 provide an analagous analysis for normal and average overtime hours worked per week. It is clear from Table 11.8 that about 1.5 hours of the total reduction for all industries and services was attributable to reductions in normal hours. Less than half of this (0.6) was

Table 11.7. *Shift-share analysis of total weekly hours (hours per week)*

	1970–3	1973–9	1979–82	1970–82
All industries and				
services				
Total change	−0.38	−0.96	−1.63	−2.97
Hours effect	−0.11	−0.35	−1.18	−1.64
Industrial effect	−0.07	−0.40	−0.39	−0.86
Compositional effect	−0.20	−0.21	−0.06	−0.47
of which:				
Gender effect	−0.07	−0.05	−0.05	−0.17
Part-time effect	0.04	−0.12	0.05	−0.03
Occupational effect	−0.18	−0.04	−0.06	−0.27
Manufacturing				
Total change	—	−0.17	−1.63	−1.80
Hours effect	−0.11	−0.24	−1.79	−2.13
Industrial effect	0.01	0.03	−0.02	0.02
Compositional effect	0.10	0.03	0.18	0.31
of which:				
Gender effect	0.01	0.09	0.02	0.11
Part-time effect	0.05	−0.08	0.25	0.22
Occupational effect	0.03	0.02	−0.08	−0.03

Notes: For details of methodology see Appendix 11.1 and main text.
Components may not sum to totals due to rounding.

Source: NES data base.

due to the average reductions in hours within each category. The effects of structural and composition changes accounted for 0.6 and 0.3 respectively. In the case of overtime hours, however, approximately two-thirds of the decline of 1.5 hours in total hours was due to lower average overtime hours worked.

The contrast for manufacturing is quite dramatic. Overall, normal hours showed no change between 1970 and 1982 (although this disguises a rise between 1970 and 1979 of a quarter of an hour followed by a subsequent decline). The negative hours effect (0.4) was almost as powerful as in all industries and services but this was offset by a compositional effect (associated mainly with the change in the mix of full-time and part-time workers) which raised the average level of normal hours by 0.3 between 1970 and 1982. Nearly all of the decline in hours in manufacturing over this period was attributable to reductions in overtime hours, especially after 1979 (see Table 11.9). Almost all of this was, in turn, due

Table 11.8. *Shift-share analysis of normal weekly hours (hours per week)*

	1970–3	1973–9	1979–82	1970–82
All industries and services				
Total change	−0.21	−0.57	−0.67	−1.46
Hours effect	−0.02	−0.19	−0.39	−0.61
Industrial effect	−0.04	−0.26	−0.27	−0.56
Compositional effect	−0.15	−0.12	−0.02	−0.29
of which:				
Gender effect	−0.05	−0.04	−0.04	−0.13
Part-time effect	0.03	−0.13	0.04	−0.07
Occupational effect	−0.12	0.05	−0.02	−0.09
Manufacturing				
Total change	0.18	0.04	−0.28	−0.05
Hours effect	0.12	−0.02	−0.49	−0.39
Industrial effect	—	0.02	−0.02	−0.01
Compositional effect	0.06	0.05	0.24	0.34
of which:				
Gender effect	—	0.05	0.01	0.06
Part-time effect	0.05	−0.04	0.24	0.25
Occupational effect	0.01	0.04	−0.02	0.03

Notes: For details of methodology see Appendix 11.1 and main text.
Components may not sum to totals due to rounding.
Source: NES data base.

to reductions in overtime hours across the board. Structural and compositional factors were of little significance.

The same technique can be used to analyse developments in pay. Table 11.10 provides results for average hourly pay deflated by the retail price index into 'real' 1979 prices. This analysis suggests that both for all industries and services and for manufacturing the bulk of the increase in hourly pay is attributable to an hourly *pay effect* (defined analogously to the hours effect above). Structural and compositional factors appear to have been relatively unimportant. For all industries and services the compositional effect is more important than the structural effect, with a positive impact due to shifts in occupational structure. This is also true for manufacturing where this influence is rather stronger, albeit still fairly small, only contributing about 5p of the total increase of 45p in real hourly pay between 1970 and 1982. It is also interesting to note that for all industries and services the shift in employment structure towards part-timers actually raised average hourly earnings *ceteris paribus*.

Table 11.9. *Shift-share analysis of overtime hours (hours per week)*

	1970–3	1973–9	1979–82	1970–82
All industries and services				
Total change	−0.17	−0.39	−0.96	−1.51
Hours effect	−0.08	−0.16	−0.78	−1.03
Industrial effect	−0.02	−0.14	−0.13	−0.29
Compositional effect	−0.06	−0.09	−0.04	−0.18
of which:				
Gender effect	−0.02	−0.01	−0.01	−0.04
Part-time effect	0.02	0.01	0.01	0.04
Occupational effect	−0.06	−0.09	−0.04	−0.19
Manufacturing				
Total change	−0.19	−0.22	−0.35	−1.75
Hours effect	−0.23	−0.21	−1.30	−1.74
Industrial effect	0.01	0.01	—	0.02
Compositional effect	0.03	−0.02	−0.05	−0.03
of which:				
Gender effect	—	0.04	0.01	0.05
Part-time effect	0.01	−0.04	—	−0.03
Occupational effect	0.02	−0.02	−0.06	−0.06

Notes: For details of methodology see Appendix 11.1 and main text.
Components may not sum to totals due to rounding.

Source: NES data base.

Overall trends in hourly pay and hours have been in opposite directions. Changes in gross weekly pay reflect these two opposing forces of rising real wage rates and falling average weekly hours. In addition however it is clear that structural and compositional effects on pay can in principle work in precisely the opposite direction to their impact on hours worked. The overall impact on weekly pay will therefore reflect the net outcome of these various offsetting effects.

In Table 11.11 we present an analysis of changes in gross weekly pay (again in 1979 prices). Between 1970 and 1982 average weekly pay rose by £12.1 in all industries and services. This was more than accounted for by a £13.6 increase due to the pay effect. The latter incorporates an effect attributable to changes in average weekly hours over the period *ceteris paribus*. In fact because the hours change was negative the *hourly* pay effect was even larger at £17 per week. Structural and compositional factors were less important, to some extent reflecting the offsetting

Table 11.10. *Shift-share analysis of hourly pay (£ 1979)*

	1970–3	1973–9	1979–82	1970–82
All industries and services				
Total change	0.1821	0.1042	0.1739	0.4602
Hourly pay effect	0.1800	0.0924	0.1645	0.4369
Industrial effect	0.0035	−0.0063	−0.0017	−0.0044
Compositional effect	−0.0015	0.0181	0.0111	0.0277
of which:				
Gender effect	−0.0116	−0.0019	−0.0061	−0.0195
Part-time effect	0.0108	0.0007	0.0063	0.0178
Occupational effect	−0.0007	0.0192	0.0109	0.0295
Manufacturing				
Total change	0.1822	0.1380	0.1286	0.4488
Hourly pay effect	0.1840	0.1075	0.0900	0.3815
Industrial effect	0.0001	0.0117	0.0043	0.0162
Compositional effect	−0.0020	0.0188	0.0343	0.0512
of which:				
Gender effect	0.0009	0.0079	0.0012	0.0101
Part-time effect	0.0006	−0.0070	0.0015	−0.0049
Occupational effect	−0.0035	0.0179	0.0316	0.0460

Notes: For details of methodology see Appendix 11.1 and main text.
Components may not sum to totals due to rounding.
Source: NES data base.

tendencies noted above. The industrial effect resulted in a decline of −£1.8 per week. The compositional effects were offsetting, the gender effect of −£0.9 was countered by +£0.6 each for the part-time and the occupational effects.

A similar pattern emerges in manufacturing. Of the total increase in pay of £14.2, £11.2 is attributable to the overall pay effect. Of the latter changes in hours reduced pay by £4.6, and so the hourly pay effect was £15.9. Changes in industrial structure were of less significance than for all industries and services, but compositional factors within industries were more important. The latter contributed £2.3 to the increase in total, the most important factor being changes in occupational composition towards higher paid groups. It is notable that in manufacturing the occupational compositional effects on both hours worked and hourly pay were reinforcing whereas in all industries and services they worked in opposite directions (see Tables 11.7 and 11.10).

Table 11.11. *Shift-share analysis of total weekly pay (£ 1979)*

	1970–3	1973–9	1979–82	1970–82
All industries and services				
Total change	6.91	2.05	3.18	12.12
Pay effect	7.19	2.72	3.72	13.63
of which:				
Due to hours	−0.19	−0.63	−2.59	−3.39
Due to hourly rates	7.38	3.35	6.31	17.02
Industrial effect	0.01	−0.95	−0.81	−1.75
Compositional effect	−0.29	0.26	0.27	0.23
of which:				
Gender effect	−0.53	−0.14	−0.30	−0.93
Part-time effect	0.52	−0.19	0.30	−0.63
Occupational effect	−0.29	−0.59	0.27	0.58
Manufacturing				
Total change	7.77	5.07	1.38	14.21
Pay effect	7.68	3.81	−0.27	11.22
of which:				
Due to hours	−0.24	−0.45	−3.95	−4.64
Due to hourly rates	7.92	4.26	3.68	15.86
Industrial effect	0.01	0.53	0.12	0.67
Compositional effect	0.08	0.73	1.52	2.33
of which:				
Gender effect	0.05	0.47	0.08	0.61
Part-time effect	0.09	−0.45	0.40	0.03
Occupational effect	−0.06	0.71	1.04	1.68

Notes: For details of methodology see Appendix 11.1 and main text.
Components may not sum to totals due to rounding.

Source: NES data base.

As in the case of hours, the overall change in pay can be divided into the changes relating to basic pay and overtime pay. The analysis for these two components is shown in Tables 11.12 and 11.13. In all industries and services real basic pay increased by £9.1 between 1970 and 1982. Of this, £9.6 was attributable to increases in real hourly wage rates. Changing hours resulted in a fall of £1.1 while changes in industry structure resulted in a decline of £0.3. Compositional effects resulted in increases in pay of £0.9, although this represented a negative gender effect and positive part-time and occupational effects. For manufacturing, compositional

Table 11.12. *Shift-share analysis of basic (residual) weekly pay (£ 1979)*

	1970–3	1973–9	1979–82	1970–82
All industries and services				
Total change	0.48	3.02	5.60	9.09
Pay effect	0.55	2.66	5.28	8.50
of which:				
Due to hours	−0.01	−0.31	−0.79	−1.10
Due to hourly rates	0.56	2.97	6.07	9.60
Industrial effect	0.06	−0.21	−0.13	−1.28
Compositional effect	−0.13	0.56	0.44	0.87
of which:				
Gender effect	−0.48	−0.10	−0.26	−0.83
Part-time effect	0.46	−0.23	0.23	0.46
Occupational effect	−0.12	0.89	0.46	1.24
Manufacturing				
Total change	−2.94	5.94	5.86	8.87
Pay effect	−2.78	4.63	3.78	5.63
of which:				
Due to hours	0.21	−0.03	−0.97	−0.79
Due to hourly rates	−2.99	4.66	4.75	6.42
Industrial effect	−0.01	0.49	0.34	0.82
Compositional effect	−2.99	4.66	4.75	6.42
of which:				
Gender effect	−0.01	0.33	0.04	0.37
Part-time effect	0.08	−0.32	0.35	0.11
Occupational effect	−0.23	0.82	1.35	1.94

Notes: For details of methodology see Appendix 11.1 and main text.
    Components may not sum to totals due to rounding.
Source: NES data base.

effects (especially the occupational effect) were much more significant accounting for £2.4 of the overall increase of £8.9.

In contrast Table 11.13 shows that overtime pay for all industries and services fell by £1.9. This was more than accounted for by reductions in hours of overtime (which resulted in a fall of £2.5). However this was in turn partly offset by the growth in hourly rates of pay. Structural and compositional effects also account for a significant part of the observed fall. In manufacturing, overtime pay fell by £2. Again the effect of hours was negative, resulting in a decline of £4.4, but this was partly offset by

Table 11.13. *Shift-share analysis of weekly overtime pay (£ 1979)*

	1970–3	1973–9	1979–82	1970–82
All industries and services				
Total change	0.78	−1.02	−1.68	−1.92
Pay effect	0.95	−0.50	−1.29	−0.84
of which:				
Due to hours	−0.22	−0.31	−1.96	−2.49
Due to hourly rates	1.17	−0.19	0.67	1.65
Industrial effect	−0.04	−0.34	−0.30	−0.69
Compositional effect	−0.12	−0.18	−0.10	−0.39
of which:				
Gender effect	−0.04	−0.03	−0.03	−0.10
Part-time effect	0.04	0.03	0.03	0.10
Occupational effect	−0.12	−0.18	−0.10	−0.40
Manufacturing				
Total change	1.20	−0.46	−2.70	−1.96
Pay effect	1.09	−0.50	−2.60	−2.02
of which:				
Due to hours	−0.56	−0.48	−3.35	−4.39
Due to hourly rates	1.65	−0.02	0.75	2.37
Industrial effect	0.02	0.07	0.01	0.10
Compositional effect	0.08	−0.03	−0.11	−0.05
of which:				
Gender effect	0.01	0.10	0.02	0.13
Part-time effect	0.01	−0.10	0.01	−0.08
Occupational effect	0.06	−0.03	−0.13	−0.01

Notes: For details of methodology see Appendix 11.1 and main text.
Components may not sum to totals due to rounding.
Source: NES data base.

the growth in hourly rates. In this case structural and compositional factors were of minor significance.

11.6. Conclusions

The initial analysis of both the published and unpublished NES data reveals important movements in hours of work, confirming and elaborating on changes outlined elsewhere in the literature. The subsequent discussion highlighted the decline in normal hours, the growth of part-time working, and the partly cyclical movements in hours of overtime. It was argued that such changes could have significant effects on the level and distribution of pay across individuals. The shift-share analysis indicated that the main determinant of changes in pay over the 1970–82 period (apart from general inflation) was the overall increase in real hourly pay rates. Changes in hours worked over this period have in general had a negative impact on pay. The latter reflects the long-term decline in normal hours but more especially the decline in overtime hours worked over this period. Structural and compositional factors were often offsetting. Changes in industrial structure (for example, the switch from manufacturing to services) have tended to reduce average hours and overall pay levels. In contrast compositional changes in favour of certain occupations (e.g. professional white-collar as opposed to lower-skilled blue-collar workers) have tended to raise pay levels, while at the same time tending to reduce average weekly hours. Thus, while the compositional effect on hourly earnings has worked in one direction, this has been cancelled out at least in part by an offsetting impact on weekly hours. In addition, different components of the compositional effect due to gender, employment status, and occupation, while individually significant, have often worked in opposite directions in affecting both hours and pay.

Appendix 11.1. Methodology for Calculating Contributions of Different Effects to the Total Change in Average Hours and Pay

The level of average weekly hours in all industries and services is a weighted average of the values across industries and across categories in the labour force. The current weighted value in year t is given by,

$$CW_t = \sum_{j=1}^{20} \sum_{i=1}^{8} \frac{H_{ijt}{}^*E_{ijt}{}^*E_{jt}}{\dfrac{\displaystyle\sum_{i=1}^{8} E_{ijt}}{\displaystyle\sum_{j=1}^{20} E_{ijt}}} \qquad (11.1)$$

where H_{ijt} and E_{ijt} are the level of hours and employment respectively in industry j and category i in period t and E_{jt} is the total employment in industry j (i.e. $\sum_{i=1}^{8} E_{ijt}$ ($j=1$, 8, $i=1$, 20 say)

$$BW_t = \sum_{j=1}^{20} \sum_{i=1}^{8} H_{ijt} {}^* E_{ij,t-n} {}^* E_{j,t-n} \frac{\dfrac{}{\sum\limits_{i=1}^{8} E_{ij,t-n}}}{\sum\limits_{j=1}^{20} E_{ij,t-n}} \tag{11.2}$$

gives BW_t the corresponding value of average hours calculated using base year $(t - n)$ employment weights. Finally,

$$BWI_t = \sum_{j=1}^{20} \sum_{i=1}^{8} H_{ij,t-1} {}^* E_{ij,t-n} {}^* E_{jt} \frac{\dfrac{}{\sum\limits_{i=1}^{8} E_{ij,t-n}}}{\sum\limits_{j=1}^{20} E_{jt}} \tag{11.3}$$

gives the level of hours that would have been worked in period t had both the composition of the workforce in each industry and the level of hours in each category remained fixed and only the relative levels of industrial employment had altered.

The total change in average hours between $t - n$ and t is therefore,

$$TC_{t,t-n} = CW_t - CW_{t-n} \tag{11.4}$$

The change attributable to changes in industrial structure alone $IC_{t,t-n}$ is given by,

$$IC_{t,t-n} = BWI_t - CW_{t-n} \tag{11.5}$$

The change due to changes in both hours and industrial effects is,

$$CC_{t,t-n} = BW_t - CW_{t-n} \tag{11.6}$$

Of this the component attributable to changes in hours is,

$$HC_{t,t-n} = CC_{t,t-n} - IC_{t,t-n} \tag{11.7}$$

The residual is then attributed to changes in the composition of the workforce within each industry,

$$SC_{t,t-n} = TC_{t,t-n} - CC_{t,t-n} \tag{11.8}$$

Using a similar approach the compositional effect *SC* can be further subdivided into components attributable to changes in sexual composition, occupational composition, and full-time/part-time status.

The results obtained are not independent of the precise method used for calculation. The change due to changes in hours, or the industrial change, could be obtained as the residual. However, the method adopted here seems the most appropriate. Pay can be analysed in an analogous manner except that here the *pay effect* analogous to the effect due to changes in hours in equation (11.7) above can be split into two parts; first, a component due to changes in hours worked (which may be total, basic, or overtime hours as appropriate); and second the difference between this and the total pay effect. This is termed as 'hourly pay effect' in the tables.

Notes

1. See for example Bosworth and Dawkins (1981: 23–5), Wilson *et al.* (1985), Blyton (1985), and Whybrew (1968).
2. Some of the early literature on worksharing is discussed in Bosworth and Dawkins (1981: 230–6). See also Dankert (1965: 162–3), Whitley and Wilson (1986), and Wilson *et al.* (1985).
3. Hours of work formed a sub-model of the Ball and St. Cyr (1966) short-run factor demand model. Nadiri and Rosen (1969) and, later, Briscoe and Peel (1975) extended this work to interrelated factor demand systems, where hours of work are one of the four primary dimensions of factor services (i.e. capital, capital utilization, labour, and hours). More recently, however, Bosworth and Westaway (1987) have emphasized the heterogeneity of hours, which are averaged over both short-time and overtime working. In addition, interest has been growing about the relationship between employment, shiftwork, and hours (Bosworth 1981, Harris 1983, and Bosworth and Pugh 1985*a*), and employment, hours, and inventories (Topel 1982, Medoff 1983, Rossana 1983, 1985).
4. See for example Gronau (1977), Gershuny (1983), and Wilson and Bosworth (1986).
5. See for example Hakim (1984*a*, 1984*b*, 1985), Blanchflower and Corry (1986*a*), and Wilson and Bosworth (1986). This literature has close connections with the work on multiple job holdings (Alden 1977) and the informal economy (Handy 1984, Heertje *et al.* 1980, Wilson and Bosworth 1986).
6. Sawyer (1973), Hood and Rees (1974), and Mulvey and Foster (1976) all report functions explaining average earnings, for manual male workers, estimated across MLHs (see also Mulvey and Abowd 1980). Pencavel (1974) examined analogous functions for all manual workers, estimated using SIC Orders level data, including the non-manufacturing sector.
7. Metcalf, Nickell, and Richardson (1976), estimated at MLH level.
8. Wabe and Leech (1978), estimated at MLH level within the manufacturing sector.
9. Adaptive and rational expectations are discussed at length in Lucas and Sargent (1981*b*). A rational expectations model of employment, stock building, investment, and wages is contained in Hall and Henry (1985). See also Henry (1981).
10. See Mitchell (1985) and Bosworth (1986*b*).
11. See for example Gregory and Smith (1983), Dawkins and Wooden (1985), and Bosworth (1986*b*).
12. See for example Department of Employment, *NES* (1979: Part F, T147, pp. F5–31).
13. Part-time working has, at least until recently, traditionally been defined around normal hours of 30 per week, with certain provisos (see for example *NES* (1978: Part A, 'Report and Key Results', Appendix 5, p. A58)). However, it did not make sense to define full-time workers around normal hours and, for consistency, we have adopted the same measure (i.e. total hours) for dividing the part-time sample. The problems introduced by this can be checked by examining the difference between basic and total hours in the part-time sample.
14. See for example the data contained in DE, *Time Rates* (annual).
15. See for example the findings of Bodo and Giannini (1985) and Bosworth and Westaway (1985, 1987).

16. The data are taken from Department of Employment, 'Overtime and Short Time Working of Operatives', *DE Gazette* (monthly).
17. See for example the description of overtime and short-time working in chemicals (Bosworth 1987), engineering (Bosworth *et al*. 1987*b*), and textiles (Bosworth and Westaway 1986).
18. See for example Wilson and Bosworth (1986).

12
Shift-working and Pay[1]
D. Bosworth and R. Wilson

12.1. Introduction

Shift-working remains a relatively under-researched aspect of the labour market. One of the main reasons for this has been the lack of suitable data to test the theoretical models that started to emerge in the 1970s. This paper considers the new information that the New Earnings Survey data provide about developments in shift-working activity and about the impact of changes in shift-working on earnings since 1973.

Shift-work impinges on earnings in two main ways: first, through changes in the incidence of shift-working (at given premium levels); second, through changes in premium rates (at given incidence levels). The first of these dimensions touches on a long-standing debate, and the newly available data are used in conjunction with other sources in an attempt to reveal the longer-term trends in the incidence of shift-working. This is followed by a shift-share analysis which examines the impact of changes in industrial and occupational structure on shift-work. In addition, we investigate the new evidence regarding the role of changes in shift premiums over time for the development of pay over this period.

Unlike hours of work, shift-working is not a primary dimension used to organize the published data in the NES and there are no separate published tables for this aspect of work patterns. The improvement to our existing level of knowledge about shift-working from analysing the new data tapes is therefore greater and more immediate. However, it should be borne in mind that there are some limitations associated with the definition of shift-working in the NES, namely that persons are classified as shift-workers or not according to whether they receive shift premiums.[2] The potential problems that this gives rise to are discussed in detail elsewhere (Bosworth and Dawkins 1981: 89–91), but it is worth noting that the definition may include certain 'unsocial hours' payments and exclude some workers on shifts or working unsocial hours who are not paid an explicit premium. A direct consequence of the adopted definition is the lack of a breakdown of shift-working by type of shift.[3]

The stratification adopted for the shift-working data parallels that of hours of work (see Chapter 11), with the exception that, in this instance, the hours bands have been replaced by a simple (1, 0) breakdown, according to whether the person in question was in receipt of a shift premium or not. Stratification took place in the following order: (1) individuals with no loss of pay; (2) full-time/part-time; (3) male/female; (4) receives premium pay; (5) receives incentive pay; (6) covered by collective agreement or Wages Council; (7) industry subdivision; (8) socio-economic group. The shift-work data base is restricted to individuals whose pay is not affected by sickness or absence.

Section 12.2 presents a review of the shift-work literature. Section 12.3 outlines the possible role of shift-work in influencing changes in the level of pay. Section 12.4 uses the NES data to examine the longer-term trends in shift-working and attempts to resolve the contradictory micro- and macro-views about the growth in shift-work. Sections 12.5 and 12.6 focus on the role of shift-work in developments in pay over the period 1973 to 1982. The first of these two sections deals mainly with the incidence of premium payments and the second section with the composition of pay. Section 12.7 examines changes in the composition of pay in greater detail. Finally, section 12.8 provides some conclusions.

12.2. Review of the Shift-work Literature

Several detailed reviews of the shift-work literature are now available.[4] These indicate that, while there is some overlap in the development of hours and shift-working research, there are also significant differences. The stimulus to the research on shift-working has come from two main areas. First, the welfare implications of unsocial times of work.[5] Second, the research on optimal capital utilization. Given that capital has to be manned at various times during its operating hours, this has direct implications for the hours and shift-work patterns adopted.[6] Given the interrelatedness of factor demands, this automatically implies the need to extend traditional factor demand models to incorporate shift-working.[7]

Most of the research focusing on shift-work patterns and earnings has looked at the reasons why shift premiums are paid. It was realized from an early stage that the magnitude of shift premiums reflects the extent to which the employees' hours fall outside of the normal times of work (i.e. 9 a.m. to 5 p.m., Monday to Friday) (Sergeant *et al.* 1969). More recently it has been recognized that they are payments for the unsocial length as well as the unsocial timing of work (Bosworth and Dawkins 1980). Subsequent research has found that shift-work is often also associated with other unsocial aspects of work, including unhealthy working conditions, higher risk, greater noise, etc. (PROSA 1981, Bosworth and Dawkins 1984).

A number of commentators see the relationship between shift-work and wage costs as a particularly important consideration (Income Data Services 1973*a*, 1973*b*, 1973*c*, 1975, 1977, 1979*a*, 1979*b*, 1982, 1983, 1985*a*, 1985*b*); however, the implications of changes in work patterns for wage costs and earnings have been less well researched in the academic literature. There has been some discussion about the effects of a switch from a high hours/low shift-working intensity to a low hours/high shift-working intensity regime for both labour costs and earnings (Bosworth and Dawkins 1981: 150–8; Bosworth 1982). These discussions have tended to be relatively abstract, however, and little or no attention has been paid to the actual changes in shift-working which have taken place over time and how this has affected earnings. Thus, to date, the inter-relationships between employment, hours, and shift-working have still not been fully explored.[8] In certain respects, the debate about work patterns has tended to move away from shift-working *per se* and has more recently focused on part-time working, homeworking, outworking, free-lance workers, and the casualization of labour (Hakim 1984*a*, 1984*b*, 1985, Blanchflower and Corry 1986*a*, Wilson and Bosworth 1986). However, shift-work and unsocial hours remain an important dimension of work patterns, for example, amongst part-time and casual workers (Blanchflower and Corry 1986*b*).

The incidence of shift-working in the early literature was seen as essentially determined by the real shift wage. The idea stemmed from the argument that minimization of the wage bill would tend to result not only in achieving the minimum point on the long-run wage–hours relationship (Garbarino 1964, Ball and St. Cyr 1966, Hart and Sharot 1978, Bosworth 1982), but also in ensuring that production was focused on the least-cost times of day, even if other influences (such as the need fully to utilize costly capital equipment) caused the production period to spill over into more unsocial times (Cook 1962, Foss 1963, Bosworth and Dawkins 1981: 137–66). More recently, however, it has been realized that other factors may also exhibit rhythmically varying prices, not least of which is the electricity input used to power capital.[9] Finally, the literature is moving towards a more comprehensive framework which integrates multiple rhythmically varying factor prices alongside rhythmically varying product prices, thereby providing a synthesis between the work pattern and peak load pricing literatures (Bosworth and Pugh 1985*b*, Bosworth 1987).

There are therefore a number of largely unresolved issues in the shift-work literature. First, there is the long-running debate about the extent to which the use of shift-working has changed in the economy. Second, there is a need for more detailed information about the extent to which various groups in the labour force (i.e. male/female, manual/non-manual, part-time/full-time, etc.) undertake shift-work. Third, there is little des-criptive information about the relationship between shift-work and estab-lishment and company size (a positive relationship is hypothesized), although this issue is not considered here.[10] Finally, there is an important question about the contribution of shift-work to pay and, thereby, its influence on wage drift as shift premiums drive average wages away from basic rates (i.e. because of the growth in the incidence of shift-working and because of increases in shift premiums). The remainder of this chapter attempts to throw some light on these issues.

12.3. Shift-work and Pay

Shift-work payments prove to be somewhat smaller in absolute importance than overtime premiums for two reasons. First, the incidence of shift-work is, overall, lower than the incidence of overtime working. In 1980, for example, the published data indicate that 54.6 per cent of full-time manual men received overtime premiums in manufacturing, compared with 24.8 per cent who received shift premiums.[11] The analogous overtime and shift figures for non-manual men, manual, and non-manual women were 22.6 and 4.6, 16.4 and 7.1, and 11.2 and 1.3 per cent respectively. Second, on average, shift premiums tend to be a lower percentage of the equivalent basic rate than overtime premiums. The top rate for shift-work is generally for permanent night work, which is typically around 33 per cent. This percentage rate often forms the lowest rung of the overtime ladder, although some agreements start lower (e.g. there are a number at 25 per cent).[12] Thus, returning to the published 1980 data, overtime forms about 13.5 per cent of gross weekly earnings for full-time manual males in manufacturing, while shift premiums form about 4.2 per cent of gross weekly earnings. The equivalent percentages for non-manual males and manual and non-manual females are 3.9 and 0.6, 3.0 and 1.3, and 1.7 and 0.3 per cent respectively.

While the importance of changes in shift-work should be seen in this broader context and kept in perspective, nevertheless, it would be wrong to dismiss them as a relatively insignificant influence on pay for a number of reasons. First, the early evidence suggested that shift-working amongst manual workers almost trebled in importance from 1954 to 1978.[13] Second, the overall manufacturing percentages tend to hide a considerable diversity of experience across industries and occupations (Bosworth and Dawkins 1981: 91–8). There are a considerable number of industries in which shift-work premiums form over 5 per cent of the gross weekly earnings of manual males, and some that exceed 10 per cent. There are even examples in the published data where shift premiums form a more important component than overtime premiums (i.e. cans and metal boxes for manual males). Even more examples of this type can be found amongst the detailed occupational groups.[14] Finally, although a fairly obvious point, as in the case of overtime payments, shift premiums form a more important component of pay amongst those who receive them than the average across all employees would suggest.

Before leaving this discussion, it is worth adding that shift-work not only appears to exhibit a long-run trend, it also shows year-on-year variations. After all, shift-work is intimately linked with capital utilization and firms tend to move from more to less intensive patterns during a recession, and towards more intensive patterns as the demand for the industries' products improves. Thus, the shift premium component of gross weekly earnings may have both important trend and cyclical components.

12.4. Long-Run Trends in the Incidence of Shift-Work

Until recently, with the lack of comparable surveys, the longer-term trends in shift-work remained the source of some uncertainty.[15] The availability of a considerable time series of information from the NES, coupled with data from new sources such as the Workplace Industrial Relations Survey, 1980, help to throw some further light on this question.

Early evidence from three broadly comparable surveys suggested a significant upward trend in the incidence of shift-working, from 12.5 per cent in 1954 to 20.0 per cent in 1964 and 34.5 per cent in 1978.[16] At that stage only the first few years of the published NES data were available as the shift-work data did not start on an annual basis until 1973. The NES data for 1973 to 1979 appeared to show some evidence of an upward trend, although the incidence levels from the survey were much lower and the increase much smaller than the other sources had suggested. The different levels of shift-work were attributed at the time to differences in definition between the sources, the differences in the scope of the surveys and the different time periods involved (Bosworth and Dawkins 1981: 89–91).

In retrospect, the high incidence reported in the IFF (1978) survey now appears suspect in the light of evidence from both WIRS 1980 and the more complete time series of data from the NES. The former suggests that the overall incidence of shift-work amongst all full-time workers in all industries and services is probably about 16 per cent, compared with the equivalent NES figure of 14 per cent, a difference of only 2 per cent. On the other hand, the information about the relative importance of various types of shift systems contained in both the spot surveys was broadly similar and may be used to provide additional insights to the crude incidence levels available from the NES, at least until the Labour Force Survey information for 1986 becomes available.

The second factor that now suggests the NES figures are perhaps closer to the true level than was first imagined concerns the scope of the definition of shift-working. The NES incidence was thought to be depressed by the exclusion of individuals who worked shifts but did not receive an explicit shift premium (Bosworth and Dawkins 1981). On the other hand, it now seems likely that, in at least one respect, the NES definition is wider than that adopted in the earlier surveys. In particular, the NES category includes those in receipt of unsocial hours payments and subsequent evidence has indicated the growth in this type of payment since the stimulus given to it by Stage III of the Heath government incomes policy.[17] The earlier surveys excluded such workers since they defined shift-working as a system in which one worker replaced another within a 24-hour period, and not all workers in receipt of unsocial hours payments are shift-workers according to this definition.[18]

Table 12.1 summarizes and updates the published NES information first reported in Bosworth and Dawkins (1981: 89–98). If the overall average NES incidence levels for the period 1970 to 1985 are taken at face value, they appear to indicate a much lower level of shift-working in the 1970s and early 1980s than formerly thought, and, by implication, a much slower growth in shift-work over the period from 1964. The average value for manual workers in manufacturing industries in 1978 is 21.7, and this seems to indicate that the incidence of shift-working has only grown by about 1 percentage point or so over its 1964 level. The figures for all manufacturing and for manual workers in manufacturing both indicate that the incidence may have peaked around 1970. The NES evidence by itself is perhaps too flimsy to support this argument. However, supportive evidence can be found in the chemicals sector,[19] which is the only industry for which regular information is published over the period 1963 onwards. Both the incidence and premium rates for the chemicals industry peak in the late 1960s–early 1970s. On the other hand, the general feeling from the literature is that shift-working is still an increasingly important phenomenon. In the discussion which follows, we attempt to use the detailed breakdown of shift-working to reconcile the slow aggregate growth with the more rapid growth suggested by case-study and micro-evidence (IDS 1985*a*).

12.5. Major Dimensions in the Incidence of Shift-Working

(*a*) Overall picture

The overall incidence of shift-working amongst all workers in all industries is shown in the total rows of the final column of Table 12.2. A

Table 12.1. *Trends in the incidence of shift-working, 1970–1985*

Percentage of employees working shifts

	All industries and services					Non-manufacturing	Manufacturing	
	Manual	Non-manual	Male	Female	All	All	All	Manual
1970	(19.6)	(4.7)	(15.1)	(7.4)	(12.9)	(10.4)	(16.4)	(22.8)
1973	16.6	4.9	12.9	7.0	11.2	9.5	13.9	19.0
1974	17.9	5.3	14.0	7.1	12.0	10.2	14.6	19.8
1975	20.6	6.4	15.9	8.0	13.6	12.8	14.9	20.4
1976	21.2	6.9	16.1	9.3	14.1	13.5	15.1	20.9
1977	20.4	6.7	15.4	9.2	13.5	12.7	14.9	20.3
1978	22.1	7.6	15.9	9.2	13.9	12.6	16.0	21.7
1979	21.5	7.3	16.1	10.0	14.2	13.1	16.2	21.9
1980	21.0	7.3	15.5	9.9	13.8	12.9	15.4	21.3
1981	21.1	7.4	15.1	10.3	13.6	13.1	14.5	20.9
1982	21.2	7.7	15.0	10.9	13.7	13.5	14.1	20.3
1983	23.2	9.3	16.8	12.3	15.3	15.1	15.9	22.5
1984	22.0	8.9	15.8	12.2	14.7	14.4	15.4	21.5
1985	22.4	9.2	16.2	12.3	14.9	14.7	15.5	22.1
1986	22.0	9.2	16.0	12.2	14.8	15.5	15.3	21.7

Note: Estimates for 1970 are not directly comparable with those for later years.

Source: New Earnings Survey and Wilson and Bosworth (1986).

Table 12.2. *Incidence of shift-work by category of employee* (%)

	Year	Full-time		Part-time		All				
		Manual	Non-manual	Manual	Non-manual	Manual	Non-manual	Full-time	Part-time	All
Males	1973	17.4	3.6	0.5	1.0	17.0	3.5	12.2	0.6	12.0
	1974	18.9	3.9	0.9	0.0	18.5	3.9	13.2	0.6	13.0
	1975	21.6	5.1	2.2	1.2	21.1	5.0	15.1	1.8	14.7
	1976	22.0	5.1	2.2	2.0	21.4	5.0	15.2	2.1	14.8
	1977	21.2	4.9	1.4	0.7	20.7	4.7	14.6	1.1	14.1
	1978	22.2	5.1	1.7	0.7	21.7	4.9	15.2	1.2	14.7
	1979	22.1	5.2	1.4	2.0	21.6	5.0	15.0	1.7	14.7
	1980	21.8	5.2	1.6	0.7	21.3	5.0	14.7	1.2	14.3
	1981	21.5	5.3	3.0	1.2	21.0	5.1	14.3	2.0	13.9
	1982	21.8	5.4	2.8	1.4	21.3	5.3	14.4	2.0	14.0
Average		21.0	4.9	1.8	1.2	20.5	4.8	14.4	1.5	14.0
Females	1973	7.4	6.1	4.7	7.1	6.1	6.3	6.5	5.7	6.2
	1974	7.5	6.2	5.2	5.8	6.4	6.1	6.6	5.5	6.2
	1975	8.9	7.2	7.0	7.5	8.0	7.3	7.7	7.2	7.5
	1976	10.3	8.4	7.2	8.9	8.7	8.5	8.9	8.0	8.6
	1977	10.0	8.3	6.6	8.8	8.3	8.4	8.7	7.6	8.4
	1978	9.9	8.3	6.8	8.4	8.3	8.3	8.7	7.6	8.3
	1979	10.3	9.1	7.3	9.1	8.7	9.1	9.4	8.2	9.0
	1980	10.5	9.1	8.2	9.3	9.2	9.2	9.5	8.7	9.2
	1981	11.5	9.4	9.5	9.8	10.4	9.5	9.9	9.6	9.8
	1982	11.7	10.0	9.2	10.4	10.4	10.1	10.4	9.8	10.2
Average		9.7	8.3	7.2	8.6	8.4	8.4	8.7	7.9	8.4
Total	1973	15.8	4.6	4.2	6.6	14.0	4.9	10.6	5.2	9.9
	1974	17.0	4.9	4.7	5.4	15.1	4.9	11.4	5.0	10.5
	1975	19.7	6.0	6.3	6.6	17.8	6.0	13.0	6.5	12.1
	1976	20.2	6.5	6.5	7.9	18.1	6.7	13.4	7.2	12.5
	1977	19.4	6.3	6.0	7.7	17.3	6.5	12.9	6.8	12.0
	1978	20.3	6.4	6.2	7.5	18.0	6.6	13.3	6.8	12.3
	1979	20.2	6.8	6.7	8.3	18.0	7.1	13.4	7.5	12.5
	1980	19.9	6.9	7.4	8.3	17.8	7.1	13.1	7.9	12.3
	1981	19.9	7.1	8.8	8.8	18.0	7.3	12.9	8.8	12.3
	1982	20.2	7.4	8.6	9.3	18.2	7.7	13.2	8.9	12.5
Average		19.3	6.3	6.6	7.6	17.2	6.5	12.7	7.1	11.9

comparable total does not exist in the published data (see Table 12.1). It rises from 9.9 per cent in 1973 to a peak of 12.5 per cent in 1976. While the incidence falls back to 12.0 per cent in 1977, it then maintains a fairly steady level of around 12.5 per cent throughout the remainder of the period to 1982. This net increase of 2.5 percentage points between 1973 and 1982 represents a 25 per cent increase in the incidence rate over the period as a whole. A number of differences can be found between the analogous figures reported in Tables 12.1 and 12.2. These are the result partly of the aggregation process, but also of restrictions placed on individuals in the new data base (i.e. the exclusion of those whose pay is affected by sickness or absence, as outlined in section 12.1 above).

(b) Male and female shift-work

The literature has suggested major differences in the incidence of shift-work between the sexes because of differences in the male and female supply of labour functions.[20] The data shown in Table 12.2 are clearly consistent with this finding, although this is not sufficient to demonstrate that it is a feature of supply rather than demand. It might, for example, be the result of the occupational segmentation of the labour force. The final column of the Table shows that, at the beginning of the period, males were twice as likely as females to receive shift premiums (i.e. the incidence rates in 1973 were 12.0 and 6.2 per cent respectively). By 1982, the incidence rates for males and females were somewhat closer (14.0 and 10.2 per cent respectively), a feature caused by the fact that the male incidence levelled off and even fell back from its 1975–6 value, while the female rate carried on growing fairly steadily throughout the period. Over the period as a whole, the female rate increased by about 65 per cent over its 1973 value, compared with a rise of 17 per cent for males. Examination of the interior of the Table points to the rise in shift-working amongst all female categories, although the increase was particularly marked amongst part-time female manual workers (we return to this below).

(c) Shift-working amongst part- and full-time employees

Unlike the earlier surveys, the NES contains information about shift-working amongst both part- and full-time employees. The main features are again summarized in Table 12.2. It is worth noting from the outset that the incidence of part-time working is low amongst males and, therefore, given shift-working is anyway a minority activity, this gives rise to very small sample sizes for part-time male shift-workers. This makes any trend information for this group suspect, although the incident rate *vis-à-vis* other groups is apparent from the all-year averages.

Overall, for males and females combined, the incidence of shift-working is considerably higher amongst full-time than part-time employees. The incidence rates were 10.6 and 5.2 per cent in 1973 respectively, and 13.2 and 8.9 per cent in 1982. Despite the small sample sizes for males, the data point to a considerably higher incidence rate amongst part-time females than part-time males. In both instances, however, there appears to have been a substantial increase in the incidence between 1973 and 1982 (bearing in mind the problems of small sample size for males). Although the incidence rates for full-time workers do not show such marked changes, they do exhibit increases over the period taken as a whole, from 12.2 to 14.4 per cent for males and from 6.5 to 10.4 per cent for females. However, where the growth in the incidence of shift-work for both female full- and part-time employees was fairly steady over the whole period, the male full-time growth took place mainly in the period 1973 to 1976 (12.2 to 15.2 per cent), before levelling off and even declining towards the end of the period.

(d) Shift-work amongst manual and non-manual employees

Empirical explorations of shift-working have emphasized the potential differences in supply functions between manual and non-manual workers.[21] The NES evidence reported in Table 12.2 appears consistent with this hypothesis, with incidence levels for the combined male and female groups around three times as large for manual as for non-manual workers (14.0 compared with 4.9 per cent in 1973 and 18.2 compared with 7.7 per cent in 1982). The incidence of shift-working increased proportionately more over the period as a whole for the non-manual group (57 per cent) than for the manual group (30 per cent). However, examination of the differences between male and female workers reveals that the incidence rates were more similar for manual and non-manual females than for manual and non-manual males. Both female series exhibited considerable growth (i.e. 70 per cent for manual and 60 per cent for non-manual workers over the period as a whole). The incidence rates for males, however, differed significantly, with the manual males having an incidence of over four times the non-manual group (17.0 compared with 3.5 in 1973 and 21.3 compared with 5.3 in 1982).

(e) Manufacturing versus non-manufacturing

The incidence of shift-working was quite different in the manufacturing and non-manufacturing industries in 1973. Table 12.1 shows that the incidence of shift-work amongst all workers in manufacturing was 13.9 per cent in 1973, compared with 9.5 per cent in non-manufacturing industries. However, by the end of the period, there was little difference between the two sectors. While the incidence of shift-work in manufacturing had increased only slightly to 15.3 per cent by 1986, growth in non-manufacturing was more rapid and sustained, reaching 15.5 per cent.

(f) Shift-work and structural changes

The discussion of this section considers how the slow overall growth in the incidence of shift-working shown in Table 12.1 can be reconciled with the widely held belief that there have been significant increases in shift-working in recent years. Table 12.2 shows that, taken over the period as a whole, the incidence of shift-work has increased in all of the groups distinguished: manual and non-manual, full- and part-time, males and females, manufacturing and non-manufacturing industries. In some instances, such as part-time manual females, this growth has been considerable (i.e. almost 100 per cent in ten years). On the other hand, on aggregating across all of these groups, the overall growth has been comparatively slow (26 per cent). For males, the net increase in incidence has been below average for those groups growing fastest (e.g. non-manual occupations, part-time workers, and service industries). For females the net increase in incidence over the period 1973–82 has been of the same order of magnitude as that for full-time manual men (about 4½ percentage points). However, the levels of incidence for females remain less than half the figure of about 20 per cent for the latter group. Thus the slow overall growth in shift-working seems likely to be associated with changes in the structure of employment (i.e. the increasing ratios of non-manual to manual male workers, part- to full-time female workers, and non-manufacturing to manufacturing industries). In practice, however, the shift-share analysis reported below does not give quite such strong support for this hypothesis.

In Chapter 11 we provide evidence on the extent to which changes in *hours worked* observed over the period 1970–82 could be attributed to changes in industrial structure and employment composition over this period. Table 12.3 reports a corresponding shift-share analysis of the proportion of people working shifts for the period 1973–82. In all industries and services the proportion of those working shifts increased by 2.6 percentage points. The bulk of this was explained by a growth in the percentage of those doing shift-work *ceteris paribus* (henceforth the incidence rate effect). Had industrial structure remained the same as in 1973 and had the composition of employment remained unaltered, then there would have been an increase of 3.4 percentage points. The differ-

Table 12.3. *Shift-share analysis of changes in the incidence of shift-work (% points)*

	1973–6	1976–9	1979–82	1973–82
All industries				
Total change	2.62	−0.04	−0.02	2.60
Industry effect	−0.15	0.02	−0.31	−0.44
Incidence rate effect	2.86	0.07	0.50	3.43
Compositional effect	−0.09	−0.13	−0.17	−0.39
of which:				
Gender	0.04	0.02	—	0.06
Part-time	−0.09	−0.02	−0.02	−0.13
Occupation	−0.05	−0.12	−0.16	−0.33
Manufacturing				
Total change	0.83	0.78	−1.50	0.10
Industry effect	0.04	0.02	−0.32	−0.26
Incidence rate effect	0.85	0.83	−0.83	0.88
Compositional effect	−0.06	−0.08	−0.35	−0.52
of which:				
Gender	0.16	−0.10	0.05	0.11
Part-time	−0.20	0.12	−0.02	−0.09
Occupation	−0.03	−0.12	−0.39	−0.54
Services				
Total change	3.71	−0.40	0.74	4.05
Industry effect	−0.05	0.05	−0.18	−0.18
Incidence rate effect	3.86	−0.30	1.02	4.58
Compositional effect	−0.10	−0.15	−0.10	−0.15
of which:				
Gender	−0.01	0.07	−0.02	0.04
Part-time	−0.03	−0.09	−0.02	−0.14
Occupation	−0.06	−0.13	−0.07	−0.25

Notes: The methodology adopted for the shift-share analysis is analogous to that used for hours worked in Chapter 11. Details are given in the appendix to that chapter.

Source: NES data tapes.

ence (−0.8 percentage points) was largely attributable to changing industrial structure. Compositional factors were to some extent offsetting although amounting to 0.4 percentage points in total over the period 1973–82. Most of the negative effects due to changing industrial employment structure and changing employment composition within industries occurred towards the end of the period. In contrast the main growth due to the incidence rate effect occurred in the 1973–6 period.

The patterns within manufacturing and services were rather different. In manufacturing, the total change was almost zero, while for services there was a 4.1 percentage point rise in the proportion working shifts. For the latter the largest effect was a 3.9 percentage point increase during 1973–6, due to the incidence rate effect. Structural and compositional effects were of relatively minor consequence over this period. Subsequently they increased in relative importance, but even over the period 1973–82 as a whole only knocked about half a percentage point off the overall growth in the proportion working shifts. In manufacturing incidence rates rose up to 1979 and then fell. The incidence rate effect was the prime factor here, probably reflecting cyclical changes in the use of shift-work. During the 1979–82 period however structural and compositional factors (notably change in occupational composition) strongly reinforced the incidence rate effect.

Given the relatively small changes in the proportion of those working shifts it is not surprising that a shift-share analysis of the effects on pay (not shown) reveals that this phenomenon did not have any significant impact on total pay levels during this period.

12.6. Changes in Pay

(a) Basic pay

Table 12.4 presents data on the ratio of basic pay of shift- to non-shift-workers. The idea of the Table is to show whether shift-workers are located in inherently better-paid jobs than their non-shift counterparts, excluding access to overtime, incentive payments, etc.

The results in the final rows of columns 5 and 6 of the Table show important differences between manual and non-manual workers. It should be noted that the aggregates, such as the ratios in the total (all male and female) rows, are a complex weighted average.[22] In particular, manual shift-workers have higher basic rates than non-shift-workers. This is consistent with the results of earlier empirical work which shows that shift-work is associated not only with unsocial hours, but also with other unsocial aspects of employment (such as noise, riskiness, etc.).[23] The shift–non-shift differences are particularly marked amongst manual women workers, and non-manual men. Until 1978, for example, basic pay for full-time female manual shift-workers was over 20 per cent higher than for non-shift-workers. This difference diminishes in later years, falling to around 12 per cent by the end of the period. On the other hand, while basic pay does not differ greatly between manual male shift- and non-shift-workers (rising to a maximum of about 7 per cent in 1976),

Table 12.4. Ratio of shift–non-shift basic pay by category of employee

	Year	Full-time		Part-time		All		Full-time	Part-time	All
		Manual	Non-manual	Manual	Non-manual	Manual	Non-manual			
Males	1973	98.9	78.0	115.4	37.2	100.6	78.3	80.6	69.8	81.6
	1974	99.3	77.8	137.0	—	101.1	78.6	80.9	97.6	82.1
	1975	104.2	81.9	128.2	91.2	106.3	83.5	85.7	105.1	87.5
	1976	105.0	81.0	114.1	88.0	107.2	82.3	85.4	98.0	87.3
	1977	103.9	82.6	155.1	46.2	106.1	84.4	85.1	104.1	87.0
	1978	102.9	77.7	119.0	104.4	104.9	79.5	82.7	105.5	84.5
	1979	99.9	78.3	108.6	61.7	101.7	79.3	81.5	79.8	83.0
	1980	100.5	81.3	86.9	58.4	102.4	83.0	81.6	72.9	83.3
	1981	101.1	78.7	109.6	109.0	102.8	80.4	80.1	100.2	81.7
	1982	102.3	77.8	105.9	94.3	104.0	79.5	80.0	94.2	81.7
Average		101.8	79.5	116.9	72.9	103.7	80.8	82.4	90.1	83.9
Females	1973	113.9	92.5	115.8	117.2	123.2	94.2	96.7	120.3	102.9
	1974	114.6	87.2	118.5	110.5	122.5	90.8	93.1	115.0	99.7
	1975	118.3	101.2	116.9	125.5	122.3	104.0	103.8	121.9	108.0
	1976	113.7	96.9	121.9	121.5	123.2	99.5	99.4	122.8	105.5
	1977	112.3	96.3	119.5	121.8	122.5	99.0	98.8	122.8	105.2
	1978	110.6	89.5	117.8	114.0	120.1	92.6	93.4	116.9	99.8
	1979	106.9	88.6	116.9	111.1	116.7	91.8	92.0	115.0	98.4
	1980	106.3	91.5	115.7	115.8	114.5	94.7	93.9	116.7	99.5
	1981	104.0	90.1	114.9	119.9	111.8	93.8	91.5	118.2	96.9
	1982	103.7	88.6	116.1	120.0	112.9	92.5	90.4	119.6	96.6
Average		110.4	92.3	117.4	117.9	118.5	95.3	95.3	119.1	101.1
Total	1973	104.1	77.3	114.7	105.5	113.9	76.4	86.5	114.1	92.0
	1974	104.5	76.4	118.9	104.2	114.2	77.0	86.5	112.3	92.6
	1975	108.7	85.3	118.3	121.3	116.9	86.5	91.7	120.3	97.3
	1976	108.6	82.7	122.4	117.0	118.0	83.1	90.4	120.7	96.1
	1977	107.5	83.3	120.5	117.6	117.4	83.8	89.9	120.8	95.8
	1978	106.5	77.9	117.6	111.3	116.5	78.7	87.2	115.2	93.2
	1979	103.4	77.2	115.8	106.4	113.1	77.5	85.8	111.8	91.3
	1980	103.8	80.0	113.6	113.2	113.0	80.4	86.2	114.2	91.5
	1981	103.9	78.1	113.1	115.9	112.4	78.7	84.2	114.7	88.9
	1982	105.1	76.5	114.0	116.0	114.1	77.2	83.9	116.0	88.7
Average		105.6	79.5	116.9	112.8	115.0	79.9	87.2	116.0	92.7

non-manual male shift-workers have significantly lower basic rates than their non-shift counterparts. The differential in basic rates for this group is more than 20 per cent in some years.

The disaggregated information for part- and full-time manual and non-manual, male and female workers also reveals important variations in the ratio over time. The ratio for full-time manual males rises from 98.9 per cent to 105.0 per cent in a period of four years, and then falls back to parity by 1979, before rising again towards the end of the period. The equivalent ratio for females shows that the fairly large and growing differential for full-time manual females between 1973 and 1975 (14 per cent to 18 per cent) is largely eroded by the end of the period.

(b) Gross pay

While information about basic pay gives some indication about whether the jobs of shift-workers are inherently better paid than those of non-shift-workers, the shift-working premium may be one way in which the gap is further extended (where the shift-working basic pay is higher) or narrowed (where it is initially lower). In addition, shift-working may itself be associated with better or worse access to other types of premiums which can affect the relative pay levels of shift- and non-shift-workers. In the first instance, this question is explored by comparing the gross pay of the two categories of workers (see also section 12.7).

Table 12.5 shows certain similarities with the comparison of basic rates reported in Table 12.4 above. The final rows of columns 5 and 6 show the ratio of gross pay of shift to non-shift for all manual and all non-manual workers. The higher basic rates of the manual shift category are augmented by premium payments, leading to a differential of 36 to 41 per cent. In the case of non-manual workers the higher premium payments of the shift-work group reduce the (negative) differential in gross pay by more than 10 percentage points in some instances. Thus, while non-manual shift-workers tend to be in relatively poorly paid jobs, shift and other premium payments go some way to closing the gap between them and non-shift-workers.

This conclusion carries over to the separate results for males and females. In the case of female non-manual workers, for example, the largely negative differential in basic rates is reversed to a positive differential in favour of shift-workers in terms of gross pay. The manual male gross pay differential rises from 19 per cent in 1973 to 26 per cent in 1982. Manual female shift-workers, on the other hand, saw their advantage eroded from 42 per cent in 1973 down to 35 per cent in 1982. Finally, there is some evidence of a cyclical movement in the manual and non-manual differentials for both males and females, with peaks in 1975 in the

Table 12.5. *Ratio of shift–non-shift gross pay*

	Year	Full-time		Part-time		All				
		Manual	Non-manual	Manual	Non-manual	Manual	Non-manual	Full-time	Part-time	All
Males	1973	116.9	93.5	70.3	47.7	118.9	94.0	104.7	62.8	106.1
	1974	117.5	94.3	61.3	—	119.4	95.3	105.4	54.9	106.9
	1975	120.9	99.5	64.8	108.8	122.9	101.5	108.4	79.5	110.5
	1976	122.7	97.1	138.8	105.2	125.5	98.7	108.1	118.3	110.5
	1977	120.8	99.1	46.1	69.2	122.1	101.3	107.2	55.0	109.0
	1978	120.7	95.1	64.2	120.0	122.7	97.3	106.0	80.2	108.1
	1979	120.5	102.9	84.0	80.0	122.7	104.2	110.6	82.7	112.6
	1980	122.3	102.1	93.7	78.1	124.7	104.3	107.8	86.2	110.1
	1981	123.7	98.0	77.1	142.4	125.5	100.2	104.8	98.2	106.8
	1982	125.1	98.5	74.9	119.0	127.1	100.6	105.7	91.8	107.7
Average		121.1	98.0	73.7	92.1	123.2	99.7	106.8	79.5	108.8
Females	1973	129.4	100.9	134.0	135.2	141.9	103.8	108.4	138.2	115.9
	1974	128.8	95.8	138.3	130.6	140.0	100.9	104.9	135.0	113.2
	1975	133.6	111.0	135.2	143.1	139.6	114.8	116.0	139.7	121.2
	1976	129.9	105.1	138.8	138.6	141.4	108.9	110.5	139.7	117.8
	1977	127.3	103.2	134.8	138.6	139.5	107.2	102.5	138.8	116.3
	1978	123.9	96.1	134.4	129.4	136.2	100.4	102.6	132.8	110.4
	1979	122.0	97.4	135.5	129.4	134.5	101.9	103.0	133.4	111.0
	1980	126.3	104.3	138.4	143.0	136.7	109.5	108.9	142.0	116.6
	1981	123.6	102.2	138.5	149.4	133.8	108.4	105.6	145.2	113.4
	1982	123.4	100.2	141.1	149.0	135.4	106.5	104.0	147.2	112.8
Average		126.8	101.7	136.9	138.9	137.9	106.4	107.2	139.3	114.9
Total	1973	123.8	88.5	126.7	122.1	136.3	87.5	111.5	128.2	118.2
	1974	124.3	88.7	129.2	123.4	136.6	89.5	112.0	120.4	119.6
	1975	127.0	99.1	126.0	138.6	137.0	100.2	115.3	132.7	121.9
	1976	127.7	94.3	140.0	133.6	139.7	94.7	113.0	137.7	120.0
	1977	125.7	94.5	117.1	134.2	136.9	95.0	111.6	127.0	118.2
	1978	125.7	89.6	124.5	126.4	138.1	90.3	110.3	126.2	117.4
	1979	125.4	93.7	130.8	124.4	138.0	93.8	113.6	128.5	120.3
	1980	127.2	95.6	134.3	139.9	139.5	96.3	112.0	138.3	118.7
	1981	127.5	92.5	130.4	144.8	138.3	93.7	108.1	138.6	113.8
	1982	129.2	91.4	131.8	144.4	140.7	92.5	108.4	140.1	114.2
Average		126.3	92.8	129.1	133.2	138.1	93.4	111.6	131.8	118.2

non-manual male and female series and 1976 in both the manual male and female series.

The interior detail of the Table contained in the first four columns is also interesting. The slight differential in basic pay in most years in favour of full-time manual males and females is accentuated further by the additional premium payments. The differential in gross pay for full-time manual males rises from 17 per cent in 1973 to 25 per cent in 1982, while the equivalent female series peaks at 34 per cent in 1975 before falling back to just over 23 per cent. The premium payments close the gap between the full-time male non-manual shift-workers and non-shift-workers, while the series for the equivalent female group now cycles above and below 100. The part-time female manual and non-manual differentials are now even more strongly in favour of shift-workers. The manual series for part-time females rises from 34 to 41 per cent over the period as a whole and the equivalent non-manual series increases even more strongly from just over 35 to 49 per cent (and from 31 to 49 per cent over the period 1974 to 1982).

12.7. Shift-work and Other Premium Payments

(a) Shift-work and overtime

The concept of the labour cost-utilization envelope suggests that shift-work and hours of work are substitutes to the extent that the firm could move from a less intensive shift system with long hours of work per employee to a more intensive system with lower hours of work per employee.[24] Nevertheless, the discrete nature of the envelope function implies that, in the short-run, some element of overtime would be the norm rather than the exception on all shift patterns operated.[25] The anticipated relationship between shift-work and hours may be reversed when we consider the effects of the costs of adjusting the size of employment. The adoption of more intensive shift systems coupled with lower hours raises not only the labour intensity of the firm's overall operations but also the costs of adjusting the size of the labour force. Thus, the final outcome appears to be a largely empirical question.

Table 12.6 compares the incidence of overtime working amongst shift- and non-shift-workers, based on individuals either in receipt of overtime premiums or those whose overtime hours were greater than zero. The results are quite striking. Compare, for example, the incidence of overtime amongst shift-workers and non-shift-workers given in the final set of rows. Incidence levels were on average around 25 percentage points higher for shift- than for non shift workers (i.e. averaging 73 per cent

Table 12.6. *Percentage of workers on overtime*

	Year	Shift-workers			Non-shift-workers			All workers		
		Full-time	Part-time	All	Full-time	Part-time	All	Full-time	Part-time	All
Males	1973	88.5	50.0	88.4	71.5	16.6	70.3	73.6	16.9	72.5
	1974	89.6	25.0	89.5	70.6	13.5	69.2	73.1	13.5	71.9
	1975	87.8	42.9	87.6	67.0	13.4	65.4	70.2	13.9	68.7
	1976	87.3	50.0	87.1	65.1	13.7	63.4	68.5	14.4	67.0
	1977	90.3	44.4	90.2	66.2	15.3	64.6	69.8	15.6	68.3
	1978	90.0	36.4	89.8	66.7	15.9	65.2	70.3	16.2	68.9
	1979	91.0	10.0	90.8	67.1	15.1	65.6	70.7	15.0	69.3
	1980	88.8	40.0	88.7	65.5	17.5	64.0	68.9	17.8	67.6
	1981	86.6	27.8	86.3	58.7	15.4	57.5	62.7	15.7	61.5
	1982	86.4	29.4	86.2	60.3	15.2	59.0	64.1	15.6	62.8
Average		88.6	35.6	88.5	65.9	15.2	64.4	69.2	15.5	67.8
Females	1973	37.1	19.6	31.7	32.5	21.9	28.9	32.8	21.8	29.1
	1974	42.2	23.7	36.4	31.5	20.9	27.7	32.2	21.0	28.2
	1975	37.7	21.0	32.5	28.6	18.9	25.4	29.3	19.0	25.9
	1976	34.4	19.0	29.4	25.3	18.5	22.9	26.1	18.5	23.5
	1977	33.7	17.1	28.3	27.3	18.8	24.3	27.9	18.6	24.6
	1978	35.1	18.5	29.7	28.9	18.6	25.2	29.4	18.6	25.6
	1979	37.5	19.3	31.5	29.1	20.2	25.9	29.9	20.2	26.4
	1980	42.9	17.8	34.3	28.5	19.4	25.2	29.8	19.3	26.0
	1981	37.9	20.9	31.8	26.7	19.6	24.1	27.8	19.7	24.9
	1982	35.6	16.6	29.0	28.1	21.8	25.9	28.9	21.3	26.2
Average		37.4	19.4	31.5	28.6	19.9	25.5	29.4	19.8	26.0
Total	1973	79.6	19.9	75.3	60.0	21.4	54.4	62.1	21.3	56.5
	1974	82.0	23.7	77.9	59.0	20.1	53.1	61.6	20.3	55.7
	1975	79.5	21.8	75.4	55.6	18.2	50.3	58.8	18.4	53.4
	1976	77.3	20.1	72.4	53.2	17.8	47.7	56.5	18.0	50.8
	1977	79.2	17.6	73.9	54.4	18.4	48.7	57.6	18.3	51.7
	1978	79.5	18.9	74.3	55.1	18.3	49.2	58.3	18.4	52.3
	1979	79.9	19.1	74.2	55.4	19.7	49.5	58.6	19.7	52.6
	1980	78.9	18.2	72.7	53.9	19.2	48.2	57.2	19.1	51.2
	1981	75.3	21.1	69.0	48.6	19.2	43.7	52.1	19.3	46.9
	1982	74.0	16.9	67.3	50.0	21.1	45.2	53.2	20.7	48.0
Average		78.5	19.7	73.3	54.5	19.3	49.0	57.6	19.4	51.9

compared with 49 per cent). The overall incidence levels for all part-time shift and non-shift were very similar (both averaging around 19 per cent). These levels differed significantly from full-time workers, where shift-workers were significantly higher than non-shift (78 compared with 54 per cent).

The interior of the Table reveals that the vast majority of full-time male shift-workers (on average of 88.6 per cent) also work overtime. In addition, there is comparatively little variation over the ten-year period, with a low of 86.4 per cent in 1981 compared with a peak of 90.9 per cent in 1979. The corresponding average for full-time male non-shift-workers is only 65.5 per cent. Not only is the figure lower for this group, but the variation in the incidence of overtime is also higher, ranging from 58.4 per cent in 1981 to 71.1 per cent in 1973. The downward movement in the incidence is much more marked in the case of non-shift-workers. This almost certainly reflects differences in the need to maintain high levels of capital utilization in the industries working shifts. A similar result applies in the case of full-time women workers, although the differences in the incidences between shift and non-shift are less marked. Female part-time workers have the lowest overtime hours of any group with the exception perhaps of part-time males, although the sample numbers in the latter group are very small. The low incidence for part-time females probably reflects the difficulties of overtime working for groups such as twilight workers.

Table 12.7 reports the results of comparing the overtime hours of shift with equivalent non-shift employees, in broadly the same way as in section 12.5 above. The most immediate feature of the Table is probably the fact that on average, over the ten-year period, the overtime hours of shift-workers exceed those of non-shift-workers for almost every group (i.e. male and female, manual and non-manual, etc.), with the exception of part-time non-manual workers. Thus, the higher overall incidence of overtime amongst shift-workers (shown in Table 12.6) is also associated with a higher number of overtime hours per worker on overtime.

In addition, the detail of the Table reveals marked independent variation in the overtime working of shift- and non-shift-workers, which causes the ratio of the two to change significantly over time. Hours have always been recognized as a somewhat less volatile element of overtime working than the incidence of overtime.[26] In the case of all full-time manual workers shown in the final rows of column 1, however, the ratio varies from a 10.6 per cent higher level of overtime amongst shift-workers in 1973 up to 41.5 per cent higher in 1981. Other, even greater differences can be found in the main body of the Table.

The results also reveal that, for the aggregate manual and non-manual groups (and for all workers), longer overtime is worked by both male and

Table 12.7. Ratio of shift–non-shift overtime hours

	Year	Full-time		Part-time		All				
		Manual	Non-manual	Manual	Non-manual	Manual	Non-manual	Full-time	Part-time	All
Males	1973	106.2	166.3	68.5	—	106.6	166.2	118.7	74.1	119.0
	1974	113.9	184.0	105.9	—	114.2	184.5	127.6	113.7	128.0
	1975	116.3	195.1	142.5	—	116.7	195.2	130.7	132.7	131.1
	1976	123.1	190.4	180.4	—	123.6	189.4	137.7	119.0	138.1
	1977	122.0	195.9	281.8	—	122.5	196.0	138.0	283.2	138.5
	1978	123.8	189.7	169.5	—	124.3	190.0	140.2	180.3	140.7
	1979	126.8	187.8	24.2	—	127.3	188.1	143.0	25.7	143.5
	1980	126.8	221.7	39.9	—	127.1	221.9	146.1	43.5	146.3
	1981	138.8	215.3	37.7	—	139.2	215.0	158.1	68.6	158.4
	1982	130.8	213.6	240.2	—	131.3	213.8	150.8	219.9	151.3
Average		122.9	196.0	129.0	—	123.3	196.0	139.1	126.1	139.5
Females	1973	164.7	141.3	90.6	69.3	161.0	122.7	171.4	81.0	154.0
	1974	155.6	175.8	117.5	140.7	152.8	166.7	168.2	126.9	160.1
	1975	151.4	169.4	134.5	76.0	152.2	144.8	170.4	103.5	154.3
	1976	165.5	140.3	139.5	104.1	166.1	130.3	163.7	123.3	154.4
	1977	163.9	148.5	131.3	108.8	166.6	138.0	168.0	119.5	157.5
	1978	165.7	164.1	105.2	89.7	158.7	145.4	175.7	98.5	159.3
	1979	170.6	117.7	156.0	94.4	172.7	111.1	147.9	124.7	143.4
	1980	155.4	143.2	110.8	92.1	151.5	132.0	153.6	102.8	144.3
	1981	156.6	136.8	120.2	112.1	151.3	128.9	151.2	115.5	141.7
	1982	136.2	152.3	145.8	108.4	143.6	140.4	149.8	128.0	145.1
Average		158.6	148.9	125.1	99.6	157.7	136.0	162.0	112.4	151.4
Total	1973	110.6	169.0	88.1	69.2	113.8	163.8	127.5	79.7	130.4
	1974	118.6	183.6	116.2	141.5	121.8	182.6	136.2	126.2	139.5
	1975	119.5	199.1	135.1	76.6	122.1	193.0	139.4	105.9	141.8
	1976	126.3	182.4	141.2	104.5	129.5	179.1	144.6	125.2	147.7
	1977	125.6	191.0	150.0	105.9	129.3	186.5	146.1	126.6	149.5
	1978	128.2	189.1	108.0	88.7	131.1	186.2	149.5	100.6	152.6
	1979	131.1	170.8	143.8	94.3	134.5	168.4	149.9	120.1	153.5
	1980	130.0	196.9	95.1	90.0	132.5	194.5	151.4	94.0	154.3
	1981	141.5	193.6	111.6	109.6	144.2	187.9	163.5	110.3	165.6
	1982	133.5	197.7	151.0	108.2	137.2	195.0	157.3	131.9	161.4
Average		126.5	187.3	124.0	98.9	129.6	183.7	146.5	112.1	149.6

female shift-workers than by non-shift-workers in almost all of the years
from 1973 to 1982. This differential is more marked amongst non-manual
than manual workers, although the detailed results by gender in columns
5 and 6 show that this finding is more true of males than females. Again,
the further breakdown by full-time and part-time shows that the ratio was
highly volatile. In the case of part-time manual females, for example, the
ratio underwent a major cycle from 1973 to 1978, with a notable jump in
1979.

(b) Shift and other premium payments

Tables 12.8–12.10 provide information about the composition of income
for shift- and non-shift-workers. The tables focus on full-time workers,
although interesting differences also exist in the composition of pay for
part-time workers.

Table 12.8 shows the important differences in composition for manual
workers. On average, only 65.2 per cent of the gross pay of full-time
manual male shift-workers is attributable to basic pay, compared with
77.5 per cent for the equivalent non-shift-work group. Shift payments
form nearly 12 per cent of income for this group. Far from substituting
for shift premium payments, on average overtime pay also forms a higher
percentage of gross income for shift-workers than for non-shift-workers.
However, incentive payments form a somewhat larger proportion of gross
income for the non-shift group. This result is even more clearly illustrated
in the case of full-time female manual workers. The main differences
from the equivalent male workers are the smaller contribution of overtime pay, and the larger contribution of shift pay for shift-workers. A
larger percentage of non-shift-working female earnings are contributed by
incentive pay. There are no major trends in the contribution of shift
payments to gross earnings in the case of manual males or manual
females, although there are a number of important year-to-year variations.

Table 12.9 shows that broadly similar results occur in the case of
full-time non-manual workers. Shift payments form a smaller percentage
of gross earnings for both males and females than in the case of manual
workers. However, perhaps the major differences between the manual
and non-manual groups are in the contributions of overtime and incentive
premiums to gross earnings, particularly in the case of female non-manual
shift-workers, where overtime premiums make an average contribution of
only 1.8 per cent of the gross pay. Table 12.10 is included to complete the
picture, giving the results for all full-time workers.

The changing composition of the workforce has also resulted in important movements in the overall composition of pay. A number of these

Table 12.8. *Components of gross pay: full-time manual workers (%)*

	Year	Shift-workers				Non-shift-workers		
		Residual	Overtime	Shift-work	Incentive	Residual	Overtime	Incentive
Male	1973	62.7	15.3	12.5	9.5	74.1	16.4	9.5
	1974	62.7	16.2	12.0	9.1	74.3	15.8	10.0
	1975	66.6	14.7	11.7	7.0	77.3	13.9	8.8
	1976	67.3	14.5	11.8	6.4	78.7	12.8	8.5
	1977	67.5	15.0	11.1	6.4	78.4	13.0	8.6
	1978	65.7	15.0	11.2	8.1	77.1	13.8	9.1
	1979	63.3	16.0	11.7	9.0	76.3	14.3	9.3
	1980	63.9	15.5	12.4	8.2	77.8	13.4	8.8
	1981	66.3	14.7	11.9	7.2	81.0	11.0	8.0
	1982	65.7	14.6	12.0	7.6	80.4	12.0	7.6
Average		65.2	15.2	11.8	7.9	77.5	13.6	8.8
Female	1973	73.5	7.8	13.0	5.7	83.5	3.4	13.1
	1974	74.0	6.7	12.0	7.3	83.2	3.5	13.4
	1975	77.2	5.3	13.4	4.1	87.2	2.5	10.4
	1976	76.7	4.7	13.8	4.8	87.6	2.2	10.1
	1977	77.7	5.0	12.6	4.6	87.6	2.4	10.0
	1978	77.0	5.7	13.3	4.0	86.4	3.1	10.5
	1979	75.3	6.2	13.7	4.8	86.1	3.3	10.6
	1980	73.9	6.5	14.9	4.8	87.9	3.0	9.1
	1981	74.8	5.4	15.5	4.3	89.1	2.9	8.0
	1982	75.1	5.2	16.0	3.7	89.4	3.3	7.3
Average		75.5	5.8	13.8	4.8	86.8	2.9	10.3
Total	1973	63.2	15.0	12.5	9.3	75.1	15.0	9.9
	1974	63.2	15.8	12.0	9.0	75.3	14.4	10.3
	1975	67.1	14.3	11.8	6.9	78.4	12.7	9.0
	1976	67.8	13.9	11.9	6.3	79.7	11.6	8.7
	1977	68.0	14.5	11.2	6.3	79.5	11.8	8.7
	1978	66.3	14.5	11.3	7.9	78.2	12.4	9.3
	1979	63.9	15.5	11.8	8.8	77.5	13.0	9.5
	1980	64.5	15.0	12.6	8.0	79.0	12.1	8.9
	1981	66.8	14.1	12.1	7.0	82.0	10.1	8.0
	1982	66.3	14.1	12.2	7.4	81.5	11.0	7.5
Average		65.7	14.7	11.9	7.7	78.6	12.4	9.0

Table 12.9. *Components of gross pay: full-time, non-manual workers (%)*

	Year	Shift-workers				Non-shift-workers		
		Residual	Overtime	Shift-work	Incentive	Residual	Overtime	Incentive
Male	1973	78.8	10.1	10.5	0.6	94.5	2.8	2.7
	1974	78.0	11.4	10.1	0.5	94.6	2.8	2.6
	1975	78.6	10.9	9.8	0.7	95.5	2.5	2.0
	1976	79.6	9.5	9.7	1.2	95.5	2.4	2.1
	1977	79.3	9.9	10.1	0.7	95.2	2.5	2.3
	1978	77.2	10.1	10.4	2.2	94.6	2.7	2.8
	1979	76.1	11.6	9.8	2.4	94.3	3.0	2.8
	1980	75.2	11.4	11.0	2.3	94.5	3.0	2.6
	1981	76.3	10.9	11.2	1.6	95.0	2.3	2.7
	1982	75.3	11.6	11.8	1.3	95.3	2.5	2.2
Average		77.5	10.7	10.5	1.3	94.9	2.6	2.5
Female	1973	90.0	1.5	8.5	0.0	98.3	1.1	0.6
	1974	89.5	2.6	7.8	0.1	98.4	1.1	0.5
	1975	89.8	2.0	8.1	0.2	98.6	1.0	0.4
	1976	91.0	1.4	7.3	0.2	98.7	0.8	0.4
	1977	91.8	1.4	6.6	0.1	98.6	0.9	0.5
	1978	91.2	1.7	6.8	0.3	98.0	0.9	1.0
	1979	89.0	1.9	8.8	0.4	97.9	1.2	1.0
	1980	85.9	2.1	11.8	0.2	98.0	1.1	0.9
	1981	86.2	1.8	11.7	0.3	98.0	1.1	1.0
	1982	86.4	2.1	11.2	0.3	97.9	1.1	1.0
Average		89.1	1.8	8.9	0.2	98.2	1.0	0.7
Total	1973	83.4	6.6	9.7	0.3	95.5	2.3	2.1
	1974	82.4	8.1	9.2	0.3	95.6	2.3	2.1
	1975	83.0	7.4	9.1	0.5	96.4	2.1	1.5
	1976	84.6	6.0	8.7	0.8	96.4	1.9	1.6
	1977	84.8	6.2	8.6	0.4	96.2	2.0	1.8
	1978	83.1	6.6	8.9	1.4	95.6	2.1	2.3
	1979	81.8	7.3	9.4	1.5	95.3	2.4	2.2
	1980	80.0	7.3	11.4	1.4	95.5	2.4	2.1
	1981	80.8	6.7	11.4	1.0	95.9	1.9	2.2
	1982	80.4	7.2	11.5	0.8	96.1	2.1	1.8
Average		82.4	6.9	9.8	0.8	95.9	2.2	2.0

Table 12.10. *Components of gross pay: all full-time workers (%)*

Year	Shift-workers				Non-shift-workers		
	Residual	Overtime	Shift-work	Incentive	Residual	Overtime	Incentive
Male							
1973	64.5	14.7	12.3	8.5	83.8	9.9	6.2
1974	64.5	15.6	11.8	8.1	84.0	9.5	6.4
1975	68.3	14.2	11.4	6.1	86.4	8.2	5.4
1976	69.0	13.8	11.5	5.7	87.3	7.4	5.2
1977	69.2	14.3	11.0	5.6	87.1	7.6	5.3
1978	67.3	14.3	11.1	7.3	86.4	7.9	5.8
1979	65.2	15.4	11.4	8.0	85.7	8.4	5.9
1980	65.8	14.8	12.2	7.2	86.9	7.7	5.4
1981	68.1	14.0	11.8	6.2	89.1	6.0	4.9
1982	67.5	14.1	12.0	6.5	89.1	6.4	4.4
Average	66.7	14.6	11.6	7.0	86.5	7.9	5.5
Female							
1973	84.0	3.8	10.1	2.1	94.4	1.7	3.9
1974	83.7	4.1	9.4	2.8	94.4	1.7	3.9
1975	85.8	3.0	9.8	1.4	95.9	1.3	2.8
1976	86.5	2.5	9.4	1.7	96.2	1.2	2.6
1977	87.5	2.5	8.5	1.5	96.1	1.3	2.7
1978	86.7	2.9	8.9	1.5	95.4	1.4	3.2
1979	85.0	3.1	10.2	1.7	95.2	1.6	3.1
1980	82.6	3.3	12.7	1.5	95.8	1.5	2.6
1981	83.4	2.7	12.6	1.3	96.4	1.4	2.2
1982	83.7	2.8	12.4	1.1	96.4	1.5	2.1
Average	85.0	3.0	10.4	1.6	95.7	1.5	2.8
Total							
1973	66.6	13.5	12.0	7.8	85.8	8.4	5.8
1974	66.4	14.5	11.6	7.5	86.1	8.0	6.0
1975	70.3	12.9	11.2	5.6	88.4	6.8	4.8
1976	71.4	12.2	11.2	5.2	89.3	6.1	4.7
1977	71.8	12.6	10.6	5.0	89.1	6.1	4.7
1978	69.9	12.9	10.8	6.5	88.4	6.4	5.2
1979	67.9	13.7	11.3	7.1	87.8	6.9	5.3
1980	68.3	13.1	12.3	6.3	88.9	6.3	4.8
1981	70.7	12.1	11.9	5.4	90.8	4.9	4.3
1982	70.3	12.1	12.0	5.5	90.8	5.3	3.9
Average	69.4	13.0	11.5	6.2	88.6	6.5	4.9

changes are clear from the preceding Tables. First, the general trend towards shift-working within most groups will have tended to raise the importance of this component of pay, although, as noted in Table 12.3 when discussing incidence rates, the compositional effects of a movement from males to females, from full-time to part-time, from manual to non-manual, and from manufacturing to services appear likely to have worked in the opposite direction. The changing composition of the work-force will not only change the incidence of shift-working (in effect, moving individuals between the shift and non-shift categories), but will also move individuals from high to low premium payment categories (and vice versa). As shift payments occur alongside overtime and incentive payments, the compositional effects appear likely to have reduced the importance of all premium payments, increasing the relative share of basic pay within the total across the workers as a whole, at least amongst full-time employees.

12.8. Conclusions

This paper has explored the contribution of shift premium payments to gross pay. In doing so, it has reviewed the long-standing debate about the incidence of shift-work. The earlier evidence of a rapid growth in the overall incidence of shift-working has been called into question. This has resulted in an anomaly between the anecdotal evidence of rapid growth at the micro-level and the much slower rates suggested by the aggregate NES data. The changing composition of the workforce provides a partial explanation. In practice, almost every group within the population has experienced a growth in the incidence of shift-work. On the other hand, there are significant differences in the incidence of shift-work between groups, and the compositional shifts in the workforce have, on balance, been away from high and towards low incidence groups. The second major area of interest concerned the magnitude of the shift premiums, and the relationship between shift and other premium payments. It has been shown that, at least for certain groups, such as manual males, there is no evidence that high incidence levels of shift-work are associated with a lower incidence of overtime. If anything, the two appear to be positively related. Examination of the component parts of gross pay reveals that, on balance, overtime pay forms a larger proportion of gross pay amongst shift-workers than amongst non-shift-workers. In addition, for those who receive shift pay, across all groups taken as a whole, shift-work contri-butes almost as large a percentage to gross pay as does overtime. Shift pay has tended broadly to maintain its share of gross pay over time across all groups. However, if anything, the premium rates (represented by the ratio of shift to basic pay) have fallen slightly, possibly reflecting the cumulative effects of recession on premium payments over this period.

Notes

1. The authors would like to thank the ESRC for funding the collection of the data, the IER for its support in undertaking this research, and Ruth Hermitage and Peter Millar for their help with the computing. Thanks also to Peter Dawkins who was involved in the early stages of the design of this work.
2. This is defined as *shift etc. premium payments*—'the premium element of payments, within the employee's total gross earnings for the survey pay period, for shift work or night work or weekend work which was not treated as overtime work' (DE, *NES* (1978: A60)).
3. Despite the fact that such detail is now available in other surveys, such as IFF (1978), DE, Workplace Industrial Relations Survey 1980 and 1984, and the Labour Force Survey 1986.
4. See for example Betancourt and Clague (1981), Bosworth and Dawkins (1981), Carter and Corlett (1982) and Bosworth (1983, 1986*a*), all of which include discussions of the statistics of shift-working as well as the theoretical literature.
5. See particularly the work of the European Foundation for the improvement of Living and Working Conditions: a list of references can be found in European Foundation (1983). See also Harrington (1979).
6. The pioneering work of Marris (1964) focused primarily on optimal capital utilization. More recently, however, see Winston and McCoy (1974), Bosworth and Pugh (1985*a*), and Bosworth (1986*a*).
7. Bosworth (1981) introduces shift-working within a factor demand model based on a Cobb–Douglas technology, Harris (1983) extends this to a CES world, and Bosworth and Pugh (1985*a*) report on a nested CES function.
8. This forms the basis of part of the discussion of new areas of employment growth in Wilson and Bosworth (1986).
9. Chung and Aigner (1981) examine changes in electricity tariffs and Bosworth and Pugh (1984 and 1985*b*) explore the consequences of joint rhythmically varying prices.
10. See Sloane (1978). The only current descriptive evidence of this appears to be Blanch-flower and Corry (1986*a*), drawn from the Workplace Industrial Relations Survey (Daniel and Millward 1983), although size has been used as an explanatory variable in a number of studies, such as Bosworth, Dawkins, and Westaway (1981*a*, 1981*b*), Ingram and Sloane (1985).
11. Department of Employment, 'Analyses by Industry', *NES* (1980: Part C, T79–82, pp. C43–50).
12. A broad check on this observation can be obtained from Department of Employment, *Times Rates* (annually).
13. Ministry of Labour (1954, 1965) 'Shiftwork' surveys of 1954 and 1964, and the IFF (1978) survey of the manufacturing sector. A discussion can be found in Bosworth and Dawkins (1981: 89–91).
14. Department of Employment, 'Analysis by Occupation', *NES* (1980: Part D, T99–100, pp. D33–6).
15. Further discussion of the trends in work patterns can be found in Wilson and Bosworth (1986).
16. See n. 13.
17. See for example the discussion of the development of 'unsocial hours' payments in IDS (1979*b*). Note also that here we interpret the term 'unsocial hours' to relate essentially to the timing of work rather than to its length. In certain instances, length may be an

important element, although, where it is, it will generally spill over into unsocial times as well.

18. Other authors have adopted somewhat broader definitions of shift-work, for example, to incorporate any workers employed at unsocial times of work (Walker 1978).
19. This is discussed in more detail in Bosworth (1986*a*, 1987) and Wilson and Bosworth (1986: 24–9) and is the subject of ongoing research.
20. This argument can be traced to Mott *et al.* (1965). See also Bosworth *et al.* (1981*a*, 1981*b*).
21. See Bosworth *et al.* (1981*a*, 1981*b*) and Bosworth and Dawkins (1981: 171–6).
22. For example, the total (male and female combined) ratios include weights for male and female shift- and non-shift-workers. The resulting overall expression can be shown to be:

$$\frac{X_S(M) \cdot \dfrac{N_S(M)}{N_s(M) + N_S(F)} + X_S(F) \cdot \dfrac{N_S(F)}{(N_S(M) + N_S(F))}}{X_{NS}(M) \cdot \dfrac{N_{NS}(M)}{(N_{NS}(M) + N_{NS}(F))} + X_{NS}(FS) \cdot \dfrac{N_{NS}(F)}{(N_{NS}(M) + N_{NS}(F))}}$$

where: X denotes the pay variable in question; N refers to the number of workers; M and F denote male and female; S and NS refer to shift- and non-shift-workers.

23. See PROSA (1981) and Bosworth and Dawkins (1984).
24. See Garbarino (1964), Ball and St Cyr (1966), Hart and Sharot (1978), and Bosworth (1982).
25. There is the possibility that normal hours will be extended on these shifts and what would normally be overtime pay will appear as higher basic pay or shift premiums.
26. See for example Bosworth and Westaway (1987).

13

National Wage Agreements[1]

R. F. Elliott and P. D. Murphy

13.1. Introduction

The New Earnings Survey records that in 1973 the pay and conditions of
72.8 per cent of all male manual workers and 61.6 per cent of all female
manual workers were affected by a national agreement. According to the
NES 56 per cent of this male total were affected by only a national
agreement while the remaining 44 per cent were affected by a national
agreement and some form of supplementary bargaining. The corresponding figures for females were 59 and 41 per cent respectively (Table 13.1).
The NES therefore suggests that the pay and conditions of a considerable
number of men and women were affected by national agreements in 1973.
Similar enquiries in 1978 revealed that the proportion of manual workers
affected by national agreements had dropped to 65.7 per cent in the case
of males and 58.5 per cent in that of females (Table 13.1).

More recently the Workplace Industrial Relations Surveys of 1980 and
1984 revealed that in 1980 national agreements were the basis for the
most recent pay increase in 34 per cent of all establishments employing
manual workers and 30 per cent of all those employing non-manual
workers (Table 13.2) and that between 1980 and 1984 'there was an
increase in the proportion of workplaces where pay was regulated by
national or industry-wide agreements' (Millward and Stevens 1986: 226).
Since, however, these tend to be the smaller establishments the number
of workers whose pay is so determined is smaller than these proportions
suggest but once again this survey reveals an important role for national
agreements in the pay determination process. Yet to admit that pay and
conditions are 'affected by' or that national agreements 'served as the
basis for the most recent pay increase', tells us little about the precise
linkages between the rates of pay that are negotiated and established
within the more than 300 national agreements that exist in the UK and
the wages that are eventually paid at the workplace.

In the middle 1970s the received wisdom was that most national agreements in the private sector no longer set the rates individuals were paid;
rather they set minima which established a safety-net below which their
pay would not be allowed to fall (see Brown and Terry 1978). Yet even at
this time it was undoubtedly the case that a large number of national

Table 13.1. *Percentages of full-time male workers whose pay and conditions were affected by various types of collective agreements*

	Manual		Non-manual	
	1973	1978	1973	1978
National only	40.6	36.4	39.6	38.5
National and supplementary	32.2	29.3	11.4	11.7
Company or local only	10.4	12.6	9.5	9.4
No collective agreement	16.8	21.7	39.6	40.5

Table 13.2. *Percentages of establishments whose pay was affected by various types of collective agreements in 1980*

	Manual		Non-manual	
	1980	1984	1980	1984
National/regional	34	40	30	36
Company and plant	23	20	18	17
Wages Council	6		4	
No collective agreement	33	38	45	46
No information and other answer	4	2	3	1

Sources: Daniel and Millward (1984: Table VIII.1); Millward and Stevens (1986: Table 9.1).

agreements in the public sector continued to set the actual rates that individuals were paid and there were several agreements in the private sector for which this was also true (see Brown and Terry 1978: 125). Moreover, even in those agreements which had long been regarded as establishing only minima, a not inconsiderable proportion of employees were at or near the minima at any one time (see Elliott 1981*b*: 371). There was also the suspicion that even in those cases where individuals were paid well above the minima changes in the minima led to changes in the rates for these workers, either because negotiators sought to re-establish some fixed relationship with the nationally agreed rate or because the change in the national rate was itself the agreed signal for changes in all workplace rates. Obviously when national agreements establish the rates paid to some or all of the workers covered by a national agreement or where they are the cause of changes in the rates of pay of those above the minima they play an important role in the wage determination process. It is for this reason that they continue to attract the attention of those analysts concerned with the workings of the wage determination system in the UK.

13.2. Single- and Multi-employer Agreements

In the early 1970s when the role of national agreements in the pay determination process was the subject of considerable debate it was usual to distinguish between workers whose pay was determined by national negotiations and those whose pay was determined by negotiations at the plant and company level. Brown and Terry (1978) have suggested that this distinction is misleading. They suggest that most plant and company and some national agreements are better understood as single-employer agreements and that those national agreements that remain are then most accurately described as multi-employer agreements. According to Brown and Terry it is the single-employer agreements that set the actual rates that individuals are paid while the role of multi-employer agreements in the pay determination process is diminishing. Moreover they argue that this distinction between single- and multi-employer agreements reveals the marked similarities that now exist in the procedures for establishing pay in wide areas of both the private and public sectors. It recognizes that in recent years private-sector wage drift has been contained and that formal negotiations once again establish effective rates of pay in this sector as they had always done in the public sector. As Brown and Terry put it, 'Managers have buried wage drift' (1978: 132).

Yet it is important to retain the distinction between national and plant and, perhaps, company bargaining, for in many circumstances the fact that a national agreement is also a single-employer agreement may be of little consequence. Of concern is the extent to which the wage rates established in any agreement reflect the circumstances in the different labour markets covered by the agreement. This is evidently not the case in a national agreement which imposes uniform conditions across a range of different labour markets. Nor is the existence of a single-employer agreement any guarantee that the rates will reflect the specific circumstances of different labour markets either. Single-employer agreements with national coverage again, typically, impose uniform pay and conditions across a range of different labour markets.

Multi-employer agreements reflect the average experience of those employers who are party to the agreement, not the circumstances of any employer or labour market in particular. Similarly, single-employer agreements often reflect the average experience of the several plants, often operating in quite distinct labour markets, that, together, comprise a company. It is such national agreements, be they single- or multi-employer, that have recently been subject to criticism. They are, it is argued, becoming less tenable because of the increasingly diverse experience of the several labour markets they cover and hence of the parties involved. Yet this thesis in turn overlooks the considerable unanimity of view over matters of pay that still binds large numbers of employers together in many industries. It ignores the advantages to employers of combining to set rates of pay—something Adam Smith recognized some time ago (Smith 1776: 1937 edition, ch. VIII)—and to a single employer of setting a uniform national rate for all his employees. For these reasons national agreements of the multi-employer and single-employer type may continue to play an important role in the wage determination process.

National agreements in the public sector are of the single-employer type and it is generally assumed that the rates they establish are the effective rates paid at the workplace. However there is now evidence that their role is changing and that the rates they set no longer influence earnings to the degree they did in the past. So what has been happening in recent years? Is there evidence to support the Brown and Terry thesis of the diminishing importance of national agreements in the private sector and what of recent developments in the public sector? What too of the rates determined by the Wages Councils? These were always regarded as minima but have rates of pay at the workplace converged or diverged from these in recent years? These are the questions we address in this chapter.

13.3. Methodology

The detailed NES files together with data we have extracted from other Department of Employment publications offer a unique opportunity to cast light on these issues. They enable us to compare the exact rates of pay for specific occupations which were established in national agreements with the basic rates of pay for these same occupations as recorded in the NES over the period 1973 to 1982. The former are taken from the annual Department of Employment publication *Time Rate of Wages and Hours of Work* (*TRWHW*) and the latter from the NES tapes made available to us. The earlier analysis (Brown and Terry 1978, Elliott 1981*b*) was unable to match the occupations shown in *TRWHW* to those in the NES as we have done, for the published NES data only provides details of earnings by occupations at the broad occupational group level, not the detailed occupational level which is required for this exercise. However not infrequently we still found that either *TRWHW* or the NES failed to record the occupational details we required so that in the end our sample comprised the agreements noted in Appendix A. From *TRWHW* we extracted the hourly rates of pay (NHR) for the principal occupations in each agreement recorded there and we then matched these to the basic rates of pay for the same occupations within the same agreement as recorded in the NES. The NES reported their standard hourly earnings (hourly earnings net of overtime pay) (SHE) and basic hourly rates of pay (BHR), this latter being basic hourly earnings net of overtime, shift, and incentive pay, once recorded as residual pay in the NES.

Our initial analysis focuses on a set of male manual occupations chosen to represent the position in each of the major collective agreements recorded in Appendix 13.1.[2] We were able to match occupations and obtain pay data for some 28 national agreements covering male manual workers. The agreements cover both the public and private sectors and together accounted for some 61 per cent of all the male manual employees who were covered by a national agreement, that is by either a national agreement only or a national plus supplementary agreement, in 1973. In addition we were able to match occupations within 10 Wage Boards and Councils. Together these accounted for 50 per cent of all manual males covered by these institutions in 1973. The analysis covers the period since 1973, the year in which the new occupational classification was first introduced.

For the analysis we calculated two ratios. First the ratio of standard hourly earnings (gross hourly earnings less overtime) for occupation i, in agreement j, SHEij, as reported in the NES, to the national hourly rates of pay, for this same occupation and agreement, NHRij, as reported in *TRWHW*. The average of these (SHE/NHR) was then found by weighting each of these by the proportion of total employment accounted for by occupation i, in agreement j, Fij, and the proportion of total employment in all agreements accounted for by agreement j, Aj. Thus our all-industry average reflects the proportion of employment accounted for by each of the industry agreements. Thus

$$\frac{\text{SHE}}{\text{NHR}} = \sum_{j=1}^{n} \sum_{i=1}^{m} A_j \, F_{ij} \left(\frac{\text{SHE}}{\text{NHR}}\right)_{ij} \tag{13.1}$$

Second we calculated the ratio of the basic hourly rates, BHRij, reported in the NES to the national hourly rate, NHRij, reported in *TRWHW* in a similar way. Thus

$$\frac{\text{BHR}}{\text{NHR}} = \sum_{j=1}^{n} \sum_{i=1}^{m} A_j \, F_{ij} \left(\frac{\text{BHR}}{\text{NHR}}\right)_{ij} \tag{13.2}$$

Of course the number of employees covered by any single national agreement has changed over the period. Some have grown in size, others contracted. This feature together with the nature of random sampling means that the same occupations are not necessarily picked up each year in the NES. Accordingly in the first instance we constructed indices using the above formula which allowed for the unrestricted entry of new occupations and for a change in the weights attaching to existing occupations as occupations diminished or increased in importance over the period. The occupations represented in this index and the weight attached to them may therefore change from year to year according to whether or not they are captured in the NES sample; these indices we term those constructed with the *full file*. To check the bias, if any, that such a procedure produces we also constructed an index comprising only those occupations reported in every year. This enabled us to establish what had happened to the ratios for a fixed set of agreements and occupations. These restrictions of course resulted in a greatly reduced number of agreements and occupations and the indices constructed on this basis we term the *matched sample*. Early comparison of the two series revealed that they produced similar patterns and therefore below we report only the results for the full file.

13.4. Sectoral Developments

The general results from the analysis of the full file are illustrated in Fig. 13.1. This reveals that the ratios of standard hourly earnings and basic hourly rates to nationally negotiated rates increased in 1974 and 1975 but in the following year declined sharply and thereafter reveal no discernible trend. Behind this general picture the experience of the public, private, and Wages Council sectors are quite different. The principal results of the sectoral analysis are detailed in Table 13.3. These reveal that the average of the ratio of standard hourly earnings to national rates of pay for the period from 1973 to 1982 was highest at 145.9 in the private sector and lowest at 128.6 in the Wages Council sector. In part these differences reflect the greater dependence on incentive pay of those in the private sector for most of this period but it is noteworthy that the difference between the public and private sectors has diminished over the years as the share of earnings accounted for by incentive pay in private-sector agreements declined while that in the public sector increased (see Table 13.4 for evidence of the share of earnings accounted for by incentive pay in each sector). Between 1973 and 1982 standard hourly earnings have fallen as a proportion of national rates of pay from 151.8 to 145.7 per cent in the private sector but risen from 120.6 to 149.0 per cent in the public sector. 1974 and 1975 represent the peak years for the ratio in the private

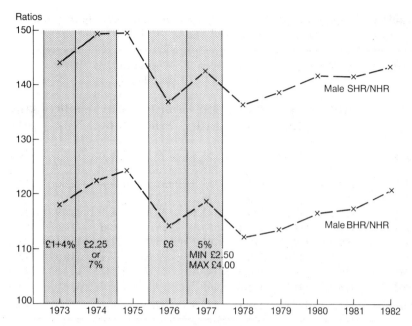

Fig. 13.1. The ratio of standard hourly earnings and basic hourly rates to nationally negotiated hourly rates

sector and while the whole of the decline occurred in the following year, 1976, this was largely sustained to the end of the period. In contrast in the public sector the ratio has increased steadily throughout the period. Again in Wages Boards and Councils there has been a decline in the ratio from 138.2 per cent in 1973 to 126.0 by 1982, most of this also accounted for by the decline in 1976.

As we might expect the ratio of basic hourly rates to national hourly rates is much lower than is the ratio of standard hourly earnings to national hourly rates. The former ratio not only controls for overtime pay but also removes the effects of shift and incentive pay and thereby reflects more closely effective rates of pay at the workplace. How has this changed over the period? Table 13.3 reveals that the ratio is on average lowest in the public sector at 111.5 and highest in Wages Boards and Councils at 122.5. No doubt this outcome in part reflects the absence of supplementary bargaining in the public sector, and the practice of plant and company bargaining in the private sector together with payments above the minimum rates stipulated in the orders in the Wages Council area. However it is now noticeable that while there is once again a steady widening in the ratio in the public sector and a narrowing in the ratio in the Wages Council sector (again largely accounted for by the decline in

Table 13.3. *Ratio of standard hourly earnings and basic hourly rates to national hourly rates for manual males, 1973–1982 (full sample)*

Year	Public sector		Private sector		Wages Councils and Boards		All	
	BHR / NHR	SHE / NHR	BHR / NHR	SHE / NHR	BHR / NHR	SHE / NHR	BHR / NHR	SHE / NHR
1973	101.3	120.6	121.8	151.8	130.1	138.2	118.1	144.4
1974	105.9	127.0	125.8	155.8	133.1	140.9	122.7	149.8
1975	107.9	132.6	128.7	156.0	131.2	136.8	124.6	149.7
1976	109.6	133.0	115.3	139.7	117.5	123.7	114.2	137.0
1977	113.4	137.3	120.5	147.1	122.5	128.1	118.9	142.8
1978	116.6	144.6	109.8	135.1	116.4	120.6	112.1	136.2
1979	109.0	137.1	115.2	142.3	115.7	121.6	113.6	138.8
1980	116.1	147.4	116.1	142.9	122.6	127.4	116.9	142.3
1981	116.1	148.2	118.3	142.4	116.6	123.2	117.3	141.6
1982	118.5	149.0	123.0	145.7	119.6	126.0	121.0	144.0
All years	111.5	137.4	119.5	145.9	122.5	128.6	117.9	142.7

Table 13.4. *The proportion of standard hourly earnings of those male manual workers covered by national agreements in the public and private sectors and in Wages Councils which is accounted for by incentive pay, 1973–1982 (males, full sample)*

Year	Private sector	Public sector	Wages Boards and Councils
1973	16.2	12.1	5.6
1974	16.4	12.8	5.1
1975	14.7	13.5	4.1
1976	14.3	12.8	3.9
1977	15.2	13.1	3.9
1978	15.9	14.7	3.2
1979	16.0	16.0	4.8
1980	15.2	16.2	3.1
1981	13.9	16.9	5.0
1982	12.7	15.7	4.1

1976) there is now no discernible trend in the ratio in the private sector as there was before.

In the public sector it appears that the practice of awarding pay supplements on top of the minima stipulated in national agreements has grown over the period. The ratio has risen from almost equality, 101.3, to 118.5 per cent over the same period. In the Wages Council sector the ratio of basic hourly to national, i.e. Wages Council, rates has fallen from 130.0 in 1973 to 119.6 in 1982. Most obvious of all is the convergence of the three sectors with basic hourly rates of pay exceeding the rates set in national agreements or Wages Council minima by around 20 per cent in all three sectors by the early 1980s.

Interestingly the picture painted by Table 13.3 confirms the general picture reported by Elliott in 1979. It emphasizes that 1975 is a rather untypical year. For while in the private sector the ratio of basic hourly to national hourly rates rose over the period to 1975, as indeed did the ratio of standard hourly earnings to national hourly rates, in the following year it fell back sharply and thereafter generally fluctuated around a mean value that was less than that reported in 1973.

13.5. Earnings and Wage Drift

Looked at in terms of earnings and wage drift, the former measured by the proportional change in the ratio SHE–NHR and the latter by the proportional change in BHR–NHR the picture is one of considerable variation over the period.[3] Table 13.5 reveals that in the Wages Council and private sectors the years from April 1975 to April 1976 and again from April 1977 to 1978 witnessed substantial negative earnings and wage drift. In the remaining years there was positive drift but these two years dominated, so that over the period as a whole the annual average rate of both wage and earnings drift was negative. In contrast both wage and earnings drift were generally positive in the public sector. Only in the twelve months to April 1979 was drift negative but the magnitude of this was not sufficient to offset developments in surrounding years. In none of the three sectors is there a discernible trend in either wage or earnings drift; on the contrary there is substantial year-on-year variation in the rates of both of these in all three sectors.

13.6. Incomes Policies

The period to April 1976 exhibits the most marked negative wage drift in the private and Wages Council sectors, as illustrated in Fig. 13.1. This

Table 13.5. *Annual wage and earnings drift, 1973–1982 (males, full sample)*

	Public sector		Private sector		Wages Councils and Boards		All sectors	
	Earnings drift[a]	Wage drift[b]	Earnings drift[a]	Wage drift[b]	Earnings drift[a]	Wage drift[b]	Earnings drift[a]	Wage drift[b]
1973/4	5.7	4.5	2.7	3.3	1.9	2.3	3.7	3.9
1974/5	4.4	1.9	0.1	2.3	-2.4	-1.4	-0.1	1.5
1975/6	0.3	1.6	-10.5	-10.4	-9.6	-10.5	-8.5	-8.3
1976/7	3.3	3.5	5.3	4.6	3.5	4.3	4.2	4.1
1977/8	5.3	2.8	-8.2	-8.9	-5.8	-5.0	-4.6	-5.7
1978/9	-5.2	-6.5	5.3	5.0	0.8	-0.5	1.9	1.3
1979/80	7.5	6.5	0.5	0.8	4.7	5.9	2.5	2.9
1980/1	0.6	0.0	-0.4	1.9	-3.3	-4.9	-0.5	0.4
1981/2	0.5	2.1	2.3	3.9	2.3	2.6	1.7	3.2
All years	2.5	1.8	-0.3	-0.3	-0.9	-0.8	0.0	+0.4

[a] Earnings drift over the previous twelve months is calculated as

$$\left[\left(\frac{\text{SHE}}{\text{NHR}} \right)_t \Big/ \left(\frac{\text{SHE}}{\text{NHR}} \right)_{t-1} \right] - 1 \cdot 100$$

where t represents the current year and $t-1$ is the previous year.
[b] Wage drift over the previous twelve months is calculated as

$$\left[\left(\frac{\text{BHR}}{\text{NHR}} \right)_t \Big/ \left(\frac{\text{BHR}}{\text{NHR}} \right)_{t-1} \right] - 1 \cdot 100$$ where the notation is as before.

coincides in large part with the period of the flat-rate £6 per week wage award under phase I of the Social Contract. In general we would expect a flat-rate policy adding an equal money sum to national and basic hourly rates to narrow the proportional difference between these two series, i.e. to result in negative wage drift. This effect alone however cannot account for the magnitude of the negative drift shown in the Wages Council and private sectors in the year to April 1976. Closer scrutiny of the individual agreements underpinning each sector reveals that while there was a £6 increase in national rates in most agreements it was not fully reflected in the rates of pay of those paid in excess of the minima nor was it fully reflected in the earnings of workers in the Wages Council or private sectors. 1976 was a year in which unemployment rose sharply in Britain following the fall in output in the previous year and this appears to be the reason why the full £6 was not conceded in supplementary bargaining and why earnings rose by less than this amount at this time.

It is clear that incomes policy alone is not the explanation for developments over this period; there were other forces at work. Indeed in both the private and Wages Council sectors the negative drift of the year to April 1976 resulted in a *permanent* drop in the ratio of standard hourly earnings and basic hourly rates to national hourly rates.

13.7. Supplementary Plant and Company Bargaining

Supplementary plant and company bargaining is the principal but not the sole reason why the hourly rates of pay reported in the NES for agreements in the private sector exceed the rates we have extracted from *TRWHW*. For in addition to local bargaining the national basic rates that we have recorded will be adjusted upwards due to special payments which are also laid down in national agreements. National agreements, for example, award tool money, dirt money, and age and other special allowances on top of basic rates, but it was not possible to incorporate all of these in the national hourly rates we recorded for they apply to only some workers and we cannot distinguish who they are. None the less the magnitude of these payments must be considerable, for when we compare the basic hourly rates of pay from the NES to the nationally negotiated rate of pay from *TRWHW* for those workers covered by a national agreement *only*, that is for those who do not enjoy supplementary or workplace bargaining, we find that a substantial gap still exists.

In 1973 and again in 1978 the New Earnings Survey recorded the pay of those workers affected by only a national agreement and those affected by a national plus a supplementary agreement. Table 13.6 reports this information for the private sector and reveals that while in general basic

Table 13.6. *Ratios of hourly earnings to nationally negotiated hourly rates of pay in the private sector (full file)*

Ratio of	National agreements only		National plus supplementary agreement	
	1973	1978	1973	1978
Basic hourly–national hourly rates	112.2	111.6	122.6	111.2
Standard hourly earnings–national hourly rates	133.8	134.6	155.6	139.4

hourly and standard hourly rates exceed nationally negotiated rates most where there is supplementary plant and company bargaining there is still a substantial difference between these ratios even where there is no supplementary bargaining. Moreover if the extent of this under-recording of the rates of pay established in national agreements is the same in the presence of supplementary bargaining as it is when workers are covered by a national agreement only, it is evident that it accounts for the major part of the gap between basic hourly and national hourly rates in this sector also. Table 13.6 suggests that in 1973 perhaps as much as 12.2 of the 22.6 per cent difference between the basic hourly rates recorded in the NES and the national hourly rates we extracted from *TRWHW* is accounted for by special payments provided for within national agreements. Table 13.6 also suggests that over the five-year period recorded here there was a substantial fall in the extent to which supplementary bargaining added to the rates of pay negotiated in national agreements, for the ratio of basic hourly to national hourly rates fell from 122.6 to 111.2, until at the later date this ratio was not substantially different from the ratio where workers were covered by national agreements only.

It is equally evident that incentive payments have declined in importance in this sector. Standard hourly earnings fell as a proportion of national rates from 155.6 in 1973 to 139.4 in 1978 among those national agreements affected by supplementary bargaining, although where workers were covered by a national agreement only the ratio was little changed at 133.8 per cent in 1973 and 134.6 per cent in 1978 (full file).

Generally the movements which took place within both national only and national and supplementary agreements over the five-year period from 1973 to 1978 were again such as to bring the two bargaining types more closely into line with one another. This convergence appears to coincide with a deepening of the recession from the middle 1970s onwards.

13.8. The Effects of Changes in the Distribution of Employment

Part of the changes we have observed occurring over the period will be accounted for by changes in the occupational composition and coverage of particular national agreements. Thus the widening of the gap between nationally negotiated hourly rates and basic hourly rates in the public sector and the narrowing of the same ratio in wages councils over the period 1973 to 1983, as detailed in Tables 13.3 and 13.5, could be accounted for by any one or all of three compositional changes: by changes in the number of occupations sampled, or in the number of workers covered by an agreement, or finally by changes in the number of workers covered by each of the occupations sampled. To distinguish these effects we calculated the proportionate change in the wage gap, the ratio of BHR to NHR, that would have occurred between the years 1973 and 1982 in three ways:

(1) We allowed no change in the occupations sampled within an agreement, although we allowed the numbers covered by each occupation to reflect the changes in the share of employment accounted for by each occupation over the period. Thus the difference between this hypothetical measure of drift and that which actually occurred represents that part of the overall change which is due to the changing occupational composition of agreements (composition in terms of the inclusion of new KOSs and exclusion of old);

(2) We start from the position reached in (1) above where we have controlled for the KOS composition of each agreement and now control for the distribution of workers between each of the national agreements and Wages Councils common to these two years. Thus the difference between this hypothetical measure of drift and that which we had previously calculated under (1) above represents that part of the overall change which is attributable to the changing distribution of employment and hence coverage of our sample of agreements between the years 1973 to 1982;

(3) Now we start from the position reached in (2) above when we had controlled for both changes in the KOSs sampled and the coverage of agreements and now further control for the number of employees in each of the matched occupations. The difference between that calculated in (2) above and this hypothetical measure of drift represents that part of the overall change which is due to

the changing size of occupations within an agreement. This last
of the three most fully abstracts from the changing pattern of
employment over the period.

The results of the above exercise are shown in Table 13.7. They reveal
(Part (a)) that the entry of new occupations and the fall-out of occupations of diminishing significance had no impact on the wage gap in the
public sector (column (7)). On the other hand, although changes in the
wage gap were smaller in both the private and Wages Board and Council
sectors, in both cases the changing KOS composition accounted for part of
the change. It reduced the increase in the wage gap in the private sector
and exaggerated the reduction in the wage gap that occurred between the
years 1973–82 in the Wages Councils and Board sector.

Changes in the coverage, the size of national agreements, accounted
for a larger part of the changes we observe as revealed in Part (b) of
Table 13.7. Here we take the hypothetical or controlled values calculated
in Part (a), column (4), these appear in column (9) of Part (b), and
contrast these with the index values we obtain after further controlling for
the changing coverage of national agreements. Now we find, column (13),
that the changing size of national agreements has arrested the widening of
the gap that occurred in the public and private sectors. Although this
latter was of course fairly negligible, the scale of this was diminished by
one-third by the changing coverage of agreements in this sector. In the
Wages Council sector there was a narrowing of the wage gap which was
exaggerated by the changing coverage of the Wages Boards and Councils.
In other words, between the years 1973 to 1982 employment was being
concentrated on those councils which had the lowest wage gap.

Finally we have taken the controlled values in column (10) of Part (b)
(these appear as column (15) of Part (c)), and further controlled for the
changes in the number of workers covered by each of the occupational
groups for which we had matched NES to *TRWHW* data. The results of
this appear in column (16) of Part (c). Now we find that the changing
occupational composition of employment within an agreement accounts
for 2 of the 17.7 percentage point growth in the wage gap in the public
sector between these years. More significantly, it accounts for the whole of
the small widening that occurred in the private sector; indeed had these
changes not occurred the wage gap would have narrowed. Again in the
Wages Board and Council sector the changing occupational distribution
served to reduce the narrowing of the wage gap that occurred in this
sector.

We can find the impact of all three of the above effects taken together
by summing the entries in columns (7) in Part (a), (13) in Part (b) and (19)
in Part (c). Thus we find that taken together they accounted for 1.3 of the

17.0 percentage points widening of the wage gap that occurred in the public sector, so they exaggerated the widening that occurred here. The small widening in the wage gap that occurred in the private sector is revealed to be entirely due to these effects; indeed had they not occurred the gap would have narrowed by 1.7 per cent. Finally in the Wages Board and Council sector in aggregate these separate effects cancel out. When netted out they are revealed to have had no impact on the narrowing of the wage gap that occurred in this sector.

13.9. Differences by Level of Skill

It seems probable that the basic rates established in national agreements and Wages Councils respond less to conditions in the labour market than do the additions to these rates resulting from supplementary bargaining or awarded at management's discretion. It seems possible therefore that the gap between the basic hourly rates which incorporate these additions and nationally negotiated rates might vary positively according to the degree of tightness in local markets. One of the features of recent years has been the coexistence of a considerable over-supply of unskilled labour together with a continued shortage of some types of skilled labour. We might therefore expect to find the basic hourly rates of pay of the unskilled, the rates paid at the workplace, converging toward the nationally negotiated rates of pay. Conversely we might expect the opposite among some skilled occupations with basic hourly rates of pay moving further away from nationally negotiated rates over the period.

Tables 13.8 and 13.9 detail the proportions of workers with different skills covered by a national agreement (national agreement only and national and supplementary) and in line with Table 13.1 reveal that these have fallen for all three skill groups. Table 13.9 also suggests that local supplements are more important for skilled workers. However Fig. 13.2 indicates that in the period since 1973 there has been no significant trend in the wage gap for any of the three groups of workers. By the end of the period the ratios for all three groups appear to exhibit a similar pattern of change. It seems clear that if supplementary bargaining or local additions to national rates were used to counter skill shortages the shortages were not sufficiently general to produce wage drift for the group as a whole. In fact we report in Chapter 3 above that unemployment rates rose relatively faster amongst the skilled than they did amongst the unskilled during large parts of the period analysed here.

Fig. 13.2 also fails to reveal any systematic attempt by the higher-skilled groups to circumvent the equalizing effects of the several incomes policies which caused a narrowing of the proportional differential

Table 13.7. *Changes in the wage gap due to changes in the size and composition of national agreements and Wages Councils, 1973–1982 (males)*

(a) *Occupation entry and exit in agreements*

	Ratio of BHR–NHR		Controlled KOS		Proportional increase in the wage gap[a]		
	Actual				Actual	Controlled	Part due to changing KOS composition of agreements
	1973 (1)	1982 (2)	1973 (3)	1982 (4)	(5)	(6)	(7)
Public sector	101.3	118.5	101.1	118.3	17.0	17.0	0.0
Private sector	121.8	123.0	121.5	123.0	1.0	1.2	−0.2
Wages Boards and Councils	130.0	119.6	128.4	118.8	−8.0	−7.5	−0.5

(b) *Part (a) above plus the changing coverage of agreements*

	Ratio of BHR–NHR			Proportional increase in the wage gap		
	Actual		Controlled	Actual: col. (6) above	Controlled	That part due to the changing size of agreements
	Col. (3) above 1973	Col. (4) above 1982	1982			
	(8)	(9)	(10)	(11)	(12)	(13)
Public sector	101.1	118.3	119.0	17.0	17.7	−0.7
Private sector	121.5	123.0	123.7	1.2	1.8	−0.6
Wages Boards and Councils	128.4	118.8	121.0	−7.5	−5.8	−1.7

(c) *Parts (a) (b) above plus the changing occupational distribution of employment within agreements*

	Ratio of BHR–NHR			Proportional increase in the wage gap		
	Actual		Controlled	Actual: col. (12) above	Controlled	That part due to the changing occupational composition
	Col. (8) above 1973	Col. (10) above 1982	1982			
	(14)	(15)	(16)	(17)	(18)	(19)
Public sector	101.1	119.0	117.0	17.7	15.7	2.0
Private sector	121.5	123.7	119.4	1.8	−1.7	3.5
Wages Boards and Councils	128.4	121.0	118.1	−5.8	−8.0	2.2

Table 13.8. *Coverage of agreements by skill group*

	Skilled	Semi-skilled	Unskilled
National only			
1973	41.0	36.9	47.0
1978	35.8	35.0	43.3
National and supplementary			
1973	35.3	29.4	28.2
1978	31.6	26.7	24.6
Company and local only			
1973	9.8	11.3	8.4
1978	12.1	13.7	9.7
No collective agreement			
1973	13.8	22.4	16.4
1978	20.4	24.6	22.4

Table 13.9. *Ratio of basic hourly rates to national hourly rates by skill group (full sample, males)*

	Skilled	Semi-skilled	Unskilled
1973	119.3	115.0	105.7
1974	123.8	119.0	109.5
1975	128.3	118.6	114.0
1976	115.5	111.2	115.2
1977	122.0	116.4	111.5
1978	109.7	110.6	121.0
1979	115.1	109.7	105.0
1980	117.5	115.4	114.3
1981	118.8	114.9	113.3
1982	122.9	118.1	114.6
Average for all years	119.3	114.9	112.4
Average no. of observations	6,196	2,970	1,806

between the nationally negotiated rates of the three groups. Certainly there is a widening of the ratio between basic hourly and national hourly rates for skilled workers during and after the 1973–4 policy and again in 1977, but following this last policy the ratio is reduced and although it climbs back up over the period to 1982 it never reaches the level it attained in 1975 and is merely on the same path as the ratio for lower-paid and less-skilled workers.

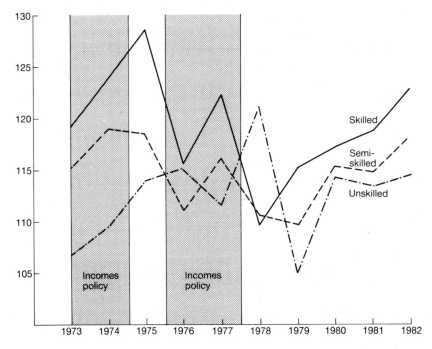

Fig. 13.2 Ratio of basic hourly rates to national hourly rates (males)

13.10. The Proportion of Workers Paid at or near the National Rate

We have seen (Table 13.3) that in each of the public, private, and Wages Council sectors the rates paid at the workplace, the basic hourly rates of pay, on average, exceeded those negotiated in national agreements. The reasons for this were that around 30 per cent of male manual workers were covered by supplementary plant and company bargaining and it was the policy of many employers in the Wages Council sector to pay above the Wages Council minimum. However we saw that the 40 per cent of manual males who were covered by a national agreement only also received supplements to their basic rates, and although these were often specified in the national agreements we were not able to quantify these. In Table 13.6 we saw that in the private sector by 1978 the basic rates of pay for those covered by only a national agreement exceeded the national rates we had recorded to a degree similar to that which occurred in the presence of supplementary bargaining. This under-recording of the rates

Table 13.10. *The distribution of basic hourly rates with respect to nationally negotiated rates of pay*

	Ratio of BHR–NHR					
	100	101–5	106–10	111–30	131–50	151+
Public sector						
1973	53.0	33.4	8.1	5.3	0.2	—
1975	13.8	9.0	54.0	20.0	3.2	—
1982	9.0	12.2	23.1	42.0	1.0	12.7
Private sector						
1973	4.6	7.2	15.5	45.5	24.7	2.5
1975	2.5	2.0	0.8	59.0	29.4	6.3
1982	1.1	7.4	15.8	47.6	25.1	3.0
Wages Boards and Councils						
1973	20.0	20.2	11.1	8.3	13.7	26.6
1975	5.7	48.8	12.5	2.9	12.8	24.8
1982	8.4	32.5	13.0	13.9	16.8	13.4

laid down in national agreements in the private sector meant that we were overstating the gap between basic hourly and national hourly rates and may well have also been overstating the magnitude of drift in this sector.

Having said this there remain substantial numbers of workers who are paid at or near the national minima we have recorded. Table 13.10 gives us some indication of this. It reveals that the proportion of employees paid at or very near the basic rates established in national agreements was largest in the public sector in 1973. At that time 94.5 per cent of all males enjoyed rates of pay which exceeded those laid down in the relevant national agreement by no more than 10 per cent. Since that date this proportion has reduced substantially and by 1982 only 44.3 per cent of all male manual employees in this sector were paid within 10 per cent of the national rates. This has been the most substantial change over the period.

In the private sector around 25 per cent received basic rates within 10 per cent of the national minimum rate in both 1973 and 1982 while in the Wages Council sector the proportion in this category is much higher at 54 per cent in 1982 but has changed little since 1973. Again Table 13.10 reveals that in the public sector in 1973 there were practically no employees with basic rates 30 per cent greater than the appropriate national rate but that by 1982 12.7 per cent of all employees in this sector were in this position. In the private sector the basic rates of pay of 27 per cent of all employees exceeded the national rates by 30 per cent in 1973 but the proportion was practically unchanged at 28 per cent in 1982. Thus the picture is of a fairly stable distribution with respect to national rates in the private sector, but of an increasing proportion of employees in the public sector enjoying substantial additions to national rates by 1982.

Developments in the Wages Council sector point to a trend in the other direction to that which has occurred in the public sector. Here the proportion enjoying rates in excess of 30 per cent of the Wages Council minimum has declined from 40.3 to 30.2 over the period 1973 to 1982.

13.11. Conclusions

The above analysis suggests a slow but growing convergence between the practices in the public and private sectors of the economy. The national rates we recorded evidently understate the rates of pay resulting from national negotiations, for we could not include all the many special payments such agreements provide. None the less it appeared that supplements to nationally negotiated rates of pay were an increasing feature of the public sector in the period to 1982. In the private sector such supplements, largely resulting from supplementary bargaining, were significant but, after the aberration of the mid-1970s, had changed little in magnitude since 1973. Indeed once we controlled for compositional changes there was a slight narrowing of the wage gap. Most significantly in both the private and public sectors in 1982 there was still a sizeable minority of employees, 44 and 24 per cent respectively, who received basic rates which were within 10 per cent or less of the recorded nationally negotiated minimum rates.

Developments in the Wages Council sector were most interesting of all. Here we found that employment was becoming more concentrated in those industries which paid the least above council rates. By 1982, 54 per cent of all manual males were paid within 10 per cent of the Wages Council minima while the proportion paid 50 per cent or more of the council minima had reduced from almost 27 per cent in 1973 to 13 per cent in 1982. This had been reflected in a fall in the ratio of basic hourly to national hourly rates for workers in this sector from 30 per cent in 1973 to 19.6 per cent in 1982 (Table 13.3).

We also found that basic pay had drifted to a small degree from the national minima stipulated for unskilled workers, amongst whom we might expect to find many Wages Council workers. It seems that this move to supplement national rates of the unskilled is occurring most in the public sector while in the Wages Council sector such supplements as once existed are now being steadily reduced. The deteriorating economic conditions throughout the period we survey do not appear to have arrested the move to supplement national rates in the public sector or caused any change in the practice of the private sector. Thus there seems to be a growing gap between their experience and that of the Wages Council sector. For in the Wages Council sector there was evidence of negative drift and of an increased role for the minimum rates stipulated in the council orders.

Appendix 13.1. National Agreements and Wages Boards and Councils Included in Analysis

Private sector

Engineering UK
Building brick and allied industries
Electrical contracting
Chemicals and allied industries
Cotton spinning and weaving
Wool textile industry
Hosiery (knitting) trade
Shipbuilding
Building industry
Paper making, paper coating, paper board, and building board
Civil engineering construction
Heating and ventilating
Furniture trade
Sawmilling
Motor vehicle retail and repair
Retail co-operative societies
Wholesale grocery and provisions
Cast stone and concrete
Retail multiple footwear

Public sector

Railway service
London Transport (road passenger transport)
Road passenger transport (municipal)
Water supply
Health services
Local authority services

Railway workshops
British Road Services

Wages Boards and Councils

Agriculture
Retail drapery
Retail furnishing
Retail food trade
Ready made and wholesale bespoke tailoring
Shirtmaking
Licensed residential establishments
Licensed non-residential establishments
Wholesale mantle
Retail bookselling and stationery

Notes

1. Thanks are due to the ESRC for providing funds to support this research. We are similarly indebted to Sophie Houston whose considerable computing expertise made this whole exercise possible and to Andrew Thomson and Mary Gregory for their initiative in bringing this group of researchers together and for their continuing efforts to administer and co-ordinate the whole enterprise. Back in Aberdeen we also benefited from a small grant from the University of Aberdeen Advisory Committee on Research to whom we extend our thanks. Thanks are also due to Hector Williams for his first-class computational and computing assistance; to Philip Hemmings, Donald Scobie, Angela Houston, and Marie Westoby for their help at various stages of the project; and to Winnie Sinclair for typing the several drafts through which this paper has proceeded.
2. We have excluded females from this analysis for two reasons. (1) In the period to 1976 the national rates for females were affected by the stages of the Equal Pay Act and we were unable to distinguish the precise magnitude of these effects. (2) We found that *TRWHW* frequently did not report female rates of pay in the detail we required—hence we were unable to calculate precisely the rates that were negotiated for them in national agreements.
3. Strictly speaking wage drift refers to a rise in the 'effective rate of pay per unit of labour input ... by arrangements that lie outside the control of the recognised procedures for scheduling rates of pay' (Phelps Brown 1962: 340). See Elliott (1981a) for a detailed discussion of wage drift.

14
Collective Bargaining and Relative Wages[1]

P. B. Beaumont and R. I. D. Harris

14.1. Introduction

There has been much discussion and debate over the broad question of whether the introduction and maintenance of *formal* institutional arrangements in the labour market make a difference to market outcomes. In other words, does a change of form or process also constitute a change of substance? The particular market outcome that has been the subject of most discussion has been wages, while the formal, institutional arrangements that are alleged to be not just neutral (impact) transmission mechanisms but 'things' of substantive importance are (1) the existence of a collective bargaining relationship, (2) the extent of union density or collective bargaining coverage, (3) the nature of bargaining structure, and, to a lesser extent, (4) the availability and usage of arbitration arrangements.

The case for the view that formal institutional arrangements, particularly collective bargaining, do make a difference to wage outcomes has evolved through three stages or types of argument. The first stage was an a priori or *assertive* type of argument. An excellent example of this type of argument was Arthur Ross's claim that rationalization and consolidation has led to the emergence of large-sized decision-making units (i.e. firms and trade unions) whose decision-making processes involve a sufficiently sizeable element of discretion such that human agents attain mastery over market forces.[2] As a result of this movement away from the small-sized decision-making units of the perfectly competitive economy, Ross claimed that 'there is real decision-making power in collective bargaining today' (1985: 306). The second type of argument to the effect that institutions matter was more one of *inference*. This type of argument pointed to the existence of certain important and long-standing features of the wage structure that were inconsistent with the predictions of competitive theory (e.g. the sizeable variation in wages that existed for a single job between establishments operating in the same local labour market area) and hence, by inference, were seen as having derived from institutional (such as internal labour market and/or collective bargaining) arrangements.[3] The third and final stage of the argument involved a *positive* case being made that institutions do matter. This work, which involved the estimation of union–non-union wage differentials, largely had its origins in the United States in the 1960s and spread across to Britain in the 1970s, mainly as a result of the availability of relevant information contained in the New Earnings Survey.

The next section of this chapter briefly reviews some of the major findings of existing studies of the size of the union–non-union wage differential in the United States and Britain, considers some of the criticisms frequently made of this estimation work, and outlines some of the differences in the institutional arrangements of the British and US systems of industrial relations which would appear to have implications for the respective sizes of the union relative wage effect in them. This is then followed by our use of the disaggregated information contained in the 1973 and 1978 New Earnings Surveys to produce new estimates of the size of the union relative wage effect.

14.2. The Existing Studies

The union relative wage effect (variously referred to as the 'union mark-up' or 'wage gap') concerns the size of the wage advantage that unionized workers enjoy over non-unionized workers, everything else held constant. The earliest work along these lines in the United States estimated this effect indirectly by comparing the average wage of more organized groups of workers with the average wage of less organized groups with the revealed wage difference being attributed to the extent of unionization.[4] In more recent years, however, it has been possible to estimate this effect directly in the United States as a result of the availability of micro-data sets in which the unit of observation is either the individual employee or the individual establishment.[5] The available evidence for the United States suggests that the size of the union relative wage effect has risen substantially through the course of time from some 10–15 per cent in the 1950s and 1960s to 25–30 per cent by the end of the 1970s (Freeman and Medoff 1984: 44–6). The reasons for this rise through time are not entirely clear, although a macroeconomic environment of rising unemployment has clearly played a part (Freeman and Medoff 1984: 54). Furthermore, economists have argued that this large and rising union relative wage effect goes a long way towards explaining the current extent of employer opposition to unions in the United States (Freeman and Medoff 1984: 239).

There are a number of both long-standing and more recent concerns about, not to say criticisms of, the estimation work concerning the union relative wage effect, which transcend the institutional details of any one system of industrial relations.[6] There is, firstly, the problem posed by the fact that unions can potentially influence non-union wages, in either a positive or negative fashion. This may occur through normal market channels (i.e. changes in the relative demand for and supply of labour between the two sectors) or through the 'threat effect', which involves non-union employers seeking to minimize any threat of unionization among their employees by paying the relevant unionized rate; this effect causes empirical estimates of the union relative wage effect to under-estimate the extent of the full effect. A second issue has been the concern that existing estimates of the union relative wage effect may contain an upward bias due to a failure adequately to control and account for other relevant wage determinants that are themselves significantly correlated with the extent of unionization. The particular concern expressed here is that an element of the estimated effect may be more of a 'compensating' differential deriving from a failure fully to account for differences in labour quality and working conditions between the unionized and non-unionized groups of workers. A further line of criticism contends that there is not a single, straightforward line of causation from unions to higher wages, hence the union relative wage effect cannot be appropri-ately estimated by an ordinary least squares regression equation in which unionism is an exogenous factor because the level of unionism is as much a function of higher wages as a cause of them. This particular criticism has, however, been subject to considerable counter-criticism on both theoretical and empirical grounds.[7] More recently, Lewis (1983) has argued that it is union status, rather than the extent of unionism, which is the critical variable that must be present in estimates of the union relative wage effect.

This latter observation is particularly important in Britain in view of the fact that the existing studies of the union relative wage effect based on the New Earnings Survey data have not in fact contained a union status variable. These inter-industry studies, which tended to produce relatively high estimates (i.e. at least 25–30 per cent) of the wage return associated with the extent of collective bargaining coverage, have also been subject to a number of other critical comments (Geroski and Stewart 1982). Moreover, recent British studies which have utilized a different data source (e.g. the National Training Survey) from that of the New Earnings Survey and included a union status variable have estimated a much smaller-sized union wage gap of only some 8 per cent in the 1970s (Stewart 1983); some extensions to this particular piece of work have suggested that the union relative wage effect in Britain was some 5 per cent in the 1960s, 8 per cent in the 1970s, and 11 per cent in the early 1980s (Metcalf and Nickell 1985).

The results of individual British and US studies are not always strictly comparable because, for example, the British studies have been much more narrowly confined to male workers in the manufacturing sector. At a general level, however, it would appear from the most recent work in the two systems that the relative wage effect in the US (i.e. 25–30 per cent) was considerably greater than that in Britain (i.e. 8 per cent) in the 1970s despite the fact that the overall level of union organization in the US was relatively low (i.e. less than 25 per cent overall union density) and falling whereas in Britain it was relatively high (i.e. more than 50 per cent overall union density) and rising in that decade. The 1970s witnessed Britain moving much closer to the US system of industrial relations in the sense of being increasingly based on single-employer (i.e. plant and company level) bargaining structures, but there were (and remain) important institutional differences between the two systems which could have important implications for the respective sizes of the union relative wage effect. These differences include the following:

1. The threat effect (mentioned earlier) can to some extent be institutionalized in a national system of industrial relations by the passage of laws and regulations that require the payment of the going industry (collectively bargained) wage. Such institutionalization has been much more a feature of the British than the American system of industrial relations with the Terms and Conditions of Employment Act 1959, Schedule 11 of the Employment Protection Act 1975, and the 1946 Fair Wages Resolution of the House of Commons all being operative during the decade of the 1970s.

2. Collective agreements in the US are legally enforceable and typically of some three years' duration, a structural feature of the system that makes collectively bargained wages considerably less cyclically sensitive than their non-union counterparts; the resulting ratchet effect is why the size of the union relative wage effect in the US rises as unemployment increases. This structural explanation of an anti-cyclical–size of union relative wage effect relationship would appear to have much less applicability in the more informal, open-ended collective bargaining system of Britain where there are annual negotiations whose results are not legally enforceable.

3. The relatively high level of union security arrangements in collective agreements in the United States means that there is relatively little difference between the extent of unionization and that of collective bargaining coverage. In Britain there is a considerable size difference between these two measures so that researchers concerned to estimate the size of the wage gap cannot use these two terms or measures interchangeably as tends to be the practice in the United States. Indeed it needs to be

explicitly acknowledged at this stage that the level of overall union density in Britain increased quite substantially in the 1970s, but such a change was not reflected in our collective bargaining coverage figures for 1973 and 1978; there was no substantial, overall increase in the extent of agreement coverage in these years (if anything, the opposite tendency was apparent). It is, of course, possible for union density to increase, but collective bargaining coverage to show little change if the new union members were overwhelmingly employed in already recognized bargaining units. This undoubtedly occurred to some extent during the 1970s, as the major union gains of that decade were concentrated in the public and manufacturing sectors where union recognition was already well established. However, this occurrence may not constitute a completely adequate explanation, so that here we can simply note, as opposed to explain, the divergent movements in the two series of figures during these years.

This completes our background discussion of previous union relative wage studies so that we can now turn to the analysis and findings of the empirical work that we have conducted for this chapter. The results of this work will in fact be presented in three basic sections. The first section presents our basic data on wages and collective bargaining coverage; this is done to provide the reader with a 'feel' for the nature of the available data and to identify any relevant aggregate relationships that can provide a useful starting-point for our subsequent, more detailed analysis. The second section involves very much a 'micro' approach whereby we disaggregate the NES data for 1973 and 1978 into separate industries and occupations and test for the significance of a wage differential *within* each sub-group. Following this analysis we move to the more conventional 'macro' approach which involves obtaining estimates of the size of the wage differential from an equation containing various proxies for the sources of bargaining power. As such, the latter approach tests for the significance of a wage differential *between* sub-groups.

14.3. Bargaining Coverage and Wages: The Overall Pattern

In Table 14.1 we set out our basic figures for collective bargaining coverage (including type) and average hourly earnings for male workers at the industry level for both 1973 and 1978. This Table indicates an overall growth in the extent of supplementary-only agreements between 1973 and 1978, although in the context of an overall fall in the extent of coverage by all agreements for nearly every industry; recall here our earlier reference to the divergent movements in union density and agreement coverage in these years. The Table also indicates the dominant

Table 14.1. *Coverage by collective agreement (males) by industry, 1973 (1978)*

Industry (SIC Order)	Average hourly earnings (£)	Percentage covered by			
		Any collective agreement	National plus supplementary agreement	National agreement only	Supplementary agreement only
1. Agriculture etc.	0.60(1.35)	41.8(36.0)	13.9(8.0)	22.6(24.6)	5.2(3.3)
2. Mining and quarrying	0.93(2.36)	95.3(94.0)	4.0(7.1)	88.9(82.5)	2.4(4.3)
3. Food, drink, and tobacco	0.91(1.97)	65.8(64.9)	17.3(14.7)	20.0(17.0)	28.5(23.2)
4. Coal and petroleum	1.01(2.78)	74.4(68.7)	10.9(22.0)	15.3(12.1)	48.2(34.6)
5. Chemicals	1.06(2.31)	58.1(59.9)	27.2(16.8)	17.4(13.0)	13.4(30.2)
6. Metals	0.95(2.15)	89.2(84.2)	59.6(55.4)	20.9(20.3)	8.6(8.6)
7. Mechanical engineering	0.93(2.05)	72.2(64.6)	41.9(39.9)	20.9(13.3)	9.3(11.4)
8. Instrumental engineering	0.93(2.20)	55.0(43.7)	28.3(16.6)	15.9(12.2)	10.7(14.9)
9. Electrical engineering	1.01(2.17)	71.0(62.6)	39.9(32.3)	18.0(10.9)	13.0(19.5)
10. Shipbuilding	0.90(1.96)	94.3(89.1)	70.6(62.8)	20.5(15.1)	3.2(11.3)
11. Vehicles	1.05(2.10)	90.3(83.2)	52.2(39.7)	14.2(14.8)	23.9(28.7)
12. Other metals	0.89(1.97)	66.1(61.5)	35.7(31.3)	19.1(14.9)	11.3(15.2)
13. Textiles	0.84(1.76)	72.9(73.8)	25.6(25.5)	28.7(26.8)	18.6(21.4)
14. Leather goods	0.69(1.68)	73.6(62.5)	30.6(41.7)	37.5(16.7)	5.6(4.1)
15. Clothing and footwear	0.85(1.79)	52.8(53.1)	12.9(13.3)	33.3(34.4)	6.5(5.3)
16. Bricks, pottery, glass	0.90(1.96)	73.6(70.7)	29.7(31.7)	25.5(20.6)	18.4(18.4)
17. Timber, furniture	0.86(1.84)	69.4(63.7)	25.3(23.6)	37.1(31.1)	7.1(9.1)
18. Printing	1.07(2.19)	73.5(70.1)	36.6(39.3)	30.6(25.1)	6.4(5.7)
19. Other manufacturing	0.92(1.95)	64.3(58.1)	26.9(19.8)	15.7(3.7)	21.7(34.6)
20. Construction	0.89(1.88)	80.5(71.8)	21.9(17.9)	55.8(51.0)	2.8(2.9)
21. Utilities	1.03(2.20)	99.3(99.0)	21.4(15.6)	77.3(83.1)	0.6(0.2)
22. Transport and communication	0.91(1.94)	87.7(84.4)	14.3(15.4)	63.6(59.3)	9.8(9.8)
23. Distribution	0.85(1.88)	42.5(35.1)	10.0(9.6)	18.7(14.7)	13.8(10.8)
24. Insurance, banking	1.41(2.99)	41.5(40.9)	12.6(14.6)	15.6(13.5)	13.3(12.8)
25. Professional services	1.23(2.64)	81.5(80.6)	10.3(11.4)	70.1(67.7)	1.1(1.6)
26. Miscellaneous services	0.81(1.78)	49.1(45.1)	11.0(12.0)	28.3(22.9)	9.8(10.3)
27. Public administration	1.02(2.26)	98.8(98.7)	16.3(16.2)	82.1(82.3)	0.4(0.2)

position of national-only bargaining in the public sector, and the very considerable extent of two-tier bargaining (national plus supplementary) in the manufacturing sector; the nature of our data cannot tell us the relative importance of these two tiers, although it is generally held that it is very much the supplementary (as opposed to the national) tier that is of increasing importance. The figures also indicate that single employer bargaining (supplementary only) is most favoured in food, drink, and tobacco, coal and petroleum products (and chemicals by 1978), vehicles, and other manufacturing (by 1978). And finally, simple correlation analysis failed to yield any statistically significant coefficients between coverage (including types) and earnings at the industry level for male workers in 1973 or 1978.

Table 14.2 produces the same body of data for female workers. This Table reveals a number of movements contrasting with those for male workers. For example, here we find a growth in overall agreement coverage in a significant proportion of industries between 1973 and 1978, although the particular development of supplementary-only bargaining was less than that which was observed for male workers. And here we also find, in contrast to the position for males, significant correlation coefficients between average hourly earnings and (1) overall bargaining coverage, (2) national-only bargaining, and (3) national plus supplementary bargaining; the coefficient between earnings and national-only bargaining was a particularly strong one ($r = 0.67$) for females.

In Table 14.3 we present the second way in which our basic data are grouped or classified, namely along socio-economic lines. This particular set of data, which is for male workers only, indicates that national-only bargaining was the predominant form for males classified along these lines in 1973, and although this had not changed by 1978 there was an increase in the proportion of the male manual groups that were covered by supplementary bargaining only. The correlation results indicated a significant, *negative* relationship between average hourly earnings and agreement coverage in 1973 (clearly as one moves up the skill hierarchy we encounter both higher wages and a smaller incidence of collective bargaining) although by 1978 this relationship was weak and insignificant ($r = -0.09$).

Finally, Table 14.4 contains the relevant basic figures for female workers classified into socio-economic groups. In this case national-only bargaining was very much the dominant form of bargaining structure in both 1973 and 1978. The strongest feature of the data here was the *positive* association between earnings and coverage, which is largely associated with coverage by national agreements only ($r = 0.71$). In general, there is not the spread in average hourly earnings for the female socio-economic groupings that characterized the data for males.

Table 14.2. Coverage by collective agreement (females) by industry, 1973 (1978)

Industry (SIC Order)	Average hourly earnings (£)	Percentage covered by			
		Any collective agreement	National plus supplementary agreement	National agreement only	Supplementary agreement only
1. Agriculture etc.	0.43(1.17)	29.9(22.5)	10.3(3.4)	12.4(15.7)	7.2(3.4)
2. Mining and quarrying	0.68(1.54)	72.5(87.5)	0.0(2.1)	64.8(83.3)	7.7(2.1)
3. Food, drink, and tobacco	0.55(1.36)	68.5(65.7)	17.6(17.7)	25.7(17.7)	25.2(30.3)
4. Coal and petroleum	0.59(1.94)	80.0(29.2)	0.0(20.8)	0.0(0.0)	80.0(8.3)
5. Chemicals	0.57(1.45)	36.2(44.1)	11.2(8.6)	10.2(6.0)	14.8(29.4)
6. Metals	0.55(1.51)	67.9(74.1)	35.7(32.2)	22.3(27.6)	9.8(14.4)
7. Mechanical engineering	0.54(1.39)	59.8(56.8)	32.6(29.6)	15.3(11.9)	11.9(15.4)
8. Instrumental engineering	0.53(1.36)	58.5(50.0)	30.6(19.0)	17.5(13.2)	10.4(17.8)
9. Electrical engineering	0.55(1.36)	75.5(66.2)	42.5(37.6)	21.0(11.2)	12.9(17.4)
10. Shipbuilding	0.50(1.56)	72.3(80.7)	38.9(54.8)	16.7(3.2)	16.7(22.6)
11. Vehicles	0.62(1.53)	84.3(76.7)	49.4(42.9)	12.3(14.9)	22.5(18.9)
12. Other metals	0.50(1.33)	60.3(63.2)	30.5(27.8)	20.3(18.7)	9.4(16.7)
13. Textiles	0.50(1.22)	74.4(73.3)	23.2(28.2)	35.3(28.1)	15.9(17.0)
14. Leather goods	0.49(1.07)	66.7(40.7)	24.2(7.4)	30.3(18.5)	12.1(14.8)
15. Clothing and footwear	0.49(1.15)	54.4(57.9)	18.2(19.4)	29.6(32.7)	6.5(5.9)
16. Bricks, pottery, glass	0.51(1.35)	66.7(75.0)	23.1(22.8)	29.1(35.1)	14.5(17.1)
17. Timber, furniture	0.57(1.26)	50.0(36.1)	11.9(13.9)	19.6(13.0)	18.4(9.3)
18. Printing	0.59(1.47)	55.5(58.3)	19.1(24.0)	25.3(24.8)	11.1(9.5)
19. Other manufacturing	0.50(1.23)	50.6(47.0)	18.3(19.6)	16.0(5.3)	16.4(22.0)
20. Construction	0.55(1.30)	24.2(20.0)	3.7(4.4)	9.9(8.8)	10.6(6.9)
21. Utilities	0.65(1.54)	98.8(99.5)	22.5(21.6)	75.6(77.9)	0.6(0.0)
22. Transport and communication	0.67(1.55)	78.3(76.1)	5.6(7.7)	64.5(61.4)	8.2(6.9)
23. Distribution	0.47(1.17)	39.7(37.4)	8.4(7.4)	20.8(19.9)	10.4(10.1)
24. Insurance, banking	0.68(1.61)	47.1(49.3)	13.6(16.9)	21.3(20.2)	12.2(12.2)
25. Professional services	0.80(1.88)	87.4(87.2)	6.5(10.6)	79.7(75.8)	1.1(0.9)
26. Miscellaneous services	0.50(1.29)	45.2(51.1)	10.2(13.7)	26.0(29.4)	9.0(8.0)
27. Public administration	0.68(1.60)	98.5(99.1)	9.5(10.3)	88.7(88.4)	0.3(0.4)

Table 14.3. *Coverage by collective agreement (males) by socio-economic group, 1973(1978)*

SEG	Average hourly earnings (£)	Percentage covered by			
		Any collective agreement	National plus supplementary agreement	National agreement only	Supplementary agreement only
1. Managers	1.54(3.14)	44.7(39.7)	8.9(9.3)	25.4(21.2)	10.4(9.3)
2. Professionals	1.47(3.07)	63.3(63.3)	12.9(11.9)	42.8(43.0)	7.6(8.4)
3. Intermediate non-manual	1.20(2.51)	66.6(66.0)	8.2(10.7)	49.8(46.6)	8.7(8.7)
4. Junior non-manual	0.87(1.87)	68.2(69.2)	14.8(14.5)	44.3(46.0)	9.0(8.8)
5. Foremen	0.96(2.02)	75.4(67.9)	21.4(21.3)	42.0(30.6)	12.0(16.0)
6. Skilled manual	0.87(1.84)	86.4(79.7)	35.4(31.6)	41.3(36.1)	9.8(12.0)
7. Semi-skilled manual	0.76(1.65)	78.0(75.6)	29.4(26.5)	37.3(35.5)	11.2(13.6)
8. Unskilled manual	0.70(1.52)	84.0(79.1)	27.9(24.4)	48.1(45.2)	8.1(9.5)

Table 14.4. *Coverage by collective agreement (females) by socio-economic group, 1973(1978)*

SEG	Average hourly earnings (£)	Percentage covered by				
		Any collective agreement	National plus supplementary agreement	National agreement only	Supplementary agreement only	
1. Managers	0.98(2.12)	53.0(42.3)	2.4(8.5)	40.8(28.2)	9.8(5.6)	
2. Professionals	1.06(2.23)	78.9(80.1)	12.1(17.6)	64.0(58.6)	2.8(3.9)	
3. Intermediate non-manual	0.95(2.13)	88.3(87.4)	5.4(10.2)	80.5(74.4)	2.5(2.8)	
4. Junior non-manual	0.57(1.38)	57.1(58.6)	10.3(11.1)	37.6(38.8)	9.2(8.7)	
5. Foremen	0.56(1.34)	62.7(65.3)	17.5(16.4)	33.4(37.8)	11.7(11.1)	
6. Skilled manual	0.51(1.24)	75.5(70.7)	30.6(28.0)	37.0(36.3)	7.8(6.5)	
7. Semi-skilled manual	0.50(1.25)	69.2(68.2)	26.5(25.6)	32.9(29.8)	9.8(12.8)	
8. Unskilled manual	0.46(1.20)	72.5(76.4)	16.5(19.7)	45.1(44.7)	10.9(12.0)	

14.4. The Intra-group Effect

In a paper by Metcalf and Nickell[8] it has been demonstrated that, in an inter-industry framework of analysis, the union–non-union differential is comprised of three elements: (1) the differential across industries, (2) the differential across individuals within an industry, and (3) the effect of the degree of industry coverage on the differential itself. In this particular section of our work we are specifically concerned with element (2) above. The potential importance of this particular element is suggested by existing criticisms of previous union relative wage studies at the industry level in Britain, namely that there has been little tendency to look beyond the estimation of an average differential that is assumed to be essentially constant across industries. It is worth pursuing this point somewhat further. The fact of the matter is that any evidence of a positive wage return to collective bargaining across industries could involve a number of quite different patterns. There could, for example, be a large, positive differential in a small number of large-sized industries which more than offsets the lack of a differential (or even small negative differentials) in the other industries. Alternatively, there could be a positive differential in most industries which are of approximately similar size or which in fact may be quite different in size terms. It is these (and other) possible patterns that provide the rationale for the exercise undertaken here.

However, before presenting our relevant findings, it is important to recall some of our earlier observations which would seem to suggest the likelihood of relatively few significant intra-industry differentials being observed in practice. This expectation follows, firstly, from the existence of legislation consciously designed to spread the industry, collectively bargaining wage to all relevant employees; and secondly, from the likelihood that the union threat effect will be of relatively greater strength within individual industries as opposed to across industries. Moreover, the general pressures for wage comparability (i.e. Ross's 'orbits of coercive comparison'), deriving from both efficiency and equity considerations, are likely to be especially strong within individual industries. The likelihood of collectively bargained wage increases being spread to other groups of employees seems particularly strong in the case of multi-plant companies where the extent of union organization and bargaining coverage can vary quite considerably between their constituent elements; and it is large organizations of this type that account for such a sizeable proportion of employment, at least in the case of certain manufacturing sector industries.

With these cautionary points in mind, we turn to present some relevant results for this matter. Those industries and occupations which record a significant wage differential between those covered and those not covered by a collective agreement[9] are summarized in Tables 14.5 and 14.6. The numbers refer to *t* values and cover both 1973 and 1978. Separate details are given for each of the male manual socio-economic groupings for which information is available, as well as an overall summary for manual and non-manual groups.

The basic point to make here is that, rather as anticipated, relatively few industries record significant differentials. However, a number of additional comments on the findings are appropriate. First, collective bargaining coverage tends to be associated with significantly *lower* earnings levels in the case of male non-manuals, whereas a generally positive wage differential is associated with collective bargaining coverage among female non-manuals; this difference between males and females might suggest that variations in age, experience, and qualifications between the covered and non-covered groups in the non-manual occupations are different (quite systematically so) between the sexes. Secondly, in the case of manual workers, both male and female, significant differentials, where they occur, are generally positive, although there is considerable variation in the number that actually do occur. There are clearly considerably more significant differentials for semi-skilled manual workers (males) than is the case, for example, among foremen; this particular finding is very much in line with that obtained from a recent analysis (Blanchflower 1986) of a different data source (i.e. the 1980 Workplace Industrial Relations Survey). Finally, it is important to note that significant earnings differentials were sometimes only apparent when comparisons were made on the basis of average gross *weekly* earnings, as opposed to average hourly earnings.

This result is clearly not inconsistent with the fact that the level and allocation of overtime working has long been one of the key subjects of collective bargaining in Britain; for skilled males in food, drink, and tobacco manufacturing, for example, the 1978 overtime hours differential between the covered and non-covered groups was 9.82 to 7.7 hours (i.e. nearly 28 per cent).

As to the orders of magnitude involved, Tables 14.7 and 14.8 present ratios of covered–non-covered earnings for those groups which had a significant differential (Tables 14.5 and 14.6).

The contents of Tables 14.7 and 14.8 reveal that the largest-sized differentials tend to be the negative ones for male non-manual employees. Secondly, that for male manual workers, positive differentials range between 1.04 and 1.61, with most around 1.1 and 1.2; the differentials for female workers also tend to fall within the range 1.1–1.2. Thirdly, where differentials exist for an SEG in an industry for both 1973 and 1978 they will often vary quite sizeably between the two years. And

Table 14.5. *Significant intra-industry differentials between covered and non-covered male workers, 1973 and 1978 (1968 SIC)*

Industry (SIC Order)	Non-manual		Manual								Total	
			SEG 5: foremen		SEG 6: skilled		SEG 7: semi-skilled		SEG 8: unskilled			
	1973	1978	1973	1978	1973	1978	1973	1978	1973	1978	1973	1978
1. Agriculture								3.4				
2. Mining, quarrying	-2.6	-3.9	n/a		5.7	7.4	2.2				4.5	5.9
3. Food, drink						2.2[a]	2.5[a]	-2.2				-2.1[b]
4. Coal, petroleum	-2.6	-2.7	—						2.9			-2.1[b]
5. Chemicals	-2.5			2.3			2.3	3.7	2.9			2.2
6. Metals					2.3		n/a					
7. Mechanical engineering	-9.3	-6.4	2.6[a]		3.7	3.0		3.9	2.7[a]		2.5	
8. Instrument engineering	-2.7								n/a			
9. Electrical engineering	-8.0	-6.9										
10. Shipbuilding	-3.9	-3.1	n/a	-4.7			n/a	n/a	n/a			-3.7[b]
11. Vehicles	-3.1	-4.1	2.3	2.5	3.9		3.0				4.0	2.7
12. Other metals	-2.8						2.3			2.0		
13. Textiles				2.1[a]		1.9	2.4			n/a		
14. Leather goods			—	—	—		3.3		-2.3	—		
15. Clothing								2.2				2.9[a]
16. Bricks, glass						2.2[a]	3.1	3.0	4.1	n/a	3.3	
17. Timber	-2.5					2.7	2.1[a]	2.1[a]		n/a	2.2[a]	2.6
18. Printing		-2.5					4.5	5.0			2.8	3.8
19. Other manufacturing							2.1	2.1[a]			2.9[a]	2.4
20. Construction	-2.2[a]			2.0[a]	2.0[a]	3.5	2.1	2.1[a]	2.1[a]	2.1	2.8	2.4
21. Utilities	n/a	n/a		n/a	n/a	n/a	n/a	n/a	n/a	n/a	n/a	n/a
22. Transport	-4.2[b]	-2.8[b]	2.1		4.7	3.8				3.0	4.3	2.1
23. Distribution	-6.2	-4.4	-2.0[b]		3.0	3.7	3.9	6.1	2.5	2.4[a]	4.4	5.3
24. Insurance	-5.8	-4.2		4.1[a]	-2.5[b]			2.9				2.3
25. Professional services	7.9	10.1	n/a	n/a			3.0[a]	1.97[a]	3.0		3.1[a]	2.5[a]
26. Miscellaneous services						2.9	2.6	3.22[a]	2.8[a]		5.8	3.7
27. Public administration	n/a	n/a	n/a		n/a	n/a	n/a	n/a	n/a	n/a	n/a	n/a

For Notes see under Table 14.6.

Table 14.6. *Significant intra-industry differentials between covered and non-covered female workers, 1973 and 1978*

Industry (SIC Order)	Non-manual		Manual	
	1973	1978	1973	1978
1. Agriculture	—	—		
2. Mining and quarrying	2.1^a	4.0	—	—
3. Food, drink, and tobacco	2.0^a		3.2	2.8
4. Coal and petroleum			—	—
5. Chemicals				
6. Metals				n/a
7. Mechanical engineering		2.1^a	2.0	2.8
8. Instrument engineering				4.9
9. Electrical engineering			2.5	3.7
10. Shipbuilding			—	—
11. Vehicles	2.1^a			
12. Other metals	−2.2		4.3	4.0
13. Textiles			2.1	
14. Leather goods				
15. Clothing, footwear			2.0^a	2.4
16. Bricks, pottery, glass			n/a	n/a
17. Timber, furniture				2.4
18. Printing	2.6			3.0
19. Other manufacturing		2.0^a	3.3	
20. Construction	2.0		—	—
21. Utilities	n/a	n/a	—	—
22. Transport, communications	5.9	6.6		
23. Distribution	−3.7	−4.6	2.8	
24. Insurance, banking	−2.6		2.4^a	
25. Professional services	11.4	13.0	4.6	3.1
26. Miscellaneous services	6.4	10.0	8.9	8.9
27. Public administration	n/a	n/a	n/a	n/a

Notes: All values are *t*-statistics significant at the 5% level or higher.

n/a No comparison is meaningful as most (or all) workers are covered by a collective agreement.

[a] Refers to a comparison based on average gross weekly pay, indicating that the test proved insignificant when average hourly pay was used.

[b] Coefficient becomes insignificant when average gross pay is used in the test—insufficient data available for a comparison.

Table 14.7. *Size of intra-industry differentials between covered–non-covered male workers, 1973 and 1978 (1968 SIC)*

Industry (SIC Order)	Non-manual		Manual — SEG 5: foremen		SEG 6: skilled		SEG 7: semi-skilled		SEG 8: unskilled		Total	
	1973	1978	1973	1978	1973	1978	1973	1978	1973	1978	1973	1978
1. Agriculture								1.05				
2. Mining, quarrying		0.81			1.36	1.61	1.25				1.21	1.39
3. Food, drink	0.87	0.73				1.10		0.74				0.97
4. Coal, petroleum												0.82
5. Chemicals	0.83		0.83	1.14			1.07	1.13	1.27			1.06
6. Metals	0.88				1.11							
7. Mechanical engineering	0.76	0.72	1.12		1.06	1.04		1.15	1.24		1.04	
8. Instrument engineering	0.82											
9. Electrical engineering	0.70	0.77										
10. Shipbuilding		0.79		0.62								
11. Vehicles	0.91		1.13	1.26	1.35		1.33				1.34	1.05
12. Other metals	0.77	0.65					1.13			1.12		
13. Textiles	0.75			1.13		1.07	1.10					
14. Leather goods							1.16					
15. Clothing								1.25	0.77			1.28
16. Bricks, glass						1.25			1.25			
17. Timber						1.17	1.28	1.20			1.17	1.11
18. Printing	0.82	0.71					1.16	1.17			1.28	
19. Other manufacturing							1.17	1.18			1.07	1.12
20. Construction	0.91			1.08	1.07	1.19	1.09	1.24	1.08	1.16	1.10	1.04
21. Utilities												
22. Transport	0.89	0.95			1.15	1.09	1.12	1.14		1.23	1.09	1.12
23. Distribution	0.71	0.78			1.07	1.13		1.24	1.14	1.33	1.12	1.11
24. Insurance	0.79	0.85		1.74	0.81							1.26
25. Professional services	1.21	1.26					1.17	1.16	1.18		1.24	1.11
26. Miscellaneous services						1.16	1.15	1.11	1.18		1.21	1.14
27. Public administration												

Table 14.8. *Size of intra-industry differences between covered–non-covered female workers, 1973 and 1978*

Industry (SIC Order)	Non-manual		Manual	
	1973	1978	1973	1978
1. Agriculture				
2. Mining and quarrying	1.14	1.44		
3. Food, drink, and tobacco	1.14		1.15	1.13
4. Coal and petroleum				
5. Chemicals				
6. Metals				
7. Mechanical engineering		1.05	1.09–1.82	1.15–1.42
8. Instrument engineering				1.19
9. Electrical engineering			1.07	1.15
10. Shipbuilding				
11. Vehicles	1.15			
12. Other metals	0.91		1.14	1.23
13. Textiles			1.18	
14. Leather goods				
15. Clothing, footwear			1.03	1.05
16. Bricks, pottery, glass				
17. Timber, furniture				1.19–1.54
18. Printing	1.15			1.14–1.29
19. Other manufacturing		1.11	1.12	
20. Construction	1.18			
21. Utilities				
22. Transport, communications	1.25	1.24		
23. Distribution	0.92	0.86	1.09	
24. Insurance, banking	0.95		1.59	
25. Professional services	1.52	1.44	1.22	1.13
26. Miscellaneous services	1.36	1.33	1.44	1.22
27. Public administration				

Note: All figures are ratios of covered–non-covered earnings.

finally, there is little evidence of a small number of industries consistently yielding high differentials for all SEGs across the two years.

From these 'micro' results we turn to our macro estimates to provide a perspective on inter-group differences.

14.5. The Inter-group Effect

Following the more recent work of Lewis (1983) in the United States, equations of the following form were estimated at the level of the individual:

$$Lnw_{ij} = a_n + a_x X_{ij} + a_y Y_j + (a_a - a_n) U_{ij}$$

where i refers to the ith individual in the jth bargaining group; w is hourly wages; X the vector of explanatory variables; Y is the 'extent of coverage' variable and refers to coverage by collective agreement in the jth bargaining group; U is a dummy variable (0, 1) indicating whether the individual is covered by a collective agreement. Hence the wage gap is estimated as $100 \left[e^{(a_u - a_n)} - 1 \right]$.

There has always been concern and criticism expressed about the adequacy of the content of the X vector of 'other explanatory variables' in estimation work of this nature. In choosing our own particular set we were much influenced by Kochan's recent comprehensive discussion of the sources of bargaining power in wage determination which identified variables under the subheadings of economic, structural, organizational, and negotiation process sources of power (1980: 311–16). Individual variables under all of these subheadings are in fact present in our equations, although (as always) the problem of data availability imposed certain limitations on us; in particular our 'labour quality' variables were limited in number.[10] The basic estimating equations, whose dependent variable was the natural logarithm of average hourly earnings (AHE) for each individual,[11] comprised variables associated with individual characteristics, which were:

1. a dummy variable to indicate the socio-economic group of the individual (SEG);
2. the average age of the individual (AGE);
3. a dummy variable to indicate whether the individual had been employed for more than 12 months by the same firm (NE12M);
4. a dummy variable to denote whether the individual worked in the public sector or not (TPUB);
5. dummy variables for each standard region (REG 1 to REG 11);
6. a dummy variable to denote if the individual worked under a payment-by-results scheme (PBR).

The other independent variables, which were constructed on an industry-by-industry basis,[12] were as follows:

1. percentage of manual workers covered by a collective agreement for each industry (COVER);
2. number of working days lost per 1,000 employees (NDLPM);
3. number of workers involved in a dispute as a percentage of all employees (NWIPM);
4. number of strikes per 1,000 employees (STRPM);
5. total resources available per employee to meet pay demands (defined as total real income (GDP) less real gross investment expenditure, all divided by total employment (RESOURCE));
6. real gross investment per employee (GIPM);
7. employment growth (EMPG);
8. growth of real output (YGROWTH);
9. growth of productivity (PRODG);
10. average establishment size (total net output of the industry divided by the Herfindahl index of the number of equivalent size establishments in the industry) (ESTSIZE);
11. average enterprise size (total net output of the industry divided by the Herfindahl index of the number of equivalent size enterprises in the industry) (ENTSIZE);
12. number of multi-plant establishments controlled by the 'typical' enterprise in the industry (MULTI).

Each industry-by-industry proxy is an average of data for the five years up to and including the year of interest (i.e. 1968–73 or 1974–8) except for variables (1), (10)–(12), which refer to either 1973 or 1978. Only data for manufacturing industries are available for the following variables: (10)–(12). Various permutations were tried involving males and females separately; manual workers only; manufacturing industry only.

In order to provide the reader with some appreciation of the data set utilized, Table 14.9 presents a summary statement of the information used for 1978—split into the covered and non-covered groups. The value of this exercise is further enhanced by the earlier noted observation that agreement coverage is likely to be systematically related to other relevant wage determining factors.

The salient features in Table 14.9, which provide arithmetic means of the variables for the various groups involved, are as follows. Firstly, industrial action occurred more frequently in industries with larger proportions of covered workers, and this was especially true when the public sector is included (namely, columns 3–4 and 7–8 of the data). It is also noticeable that the growth of output and productivity growth was generally lower in 'high coverage' industries, while employment loss was faster in

Table 14.9. *Summary of 1978 data used in regression equations (manual workers)*

Variables	Male				Female			
	Manufacturing		All		Manufacturing		All	
	Covered workers	Not-covered workers	Covered workers	Not-covered workers	Covered workers	Not-covered workers	Covered workers	Not-covered workers
AHE (£)	1.84	1.77	1.75	1.59	1.28	1.17	1.26	1.10
COVER (%)	79.1	75.2	80.7	63.7	73.4	65.8	76.0	57.1
STRPM	0.243	0.228	0.199	0.128	0.175	0.154	0.114	0.089
NWIPM (per 1,000)	129.3	102.0	90.5	49.7	75.9	60.8	50.8	33.4
NDLPM (per 1,000)	1004.4	794.5	695.2	381.3	578.0	444.9	366.9	242.8
YGROWTH (%)	−1.1	−0.5	0.2	0.1	−0.3	0.6	0.8	0.9
EMPG (%)	−1.4	−1.2	−0.8	−0.4	−1.8	−1.8	−0.3	−0.1
RESOURCE (£000)	0.37	0.43	0.48	0.91	0.47	0.49	0.41	0.68
PRODG (%)	0.3	0.7	1.1	0.6	1.6	2.4	1.1	1.1
GIPM (£000)	0.51	0.46	0.88	0.63	0.41	0.38	0.46	0.43
NE12M (%)	84.0	81.3	83.2	80.4	81.6	79.2	82.4	77.5
AGE (yrs.)	42.3	41.7	42.3	40.8	39.6	39.0	41.3	38.2
PBR (%)	49.5	22.5	48.8	16.6	48.9	25.9	35.6	18.6
ENTSIZE (£m.)	195.4	140.7	n/a	n/a	129.2	93.5	n/a	n/a
MULTI	13.9	12.8	n/a	n/a	16.2	12.7	n/a	n/a
ESTSIZE (£m.)	25.8	17.5	n/a	n/a	11.0	7.23	n/a	n/a
TPUB (%)	8.7	2.6	34.5	2.0	1.0	0.0	35.8	2.9

Note: Variables are defined in Appendix 14.2; n/a denotes not available.

these same industries. (This is no doubt associated with the higher gross investment-per-head figures, suggesting higher factor substitution rates in the high coverage sectors.) The variable reflecting the amount of resources (profits) available for distribution was lower in the high coverage sectors. Another relevant observation is the greater length of employment in high coverage sectors; typically, the percentage of workers having been with the same firm for more than twelve months was three percentage points higher. This is also highlighted by the average age of workers: a higher value was recorded by covered workers. Payment-by-results schemes are more popular in covered sectors, while in manufacturing, establishment and firm size are significantly larger. Finally, and as expected, high coverage by collective agreements is associated more with the public sector.

The full results of our estimation work are reported in Appendix 14.2, while Appendix 14.3 contains a full listing (with sources) of the variables utilized. The multiple regression equations contain a number of individual results that should be particularly highlighted. Those we would particularly wish to emphasize are as follows:

1. the negative coefficient on TPUB, indicating lower wages in the public sector, although not for females;
2. the negative coefficient on AGE for males and positive value for females (the chapter on age differentials shows that for male manual workers, the age–earnings profile falls after about 35 years, while the average approximate age for our sample is 42 years);
3. the bigger 'strike' effect in the public sector;
4. the significance of PBR for unionized workers (a failure to account for this would seriously bias upwards the estimates of UNION);
5. the larger effect for females of collective bargaining.

The wage gap (or covered–non-covered differential) is measured as $100(e^{a_u - a_n} - 1)$ where $(a_u - a_n)$ is the coefficient on UNION, while the 'extent of coverage' is $100(e^{a_y} - 1)$, where a_y is the coefficient on COVER. Hence our results are as follows:

	Male manual manufacture	Male manual	Female manual manufacture	Female manual
Wage gap				
1973	2.46	4.15	4.78	7.00
1978	2.16	3.83	5.33	7.10
Extent of coverage				
1973	46.00	54.98	—	11.20
1978	30.66	12.02	16.28	—

14.6. Conclusions

This study has been the first one in Britain to use a union status variable in an analysis of the New Earnings Survey data. The results obtained indicate a much smaller relative wage effect associated with this particular variable than with the extent of coverage variable in this and previous studies. The way in which our data has been grouped produces a downward bias in the size of our estimate (see Appendix 14.1) so that once allowance is made for this fact our wage gap estimates for the 1970s from the New Earnings Survey seem highly consistent with the size of the relative wage effect that Stewart obtained in his analysis of the National Training Survey data. This downward revision of the size of the union relative wage effect is an important finding which may go some way towards explaining why British employers are not currently displaying anything like the same extent of opposition to unions than is the case with their counterparts in the United States.

Appendix 14.1

This appendix discusses the effect on our estimates of the 'wage gap' of using observations treated as being in the 'covered' or 'not-covered' sector when 50 per cent or more of the individuals in each cell belong to one or other category. Using the 1973 and 1978 data bases, we compared the average hourly earnings figures for each group (broken down into industry and SEG—see Table 14.10) with the earnings estimates that are obtained when only unique cases (i.e., where all 3–5 individuals in each observation are either 'covered' or 'not covered') are used. Note, for adult full-time males around 39 per cent of the observations in the data bases for the two years were not unique. Table 14.10 shows that estimates of average hourly earnings are generally similar whichever method is used although there is some tendency for the earnings of 'not-covered' workers to be generally higher when all cases (based on the 50 per cent rule) are used, as compared to the situation when only unique cases are included. This is in line with expectations (as is the tendency for 'covered' earnings to be underestimated when all cases are used), since if there is a positive 'wage gap', then using cases based on the 50 per cent rule underestimates the true value of the gap.

Finally, it is worth pointing out that estimates similar to those given in Table 14.10 were obtained when (comparable) 1973 data was used.

Table 14.10. *Ratio of average hourly earnings for full-time adult males for observations based on the '50% rule' to observations based on unique cases, 1978, by industry division and socio-economic grouping*

Division	SEG 1: managers	SEG 2: professionals	SEG 3: intermediate non-manual	SEG 4: junior non-manual	SEG 5: foremen	SEG 6: skilled manual	SEG 7: semi-skilled manual	SEG 8: unskilled manual
0. Agriculture	1.0 *(1.0)*		1.04 *(0.97)*	1.0	0.92	0.99	1.01 *(1.03)*	1.01 *(0.98)*
1. Energy	1.0 *(1.02)*	0.98 *(1.0)*	1.05 *(1.02)*	0.98 *(1.01)*	*(1.01)*	*(1.0)*	0.99 *(1.01)*	1.20 *(1.0)*
2. Metals and chemicals	0.96 *(1.02)*	0.97 *(0.98)*	0.98 *(0.97)*	1.01 *(0.99)*	1.02 *(0.99)*	1.03 *(0.99)*	1.01 *(0.98)*	0.88 *(0.98)*
3. Engineering and vehicles	0.98 *(1.05)*	1.01 *(1.01)*	1.01 *(1.0)*	1.01 *(1.0)*	1.03 *(0.98)*	1.0 *(0.99)*	1.05 *(0.99)*	1.03 *(0.97)*
4. Other manufacturing	0.98 *(0.99)*	0.98 *(1.05)*	1.0 *(0.99)*	0.99 *(0.98)*	1.02 *(0.99)*	0.99 *(0.98)*	0.98 *(0.97)*	1.15 *(0.99)*
5. Construction	0.99 *(0.96)*	1.03 *(0.98)*	0.97 *(0.99)*	0.97 *(0.98)*	0.94 *(1.02)*	1.10 *(1.0)*	1.10 *(0.99)*	1.07 *(0.99)*
6. Distribution	0.97 *(1.05)*	0.90	0.95 *(1.08)*	0.98 *(1.07)*	0.98 *(0.98)*	1.02 *(0.96)*	1.0 *(0.97)*	1.04 *(0.91)*
7. Transport and communications	1.09 *(1.02)*	1.32 *(0.99)*	0.85 *(1.0)*	1.03 *(1.0)*	1.10 *(1.01)*	1.02 *(0.99)*	1.16 *(1.01)*	1.09 *(1.02)*
8. Banking, etc.	1.03 *(0.97)*	1.06 *(1.15)*	1.03 *(0.95)*	1.0 *(0.96)*	1.05	1.02 *(1.05)*	1.01 *(0.99)*	1.07 *(0.96)*
9. Other services	0.96 *(1.0)*	1.04 *(1.01)*	1.03 *(0.99)*	1.0 *(1.0)*	1.07 *(0.98)*	1.08 *(1.0)*	0.97 *(1.0)*	1.06 *(0.99)*

Note: Figures in italics refer to workers whose pay was covered by a collective agreement; other figures refer to workers whose pay was not covered by an agreement.

Source: NES.

Table 14.11. *Regression equations of individual log of hourly earnings, 1973 and 1978 (manual workers)*

Variable	Male		Female	
	Manufacturing	All	Manufacturing	All
1973				
UNION	0.024(4.1)	0.041(9.5)	0.047(5.0)	0.067(8.2)
COVER	0.378(5.9)	0.438(23.0)	−0.068(0.7)	0.090(2.1)
STRPM	—	0.153(5.3)	0.174(1.9)	0.352(4.0)
NWIPM ($\times 10^2$)	−0.023(3.1)	0.017(4.4)	—	0.044(3.9)
NDLPM ($\times 10^3$)	—	0.021(5.6)	—	0.037(1.6)
YGROWTH	—	—	—	1.865(6.0)
EMPG	2.883(6.6)	1.839(9.1)	−0.060(0.1)	−0.918(2.5)
RESOURCE	−0.008(0.5)	0.053(15.0)	0.190(3.9)	0.035(2.6)
PRODG	−1.462(6.8)	1.553(10.0)	1.797(3.1)	—
GIPM	0.037(1.9)	0.003(0.8)	−0.106(2.6)	0.025(1.9)
SEG	−0.096(37.1)	−0.103(60.7)	−0.057(8.3)	−0.053(10.0)
NE12M	0.110(12.9)	0.067(11.3)	0.118(8.0)	0.092(7.5)
PBR	0.053(14.2)	0.079(28.5)	0.086(12.1)	0.091(13.6)
ENTSIZE ($\times 10^2$)	0.027(5.2)	n/a	−0.027(1.5)	n/a
MULTI	−0.001(2.5)	n/a	−0.001(0.9)	n/a
ESTSIZE	—	n/a	0.009(4.0)	n/a
TPUB	−0.029(3.4)	−0.049(11.1)	0.039(0.5)	0.159(9.6)
Constant	6.989(135.4)	6.777(340.2)	6.330(86.3)	6.183(125.7)
R^2	0.31	0.41	0.22	0.34
DW	2.0	1.8	1.9	1.9
n	8,325	17,148	1,994	3,337

1978

UNION	0.214(4.3)	0.038(10.3)	0.052(6.1)	0.057(7.5)
COVER	0.267(3.7)	0.113(7.0)	0.151(1.8)	0.027(0.8)
STRPM	0.170(2.9)	0.619(23.3)	-0.145(0.9)	0.445(5.5)
NWIPM ($\times 10^3$)	—	0.042(1.3)	—	—
NDLPM ($\times 10^3$)	—	—	0.048(1.2)	0.051(4.5)
YGROWTH	—	—	—	-1.410(3.7)
EMPG	2.223(6.6)	0.883(6.4)	2.248(2.3)	—
RESOURCE	-0.019(3.9)	0.022(9.0)	0.049(1.5)	0.060(5.1)
PRODG	-0.006(0.1)	-0.852(8.8)	-1.231(2.1)	0.857(2.1)
GIPM	0.153(8.8)	0.010(3.0)	0.063(1.2)	0.010(0.8)
SEG	-0.087(33.6)	-0.092(53.9)	-0.050(7.9)	-0.043(8.7)
AGE ($\times 10^2$)	-0.134(6.7)	-0.097(6.8)	0.030(0.8)	0.080(2.6)
NE12M	0.052(6.4)	0.041(7.1)	0.044(3.0)	0.026(2.1)
PBR	0.051(13.7)	0.074(26.4)	0.077(10.9)	0.085(13.1)
ENTSIZE ($\times 10^2$)	0.002(0.6)	n/a	0.009(0.5)	n/a
MULTI	-0.001(2.2)	n/a	-0.005(3.7)	n/a
ESTSIZE	—	n/a	—	n/a
TPUB	-0.027(3.2)	-0.027(6.1)	0.803(0.1)	0.181(12.0)
Constant	7.786(133.2)	7.819(445.3)	7.342(85.0)	7.128(164.2)
R^2	0.27	0.40	0.32	0.36
DW	2.0	1.9	2.1	1.9
n	7,250	15,235	1,589	2,815

Note: coefficients for regional dummy variables are omitted; t-statistics in parenthesis; R^2 is the adjusted coefficient of determination; DW is the Durbin–Watson statistic; n represents the sample size.

Appendix 14.2

From a statistical viewpoint, each regression equation was examined with regard to certain classical assumptions invoked when using the ordinary least squares (OLS) approach. The Durbin–Watson (DW) statistic suggests that serial correlation is not a serious problem in our equations. As to whether the assumption of homoskedacity is violated, plots of studentized residuals (i.e. a residual divided by an estimate of its standard deviation) against the predicted values for the dependent variable did not suggest increasing variance. The latter was also used to confirm the assumption that the relationship between the independent and dependent variables is linear. The normality assumption concerning the distribution of residuals was tested visually using a histogram plot of the studentized residuals against expected 'normal' distribution. Finally, the influence of outliers, and whether these significantly affected the parameter results obtained, were examined, using Cook's Distance measure. No significant outliers were found, so our results are not biased in any particular direction because, for example, of the influence of a particular industry.

Regression equations were also estimated for all workers, including non-manual workers (Table 14.11). The 'wage gap' in this instance was not significantly different from a value of zero. Hence, results are not reported.

Appendix 14.3. Data Appendix

Sources and definitions

COVER	Percentage covered by a collective agreement in each industry (males or females) (NES estimate)
UNION	Individual coverage by collective agreement (0.1) (NES estimate)
STRPM	Number of strikes starting in a given year divided by employees in employment (measured in thousands of employees) (DE estimates)
NWIPM	Number of actual employees involved in industrial disputes divided by employees in employment (per thousand) (DE estimates)
NDLPM	Number of actual days lost due to industrial disputes divided by employees in employment (per thousand) (DE estimates)
YGROWTH	Percentage change in the index of industrial production (1975 = 100) (NIBB estimate)
EMPG	Percentage change in employees in employment (DE estimate)
RESOURCE	GDP (in £m.) minus income from employment (£m.) minus gross investment (£m.) all in constant 1975 prices (NIBB estimates)
PRODG	Percentage change in index of industrial production divided by employees in employment (normalized 1975 = 100) (NIBB and DE estimates)

GIPM   Gross investment (£m. 1975 prices) divided by employees in employment (per thousand) (NIBB and DE estimates)

NE12M   Whether individual has worked for more than 12 months for the same firm (NES estimate)

AGE   In years (NES estimate)

PBR   Whether individual covered by a payment-by-results scheme

ENTSIZE   Total industry net output (in 1975 £m. prices) divided by the Herfindahl index of the number of equivalent size enterprises (based on 1973 and 1978 net output enterprise size band information in 1975 £m. prices, available from the Census of Production 1973 and 1978)

ESTSIZE   Total industry net output (in 1975 £m. prices) divided by the Herfindahl index of the number of equivalent size establishments (same sources ENTSIZE)

MULTI   ESTSIZE/ENTSIZE

TPUB   Whether individual in public sector or not

SEG   Takes on value 5 to 8 depending upon socio-economic group

Notes

1. A number of thoughtful and helpful comments by Bob Elliott on an earlier draft are gratefully acknowledged.
2. See Ross (1985: 305–6).
3. See for example Dunlop (1984).
4. The major work here is that of Lewis (1963).
5. See for example Freeman and Medoff (1984: ch. 3).
6. For a useful summary statement see Mitchell (1980: ch. 3).
7. See for example Kochan and Helfman (1981: 332) and Freeman and Medoff (1981: 86).
8. See Appendix by Metcalf and Nickell to Metcalf (1977).
9. The nature of our data base involves individuals being aggregated into cases of between three and five employees. We treat a case as belonging to the 'covered' group if 50% or more of its members are covered. This basis lessens the accuracy of our estimates but we have carried out tests, using only those cases that are uniquely in each group, to ensure that our results are not misleading. See Appendix 14.1.
10. Perhaps we can at least draw some comfort here from the fact that even the more sophisticated human capital models have not been particularly successful in accounting for earnings differences.
11. Note that due to the way the data base has been set up, an 'individual' refers to the average of each case of three, four, or five people.
12. This procedure of using the average characteristics of each industry necessarily reduces the variance in these independent variables and therefore results in measurement error which may reduce the efficiency of our estimates.

15
The Use of Incentive Payment Schemes, 1977

Angela M. Bowey

In 1977, and only in that year, a special question was included in the New Earnings Survey which asked for more detail than is usually sought about incentive pay. As a result we know whether each individual in that Survey received incentive pay, what kind of incentive scheme this derived from, and how much the incentive pay was. From this question it is possible to learn details about the kind of circumstances in which different types and amounts of incentive pay were used and the outcome in terms of pay; in other words, what kinds of scheme are used for particular types of works, particular industries, in conjunction with large or small amounts of other types of pay (overtime, basic wage). There are many theories about such relationships, but this is the first time that a large-scale sample has been made available on which to test some of them. The results have not always upheld prevailing theories, and parts of the information discussed below will require specialists in this field to rethink some of their theories.

15.1. Coverage of Different Types of Incentive Schemes

In the total sample covered by the New Earnings Survey in 1977, 17 per cent of individuals were reported as receiving some kind of incentive pay. For approximately a quarter of these cases (27 per cent) the kind of incentive scheme was not reported. This still left over 5,500 individuals for whom details of the type of incentive scheme were available, a very substantial sample and large enough for the results to be taken as representative of the usage of incentives in 1977.

The most common kinds of schemes were individual based (41 per cent) and the next most common were schemes based on the performance of a group of people (27 per cent). Company-wide incentive schemes were uncommon in 1977 (only 4 per cent of those receiving incentives were paid on the basis of company performance). The effects of the incomes policy current at that time, which prohibited wage or salary increases above 10 per cent unless they were derived from a 'self-financing productivity scheme', coupled with the fashion for 'added value'

Table 15.1. *Occurrence of different kinds of incentive scheme, 1977*

Type of scheme	Percentage covered
Individual schemes	
Piecework or incentive pay for number of pieces	10
Incentive pay based on time allowed	16
Incentive pay based on value of work or sales	10
Other individual-based schemes	6
Incentives based on group performance	
On number of pieces	8
On allowed times	13
On value of work or sales	4
Some other group measure of performance	3
Incentives based on whole organizations' performance	
All men covered by such schemes	4
All women covered by such schemes	1
Type of incentive scheme not reported	27

schemes in the late 1970s and for profit-sharing schemes in the 1980s has no doubt changed this picture, with more people now being covered by company-wide incentive schemes. The question about incentive schemes has not been repeated in the New Earnings Survey since 1977, and therefore such trends in types of scheme can only be identified from later, smaller-scale studies (Bowey and Thorpe with Hellier 1986, White 1984).

Table 15.1 shows the frequency of occurrence of the various different types of scheme in the New Earnings Survey sample. In the total sample, 83 per cent were not covered by an incentive scheme or did not receive any money from one. The range of incentive pay earned by those who were affected by these systems varied considerably, with 29 per cent of them earning £5 or less per week incentive pay while 21 per cent earned more than four times that amount. Fig. 15.1 shows the distribution of incentive pay recipients according to the amounts they received from the schemes.

15.2. Relationship Between Type of Incentive and Amount of Incentive Pay

One of the questions which can be asked from a sample of this size is whether certain types of incentive scheme tend to pay employees more than others do. There are two reasons why this might be so. Firstly certain schemes may be more easily manipulated by employees to

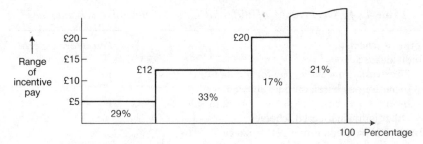

Fig. 15.1. Percentages of those receiving incentive pay according to amount received weekly

increase their earnings. And secondly employers may allow certain kinds of scheme to make up more of the pay packet than others, on such grounds as the amount of trust they put in the scheme to lead to improved performance.

From Table 15.2 it can be seen that the kind of scheme which most commonly led to high incentive earnings was individual piece-work, where 48 per cent earned more than £20 per week from their scheme. No other scheme came out clearly as producing high earnings. This result can be interpreted in three ways. One possibility is that these schemes, which are of a type which has been used for many decades and therefore many of them may have been in operation for a number of years, could be being manipulated by the employees to ensure that high earnings are achieved. The second possibility is that employers have more faith in this kind of scheme actually producing improved performance in response to high incentive earnings potential, and therefore design their schemes to pay more money than other schemes. The third possibility is that these schemes have been in operation longer than others and were introduced at a time when it was the norm to design an incentive scheme to pay one-third of basic pay in return for a one-third improvement in perform-ance. That norm has changed in more recent years, and many recently introduced schemes have much smaller levels of incentive. It is likely that there is some truth in each of these explanations, as research on smaller samples would suggest (Bowey *et al.* 1986).

The kinds of incentive scheme which most commonly led to low incen-tive pay were individual schemes in the 'other kinds' category, where 63 per cent earned £5 or less, group schemes in the 'other kinds' category, where 45 per cent earned £5 or less, and organization-wide incentive schemes particularly those applied to female employees, 63 per cent of whom earned less than £5 per week from their scheme. One possible interpretation of the low incentive earnings from 'other' kinds of schemes

Table 15.2. *Effect of type of scheme on levels of incentive earning*

Category of scheme	% of category who were earning:				Total (%)
	£5 or less	£5–£12	£12–£20	£20+	
Individual schemes					
Payment by the piece	14	22	16	48	10
Based on allowed times	22	38	22	19	16
Based on value of work	31	27	13	28	10
Other individual schemes	60	24	9	5	6
Group schemes					
Based on no. of pieces	21	36	21	23	8
Based on allowed times	24	44	19	13	13
Value of work or sales	32	33	16	18	4
Other group schemes	45	37	12	6	3
Company- or organization-wide schemes					
Men in such schemes					
Based on items completed	35	37	16	12	1
Profit share/added value	33	33	10	25	1
Other company-wide schemes	46	45	8	1	2
Women in such schemes					
All company-wide schemes	63	25	2	10	1
Type not reported	31	32	18	19	26

may be that some basis which has not been identified by the Survey has particularly poor earnings potential. However it is more likely that this category includes a wide range of informal schemes and special one-company schemes which are low-paying.

The likelihood that more recent schemes, many of which will have been organization-wide schemes, were designed to pay smaller sums is consistent with this set of findings also. There is a clear suggestion in these figures that sex may have been a factor explaining the difference in incentive earnings, and this will be examined further.

15.3. Relationship between Sex and Types of Incentive Scheme

Of the people for whom the sample gave both sex and information about the incentive scheme, 21 per cent were women and 79 per cent men; in other words 21 per cent of those receiving incentive pay of some kind were women. The incentive scheme most commonly applied to female employees in 1977 was individual piece-work or payment by the piece (18 per cent), although a higher number were covered by incentive schemes which fell into the category 'type not reported' (27 per cent). This was the category making up the highest proportion of the lowest-paid classification of incentive pay. Thirty-one per cent of the category 'unreported type' were receiving less than £5 per week from their incentive schemes. The two next most common types of scheme applied to female employees were individual schemes based on allowed times (14 per cent) and group schemes based on allowed times (12 per cent).

The type of scheme most commonly applied to men was individual schemes based on allowed times, but again the 'type not reported' category had an even higher proportion of recipients. Fig. 15.2 shows the distribution of men and women across the spectrum of types of scheme.

In terms of the numbers of people affected, there were over 1,500 men receiving more than £20 per week incentive pay, while only 294 women received as much as this. Since women made up approximately 40 per cent of the workforce in 1977, this reflects both less favourable opportunities to earn incentive pay and less favourable payments under these schemes for women.

Are incentives used as compensation for low pay? Do individuals receiving incentive pay fall behind in terms of their overall earnings? Or is incentive pay a means by which employees can ensure they are more highly paid?

These are questions which are often asked about incentive schemes, and the answer is that at least in 1977, the higher the incentive earnings the higher the pay per hour, excluding overtime (Table 15.3). Hourly

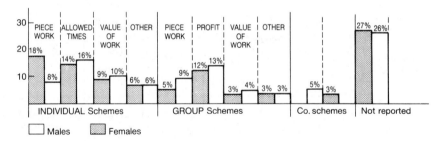

Males Females

Fig. 15.2. Distribution of types of incentive scheme by sex

Table 15.3. *Hourly earnings and incentive earnings for people receiving incentive pay whose hourly earnings were reported*

Range of hourly earnings	% in each range receiving this amount of incentive pay				Total this range as % of total
	<£5	£5.01–£12	£12.01–£20	£20+	
<£1.10	67	20	3	10	13
£1.10 – £1.50	35	45	14	6	42
£1.51 – £1.90	15	35	29	21	29
£1.90+	8	15	16	60	16

earnings for this analysis were divided into four categories, namely £1.10 or less; £1.10–£1.50; £1.51–£1.90; over £1.90. Hourly earnings were not reported for 9 per cent of the sample. The modal hourly earnings for those not earning incentive pay were £1.10–£1.50, but there were almost as many earning less than this (21 per cent and 26 per cent respectively). The modal hourly earnings for those with the lowest level of incentive earnings were the same, but with a much higher percentage above the £1.10 level (69 per cent). The same was true again for the next higher category of incentive pay, with 54 per cent earning £1.10–£1.50 per hour and a further 37 per cent earning more. The modal hourly earnings for the next level up in incentive pay were £1.51–£1.90; and for the highest level of incentive pay they were over £1.90.

Further light is shed on this picture if we consider the range of incentive pay earned by men and by women. For women the most common level of incentive pay was the lowest category, less than £5 per week. More than half of the women fell into this group. For men the most common range of incentive earnings was between £5 and £12; and in

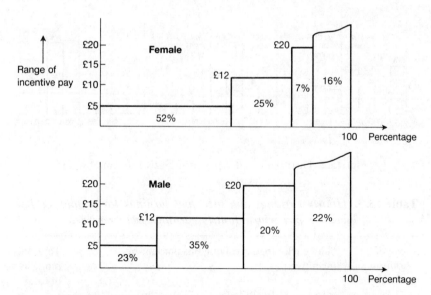

Fig. 15.3. Distribution by sex across levels of incentive pay

addition the men were more spread across the range of incentive earnings, with almost as many in the highest category as in the lowest. Fig.
15.3 shows the distribution for men and women across the four levels of
incentive pay.

Although the picture is undoubtedly affected by the fact that female
employees tend to be both low paid and low incentive earners, there is
evidence here that those employees who receive the highest amounts of
incentive pay are also the ones receiving the highest wages or salaries.
Either this is because their employers value them more than other employees, and for this reason reward them well; or because access to
incentive pay enables employees to raise their hourly earnings above what
they might otherwise have been in non-incentive conditions.

15.4. Relation between Hours Worked and Incentive Payments

An examination was made of the links between hours worked and incentive payments. There were five categories of workers used in this analysis,
namely part-time workers whose actual hours were not reported, of
whom there were very few and hardly any of them received incentive

payments; employees who worked less than a full 35-hour week (of whom 97 per cent were female); full-time workers doing little or no overtime; full-time workers who worked overtime; and full-time workers whose hours were not reported, possibly because their hours were not recorded and they therefore could not have been paid for overtime. The purpose of this analysis was to find out whether different types of scheme tend to be used for part-time workers from those for full-time workers; and most significantly to test whether there is truth in the argument that employees will substitute overtime earnings for incentive earnings by stretching the work out to justify overtime rather than completing it swiftly to earn higher incentive pay. If this were the case then one might expect to find employees working overtime to be receiving less incentive pay than those only working standard hours.

The first point to note from Table 15.4 is that it is relatively rare to pay incentives to employees who only work part-time (i.e. less than a full 35-hour week). Only 6 per cent of the 9,728 employees working less than 35 hours a week received any incentive pay at all. Ninety-seven per cent of these people were women; and it appears from these figures that female part-time employees have virtually no access to incentive payments. It is far more common to pay incentives to full-time workers, and especially to those working overtime. Thirty per cent of those working more than 42 hours received incentive pay, compared with 15 per cent of those working 35–42 hours. Amongst those full-time employees whose hours were not reported, 11 per cent received incentive earnings, and these were mostly based on individual value of work and fell into the highest range of incentive pay.

For part-time workers the most common kinds of incentive schemes which were applied were individual piece-work-type schemes and group schemes based on allowed times. For full-time workers the most common types of schemes were based on individual allowed times. Seventeen per cent of the full-time recipients of incentive earnings came under such schemes, excluding those whose hours were not recorded.

In terms of the amount of incentive pay, this was lowest for those working less than a full week, but showed very little difference between those working a more or less standard week and those working more than 42 hours.

Table 15.4 shows the range of earnings for the various categories of employees by hours worked. There is no evidence here that individuals substitute incentive pay for overtime opportunities. Indeed it is possible to interpret the results as meaning that employers who need more work from a particular group of employees are likely to use both overtime working and incentive payments to achieve this objective.

Table 15.4. *Hours worked and incentive earnings*

Category of hours worked weekly	% of those receiving incentive pay				Total this category as % of total	% receiving no incentive pay	% females receiving any incentive pay
	<£5	£5.01 – £12	£12.01 – £20	£20+			
<35	74	14	2	9	7	94	97
35–42	26	35	16	22	49	85	24
42+	25	36	21	18	40	70	3
FT hours not reported	17	16	12	55	4	89	9

15.5. Incentive Pay in Different Industries

There were considerable variations between industries in the types and amounts of incentives paid. The industries in which the highest proportions received high incentive pay were banking, finance, insurance, and business services, where 57 per cent earned over £20 per week from incentives; and agriculture, forestry, and fishing, 44 per cent with over £20 per week incentive pay, although the numbers were very small. Also paying fairly high incentives to a high proportion was construction, with 51 per cent with over £12 per week incentive pay. In the latter two categories there were no women.

Excluding the 'other' category, where 84 per cent received less than £12 per week incentive pay, the industries paying the lowest amounts of incentives were distribution, hotels, catering, and restaurants (36 per cent below £5 and a further 30 per cent below £12), and transport and communications (35 per cent below £5 and a further 35 per cent below £12). Industries falling between these extremes were energy and water supply (58 per cent received between £5 and £12), mineral extraction (35 per cent received between £5 and £12 and the rest spread across the range), and metal goods, engineering, and vehicle manufacture (spread fairly evenly across the range).

The variations between industries in the kinds of incentive schemes which were most common were interesting. Some were fairly predictable, such as that the industries making most use of individual schemes based on allowed times were in the metal goods, engineering, and vehicles sector (32 per cent of all people covered by that kind of scheme were in these industries), closely followed by 'other manufacturing industries' (a further 17 per cent) and construction (16 per cent). Schemes based on allowed times were developed in engineering industries where the individual's output could not easily be counted (for piece-work purposes). Work study was used to judge allowed times and thence to calculate effort rating. A different form of 'allowed times' scheme may be reflected in the figures from the construction industry, where workers are often given a time within which to complete a job in order to earn either their normal bonus or some agreed sum.

The industries making most use of group piece-work-type incentives were in the metal goods, engineering, and vehicles sector (29 per cent of all those receiving this kind of incentive) and the metal extraction sector (a further 24 per cent) closely followed by 'other manufacturing' (21 per cent). Such schemes appeared to be little used in any other sector. They are used where the output can be readily counted or measured, such as where individuals are repeating the same tasks or producing large numbers of the same items. This makes them suited (along with individual piece-work-type incentives) to employees working on assembly lines and to people making long runs of repeat items (such as garments). Group piece-work-type schemes are also suited to mining industries where team output can be measured in tonnes.

A very high proportion of recipients of incentive pay in the banking, finance, insurance, and business services sector were paid according to the value of their individual contribution (82 per cent of them), as were 55 per cent of recipients of incentives in the distribution, hotel, catering, and restaurant industries and 20 per cent of those in the transport and communications sector. These kinds of schemes are most likely to be found in service industries where the value of work done is one of the few ways of measuring individual performance.

Group profit-sharing schemes were most common in metal goods, engineering, and vehicles (25 per cent of all people covered by such schemes) and in energy and water supply (a further 14 per cent, representing 44 per cent of those in this industry for whom the kind of scheme was reported). Table 15.5 shows the percentages in each industrial sector covered by the main kinds of incentive schemes (as percentage of those in that sector for whom the kind of incentive was reported). Other kinds of scheme were either not specifically named (i.e. covered by the category 'other') or had relatively small numbers from all sectors.

Apart from identifying in a fairly crude way which kinds of incentive schemes are most common in which industries, it is also evident from these figures that certain industries use incentive schemes far more than others. In the construction industry 41 per cent of those people covered by the New Earnings Survey were receiving incentive payments. This was substantially higher than any other industry. The manufacturing industries together with mining and energy and water supply industries all ranged between 26 per cent and 31 per cent of their workforces receiving incentive payments. And the industries showing the least tendency to make incentive payments were agriculture, forestry, and fishing (5 per cent) and banking, finance, insurance, and business services (5 per cent).

15.6. Incentive Pay and Age

In order to examine whether age was a factor affecting either the kind of incentive scheme or the amount of incentive earnings, the people in the survey were divided into those under 25 years (of whom there were 9,453, 18 per cent of the total), those between 25 and 40 (16,328, or 32 per cent of the total), and those 40 and over (25,514, or 50 per cent of the total).

Age made no significant difference to the kind of incentive scheme

Table 15.5. *Most common incentive schemes in various industrial sectors* (%)

Type of incentive scheme	Agriculture, forestry, fishing	Energy and water supply	Mineral extraction	Metal goods, engineering and vehicles	Other manufacturing	Construction	Distribution, hotel, catering, and restaurants	Transport and communication	Banking, finance, insurance, business services
Individual									
Per piece	79			18	26				
Allowed times		33				28		18	
Value				26	20		55	20	82
Group									
Per piece			25	12	13				
Allowed times		44		18					

Table 15.6. *Incentive earnings for different age groups*

Age group	% in each age group receiving this amount of incentive pay				Total this age group as % of total
	<£5	£5.01–£12	£12.01–£20	£20+	
<25	37	32	14	17	15
25–39	25	31	19	26	33
40+	30	35	17	19	52

which was applied to these people. The proportions of each age group receiving each type of incentive was in balance with the proportions of that age group in the total sample.

On the other hand, the amount of incentive pay received was affected by age. Younger workers tended to receive the lowest amounts of incentive pay, while those in the middle band (between 25 and 40) earned the most. Table 15.6 shows the relation between age and incentive pay.

It has sometimes been suggested that younger people work harder under incentive conditions than older people, because young people have more commitments in terms of mortgage payments, children to support, etc., whereas older workers may have already repaid their mortgage and their children may have grown up. The youngest age group (under 25) did not fit this pattern, although this could be interpreted as arising because they had not yet acquired these commitments, while their colleagues in the age range 25 to 40 had. Certainly in the older age group (40 and over), a lower proportion were high incentive earners. This is inconsistent with such considerations as older people having more familiarity with the means of making the most out of an incentive scheme due to their experience; and older people having the benefits of seniority to acquire the most rewarding tasks. It would seem that either people do lose interest in incentive payments over the age of 40, or else they do not have such good access to high incentive payments as their colleagues.

A check was made on whether sex had an effect on the relation between incentive pay and age. There was no significant difference in the proportions of women incentive earners in the different age bands.

15.7. Conclusions

This chapter has considered newly available information about the kinds of people and situations to which various types and amounts of incentive pay are applied.

Of the total sample just under 17 per cent received incentive pay of some kind. The most common types of schemes were individual-based, with schemes based on individual allowed times being the most common (covering 16 per cent of those receiving incentives), closely followed by group schemes based on allowed times (covering 13 per cent of the total). One industry, the construction industry, had a very much higher proportion of its employees receiving incentives (41 per cent) than others, and since this industry most commonly used schemes based on individual allowed times, this contributed greatly to the high figures for these schemes.

Twenty-one per cent of those receiving incentive pay in 1977 were women, and the scheme most commonly applied to women was individual payment by the piece. Forty-one per cent of the women in the total sample worked less than 35 hours per week, and they comprised 97 per cent of this category. These part-time workers had particularly poor access to incentive pay, with only 6 per cent receiving any kind.

The highest levels of incentive pay were earned by those workers whose earnings per hour were the highest. Incentives were therefore not typical of low-paying industries; rather the reverse.

The kind of incentive scheme which most commonly led to high incentive earnings was individual payment by the piece, where 48 per cent earned more than £20 incentive pay per week. At the other extreme, the kinds of schemes which most commonly led to low incentive earnings were the ones which were not classified into any of the proffered categories (possibly because they were tailor-made or informal schemes).

Women fared particularly badly in relation to incentive payments. More than half of those receiving any incentive pay at all fell into the lowest category and earned less than £5 a week from this source (compared to 23 per cent of the men). Of the people receiving over £20 per week from an incentive scheme, only 15 per cent were women.

There was no evidence that employees working overtime substituted overtime pay for incentive pay, since there was very little difference in the ranges of incentive pay earned by those working a normal (35–42 hours) week and those working longer.

16

The New Earnings Survey Panel

Rebecca Endean and William Smith

16.1. Introduction

At the same time the grouped New Earnings Survey data was being developed for the researchers working on the ESRC project, the Employment Market Research Unit (EMRU) at the Department of Employment started working on a plan to link the separate years of information from the NES. This has involved the creation of a large panel file such that the NES information is stored, by individual records, for each year they appear in the Survey. From this panel file a series of different cohorts can be extracted.

The panel data set of NES records has been possible because the sample is based on all employees with a National Insurance number ending in the same two digits in every year. Linking the information for each year the individual is present enables us to follow individuals over time as well as to analyse the information collected about them in each year's Survey.

The data set is planned to cover the period from 1975 to 1986. A starting year of 1975 was chosen rather than 1970 (when the NES began) because of the change in the sample selection method which took place in 1975, resulting in a maximum sample overlap of only 25 per cent between these two dates. However, at the time of writing, we have only produced analysis for the period up to 1984; but the analysis for 1985 and 1986 will be conducted in the near future. The present size of the panel over 1975–84 is around 350,000 individuals and for the whole period is in the region of 370,000 individuals. The discussion in this chapter refers to the period 1975 to 1984 only, and because only the consistent[1] records have been used any results must be regarded as for purposes of illustration alone. EMRU is intending to conduct a significant amount of research using this data set over the next few years and any results given here are of a provisional nature.

16.2. Advantages of NES Panel Data

This panel data set is—for Great Britain—quite unique and although the NES was never purposefully designed with this end, its construction provides certain advantages: panel data enable researchers to answer questions which cannot be answered in any other way. For example, the NES panel will enable, for the first time, construction of accurate age–earnings profiles where account can be taken of the effect of cohort size and time-specific events. Similarly, the extent and importance of occupational and earnings mobility can be evaluated.

Also panel data sets, in economic research, have several major advantages over conventional cross-sectional or time series sets. The large number of observations will maintain the degrees of freedom and, since panel data follow individuals over time, modelling of complicated dynamic structures can be attempted at an individual level. In particular, it becomes possible to model occupational mobility while controlling for many different individual characteristics.

The panel data file incorporates the majority of the information held on each year of the NES (i.e. detailed information on earnings, hours, occupation, industry, region, and collective bargaining structure) as well as all the information gathered in specific years from the special questions. The possibilities for research on the data set are obviously very large but among the most important are: analyses of earnings mobility, occupational mobility, regional mobility, age–earnings profiles, and earnings patterns following breaks from continuous employment.

However, panel data analysis is not without its problems. The sheer size, and complexity, of the data set may make it difficult and time consuming to analyse. In addition there is the problem of how to cope with non-continuous strings of observations over time. The NES panel has relatively few individuals who are present for the entire period and two main reasons why people have breaks from the panel data set can be identified:

1. *Attrition*. Individuals may leave the population sector covered by the NES. This can be as a result of unemployment, leaving the labour force, becoming self-employed, or moving into employment in one of the groups not covered (such as the armed forces or domestic service).
2. *Non-response*. The individual may be working in a sector of employment which is covered by the NES, but in a particular year does not get included. This could happen if they are earning less than the NI limit or have recently changed jobs. They may simply be working for an employer who does not comply with the legal requirement to return the information.

It is impossible to determine which, if any, of the above reasons is the cause of a break from the panel. If the probability of being out of the sample is related to any dependent variables then there will be sample selection bias. Techniques to counteract this bias can be utilized (i.e.

modelling the probability of appearing in the sample), but the main difficulty with the NES panel is that the reasons why individuals do not appear cannot be identified.

16.3. Individual Time Inconsistencies

On examining the NES panel file over the period 1975–84 33,938 records were found to be sex and/or age inconsistent over the time period. Of these 28,476 were age inconsistent, 1,495 sex inconsistent, and 3,967 were age and sex inconsistent simultaneously. The records which are inconsistent in either age or sex alone are at present being made consistent where possible.[2] However the records that are inconsistent in both sex and age together will not be corrected because there are doubts about whether they refer to one person.

The existence of such a large number of age inconsistent records in the panel should not be too surprising, since the year of birth is estimated by the employer if the correct age is not known. The existence of so many records that are both age and sex inconsistent is more disturbing. The most probable explanation is that two people have been assigned the same National Insurance number in two different years which, in turn, suggests two further possible errors may have occurred, with implications for future analyses. Firstly; there could be a number of records in the panel which are only inconsistent in age but are, in fact, two people of the same sex. Secondly individuals may in one year be assigned an incorrect National Insurance number—which has no duplicate present—and there will therefore be two records in the panel for the same individual: one where there is an observation incorrectly missing and one where there is only one observation.

16.4. Numbers in the Panel Data Set

Table 16.1 gives the number of individuals in the panel classified by age, sex, and 'consistency'. The numbers present in each year are slightly different from the numbers contained in the annual published NES tables because some individuals are included in the panel file whose questionnaires were returned too late to be used in the NES reports. This is particularly obvious for 1979 when the proportion of late returns was significantly larger than usual.

Three main trends in the appearance of individuals over time can be observed:

1. The proportion of part-timers (both male and female) in the panel has increased. The increase in part-time employment throughout the

Table 16.1. *Numbers present in each year in the NES cohort*

| | Males | | | | | | Females | | | | | |
| | Consistent | | Age inconsistent | | | | Consistent | | Age inconsistent | | |
	Number	Part-time (%)	Number	Part-time (%)			Number	Part-time (%)	Number	Part-time (%)
1975	89,601	2.6	9,163	4.3			50,035	31.1	5,679	40.1
1976	95,880	2.8	8,769	4.8			56,691	32.9	5,600	42.9
1977	95,797	2.4	9,323	5.2			58,312	33.1	6,113	43.8
1978	95,847	2.4	9,234	5.0			59,090	33.4	6,131	43.8
1979	94,542	2.5	9,743	5.7			59,808	33.8	6,659	45.7
1980	93,460	2.4	10,257	4.6			60,216	33.6	6,941	46.4
1981	93,865	2.6	9,792	5.1			61,306	33.9	6,752	47.1
1982	90,382	2.5	9,466	5.0			60,375	33.8	6,539	47.0
1983	87,575	2.7	8,793	5.1			60,157	34.0	5,949	46.5
1984	86,386	3.1	8,517	4.9			59,964	34.5	5,778	47.4
TOTAL	180,907		16,617				134,945		11,859	

Note: The number in each year refers to the individual records. The total refers to the number of individual records over the whole period and this reflects multiple occurrences for most individuals.

economy will have been the underlying cause of this, but it is also possible that the proportion of part-timers covered by the NES may itself have increased over the period.

2. The proportion of the panel (males and females) present in any particular year is noticeably low for 1975 which may reflect a higher non-response in the first year of the new sampling method.

3. The inconsistent records with at least one inconsistent observation are much more likely to be working part-time; which may be related to an age factor, or due to administrative records being poorer for part-time employees. The inconsistent observations seem more likely to appear in 1975 and between the years 1979 to 1982.

Fig. 16.1 gives the percentage of the whole panel (male or female) which is present in each year by age group. The age grouping used is the age in each year.[3] This enables us to compare the percentage present of each age for the same age groups over time. By looking at males aged between 25 and 39, we can assume there will be relatively few entries and exits (for demographic reasons) from the labour market, and therefore the proportion present will depend primarily on unemployment, transfers into self-employment and non-response. 1975 has the lowest proportion which is probably a reflection of the poorer response rate in that year. The proportion present gradually decreases between 1976 and 1979 but despite a slight increase in 1981 it decreases quite sharply thereafter.

The decrease in response after 1981 is almost certainly explained by both increasing unemployment and greater self-employment. However it is not so easy to explain the slight increase in the proportion present in 1981, considering the increase in unemployment after 1980. The proportion of employed people covered by the NES rose between 1980 and 1981 and it may be this factor which has caused the slight increase in the proportion present. Since one of the possible causes of non-response in the NES is the level of turnover in the economy, it may be that a reduction in turnover, accompanying the recession after 1980, could have led to a decrease in non-response.

The pattern for females is rather different since after 1975 there is a fairly constant response rate but the difference between the age groups is more marked, with a much higher proportion of older females being present in any one year than of the younger age group.

16.5. Time Spent in the Panel Data

Table 16.2 indicates the length of time spent in the cohort. There is a surprisingly high proportion of individuals who spend only one year in the

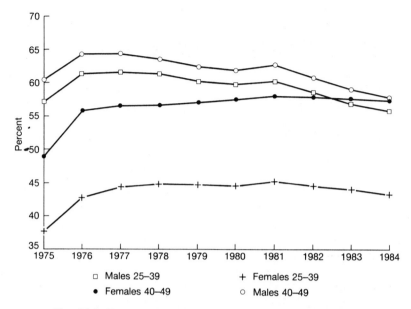

Fig. 16.1. Percentage present in each year (by age group)

panel (23 per cent of age consistent males and 26 per cent of age consistent females) compared with those who spend two or three years. We would expect—and it is confirmed—that there is a smaller proportion of females who spend all their time in the Survey than males.

On examining the total number of years present (Basis A)[4] with the number of consecutive years (also Basis A), we found that for those who spend close to the maximum number of years in the Survey, the spell is more likely to be broken than to be consecutive.

Tables 16.3 to 16.8 show the number of years present by sex and age group in 1975. Males aged between 25 and 50 stay for much longer periods in the panel—on average 16 per cent stay for the whole ten years as compared with 10 per cent for all those in the file. Only 1 per cent of prime age males spend no time in full-time employment compared to 22 per cent of those aged over 60.

The female pattern may also reflect movements in and out of the labour force. For ages below 25 there are very few females who stay in the Survey for more than six years. However for the age group 25–49 there are substantially larger numbers who stay for 8, 9, and 10 years. After the age of 50 the number of years spent in the Survey declines.

This pattern changes if only full-time jobs are considered. For females between the ages of 25 and 60, 37 per cent spend no time in full-time

Table 16.2. *Number of years present in the NES cohort*

Number of years	Males				Females				Sex inconsistent	
	Age consistent		Age inconsistent		Age consistent		Age inconsistent			
	Number	%	Number	%	Number	%	Number	%	Number	%
1	42,080	23	0	0	35,290	26	0	0	0	0
2	14,663	8	1,856	11	15,341	11	1,616	14	226	15
3	12,725	7	2,012	12	12,912	10	1,642	14	236	16
4	12,935	7	2,037	12	12,301	9	1,707	14	207	14
5	13,355	7	2,236	13	11,391	8	1,650	14	218	15
6	13,767	8	2,164	13	10,691	8	1,604	14	201	13
7	15,311	8	2,242	13	9,872	7	1,380	12	160	11
8	17,623	10	2,002	12	9,950	7	1,093	9	129	9
9	20,004	11	1,393	8	9,715	7	793	7	82	6
10	18,444	10	675	4	7,481	6	374	3	30	2
TOTAL	180,907	100	16,617	100	134,944	100	11,859	100	1,489	100

Table 16.3. *Percentage of age group who are present (Basis A) by number of years (males: consistent age)*

Number of years	Age group						
	Under 15	15–24	25–39	40–9	50–9	60+	Total
1	36	21	20	20	21	37	23
2	18	7	5	4	6	21	8
3	13	7	4	4	7	16	7
4	12	7	5	4	8	12	7
5	10	8	5	5	11	7	7
6	7	9	7	7	12	3	8
7	3	10	9	10	10	2	8
8	1	11	13	13	10	1	10
9	0	12	16	16	8	1	11
10	0	9	16	17	7	0	10
TOTAL	20,744	37,209	50,229	30,381	28,848	13,496	180,907

Table 16.4. *Percentage of age group who are present full-time (Basis A) by number of years (males: consistent age)*

Number of years	Age group						
	Under 15	15–24	25–39	40–9	50–9	60+	Total
1	34	20	19	19	20	30	22
2	17	7	5	4	7	18	8
3	13	7	4	4	7	14	7
4	12	7	5	4	9	9	7
5	9	8	5	5	11	4	7
6	6	9	7	7	12	1	8
7	3	10	9	10	10	0	8
8	1	11	13	13	9	0	10
9	0	12	16	16	8	0	11
10	0	9	15	17	6	0	10
Missing[a]	4	1	1	1	2	22	3
TOTAL	20,744	37,209	50,229	30,381	28,848	13,496	180,907

[a] 'Missing' refers to those who are in the cohort file (i.e. Basis A) but not necessarily full-time or with earnings unaffected by absence (Basis D).

Table 16.5. *Percentage of age group present full-time (Basis D) by number of years (males: consistent age)*

Number of years	Age group						
	Under 15	15–24	25–39	40–9	50–9	60+	Total
1	33	19	18	18	20	30	21
2	18	8	5	5	8	18	9
3	13	8	5	5	9	13	8
4	11	9	6	6	10	7	8
5	8	9	7	7	11	3	8
6	4	10	9	9	11	1	8
7	2	10	11	12	9	0	9
8	0	9	13	13	8	0	9
9	0	8	13	12	6	0	8
10	0	4	9	9	3	0	5
Missing[a]	11	5	4	4	5	27	7
TOTAL	20,744	37,209	50,229	30,381	28,848	13,496	180,907

[a] 'Missing' refers to those who are in the cohort file (i.e. Basis A) but not necessarily full-time or with earnings unaffected by absence (Basis D).

Table 16.6. *Percentage of age group who are present (Basis A) by number of years (females: consistent age)*

Number of years	Age group						
	Under 15	15–24	25–39	40–9	50–9	60+	Total
1	35	24	24	23	25	41	26
2	20	11	9	6	11	21	11
3	14	10	8	6	10	14	10
4	12	10	8	6	10	10	9
5	9	9	8	6	10	6	8
6	6	9	8	7	10	3	8
7	3	8	8	9	8	2	7
8	1	7	9	12	7	1	7
9	0	6	10	13	5	1	7
10	0	4	8	12	3	0	6
TOTAL	20,306	32,152	37,282	23,228	17,422	4,554	134,944

Table 16.7. *Percentage of age group who are present full-time (Basis A) by number of years (females: consistent age)*

Number of years	Age group						
	Under 15	15–24	25–39	40–9	50–9	60+	Total
1	32	22	18	16	17	17	20
2	18	11	7	5	8	8	10
3	13	10	6	4	7	5	8
4	12	9	5	4	7	3	7
5	9	8	5	5	6	2	6
6	5	8	4	5	6	1	5
7	2	7	4	5	4	0	5
8	1	6	4	6	3	0	4
9	0	5	5	7	2	0	4
10	0	3	4	6	1	0	3
Missing[a]	8	10	37	37	38	63	27
TOTAL	20,306	32,152	37,282	23,228	17,422	4,554	134,944

[a] 'Missing' refers to those who are in the cohort file (i.e. Basis A) but not necessarily full-time or with earnings unaffected by absence (Basis D).

Table 16.8. *Percentage of age group present full-time (Basis D) by number of years (females: consistent age)*

Number of years	Age group						
	Under 15	15–24	25–39	40–9	50–9	60+	Total
1	31	22	17	15	17	17	20
2	18	12	7	6	9	8	10
3	13	10	6	5	8	4	8
4	11	9	5	5	7	3	7
5	7	8	5	5	6	1	6
6	4	7	4	5	5	1	5
7	2	6	4	5	4	0	4
8	0	5	4	6	3	0	4
9	0	4	4	5	2	0	3
10	0	2	3	4	1	0	2
Missing[a]	14	14	40	40	41	66	31
TOTAL	20,306	32,152	37,282	23,228	17,422	4,554	134,944

[a] 'Missing' refers to those who are in the cohort file (i.e. Basis A) but not necessarily full-time or with earnings unaffected by absence (Basis D).

employment compared with 10 per cent of those aged below 25. Also, the proportions who spend 8, 9, and 10 years in full-time employment are fairly similar across the ages of 15 to 50, which together suggests that a large proportion of this age group spend long periods of time in the Survey working part-time. The proportion of women who spend long periods of time employed in full-time jobs is relatively small and does not differ significantly across age groups.

The majority of these figures are consistent with expected employment patterns by age, but a major problem with this panel data is the large percentage of individuals who are present for one year only. It is possible that errors in National Insurance numbers could be a cause.

16.6. Entry and Exit from the Panel Data

Part of the interest in the panel is to see how far earnings are affected by changes in employment patterns over time. A preliminary step in the analysis of the panel is to establish how far expected employment patterns are reflected in length of time spent in the panel.

Figs. 16.2 and 16.3 show the proportion in each year who are absent in the preceding year (i.e. they join the panel in that year but possibly not for the first time). Not surprisingly there is always a higher proportion of the younger age groups joining in any particular year. After 1975 the proportion entering remains constant until 1981 whereupon it decreases quite sharply.

If we consider those who are present in any particular year but are missing the following year, we find that—as expected—the proportion of people leaving the panel increases with age but (except for those over 50) the proportion leaving the panel declines after 1979.

Below the age of 40 a much higher proportion of females join and leave the panel in any particular year than males confirming that they are more likely to take breaks from employment.

An interesting feature is the decline in the numbers entering and exiting from the panel after 1980. The higher response rate to the NES after 1980 may mean that there will be fewer individuals who enter and exit from the panel from year to year. The recession itself may have led to a lower overall turnover in employment, through its effect on employment patterns.

16.7. Preliminary Analysis of Earnings Mobility

Although some work concerned with the age/time inconsistencies in the individual records has been undertaken, the analysis of earnings which is

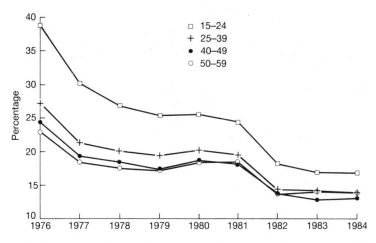

Fig. 16.2. Those absent in preceding year as percentage of those present (males)

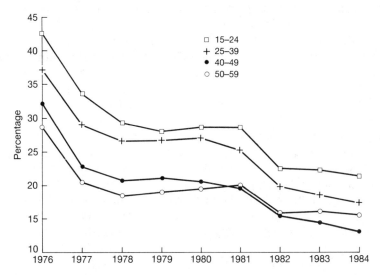

Fig. 16.3. Those absent in preceding year as percentage of those present
(females)

discussed here is based only on consistent records. The Tables we have
provided are for purposes of illustration only. All males aged 25, 35, and
45 were extracted from the panel file and their earnings over time have
been examined.

Changes in the level of decile positions are frequently used in the
literature, to describe changes in the earnings of particular groups of

people over time. The position of the upper decile and the lower decile have been used to describe the position of the relatively rich and poor. The top and bottom decile, however, do not consist of the same people over time, as people not only move within the distribution, but also enter and leave the distribution completely.

With panel data, however, it is possible to provide an indication of the earnings of actual groups of individuals over time. It is also possible to provide an indication of the effect of 'gaps' (i.e. non-appearance) from the survey as well as the effect of being part of a relatively large cohort who enter the distribution at the same time. For example, the whole shape of the distribution may be substantially changed, as members of a particular generation enter the labour market.

Although the sample which we have selected includes people who are not necessarily present for the entire period, it can only provide an indication of the earnings mobility of those individuals who are in the panel in a particular year.

This analysis may be compared with that of the Royal Commission,[5] where a matched sample from the 1978 NES was used to examine earnings mobility by looking at their position in the earnings distribution in the previous two years. One of their main conclusions was that a large proportion of any percentile group were found in a different group in earlier years (i.e. significant mobility within the distribution). However they noted that many individuals could not be traced in the earlier years possibly causing bias to their results. With the NES panel it is possible to locate an individual's position in the earnings distribution if they ever reappear in the distribution at any time.

Individuals were assigned to a percentile position[6] calculated from the distribution for all age groups taken from the published NES tables.[7] Table 16.9 shows how the distribution of the three age cohorts (25, 35, and 45 in 1975) differs from the distribution for all ages. The 25-year-olds are concentrated at the bottom end of the distribution in 1975 but as a group they tend to move significantly up the distribution as they get older.

The 35-year-olds are relatively concentrated towards the top of the distribution, with only 5 per cent present in the bottom decile but 14 per cent in the top decile, for 1984. These distributions, across the percentile groups, reflect previously estimated age–earnings profiles but we might expect different cohorts to be affected differently by time specific events.

In all these illustrations, only those individuals who have earnings unaffected by absence and are working full-time have been included. Any individuals with time inconsistent observations have not been selected. An examination of the inconsistent records however found that they have, on average, lower gross pay and spend fewer years in the panel.

Table 16.9. *Proportions in each percentile group: full-time males with earnings unaffected by absence*

Percentile position	Year									
	1975	1976	1977	1978	1979	1980	1981	1982	1983	1984
Males aged 25 in 1975										
(Age)	(25)	(26)	(27)	(28)	(29)	(30)	(31)	(32)	(33)	(34)
0–9	10.2	8.7	8.0	6.9	7.5	6.2	6.8	5.5	6.1	5.2
10–24	19.1	16.1	14.8	12.8	12.2	10.7	11.6	10.6	10.2	9.6
25–49	30.8	31.6	29.1	28.4	26.2	25.7	23.7	23.2	22.4	22.6
50–74	26.8	26.4	30.1	30.1	29.1	30.9	28.9	30.9	28.9	29.2
75–89	9.6	13.3	13.3	15.2	17.0	17.4	19.6	19.6	20.4	21.4
90–100	3.4	4.0	4.7	6.7	8.1	9.1	9.4	10.2	12.1	12.0
Males aged 35 in 1975										
(Age)	(35)	(36)	(37)	(38)	(39)	(40)	(41)	(42)	(43)	(44)
0–9	5.9	6.2	5.2	5.7	4.3	4.3	5.0	5.4	5.8	5.5
10–24	9.6	10.3	8.2	10.7	9.9	8.8	10.5	11.2	10.7	10.9
25–49	23.3	20.1	22.9	22.0	22.1	23.0	23.3	22.8	23.3	22.5
50–74	28.6	27.9	27.7	27.7	27.3	28.4	26.0	25.2	26.5	27.2
75–89	19.7	20.8	20.5	18.2	19.3	19.8	19.7	19.2	18.2	19.8
90–100	13.0	14.6	15.4	15.8	17.1	15.7	15.5	16.2	15.6	14.2
Males aged 45 in 1975										
(Age)	(45)	(46)	(47)	(48)	(49)	(50)	(51)	(52)	(53)	(54)
0–9	6.9	7.2	7.7	7.9	8.0	8.0	8.9	8.3	8.1	8.6
10–24	10.1	11.7	11.3	13.3	14.4	14.4	14.0	14.1	15.0	14.3
25–49	23.3	23.8	22.9	23.3	24.0	23.1	22.6	26.3	25.0	25.5
50–74	27.0	25.8	28.4	24.3	24.5	25.1	25.0	22.7	24.5	24.3
75–89	17.7	18.3	17.0	17.0	16.0	17.0	15.5	16.5	15.1	15.1
90–100	15.0	13.2	12.7	14.2	13.0	12.5	13.9	12.2	12.3	12.2

Note: Figures for the percentile positions are taken from the published NES tables for all age groups.

This is not surprising since the majority of these cases are probably caused by inaccuracies, or employers estimating the year of birth; both of which will occur more frequently in jobs where records are not well kept, or are of short duration. These tend to be more common at the bottom end of the earnings distribution and indicate the bias that can exist by not allowing for the inconsistent cases.

Tables 16.10 and 16.11 show the position in 1976, 1979, and 1984 of all individuals who were in the bottom and top decile in 1975. The Tables

Table 16.10. *Movement between percentile groups in selected years for those in the bottom decile in 1975*

Percentile position	1976			1979			1984			Average position		
	Number	(%)	Valid (%)	Number	(%)	Valid (%)	Number	(%)	Valid (%)	Number	(%)	Valid (%)
Males aged 25 in 1975												
0–9	63	35	52	37	20	33	25	14	27	84	46	52
10–24	32	18	26	28	15	25	21	12	23	39	22	24
25–49	20	11	16	27	15	24	22	12	24	30	17	18
50–100	7	4	5	20	11	18	24	13	26	10	6	6
Not present	59	33		69	38		89	49		18	10	
TOTAL	181	100	100	181	100	100	181	100	100	181	100	100
Males aged 35 in 1975												
0–9	32	34	52	17	18	33	22	24	48	30	32	36
10–24	17	18	28	16	17	31	5	5	11	25	27	30
25–49	6	6	10	8	9	15	13	14	28	18	19	22
50–100	6	6	10	11	12	21	6	6	13	10	11	12
Not present	32	34		41	44		47	51		10	11	
TOTAL	93	100	100	93	100	100	93	100	100	93	100	100
Males aged 45 in 1975												
0–9	43	38	61	44	39	59	31	28	50	56	50	55
10–24	15	13	21	21	19	28	14	13	23	27	24	27
25–49	10	9	14	6	5	8	13	12	21	12	11	12
50–100	3	3	4	4	4	5	4	4	6	6	5	6
Not present	41	37		37	33		50	45		11	10	
TOTAL	112	100	100	112	100	100	112	100	100	112	100	100

Note: Figures for the percentile positions are taken from the published NES tables for all age groups.

Table 16.11. *Movement between percentile groups in selected years for those in the upper decile in 1975*

Percentile position	1976			1979			1984			Average position		
	Number	(%)	Valid (%)	Number	(%)	Valid (%)	Number	(%)	Valid (%)	Number	(%)	Valid (%)
Males aged 25 in 1975												
0–49	5	8	12	5	8	16	5	8	16	4	7	7
50–74	6	10	14	5	8	16	1	2	3	11	18	19
75–89	8	13	13	8	13	25	9	15	29	14	23	24
90–100	24	39	56	14	23	44	16	26	52	29	48	50
Not present	18	30		29	48		30	49		3	5	
TOTAL	61	100	100	61	100	100	61	100	100	61	100	100
Males aged 35 in 1975												
0–49	5	2	3	7	3	5	4	2	3	5	2	3
50–74	16	8	10	9	4	7	24	12	15	21	10	11
75–89	28	14	14	24	12	18	45	22	29	33	16	17
90–100	115	56	70	91	44	69	83	40	53	134	65	69
Not present	43	21		76	37		51	25		14	7	
TOTAL	207	100	100	207	100	100	207	100	100	207	100	100
Males aged 45 in 1975												
0–49	3	1	2	9	4	5	14	6	9	8	3	3
50–74	12	5	7	10	4	6	14	6	9	17	7	7
75–89	28	11	11	42	17	25	30	12	19	44	18	19
90–100	138	57	76	105	43	63	97	40	63	159	65	69
Not present	63	26		78	32		89	36		15	6	
TOTAL	244	100	100	244	100	100	244	100	100	244	100	100

Note: Figures for the percentile positions are taken from the published NES tables for all age groups.

show a considerable movement out of the bottom and top deciles. Part of this can, of course, be thought of as a pure ageing effect since we would expect the 25-year-olds to be more inclined to move out of the bottom decile than the 35-year-olds, who are, in turn, more upwardly mobile than the 45-year-olds. The Tables indicate, for our sample, greater movement out of the bottom decile than out of the top.

Another important feature of the Tables is the substantial numbers leaving the earnings distribution in each year. This does not mean leaving the NES sample totally, because a move into part-time work and/or having pay affected by absence will also count as missing in the Tables, which accounts for around 20 per cent of those who are missing for any reason.

This analysis suggests that 'decile' groupings do not apply to the same individuals over time and therefore should not be used to define the well-being of specific individuals over time. The decile groups examined here do not contain the same people over time and the earnings distribution is much more fluid than bench-mark measures might suggest. However until we can establish the extent to which periods out of the Survey affect the mobility of individuals it is not possible to establish whether there are distinct groups of high-paid or low-paid individuals.

16.8. Conclusion

This, as a preliminary exercise, provides some insight into the earnings distribution. We will, at a later date, be able to examine the whole of the earnings distribution and to see whether the narrowing (mid to late 1970s) and widening (early 1980s) has been reflected in the earnings of specific groups of individuals. We will also hope to examine the effect that the large changes in the employed labour force have had on the summary statistics used to describe the distribution. The analysis of entries and exits over time indicates that the recession has had quite an impact and the shake-out from employment, during the early 1980s, is clearly marked.

Notes

1. In this context, consistent is defined with regard to age and sex over time.
2. Where a series of observations exists it is often the case that just one is inconsistent with the rest. Routines have been used to produce a consistent series as well as recording the magnitude of the inconsistency. When these fall within 'reasonable' limits the records will be used in the analysis.

3. In the Tables and Figures used in the rest of this chapter individuals are referred to by their age in 1975.

4. The NES uses different categories for the information obtained on the employees. Basis A essentially denotes that a return with some information on it has been received although the individual may not have had any earnings during the sample week. Basis D is the most often used category of earnings information because it indicates that individuals were working full-time and their earnings were not affected by absence.

5. See Royal Commission on the Distribution of Income and Wealth (1979: 106–16).

6. The actual positions chosen were the 10th, 25th, 50th, 75th, and 90th.

7. The individual's position in the overall published adult, Basis D, distribution has been used to indicate how they have moved relative to the whole NES sample.

17

A Perspective on Pay

Mary B. Gregory

17.1. An Overview of Pay, 1970–1982

The preceding chapters have given a descriptive and analytical view of many of the dimensions of pay in Britain over the period 1970–82 as revealed through the annual New Earnings Surveys. This final chapter aims to draw these together into an overall perspective on developments in pay, and to link the evidence which they provide on patterns and trends in pay outcomes to current themes in the theory of wage determination.

Three major developments shaped the context of pay-setting over the period. The most important of these was the emergence of high and variable inflation as one of the predominant features of the macroeconomic and microeconomic environments. The rates of inflation which occurred, ranging from 6 to 24 per cent annually, set a new and testing context for pay bargaining. While in many countries some form of indexation came to be adopted as at least a partial shield for wage-earners against inflation and in particular its unpredictability, in Britain the entire adjustment had to be effected through the plethora of individual settlements which make up the pay-setting process. Achieving the appropriate level of pay in real terms against fluctuating nominal values became the dominant challenge in pay-setting, with the size and timing of successive pay settlements becoming of crucial importance. Moreover, in the general inflationary environment pay bargaining outcomes became of central concern not only to those directly involved but also in the aggregate. The perceived interaction of pay and price increases and the widespread view of pay as a major part of the transmission mechanism of inflation, if not as the prime mover in the inflation process, gave rise to frequent government intervention in pay outcomes with the objective of restraining the growth of pay at least in nominal terms. Repeated resort to incomes policies as a global constraint on pay increases was a major feature of pay-setting in the 1970s (as to a lesser extent in the 1960s) with little historical precedent in peacetime. The formal use of these policies was, however, discontinued in 1980–2. The third major feature is a more general one; pay-setting takes place in a particular legislative and institutional framework and set of product and labour market conditions which dispersion of earnings within them remains relatively constant, with change occurring only gradually, even in the face of the substantial external shocks experienced during the period.

The most striking example of the resilience of pay relativities in the face not only of inflationary disturbances but of deliberate intervention can be seen in the case of public-sector pay (Chapter 6). At the forefront of government attempts to restrain the rate of growth of incomes for much of the period, the pay of public-sector groups was on several occasions forced substantially out of line with private-sector pay, the deviations often being between 10 and 20 per cent, and on occasion even greater. The size of the fluctuations in the manual skill differentials cited above underlines the extent of the pay distortion forced on (and, on at least one occasion, by) public-sector groups. In almost all cases, however, these deviations were adjusted at a later date, when incomes policy was relaxed, leading to a cyclical movement of several years' duration. Even the commitment of successive governments to macroeconomic goals and policies involving intervention in the pay structure eventually had their admittedly largely incidental, effects on relative pay frustrated by the pay-setting processes themselves.

The dominance of stability over change in established relativities was not, however, universal over the period. The relative pay of women, which had maintained a high degree of constancy over previous decades, apart from wartime years, increased from 67 per cent of male earnings in 1970 to 75 per cent latterly, the major part of the change occurring over the first half of the period, in particular around 1974–6, with the movement towards convergence ceasing after 1978 (Chapter 5). This narrowing of the differential coincided with the implementation of the legislation on equal pay, passed in 1970 and requiring compliance from employers by 1975. The unsettled question is how far the observed narrowing was due to the legislative change, the move towards convergence peaking as its provisions came into force and ceasing thereafter, and how far structural change in the economy of itself brought a change in pay relationships. The analysis reported in Chapter 5 indicates that, while the importance of the legislative change is clearly detectable in the reduced differences in the levels of pay for men and women within the same group, the sex differential was an area where structural change, in this case in the pattern of women's employment as they moved into higher-paying industries and occupations, also contributed significantly to the change in a major differential.

A further instance of a significant change in pay structures to emerge during the period was in the age–earnings profile for men, where a rise in the relative pay of juveniles brought a flattening of the profile for men, both non-manual and manual, in the first half of the period, which was

checked and partially reversed after 1977 (Chapter 9). Legislative changes
are again relevant. The reduction in the age of majority from 21 to 18 in
1969 encouraged the earlier payment of adult rather than juvenile rates,
while the raising of the minimum school-leaving age from 15 to 16 in 1972
brought a one-year interruption to the number of school-leavers entering
the labour market, temporarily altering the balance of supply and demand there. While these changes should arguably have affected the
position of girls in a similar way, the age–earnings profile for females did
not show a corresponding flattening, possibly because adult rates were
already more widely paid at 18. As with the sex differential, the combination of legal and structural changes seems to have produced an instance of
the flexibility in apparently established relativities emphasized by Saunders and Marsden (1981).

This high level of stability in the macro-structures of pay is accompanied by very substantial movement at the micro-level. The exploratory
study using the panel element in the NES (Chapter 16) provides important evidence of the extent to which individuals move upwards through
the earnings distribution at different ages and the relatively small number
whose position remains static within the distribution.

Turning to the impact of collective bargaining, the evidence again for
the most part shows patterns of stability or convergence. Wage drift, the
gap between actual earnings and negotiated rates, often seen in the 1960s
and 1970s as an indicator of the role of wages in inflation, is found to
have stabilized for the private sector, while the public sector moved
towards the private-sector pattern of increased use of pay supplements. In
the Wages Council sector, on the other hand, there was an increasing
tendency for actual pay to correspond to the prescribed minima (Chapter
13). A re-examination of the relationship between the union status of the
employee and his pay indicates that the mark-up associated with unionization is small (Chapter 14).

The striking evidence adduced on the positive association between
average earnings and plant and company size documented in Chapter 10
unfortunately relates only to the single year 1979, but invites speculation
and further research on the effects on pay across the period as a whole of
changes in the size–structure of plants and companies consequent on developments in technology, industrial structure, and mergers and take-
overs.

Developments in pay cannot be treated in isolation from the number of
hours worked to obtain it. The record of the period on hours of work is
straightforward, although the relationship of hours to pay is an ambiguous one. Although modal hours worked remained at 40 for men
throughout the period and fell for women from 40 to 37½ only in 1982,
average hours worked fell (Chapter 11). All three main influences on the

average contributed to a reduction. Normal basic hours declined slowly but steadily; the incidence of overtime, affecting predominantly the male manual workforce, showed a significant trend decline in addition to its cyclical variability; and the changing structure of employment involved the growth of non-manual occupations and services where hours are generally lower, at the expense of manual occupations particularly in industry where hours have traditionally been longer. The lower hours had, in general, a negative effect on the growth of earnings, part of the gain in real standard of living due to higher hourly earnings being taken in the form of increased leisure. Structural changes, on the other hand, were often ambiguous in effect. The shift in the industrial structure of employment, from manufacturing to services, and the increased role of women in the labour force, both tended to reduce average pay and average hours of work, while the shift from manual to white-collar jobs tended to increase average pay and reduce hours worked. In these and other ways the impact on pay of changes in the economy was often at least partially offset through their impact on hours of work. A similar stabilizing effect from structural change has been established through the role of shift-working, where the incidence increased almost universally, measured on a group-by-group basis, with the overall effect cancelled out by the decline of high-incidence sectors (males, manufacturing) relative to low-incidence sectors (women, services). These developments are detailed in Chapter 12.

17.2. Approaches to the Theory of Pay

The debate on the determinants of pay is often presented as a two-, even three-cornered one, between the market approach, emphasizing the role of wages in balancing the supply and demand for different types of employee, on the one side, and on the other a more sociological view, emphasizing the influence of social pressures in the form of custom underpinned by a sense of justness or fairness, while yet others give priority to the role of collective bargaining and other institutional features of the wage-setting process. For the most part economists tend to give pride of place to the role of market forces as both the proximate and the fundamental determinants of wages. Labour demand encapsulates all the influences on marginal productivity, product market conditions, the prices and availability of other inputs, technology, and the possibilities of factor substitution, while labour supply reflects income–leisure preferences, household and demographic structures, and ultimately all the determinants of occupational choice. In its traditional form this view treats the labour market as functioning in a similar way to any other

market, with the wage as the price fulfilling a signalling and allocative
role. Moreover, it is straightforward to at least seem to incorporate other
factors, such as the influence of custom and institutional arrangements, as
modifiers of these basic forces. Phelps Brown, for example, offers this
conclusion from his extended review of the structure of pay both across
countries and over time:

The discussion of this and the preceding chapter has left us with a view of
differences of pay as determined in the main by market forces, though this
determination has limits of tolerance within which other forces take their effect.
Certain of these other forces, again, may be the immediate causes of changes that
are compatible with underlying shifts of supply and demand. The other forces are
national culture and tradition; custom; trade unions; and the policy of governments or pay-negotiating bodies. (1977: 100)

Others, however, including a number of close observers of the pay
scene, reject what Routh has termed this 'orthodox view':

that views economies as orderly systems in which market equilibria are established between supply and demand through the medium of price ...
   After three centuries of this doctrine, it is difficult for modern man and woman
not to believe that demand-and-supply are beavering away out there, tirelessly
regulating rewards, optimising allocation and maximising profits and utility ...
   I searched for cases that would illustrate this process. I followed up many false
clues ...
   If demand and supply are at work, their influence is but dimly discerned. (1980:
205, 208)

His preferred view is that 'Orderly patterns were maintained through the
tensions of perpetual disequilibrium, the system powered by *moral* energy: the pursuit of what is right and fair' (1980: 204–5). Wood (1978) has
sought to integrate the notion of 'fairness' as a central element in a theory
of pay determination which in other respects draws strongly on conventional economic analysis.

   Both of these approaches can allow a role for the process of collective
bargaining and other institutional practices in wage-setting to influence
pay outcomes. However, both would tend to see institutional arrangements as the vehicles through which in the one case market forces and in
the other feelings of custom and fairness found expression. In this respect
the differences between them and the institutional approach are differences of degree rather than kind.

   It is clear, explicitly or implicitly, from a number of the preceding
chapters that the process of change in the labour market takes place more
importantly through employment than wage changes, and that the adjust-

ment of wages in the face of changes in the balance of supply and demand in the labour market has frequently been on a relatively minor scale, with employment changes effecting the major part of the adjustment. The cyclical insensitivity of skill differentials is clearly one such instance. More generally, as was widely noted at the time and can be formally confirmed from each of the dimensions of pay discussed, as the recession deepened and unemployment accelerated in 1980–2, neither real nor nominal wages responded to the upsurges of excess supply with the downward adjustments which market forces would predict.

In contemporary conditions, where the typical job may be of twenty years' duration, the labour market is an internal labour market as importantly as a traditional one. The developments in the analysis of wage and employment relationships which stem from this tend to show that the implied conflict between the three viewpoints outlined above is largely illusory, and that it is increasingly possible to set all three within a common framework.

The two developments making the greatest contribution to the emergent theory of wages (and employment and unemployment), 'insider–outsider' and 'efficiency wage' models, are best viewed as complementary rather than competing theories. Each starts from a different, but important, aspect of labour as a factor of production. In the case of insider–outsider models the crucial element is labour's capacity to learn and so to benefit, in terms of enhanced marginal productivity, from training and work experience; with efficiency wage models it is labour's capacity to be motivated and so to determine its own productivity. What both share is a focus on wage-setting within the firm as part of an ongoing employment relationship which is largely insulated from the operation of market forces on the traditional pattern. Since these theories are widely discussed elsewhere and their detailed formulation is currently the subject of rapid development we will highlight only the essential ideas and the ways in which they illuminate the practical view of pay developments since 1970.

Where the traditional model of wage determination through market forces followed the dichotomy of the Marshallian short run, where labour is the variable factor of production, with zero costs of adjustment, and capital as the fixed factor, implicitly with infinite costs of adjustment in the short run, the insider–outsider approach starts from the recognition that labour turnover is costly to the firm, through hiring and firing costs and, particularly, through the sacrifice of the future return from the enhanced productivity of current employees which is the outcome of training and work experience. These turnover costs make the incumbent employee, the insider, imperfectly replaceable by a new recruit from the outside labour market. The rent from the enhanced marginal productivity available within the present employment situation, since training and experience relate there, gives the employer an interest in the continuity of the employment relationship thus conferring market power on the insider. The wage is then the cement for this continuing employment contract, its level reflecting the market power of the insider. The wage–employment relationship then becomes largely impervious to developments in the external labour market, notably any emergence of excess supply, as insiders are protected from any underbidding by outsiders by the presence of turnover costs and the rent from their enhanced productivity. A natural role emerges for the union, in mobilizing the collective power of the insiders to capture a share of the rent.

The concept of efficiency wages likewise can be traced back to Marshall, this time to his analysis of 'the economy of high wages', where the payment of wages in excess of the minimum which the market required could be self-validating through the enhanced productivity derived from improved nutrition and health levels. Efficiency wage theories take as their starting-point the recognition that workers are heterogeneous in ways which may be difficult to detect at recruitment, and that employees' productivity is not a datum but will respond to the motivation expressed through the wage. Typically, the employer is envisaged as a wage-setter, with the same incentive as in the insider–outsider approach to use the wage to reduce quitting. In addition the firm perceives that a higher wage encourages better-quality applicants and motivates current employees. The wage is not constrained by its market-clearing level, and the adverse effects on productivity prevent wage reductions in response to excess supply in the external labour market.

In both insider–outsider and efficiency wage theories parts of the story can easily be told in terms of fairness. In order for the wage–employment relationship to be a continuing one certain commitments and expectations must be entertained on both sides; fair dealing implies respect for implicit as well as explicit commitments.

It is easily accepted that turnover costs are an increasingly important consideration for employers, with the growth of employment protection provisions, the increasing sophistication of many work processes, and the declining role of unskilled labouring jobs. Internal labour markets are now widespread and likely to increase in importance. The implication is that the wage structure increasingly serves to regulate the ongoing employment relationship between firm and worker rather than to equilibrate the external labour market. The role of flexibility then centres on internal wage structures and the relativities which they embody rather than the external market. This argues for analysis at the level of the individual employee and the firm, and of the individual in the context of his ongoing employment experience, for which the NES has much to offer.

Appendix A.
The Survey Questionnaire, 1982

Dear Sir(s)

NEW EARNINGS SURVEY 1982

—NOTICE UNDER SECTION 1 OF STATISTICS OF TRADE ACT 1947

I am writing on behalf of the Secretary of State for Employment to require you to supply the information asked for in respect of the employee(s) named on the enclosed form(s). The information is needed to provide statistics of the earnings of various groups of employees and other related matters as part of a statistical service for industry and Government Departments.

Completion of Returns

A form is enclosed for completion for each employee in the sample who is in your employment. Please provide information only about the employee named on the perforated tear-off at the top of the form, even though the individual may not seem typical and even though you may not be the employee's main employer. As in previous years, the survey is being restricted to the earnings of a relatively small number of individual employees and it is, therefore, very important that forms should be completed for everyone in the sample.

You should return the endorsed or completed forms within the next month to the local office of the Department at the address shown at the head of this letter. A business reply label is enclosed. If you prefer, the forms may be sent direct to the Department of Employment, Statistics Division A5, Orphanage Road, Watford, Herts WD1 1PJ.

If you need a little longer to complete the form, please consult that local office. To enable us to get the survey results out as early as possible, prompt returns are appreciated.

If the employee's workplace is in Northern Ireland, we should be grateful if you would complete the return and agree to its transfer to the Department of Manpower Services, Belfast, for inclusion in their corresponding survey of employees in Northern Ireland. Please enter Northern Ireland and the town or district in reply to question 3.

Further guidance

The following pages provide information on the purposes of the survey, changes from the 1981 survey, the employees covered or exempted, working proprietors and company directors, confidentiality and the survey results. It also includes lists and other information to which you will need to refer in completing the form. Should you need further information or guidance, the staff at the local office of the Department or at the Watford address (telephone: Watford 28500, ext 530 or 578) will be pleased to do all they can to help.

Yours faithfully
A. G. CARRUTHERS
Director of Statistics

Confidential   Department of Employment—New Earnings Survey 1982

FOR OFFICIAL USE		MLH
	Sheet ... Line ...	..... A ....
		..... O ....
		..... C ....
B/Seq. No..		..... J ....
		..... E ....
NI No.	1 4	SICR

Please provide the following information about the employment, earnings and hours of the employee named above for the pay-week (or other longer period used for pay purposes) which included Wednesday, 28th April 1982.

If the employee was not in your employment at any time during the pay-period which included 28th April, please give information for another pay-period ending after 28th February 1982.

*Please answer questions marked * by putting a circle round the number to the right of the answer which applies, (e.g. In answer to question 1(a), put ① for a male but ② for a female).

1. Sex and year of birth
   *(a) Please indicate the sex of this employee.   *(a) male   ... 1 / female ... 2

   (b) Please enter the employee's year of birth. (If this   (b) |1|9| | |
       question presents difficulty please give an estimate).

2. Occupation
   Please refer to the notes on page 3 of the accompanying leaflet and enter both:–
   (a) the employee's job title
   (b) a brief description of the work, and indicate

   (a) Job title
   (b) Description of work

   *(c) whether the employee has been doing work of the kind described for at least *(c) At least 12 months .... 1 / Under 12 months 2
       12 months in your employment.

3. Location of workplace
   Please refer to list 1 in the accompanying leaflet and enter the name of the London Borough or the names of the town or district and also the county etc., in which the employee works or, if mobile, is based together with the appropriate Post Code.
   (a) In Greater London, the Borough of ....⎫ Post
   (b) In England or Wales, ... Town/District in .... County ⎬ Code
   (c) In Scotland, ... Town/District in .... Region ⎭ ....

4. Wages Board or Council/Collective agreement
   (a) If this employee is within the scope of a statutory **Wages Board or Council** (even though other negotiated arrange-

ments may more directly affect the pay and conditions of
employment of the employee) please enter its number from
list 2 in the accompanying leaflet.   Otherwise, enter 'NA' ⬚⬚⬚
(b) If one of the major **Collective agreements** in list 3 in the
accompanying leaflet affects the pay and conditions of
employment of this employee, *either directly or indirectly,*
please enter its number from the list.   Otherwise, enter 'NA' ⬚⬚⬚

5. **Normal basic hours**

	Hours	Min
(a)		

(a) Please enter the number of hours which this employee (a)
is expected to work in a normal week
excluding main meal breaks and
excluding all overtime hours, even if some of these are
worked regularly or contractually, but including hours
not worked for which the employee was available and
guaranteed payments were paid.

*(b) If, however, it is not possible to give a specific
number of hours because of the nature of job   *(b)
please indicate whether the employee is regarded
as a full-time or part-time worker.

full-time . . . 1
part-time . . 2

6. **Total earnings for the specified period**
specified period

*(a) Please indicate the length
of the period to which   *(a)
the earnings entered at
(c) below relate.

one week ..1 two weeks..2 three weeks 3
four weeks..4 five weeks..5 one calendar month..6
other period (please specify) 7

*(b) Were the employee's earnings for
this particular period affected by
— sickness absence
— other absence (ignore losses   *(b)
of overtime)
— holidays
— short-time working
— or the employment lasting for
only part of the period?

earnings affected 1
earnings not affected 2

(c) Please enter the employee's total gross (c) total gross
earnings **for this period** *before*   earnings
deducting PAYE, national
insurance, pension scheme and If none, enter 'Nil'
any voluntary deductions.

£	p

Include in (c)

(1) All payments (whenever paid)
relating to this period, including
any overtime pay, shift premium,
bonus, commission, etc.

(2) Where bonuses or similar

Exclude from (c)

(5) Any amounts paid in this period
but relating to other periods, such
as arrears (including the
retrospective element of pay
settlements implemented in the

payments are not paid in each pay period, include the proportionate amount for one pay period based on the last payment, or next payment if known (e.g. one-third of a quarterly bonus for a monthly pay period or one-quarter of a monthly bonus for a weekly pay period). This estimate should also be separately reported at question 7(b)(2) below.

(3) Salaries paid to company directors.

(4) For agricultural and catering workers only the reckonable value (laid down in the appropriate Wages Order) of accommodation, meals, etc., provided by the employer.

period), advances of pay for holidays or sickness absence outside this period.

(6) If a periodical bonus relating to a longer period was paid in this period, *exclude* the proportionate amount relating to more than one pay period (e.g. two-thirds of a quarterly bonus paid in a monthly pay period).

(7) The value of benefits in kind except at (4) aside.

(8) Reimbursements or payments of travelling, subsistence, etc., expenses incurred in carrying out the employer's business.

(9) Payments to company directors other than salaries.

7. Make-up of earnings

Please enter any payments of the following kind included in the total earnings for this period at question 6(c) above.

(a) Overtime earnings and hours

    (1) The full amount of over-time earnings for this period—not just the premium element.   If none, enter 'NIL' (a)(1)

    (2) The actual hours of overtime worked (e.g. if 4 hours worked at time and a half enter 4 not 6).   If none, enter 'NIL' (a)(2)

(b) Incentive payments

Payment by results (e.g. piecework), bonuses (including profit sharing), commission, productivity and other incentive payments.

    (1) Where made in each pay period, enter the amount paid for this period.   If none, enter 'NIL' (b)(1)

    (2) Where made less frequently than each pay period, enter the proportionate amount for one pay period based on the latest payment, or next payment if known (see note 2 under question 6(c) above).   If none, enter 'NIL' (b)(2)

(c) Shift premium etc.

Premium payments (not total pay) for shift work, and for night work or weekend work where these are not treated as overtime.   (c)

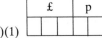

Please nominate a person to deal with any queries about this completed form

Name Mr/Mrs/Miss .... Telephone ....
(Block letters)

Date .... Signed on behalf of employer ....

NES 1982   SPS Ltd/Dd 8308467/310m/1.82

Counties and Other Areas—List 1 (Question 3)

England

SOUTH EAST ENGLAND Greater London	BOROUGHS AND CITIES		
	City of London	Haringey	Newham
	Barking	Harrow	Redbridge
	Barnet	Havering	Richmond-upon-
	Bexley	Hillingdon	Thames
	Brent	Hounslow	Southwark
	Bromley	Islington	Sutton
	Camden	Kensington &	Tower Hamlets
	Croydon	Chelsea	Waltham
	Ealing	Kingston-upon-	Forest
	Enfield	Thames	Wandsworth
	Greenwich	Lambeth	City of
	Hackney	Lewisham	Westminster
	Hammersmith	Merton	

	COUNTIES (*indicates Metropolitan County)		
Remainder of the South East	Bedfordshire	Essex	Kent
	Berkshire	Hampshire	Oxfordshire
	Buckinghamshire	Hertfordshire	Surrey
	East Sussex	Isle of Wight	West Sussex
EAST ANGLIA	Cambridgeshire	Norfolk	Suffolk
SOUTH WEST ENGLAND	Avon	Dorset	Somerset
	Cornwall	Gloucestershire	Wiltshire
	Devon		
WEST MIDLANDS	*West Midlands	Hereford and Worcester	Staffordshire
		Shropshire	Warwickshire
	Derbyshire	Lincolnshire	Nottinghamshire
EAST MIDLANDS	Leicestershire	Northampton- shire	
YORKSHIRE & HUMBERSIDE	*South Yorkshire *West Yorkshire	Humberside	North Yorkshire
NORTH WEST ENGLAND	*Greater Manchester *Merseyside	Cheshire	Lancashire
NORTHERN ENGLAND	*Tyne and Wear	Cleveland Cumbria	Durham Northumberland

Wales	Clwyd—West	Gwent	Mid-Glamorgan
	Clwyd—East	Gwynedd	South Glamorgan
	Dyfed (excluding Llanelli)	Powys	West Glamorgan (including Llanelli)

Scotland	REGIONS		
	Borders	Grampian	Tayside
	Central	Highland	Orkney,
	Dumfries and Galloway	Lothian	Shetland,
		Strathclyde	Western Isles
	Fife		

Wages Boards and Councils—List 2 (Question 4(a))

Clothing etc. manufacturing
  Clothing Manufacturing
201 Dressmaking and women's light clothing—England and Wales
202 Dressmaking and women's light clothing—Scotland
203 Wholesale mantle and costume
204 Ready-made and wholesale bespoke tailoring
207 Rubber-proofed garment
208 Shirtmaking
209 Corset
  Other
205 Retail bespoke tailoring
210 Hat, cap and millinery
Textile etc. manufacturing
211 Lace finishing
212 Linen and cotton handkerchief and household goods and linen piece goods
213 Made-up textiles
214 Fur
215 Ostrich and fancy feather and artificial flower
216 Flax and hemp
217 Rope, twine and net
218 Sack and bag
Other manufacturing
219 Aerated waters—England and Wales
220 Aerated waters—Scotland
221 Button
223 Coffin furniture and cerement making
224 Perambulator and invalid carriage
225 Toy
Agriculture
226 Agriculture—England and Wales
227 Agriculture—Scotland

Retail distributive trades
  Retail food and allied trades
228 Retail food (England and Wales) sector
229 Retail food (Scotland) sector
230 Retail bread and flour confectionery (England and Wales) sector
231 Retail bread and flour confectionery (Scotland) sector
232 Retail newsagency, tobacco and confectionery (England and Wales) sector
233 Retail newsagency, tobacco and confectionery (Scotland) sector
  Retail trades (Non-food)
234 Retail bookselling and stationery sector
235 Retail drapery, outfitting and footwear sector
236 Retail furnishing and allied trades sector
Catering
237 Licensed residential establishment and licensed restaurant
238 Licensed non-residential establishment
239 Unlicensed place of refreshment
Other Services
241 Boot and shoe repairing
242 Hairdressing undertakings
243 Laundry
244 Cotton waste reclamation
245 General waste materials reclamation

Major Collective Agreements—List 3 (Question 4(b))

Public Sector

Coalmining
401 Management and clerical staff
402 Mining officials and weekly-paid industrial staff
403 Underground mineworkers
404 Surface mineworkers

Iron and steel
405 Iron and steel and pig iron manufacture

Gas
406 Gas staffs, and senior officers NJC (NOT to include Higher Management NJC)
407 Gas plant maintenance craftsmen (CSEU)
408 Gas workers NJIC

Electricity supply
409 Administrative and clerical grades NJC
410 Technical engineering staff NJB
411 Building operatives NJ (B & CE) C
412 Workers other than building operatives NJIC

Water
460   Water service staffs NJC
461   Water service—craftsmen
462   Water service NJIC—non craftsmen

Shipbuilding
464   Shipbuilding and ship repairing

British Airways
414   Engineering and maintenance grades NJC
415   Ground services NJC

British Rail
416   Salaried staff
417   Railway workshops
418   Footplate staff
419   Conciliation staff (other than footplate staff) and miscellaneous grades

London Transport
420   Railways, general and operating grades
421   Road passenger transport, drivers and conductors
422   Garages: maintenance staff

British Road Services
423   Engineering maintenance and repair grades NJNC
424   Operating and other wages grades NJNC

Other Transport
425   Road passenger transport: municipal undertaking NJIC
426   Omnibus industry: National Council undertakings

National Health Service
431   Administrative and clerical staffs Whitley Council
432   Nurses and midwives Whitley Council
433   Ancillary staffs Whitley Council
434   Maintenance staff
463   Ambulancemen Whitley Council

Teaching
  England and Wales: Burnham Committee
435   Primary, secondary and special schools
436   Establishments for further education

  Scottish Teachers Salaries Committee
437   Primary and secondary schools
438   Establishments for further education

Universities
466   Academic staff (non-clinical)
  Non-teaching staff
467   Clerical and certain related administrative staff JC
468   Technical staff JC
469   Manual and ancillary staff JC

British Broadcasting Corporation
465 Non-manual workers

Local authorities' services
  England and Wales
439 Administrative, professional, technical and clerical NJC
440 Building and civil engineering workers JNC
441 Engineering craftsmen and electricians JNC
442 Manual workers NJC

  Scotland
443 Administrative, professional, technical and clerical NJC
444 Building and civil engineering workers
445 Engineering craftsmen
446 Electricians and plumbers JNC
447 Manual workers NJC

National Government
448 Prison Officers
449 Government industrial establishments JCC

  Civil Service National Whitley Council
450 Administration group: middle and higher grades
451 Administration group: clerical grades
452 Professional and technology group
453 Science group
454 Secretarial, typing and data processing grades
455 Paper-keeping and messengerial grades

Other services
456 Police service (ranks below superintendent only)
458 Fire services—operational ranks from station officer to senior divisional officer
457 Fire services—operational ranks below station officer
459 Fire services—control room and non-operational staff

Private Sector

Quarrying
601 Roadstone quarrying NJIC

Food, drink and tobacco manufacturing
602 Bacon curing NJIC
603 Baking industry NJC—England and Wales
604 Baking industry NJC—Scotland
605 Master bakers—England and Wales
606 Biscuit JIC
607 Cocoa, chocolate and confectionery JIC
608 Corn trade NJIC
609 Flour milling NJIC
610 Food manufacture JIC

611 Milk product/milk processing and distribution NJNC—England and Wales
612 Tobacco NJNC

Chemical manufacturing
613 Chemical industries—maintenance craftsmen
614 Chemical and allied JIC—other workers
676 Drug and fine chemical JC
615 Paint, varnish and lacquer NJIC

Metal manufacturing and metal using industries
616 Light metal trades
619 Engineering—manual workers
621 Vehicle building—England and Wales
622 Vehicle building—Scotland
623 Electrical cable making JIC
624 Wire and wire rope NJIC

Textiles, clothing and footwear manufacturing
625 Cotton and man-made fibres spinning and weaving
626 Woollen and worsted spinning and weaving—Yorkshire
627 Textile bleaching, dyeing, printing and finishing
628 Silk JIC (including Leek and Macclesfield)
629 Carpet NJC
630 Clothing
631 Hosiery (knitting) trade NJIC
632 Footwear

Brick, ceramics, glass etc. manufacturing
633 Building brick and allied NJC—England and Wales
634 Cast stone and cast concrete products NJIC—England and Wales
635 Ceramic industry NJC
636 Glass container NJIC

Timber, furniture etc. manufacturing
637 Sawmilling—England and Wales
638 British furniture trade JIC
675 Timber container JIC

Paper and printing industries
639 Paper making, paper coating, paper board and building board making
640 Fibreboard packing case making
641 Newspapers: Newspaper Society—England and Wales
642 Newspapers: NPA—London and Manchester
643 Newspapers: Scotland
644 General printing—England and Wales excluding London
645 General printing—London
646 General printing—Scotland
647 Journalists—provincial newspapers

Construction
649 Civil engineering construction CB
650 Mechanical construction engineering

651   Building industry—road haulage workers
652   Building industry NJC: operatives etc.—England and Wales
653   Building industry NJC: operatives etc.—Scotland
654   Electrical contracting JIB—England and Wales
655   Electrical contracting JIB—Scotland
656   Plumbing mechanical engineering services JIB—England and Wales
657   Plumbing JIB—Scotland
658   Heating and ventilating
674   Environmental engineering NJIC

Distributive trades
659   Wholesale grocery and provision trade JIC—England and Wales
660   Wholesale grocery trade JC—Scotland
673   Slaughtering Industry JIC
661   Retail co-operative societies
662   Retail multiple grocery and provisions trade JC
663   Retail meat trade JIC—England and Wales
664   Retail meat trade JIC—Scotland
665   Retail multiple footwear trade
666   Retail pharmacy NJIC—England and Wales

Other services
667   Banking JNC—England and Wales
668   Banking JNC—Scotland
669   Port transport (dockworkers) NJC
670   Motor vehicle retail and repair industry NJC
671   Merchant Navy officers
672   Merchant Navy seamen

Abbreviations

(N) JIC   —(national) joint industrial council
(N) JNC   —(national) joint negotiating committee/council
NJB   —national joint board
NJC   —national joint committee/council
JC   —joint committees or joint conference
JCC   —joint co-ordinating committee
JIB   —joint industry board
CB   —conciliation board
B & CE   —building and civil engineering
CSEU   —Confederation of Shipbuilding and Engineering Unions
NPA   —Newspaper Publishers Association

Appendix B.
The Classification of Occupations

The KOS/CODOT System, 1973–1982

Since 1973 the classification of occupations in the New Earnings Survey has followed the KOS/CODOT system. CODOT (the Classification of Occupations and Directory of Occupational Titles) is a comprehensive directory of occupations which formed the basis for occupational definitions used throughout the Department of Employment. Its index contains some 12,000 job titles, covering the 3,800 individual occupations which it recognizes. KOS (Key Occupations for Statistical Purposes) is the much smaller list of just over 400 occupations for which national statistics are collected and published. Occupations are included in the key list on the basis of their importance to statisticians, policy-makers and organizations consulted over the composition of the key list. The KOS system builds on the CODOT classification, each KOS occupation being constructed from one or more CODOT references.

CODOT comprises a four-tier structure, aimed at capturing the various dimensions of similarity in different jobs. In the words of the Department of Employment: 'The basic principle of CODOT is the classification by work content or job activity. Occupations are defined according to what the worker does, and are grouped according to similarity of the work done' (Department of Employment 1972a: 3). At the highest level of aggregation, occupations are grouped into 18 broad divisions known as major groups. These are:

   I Managerial (general management)
  II Professional and related supporting management and administration
 III Professional and related in education, welfare, and health
 IV Literary, artistic, and sports
  V Professional and related in science, engineering, technology, and similar fields
 VI Managerial (excluding general management)
 VII Clerical and related
VIII Selling
 IX Security and protective service
  X Catering, cleaning, hairdressing, and other personal service
 XI Farming, fishing, and related
 XII Materials processing (excluding metal)
XIII Making and repairing (excluding metal and electrical)
XIV Processing, making, repairing, and related (metal and electrical)
 XV Painting, repetitive assembling, product inspecting, packing, and related
XVI Construction, mining, and related not identified elsewhere
XVII Transport operating, materials moving and storing, and related
XVIII Miscellaneous

As the Department of Employment explains:

This general structure of the major groups is based on the organisational pattern of many large manufacturing firms, with top management first, followed by the supporting professional and technical specialists, and then by line management and the production and service occupations under their control. (Department of Employment 1972a: 4).

Each major group is divided into a series of minor groups, reflecting a common area of activity. These are coded at the two-digit level; for example,

10 Social science, welfare, and religious occupations
77 Pipe, sheet, and structural metal working and related

The minor groups are then subdivided into unit groups of occupations more narrowly defined, to give the three-digit level of disaggregation:

101 Social scientists
102 Welfare occupations

773 Metal plate working and riveting
779 Pipe, sheet, and structural metal working not classified elsewhere.

Finally, the individual occupations are defined within the unit groups, and represented by a two-digit suffix to the unit-group code:

101.10 Sociologist
101.40 Historian

102.14 Childcare officer
102.38 Mental welfare officer

773.08 Boiler plater
773.18 Caulker

779.10 Ornamental metal worker
779.50 Rivet heater.

The KOS list of key occupations comprises 404 individual occupations. For use in the NES these were expanded to 445 categories (441 from 1973 until 1978, 442 in 1979 and 1980). The individual KOS occupations are made up of one or more unit groups and/or occupations from the CODOT list, and classified into the 18 major groups. Each KOS occupation is defined as either exclusively manual or exclusively non-manual, although the division between non-manual and manual is not strictly maintained at the level of the 18 main groups.

When the NES returns are being processed, responsibility for identifying the appropriate KOS/CODOT reference from the job title and work description given by the employer, and for coding the Survey return accordingly, lies with Statistics Division of the Department of Employment at its Watford office. While the CODOT list, particularly in its index form with 11,000 entries, is intended to be sufficiently comprehensive to minimize the judgemental element involved in identifying and coding occupations, the complexity of job classifications and the potentially subjective nature of the job description given by the employer or his representative in completing the questionnaire may leave considerable residual responsibility for identifying the employee's occupation with the DE's officers.

The full list of KOS occupations accompanying the 1982 NES Survey is appended in Table B.1. The CODOT system is described in Department of Employment (1972*a*), and the KOS system in Department of Employment (1972*b*).

The Socio-economic Groups, 1973–1982

Since the occupational classification in KOS/CODOT is based on job content or similarity of work done, as the DE points out: 'Occupations are not, therefore, grouped on the basis of qualifications, status, level of skill or industry' (Department of Employment 1972*a*: 3). In particular, the KOS/CODOT system does not use a 'multi-axial' method of classification:

The basic difficulty is a practical one, resulting from the limited amount of information which is available to a clerk coding a census return or to the clerks who fill in statistical returns in the great majority of companies. The main problems are:

(a) It is not possible to obtain reliable information about skills and levels of authority from the self-descriptions which individuals put on their census returns.

(b) The multi-axial classifications use highly sophisticated concepts (job function, job knowledge, job skill, job authority, discipline and level of qualification) which are not familiar to many of the people who have to fill in statistical returns. (Department of Employment 1972*b*: 799)

The KOS/CODOT system is thus not designed to capture the socio-economic identity which attaches to individual occupations or the elements of social and economic hierarchy often relevant in the analysis of pay.

In a previous study based on the NES (Gregory and Thomson 1981) a system of socio-economic categories was devised to capture the socio-economic status attaching to individual occupations in a broad-banded way. The same set of categories are applied again in the present work. Eight socio-economic groups are used, based on a reaggregation of the individual KOS occupational titles, while retaining the main manual/non-manual division used pervasively in the published results for the NES Surveys. Groups 1–4 are non-manual and groups 5–8 manual. The general principles of the classification are:

1. *Managers.* Those in occupations where the primary function is the exercise of managerial or administrative responsibilities, and where the scope of these is substantial. These may be in either the public or the private sector.
2. *Professionals.* Members of recognized professions requiring high academic or professional qualifications.
3. *Intermediate non-manuals.* Those in occupations involving significant responsibility, but lower levels of formal qualification than for professional posts.
4. *Junior non-manuals.* Those in occupations involving little in the way of responsibility or qualifications.
5. *Foremen and supervisors* (manual). Largely self-defined, as in charge of groups of production workers.
6. *Skilled manuals.* Those in jobs requiring traditional craft-type skills or a minimum of six months' training.
7. *Semi-skilled manuals.* Those in jobs requiring training, of at least one

month's but less than six months' duration, much of which typically take the form of supervised on-the-job training and work experience. These jobs typically involve repetitive work, often in process or service industries.

8. *Unskilled manuals*. Those in jobs requiring minimal training and expertise, where proficiency does not increase significantly with job experience.

Table B.2 below gives the allocation of the KOS occupations among these socio-economic groups, with the job titles following the KOS list.

The Occupational Classification, 1970–1972

Before the introduction of KOS/CODOT in 1973 the NES used its own occupational classification, specially designed for the Survey, and originally introduced in 1968. After revisions in 1970 this comprised sixteen main groups with 189 individual occupations. The full list is appended as Table B.3. As with its successor KOS/CODOT system, the main basis for the classification was the job title, although with particular attention to level of skill for manual workers and degree of responsibility for non-manual workers. The general criterion for a skilled occupation was a period of apprenticeship, or a minimum of six months' training, or considerable experience. Semi-skilled occupations were defined as requiring at least one month's training or experience to attain proficiency. Clerks (group 8), were classified to senior level if the work required a significant degree of individual responsibility, discretion, initiative or judgement, or specialized knowledge, or the application of a professional technique. Routine or junior-level work took place within well-defined rules, required only brief training and was subject to close supervision and checking.

The mapping of these occupations into the eight socio-economic groups is shown in Table B.4. Although the same categories are used, the discontinuities in the constituent occupations before and after 1973 make differences in the composition of the groups inevitable.

A Comparison with Routh's Occupational Classes

A concept similar to our socio-economic groups has been applied by Routh (1965 and 1980) in his studies of occupation and pay. Routh's occupational classification, however, is that used in the Census of Population, which pre-dates KOS/CODOT and places much greater emphasis on industry and employment status in establishing occupational definitions. Routh uses nine 'occupational classes':

1A Higher professional
1B Lower professional
2A Employers and proprietors
2B Managers and administrators
3   Clerical workers

4   Foremen, supervisors, inspectors
5   Skilled manual
6   Semi-skilled manual
7   Unskilled manual.

In devising this structure he combines the Census categorization by social class with the definition of occupation. A professional allocated by the Census to social class I is allocated by Routh to occupational class 1A, one from social class II to 1B. Manual workers from Census social class III are allocated to occupational class 5 (skilled manual), those from class IV to class 6 (semi-skilled), and those from class V to 7 (unskilled). Noting that Routh's class 2A, employers and proprietors, are excluded from the NES sample base of employees in employment, our system and Routh's can be seen to be extremely similar in concept, with our socio-economic group 3, intermediate non-manuals, replacing Routh's class 1B, lower professionals.

Since they are derived from different lists of occupations the two socio-economic classifications can be compared only somewhat indirectly on the basis of occupational title. The overall correspondence is, however, close, with the majority of occupations classified identically in the two systems. Three main sources of discrepancy occur. Firstly, most of the KOS main groups include a residual 'all other' category, classifiable only by guesswork, and therefore left out of the discussion. Secondly, 12 occupations which Routh classifies as manual are non-manual in the KOS/NES system and therefore allocated to a non-manual group by Gregory and Thomson. These are

KOS occupation	Gregory and Thomson	Routh
Supervisors of clerks	3	4
Supervisors of typists	3	4
Supervisors of office machine operators	3	4
Supervisors of postmen and messengers	3	4
Sales supervisors	3	4
Supervisors (police sergeants, fire, etc.)	3	4
Retail shop cashiers	4	6
Retail shop check-out operators	4	6
Salesmen and shop assistants	4	6
Policemen (below sergeant)	4	5
Firemen	4	5
Prison officers below principal officer	4	5

Thirdly, 102 occupations are allocated to different socio-economic groups in the two systems, most commonly to an adjacent group. These may be grouped as follows: among non-manuals, differing interpretations of the boundary between managers and professionals, and between these and intermediate or junior non-manual occupations; in the role of inspectors; and among manuals between skilled and semi-skilled, and between semi-skilled and unskilled.

KOS occupation	Gregory and Thomson	Routh
Managerial/professional		
O & M, work study	1	1A
Aircraft flight deck officers	1	1B
Air traffic planners and controllers	1	1B
Ship's masters, deck officers, pilots	1	1B
Ship's engineer officers	1	1B
Ship's radio officers	1	1B
Secretaries of trade associations etc.	2	1B
Systems analysts and programmers	2	1B
Librarians and information officers	2	1B
University academic staff	2	1B
Teachers in further and higher education	2	1B
Welfare workers	2	1B
Veterinarians	2	1B
Actors, musicians, entertainers	2	1B
Estimators, valuers, and assessors	2	2B
Finance, investment, tax specialists	2	2B
Public health inspectors	2	2B
Other statutory inspectors	2	2B
Non-manual/managerial/professional		
Nurse administrators and executives	3	2B
Site managers, clerks of works	3	2B
Branch managers of shops	3	2B
Managers of independent shops	3	2B
Hotel and residential club managers	3	2B
Publicans	3	2B
Catering managers	3	2B
Entertainment and sports managers	3	2B
Farm managers	3	2B
Technical sales representatives	3	2B
Sales representatives (wholesale)	3	2B
Other sales representatives	3	2B
Nursing auxiliaries	4	1B
Window dressers	4	1B
Professional sportsmen and officials	4	1B
Engineering draughtsmen	4	1B
Architectural draughtsmen	4	1B
Manual/foremen		
Inspectors and testers	6	4
Viewers (metal and electrical engineering)	7	4
Waste inspectors (water supply)	7	4

KOS occupation	Gregory and Thomson	Routh
Skilled/semi-skilled		
Chefs, cooks	6	6
Bread bakers (hand)	6	6
Printing machine minders (letterpress)	6	6
Printing machine minders (lithography)	6	6
Printing machine minders (photogravure)	6	6
Printing machine assistants	6	6
Cutting machine operators (paper)	6	6
Case and box makers	6	6
Woodworking machinists (setters)	6	6
Other woodworking machinists	6	6
Dental mechanics	6	6
Other welders	6	6
Bus and coach drivers	6	6
Heavy goods drivers	6	6
Mechanical plant drivers	6	6
Crane drivers	6	6
Fork lift and mechanical truck drivers	6	6
Electricity power plant operators	6	6
Turncocks (water supply)	6	6
Security officers and detectives	7	5
Travel stewards	7	5
Ambulancemen	7	5
Preparatory fibre processors	7	5
Flour confectioners	7	5
Bakers (not hand)	7	5
Beatermen (paper making)	7	5
Machinemen, dryermen, calendarmen	7	5
Masticating millmen	7	5
Rubber mixers	7	5
Calendar machine operators	7	5
Man-made fibre makers	7	5
Other clothing cutters	7	5
Hand sewers	7	5
Linkers	7	5
Sewing machinists	7	5
Footwear lasters	7	5
Leather sewers	7	5
Tyre builders	7	5
Annealers	7	5
Metal polishers	7	5
Fettlers	7	5

KOS occupation	Gregory and Thomson	Routh
Railway lengthmen	7	5
Mains layers, pipe jointers	7	5
Tunnellers	7	5
Deck and engine room hands	7	5
Bargemen, tugmen	7	5
Railway guards	7	5
Railway signalmen	7	5
Storekeepers, warehousemen	7	5
Stevedores, dockers	7	5
Unskilled/semi-skilled		
Petrol pump attendants	8	6
Counterhands, assistants	8	6
Home helpers, maids	8	6
School helpers	8	6
Railway stationmen	8	6
Lift and car park attendants	8	6
General farm workers	8	6
Packers, bottlers, canners, fillers	8	6
Asphalt road surfacers	8	6
Furniture removers	8	6

In many cases the job titles are not identical between the KOS and Census lists, introducing a degree of bias in the selection of skill category. In others, the skill category is inherently ambiguous, as the occupational title must cover differing levels of skill, as with chefs and cooks, hand sewers, or machine setter-operators and operators. Skill levels themselves respond to the economic environment, as studies of dilution have shown, while the breakdown of the craft apprenticeship system and the growth of multi-skilling make traditional definitions less relevant. For these various reasons, no set of rules can generate a unique socio-economic classification, making some element of judgement inescapable. The reassuring feature is that from separate bases two independent classifications have reached a large measure of coherence.

Table B.1. Grouped List of Occupations used in the NES 1973–1982
(As appended to the Survey questionnaire)

The occupations are arranged in 18 main groups. Those in groups I to IX are classified as **non-manual** with six exceptions, marked with an 'm' in groups VII, VIII and IX. These six and all occupations in groups X to XVIII are classified as **manual**. As explained in Chapter 2, where occupations are bracketed in the list, results are presented in the occupational analyses only for the combined group of occupations, but not for the separate occupations. In the analysis by occupation, shorter titles are used for some occupations and groups of occupations, particularly those bracketed in the list.

Group I—managerial (general management)

Top managers—national government and other non-trade organisations
General, central, divisional managers—trading organisations

Group II—professional and related supporting management and administration

Judges, barristers, advocates and solicitors
Company secretaries
Town clerks and other clerks to local authorities
Secretaries of trade associations, trade unions, professional bodies and charities
Accountants
Estimators, valuers and assessors
Finance, investment, insurance and tax specialists
Personnel and industrial relations officers and managers
Organization and methods, work study and operational research officers
Economists, statisticians and actuaries
Systems analysts and computer programmers
Marketing and sales managers and executives
Advertising and public relations managers and executives
Purchasing officers and buyers
Property and estate managers
Librarians and information officers
{ Public health inspectors
{ Other statutory and similar inspectors
General administrators—national government
General administrators—local government
All other professional and related supporting management and administration

Group III—professional and related in education, welfare and health

University academic staff
Teachers in establishments for further and higher education
Secondary teachers
Primary teachers
{ Pre-primary teachers
{ Special education teachers
Vocational/industrial trainers
Directors of education, education officers, school inspectors
Social and behavioural scientists
Welfare workers—social, medical, industrial, educational and moral
Clergy, ministers of religion
Medical practitioners
Dental practitioners
Nurse administrators and nurse executives
State registered and state enrolled nurses and state-certified midwives
Nursing auxiliaries and assistants

Pharmacists
Medical radiographers
Ophthalmic and dispensing opticians
Remedial therapists
Chiropodists
Medical technicians and dental auxiliaries
Veterinarians
All other professional and related in education, welfare and health

Group IV—literary, artistic and sports
Journalists
Artists, commercial artists
Industrial designers
Actors, musicians, entertainers, stage managers
{ Photographers and cameramen
{ Sound and vision equipment operators
Window dressers
Professional sportsmen, sports officials
All other literary, artistic and sports, including authors and writers

Group V—professional and related in science, engineering, technology and similar fields
Biological scientists and biochemists
Chemical scientists
Physical and geological scientists and mathematicians
Civil, structural and municipal engineers
Mechanical engineers
{ Electrical engineers
{ Electronic engineers
{ Electrical/electronic engineers
Production engineers
Planning and quality control engineers
{ Mining, quarrying and drilling engineers
{ Aeronautical engineers
{ Chemical engineers
{ Heating and ventilating engineers
{ General and other engineers
{ Metallurgists
{ All other technologists
Architectural draughtsmen
Engineering and other draughtsmen
Laboratory technicians—scientific and medical
Engineering technicians and technician engineers
Architects and town planners
Town planning assistants, architectural and building technicians
Quantity surveyors
Building, land and mining surveyors
Aircraft flight deck officers

Air traffic planners and controllers

{ Ships' masters, deck officers and pilots
Ships' engineers officers
Ships' radio officers

All other professional and related in science, engineering and other technologies and similar fields

Group VI—managerial (excluding general management)

Production managers, works managers, works foremen

Engineering maintenance managers

Site and other managers, agents, clerks of works, general foremen (building and civil engineering)

Managers—underground mining and public utilities

Transport managers—air, sea, rail, road, harbour

Managers—warehousing and materials handling

{ Office managers—national government
Office managers—local government
Other office managers

Managers—wholesale distribution

Managers—department store, variety chain store, supermarket and departmental managers

Branch managers of shops other than above

Managers of independent shops (employees)

{ Hotel and residential club managers
Publicans (employees)
Catering and non-residential club managers

Entertainment and sports managers

Farm managers (employees)

{ Police officers (inspectors and above)
Fire service officers

Prison officers (chief officers and above)

All other managers

Group VII—clerical and related

Supervisors of clerks

Costing and accounting clerks

Cash handling clerks

Finance, investment and insurance clerks

Production and materials controlling clerks

Shipping and travel arranging clerks

Records and library clerks

General clerks and clerks not identified elsewhere

Retail shop cashiers

Retail shop check-out and cash and wrap operators

Receptionists

Supervisors of typists etc.

Personal secretaries, shorthand writers and shorthand typists

Other typists

Supervisors of office machine operators
Accounting and calculating machine operators
Key punch operators
Automatic data processing equipment operators
Office machine operators not identified elsewhere
Supervisors of telephonists, radio and telegraph operators
Telephonists
Radio and telegraph operators
m Supervisors of postmen, mail sorters and messengers
m Postmen, mail sorters and messengers

Group VIII—selling

Sales supervisors
Salesmen, sales assistants, shop assistants, and shelf fillers
m Petrol pump/forecourt attendants
m Roundsmen and van salesmen
Technical sales representatives
Sales representatives (wholesale goods)
Other sales representatives and agents

Group IX—security and protective service

Supervisors (police sergeants, fire fighting and related)
Policemen (below sergeant)
Firemen
Prison officers below principal officer
Security officers and detectives
m Security guards, patrolmen
Traffic wardens
m All other in security and protective service

Groups X to XVIII: manual. A few occupations, prefixed with letter 'm' in groups VII, VIII and IX are also classified as manual

Group X—catering, cleaning, hairdressing and other personal service

Catering supervisors
Chefs, cooks
Waiters, waitresses
Barmen, barmaids
Counter hands/assistants
Kitchen porters/hands
{ Supervisors—housekeeping and related
{ Supervisors/foremen—caretaking, cleaning and related
Domestic housekeepers
Home and domestic helpers, maids
School helpers and school supervisory assistants
Travel stewards and attendants
Ambulancemen

Hospital/ward orderlies
Hospital porters
Hotel porters
Caretakers
Road sweepers (manual)
Other cleaners
Railmen, stationmen
Lift and car park attendants
Garment pressers
Hairdressing supervisors
Hairdressers
All other in catering, cleaning, hairdressing and other personal service

Group XI—farming, fishing and related

Foremen—farming, horticulture, forestry
General farm workers
⎧ Dairy cowmen
⎨ Pig and poultrymen
⎩ Other stockmen
Horticultural workers
Domestic gardeners (private gardens)
Non-domestic gardeners and groundsmen
Agricultural machinery drivers/operators
Forestry workers
Supervisors/mates (fishing)
Fishermen
All other in farming, fishing and related

Group XII—materials processing (excluding metal)

(Hides, textiles, chemicals, food, drink and tobacco, wood, paper and board, rubber and plastics)
Foremen—tannery production workers
Tannery production workers
Foremen—textile processing
Preparatory fibre processors
Spinners, doublers/twisters
Winders, reelers
Warp preparers
Weavers
Knitters
Bleachers, dyers and finishers
Burlers, menders, darners
Foremen—chemical processing
Chemical gas and petroleum process plant operators
Foremen—food and drink processing
⎧ Bread bakers (hand)
⎩ Flour confectioners

Butchers and meat cutters
Foremen—paper and board making
{ Beatermen, refinermen—paper and board making
{ Machinemen, dryermen, calendermen, reelermen—paper and board making
Foremen—processing—glass, ceramics, rubber and plastics etc.
Glass and ceramic furnacemen and kilnmen
Kiln setters
Masticating millmen—rubber and plastics
Rubber mixers and compounders
Calender and extruding machine operators—rubber and plastics
Man-made fibre makers
Sewage plant attendants
All other in materials processing (other than metal)

Group XIII—making and repairing (excluding metal and electrical)

(Glass, ceramics, printing, paper products, clothing, footwear, woodworking, rubber and plastics)
Foremen—glass working
Glass formers and shapers
Glass finishers and decorators
Foremen—clay and stone working
{ Casters and other pottery makers
{ Cutters, shapers and polishers—stone
{ Foremen—printing
{ Foremen—paper products making
{ Foremen—bookbinding
Compositors
Electrotypers, stereotypers
Other printing plate and cylinder preparers
{ Printing machine minders (letterpress)
{ Printing machine minders (lithography)
{ Printing machine minders (photogravure)
Printing machine assistants (letterpress, lithography and photogravure)
Screen and block printers
Bookbinders and finishers
Cutting and slitting machine operators (paper and paper products making)
Foremen—textile materials working
{ Bespoke tailors and tailoresses
{ Dressmakers
{ Clothing cutters and makers (measure)
Other clothing cutters and makers
{ Coach trimmers
{ Upholsterers, mattress makers
Milliners
Furriers
Hand sewers and embroiderers
Linkers

Sewing machinists (textile materials)
Foremen—leather and leather substitutes working
{ Boot and shoe makers (bespoke) and repairers
Leather and leather substitutes cutters
Footwear lasters
Leather and leather substitutes sewers
Footwear finishers
Foremen—wood working
Carpenters and joiners (construction sites and maintenance)
{ Carpenters and joiners (ship and stage)
Carpenters and joiners (other)
{ Cabinet makers
Case and box makers
Wood sawyers and veneer cutters
Woodworking machinists (setters and setter operators)
Other woodworking machinists (operators and minders)
Patternmakers (moulds)
Labourers and mates to woodworking craftsmen
Foremen—rubber and plastics working
Tyre builders
Moulding machine operators/attendants (rubber and plastics)
Dental mechanics
All other in making and repairing (excluding metal and electrical)

Group XIV—processing, making, repairing and related (metal and electrical)

(Iron, steel and other metals, engineering (including installation and maintenance) vehicles and shipbuilding)
Foremen—metal making and treating
{ Blast furnacemen
Furnacemen (steel smelting)
Other furnacemen—metal
Rollermen (steel)
{ Moulders and moulder/coremakers
Machine moulders, shell moulders and machine coremakers
Die casters
Metal drawers
Smiths, forgemen
Electroplaters
Annealers, hardeners, temperers (metal)
Foremen—engineering machining
Press and machine tool setters
Roll turners, roll grinders
Other centre lathe turners
Machine tool setter-operators
Machine tool operators (not setting up)
Press and stamping machine operators
Automatic machine attendants/minders

Metal polishers
Fettlers/dressers
Foremen—production fitting (metal)
Toolmakers, tool fitters, markers out
Precision instrument makers
Metal working production fitters (fine limits)
Metal working production fitter-machinists (fine limits)
Other metal working production fitters (not to fine limits)
Foremen—installation and maintenace—machines and instruments
Machinery erectors and installers
Maintenance fitters—non-electrical plant and industrial machinery
Knitting machine mechanics (industrial)
Motor vehicle mechanics (skilled)
Other motor vehicle mechanics
Maintenance and service fitters—aircraft engines
Watch and clock repairers
Instrument mechanics
Office machinery mechanics
Foremen—production fitting and wiring (electrical/electronic)
Production fitters—electrical/electronic
Production electricians
Foremen—installation and maintenance (electrical/electronic)
Electricians—installation and maintenance (plant and machinery)
Electricians—installation and maintenance (premises, ships)
Telephone fitters
Radio, television and other electronic maintenance fitters and mechanics
Cable jointers and linesmen
Foremen/supervisors—metal working—pipes, sheets, structures
Plumbers, pipe fitters
Heating and ventilating engineering fitters
Gas fitters
Sheet metal workers
Platers and metal shipwrights
Caulker burners, riveters and drillers (constructional metal)
General steel workers—shipbuilding and repair
⎧ Steel erectors
⎨ Scaffolders, stagers
⎩ Steel benders, bar benders and fixers
Welders—skilled
Other welders
Foremen—other processing, making and repairing (metal and electrical)
Goldsmiths, silversmiths and precious stone workers
Engravers and etchers (printing)
Coach and vehicle body builders/makers
Aircraft finishers
Maintenance and installation fitters—mechanical and electrical
Setter operators of woodworking and metal working machines

{ All other skilled in processing, making and repairing (metal and electrical)
{ All other non-skilled in processing, making and repairing (metal and electrical)

Group XV—painting, repetitive assembling, product inspecting, packaging and related

Foremen—painting and similar coating
Painters and decorators
Pottery decorators
{ Coach painters
{ Other spray painters
French polishers
{ Foremen—product assembling (repetitive)
{ Foremen—product inspection
Repetitive assemblers (metal and electrical goods)
Inspectors and testers (skilled)—metal and electrical engineering
Viewers—metal and electrical engineering
Foremen—packaging
Packers, bottlers, canners, fillers
All other in painting, repetitive assembling, product inspecting, packaging and related

Group XVI—construction, mining and related not identified elsewhere

Foremen—building and civil engineering not identified elsewhere
Bricklayers
Fixer—walling masons
Plasterers
Floor and wall tilers, terrazzo workers
Roofers and slaters
Glaziers
Railway trackmen and platelayers
{ Asphalt and bitumen road surfacers
{ Other roadmen
Concrete erectors/assemblers
Concrete levellers/screeders
General builders
{ Sewermen (maintenance)
{ Mains and service layers and pipe jointers (drainage, gas, oil, water)
Waste inspectors (water supply)
Craftsmen's mates and other builders labourers not identified elsewhere
Civil engineering labourers
Foremen/deputies—coalmining
Face-trained coalmining workers
Tunnellers
All other in construction, mining, quarrying, well drilling and related not identified elsewhere

Group XVII—transport operating, materials moving and storing and related

    { Foremen—ships, lighters and other vessels
    { Foremen—rail transport operating
    { Foremen—road transport operating
    { Deck and engine room hands (sea-going)
    { Bargemen, lightermen, boatmen, tugmen
    Locomotive drivers, motormen
    Secondmen (railways)
    Railway guards
    Railway signalmen and shunters
    Bus inspectors
    Bus and coach drivers
    Heavy goods drivers (over 3 tons unladen weight)
    Other goods drivers
    Other motor drivers
    Bus conductors
    Drivers' mates
    Foremen—civil engineering plant operating
    Mechanical plant drivers/operators—earth-moving and civil engineering
    Foremen—materials handling equipment operating
    Crane drivers/operators
    Fork lift and other mechanical truck driver/operators
    Foremen—materials moving and storing
    Storekeepers, warehousemen
    Stevedores and dockers
    Furniture removers
    Warehouse, market and other goods porters
    Refuse collectors/dustmen
    All other in transport operating, materials moving and storing and related not identified elsewhere

Group XVIII—Miscellaneous

    Foremen—miscellaneous
    Electricity power plant operators and switchboard attendants
    Turncocks (water supply)
    { General labourers—engineering and shipbuilding
    { Other general labourers
    All other in miscellaneous occupations not identified elsewhere

Table B.2. The Allocation of KOS Occupations into Socio-economic Groups 1973–1982

1. Managers

Group I

Top managers—national government and other non-trade organizations
General, central, divisional managers—trading organizations

Group II

Company secretaries
Town clerks and other clerks to local authorities
Personnel and industrial relations officers and managers
Organization and methods, work study, and operational research officers
Marketing and sales managers and executives
Advertising and public relations managers and executives
Purchasing officers and buyers
Property and estate managers
General administrators—national government
General administrators—local government

Group III

Directors of education, education officers, and school inspectors

Group V

Aircraft flight deck officers
Air traffic planners and controllers
Ships' masters, deck officers, and pilots
Ships' engineers officers
Ships' radio officers

Group VI

Production managers, works managers, and works foremen
Engineering maintenance managers
Managers—underground mining and public utilities
Transport managers—air, sea, rail, road, harbour
Managers—warehousing and materials handling
Office managers—national government
Office managers—local government
Other office managers
Managers—wholesale distribution
Managers—department store, variety chain store, supermarket, and departmental managers
Police officers (inspectors and above)
Fire service officers
Prison officers (chief officer and above)
All other managers

2. Professionals

Group II

Judges, barristers, advocates, and solicitors
Secretaries of trade associations, trade unions, professional bodies, and charities
Accountants
Estimators, valuers, and assessors

Finance, investment, insurance, and tax specialists
Economists, statisticians, and actuaries
Systems analysts and computer programmers
Librarians and information officers
Public health inspectors
Other statutory and similar inspectors
All other professional and related supporting management and administration

Group III

University academic staff
Teachers in establishments for further and higher education
Social and behavioural scientists
Welfare workers—social, medical, industrial, educational, and moral
Clergy, ministers of religion
Medical practitioners
Dental practitioners
Veterinarians
All other professional and related in education, welfare, and health

Group IV

Journalists
Actors, musicians, entertainers, stage managers

Group V

Biological scientists and biochemists
Chemical scientists
Physical and geological scientists and mathematicians
Civil, structural, and municipal engineers
Mechanical engineers
Electrical engineers
Electronic engineers
Electrical/electronic engineers
Production engineers
Planning and quality control engineers
Mining, quarrying, and drilling engineers
Aeronautical engineers
Chemical engineers
Heating and ventilating engineers
General and other engineers
Metallurgists
All other technologists
Architects and town planners
Quantity surveyors
Building, land, and mining surveyors
All other professional and related in science, engineering, and other technological and similar fields

3. Intermediate non-manuals

Group III

Secondary teachers
Primary teachers
Pre-primary teachers
Special education teachers
Vocational/industrial trainers
Nurse administrators and nurse executives
State registered and state enrolled nurses and state-certified midwives
Pharmacists
Medical radiographers
Ophthalmic and dispensing opticians
Remedial therapists
Chiropodists
Medical technicians and dental auxiliaries

Group IV

Artists, commercial artists
Industrial designers
Photographers and cameramen
Sound and vision equipment operators
All other literary, artistic, and sports, including authors and writers

Group V

Laboratory technicians—scientific and medical
Engineering technicians and technician engineers
Town planning assistants, architectural and building technicians

Group VI

Site and other managers, agents, clerks of works, general foremen (building and civil engineering)
Branch managers of shops
Managers of independent shops (employees)
Hotel and residential club managers
Publicans (employees)
Catering and non-residential club managers
Entertainment and sports managers
Farm managers (employees)

Group VII

Supervisors of clerks
Supervisors of typists etc.
Supervisors of office machine operators
Supervisors of telephonists, radio and telegraph operators

Group VIII

Sales supervisors
Technical sales representatives
Sales representatives (wholesale goods)
Other sales representatives and agents

Group IX

Supervisors (police sergeants, fire fighting, and related)

4. Junior non-manuals

Group III

Nursing auxiliaries and assistants

Group IV

Window dressers
Professional sportsmen, sports officials

Group V

Architectural draughtsmen
Engineering and other draughtsmen

Group VII

Costing and accounting clerks
Cash handling clerks
Finance, investment, and insurance clerks
Production and materials controlling clerks
Shipping and travel arranging clerks
Records and library clerks
General clerks and clerks not identified elsewhere
Retail shop cashiers
Retail shop check-out and cash and wrap operators
Receptionists
Personal secretaries, shorthand writers, and shorthand typists
Other typists
Accounting and calculating machine operators
Key punch operators
Automatic data processing equipment operators
Office machine operators not identified elsewhere
Telephonists
Radio and telegraph operators

Group VIII

Salesmen, sales assistants, shop assistants, and shelf fillers

Group IX

Policemen (below sergeant)
Firemen
Prison officers below principal officer
Security officers and detectives
Traffic wardens

5. Foremen and supervisors

Group VII

Supervisors of postmen, mail sorters, and messengers

Group X

Catering supervisors
Supervisors—housekeeping and related
Supervisors/foremen—caretaking, cleaning, and related
Hairdressing supervisors

Group XI

Foremen—farming, horticulture, forestry
Supervisors/mates (fishing)

Group XII

Foremen—tannery production workers
Foremen—textile processing
Foremen—chemical processing
Foremen—food and drink processing
Foremen—paper and board making
Foremen—processing—glass, ceramics, rubber, and plastics, etc.

Group XIII

Foremen—glass working
Foremen—clay and stone working
Foremen—printing
Foremen—paper products making
Foremen—bookbinding
Foremen—textiles materials working
Foremen—leather and leather substitutes working
Foremen—wood working
Foremen—rubber and plastics working

Group XIV

Foremen—metal making and treating
Foremen—engineering machining
Foremen—production fitting (metal)
Foremen—installation and maintenance—machines and instruments
Foremen—production fitting and wiring (electrical/electronic)
Foremen—installation and maintenance (electrical/electronic)

Foremen/supervisors—metal working—pipes, sheets, structures
Foremen—other processing, making, and repairing (metal and electrical)

Group XV

Foremen—painting and similar coating
Foremen—product assembling (repetitive)
Foremen—product inspection
Foremen—packaging

Group XVI

Foremen—building and civil engineering not identified elsewhere
Foremen/deputies—coal-mining

Group XVII

Foremen—ships, lighters, and other vessels
Foremen—rail transport operating
Foremen—road transport operating
Bus inspectors
Foremen—civil engineering plant operating
Foremen—materials handling equipment operating
Foremen—materials moving and storing

Group XVIII

Foremen—miscellaneous

6. Skilled manuals

Group X

Chefs, cooks
Hairdressers

Group XII

Warp preparers
Weavers
Knitters
Bleachers, dyers, and finishers
Burlers, menders, and darners
Bread bakers (hand)
Butchers and meat cutters
Glass and ceramic furnacemen and kilnmen
Kiln setters

Group XIII

Glass formers and shapers
Glass finishers decorators
Casters and other pottery makers
Cutters, shapers, and polishers—stone
Compositors
Electrotypers, stereotypers
Other printing plate and cylinder preparers

Printing machine minders (letterpress)
Printing machine minders (lithography)
Printing machine minders (photogravure)
Printing machine assistants (letterpress, lithography, and photogravure)
Screen and block printers
Bookbinders and finishers
Cutting and slitting machine operators (paper and paper products making)
Bespoke tailors and tailoresses
Dressmakers
Clothing cutters and makers (measure)
Coach trimmers
Upholsterers, mattress makers
Milliners
Furriers
Boot and shoe makers (bespoke) and repairers
Leather and leather substitutes cutters
Footwear lasters
Leather and leather substitutes sewers
Footwear finishers
Carpenters and joiners (construction sites and maintenance)
Carpenters and joiners (ship and stage)
Carpenters and joiners (other)
Cabinet makers
Case and box makers
Wood sawyers and veneer cutters
Woodworking machinists (setters and setter operators)
Other woodworking machinists (operators and minders)
Patternmakers (moulds)
Dental mechanics

Group XIV

Blast furnacemen
Furnacemen (steel smelting)
Other furnacemen (metal)
Rollermen (steel)
Moulders and moulder/coremakers
Machine moulders, shell moulders, and machine coremakers
Die casters
Metal drawers
Smiths, forgemen
Electroplaters
Press and machine tool setters
Roll turners, roll grinders
Other centre lathe turners
Machine tool setter-operators
Toolmakers, tool fitters, markers out
Precision instrument makers
Metal working production fitters (fine limits)

Metal working production fitter-machinists (fine limits)
Other metal working production fitters (not to fine limits)
Machinery erectors and installers
Maintenance fitters—non-electrical plant and industrial machinery
Knitting machine mechanics (industrial)
Motor vehicle mechanics (skilled)
Maintenance and service fitters—aircraft engines
Watch and clock repairers
Instrument mechanics
Office machinery mechanics
Production fitters—electrical/electronic
Production electricians
Electricians—installation and maintenance (plant and machinery)
Electricians—installation and maintenance (premises and ships)
Telephone fitters
Radio, television, and other electronic maintenance fitters and mechanics
Cable jointers and linesmen
Plumbers, pipe fitters
Heating and ventilating engineering fitters
Gas fitters
Sheet metal workers
Platers and metal shipwrights
Caulker burners, riveters, and drillers (constructional metal)
General steel workers—shipbuilding and repair
Steel erectors
Scaffolders, stagers
Steel benders, bar benders, and fixers
Welders—skilled
Other welders
Goldsmiths, silversmiths, and precious stone workers
Engravers and etchers (printing)
Coach and vehicle body builders/makers
Aircraft finishers
Maintenance and installation fitters—mechanical and electrical
Setter operators of woodworking and metal working machines
All other in processing, making, and repairing (metal and electrical)

Group XV

Painters and decorators
Pottery decorators
Coach painters
Other spray painters
French polishers
Inspectors and testers (skilled)—metal and electrical engineering

Group XVI

Bricklayers
Fixer/walling masons

Plasterers
Floor and wall tilers, terrazzo workers
Roofers and slaters
Glaziers
Face-trained coal-mining workers

Group XVII

Locomotive drivers, motormen
Secondmen (railways)
Bus and coach drivers
Heavy goods drivers (over 3 tons unladen weight)
Mechanical plant drivers/operators—earthmoving and civil engineering
Crane drivers/operators
Forklift and other mechanical truck drivers/operators

Group XVIII

Electricity power plant operators and switchboard attendants
Turncocks (water supply)

7. Semi-skilled manuals

Group VII

Postmen, mail sorters, and messengers

Group VIII

Roundsmen and van salesmen

Group IX

Security guards, patrolmen
All other in security and protective service

Group X

Waiters, waitresses
Barmen, barmaids
Domestic housekeepers
Travel stewards and attendants
Ambulancemen
Hospital/ward orderlies
Garment pressers
All other in catering, cleaning, hairdressing, and other personal service

Group XI

Dairy cowmen
Pig and poultrymen
Other stockmen
Horticultural workers
Domestic gardeners (private gardens)

Non-domestic gardeners and groundsmen
Agricultural machinery drivers/operators
Forestry workers
Fishermen
All other in farming, fishing, and related

Group XII

Tannery production workers
Preparatory fibre processers
Spinners, doublers/twisters
Winders, reelers
Chemical, gas, and petroleum process plant operators
Flour confectioners
Beatermen, refinermen—paper and board making
Machinemen, dryermen, calendermen, reelermen—paper and board making
Masticating millmen—rubber and plastics
Rubber mixers and compounders
Calender and extruding machine operators—rubber and plastics
Man-made fibre makers
Sewage plant attendants
All other in materials processing (other than metal)

Group XIII

Other clothing cutters and makers
Hand sewers and embroiderers
Linkers
Sewing machinists (textile materials)
Tyre builders
Moulding machine operators/attendants (rubber and plastics)
All other in making and repairing (excluding metal and electrical)

Group XIV

Annealers, hardeners, temperers (metal)
Machine tool operators (not setting up)
Press and stamping machine operators
Automatic machine attendants/minders
Metal polishers
Fettlers/dressers
Other motor vehicle mechanics

Group XV

Repetitive assemblers (metal and electrical goods)
Viewers—metal and electrical engineering
All others in painting, repetitive assembling, product inspecting, packaging, and
related

Group XVI

Railway trackmen and platelayers
Concrete erectors/assemblers
Concrete levellers/screeders
General builders
Sewermen (maintenance)
Mains and service layers and pipe jointers (drainage, gas, oil, water)
Waste inspectors (water supply)
Tunnellers

Group XVII

Deck and engine room hands (sea-going)
Bargemen, lightermen, boatmen, tugmen
Railway guards
Railway signalmen and shunters
Other goods drivers
Other motor drivers
Bus conductors
Storekeepers, warehousemen
Stevedores and dockers

8. Unskilled manuals

Group VIII

Petrol pump/forecourt attendants

Group X

Counter hands/assistants
Kitchen porters/hands
Home and domestic helpers, maids
School helpers and school supervisory assistants
Hospital porters
Hotel porters
Caretakers
Road sweepers (manual)
Other cleaners
Railmen, stationmen
Lift and car park attendants

Group XI

General farm workers

Group XIII

Labourers and mates to woodworking craftsmen

Group XV

packers, bottlers, canners, fillers

Group XVI

Asphalt and bitumen road surfacers
Other roadmen
Craftsmens' mates and other builders' labourers not identified elsewhere
Civil engineering labourers
All other in construction, mining, quarrying, well drilling, and related not iden-
tified elsewhere

Group XVII

Drivers' mates
Furniture removers
Warehouse, market, and other goods porters
Refuse collectors/dustmen
All other in transport operating, materials moving, and storing

Table B.3. Grouped List of Occupations used in the NES 1970–1972
(As appended to the Survey questionnaire)

Notes: The main groups are numbered from 1 to 16; within groups 1 to 10 'm'
denotes occupations classified as manual; within groups 14 to 16 'a' denotes
occupations classified as skilled and 'b' those classified as semi-skilled.

Non-manual (unless otherwise indicated)

  1. Managers
     Company chairman; director
     General manager; divisional manager (with other managers under their
     control)
     Company secretary
     Works manager/superintendent, production manager
     Marketing, advertising, sales manager
     Personnel or training manager
     Transport manager
     Office manager (including departmental office manager)
     Site or yard manager
     Retail shop manager or departmental manager
     Hotel, catering, club or entertainments manager
     Other managerial staff
  2. Supervisors and foremen
     Office supervisor
     Sales supervisor, section head, first assistant
  m Catering supervisor
     Transport Inspector
     Senior or higher level foreman (e.g. works foreman)
  m Other foreman or supervisor

3. Engineers, scientists, technologists (performing work normally requiring university degree or equivalent)
   Engineer—civil, structural or municipal
   Engineer—electrical, electronic
   Engineer—mechanical
   Engineer—planning and production
   Engineer—other
   Natural scientist (biologist, chemist, physicist, etc.)
   Social or other scientist
   Technologist
4. Technicians
   Draughtsman
   Systems analyst, computer programmer
   Technician—laboratory, scientific, medical, dental
   Technician—design, costing, production
   Other technician
5. Academic and teaching staff
   University academic staff (professors, readers, lecturers, and others)
   Teachers in establishments for further education
   School teachers—secondary, primary, nursery, special schools
   Other teachers and instructors
6. Medical dental, nursing and welfare staff
   Medical or dental practitioner
   Medical auxiliary (radiographer, physiotherapist, etc.)
   Nursing matron, sister
   Staff nurse, enrolled nurse, registered nurse, midwife
   Nursing assistant
   Welfare worker (including probation officer, children's officer, hospital almoner)
m Ambulance man, hospital or ward orderly
   Other medical, dental, nursing and welfare staff
7. Other professional and technical staff
   Accountant (professional)
   Architect, planner
   Surveyor
   Solicitor
   Author, editor, journalist
   Artist, musician, photographer, entertainer, sportsman
   Purchasing officer, buyer
   Aircrew officer, ship's officer, pilot
   Other professional and technical staff
8. Office and communications staff
   Clerk—senior level
   Clerk—intermediate level
   Clerk—routine or junior level
   Secretary, shorthand typist
   Copy/audio typist

   Receptionist
   Telephonist
   Office machine operator (including punch and telex)
m Postman, mail sorter, messenger
   Other office and communications staff not listed elsewhere

9. Sales staff
   Sales representative, traveller, agent, technical salesman
   Cashier—retail shop
   Shop salesman, sales assistant, shop assistant
m Roundsman—retail sales, van salesman
m Petrol pump attendant
   Other sales staff not listed elsewhere

10. Security staff
   Police officer (inspector and above)
   Police sergeant or constable
   Fire officer
   Fireman
   Prison officer
m Guard, watchman
m Caretaker, office keeper
m Other security staff

Manual

11. Catering, domestic and other service staff
   Chef/cook
   Steward, stewardess, hostess—aircraft, railways, ships
   Waiter, waitress
   Kitchen/counter hand, school meals helper
   Barman, barmaid
   Other catering staff
   Hairdresser, barber
   Car park attendant, lift attendant
   Cleaner, charwoman
   Housekeeper, house warden
   Maid, valet, etc., domestic gardener
   Other domestic and service staff

12. Farming, forestry and horticultural occupations
   Stockman
   Agricultural machinery driver/operator
   General farm worker
   Groundsman, gardener—non-domestic
   Horticultural worker
   Other farming, forestry or horticultural occupation

13. Transport occupations
   Railway engine driver, motorman, 2nd man
   Railway signalman

Railway guard
Railway porter, ticket collector, railman
Railway lengthman
Bus conductor
Bus or coach driver
Taxi driver, other private hire driver
Lorry or van driver (vehicles up to 5 tons)
Lorry or van driver (vehicles 5 to 10 tons)
Lorry or van driver (vehicles 10 to 15 tons)
Lorry or van driver (vehicles over 15 tons)
Deck or engine-room hand, seaman, boatman, fisherman
Docker, stevedore
Other transport occupations not listed elsewhere

14. Building, engineering, etc., occupations
a Bricklayer
a Carpenter and joiner
a Plumber, pipe-fitter
a Painter, decorator
a Plasterer
a Heating and ventilating fitter/engineer
a Steel erector, framework erector, steel bender, fixer
a Scaffolder
b Mechanical equipment operator (except crane operator)
a Electrician—building and wiring
a Electrician—maintenance
a Electrician—production
a Fitter—electrical, electronic
a Fitter—maintenance
a Fitter—production
a Fitter—toolroom, tool/die maker
a Fitter—gas
a Precision instrument maker/repairer
a Motor vehicle fitter/mechanic—skilled
b Motor vehicle mechanic—semi-skilled
a Radio or television mechanic/repairer
a Office machinery mechanic (typewriters, calculators, etc.)
a Assembler—skilled
b Assembler—semi-skilled
Assembler—other
a Machine tool setter, setter-operator
a Machine tool operator—skilled
b Machine tool operator—semi-skilled
a Machine operator, machinist (metal)—skilled
b Machine operator, machinist (metal)—semi-skilled
a Machine operator, machinist (wood)—skilled
b Machine operator, machinist (wood)—semi-skilled
Machine minder (wood or metal)

a Electroplater
a Moulder, coremaker—skilled
b Moulder, coremaker—semi-skilled
a Pattern maker (wood or metal)
a Plater, riveter
a Smith, forgeman
a Sheet metal worker
a Welder—skilled
a Welder—semi-skilled
a Linesman, cable-jointer
a Telephone installer, repairman
a Other craftsman or skilled building or engineering worker
b Other semi-skilled building or engineering worker (including craftsman's mate)
  Unskilled building or engineering worker

15. Textile clothing and footwear occupations
b Textile spinner, doubler, twister
b Textile winder, reeler
a Textile weaver
a Textile knitter, linker
a Sewing machinist—skilled
b Sewing machinist—semi-skilled
a Tailor, cutter, dressmaker (other than sewing machinist)
a Sewer (hand); embroiderer
a Finisher, presser
a Other textile, clothing or footwear worker—skilled
b Other textile, clothing or footwear worker—semi-skilled
  Unskilled textile, clothing or footwear worker

16. Other occupations not listed above
a Coalminer—underground
a Coalminer—surface
a Bookbinder, cutter, ruler
a Compositor, typesetter
a Electrotyper, stereotyper, engraver
a Printing press operator
a Crane operator
b Fork lift truck operator
a Furnaceman—skilled
b Furnaceman—semi-skilled
a Baker (table-hand), confectioner
a Butcher, meat cutter
a Inspector, viewer, examiner, checker—skilled
b Inspector, viewer, examiner, checker—semi-skilled
  Other inspector, viewer, examiner, checker
a Storekeeper, storeman, warehouseman—skilled
b Storekeeper, storeman, warehouseman—semi-skilled
  Packer, bottler, canner

a Skilled worker not specified elsewhere
b Semi-skilled worker not specified elsewhere
Labourer or unskilled worker not specified elsewhere

Table B.4. The Allocation of Occupations into Socio-economic Groups, 1970–1972

1. Managers

Group 1

Company chairman; director
General manager; divisional manager (with other managers under their control)
Company secretary
Works manager/superintendent, production manager
Marketing, advertising, sales manager
Personnel or training manager
Transport manager
Office manager (including departmental office manager)
Other managerial staff

Group 7

Purchasing officer, buyer
Aircrew officer, ship's officer, pilot

Group 10

Police officer (inspector and above)

2. Professionals

Group 3

Engineer—civil, structural, or municipal
Engineer—electrical, electronic
Engineer—mechanical
Engineer—planning and production
Engineer—other
Natural scientist (biologist, chemist, physicist, etc.)
Social or other scientist
Technologist

Group 4

Systems analyst, computer programmer

Group 5

University academic staff (professors, readers, lecturers, and others)
Teachers in establishments for further education

Group 6

Medical or dental practitioner
Welfare worker (including probation officer, children's officer, hospital almoner)

Group 7

Accountant (professional)
Architect, planner
Surveyor
Solicitor
Author, editor, journalist
Other professional and technical staff

3. Intermediate non-manuals

Group 1

Site or yard manager
Retail shop manager or departmental manager
Hotel, catering, club, or entertainments manager

Group 2

Office supervisor
Sales supervisor, section head, first assistant
Transport inspector

Group 4

Technician—laboratory, scientific, medical, and dental
Technician—design, costing, production
Other technician

Group 5

School-teachers—secondary, primary, nursery, special schools
Other teachers and instructors

Group 6

Medical auxiliary (radiographer, physiotherapist, etc.)
Nursing matron, sister
Staff nurse, enrolled nurse, registered nurse, midwife

Group 7

Artist, musician, photographer, entertainer, sportsman

Group 8

Clerk—senior level
Clerk—intermediate level

Group 9

Sales representative, traveller, agent, technical salesman

Group 10
Fire officer

4. Junior non-manuals

Group 4
Draughtsman

Group 6
Nursing assistant
Other medical, dental, nursing, and welfare staff

Group 8
Clerk—routine or junior level
Secretary, shorthand typist
Copy/audio typist
Receptionist
Telephonist
Office machine operator (including punch and telex)
Other office and communications staff, not listed elsewhere

Group 9
Cashier—retail shop
Shop salesmen, sales assistant, shop assistant
Other sales staff not listed elsewhere

Group 10
Police sergeant or constable
Fireman
Prison officer

5. Foremen and supervisors

Group 2
Catering supervisor
Senior or higher-level foreman (e.g. works foreman)
Other foreman or supervisor

6. Skilled Manuals

Group 11
Chef/cook
Hairdresser, barber

Group 13
Railway engine driver, motorman, secondman
Bus or coach driver

Lorry or van driver (vehicles 5 to 10 tons)
Lorry or van driver (vehicles 10 to 15 tons)
Lorry or van driver (vehicles over 15 tons)

Group 14
Bricklayer
Carpenter and joiner
Plumber, pipe-fitter
Painter, decorator
Plasterer
Heating and ventilating fitter/engineer
Steel erector, framework erector, steel bender, fixer
Scaffolder
Mechanical equipment operator (except crane operator)
Electrician—building and wiring
Electrician—maintenance
Electrician—production
Fitter—electrical, electronic
Fitter—maintenance
Fitter—production
Fitter—toolroom, tool/die maker
Fitter—gas
Precision instrument maker/repairer
Motor vehicle fitter/mechanic—skilled
Radio or television mechanic/repairer
Office machinery mechanic (typewriters, calculators, etc.)
Assembler—skilled
Machine tool setter, setter-operator
Machine tool operator—skilled
Machine operator, machinist (metal)—skilled
Machine operator, machinist (wood)—skilled
Electroplater
Moulder, coremaker—skilled
Pattern maker (wood or metal)
Plater, riveter
Smith, forgeman
Sheet metal worker
Welder—skilled
Linesman, cable-jointer
Telephone installer, repairman
Other craftsman or skilled building or engineering worker

Group 15
Textile weaver
Textile knitter, linker
Sewing machinist—skilled

Tailor, cutter, dressmaker (other than sewing machinist)
Finisher, presser
Other textile, clothing, or footwear worker—skilled

Group 16
Coal-miner—underground
Coal-miner—surface
Bookbinder, cutter, ruler
Compositor, typesetter
Electrotyper, stereotyper, engraver
Printing press operator
Crane operator
Fork lift truck operator
Furnaceman—skilled
Baker (tablehand), confectioner
Butcher, meat cutter
Inspector, viewer, examiner, checker—skilled
Storekeeper, storeman, warehouseman—skilled
Skilled worker not specified elsewhere

7. Semi-skilled manuals

Group 6
Ambulance man, hospital or ward orderly

Group 8
Postman, mail sorter, messenger

Group 9
Roundsman—retail sales, van salesman

Group 10
Guard, watchman
Caretaker, office keeper
Other security staff

Group 11
Steward, stewardess, hostess—aircraft, railways, ships
Waiter, waitress
Barman, barmaid
Housekeeper, house warden

Group 12
Stockman
Agricultural machinery driver/operator
Groundsman, gardener—non-domestic

Horticultural worker
Other farming, forestry, or horticultural occupation

Group 13
Railway signalman
Railway guard
Railway lengthman
Bus conductor
Taxi driver, other private hire driver
Lorry or van driver (vehicles up to 5 tons)
Deck or engine-room hand, seaman, boatman, fisherman
Docker, stevedore

Group 14
Motor vehicle mechanic—semi-skilled
Assembler—semi-skilled
Machine tool operator—semi-skilled
Machine operator, machinist (metal)—semi-skilled
Machine operator, machinist (wood)—semi-skilled
Machine minder (wood or metal)
Moulder, coremaker—semi-skilled
Welder—semi-skilled
Other semi-skilled building or engineering worker (including craftsman's mate)

Group 15
Textile spinner, doubler, twister
Textile winder, reeler
Sewing machinist—semi-skilled
Sewer (hand); embroiderer
Other textile, clothing, or footwear worker—semi-skilled

Group 16
Furnaceman—semi-skilled
Inspector, viewer, examiner, checker—semi-skilled
Storekeeper, storeman, warehouseman—semi-skilled
Semi-skilled worker not specified elsewhere

8. Unskilled manuals

Group 9
Petrol pump attendant

Group 11
Kitchen/counter hand, school meals helper
Other catering staff
Car park attendant, lift attendant

Cleaner, charwoman
Maid, valet, etc., domestic gardener
Other domestic and service staff

Group 12
General farm worker

Group 13
Railway porter, ticket collector, railman
Other transport occupations not listed elsewhere

Group 14
Assembler—other
Unskilled building or engineering worker

Group 15
Unskilled textile, clothing, or footwear worker

Group 16
Other inspector, viewer, examiner, checker
Packer, bottler, canner
Labourer or unskilled worker not specified elsewhere

Appendix C.
The Change in Industrial Classification, 1982

Throughout the period 1970–82 the industrial classification under which establishments were coded in the NES (as in all other data series compiled on an industry basis) was the Standard Industrial Classification (SIC), 1968. This was a two-, occasionally three-level classification, comprising 27 main Orders aggregated from 184 Minimum List Headings (MLHs) (182 before 1974). The list of these is appended. In the early 1980s the Revised Standard Industrial Classification (SIC(R)), 1980, was developed, to reflect the changes in industrial structure, such as the increased importance of the energy sector, to take advantage of the greater availability of establishment-level data on production, and to link to the General Industrial Classification of Economic Activities within the European Communities, commonly known as NACE. The SIC(R) 1980 involves an entirely different structure from SIC 1968, being based on four levels of aggregation, 10 divisions, 60 classes, 222 groups, and 334 activity headings. The SIC(R) has been adopted as the system of industrial classification in the case of the NES with effect from 1983, but with 1982 treated as the cross-over year, when the main tables were published on the old basis, but with some repeated on the new classification. While the change of classification does not introduce a discontinuity within the period of this study, since the NES is a continuing Survey and the intention in bringing the Survey data into the public domain was in part to provide a basis for future research, we considered it appropriate to establish a link between the data sets generated for 1970–82 and future Surveys.

To effect the conversion in full, by mapping the MLH and SIC system into activity headings across the period as a whole, was clearly totally impracticable, particularly as the need to establish alike individuals was precluding the use of extensive subdivisions in any classification. It was therefore decided that the most suitable way of providing continuity was by making the new classification available throughout the pre-1982 period, but only at a high level of aggregation. The 10 divisions were the obviously suitable units.

The composition of each division in terms of the MLHs of the 1968 SIC is detailed in Central Statistical Office (1980) and (1981). For the majority of MLHs the reallocation is straightforward, the MLH being assigned in its entirety to a single division. For the 46 MLHs which are divided between two or more divisions allocators had to be devised. Since the CSO publications give definitions of the content of each category but no indication of quantitative importance, evidence was adduced from three further sources:

1. Following their own reclassification exercise on the 1982 Survey, the DE at Runcorn supplied tabulations of the number of employees in that year's Survey classified by MLH and by activity head. While in principle this should have

provided the perfect allocator, other changes to the file made between the two classifications vitiated direct comparisons. In particular, a number of amendments are made to each year's file when the following year's results are processed, such that changes in numbers occurred even where an MLH mapped over in its entirety to a single activity head or group.

2. Department of Employment (1982) and (1983*b*) both give the results of the Census of Employment as at September 1981, the former on SIC 1968, the latter on SIC(R), both rounded to thousands.

3. Department of Employment (1983*b*) also reports the activity headings of SIC(R) listed by the percentage of employees in any MLH allocated to that AH. This is given by five bands of 20 per cent—0–20 per cent, 20–40, 40–60, 60–80, and 80–100. Any MLH contributing less than 5 per cent of the employees in any AH is omitted.

Since each of these sources gives relevant evidence but in an approximate form, an element of judgement had to be applied in selecting the allocator. The majority of allocators have been rounded to the most likely 10 per cent, but where the MLH is particularly large, 5 per cent has been used. The full allocation of MLHs to divisions is shown in Table C.1.

To establish the changeover in the industrial classification two versions of each data file for 1982 have been prepared. The first version, used in the analyses reported, maintains direct consistency with the years 1970–81 by constructing the allocation of individuals to divisions on the basis of their MLH. The second version applies the division codes taken directly from the DE's own reclassification work for that year, to give a direct link to later years. The two versions of the 1982 data files differ only in this respect, although the consequent changes to the incidence of small cells and hence discarding of non-alike individuals make minor differences to the numbers in the samples.

Table C.1. The Revised Standard Industrial Classification: Allocation of Employment by MLH to Divisions

The 27 SIC Orders of the SIC 1968 are:

1. Agriculture, forestry, and fishing
2. Mining and quarrying
3. Food, drink, and tobacco
4. Coal and petroleum products
5. Chemical and allied products
6. Metal manufacture
7. Mechanical engineering
8. Instrument engineering
9. Electrical engineering
10. Shipbuilding and marine engineering
11. Vehicles
12. Other metal goods
13. Textiles

14. Leather, leather goods, and fur
15. Clothing and footwear
16. Bricks, glass, pottery, and cement
17. Timber, furniture, etc.
18. Paper, printing, publishing
19. Other manufacturing industry
20. Construction
21. Gas, electricity, water
22. Transport and communications
23. Distributive trades
24. Insurance, banking, finance
25. Professional and scientific services
26. Miscellaneous services
27. Public administration

The 10 divisions of the SIC(R) 1980 are:

0. Agriculture, forestry, and fishing
1. Energy and water supply industries
2. Extraction of minerals other than fuels, manufacture of metals, of mineral goods, and chemicals
3. Metal goods, engineering, and vehicle industries
4. Other manufacturing industries
5. Construction
6. Distribution; hotels and catering; repairs
7. Transport and communications
8. Banking, finance, insurance, business services, and leasing
9. Other services

The allocation of MLHs to divisions is as follows:

SIC 1		*Allocation to division*
MLH 001	Agriculture and horticulture	0
002	Forestry	0
003	Fishing	0

SIC2		
MLH 098[a]	Coal-mining, underground	1
099[a]	Coal-mining, surface	1
100[a]	Coal-mining nes	1
101[b]	Coal-mining	1
102	Stone and slate quarrying	2
103	Chalk, clay, sand, gravel	2
104	Petroleum, natural gas	1
109	Other mining and quarrying	2

SIC 3		
MLH 211	Grain milling	4
212	Bread and flour confectionery	4
213	Biscuits	4
214	Bacon curing, meat products	4

215	Milk and milk products	4
216	Sugar	4
217	Cocoa, chocolate, confectionery	4
218	Fruit and vegetable products	4
219	Animal and poultry foods	4
221	Vegetable, animal oils and fats	4
229	Food industries nes	4
231	Brewing and malting	
232	Soft drinks	4
239	Other drink industries	4
240	Tobacco	4

SIC 4

MLH 261	Coke ovens	1
262	Mineral oil refining	1
263	Lubricating oils, greases	1

SIC 5

MLH 271	General chemicals	males: 10% to 1, 90% to 2; females: 100% to 2
272	Pharmaceutical chemicals	2
273	Toilet preparations	2
274	Paint	2
275	Soap and detergents	2
276	Synthetic resin, rubber, plastic	males and females: 60% to 2, 40% to 4
277	Dyestuffs and pigments	2
278	Fertilizers	2
279	Other chemical industries	2

SIC 6

MLH 311	Iron and steel (general)	males and females: 95% to 2, 5% to 3
312	Steel tubes	2
313	Iron castings	males and females: 10% to 2, 90% to 3
321	Aluminium and alloys	males and females: 70% to 2, 30% to 3
322	Copper, brass, and alloys	males and females: 90% to 2, 10% to 3
323	Other base metals	males and females: 90% to 2, 10% to 3

SIC 7

MLH 331	Agricultural machinery	3
332	Metal-working machine tools	3
333	Pumps, valves, compressors	3
334	Industrial engines	3
335	Textile machinery	3

336	Construction equipment	3
337	Mechanical handling equipment	3
338	Office machinery	3
339	Other plant and machinery	3
341	Industrial plant, steelwork	3
342	Ordnance and small arms	3
349	Other mechanical engineering	3

SIC 8

MLH 351	Photographic equipment	3
352	Watches and clocks	3
353	Surgical instruments	males and females: 10% to 2, 90% to 3
354	Scientific instruments, systems	3

SIC 9

MLH 361	Electrical machinery	3
362	Insulated wires and cables	3
363	Telephone apparatus, equipment	3
364	Radio, electronic components	3
365	Broadcasting equipment	3
366	Electronic computers	3
367	Radio, radar, electronic goods	3
368	Electric appliances, domestic	3
369	Other electrical goods	3

SIC 10

MLH 371^c	Shipbuilding	3
372^c	Marine engineering	3

SIC 11

MLH 380	Wheeled tractor manufacture	3
381	Motor vehicle manufacture	3
382	Motor, pedal cycle manufacture	3
383	Aerospace equipment	3
384	Locomotives	3
385	Railway carriages and wagons	3

SIC 12

MLH 390	Engineers' small tools	3
391	Hand tools and implements	3
392	Cutlery, plated tableware	3
393	Bolts, nuts, screws, rivets	3
394	Wire and wire manufactures	2
395	Cans and metal boxes	3
396	Jewellery, precious metals	4
399	Metal industries nes	3

SIC 13

MLH 411	Production of man-made fibres	2
412	Spinning cotton and flax	4

413	Weaving cotton, man-made fibres	4
414	Woollen and worsted	4
415	Jute	4
416	Rope, twine, net	4
417	Hosiery	4
418	Lace	4
419	Carpets	4
421	Narrow fabrics	4
422	Made-up textiles	4
423	Textile finishing	4
429	Other textile industries	males and females: 60% to 2, 40% to 4

SIC 14

MLH 431	Leather	4
432	Leather goods	4
433	Fur	4

SIC 15

MLH 441	Weatherproof outerwear	4
442	Men's and boys' outerwear	4
443	Women's and girls' outerwear	4
444	Overalls etc.	4
445	Dresses, lingerie	4
446	Hats	4
449	Dress industries nes	4
450	Footwear	4

SIC 16

MLH 461	Bricks and fireclay	2
462	Pottery	2
463	Glass	2
464	Cement	2
469	Abrasives, building materials nes	Males and females: 90% to 2, 10% to 3

SIC 17

MLH 471	Timber	4
472	Furniture, upholstery	4
473	Bedding	4
474	Shop and office fitting	4
475	Wooden containers	4
479	Misc. wood manufactures	4

SIC 18

MLH 481	Paper and board	4
482	Packaging products	4
483	Manufactured stationery	4
484	Manufs. of paper and board nes	4
485	Newspapers	4

486	Periodicals	4
489	Other printing, publishing, etc.	4

SIC 19

MLH 491	Rubber	4
492	Linoleum, plastic floorcovering	4
493	Brushes and brooms	4
494	Toys, games, sports equipment	4
495	Misc. stationers' goods	4
496	Plastic products nes	4
499	Misc. manufacturing industries	4

SIC 20

MLH 500	Construction	5

SIC 21

MLH 601	Gas	1
602	Electricity	1
603	Water	1

SIC 22

MLH 701	Railways	7
702	Road passenger transport	7
703	Road haulage	7
704	Other road haulage	7
705	Sea transport	7
706	Port, inland water transport	7
707	Air transport	7
708	Post and telecommunications	7
709	Misc. transport and storage	7

SIC 23

MLH 810	Wholesale food, drink	6
811	Wholesale petroleum distribution	6
812	Other wholesale distribution	6
820	Retail food, drink distribution	6
821	Other retail distribution	males: 95% to 6, 5% to 8; females: 100% to 6
831	Dealing in coal, oil, grain, etc.	6
832	Dealing in other industrial materials	males and females: 90% to 6, 10% to 8

SIC 24

MLH 860	Insurance	8
861	Banking	8
862	Other financing institutions	8
863	Property owning and management	8
864	Advertising	8
865	Other business services	males and females: 70% to 8, 30% to 9
866	Central offices nae	8

SIC 25

MLH 871	Accountancy	8
872	Education services	9
873	Legal services	8
874	Medical and dental services	9
875	Religious organizations	9
876	Research, development services	9
879	Other professional services	males and females: 90% to 8, 10% to 9

SIC 26

MLH 881	Cinema, theatre	9
882	Sport and recreation	9
883	Betting and gambling	9
884	Hotels	9
885	Restaurants, cafés	6
886	Public houses	6
887	Clubs	6
888	Catering contractors	6
889	Hairdressing	9
891[d]	Private domestic service	9
892	Laundries	9
893	Dry cleaning	9
894	Motor repairs, garages	6
895	Boot and shoe repairs	6
899	Other services	males: 10% to 4, 90% to 9; females: 100% to 9

SIC 27

MLH 901	National government	9
906	Local government	9

[a] From 1974 only.
[b] 1970–3 only.
[c] MLH 370 is not used in the NES.
[d] Not used in the NES.

References

ABRAHAM, K. G., and FARBER, H. S. (1987), 'Job Duration, Seniority and Earnings', *American Economic Review*, 77: 278–97.

ALDEN, J. D. (1977), 'The Extent and Nature of Double Job Holding in Great Britain', *Industrial Relations Journal*, 8: 14–33.

ARCHIBALD, G. C. (1969), 'The Phillips Curve and the Distribution of Unemployment', *AEA Papers and Proceedings*, 59: 124–34.

ASHENFELTER, O., and LAYARD, R. (1983), 'Incomes Policy and Wage Differentials', *Economica*, 50: 127–43.

—— —— (1986), *Handbook of Labour Economics*, Amsterdam: North-Holland.

ATKINSON, A. B. (1970), 'On the Measurement of Inequality', *Journal of Economic Theory*, 2: 244–63.

—— MICKLEWRIGHT, J., and STERN, N. H. (1981), 'A Comparison of the Family Expenditure Survey and the New Earnings Survey 1971–77. Part I: Characteristics of the Sample', Social Science Research Council Programme *Taxation, Incentives and the Distribution of Income*, Discussion Paper no. 27.

—— —— —— (1982), 'A Comparison of the Family Expenditure Survey and the New Earnings Survey 1971–77. Part II: Hours and Earnings', Social Science Research Council Programme *Taxation, Incentives and the Distribution of Income*, Discussion Paper no. 32.

BAIN, G. S. (ed.) (1983), *Industrial Relations in Britain*, Oxford: Basil Blackwell.

BALL, J. M., and SKEOCH, H. K. (1981), *Inter-plant Comparisons of Productivity and Earnings*, Government Economic Service Working Paper no. 38, May.

BALL, R., and ST CYR, E. (1966), 'Employment Models in UK Manufacturing Industries', *Review of Economic Studies*, 33: 179–207.

BEACH, B. (1985), 'Regional Earnings Convergence: The Case of Northern Ireland', *Regional Studies*, 19: 1–8.

BEACHABY, D. H., and MANNING, D. N. (1985), 'Regional Earnings Revisited', Department of Economics Working Paper 85-04, University College Swansea.

BEAUMONT, P. B. (1978), 'The Obligation of Government as an Employer in the British Civil Service', *Public Administration*, 56: 13–24.

—— and HARRIS, R. I. D. (1988), 'Sub-systems of Industrial Relations: The Spatial Dimension in Britain', *British Journal of Industrial Relations*, 26: 397–407.

BELL, F. W. (1967), 'The Relation of the Region, Industrial Mix and Production Function to Metropolitan Wage Levels', *Review of Economics and Statistics*, 49: 368–74.

BETANCOURT, R. R., and CLAGUE, C. K. (1981), *Capital Utilisation: A Theoretical and Empirical Analysis*, Cambridge: Cambridge University Press.

BLACK, B. (1985), 'Regional Earnings Convergence: The Case of Northern Ireland', *Regional Studies*, 19: 1–7.

534   *References*

BLANCHFLOWER, D. (1986), 'What Effect do Unions Have on Relative Wages in Great Britain?', *British Journal of Industrial Relations*, 15: 195–204.
—— and CORRY, B. (1986a), *Part Time Employment in Great Britain*, Research Report, Coventry: Institute for Employment Research, University of Warwick.
—— —— (1986b), 'The Determinants of Shiftworking at the Establishment Level', mimeo, Coventry: Institute for Employment Research, University of Warwick.
—— and OSWALD, A. (1988), 'The Determination of White-Collar Pay', Centre for Labour Economics, LSE, Discussion Paper no. 307.
BLINDER, A. S. (1974), *Towards an Economic Theory of Income Distribution*, Cambridge, Mass.: MIT Press.
BLYTON, P. (1985), *Changes in Working Time: An International Review*, London: Croom Helm.
BODO, G., and GIANNINI, C. (1985), 'Average Working Time and the Influence of Contractual Hours: An Empirical Investigation for Italian Industry (1970–81)', *Oxford Bulletin of Economics and Statistics*, 47: 131–52.
BOSWORTH, D. L. (1981), 'Specification of Factors Demand Models and Shiftworking', *Scottish Journal of Political Economy*, 28: 256–65.
—— (1982), 'The Wage–Utilisation Relationship and the Structure of Labour Costs', Occasional Research Paper no. 65, Loughborough: Department of Economics, Loughborough University.
—— (1983), *Economic Aspects of Shiftworking*, Report to the ILO, Geneva.
—— (1986a), *Work Patterns and Optimal Capital Utilisation in British Manufacturing Industry*, Research Report, Coventry: Institute for Employment Research, University of Warwick.
—— (1986b), *The Economics of Labour Utilisation*, Final Report to the South Australian Department of Labour and the Reserve Bank, Flinders: National Institute of Labour Studies.
—— (1987), 'Time Intensity Utilisation Rates in the UK Chemicals Industry', in Bosworth and Heathfield (1987): 406–29.
—— (1988), 'Optimal Capital Utilisation with Multiple Rhythmically Varying Factor and Product Prices', mimeo, Coventry: Institute for Employment Research, University of Warwick.
—— and DAWKINS, P. J. (1980), 'Compensation for Workers' Disutility: Time of Day, Length of Shift and Other Features of Work Patterns', *Scottish Journal of Political Economy*, 27: 80–96.
—— —— (1981), *Work Patterns: An Economic Analysis*, Aldershot: Gower Press.
—— —— (1983), 'Optimal Capital Utilisation in British Manufacturing Industry', in Eichhorn et al. (1983).
—— —— (1984), 'Shiftworking and Perceived Working Conditions: An Empirical Analysis', in Wedderburn and Smith (1984).
—— —— and WESTAWAY, A. J. (1981a), 'Explaining the Incidence of Shiftworking in Great Britain', *Economic Journal*, 91: 145–57.
—— —— —— (1981b) 'The Supply of and Demand for Shiftworkers', in Currie et al. (1981): 361–82.
—— DUTTON, P., GREEN, A., and WARREN, P. (1987a), *Engineering: Performance*

and Prospects, Research Report, Coventry: Institute for Employment Research, University of Warwick.

—— —— —— —— (1987*b*), *Review of Engineering*, Research Report, Coventry: Institute for Employment Research, University of Warwick.

—— and HEATHFIELD, D. F. (eds.) (1987), *Working Below Capacity*, London: Macmillan.

—— and PUGH, C. A. (1984), 'Rhythmical Factor Prices and the Timing of Factor Demands', mimeo, London: Faculty of Social Sciences and Business Studies, Polytechnic of Central London.

—— —— (1985*a*), 'Optimal Capital Utilisation and Shiftworking', *Scandinavian Journal of Economics*, 87: 658–67.

—— —— (1985*b*), 'Industrial and Commercial Demand for Electricity by Time of Day', *Energy Journal*, 6: 101–7.

—— and WESTAWAY, A. J. (1985), 'Hours of Work and Employment in UK Manufacturing Industry: An Empirical Analysis', in Wilson *et al.* (1985).

—— —— (1986), 'Over Time and Short Time Working in the British Textiles Industries', mimeo, Coventry: Institute for Employment Research, University of Warwick.

—— —— (1987), 'The Demand for Hours', *Scottish Journal of Political Economy*, 34: 368–87.

BOWEY, A. M., THORPE, R., and HELLIER, P. (1986), *Payment Systems and Productivity*, London: Macmillan.

BRISCOE, G., and PEEL, D. (1975), 'The Specification of the Short-Run Employment Function: An Empirical Investigation of the Demand for Labour in the UK Manufacturing Sector 1954–72', *Oxford Bulletin of Economics and Statistics*, 37: 115–42.

BROWN, W. (1976), 'Incomes Policy and Pay Differentials', *Oxford Bulletin of Economics and Statistics*, 38: 27–49.

—— (1979), 'Engineering Wages and the Social Contract 1975–77', *Oxford Bulletin of Economics and Statistics*, 41: 51–62.

—— (1981), *The Changing Contours of British Industrial Relations*, Oxford: Basil Blackwell.

—— and TERRY, M. (1978), 'The Changing Nature of National Wage Agreements', *Scottish Journal of Political Economy*, 25: 119–33.

CARTER, F. A., and CORLETT, E. N. (1982), *Review of the European Foundation's Research into Shiftwork, 1977–80: The Effect on Living and Working Conditions and Recommendations for Improvements*, Dublin: European Foundation for the Improvement of Living and Working Conditions.

Central Statistical Office (1980), *Standard Industrial Classification Revised 1980: Reconciliation with Standard Industrial Classification 1968*, London: Central Statistical Office.

—— (1981), *Indexes to the Standard Industrial Classification: Revised 1980*, London: Central Statistical Office.

—— (1985*a*), *Economic Trends*, Dec. 1985, Appendix 2.

—— (1985*b*), *U.K. National Accounts: Sources and Methods*, London: HMSO.

CHAMPERNOWNE, D. G. (1953), 'A Model of Income Distribution', *Economic Journal*, 63: 318–51.

CHATER, R. T. J., DEAN, A. J. H., and ELLIOTT, R. F. (1981), *Incomes Policy*, Oxford: Oxford University Press.

CHIPLIN, B., and SLOANE, P. J. (1974), 'Sexual Discrimination in the Labour Market', *British Journal of Industrial Relations*, 12: 371–402.

—— —— (1976), 'Male–Female Earnings Differences: A Further Analysis', *British Journal of Industrial Relations*, 14: 77–81.

—— —— (1986), 'The Effect of Britain's Anti-Discrimination Legislation on Relative Pay and Employment: A Comment', Discussion Paper 86-02, Aberdeen University, Department of Political Economy.

CHUNG, C., and AIGNER, D. J. (1981), 'Industrial and Commercial Demand for Electricity by Time of Day: A California Case Study', *Energy Journal*, 2: 91–106.

Civil Service Department (1981), *Civil Service Pay*, Factual Background Memorandum on the Non-industrial Home Civil Service, to the Enquiry into Non-industrial Civil Service Pay, London: HMSO.

Clegg Commission (1980), see Standing Commission on Pay Comparability (1980).

COOK, F. (1962), *Shiftwork*, London: Institute of Personnel Management.

COUSINEAU, H. M., and LACROIX, R. (1977), *Wage Determination in Major Collective Agreements in the Private and Public Sectors*, Ottawa: Economic Council of Canada.

COWELL, F. A. (1984), 'The Structure of American Income Inequality', *Review of Income and Wealth*, 30: 351–75.

CREEDY, J., and WHITFIELD, K. (1982), 'Professional Chemists: The First Three Jobs', *Chemistry in Britain*, 18: 352–8.

CURRAN, J., and STANWORTH, J. (1981), 'Size of Workplace and Attitudes to Industrial Relations in the Printing and Electronics Industries', *British Journal of Industrial Relations*, 14: 14–25.

CURRIE, D., PEEL, D., and PETERS, W. (eds.) (1981), *Microeconomic Analysis*, London: Croom Helm.

DANIEL, W. W., and MILLWARD, N. (1983), *Work-Place Industrial Relations in Britain*, London: Heinemann.

DANKERT, C. E. (1965), 'Automation, Unemployment and Shorter Hours', in Dankert *et al.* (1965): 161–78.

—— MANN, F. C., and NORTHUP, H. R. (eds.) (1965), *Hours of Work*, New York: Harper and Row.

DAWKINS, P. J., and WOODEN, M. (1985), 'Labour Utilisation and Wage Inflation in Australia: An Empirical Examination', *Economic Record*, 61: 516–21.

DEAN, A. J. H. (1975), 'Earnings in the Public and Private Sectors 1950–75', *National Institute Economic Review*, 74: 60–70.

—— (1980), 'Wages and Earnings', Royal Statistical Society and Social Science Research Council, *Reviews of U.K. Statistical Sources*, vol. xiii, Oxford: Pergamon.

—— (1981), 'Public and Private Sector Pay and the Economy', in Fallick and Elliott (1981*b*): 45–71.

DEATON, A., and MUELLBAUER, J. (1980), *Economics and Consumer Behaviour*, Cambridge: Cambridge University Press.

Department of Employment (1972*a*), 'New Occupational Classification', *Department of Employment Gazette*, 3–5.

—— (1972*b*), 'List of Key Occupations for Statistical Purposes', *Department of Employment Gazette*, 799–800.

—— (1981), *Review of Statistical Services in the Department of Employment and the Manpower Services Commission*, London: Department of Employment.

—— (1982), 'Census of Employment Results for September 1981', *Department of Employment Gazette*, 504–13.

—— (1983*a*), 'The Unemployed: Survey Estimates for 1981 Compared with the Monthly Count', *Department of Employment Gazette*, 266–7.

—— (1983*b*), 'Census of Employment Results for September 1981 (based on the 1980 revision of the Standard Industrial Classification)', *Department of Employment Gazette*, 91, Occasional Supplement 1.

—— (annual), *Time Rates of Wages and Hours of Work*, London: HMSO.

—— (annual), *New Earnings Survey*, London: HMSO.

DOERINGER, P. B., and PIORE, M. J. (1971), *Internal Labor Markets and Manpower Analysis*, Boston: Lexington.

DUNLOP, J. T. (1984), 'Industrial Relations and Economics: The Common Frontier of Wage Determination', *Proceedings of the Industrial Relations Research Association*, winter.

EHRENBERG, R. (ed.) (1981), *Research in Labor Economics*, Greenwich, Conn.: JAI Press.

EICHHORN, W., HENN, R., NEWMANN, K., and SHEPHARD, R. W. (eds.) (1983), *Quantitative Studies in Production and Prices*, Wurzberg, Vienna: Physics Verlag.

ELLIOTT, R. F. (1977), 'Public Sector Wage Movements 1950–73', *Scottish Journal of Political Economy*, 24: 133–50.

—— (1981*a*), 'The Diminishing Importance of Wage Drift', in Chater, Dean, and Elliott (1981): 128–45.

—— (1981*b*), 'Some Further Observations of the Importance of National Wage Agreements', *British Journal of Industrial Relations*, 19: 370–5.

—— and FALLICK, J. L. (1979), 'Pay Differentials in Perspective', *Economic Journal*, 89: 377–84.

—— —— (1981), *Pay in the Public Sector*, London: Macmillan.

European Foundation (1981), *Publications of the European Foundation to May 1981*, Dublin: European Foundation for the Improvement of Living and Working Conditions.

—— (1983), *Catalogue of Publications in Print, 1983*, Dublin: European Foundation for the Improvement of Living and Working Conditions.

FALLICK, J. L., and ELLIOTT, R. F. (1981*a*), 'Incomes Policy and the Public Sector', in Fallick and Elliott (1981*b*): 100–27.

—— —— (1981*b*), *Incomes Policies, Inflation and Relative Pay*, London: George Allen and Unwin.

FELS, A. (1972), *The British Prices and Incomes Board*, Cambridge: Cambridge University Press.

FOGEL, W., and LEWIN, D. (1974), 'Wage Determination in the Public Sector, *Industrial and Labor Relations Review*, 27: 410–31.

Foss, M. (1963), 'The Utilisation of Capital Equipment', *Survey of Current Business*, 43/6: 8–16.

Foster, N., Henry, S. G. B., and Trinder, C. (1984), 'Public and Private Sector Pay: A Partly Disaggregated Study', *National Institute Economic Review*, 107: 63–73.

Freeman, R. B., and Medoff, J. L. (1981), 'The Impact of Collective Bargaining: Illusion or Reality?', in Stieber, McKersie, and Mills (1981).

—— —— (1984), *What Do Unions Do?*, New York: Basic Books.

Garbarino, J. (1964), 'Fringe Benefits and Overtime as Barriers to Expanding Employment', *Industrial and Labour Relations Review*, 17: 426–42.

Garside, W. R. (1980), *The Measurement of Unemployment in Great Britain 1850–1979: Methods and Sources*, Oxford: Basil Blackwell.

George, K. D., McNabb, R., and Shorey, J. (1977), 'The Size of the Work Unit and Labour Market Behaviour', *British Journal of Industrial Relations*, 15: 265–78.

Geroski, P., and Stewart, M. B. (1982), 'Trade Union Wage Differentials in the UK: A Strange and Sad Story', Industrial Relations Section, Princeton University, Working Paper no. 157.

Gershuny, J. I. (1983), *Social Innovation and the Division of Labour*, Oxford: Oxford University Press.

Gibrat, R. (1931), *Les Inégalités économiques*, Paris: Sirely.

Goldthorpe, J. H. (1968), *The Affluent Worker*, Cambridge: Cambridge University Press.

Gregory, M. B., Lobban, P., and Thomson, A. W. J. (1985), 'Wage Settlements in Manufacturing 1979–84: Evidence from the CBI Pay Databank', *British Journal of Industrial Relations*, 23: 129–50.

—— and Thomson, A. W. J. (1981), 'The Coverage Mark-up, Bargaining Structure and Earnings in Britain, 1973 and 1978', *British Journal of Industrial Relations*, 19: 26–37.

Gregory, R. G., and Smith, R. E. (1983), 'Unemployment, Inflation and Job Creation Policies in Australia', paper presented to the Conference on Government Policies toward Inflation and Unemployment in Developed Countries, Macquarie University.

Gronau, R. (1977), 'Leisure, Home Production and Work: The Theory of the Allocation of Time Revisited', *Journal of Political Economy*, 85: 1101–23.

Gunderson, M. (1979), 'Earnings Differentials between the Public and Private Sectors', *Canadian Journal of Economics*, 12: 228–42.

Hakim, C. (1984a), 'Employers' Use of Homework, Outwork and Freelances', *Department of Employment Gazette*, 92: 144–50.

—— (1984b), 'Homework and Outwork: National Estimates from Two Surveys', *Department of Employment Gazette*, 92: 7–12.

—— (1985), *Employers' Use of Outwork*, Research Paper no. 44, Department of Employment, London: HMSO.

Hall, S. G., and Henry, S. G. B. (1985), 'Rational Expectations in an Econometric Model', *National Institute Economic Review*, 114: 58–68.

Handy, C. (1984), *The Future of Work*, Oxford: Basil Blackwell.

Harrington, J. M. (1979), *Shiftwork and Health: A Critical Review of the Litera-*

ture, London: TUC Centenary Institute of Occupational Health, London School of Hygiene and Tropical Medicine, University of London.

HARRIS, R. (1983), 'Specification of Factor Demand Models and Shiftworking: An Extension to the CES Case', *Scottish Journal of Political Economy*, 30: 170–4.

HART, R. A., and SHAROT, T. (1978), 'The Short Run Demand for Workers and Hours: A Recursive Model', *Review of Economics Studies*, 45: 299–309.

HEERTJE, A., ALLEN, M., and COHEN, H. (1980), *The Black Economy*, London: Pan Books.

HENRY, S. G. B. (1981), 'Incomes Policy and Aggregate Pay', in Fallick and Elliott (1981*b*): 23–44.

HOOD, W., and REES, R. D. (1974), 'Inter-industry Wage Levels in United Kingdom Manufacturing', *Manchester School*, 42: 175–85.

HUTCHENS, R. M. (1987), 'A Test of Lazear's Theory of Delayed Payment Contracts', *Journal of Labor Economics*, 5/4/2: S153–70.

IFF (1978), *Shiftwork in Manufacturing Industry: Great Britain*, Research Report to the European Foundation for the Improvement of Living and Working Conditions, Dublin, London: Industrial Facts and Forecasting.

Income Data Services (1973*a*), *Shiftwork—1*, Study no. 44, London: IDS Ltd.

—— (1973*b*), *Shiftwork—2*, Study no. 48, London: IDS Ltd.

—— (1973*c*), *Shiftwork—3*, Study no. 65, London: IDS Ltd.

—— (1975), *Shiftwork—4*, Study no. 110, London: IDS Ltd.

—— (1977), *Shiftwork—5*, Study no. 151, London: IDS Ltd.

—— (1979*a*), *Guide to Shiftwork*, London: IDS Ltd.

—— (1979*b*), *Shiftwork and Unsocial Hours Payments*, Study no. 207, London: IDS Ltd.

—— (1982), *CAD: Agreements and Pay*, Study no. 276, London: IDS Ltd.

—— (1983), *Shift and Unsocial Hours Payments*, Study no. 287, London: IDS Ltd.

—— (1985*a*), *Shift Patterns*, Study no. 335, London: IDS Ltd.

—— (1985*b*), *Shift Premiums*, Study no. 336, London: IDS Ltd.

INGHAM, G. K. (1970), *Size of Industrial Organization and Worker Behaviour*, Cambridge: Cambridge University Press.

INGRAM, A. H., and SLOANE, P. J. (1985), 'Shiftwork and Socio-economic Policy', *International Journal of Manpower*, 6/5: 3–15.

Inquiry into Civil Service Pay (1982), *Report*, Cmnd. 8590, London: HMSO (Megaw Inquiry).

JOLLY, J., CREIGH, S., and MINGAY, A. (1980), *Age as a Factor in Employment*, Department of Employment, Research Paper no. 11.

KAKWANI, N. C. (1980), *Income, Inequality and Poverty*, Oxford: Oxford University Press.

KESSLER, S. (1983), 'Comparability', in Robinson and Mayhew (1983).

KOCHAN, T. A. (1980), *Collective Bargaining and Industrial Relations*, Homewood: Irwin.

—— and HELFMAN, D. E. (1981), 'The Effects of Collective Bargaining on Economic and Behavioural Job Outcomes', in Ehrenberg (1981): 321–65.

KOSTIUK, D. F., and FOLLMAN, D. A. (1989), 'Learning Curves, Personal Characteristics and Job Performance', *Journal of Labor Economics* 7/2: 129–46.

LAZEAR, E. (1976), 'Age, Experience and Wage Growth', *American Economic Review*, 66: 548–58.

—— (1981), 'Agency, Earnings Profiles, Productivity and Hours Restrictions', *American Economic Review*, 71: 606–20.

LESTER, R. (1967), 'Pay Differentials by Size of Establishment', *Industrial Relations*, 7: 57–67.

LEWIS, H. G. (1963), *Unionism and Relative Wages in the United States*, Chicago: University of Chicago Press.

—— (1983), 'Union Relative Wage Effects: A Survey of Macro Estimates', *Journal of Labor Economics*, 1: 1–27.

LUCAS, R. E., and SARGENT, T. J. (1981a), 'After Keynesian Macroeconomics', in Lucas and Sargent (1981b), ch. 16.

—— —— (1981b), *Rational Expectations*, London: George Allen and Unwin.

McCARTHY, W. E. J. (ed.) (1985), *Trade Unions*, Harmondsworth: Penguin, 2nd edn.

McDONALD, J. B. (1984), 'Some Generalized Functions for the Size Distribution of Income', *Econometrica*, 52: 647–63.

MacKAY, R. R. (1973), 'Employment Creation: A Resurrection', *Scottish Journal of Political Economy*, 20: 175–7.

MAIN, B. (1982), 'The Length of a Job in Britain', *Economica*, 49: 325–33.

MARGINSON, P. (1984), 'The Distinctive Effects of Plant and Company Size on Workplace Industrial Relations', *British Journal of Industrial Relations*, 22: 1–14.

MARRIS, R. L. (assisted by MacLEAN, I., and BERMAN, S.) (1964), *The Economics of Capital Utilisation: A Report on Multiple Shiftwork*, Cambridge: Cambridge University Press.

MARSDEN, D. (1985), 'Youth Pay in Britain Compared with France and the FR of Germany since 1966', *British Journal of Industrial Relations*, 24: 399–414.

—— (1987a), 'Small Firms and Labour Markets in the UK', paper prepared for the International Institute of Labour Studies.

—— (1987b), 'Employment and Pay by Occupation in Some Major OECD Countries since 1970', London School of Economics, mimeo.

MARSHALL, R. C., and ZARKIN, G. A. (1987), 'The Effect of Job Tenure on Wage Offers', *Journal of Labor Economics*, 5: 301–24.

MARTIN, R. L. (ed.) (1981), *Regional Wage Inflation and Unemployment*, London: Pion.

MASTERS, S. H. (1969), 'An Inter-industry Analysis of Wages and Plant Size', *Review of Economics and Statistics*, 51: 341–5.

MAYHEW, K. (1976a), 'Regional Variations of Manual Earnings in Engineering', *Oxford Bulletin of Economics and Statistics*, 38: 11–25.

—— (1976b), 'Plant Size and the Earnings of Manual Workers in Engineering', *Oxford Bulletin of Economics and Statistics*, 38: 149–60.

MEDOFF, J. L. (1983), 'US Labor Markets: Imbalance, Wage Growth and Productivity in the 1970s', *Brookings Papers on Economic Activity*: 87–128.

Megaw Inquiry (1982), see Inquiry into Civil Service Pay (1982).

METCALF, D. (1977), 'Unions, Incomes Policy and Relative Wages in Britain', *British Journal of Industrial Relations*, 15: 157–75.

—— and NICKELL, S. (1985), 'Will Pay Cuts Bring More Jobs?', *New Society*, 28 Feb.

—— —— and RICHARDSON, R. (1976), 'The Structure of Hours and Earnings in British Manufacturing Industry', *Oxford Economic Papers*, 29: 284–303.

MICKLEWRIGHT, J., and TRINDER, C. (1981), 'New Earnings Surveys 1968–80: Sampling Methods and Non-response', Social Science Research Council Programme *Taxation, Incentives and the Distribution of Income*, Discussion Paper no. 31.

MILLWARD, N., and STEVENS, M. (1986), *British Workplace Industrial Relations: 1980–84*, London: Gower.

Ministry of Labour (1954), 'Shiftwork', *Gazette*, Oct.: 337–42.

—— (1965), 'Shiftwork', *Gazette*, Apr.: 148–55.

MITCHELL, D. J. B. (1980), *Unions, Wages and Inflation*, Washington: Brookings.

MITCHELL, W. F. (1985), 'The NAIRU, Structural Imbalance and the Macro-equilibrium Unemployment Rate, mimeo, Canberra: Bureau of Labour Market Research.

MOORE, B., and RHODES, J. (1981), 'The Convergence of Earnings in the Regions of the United Kingdom', in Martin (1981).

MORTENSEN, D. T. (1988), 'Wages, Separations and Job Tenure: On-the-Job Specific Training or Matching?', *Journal of Labor Economics*, 6: 445–71.

MOTT, P. E. *et al.* (1965), *Shiftwork: The Social, Psychological and Physical Consequences*, Ann Arbor: University of Michigan Press.

MULVEY, C., and ABOWD, J. (1980), 'Estimating Union/Non-union Wage Differentials: A Statistical Issue', *Economica*, 47: 73–9.

—— and FOSTER, J. (1976), 'Occupational Earnings in the UK and the Effects of Collective Agreements, *Manchester School*, 44: 258–75.

NADIRI, N. J., and ROSEN, S. (1969), 'Inter-related Factor Demand functions', *American Economic Review*, 59: 457–71.

PARNES, H. S. (ed.) (1963), *Planning Education for Economic and Social Development*, Paris: OECD.

Pay Board (1973), *Anomalies*, Advisory Report no. 1, Cmnd. 5429, London: HMSO.

—— (1974), *Relativities*, Advisory Report no. 2, Cmnd. 5535, London: HMSO.

PENCAVEL, J. (1974), 'Relative Wages and Trade Unions in the United Kingdom', *Economica*, 41: 194–210.

PHELPS BROWN, H. (1962), 'Wage Drift', *Economica*, 24: 339–56.

—— (1977), *The Inequality of Pay*, Oxford: Oxford University Press.

PIKE, M. (1982), 'Segregation by Sex, Earnings Differentials and Equal Pay: An Application of a Job Crowding Model to UK Data', *Applied Economics*, 14: 503–14.

PRATTEN, C. F. (1976), *Labour Productivity Differentials within International Companies*, University of Cambridge, Department of Applied Economics Occasional Paper 50, Cambridge: Cambridge University Press.

Priestley Commission (1955), see Royal Commission on the Civil Service (1955).

PROSA (1981), *Project Schichtarbeit: Gesamtergebuis der Problemanalyse*, IG Chemie-Papier-Keramik.

Rayner Review (1981), see Department of Employment (1981).

REDER, M. W. (1955), 'The Theory of Occupational Wage Differentials', *American Economic Review*, 45: 834–52.

ROBINSON, D., and MAYHEW, K. (eds.) (1983), *Pay Policies for the Future*, Oxford: Oxford University Press.

ROSS, A. M. (1985), 'Trade Unions and the Theory of Wages', in McCarthy (1985): 303–17.

ROSSANA, R. (1983), 'Some Empirical Estimates of the Demand for Hours in US Manufacturing Industries', *Review of Economics and Statistics*, 65: 560–9.

—— (1985), 'Buffer Stocks and Labour Demand: Further Empirical Evidence', *Review of Economics and Statistics*, 67: 16–26.

ROUTH, G. (1965), *Occupation and Pay in Great Britain 1906–60*, London: Macmillan.

—— (1980), *Occupation and Pay in Great Britain 1906–79*, London: Macmillan.

Royal Commission on the Civil Service (1955), *Report*, Cmnd. 9613, London: HMSO (Priestley Commission).

Royal Commission on the Distribution of Income and Wealth (1979), *Fifth Report on the Standing Reference*, Report no. 8, Cmnd. 7679, London: HMSO.

SAUNDERS, C., and MARSDEN, D. (1981), *Pay Inequalities in the European Communities*, London: Butterworth.

—— MUKHERJEE, S., MARSDEN, D., and DONALDSON, A. (1977), *Winners and Losers: Pay Patterns in the 1970s*, London: Political and Economic Planning.

SAWYER, M. C. (1973), 'The Earnings of Manual Workers: A Cross-Section Analysis', *Scottish Journal of Political Economy*, 20: 141–57.

SEN, A. (1973), *On Economic Inequality*, Oxford: Oxford University Press.

SERGEANT, R., HOWELL, D., TAYLOR, P. J., and POCOCK, S. (1969), 'Compensation for Inconvenience: An Analysis of Shift Payments in Collective Agreements in the UK', *Occupational Psychology*, 43: 183–92.

SHAPIRO, D. (1978), 'Relative Effects of Unions in the Public and Private Sectors', *Industrial and Labor Relations Review*, 31: 193–204.

SLOANE, P. (1978), 'Economic Aspects of Shift and Night Work in Industrialised Market Economies', *International Labour Review*, 117: 129–42.

SMITH, A. (1776), *The Wealth of Nations* (1937 edn.), Modern Library.

SMITH, A. D., HITCHENS, D. M. W. N., and DAVIES, S. W. (1982), 'International Industrial Productivity: A Comparison of Britain, America and Germany', *National Institute Economic Review*, 101.

SMITH, S. P. (1976), 'Pay Differentials between Federal Government and Private Sector Workers', *Industrial and Labor Relations Review*, 29: 179–97.

Standing Commission on Pay Comparability (1980), *General Report: Report no. 9*, Cmnd. 7995, London: HMSO (Clegg Commission).

STEWART, M. B. (1983), 'Relative Earnings and Individual Union Membership in the UK', *Economica*, 50: 111–25.

STIEBER, J. W., McKERSIE, R. B., and MILLS, D. Q. (eds.) (1981), *US Industrial Relations, 1950–80: A Critical Assessment*, Madison: IRRA, University of Wisconsin.

THOMAS, R. L., and STONEY, P. J. M. (1971), 'Unemployment Dispersion as a Determinant of Wage Inflation in the UK: 1925–1966', *Manchester School*, 39: 83–116.

THOMSON, A. W. J., and BEAUMONT, P. B. (1978), *Public Sector Bargaining: A Study of Relative Gain,* Farnborough: Saxon House.

—— MULVEY, C., and FARBMAN, M. (1977), 'Bargaining Structure and Relative Earnings in Great Britain', *British Journal of Industrial Relations*, 15: 176–91.

TOPEL, R. (1982), 'Inventories, Layoffs and the Short-Run Demand for Labour', *American Economic Review*, 72: 767–86.

TRINDER, C. (1981), 'The Pay of Employees in the Public and Private Sector', *National Institute Economic Review*, 97: 48–56.

WABE, S., and LEECH, D. (1978), 'Relative Earnings in UK Manufacturing: A Reconsideration of the Evidence', *Economic Journal*, 88: 296–313.

WALKER, J. (1978), *Human Aspects of Shiftwork*, London: Institute of Personnel Management.

WEDDERBURN, A., and SMITH, P. (eds.) (1984), *Psychological Approaches to Night and Shift Work: International Research Papers*, Edinburgh: Heriot-Watt University.

WEISS, A., and LANDAU, H. J. (1984), 'Wages, Hiring Standards and Firm Size', *Journal of Labor Economics*, 2: 477–500.

WEISS, L. (1966), 'Concentration and Labor Earnings', *American Economic Review*, 56: 96–117.

—— and HALL, M. (1969), 'Firm Size and Profitability', *Review of Economics*, 149.

WELLINGTON, H. H., and WINTER, R. K. (1971), *The Unions and the Cities*, Washington: Brookings Institution.

WELLS, W. (1983), *The Relative Pay and Employment of Young People*, Department of Employment, Research Paper no. 42.

WHITE, M. (1984), *Incentive Pay in Britain*, London: Gower.

WHITLEY, J. D. (1986), 'A Model of Incomes Policy in the UK 1963–79', *Manchester School*, 34: 31–64.

—— and WILSON, R. A. (1986), 'The Impact on Employment of a Reduction in the Length of the Working Week', *Cambridge Journal of Economics*, 10/1: 43–60.

WHYBREW, E. G. (1968), *Overtime Working in Britain*, Royal Commission on Trade Unions and Employers Associations, Research Paper no. 9, London: HMSO.

WILLIS, R. J. (1986), 'Wage Determinants: A Survey and Reinterpretation of Human Capital Earnings Functions', in Ashenfelter and Layard (1986): 525–602.

WILSON, R. A., and BOSWORTH, D. L. (1986), *New Forms and New Areas of Employment Growth*, Programme of Research into Actions on the Development of the Labour Market, Study no. 85397, Coventry: Institute for Employment Research, University of Warwick.

—— —— NEALE, A. J., WESTAWAY, A. J., and WHITLEY, J. D. (1985), *Hours of Work*, Coventry: Institute for Employment Research, University of Warwick.

WINCHESTER, D. (1983), 'Industrial Relations in the Public Sector', in Bain (1983): 155–78.

WINSTON, G. C., and McCOY, T. O. (1974), 'Investment and the Optimal Idleness of Capital', *Review of Economics Studies*, 41: 419–28.

WOOD, K. A. (1978), *A Theory of Pay*, Cambridge: Cambridge University Press.

WRAGG, R., and ROBERTSON, J. (1978), 'Post-war Trends in Employment', Research Paper no. 3, Department of Employment, June.

ZABALZA, A., and TZANNATOS, Z. (1985a), 'The Effects of Britain's Anti-discriminatory Legislation on Relative Pay and Employment', *Economic Journal*, 95: 679–99.

—— —— (1985b), *Women and Equal Pay: The Effects of Legislation on Female Employment and Wages in Britain*, Cambridge: Cambridge University Press.

Subject Index

Author Index